Great Cruelties Have Been Reported

Published in cooperation with the
William P. Clements Center for Southwest Studies

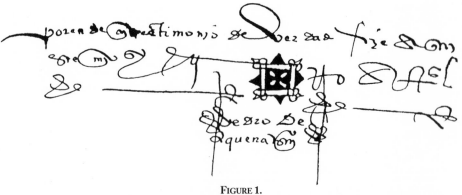

FIGURE 1.
El signo y la rubrica de Pedro de Requena, AGI, Justicia, 1021, N.2, Pieza 4, fol. 105r

---

Por ende *en* testimonio de Verdad Fize Aqui / este myo syg*no* (A)tal/ [signo] / Pedro De / R*e*quena escry*bano* [rubrica]

Therefore, in testimony of the truth [of what is recorded] I affixed here this sign of mine [made] in this way [registered device], Pedro de Requena, scribe [rubric]

Great Cruelties Have Been Reported

The 1544 Investigation
of the Coronado Expedition

RICHARD FLINT

SOUTHERN METHODIST
UNIVERSITY PRESS
Dallas

Requests for permission to reproduce material from this work should be sent to:
Rights and Permissions
Southern Methodist University Press
PO Box 750415
Dallas, Texas 75275-0415

LIBRARY OF CONGRESS CATALOGING-IN-PUBLICATION DATA

Flint, Richard.
    Great cruelties have been reported : the 1544 investigation of the Coronado Expedition
/ Richard Flint.
        p. cm.
    Includes bibliographical references and index.
    ISBN 0-87074-460-7 (alk. paper)
    1. Coronado, Francisco Vázquez de, 1510–1554—Relations with Indians. 2. Coronado,
Francisco Vázquez de, 1510–1554—Trials, litigation, etc. 3. Indians of North America—
First contact with Europeans—Southwest, New. 4. Indians of North America—Civil
rights—Southwest, New—History—16th century. 5. Indians, Treatment of—Southwest,
New. 6. Governmental investigations—Mexico—History—16th century. 7. Human
rights—Southwest, New—History—16th century. 8. Southwest, New—Discovery and
exploration—Spanish. 9. Southwest, New—Discovery and exploration—Social aspects.
10. Southwest, New—Ethnic relations. I. Title.

E125.V3 F57 2002
979'.01'092—dc21   2001042913

Jacket art by Isidoro Lucero

Jacket and text design by Tom Dawson Graphic Design

Printed in the United States of America on acid-free paper

10   9   8   7   6   5   4   3   2   1

ABOUT THE COVER: A native of Villanueva, New Mexico, artist Isidoro Lucero now lives in Granbury, Texas. For 15 years he has been designing images incorporating elements from a pictographic catechism painted in the 1520s and ascribed to fray Pedro de Gante, one of the very earliest missionaries to Mexico. The anthropomorphic elements in the image he has created for the cover derive from that source. The cartoon-like character of the images was typical of central Mexican painted manuscripts of late prehistory and the early historic period.

The large figure on the left is that of a conquistador which fray Pedro used to convey the concept *enemigo* or enemy in teaching Indians of central Mexico the prayer "O, our Lord God, with the sign of the cross, deliver us from our enemies with your hand." The ideology of the Pueblo Indians is represented by the *avanyu* or horned serpent, which is being lanced by the conquistador as his companions in arms prepare to assault a Pueblo town. The elements in the black sky are other pictograms from the prayer for deliverance, including a dual-gender representation of God and supplication of protection from his/her hand. The catechism is a remarkable example of Spanish Catholic-Native American syncretism that still was in use at the time of the Coronado expedition.

CONTENTS

Acknowledgments

Although the great bulk of my work on the *pesquisa* of 1544 has taken place since 1993, it rests on research into the expedition to Tierra Nueva that has been ongoing since 1980. During all of the last 20-plus years historian Shirley Cushing Flint has been my partner in that research, sometimes studying the same facets of the expedition, sometimes delving into other topics of special interest to her. As noted later in this study, without her parallel research in the Archivo General de Indias the important document recording testimony of *de parte* witnesses in Culiacán province would almost certainly remain undiscovered. That only begins to suggest the innumerable crucial ways in which her work has dovetailed with and reinforced mine. It has been beyond marvelous to have such a partner.

As with any undertaking, serendipity repeatedly has played a role in my work. No single happenstance has been more decisive in the course of that work than meeting Cal and Brent Riley in 1987. Colleagues and teachers who quickly became the dearest of friends, they have been extremely generous with suggestions, encouragement, and insights. Their own voluminous work on the expedition, both ethnohistorical and fictional, has been of fundamental significance to me. It continues to be an honor and a pleasure to enjoy their friendship.

In 1992, with a masters degree heavily weighted in anthropology, I sought a school and program where I could pursue and expand my researches already then underway for more than a decade. When I despaired of finding such a niche in New Mexico it was John L. Kessell who, with characteristic enthusiasm and liberality, invited me to try the History Department at the University of New Mexico. He has afforded me since many priceless opportunities, not the least of which has been to work in the Vargas Project for four years, allowing me to hone my skills in Spanish paleography and documentary editing. To have such a craftsman in the writing of history as friend and teacher is of inestimable value.

Because my work has been of such long duration there have been many, many people who have aided and assisted me along the way. From among them I must single out for special thanks Bill and Gayle Hartmann. Dialogs with them over the course of years have fine tuned my vision of the century of conquest. And a travel grant from the Hartmanns made possible research in the Archivo General de Notarías in 1996. That the late Vivian Fisher, formerly of the Bancroft Library of the University of California at Berkeley, shared a day with me in Berkeley at the very beginning of work on the pesquisa was an incomparable gift. Particular thanks are also due to Charles Cutter of Purdue University for sharing insights regarding early-modern Spanish jurisprudence. And I am grateful to friend and fellow historian Harry Myers for his work in digitally cleaning up the document facsimiles which appear as illustrations.

Much of the research that permitted my becoming acquainted in detail with the individuals involved in the 1544 investigation was done in Sevilla, Spain, during 1997–98 under a Fulbright dissertation grant, for which I will always be grateful. The Archivo General de Indias and the staff that cares for its collection are incredible. Even with all the research and writing done, this would not have become a book without the wholehearted support of David Weber of Southern Methodist University and the generosity of the Southwestern Foundation for Education and Historical Preservation, the Southwestern Missions Research Center, the William P. Clements Center for Southwest Studies at SMU, and Don Cushing Associates.

Thank you all.

Introduction

In the course of the sixteenth century scores of armed expeditions were mounted and carried out under Spanish direction throughout an expanding worldwide domain of asserted sovereignty: in Italy, Africa, the Canary Islands, South America, Central America, North America, and the Philippines. That aggressive expansion was undertaken not primarily to increase territorial limits, but first and foremost to bring all the world's people under the religious, political, and economic hegemony of a royal and noble elite that saw itself as divinely anointed and directed. Individual success in the enterprise of expansion was viewed both as progress toward the ultimate goal of universal rule and as confirmation of heavenly election. The subjugation of wealthy peoples was exquisitely confirmatory, since possession of riches was seen as a demonstration of supernatural favor. Thus the wondrously prosperous Mexica of central Mexico, Inca of Peru, Maya of Central America, and Filipinos of the Far East were all targeted and conquered during the 1500s.

Successful Spanish conquest altered radically and permanently indigenous peoples and their lifeways, sometimes eradicating both cultures and their practitioners. It also had profound effects on the conquerors themselves, remaking their society and transforming individuals. But what of the failed conquests, those ventures undertaken with equal vainglory and fervor that were frustrated and abandoned? Most attempted conquests fall into this category: expeditions led by Hernán Cortés to Honduras and Baja California, Francisco de Orellana into the Amazon Basin, Álvar Núñez Cabeza de Vaca to Paraguay, Juan Ponce de León to Florida, Pánfilo de Narváez to Florida, Juan Pardo into the Appalachians, Hernando de Soto through the American Southeast, and Francisco Vázquez de Coronado into the Greater American Southwest, to name only a few. The case of New Mexico is typical; there, four attempted conquests preceded the final successful colonization nearly 60 years after the first attempt. What effects did these transitory encounters between indigenous societies and agents of European paradigms have on both parties and how lasting were those effects? Were the events of unsuccessful conquest mere whirlwinds without persistent effect, insignificant to would-be conquerors and potential vassals alike? It is the purpose of this book to look at the myriad effects of one failed sixteenth-century Spanish expedition of conquest with just such questions in mind, the expedition launched by Antonio de Mendoza and led by Francisco Vázquez de Coronado from 1540–1542.

In 1949, the great historian and Coronado expedition scholar Herbert E. Bolton characterized Vázquez de Coronado and the expedition he led as "notably more humane" and having "a finer sense of the rights and dignity of human beings" than did other Spanish expeditions of the period. He stated categorically that "in the main the Coronado expedition had been quite exemplary—mild and gentle as compared with acts committed by Cortés, Pedrarias, Guzmán, De Soto, or the Pizarros."[1] These statements and Bolton's generally sanitized narration of the events of the expedition in his classic *Coronado, Knight of Pueblos and Plains* have given the impression to generations of readers that the native population of the Greater Southwest had little to complain about when it came to the Coronado expedition. The representation is made that the expedition caused the gentlest of ripples in the lives of native peoples of the Greater Southwest.

Nothing could be farther from the truth. Vázquez de Coronado himself may have been quite dutiful in observing the laws and directives that established a framework for Spanish conquest, but those laws and directives, even at their most humane, foresaw nothing less than the eradication of indigenous culture and the substitution of a Spanish Catholic culture, by force if necessary (which was the norm). Furthermore, Vázquez de Coronado was a very pragmatic leader, willing to suspend law and ordinance when the lives or comfort of Spaniards was at stake. And many of his subordinates disregarded laws and directives and saw to it that their leader never learned of their transgressions.

Fortunately, for the purpose at hand, an investigation into effects of the Coronado expedition to Tierra Nueva on the native peoples it sought to bring under Spanish dominion was conducted by Spanish officials in Nueva España only two years after the return of the disappointing thrust into the far north. The lengthy documents of that investigation record are at the heart of this study. The evidence from the 1544 testimony is compelling. The fact that the *maestre de campo* of the expedition was punished as a result of the investigation (very lightly though he was) attests to the official contemporary assessment of the expedition as unacceptably brutal. The investigating judge and the prosecutor lodged serious complaints. The expedition had tortured, executed, and terrorized American natives from what is today western Mexico to modern Kansas. It had destroyed native towns and scattered their populations. It had stolen and extorted possessions of Indian people. It had taken many Indian women for sexual gratification and involuntary service. By and large, the witnesses during the investigation made no attempt to disprove the complaints against the expedition. In fact, the issue of the investigation was not whether cruelty had occurred, but rather who committed and sanctioned it.

The evidence of the 1544 investigation is augmented and its scope and depth are here substantively broadened by study of dozens of other contemporary Spanish documents dealing with the expedition as a whole and with individual participants in it. Furthermore, with a goal of adding a less (or at least differently) culturally biased source of information, I also liberally employ the findings of archeologists and ethnohistorians.

What emerges is a story of conflict and attempted accommodation, resistance, and attempted disengagement which, for example, realigned the balance of regional power and territory in the Rio Grande Valley of New

Mexico, imported a significant Mesoamerican population into the Zuni pueblos, reinforced the Spanish hold on the northern fringe of Nueva España, resulted in massive death and suffering for the Tiwa Pueblos, confirmed and crystallized attitudes of the parties toward each other, discouraged and delayed Spanish designs on North America, essentially ended the career of a conscientious Spanish functionary, set the stage for establishment of privilege for a number of individuals within colonial Mexico, and consigned some participants in the expedition to lifelong poverty. The result is a cautionary tale about attempts at forced cultural transformation and the deep-seated and subtle nature of culturally based conflict.

My purpose in this book is to consider the following four questions: 1) what specifically were the immediate and long-term impacts of the Coronado expedition on the native groups it encountered (especially the Pueblos) and on the members of the expedition itself, 2) how substantial and enduring were those effects, 3) what brought on the 1544 investigation of treatment of natives of Tierra Nueva, which the "Proceso de Francisco Vázquez" records, and 4) what was accomplished by the investigation? A complex set of forces, motives, and results are delineated, both with regard to native groups and the European-led expedition. Thus, I detail a series of encounters in Tierra Nueva during the early 1540s between profoundly heterogeneous groups, encounters that had lasting effects on all the parties involved.

As a result of research into the lives of the witnesses, we have a much more detailed picture of the makeup of the expedition than has been available heretofore. We also discern some of the variety of attitudes, expectations, and allegiances that characterized the mass of the expedition. Prosopographical data on those directly concerned by the investigation and on the group of witnesses reveals the interplay of forces of political power, economic control, and assertion of a humanitarian ethos that combined to stimulate and shape the 1544 investigation. Simple and essentialized images of the expedition and resulting investigation typical of past scholarship yield to an increasingly intricate complexity. My research shows, for instance, that the viceroy and Vázquez de Coronado saw the investigation principally as a political challenge and orchestrated the investigation to assure minimal political damage.

The effects of the expedition on native groups prove to be equally as various and complex. Documentary and ethnographic evidence shows shifting results of interaction between members of the expedition and native individuals and groups. Particularly intriguing are the interactions between Mexican Indians (who, in point of fact, made up the bulk of the expedition) and Puebloans and other native peoples of Tierra Nueva. Among major geopolitical results of the encounter, I point to a significant reconfiguration of ethnic occupation of the middle Rio Grande Valley, as Keres Pueblos permanently pushed into the northern fringe of what had been Tiwa territory. A variety of strategies of contact appear to have been employed by Zunis, Keres, Tiwas, and Pecos, ranging from open confrontation to subterfuge to passive resistance to feigned submission to alliance. Furthermore, the expedition's dealings with native groups varied both from one group to another and over time, as did the responses of those indigenous people.

Chapter 1

The Historical Background

uring the 1530s, rumors and reports of town-dwelling Indians, who cultivated corn, wore cotton clothes, and possessed turquoise in abundance, reached the Viceroyalty of Nueva España from the north. That news created a sensation and stimulated competition for the right to confirm the reports. Ultimately, the Spanish king Carlos I authorized two such expeditions: one entering southeastern North America led by Hernando de Soto and a second striking northward along Nueva España's west coast. Antonio de Mendoza, viceroy of Nueva España, recommended that command of this second expedition be given to his young protege and newly appointed governor of Nueva Galicia, Francisco Vázquez de Coronado. In appointing the young captain general, the king expressed confidence that Vázquez de Coronado would "take special care in the protection and defense of the said lands [to the north] and their natives." This echoed the king's sentiments in his instructions of 1535 to Mendoza as Nueva España's first viceroy. The king had written then, "The murder, plundering, and other improper acts that have been done in the said conquest as well as capturing the Indians as slaves should cease."

With considerable caution, Mendoza dispatched two small reconnaissance parties ahead of the main expedition, which itself got underway in Feb-

FIGURE 2.
Conquistador with Banner, after *Codex Aubin*

ruary 1540. During the next 28 months, Vázquez de Coronado's force of 300-odd Europeans, an unknown number of Africans, and over 1000 Indian allies from central and west Mexico traversed the Greater Southwest, always seeking populated places. The expedition encountered many native groups, from agriculturalists in Sonora to bison-hunters on the Great Plains. Sometimes relations between the expedition and native peoples were amicable from beginning to end. But, more often than not, the expedition resorted to intimidation and violence to secure the cooperation and assistance of unwilling Indians.

Coercion, though, could not change the fact that there was no ready-to-hand wealth, according to European definitions, waiting to be appropriated from among the peoples of the Greater Southwest. Thus, in 1542, having come to that conclusion, the expedition returned to Mexico City.

With promulgation of the New Laws of the Indies, that same year marked the height of the Spanish crown's efforts to legislate humane treatment of the Indians of the Americas. In addition, 1542 saw a reading before the royal court of the first version of Bartolomé de las Casas's *Brevísima Relación de la Destrucción de las Indias*, a lurid account of 50 years of slaughter of American Indians. Certainly, many Spanish consciences were aroused. In such a climate, the expedition to Tierra Nueva was denounced to the king. In September of 1543, the king wrote, "It has been reported to us that in the expedition which Francisco Vázquez de Coronado made to the province of Cíbola, he and the Spaniards who went with him committed, both in going and returning, great cruelties against the natives of the lands through which they passed, killing large numbers of them and committing other acts and injustices to the detriment of the service of God and ours."

To investigate these allegations, the king appointed lawyer Lorenzo de Tejada, *oidor* or judge of the Royal Audiencia of Nueva España. Tejada's charge was to determine who, among the members of the expedition, had been responsible for mistreatment of Indians of Tierra Nueva. From May through September of 1544, he examined 14 witnesses in the case, both in Mexico City and in Guadalajara, seat of Vázquez de Coronado's government of Nueva Galicia. Those 14 were Francisca de Hozes and her husband Alonso Sánchez, Juan de Paradinas, Domingo Martín, Juan de Contreras, Rodrigo Ximón, Cristóbal de Escobar, Rodrigo de Frías, Melchior Pérez,[1] Pedro de Ledesma, Juan de Zaldívar, Alonso Álvarez, Vázquez de Coronado himself, and Juan Troyano. None of these, except the captain general and Zaldívar, was among the expedition's leadership. All testimony was taken in the presence of and recorded by Pedro de Requena, a scribe of the audiencia of Nueva España.

The record of the testimony taken by Tejada was forwarded to the audiencia's *fiscal* or prosecuting attorney, Cristóbal de Benavente, for assessment of whether and against whom formal charges should be lodged. On March 21, 1545, the fiscal filed criminal charges against Vázquez de Coronado for six alleged offenses that "he, and his captains and lieutenants by his command, committed."

Vázquez de Coronado and his attorney, Pedro Ruiz de Haro (who later brought suit on Vázquez de Coronado's behalf), filed rebuttal testimony, including that of four witnesses from Culiacán and three from Mexico City. With the testimony that Tejada took, Benavente's accusation, and Vázquez de Coronado's rebuttal testimony in hand, the audiencia as a whole sat in judgment and delivered its decision February 19, 1546. According to the document the audiencia issued at the time, "We find them [the fiscal's charges] and pronounce them not proven; and also that the aforesaid Francisco Vázquez de Coronado proved his exceptions and defenses."

That, however, was not the end of charges resulting from Tejada's investigation. A copy of the testimony he had taken was forwarded to the Council of the Indies in Spain. As a result, the Council's fiscal, Juan de Villalobos, lodged charges of misconduct and maltreatment of Indians against the expedition's maestre de campo or field commander, García López de Cárdenas. After lengthy judicial machinations, a decision in the case, and appeal of that decision, the Council of the Indies announced its final decision on July 18, 1551. The Council affirmed its determination of half a year earlier that the fiscal had "proved his accusation and complaint." And the Council sentenced López de Cárdenas to one year's military service on the Navarra frontier, a fine of 200 ducats, and banishment from the Indies for ten years. In November of that same year the site of López de Cárdenas's service was moved conveniently to Granada, in the jurisdiction of Antonio de Mendoza's brother, the conde de Tendilla. In total, López de Cárdenas's movements were restricted for seven years while awaiting the Council's decision and in subsequent service. He was the only member of the expedition to Tierra Nueva punished for violence committed against Indians of the Greater Southwest and that punishment was extremely light.

Throughout the various investigations, the allegations that violence had been committed went largely unchallenged. The main question at issue was who was responsible for that violence. Together, the audiencia of Nueva España and the Council of the Indies traced only a few specific violent incidents and those were laid to the maestre de campo's responsibility. (The following chronology summarizes events pertinent to the investigation.)

Chronology of the Expedition to Tierra Nueva and Investigation of Its Conduct

October 1535
Antonio de Mendoza arrived at Veracruz to take up his post as first viceroy of Nueva España. Accompanying him were Francisco Vázquez de Coronado and others.

1536
Survivors of the Pánfilo de Narváez expedition to La Florida arrived in Mexico City, telling of possible wealthy populations to the north.

March 7, 1539
Fray Marcos de Niza was dispatched to Cíbola to check rumors of wealth and large cities.

August 1539
Fray Marcos returned from Cíbola with very favorable reports.

November 1539
Melchor Díaz and Juan de Zaldívar were sent north to verify fray Marcos's reports.

January 6, 1540
Vázquez de Coronado was commissioned captain general of the expedition to Tierra Nueva.

February 22, 1540
Members of the expedition to Tierra Nueva mustered at Compostela in Nueva Galicia.

February 26, 1540
The expedition began its northward trek.

March 1540
The expedition met Melchor Díaz returning from the north with less than enthusiastic news. Maestre de campo Lope de Samaniego was killed while

pursuing Indians who refused to furnish supplies, near Chiametla, Nueva Galicia.

March 28, 1540
A mock battle was staged as welcome for the expedition at Culiacán, Nueva Galicia.

May-June 1540
Vázquez de Coronado, with an advance guard, reached the area of the modern U.S.-Mexico border without having been opposed along the way.

June 1540
The body of the expedition proceeded north to a heavily populated area known as Corazones, where an outpost called San Gerónimo was established.

July 7, 1540
The advance guard reached Cíbola where the native people refused to accede to the *requerimiento;* the pueblo was stormed and occupied by the advance guard.

July 1540
A trading/diplomatic party from the pueblo of Cicuique, including a man called "Bigotes" by the Spaniards, offered the expedition friendship and invited it to go east.

Two exploring parties journeyed west to the pueblos of Tusayán, where one pueblo was attacked and subdued.

August 1540
Fray Marcos left the expedition, heading back south with Melchor Díaz, who was to take command of San Gerónimo.

A small exploring party led by Hernando de Alvarado went eastward to the pueblos of Tiguex and Cicuique and on to the buffalo plains.

September 1540
The body of the expedition reached Cíbola, where it occupied one of the pueblos.

Alvarado was told of the wealth of Quivira far out on the eastern plains by an Indian guide called "El Turco" by the Spaniards.

Fall 1540
The expedition established winter quarters at one of the Tiguex pueblos, which had been vacated by its residents.

Alvarado imprisoned Bigotes and the cacique, important men or *principales* of Cicuique, in an attempt to discover the truth about stories of gold at Quivira.

Winter 1540–1541
Friction between the Tiguex pueblos and the expedition erupted into war; two or three pueblos were besieged; in all, 12 to 20 Tiguex pueblos were abandoned by their inhabitants and burned.

January 1541
After a battle with Indians of the Tizón River, Melchor Díaz died, leaving Diego Alcaraz in charge at San Gerónimo.

April 23, 1541
The expedition left Tiguex bound for Quivira, guided by El Turco and Ysopete.

June 1541
The expedition, "lost" on the buffalo plains, was divided, the main body returning to Tiguex and a select detachment heading north for Quivira.

July 1541
Vázquez de Coronado and the select detachment reached Quivira, finding no gold or other precious metals; the guide El Turco was garroted.

September 1541
The select detachment rejoined the main body of the expedition at Tiguex; all the Tiguex pueblos remained abandoned and Cicuique was hostile.

December 1541
Vázquez de Coronado was seriously injured in a fall.

Late 1541 or Early 1542
The Indians of the Suya Valley attacked and overran San Gerónimo.

Early 1542
Vázquez de Coronado decided to abandon Tierra Nueva and lead the expedition back to Mexico.

April 1542
The expedition began the return march to Mexico, except for fray Juan de Padilla, fray Luis, and several of their assistants, who remained in the north to preach to the Indians of Quivira and Cicuique, respectively.

Summer 1542
Juan Gallego retaliated for the destruction of San Gerónimo by burning Indian villages and hanging individuals.

On its southward journey, the expedition was attacked by Indians several times.

Autumn 1542
Vázquez de Coronado and a much-reduced following reached Mexico City.

1542
The New Laws of the Indies regarding treatment of Indians were enacted and Bartolomé de las Casas read a draft of his *Brevísima Relación de la Destrucción de las Indias* before the Spanish royal court.

September 7, 1543
Lorenzo de Tejada was commissioned to investigate allegations of mistreatment of Indians by the expedition to Tierra Nueva.

May-September 1544
Tejada took testimony from 14 witnesses in Mexico City and Guadalajara.

January-March 1545
On instructions from Vázquez de Coronado, testimony was taken from four rebuttal witnesses in the province of Culiacán; other rebuttal testimony was taken in Mexico City and probably elsewhere.

March 11, 1545

A copy of the testimony taken by Tejada was made (the *Información contra Coronado*) and forwarded to the Council of the Indies for possible prosecution of García López de Cárdenas.

March 21, 1545

Fiscal Cristóbal de Benavente filed criminal charges against Vázquez de Coronado for ordering and condoning cruelty to Indians.

January 7, 1546

In Spain fiscal Juan de Villalobos lodged charges against García López de Cárdenas for cruelty to Indians while on the expedition to Tierra Nueva.

February 19, 1546

Vázquez de Coronado was exonerated on all charges of cruelty by the audiencia of Nueva España.

January 10, 1547

A second copy of the testimony taken by Tejada was made (AGI, Justicia, 1021, N. 2, Pieza 6) and was appended to testimony taken at the request of the fiscal.

March 31, 1547

A third copy of the testimony taken by Tejada was made (the *Proceso de Francisco Vásquez*) and forwarded to the Council of the Indies.

December 20, 1549

The Council of the Indies found López de Cárdenas guilty on all charges of cruelty.

July 17, 1551

The Council of the Indies lightened López de Cárdenas's sentence to banishment from the Indies for ten years, one year's military service on the frontier of Navarra, and a fine of 200 ducats.

November 10, 1551

López de Cárdenas's place of service was changed to Granada.

Chapter 2

The Texts and Editorial Protocols

The Texts

This study is founded on the extant records of the investigation conducted by Lorenzo de Tejada from May through September 1544, along with a letter from Tejada to the king, testimony taken between January and March 1545 on behalf of Vázquez de Coronado, as well as other undated *de parte* testimony, and the final royal judgment in the case. Presented herein are Spanish transcriptions and English translations of all of those documents.

Three copies of the original record of the 1544 investigation of the Coronado expedition conducted by Lorenzo de Tejada are known to exist. The original record itself no longer survives. All three copies are preserved in the Justicia section of the Archivo General de las Indias (AGI) in Sevilla, Spain. The first, known as the *"información contra Coronado"* or simply "información," is designated as AGI, Justicia, 1021, N. 2, Pieza 4. Like the original, it was prepared by Pedro de Requena, an *escribano* or scribe of the Royal Audiencia of Nueva España. George P. Hammond and Agapito Rey extracted Vázquez de Coronado's testimony from this document and published it in English in 1940 in their *Narratives of the Coronado Expedition, 1540-1542*.[1]

Commissioned by Herbert Bolton, Rey prepared a draft transcription and a draft English translation of AGI, Justicia, 1021, N. 2, Pieza 4, which Bolton then used in writing his 1949 *Coronado, Knight of Pueblos and Plains.*[2] A second complete copy of the investigation record exists in AGI, Justicia, 1021, N. 2, Pieza 6. This copy was made in January 1547 by the scribe Sancho López de Agurto. When I began my work on Tejada's investigation I was under the impression that Justicia 1021 contained the only record of the testimony he took, two identical copies.

While searching through an index of microfilm of AGI documents held by the University of California at Berkeley's Bancroft Library, however, I ran across the following entry under Justicia, 267: "Case against Coronado for maltreatment of Indians opened May 6, 1544, by oidor Tejada."[3] Since there was no indication of how many frames of microfilm comprised the document, my expectation was that it was very brief, perhaps only a certification of the commencement of the investigation on that day. So I was extremely surprised when the film arrived in Albuquerque by Interlibrary Loan to find that Justicia, 267, N. 3 contained a third complete copy of the investigation record. In fact, the Justicia, 267 document, known as the "*proceso de* Francisco Vázquez" or "proceso," includes a considerable amount of text not present in the "información."

Although I had completed a transcription of the "información" and was nearly finished with a translation of that document, a lengthy comparison with the "proceso" and AGI, Justicia, 1021, N. 2, Pieza 6 led me to the conclusion the "proceso" and Pieza 6 (essentially contemporary identical copies) are considerably more complete and accurate than the "información." Thus, I have chosen to use the "proceso" as the basic record of the *de oficio* investigation, occasionally augmented and clarified by text from the "información." A comparison of the three documents outlines my reasons for making this choice.

The "información" was prepared in March 1545 at licenciado Tejada's request by Pedro de Requena, as a copy of the original case record, which had also been executed by Requena. It was forwarded to the Council of the Indies, so that body could investigate the actions of García López de Cárdenas, whom Tejada and the fiscal Cristóbal de Benavente found to be culpable in the case. The "información" comprises 105 folios, all in Requena's hand, except for marginal glosses probably added in Spain. The whole of Justicia, 1021, N. 2 is devoted to the investigation of López de Cárdenas and includes the accusations against him, his defenses, and the sentence rendered against him.

The "proceso" and Justicia, 1021, N. 2, Pieza 6, on the other hand, were copied out two years later, in January and March 1547. The "proceso" was prepared at the request of Francisco Tello de Sandoval, the king's *visitador* in Nueva España. The 125 folios are in the hands of two separate scribes; the first transcribed 44 folios, the other all of the remainder but the final two folios. I have not been able to identify either of these scribes, though neither is Requena. The only signature on the document is that of Antonio de Turcios, chief scribe of the audiencia of Nueva España, though his hand appears only on the last two folios of the "proceso." Requena, however, is listed as one of the witnesses who were present for correction and reconciliation of the "proceso." Justicia, 267, N. 3, which contains the "proceso," is one of a lengthy series of legajos in the AGI that record the *visitas* or extraordinary administrative reviews of scores of officials of Nueva España conducted by Tello de Sandoval.

AGI, Justicia, 1021, N. 2, Pieza 6 is a copy of the testimony prepared at the request of Cristóbal de Benavente, fiscal of the audiencia of Nueva España, on behalf of Juan de Villalobos, fiscal of the Council of the Indies. It was signed by Sancho López de Agurto, as a public scribe of the city of Mexico in January 1547, although the text of 180 folios is in a different hand.

The introductory and concluding texts of the "información" and Justicia, 1021, N. 2, Pieza 6 differ substantially and substantively from the corresponding portions of the "proceso." Much, though not all, of the variation is explained by the fact that the "información" and Justicia, 1021, N. 2, Pieza 6 were prepared for use in investigating López de Cárdenas and the concluding sections of both these documents especially deal specifically with him.

The body of the three documents, the testimony of the 14 de oficio witnesses, though, is much more consistent, but still riddled with, mostly minor, scribal differences. Having translated all three documents, I can testify that there are dozens of occasions on which the Spanish of the "información" seems clumsy and sometimes incomprehensible. Invariably those difficulties evaporate when either the "proceso" or Justicia, 1021, N. 2, Pieza 6 is consulted.

For purposes of analyzing the variation among the documents, it is less cumbersome and more appropriate to compare only two, the bodies of the "proceso" and Justicia, 1021, N. 2, Pieza 6 being, for this purpose, the same. Thus, the discussion that follows is limited to the "proceso" and the "información".

Considering only the body of the two documents, there are 215 instances in which additional words appear in the "proceso" which are absent from the "información," including six phrases of four or more words. Correspondingly, there are 185 instances in which words appear in the "información" that are not present in the "proceso," including six phrases of four or more words.[4] At first blush, this appears to indicate that the two copies are about equally "sloppy." But the extra words in the "información" are more often particles such as "a," "se," "e," "y," and "dicho," often not contributing to and even detracting from the sense of passages. The extra words in the "proceso," on the other hand, are much more frequently nouns, verbs, adjectives, and adverbs which significantly affect meaning.

In addition to such differences as these, there are hundreds of other cases in which the two versions agree on the presence of a word, but disagree as to the form of the word. The most common substantive differences in this regard between the two documents are in subject number (singular or plural) and verb tense (usually between imperfect indicative and preterit indicative and between active and passive voice). As an example of the variant readings that result from such subtle but extensive differences, I cite one example. In the testimony of Cristóbal de Escobar on folio 41v of the "información" the following is recorded: "vio que aperrearon por su mandado mas de ciento y quarenta indios que se tomaron vivos syn otros que se alançearon (he saw that, by [the general's] order, the [Spaniards] set dogs on more than *140* Indians who were captured alive [*passive voice*], without [counting] others who were lanced)." The corresponding passage from the "proceso," folio 49v, is "vio que aperrearon por su mandado mas de ciento y cinquenta Indios que tomaron vivos syn otros muchos que se alançearon (he saw that, by [the general's] order, the [Spaniards] set dogs on more than *150* Indians whom they captured alive [*shift to active voice*], without [counting] *many* others who were lanced." The cumulative effect of hundreds of such differences is a significant variation in content.

There is a hint from the scribes themselves that the "proceso" is the more complete and accurate of the two documents. At the bottoms of 32 folio sides of the "información" Requena indicated that he had to make corrections on those pages, either adding or deleting words. This is in marked contrast to the "proceso," in which such scribal correction was necessary only once. In the "información" Requena also made a large number of uncorrected errors, including several misrecorded names: Diego López instead of García López, once; Pedro de Guevara instead of Diego de Guevara, once; Pedro Troyano instead of Juan Troyano, once; and consistently, Cárdenes instead of Cárdenas. Again, significantly, these errors do not occur in the "proceso."

The rendering in the "proceso" also resolves an issue raised by the "información" that has mislead earlier scholars. While there is no indication in other known Coronado expedition documents that wheeled vehicles made the trip to Tierra Nueva, the "información," folio 49v, records Juan Troyano as saying that he returned to Cíbola from Tiguex to get "unos carros de artilleria (some artillery wagons)." Folio 59r of the "proceso," in contrast, has "unos tiros de artilleria (some artillery pieces)," thus not indicating wheeled vehicles and not conflicting with other expeditionary documents.[5]

If, as I propose, the "proceso" is to be preferred as a source over the "información," new evidence results on such points as the number of children that Francisca de Hozes and Alonso Sánchez had with them during the course of the expedition. While the "información," folio 12v, records that they had "hijos (children)," the "proceso," folio 14v, indicates that they had only one "hijo (son)." Herbert Bolton asserted that, "In the disillusioned band, now led by Cárdenas over the back track, were Alonso Sánchez, his *soldadera* wife Francisca de Hozes, and their children, of whom there were now two, one

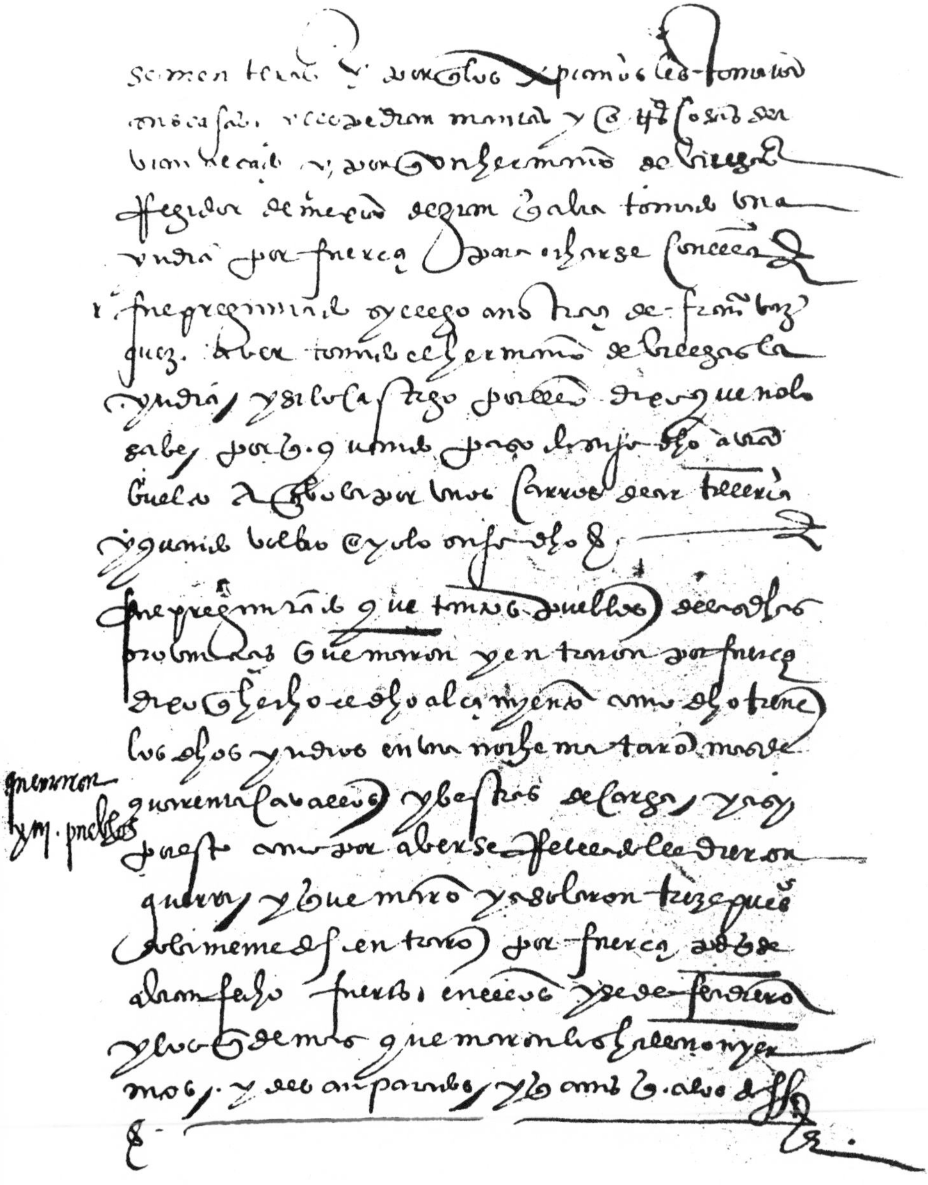

FIGURE 3.
Facsimile of Carros, AGI, Justicia, 1021, N.2, Pieza 4, fol. 49v

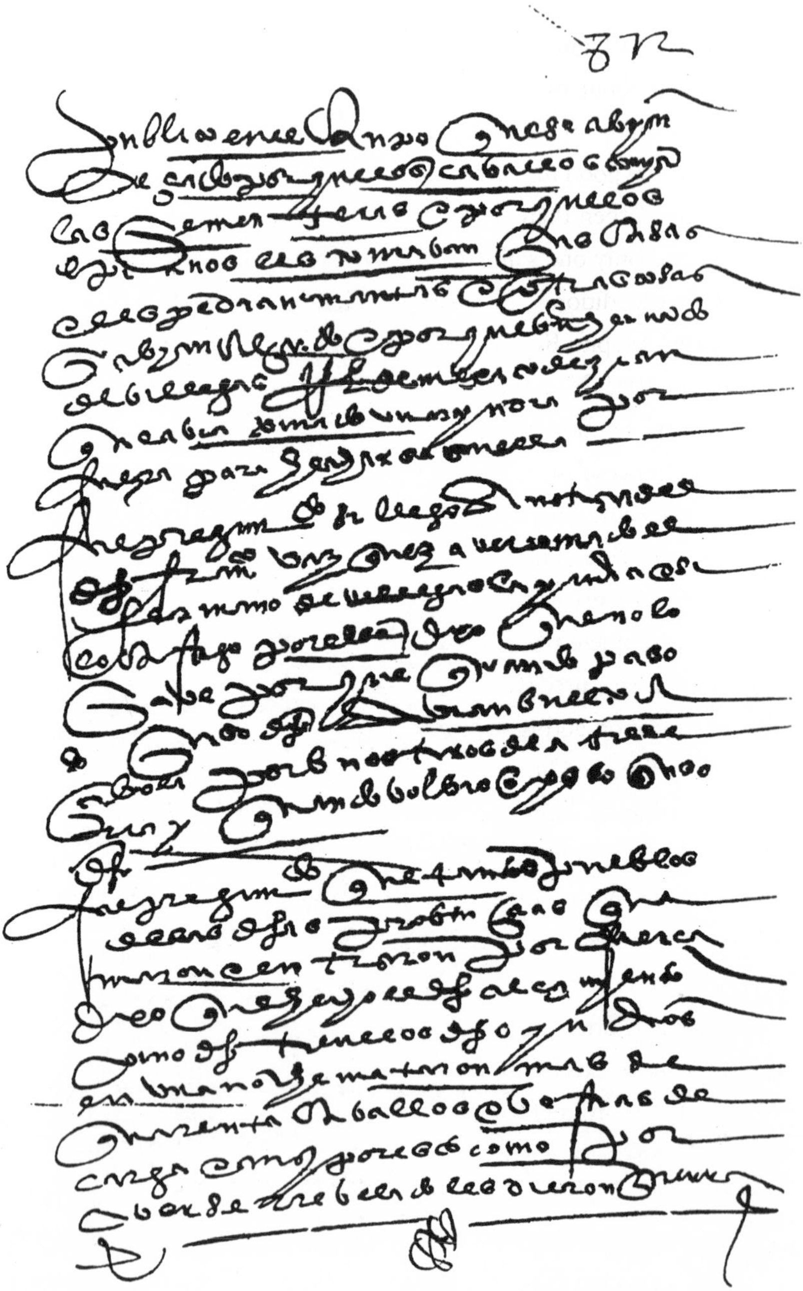

FIGURE 4.
Facsimile of Tiros, AGI, Justicia, 267, N.3, fol. 59r

having been born in Tiguex or somewhere on the trail."[6] Bolton's sole support for his statement about two children seems to have been the appearance of the plural word "hijos" in the passage in the "información" just referred to. If, as I think, there are good reasons not to accept unquestioningly the details of the "información," then there is a good chance that Francisca de Hozes and her husband had only one son with them, and he was at least a teenager at the time of the expedition.[7]

Apparently, Agapito Rey also became aware of the existence of the "proceso" or Justicia, 1021, N. 2, Pieza 6 while he was transcribing and translating the "información" for Bolton. At least, he seems to have incorporated readings from the "proceso" into his transcription on several occasions, though only very sporadically. And he never made written reference to a second or third copy of the investigation record.

In sum, then, there can be little doubt that the "proceso" is both more reliable and more complete than the "información," though it is far from flawless. Therefore, I have used the "proceso" as the principal record of the 1544 de oficio investigation and have supplemented its text in a few places where variant readings from the "información" and Justicia, 1021, N. 2, Pieza 6 seem to clarify obscurities or supply obvious lacks.

A word or two should be said about scribal drafting and copying of documents in general. With some confidence it can be said that literally identical scribal copies of the same document are all but unknown, except in the case of the very shortest of documents. Mistranscription is one source of difference. Another and often very significant source, though, is purposeful and unnoted revision of texts by copyists. Sixteenth-century Spanish scribes were definitely NOT committed to rendering verbatim copies. If the copyist was in the habit of spelling a word differently than it appeared in the original, say *"facer"* instead of *"hacer,"* he is very likely to have substituted "facer" for most, if not all, instances of "hacer" in the original. Of more substantive import, scribes readily corrected each other's work in the process of making copies, if factual error was thought to be involved. As but one of countless examples, there is the case of Antonio de Turcios, chief scribe of the audiencia of Nueva España in the 1540s. When, late in 1540, a *cédula* from the king arrived in

Mexico City directed to Vázquez de Coronado, confirming his appointment to lead the expedition to the north, Turcios prepared at least one copy. Finding that the original scribe, Juan de Sámano, had referred to Galicia instead of Nueva Galicia and had dated the cédula 1539 rather than 1540, Turcios simply corrected the errors in the copy without mentioning the fact. Sometimes this could be benign, at others the copyist, thinking to make corrections, actually introduced errors. Apropos of the case at hand, it is also clear that scribes from time to time lost their concentration and as a result their miscopying errors rose dramatically, especially when copying very long documents that they themselves had recorded in the first place. Just as an author often makes a poor proofreader of his or her own work, so too a scribe copying his own work was prone to more errors than if the copying had been done by a "fresh" scribe. This may have been the case with Pedro de Requena and may explain why his own copy of the case record he had himself originally made, the "información," is riddled with errors.

The procedure of sixteenth-century Spanish scribes has not been well studied, but one aspect of their standard practice is inferable from their products, the *autos, procesos, diligencias*, etc. that they drafted. Of primary importance for the historian is that, as a rule, scribes did not make word-for-word records of testimony. Statements were likely not even recorded at the time or in the form in which they appear in the official documents; instead, it seems, the scribe made detailed shorthand notes as witnesses replied to the questions asked and then shortly afterwards, perhaps the same day, would produce a summarized and essentialized, third-person rendition.[8] For instance, in the more than 200 folios of testimony in this case, only two short phrases in witness testimony are presented in the first person. This method of operating is part of the reason the great bulk of Spanish legal testimony of the period sounds so much alike and why, within any given case, the answers to any specific question read so similarly as to give strong evidence of the role of the scribe in their composition, a role of no less importance than that of the witnesses themselves. Pedro Requena hinted at this procedure in testimony he himself gave in the fall of 1544 regarding the residencia of officials of Nueva Galicia (including Vázquez de Coronado), for which he also served as scribe.

He stated (through another scribe) that for much of the time every day he was in a separate room from the judge, where he was writing up and executing documents ordered by the judge.[9] These various ways in which scribal renderings are not literally the words of witnesses were borne in mind as I read and studied the lengthy testimonial record.

Until recently, the only testimony known in this case was what was described earlier, the de oficio testimony, that is the statements of witnesses called by the judge Lorenzo de Tejada, recorded in AGI, Justicia, 267. However, Shirley Cushing Flint, while doing research in the AGI in an unrelated document from 1566, found incorporated at the end of it a copy of rebuttal testimony in the 1544 case: the testimony of four witnesses taken in the province of Culiacán, Nueva Galicia, January through March 1546, *por parte de*, on behalf of, Francisco Vázquez de Coronado. This copy comprises 38 folios near the end of AGI, Patronato, 216, R. 2, proceedings relative to Nuño de Chávez, Mexico City, 1566. The testimony of the four witnesses, Lorenzo Álvarez, Diego López, Luis de Figueredo, and Pedro de Tovar, together with the accompanying *interrogatorio* (doubtless formulated either by or with the participation of Vázquez de Coronado), provides valuable insight into the line of defense taken by the former captain general and his attorney. And it reveals some of the core attitudes among the settlers and conquerors of Nueva España regarding treatment of indigenous peoples. Only one copy of this testimony is known to survive, but it should be noted that it is a copy and not the original record of testimony. I provide later a transcription and translation of the record of this rebuttal testimony.

A brief summary of the testimony of three other *de parte* witnesses, García Rodríguez, Gaspar de Saldaña, and Rodrigo Maldonado, also exists in AGI, Justicia, 1021, N. 2, Pieza 2, extract from the affidavit prepared on behalf of Francisco Vázquez de Coronado, n.p., n.d. As a summary, the information it provides is at even farther remove from the original record of testimony than is the information from simple copies. Nevertheless, it provides additional important information. I have included herein a transcription and translation of that summary.

Additionally, I have included within the case record a letter written May

24, 1544 by Lorenzo de Tejada to the king. Unlike the other documents discussed so far, it is the signed original and is curated as AGI, Mexico, 68, R.
11, N. 25, letter, licenciado Tejada to the king, Mexico City, May 24, 1544. It
is important primarily because it provides an idea of the circumstances and
time constraints of the investigation and shows how it related to other, much
wider-ranging investigations going on at the same time.

The final element of the core documents used in this study is a copy of
the final judgment of the king and audiencia in the case, with regard to the
conduct of Vázquez de Coronado. The judgment was rendered December 20,
1547, while the copy was made at Vázquez de Coronado's request in 1551 as
he sought to have *encomiendas* restored to him. The document, comprising 15
folios conserved in AGI, Justicia, 336, provides the charge-by-charge refuta-
tion offered by Vázquez de Coronado of the fiscal's accusations.

A number of other documents related to and resulting from Tejada's
investigation survive. In their *Narratives of the Coronado Expedition, 1540-
1542*, Hammond and Rey published translations of the following relevant
documents:

1) "Testimony of López de Cárdenas,"

2) "Sentence of López de Cárdenas," and

3) "Amended Sentence of Cárdenas."[10]

The originals of these and a series of other related documents contained
in AGI, Justicia, 1021, N. 2, Pieza 1, concern the prosecution of López
de Cárdenas. All of these have been consulted in manuscript in the conduct
of this study. Scores of other documents from a number of archives in
Spain, Mexico, and the United States have also been used in elucidating
the events, persons, and places referred to in the course of the 1544 investigation.[11]

Transcription and Translation Protocols

In transcribing the texts, I have followed a semi-paleographic method. My
goal has been to transform difficult sixteenth-century scripts, riddled with

abbreviations, into a modern printed version, more accessible to today's readers. I have sought to retain much of the flavor of the documents as they were prepared by the various scribes and to minimize violence to the texts. Thus, I have retained scribal line and folio length, and rare marginal notes. I have, however, emended the text to the extent of expanding numerous scribal abbreviations, the legacy of a tradition of stenography already venerable in the sixteenth century.[12] Such emendations are rendered in modern spelling, rather than that of the scribes. Rare scribal punctuation and use of diacritical marks are omitted, except for ñ and ç.

As editor of the texts, I have adhered to the following typographic conventions in preparing transcriptions. All emendations, additions, and expansions, whether scribal or editorial, including interlineations, are rendered in italics, as are the infrequent Latin words and phrases present in the documents. In the case of scribal emendations, the characters or words in italics are preceded by a caret ^. Marginal notes, symbols, and marks appearing in the texts are rendered in Roman type but are enclosed between flourished brackets { }. Letters that are superscribed in the documentary texts are lowered to the main text line in the transcriptions. Both scribal and editorial deletions are preserved in the transcripts, but are identified as deletions by being enclosed between standard parentheses ( ). In the case of scribal deletions, a caret is also included within the parentheses (^). I have made editorial deletions in cases where modern orthography and sixteenth-century scribal spelling vary sufficiently to render words awkward, ambiguous, or difficult to identify for many modern readers. But, even in cases of editorial deletion, all letters present in the documentary texts appear in the transcripts. Scribal use of majuscule characters is adhered to in the transcripts.

For those unfamiliar with sixteenth-century spelling practice, a few remarks about interchange of characters may be helpful in reading the Spanish transcriptions. First, spelling was less standardized and thus more variable in the 1500s and before, than it is today. Different scribes frequently used slightly different spellings. Even a single scribe would change spelling within a document, often even within a single line of text. For the most part, though, the differences in spelling conformed to a pattern of possibilities. For example, specific pairs or sets of consonants were regularly interchanged.

Perhaps the most common interchange was between "b" and "v". Accordingly, throughout the transcriptions that follow, the Spanish equivalent of "to know" appears variously as "saber" and "saver" with equal validity. Likewise, the equivalent of "to have" is spelled either "haber" or "haver". In the original manuscripts themselves the characters "b" and "v" are nearly indistinguishable. It is my practice to transcribe as "b" or "V" such a character whose left-hand member or leg is longer than its right-hand member. When the legs are of equal length the character has been transcribed as "v".

Further complicating the transcription of "b" and "v" in sixteenth-century Spanish, the characters for "v" and "u" were orthographically interchangeable, both in miniscule and majuscule. Thus, in transcribing the characters "b", "v", and "u" I have followed the protocols in the preceding paragraph when phonetically a consonant was clearly intended. When, on the other hand, a vowel is appropriate, the character is rendered as "u" or "U".

Other common consonant interchanges in sixteenth-century Spanish include:

1) "c", "ç", "s", and "z" for the soft or sibilant "c"; thus, one sees "decir", "deçir", "desir", and "dezir" for the Spanish equivalent of "to speak or say";
2) "c", "q", and occasionally "g" for the hard "c" or "k" sound, as in "descubrir", "desgubrir", or "desqubrir";
3) "g", "j", and "x" for the fricative "h", as in "elexir", "elejir", or "elegir";
4) "m" and "n", as in "campo" or "canpo";
5) "t" and "th", as in "tener" or "thener."

There are also a few vowels that were commonly interchanged; they include:

1) "i" and "y", as in "fin" or "fyn";
2) "i" and "e", as in "ningun" or "nengun";
3) "o" and "u", as in "descubrir" or "descobrir".

In transcribing the documents of the 1544 investigation, I have not modified such interchanges unless they rendered the words in which they occurred particularly difficult to read. Ordinarily this was when the interchange occurred in the first or second syllable of the word or was compounded by other spelling irregularities.

In preparing the transcription and translation of AGI, Justicia, 267, the "proceso," I referred to transcription and translation drafts of its cognate text, AGI, Justicia, 1021, N. 2, Pieza 2, the "información," prepared by Agapito Rey in the 1930s and used by Herbert Bolton in writing his 1949 *Coronado, Knight of Pueblos and Plains*. Because of occasional errors and omissions on Rey's part, because of the multitude of differences between the two documents themselves (as outlined previously), because of shifts in scholarly knowledge and assumption in the last 60 years, and because of difference of opinion on translation and interpretation, the transcription and translation I present here vary significantly from those that Rey produced at Bolton's request.

Nonetheless, as Bolton wrote, "[the Información contra Coronado/Proceso] has added immensely to the data hitherto available regarding nearly every episode of the Coronado expedition. It is a priceless source of knowledge for many subjects formerly shadowy in the extreme or completely in the dark."[13] That statement has been rendered even more emphatic by use of the fuller and more accurate "proceso" text and the addition of rebuttal testimony, and other ancillary documents to which neither Rey nor Bolton had access.

Herbert Priestley wrote of his translation of documents in *The Luna Papers* that "effort has been made in the change from sixteenth-century Spanish idiom to twentieth-century English to lean to the side of intelligibility rather than literalness."[14] I have had the same intent in translating the testimony of the witnesses in the 1544 investigation of treatment of Indians, some of Tristán de Luna's comrades-in-arms during the expedition to Tierra Nueva under Francisco Vázquez de Coronado. Too-literal translation cripples the language and gives the misleading impression that another language is clumsy and ugly. Or, alternately, it gives the equally misleading impression that the writers of historical documents were barely literate and incapable of meeting even minimal standards of style and elegance. Furthermore, it is the first job of a translator (especially when a verbatim parallel original language text is provided, as in the present instance) to render documents in such a way that they are easily comprehended in the receiving language and sometimes this involves more interpretation than literalists are comfortable with. This last is particularly important if the historical translator wants to have any hope of reaching a wider lay audience, beyond specialists in the field (who, in any case, are unlikely to trust completely any sort of translation as evidence in their own work).

Most commonly, my interpretation has involved supplying referents for ambiguous pronouns. In the conviction that there is no one-to-one correspondence between a Spanish word and its rendition in English, I often employ a series of synonyms or closely related English words to translate a single Spanish word. This I do in the hope that the aggregate translation provides a more adequate rendering than would a mechanical repetition of a single "equivalent." Thus I translate the word *ejército* as army, armed force, company, and expedition, since the most common modern translation, army, alone connotes a full-time, professional fighting force, which the Coronado expedition decidedly was not. Further, occasionally I have inserted words or phrases to ease the flow of particularly choppy passages. In any case, my insertions are identifiable as enclosed in square brackets [] in the translations. Original foliation is indicated in the translations with numbers enclosed in square brackets [].

In the English version, I have supplied paragraphing and punctuation. I have retained archaic and variant spellings of North American non-Spanish proper names and toponyms. I consider this especially important since there is a lack of scholarly consensus about the identity of many of the places and some of the peoples referred to in Coronado expedition documents. In many cases, modernization and consistency of spelling would obscure this uncertainty and destroy possible ethnographic clues to their ultimate identification. Thus, in both transcripts and translations, the name of the pueblo besieged by the Coronado expedition for two months during the winter of 1540-1541 appears variously as Moho, Moha, Mohi, Mocha, and Macha. In the translation, scribal marginalia are enclosed and designated by flourished brackets

{}, just as in the transcripts, and are inserted at the nearest appropriate point in the text.

Rather than providing extensive information about persons and places in footnotes, I include alphabetically arranged biographical and geographical data in Appendices 2 and 3.

Abbreviations Used in This Text

AGI	Archivo General de Indias, Sevilla, Spain
AGnot	Archivo General de Notarías, Mexico City, Mexico
AGS	Archivo General de Simancas, Simancas, Spain
AHN	Archivo Histórico Nacional, Madrid, Spain
ARMS	Archeological Records Management System, Laboratory of Anthropology, Museum of New Mexico, Santa Fe

Chapter 3

Lorenzo de Tejada and the Beginning of the Investigation

Spanish Concern Over Treatment of Indians

Spanish colonization of the Caribbean islands in the last decade of the 1400s and first decades of the 1500s had a devastating effect on the native peoples of that region. By 1550 the indigenous population of the Caribbean islands was all but extinct. Most native groups elsewhere in the hemisphere experienced less drastic, but still disastrous, impacts, with death rates often running as high as 90%. Various explanations for this catastrophe have been adduced: introduction of Old World diseases; abuse, overwork, and outright slaughter; dissolution of indigenous social patterns and structures; and sexual appropriation of Indian women by European men.[1]

Many members of Spanish colonial society were astonished and bewildered by the precipitous decline of Indian populations. Some few were outraged by the brutal acts toward native peoples committed by many of their fellows. First to publicly call for an end to violence against Native Americans was fray Antonio de Montesinos on the island of Hispaniola in late 1511. Not unexpectedly, attempts were quickly made to silence the outspoken cleric. He was successful, though, in laying his charges directly before the king. The result was convocation of an ecclesiastical and civil panel for the purpose of drafting laws to remedy what the king understood as a widespread outrage. In December 1512, therefore, King Fernando issued a series of laws, known as the Laws of Burgos, regulating relations with Indians of the Americas.[2] This first code governing treatment of Indians specified the kinds and amount of labor that could be exacted from American natives held in encomienda; required that encomenderos provide food, lodging, clothing, and religious instruction to their charges; and prohibited corporal punishment of Indians except by designated justices. The Laws of Burgos, however, did not address treatment of native peoples during the course of conquest.[3] At about the same time as issuance of the Laws of Burgos, though, the practice of reading the requerimiento or official summons to submit peacefully was instituted as standard practice for expeditions of conquest. This formal document ostensibly provided justification of Spanish rule to native peoples and offered them the option of voluntarily rendering allegiance to the king.[4]

In the wake of Montesinos's agitation on behalf of more benevolent, if paternalistic, treatment of Indians, an increasingly powerful movement arose both in Spain and the New World dedicated to ameliorating the conditions and treatment of Indians. In 1530 that movement achieved a major accomplishment, the announcement of a royal decree prohibiting enslavement of Indians.[5] Though the provisions were revoked four years later, they are a barometer of the strength of the Spanish "Indian rights" movement of the time.

Its greatest champion, former *encomendero* fray Bartolomé de las Casas, forcefully and repeatedly made the case for more humane treatment of Native Americans before the royal court. In 1542, as the Coronado expedition was returning from its disappointing reconnaissance of Tierra Nueva, las Casas read before the king a draft of his virulent indictment of Spanish activities in the New World, *Brevísima Relación de la Destrucción de las Indias, A Very Brief Account of the Destruction of the Indies*. Hard on the heels of that reading, on November 20, 1542, the king issued the "Leyes y ordenanzas nuevamente hechas por su Magestad para la gobernación de las Indias y buen tratamiento y conservación de los Indios," commonly called the New Laws. This lengthy set of ordinances sought to end the encomienda system and charged government officials and the citizenry at large to take special and perpetual care to preserve and protect the Indians of the Americas. The royal courts were enjoined to "enquire continually into the excesses and ill-treatment which are or shall be done to them by governors or private persons."[6]

On the thirteenth of March 1544 a copy of the New Laws was presented before the audiencia in Mexico City. In attendance were Viceroy Antonio de Mendoza and oidores of the court Francisco Ceynos and Lorenzo de Tejada, as well as the *visitador general* Francisco Tello de Sandoval. The laws were then read aloud in public in Mexico City eleven days later.[7]

The Residencia, Visita, and Pesquisa Traditions

The sixteenth-century Spanish royal bureaucracy provided several sometimes redundant means by which malfeasance and criminality of government functionaries and common subjects could be ferreted out and punished. Civil and ecclesiastical courts abounded; virtually every governing body, from town council (*cabildo*) to provincial court (audiencia), from royal council to the king himself, exercised some form of judicial and prosecutorial authority. Government officials were subjected to administrative review (*residencia*) as a matter of course at the end of their terms of office. At any time the king could authorize a special review (visita) of the performance of officials in a region or even of entire units of government. In the face of specific charges or allegations, he might also mandate a special judicial investigation (pesquisa). Judicial jurisdictions commonly overlapped or were amorphous. Complaints and appeals could be raised at almost any level; direct access to the king was always a possibility. As Peter Bakewell has written recently:

> Officials at all levels knew, indeed, that they were expected to spy on their fellows, and should expect to be spied on. Private citizens of the colonies were quick, naturally enough, to turn this inbuilt rivalry to their own ends by allying themselves in various ways with the dominant bureaucrats of a particular moment, while sending back to Spain criticisms of others.[8]

Despite this complex web of oversight, it was rare for sixteenth-century expeditions of conquest and reconnaissance to be subjected to review or investigation, except when aspects of an expedition were examined as part of a broader inquiry into discharge of duties by an official. Thus, the pesquisa that was launched to look into the Coronado expedition's treatment of Indians was highly unusual. This is not to say that abuse of and excessive violence against American natives went unprosecuted. Indeed, besides Vázquez de Coronado, two other governors closely associated with stories of wealth to the north of Nueva España, Nuño Beltrán de Guzmán and Álvar Núñez Cabeza de Vaca, both underwent lengthy judicial proceedings because of their alleged mistreatment of Indians. Both also lost their governorships in the process. In 1537 Guzmán was absolved by the investigating judge Juan Álvarez de Castañeda of failing to see to it that Indians were well treated and failing to punish those who mistreated them.[9] This was a gross misjudgment in light of the enslavement and death of hundreds, if not thousands, of natives of Pánuco and Jalisco while Guzmán held sway there. Nine years later Cabeza de Vaca was charged with robbing, overworking, killing, and enslaving thousands of Indians in Paraguay. He was found guilty, unjustly (insists his recent biographer), and was released after eight years' imprisonment.[10]

An Investigation Is Launched

By late August or early September 1542 Vázquez de Coronado and what remained of the expedition to Tierra Nueva returned to Mexico City. A significant portion of the expeditionary force had disbanded en route, particularly at Culiacán and Compostela, as individuals picked up the threads of their former lives or pursued new possibilities. Since many, perhaps the majority, of those who went on the expedition had spent their own money and borrowed other funds to equip and outfit themselves, there was much discontent about its lack of success. And there were some, at least, who attributed the expedition's disappointing results to mistreatment of the native peoples of Tierra Nueva.

Formal complaints about treatment of Indians by the expedition were registered with the king and the Council of the Indies in the form of letters that must have been on board the earliest sailings for Spain after return of the expedition. It is even possible that accusations were dispatched before Vázquez de Coronado's return, since fray Marcos de Niza, Juan de Zaldívar, Juan Gallego, and survivors of the native uprising at San Gerónimo (to mention only those who are known) had returned south during the course of the expedition and could have made denunciations themselves or provided information to those who did make them. Another possible complainant against the expedition was fray Juan de Zamárraga, the bishop of Mexico, whose smuggled report to the king had precipitated the earlier investigation of Nuño Beltrán de Guzmán's treatment of Indians.[11]

None of the letters of denunciation is known to survive, so their substance can only be inferred from the questions asked of the first witness in the pesquisa or investigation that resulted. Francisca de Hozes, the first witness called, was asked specifically only about dogs having been set on Indians, about the execution of the expedition's guide El Turco, and about whether outrages committed against natives led to the uprising at San Gerónimo; presumably these are the items of misconduct denounced in the complaints. No other abuses were probed in the brief series of questions Francisca de Hozes was asked. Since the uprising at San Gerónimo did not occur until very late in 1541 or early 1542, the accusations are unlikely to have been made before then.

By the time denunciations of the expedition to Tierra Nueva reached Spain preparations were well underway for publication of the New Laws. This series of ordinances was promulgated with the intention of curbing and curtailing what was seen as frequent abuse and unjust treatment of the natives of the New World by Spaniards and their minions. Official publication occurred in May 1543. The climate in the royal court in Spain following formulation of the New Laws, with the ongoing sensational accusations leveled by fray Bartolomé de las Casas concerning inhumane behavior of conquistadores, was one in which fresh evidence of abuse of New World natives was taken very seriously.[12] Denunciations of the expedition to Tierra Nueva may have forcefully portrayed its behavior as flagrantly and wantonly brutal.

Whatever the case, the king and Council of the Indies were disturbed enough by what they read and heard about the expedition that in fall 1543 they ordered an investigation, *pesquisa secreta*, of its conduct. They had just acceded to years of pressure from Hernán Cortés by ordering a visita of the entire viceregal government of Nueva España. Among the many charges leveled against Antonio de Mendoza and his officials by Cortés was that they had often extorted valuable goods from Indians and used violence against them.[13] It may have seemed only natural, therefore, to submit the expedition to Tierra Nueva to the same sort of scrutiny, since it was, in fact, the viceroy's expedition, assigned to the direction of his protege.[14]

In a pesquisa secreta the *juez pesquisador* or investigating judge made public announcement of the beginning of the investigation and summoned witnesses to appear before him to answer his questions. The testimony of each witness in such investigations was to taken in closed session and kept secret from the other witnesses. Because of the potential for abuse of such secrecy by judges, pesquisas secretas were permitted only by express commission of the king, as was the case here.[15]

Rather than entrusting conduct of the pesquisa secreta of the expedition to Francisco Tello de Sandoval, the member of the Council of the Indies who had been appointed visitador general or administrative review judge of Nueva España, the king and council assigned responsibility for calling and examining witnesses in the case to licenciado Lorenzo de Tejada.[16] His commission as both judge of the investigation of the expedition and judge of the simultaneous residencia of the officials of Nueva Galicia was signed September 7, 1543.

Lorenzo de Tejada was one of the four oidores (judges) of the audiencia of Nueva España during Antonio de Mendoza's administration as viceroy. He served in that capacity from 1537–1552, at age 35 replacing Vasco de Quiroga who had been named bishop of Michoacán.[17] Tejada was a native of Santo Domingo de la Calzada in La Rioja, Spain.[18]

Eight years after his appointment as investigating judge, in the face of repeated conflict with the second viceroy of Nueva España Luis de Velasco, Tejada left the New World and took up residence in Granada, a city and province in Spain that would be administered for more than a hundred years by members of the Mendoza family. The former oidor was a *vecino* there by 1559.[19] Tejada's return to Spain in 1552 was lamented by many, though others had resented his energetic investment and building activities while oidor.[20] He employed Indians from Coyoacán, Xalataco, Xochimilco, Ecapuzalco, Tenango, Amecameca, Santiago, Mexicalcingo, Atlacubaya, Tacuba, Culiacán, Santa Fe, Tlalmanalco, Texcoco, and Otumba—hundreds at a time—in building a very large stone house; digging, clearing, and covering *acequias*; building fences of stone, adobe, and sod; killing caterpillars and locusts in his fields and vineyards; carrying vigas, bricks, lime, and *tezontle* building stone; baking bread; building a road; and supplying beds. He was later accused of having overworked and underpaid or failed to pay the Indian laborers. Other citizens of Mexico City complained that Tejada employed so many Indian laborers, carpenters, and bricklayers that others could not obtain them. And he was accused, along with his henchmen, of ill treatment of Indians working on his estate, where many died and became ill.[21] Tejada was found innocent of most of these charges, although he was fined for several cases of underpaying wages.

He complained bitterly about restrictions placed on the economic activity of audiencia officials, saying that the oidores of Nueva España ought to be allowed to have estates and grain fields like other oidores and *consejeros*, otherwise they had to live in poverty on their salaries only.[22] He made these complaints despite having been conceded in 1540 by royal cédula the right to establish a *huerta* and *arboleda* and to plant grapevines and wheat fields in Chalco and Tlacubaya.[23]

According to Arthur Aiton, Tejada was the "first great real estate promoter in the New World."[24] And certainly his acquisition of property was prodigious. A recent study by Ethelia Ruiz Medrano has detailed Tejada's ownership of at least 19 separate agricultural properties, totaling some 600 hectáreas, mostly near Tacuba. He also took control of three properties in Tlalmanalco, which he used in forced exchange with indigenous communities for land in the immediate vicinity of Mexico City, an activity which on appeal to Viceroy Mendoza was upheld as legitimate.[25] It is interesting that during 1543 and 1544, at about the time of Tejada's conduct of the investigation of the Coronado expedition, Juan de Contreras, a de oficio witness in the pesquisa, served as interpreter for Tejada in his employment of Indians from Otumba, Tacuba, and Cuautitlán to work his agricultural properties. During the same period, Pedro de Requena, *escribano* for the 1544 investigation, also served as scribe in drawing up Indian employment agreements for Tejada. The principal produce of the oidor's agricultural activities, grapes and wheat, found ready markets in stores owned by Tejada in Mexico City.[26] Importantly, Tejada served as agent for Viceroy Mendoza in the purchase of *estancias* in 1541. So also did Hernán Pérez de Bocanegra, who later established multiple links with the Vázquez de Coronado family through the marriage of three of his sons to three daughters of the former captain general.[27]

FIGURE 5.
Scribe, after *Arte Subtilissima* by Juan de Yciar, 1550

In May 1544 Tejada wrote that his commission to serve as judge of the investigation of the Coronado expedition had arrived with the same fleet that brought the visitador general Tello de Sandoval. Subsequently, the two had rancorous disputes and fought openly. As Tejada himself told it, at one meeting of the audiencia the visitador "rose from his seat, very angry with me, and, extending his arm across the table, poked his fingers in my eyes, saying now maybe I could see why he was voting to have me bound, because he was the visitador." Tejada accused Tello de Sandoval of seeking out damaging witnesses who were enemies of his and of working to take him prisoner and send him to Spain. Tejada claimed the visitador desired to destroy the viceroy and throw him out of office. As a result, according to Tejada, Nueva España was split into contending factions.[28]

Because of the impending visita by Tello de Sandoval and because of his own illness, Tejada delayed leaving for Nueva Galicia to take testimony about the expedition's treatment of Indians. Nevertheless, he managed to examine nine witnesses in the case while still in Mexico City. As it turned out, he left the seat of the audiencia July 19, 1544, and examined his first witness in Guadalajara, Melchior Pérez, on August 12.[29] To do the work of the pesquisa, Tejada took with him to Guadalajara a scribe, an *alguacil* or constable, and an interpreter.[30]

The scribe whom Tejada chose to record the investigation, as well as the residencia of officials of Nueva Galicia, was 27-year-old Pedro de Requena, a scribe of the audiencia working in the office of the chief scribe, Antonio de Turcios. Requena, a native of the *villa* of Requena in Valencia was also living in Turcios's home, along with two other scribes.[31] By 1556 he was a vecino of Mexico City and was still serving as a scribe of the audiencia as late as 1558.[32] Long after the end of Antonio de Mendoza's term as viceroy in 1550, Requena served in the staff of the audiencia and was described in 1587 as having held a commission as judge of accounts or *juez de cuentas* for many years. He had audited numerous accounts since at least 1567.[33]

Together, Tejada, Requena, and the unknown alguacil and interpreter, worked in Guadalajara for three and a half weeks securing testimony from five witnesses, including the captain general, Vázquez de Coronado. Nothing is known about relations between the leader of the expedition and the judge of the pesquisa prior to the investigation. Because Francisco Vázquez de Coronado was away from Mexico City most of the time between the new oidor's arrival in Nueva España in 1538[34] and the opening, in summer 1544, of Tejada's investigation of the expedition to Tierra Nueva, it is unlikely that the oidor had detailed personal acquaintance with the rising star of the viceroy's court before conducting the pesquisa. But afterwards they were very cordial.

When, in January 1548, *regidor* Ruy González of the cabildo of Mexico City registered a complaint about attendance of oidores and the president of the audiencia at the cabildo meetings, Vázquez de Coronado responded specifically in defense of Tejada, saying that he had not seen or heard that Tejada caused any injury or applied any force by coming to the cabildo, nor had he interfered with the regidores' right to speak and vote.[35] Given the connection of each man with the city of Granada, it is not unlikely that they or their families had known one another there or were even linked by kinship or career. This despite the fact that in 1544 Tejada found Vázquez de Coronado "more suitable to be governed than to govern anyone else."[36]

Tejada's relationships with parties to other cases in which he served as judge were not so amicable. In 1543 he conducted a residencia of all the interpreters of the audiencia. Those whom he charged with wrongdoing formed enmity against Tejada, especially Antonio Ortiz, Marcos Romero, and Francisco de Triana, all described disparagingly by Tejada as *moriscos* and Sevillanos. According to Tejada, they coached three Indians who, disguised as Spaniards, denounced Tejada to Tello de Sandoval.[37]

In addition to the charges that resulted from the investigation of the expedition against Vázquez de Coronado, Tejada also found the Vázquez de Coronado and Guzmán encomiendas in Nueva Galicia to be fraudulent. He blamed Vázquez de Coronado for lack of courts and justice in Nueva Galicia and called for establishment of a second audiencia there.[38] Four years later that suggestion became a reality with inauguration of the audiencia of Nueva Galicia in 1549 at Compostela.

As was standard practice in pesquisas or investigations, there was no interrogatorio (standard questionnaire) that guided Tejada's taking of testimony. And indeed, the set of questions recorded in the "proceso" and "información" varies from witness to witness, evolving during the course of the investigation, though there are many recurring questions. A total of 64 different questions was asked by Tejada during the investigation, but no more than half that number was ever asked of any single witness. The number of questions which witnesses were asked varied from a low of eight for Francisca de Hozes to a high of 32 for Vázquez de Coronado himself.[39] The questions followed closely the chronology of the expedition, dealing with possible cruelty to Indians first in Sonora, then in Cíbola, and successively in Tiguex and Cicuique and during the march to Quivira.

The substantive issues around which the investigation centered were seven: 1) Did the Spaniards provoke uprisings among the pueblos of Tiguex and Cicuique? 2) Did the Spaniards provoke the uprising at Señora? 3) Was the legal summons or requerimiento made to Indians before war was waged? 4) Why and by whose order were pueblos burned? 5) Why and by whose order was brutality committed against captive Indians? 6) Why and by whose order were dogs set on Bigotes and the cacique? and 7) Why and by whose order was El Turco killed? The central concern was to establish responsibility for these events and to ascertain whether the violence employed by the expedition in each case was justified within the context of sixteenth-century Spanish jurisprudence. Whether the events occurred was never at issue and no one denied that they had happened.

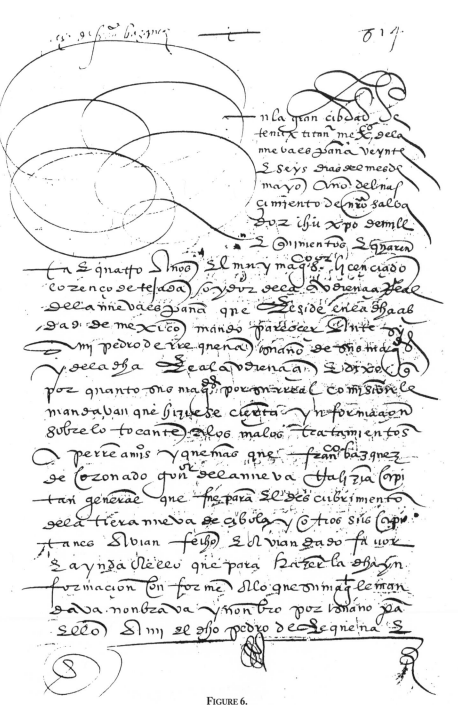

A TRANSLATION OF THE DOCUMENTARY RECORD

Investigation of Francisco Vázquez [de Coronado][40]

[1r] In the great city of Tenuxtitán-México in Nueva España on the twenty-sixth day of the month of May in the one thousand five hundred and forty-fourth year since the birth of our savior Jesus Christ, the very eminent lord licenciado Lorenzo de Tejada, judge of the Royal Audiencia of Nueva España, that has its seat in this city of Mexico, ordered that I, Pedro de Requena, their majesties' scribe and scribe of the aforesaid Royal Audiencia, appear before him. He stated that by royal commission, Their Majesties have ordered him to conduct an investigation concerning outrages, burnings, and the setting on of dogs committed by Francisco Vázquez de Coronado, governor of Nueva Galicia and former captain general for exploration of the tierra nueva of Cíbola, and his captains, who aided and assisted in that discovery. In order to conduct this investigation in conformance with what his majesty ordered, licenciado Tejada has named me, Pedro de Requena as the scribe for it, [1v] as well as for the residencia that must be conducted in Nueva Galicia relative to [Vázquez de Coronado] and the other officials there. And he signed, inscribing his customary sign and rubric.

licenciado Tejada
Witnesses: Juan de Arana
Francisco Díaz

Then the lord licenciado delivered to me a decree from His Majesty directing him to conduct the aforesaid investigation. It is written on paper stamped with the royal seal and signed by Prince Felipe, our lord, and the members of his Royal Council of the Indies. It is countersigned by Juan de Sámano, the Council's secretary, and ratified by other officials. The sum and substance of the decree is as follows.

Tejada's Commission

Don Carlos, by divine favor emperor and always-revered king of Germany; doña Juana, his mother, and don Carlos, by the same divine grace sovereigns of Castilla, León, Aragón, the two Sicilies, Jerusalem, Navarra, Granada, Toledo, Valencia, Galicia, [2r] Majorca, Sevilla, Sardinia, Córdoba, Corsica, Murcia, Jaén, the Algarves, Algeciras, Gibraltar, the Canary Islands, the Indies, and the islands and mainland of the Ocean Sea; counts of Barcelona; lords of Vizcaya and Molina; dukes of Athens and Neopatria; counts of Flanders and Tirol, etc.

Health and goodwill to you, licenciado Tejada, judge of our Royal Audiencia of Nueva España. Know that we have been informed that during the expedition that Francisco Vázquez de Coronado made to the province of Cíbola, he and the Spaniards who went with him committed great cruelties against the natives of the lands through which they passed, both in going and returning. It is said that they killed a large number of them and did other unjust things in disservice to us and God our lord.

Because we want to mete out punishment for this and because we have confidence in your uprightness, loyalty, and integrity and that you are a person who will perform well, faithfully, and diligently what we may entrust to you and direct you to do, it was agreed, with approval of the members of our Council of the Indies, that we should commend and entrust this to you, [2v] as with this letter we do commend and entrust it to you. We order you to conduct an investigation, in the province of Nueva Galicia and the city of Mexico and any other place you consider appropriate, and to find out how and in what manner what has been reported transpired. And you are to determine what cruelty, robberies, and noteworthy injustices were committed by Francisco Vázquez and the Spaniards who were with him going to and returning from the province of Cíbola. And you are to learn who and which persons perpetrated and committed them, by whose order they were done, and who provided advice, aid, and assistance.

When you have conducted the investigation and through it have learned the truth about who is guilty, you will take their persons into custody and, as prisoners, you will hear their defenses and refutations. When you have heard them, you will transmit the proceedings, including their defenses, to our Royal Audiencia of Nueva España together with the record of the investigation you made. This is so that everything can be considered there and justice can be done. You may conduct the investigation wherever you are, be it in the province of Nueva Galicia (to which we are directing that you go as judge of its residencia) [3r] or any other place you are. As was said, you will send the investigation record to our president and judges [of the audiencia], whom we are ordering to accept those you find guilty, together with the record of the investigation, the legal action you institute against them, and their defenses.

They will review what you send and proceed against those individuals they find guilty, in accordance with the laws and statutes of those kingdoms and the ordinances and decrees issued by the Catholic Sovereigns, such as those of the Emperor, my lord, for the benevolent treatment of Indians. And we order those parties whom this commission concerns and to whom it refers, as well as any others of whom you intend to make inquiry so as to learn the truth regarding this matter, to come and appear before you in response to your call and summons and to testify and make their statements within the time limits and under the penalties you may impose on them or may order imposed. By this decree we impose those same penalties and consider them imposed. You may carry out those penalties against those who refuse and do not comply.

If, in order to perform and complete what we order, you need aid and support, by this decree [3v] we order all councils and courts, and all councilmen, gentlemen, squires, officials, and high lords of all the cities, villages, and settled places in the province of Nueva Galicia and in the other parts of Nueva España to give it to you and render it under the penalties you may impose on them. By this decree we impose those penalties and consider the sentence imposed and pronounced against those who do otherwise than as we order. In order that you may carry out punishment against their persons and property and do everything else pertaining to this case, we concede to you full power with all its concomitants, adjuncts, and additional authority.

Issued in Valladolid on the seventh day of the month of September, one thousand five hundred and forty-three.

I, the prince[41]
Juan de Sámano,
Secretary of the Imperial and Catholic Majesties
 I have drafted the commission by your highness's order.

Countersigned, Uchoa de Loyando, on behalf of Chancellor Blas de
Saavedra
licenciado Gutierre Velázquez
licenciado Salmerón

Letter from Tejada to the Prince, May 24, 1544[42]

[1r]
Very exalted and very powerful lord,
 With the ships in which licenciado Tello de Sandoval, visitador of this
royal audiencia, came I received the dispatches concerning Nueva Galicia, to
which your highness ordered me sent. Those messages are: a letter from your
highness by which I am ordered to go to the province of Nueva Galicia to
conduct a residencia of Francisco Vázquez de Coronado and his lieutenants
and officials and the other justices and to make an investigation into the brutality committed during the expedition to and reconnaissance of Tierra
Nueva; the commission [granting authority] to conduct the residencia;
another cédula by which are revoked and annulled those transfers of Indians
that were made by methods that contravened the ordinances, together with
new charges against the persons who are ordered stripped of [encomiendas]
that are to be placed under royal jurisdiction; [and] the aforesaid ordinances
with another cédula according to which they are to be proclaimed and published in all the towns of that province.
 Also, with the caravel that arrived in port during this month of May I
received another directive by which [it is ordered] that no Indians, either free
or slave, may be transported by sea from one province to another and a cédula
ordering that blasphemies be punished in conformance with the laws of the
realm, notwithstanding any others that may have been promulgated to the
contrary.

I would have departed immediately in order to comply with what Your Highness orders me, but for the visita and residencia that is being conducted of us [the officials of the audiencia]. That is because it seemed to me that I should first give account of myself and afterwards take that of others. Furthermore, it seemed to me that Your Highness would not be served by my being absent at such a time. And it seemed so, too, to your viceroy, with whom I communicated about this. In addition, I was ill with a high fever and pains in my side, for which they bled me six times. That left me so incapacitated that for many days I did not deal with business.

Upon recuperating, I will depart, which, if it pleases God, will be the thirtieth of June or a week later. Before I leave, I will conduct in this city what investigation I can concerning [1v] the brutality and will make a report to Your Highness both of what is found during it and of the state in which that province is. Despite the short amount of time that has been designated [for this work], it is possible to make an accurate [determination].

Since, for promptness and efficiency of this work, it would be necessary that I take with me a scribe, an alguacil, and an interpreter, in consultation with your viceroy and the audiencia, a salary of one *peso de oro común* per day has been designated for each one of them.

May God protect Your Highness's royal person with increase of grander kingdoms and dominions. From Mexico City, the twenty-fourth of May, 1544, Your Highness's least servant, who kisses your royal feet and hands.

licenciado Tejada [rubric]

[2r] [blank]

[2v] He would respond.

To His Highness.

From licenciado Tejada, the twenty-fourth of May, 1544.

Reviewed. The response should be that he promptly send the residencia record and the report on the state of the land.

Item: salary for the officials, 2,000.

Item: Letter to the viceroy and audiencia. I include the chapter of the law which provides that what has been given to *conquistadores* and their children may be revoked by the governor and officials, in keeping with their maintenance.

To the very exalted and very powerful lord the Prince, our lord.

[3v cont'd][43] By virtue of the decree from his majesty included here, lord licenciado Tejada [4r] conducted the following investigation before me, as scribe.

The Record of the Investigation

Oaths of the Witnesses

In the great city of Tenuxtitán-México in Nueva España on the twenty-seventh day of the month of May, one thousand five hundred and forty-four, lord licenciado Tejada, judge of His Majesty's Royal Audiencia of Nueva España, by virtue of His Majesty's commission (granted so that he might conduct an investigation of what was done by Francisco Vázquez de Coronado, governor of Nueva Galicia, in the course of crossing and exploring the tierra nueva of Cíbola), ordered Francisca de Hozes, wife of Alonso Sánchez (a vecino or citizen of this city of Mexico), to appear before him. He received her oath to tell the truth about everything that she might know and be asked in this case, by God and Santa María and a representation of the cross (on which she placed her right hand) and the words of the Holy Gospels (wherever they are most fully written), fearing God and looking after her [4v] conscience and soul, as a good Christian. She is brought as a witness in this case. If she tells the truth, God our lord will help her. If, on the contrary, she replies to what she is asked like a bad Christian, then she has committed perjury and knowingly sworn by God's holy name in vain. At the conclusion of the oath she said, "Yes, I swear, amen." And she promised to tell and declare the truth about everything she might know in this case.

Afterwards, in the same city and on the same day, month, and year, lord licenciado Tejada ordered that Alonso Sánchez, a citizen of this city, appear before him for this investigation. He received his oath in legal form, which he made just as and in the same manner and form as did the first witness. At the conclusion of the oath he said, "Yes, I swear, amen." And he promised to tell the truth.

Subsequently, in the same city on the twenty-ninth day of the month of [5r] May, one thousand five hundred and forty-four, lord licenciado Tejada ordered that Juan de Paradinas, a tailor, appear before him for this investigation. He received his oath in legal form, which he made just as and in the same manner and form as did the first witness. At the conclusion of the oath he said, "Yes, I swear, amen."

After that, in the same city on the thirty-first day of the same month and year, lord licenciado Tejada ordered that Domingo Martín, a vecino of this city, appear before him for this investigation. He received his oath in legal form, which he made. At the conclusion of the oath he said, "Yes, I swear, amen."

Afterwards, in the same city on the fourth day of June of the same year, the judge lord licenciado Tejada ordered that Juan de Contreras, an interpreter for the Royal Audiencia, appear before him for this investigation. He received his oath in legal form, which he made. At the conclusion [5v] of the oath he said, "Yes, I swear, amen."

Subsequently, on the sixth day of the aforesaid month of June, one thousand five hundred and forty-four, the judge lord licenciado Tejada ordered that Rodrigo Ximón, a citizen of this city of Mexico, appear before him for this investigation. He received his oath in legal form, which he made. At the conclusion of the oath he said, "Yes, I swear, amen."

Afterwards, in the city of Mexico on the seventh day of the same month and year, the judge lord licenciado Tejada ordered that Cristóbal de Escobar, vecino of this city of Mexico, appear before him. He received his oath in legal form, which he made. At the conclusion of the oath he said, "Yes, I swear, amen." And he promised to tell the truth.

Thereafter, in the city of Mexico on the ninth day of the month of June of the same year, the judge lord licenciado Tejada ordered that Juan Troyano appear before him. He lodges in the house of [6r] Bartolomé de Écija, an artilleryman and citizen of this city of Mexico. He received his oath in legal form, which he made. At the conclusion of the oath he said, "Yes, I swear, amen."

Subsequently, in the same city on the twenty-fifth day of the same month and year, the judge lord licenciado Tejada ordered that Rodrigo Frías appear before him. He is a resident of this city who lodges in the house of doña Francisca, widow of Francisco Flores. He received his oath in legal form, which he made. At the conclusion of the oath he said, "Yes, I swear, amen."

Afterwards, in the city of Guadalajara in Nueva Galicia in Nueva España on the twelfth day of the month of August, one thousand five hundred and forty-four, the judge lord licenciado Tejada ordered that Melchior Pérez, a citizen of this city, appear before him for this investigation. He received his oath in legal form, which he made. At [6v] the conclusion of the oath he said, "Yes, I swear, amen."

Witnesses: Cristóbal de Ocanete[44] and Juan de Zaldívar

A TRANSCRIPT OF THE
DOCUMENTARY RECORD

[fol. 1r]⁴⁵

814

El proçeso de Francisco Vazquez

En la gran çiUDaD De / tenuxtitan meXico de la / nueva esPaña veynte / E
seys dias del mes de / mayo Año del naS- / cimiento de nuestro salva- / dor
Jesu cristo de mill / E quinientos E quaren- / Ta E quatro Años El muy mag-
nifico señor liçençiado / lorenço de tejada oydor de la aUdiençia Real / de la
nueVa esPaña que Reside en la dicha çiU- / dad de meXico mando paresçer
Ante sy / A mi pedro de rrequena escrivano de sus magestades / Y de la dicha
Real aUdiençia E dixo que / por quanto sus magestades por su rreal comision
le / mandaban que hiziese çierta ynformaçion / sobre lo tocante A los malostratamientos / Aperreamientos y quemas que Francisco Vazquez / de Coronado governador de la nueva Galizia Capi- / tan general que fue para El
descubrimiento / de la tierra nueVa de çibola y otros sus Capi- / tanes que
hAbian (F)hecho E hAbian dado favor / E ayuda A ello que para hazer la
dicha yn- / Formaçion Conforme A lo que su magestad le man- / daba non-
braba y nonbro por escrivano para / Ello A mi El dicho pedro de Requena E

[fol. lv]
Ansimismo para la ResiDençia / que ansimismo se ha de tomar en la dicha /
nueva Galizia A el y a los otros ofiçiales / que en ella han sido y lo senalo con la
Ru- / briCa y señal que suele hazer testigos juan de / Aranda y Francisco diaz

E luego El dicho señor liçençiado entre- / go A mi el dicho pedro de rrequena
Una / proVision de su magestad escri(p)ta en papel E / sellada Con su rreal
sello y firmada / del prinçipe don Felipe nuestro señor y de los / del su rreal
conseJo de yndias y Refren- / dada de joan de samano su secretario E librada

/ de otros ofiçiales para hazer la dicha / ynformaçion su tenor de la qual dicha pro- / Vision es este que se sygue

{La provision para / tejada}
Don carlos por la divina clemençia enpe- / Rador senper Augusto Rey de / alemañia dona Juana su madre / Y el mismo don carlos por la mesma graciA / Reyes de castilla de leon de Aragon de / las doSS seçillias de Jherusalen de naVarra / de Granada de toledo de valencia de galizia / [no number]

[fol. 2r]
815
De mallorcas De seVilla De çerdena De cor- / dova de corçega de murçia de jaen de los al- / garves de aljeziras de gibraltar de las yslas / de Canaria de las yndias yslas E tierra fir- / me del mar oçeano Condes de barçelona senores / de Vizcaya E de molina duques de Atenas / e de neopatria condes de flandes E de tirol / {mark} / E *etcera* A vos El liçençiado Tejada oydor de la / nuestra audiençia Real de la nueVa espana sa- / lud E graçia sepades que nos somos ynforma- / doSS que en la jornada que francisco Vazquez / de Cor(a)onado hizo A la provinçia de çibola / ansi a la yda como A la Vuelta El y los / espanoles que con el fueron hizieron gran- / des crueldades a los naturales de las tierras / por donde pasaron matando Gran numero / de ellos E haziendo otras cosas E ynjustiçias / en desserViçio de dios nuestro señor E nuestro E quirien- / do proveer En el castigo de ello Visto por / los del nuestro consejo de las yndias Confiando / de Vuestra Rectitud E fidilidad E Conçiençia E / que soys tal persona que bien E fiel E di- / ligentemente hareys lo que por nos Vos / Fuere mandado E Cometido fue ACordado / que os lo debiamos enComendar y Cometer

[fol. 2v]
Como por la presente Vos lo enco- / mendamos y Cometemos por que vos man- / damos que hayays ynformaçion E se- / pays Ansi en la proVinçia de galizia Como / en la çiUdad de meXico y en otras quales- / quier partes que Vieredes que ConViene como / y de que manera lo susodicho ha pasado y

pasa / E que crueldad*es* E ynjustiÇias notables E / Robos hizieron E
Cometieron El d*i*cho fran*ci*sco / Vazquez E los españoles que Con el fueron
/ y vinieron de la d*i*cha proVinçia de çibola / E quien E quales personas lo
hizieron y Co- / metieron E por cuyo mandado E quien / les dio para Ello
consejo favor E ayuda / E la d*i*cha ynformaçion *h*Avida E la verdad / sabida
A los que por ella (f)*h*allared*es* CulpadoS / les prendes los querpos E asi
presos oygays / sus desCulpas y descargos E oydos los rremi- / Tireys A la
n*u*es*t*ra aUdiençia Real de la d*i*cha nueva / esPaña Juntamente con la ynformaçion que / Vos hiziered*es* E Con los d*e*sCargos que ellos dieren / Para que
en ella Se Vea todo y se haga jus- / Tiçia la qual ynformaçion hareys don- /
dequiera que vos hallaredes Ansi en la / d*i*cha proVinçia de galizia Adonde os
man- / damos yr por n*u*es*t*ro juez de Residençia / [no number]

[fol. 3r]
816
De *e*lla Como en otra qualquier p*a*rte / donde os hallared*es* la qual Remitireys
como / d*i*cho es al d*i*cho n*u*es*t*ro presidente E oydores A / los mandamos que
rresçiban los Culpados / que ansi Vos les rremitired*es* E la ynforma- / Çion E
proçeso que Contra ellos *h*obiered*es* / hecho juntamente con sus d*e*sCargos y lo
/ Vean y proçedan contra ellos como halla- / Ren por d*e*rec*h*o E leyes de *e*stos
Reynos e a las / (h)ordenanças E proVisiones dadas por los / Reyes Catolicos
Como por el enperador mi s*e*ñor / Para el buen tratami*en*to de los indios e
manda- / mos a las p*a*rt*e*s a quien lo susod*i*cho toca e a- / tane e a otras qualesquier personas / de quien entendiered*es* ser ynformado / e Saber la Verdad
çerca de lo susod*i*cho / que vengan y parezcan Ante Vos A / V*u*est*r*os lla-
mamyentos y enplazami*en*tos y digan / sus d*i*chos y dipusiçiones a los plazos E
so / las penas que vos de n*u*es*t*ra p*a*rte les pusie- / Red*es* o mandaredes poner las
q*u*a*l*es / nos por la presente les pone(n)*m*os y *h*abemos / por puestas E las podays
(h)exeCutar en / los que rrebeldes e ynobidientes fueren / e si para hazer E
Cumplir lo susod*i*cho favor / E Ayuda *h*o(f)*b*iered*es* menester Por la pres*en*te

[fol. 3v]
ManDamos A todos los *consejos* JusTiçias E / Regidores caballeros esCuderos

ofiçiales y / homes buenos de todas las çiUdades villas / E lugares Ansi de la dicha
proVinçia de galizia / como de las otras partes de la dicha nueva / españa que os
lo den E hagan dar so las penas / que vos de nuestra parte les pusieredes las quales
/ nos por la presente les ponemos e habemos / por puestas E por condenados En
ellas lo / Contrario haziendo que para ello y para / las (h)eXeCutar en sus personas E bienes / e Para lo demas a este caso conçerniente / Vos damos poder
Cumplido con todas sus / ynçidençias E dependençias Anexidades / E Conexi-
dades dada en Valladolid A siete / dias del mes de Septienbre de mill E /
quinientos E quarenta E tres Años yo / el prinçipe yo juan de samano secretario
/ de sus çesareas e catolicas magestades la (f)hize / escribir por mandado de su
alteza Refrendada / (J)uchoa de luyando por chanciller blas de / saaVedra El
liçençiado gutierre velazquez El liçenciado / salmeron

*Carta de Licenciado Tejada*⁴⁶

[fol. 1r]
muy alto y muy / poderoso señor
en los navios en que vino el licenciado tello de sandoVal visitador de esta rreal
/ audiencia rresevi los despachos de la nueVa galicia que Vuestra alteza me
mando yn- / Viar que son una carta de vuestra alteza por la qual me manda
Vaya a la proVincia de la nueVa / galicia a tomar rresidencia a francisco
Vazquez de coronado y a sus tenyentes e o- / fficiales y a las otras justicias e
haya informacion de las crueldades que se hicieron / en la Jornada e des-
cubrymiento de la tierra nueVa la comysyon para tomar la rresydencia / otra
çedula para que Se rreVoquen E anulen las enaJenaciones de indios que se
hobieren / hecho en fraude de las (h)ordenanças y nueVos capitulos por las
personas a quyen / se mandan quytar y ponerlos en su real cabeça las dichas
ordenanças con otra çe- / dula para que se pregonen y publiquen por todos los
pueblos de aquella proVynçia / ansimesmo Recibi en la caraVela que llego al
puerto este mes de mayo otra proVysyon / para que por mar nyngunos yndios
libres ny esclavos no se lleVen de Una proVyncia a o- / tra y una çedula para
que se castiguen las blasfemyas conforme a las leyes del rreyno / syn enbargo
de otras qualesquyer que en Contrario se hayan dado yo me partiera luego / a

cumplir lo que Vuestra alteza me manda salVo por la visita y Resydencia que
se nos toma porque / me parescio que debia primero dar my quenta y despues
tomar la aJena y porque crey que Vuestra al- / teça no seria servydo que a tal
tiempo me aUsentase y asi parescio a Vuestro Visorrey con / quyen lo comun-
yque y aun porque enferme de Una fiebre estrima y dolor de costado de / que
me sangraron seis Veçes y me dexo tan maltratado que a muchos dias que no
entiendo en ne- / gocios en convaleciendo me partire que placiendo a dios sera
en treinta de junyo o andada / Una semana de el y antes que partir tomare en
esta ÇiUdad la informacion que se pudiere haver sobre

[fol. 1v]
Las dichas crueldades y hare Relaçion a Vuestra alteza ansy de lo que en esto se
hallare / como del estado en que aquella proVyncia estuViere aUnque el tiempo
que se me señala es tan bre- / Ve que con dificultad se puede de haser cosa açer-
tada y porque habia neçesidad de lleVar / conmygo escribano alguazil y naguatato
para la expedicion y buen despacho de los negoci- / os con parescer de Vuestro
Visorey e audyencia se les señalo de salario Cada sendos pesos de o- / ro comun
por dia nuestro señor la real persona de Vuestra alteza guarde con acrecen- /
tamyento de mayores reynos y señoryos de mexico xxiiij de mayo 1544

de Vuestra alteça menor cryado / que sus reales pies y manos besa /
El licenciado / teJada [rubrica]

[fol. 2r]
[blank]

[fol. 2v]
Responda / a Su alteza / del liçenciado teJada de xxiiij de mayo de / 1544

Vista y que Se Responda / que Con brevedad enVie la Resydencia / y Relacion del estado de la tierra

ytem Salario a los officiales cada iiU

ytem *cart*a al virrey y aUdi*enci*a yn*ser*to el Capitulo / de la ley P*ar*a q*ue* de lo q*ue* se quitare a go*bernad*or y / o*fficiale*s se de a conquistadores e hijos / de *e*llos congrua Sustentaçion

Al muy alto y muy poderoso / señor El p*r*incipe n*ues*t*r*o señor

[fol. 3v cont'd][47]
Por Virtud de la qual di*c*ha proVision de / su mag*esta*d susoyncorporada El di*c*ho señor / liçençiado tejada por Ante mi el di*c*ho / iii

[fol. 4r]
817
es*cri*vano Hizo La ynformaçion / siguiente

{Juramentos / de t*esti*gos}
En la gran çiUdad de tenuxtitan / mexico de la nueva esPaña veyn- / te y siete dias del mes de mayo / de mill E quinientos E quarenta E qua- / Tro Años el senor liçençiado Tejada / oydor de la aUdiençia Real de su / mag*esta*d de la nueva esPaña por Vir- / tud de la Comision de su mag*esta*d A el dada / Para hazer la ynformaçion de lo que / Fran*cis*co Vazquez de Coronado Governa- / dor de la nueva galizia hizo en la / jornada y desqubrimi*ent*o de la tierra / nueva de çibola mando paresçer ante / sy A fran*cis*ca de hozes muger de Alonso san- / chez V*ezin*o de la di*c*ha çiUdad de meXico de la / qual Fue Resçibido juramento Por / dios e Por Santa maria E por Una / Senal de cruz en que puso su mano d*erec*ha / e por las palabras de los Santos eVan- / gelios doquier que mas largamente es- / Tan es*cri*(p)tos que como buena E fiel / *cristi*ana temiendo A dios E guardando

[fol. 4v]
Su Anima y Conçiençia Dira / *ver*dad de todo aquello que supiere E / le Fuere preguntado En este caso / de q*ue* es trayda para t*esti*go e que sy asi lo / hiziese dios n*ues*t*r*o se*ñ*or le Ayudase el co*n*t*r*ario / se lo demande Como A mala *cris*-*t*iana / q*ue* se perjura A sabiendas jurando el / Santo nonbre de dyos en vano la

qual / a la confusion E Conclusion del dicho jura- / mento dixo si juro e amen
e prometio / de dezir e aclarar la verdad de todo / lo que supiese En este caso /
E despues de lo susodicho en la dicha çiUdad / en este dicho dia e mes e año
susodicho / el dicho señor liçençiado Tejada Para la / dicha ynformaçion mando
Paresçer / ante si a alonso Sanchez vecino de la dicha çiU- / dad del qual fue
Resçibido juramento / en forma de derecho y el lo hizo segun e de la / Forma E
manera que el primero testigo e a la / confusion E Conclusion del dicho juramento / dixo si juro e amen e prometio de decir / Verdad / E despues de lo
susodicho en la dicha çiUdad / veynte E nueve dias del mes de / iiii

[fol. 5r]
818
mayo Del dicho Año De mill E quinientos / E quarenta E quatro Años el
dicho / senor liçençiado tejada Para la dicha / ynformaçion mando Paresçer
ante / sy a juan de paradinis Sastre del qual / Fue Resçibido juramento en
forma de / derecho y el lo hizo Segun E de la forma E / manera que el primero
testigo E a la confusion / e Conclusion del dicho juramento dixo si juro e amen
/ E despues de lo susodicho en la dicha çiUdad / Treynta e un dias del dicho
mes e año suso- / dicho el dicho senor liçençiado tejada Para la / dicha ynformaçion mando paresçer ante sy / a domingo martin vecino de la dicha çiUdad
de mexico / del qual fue Resçibido juramento en for- / ma de derecho y el lo
hizo E a la Confusion E / conclusion del dicho juramento dixo si juro E /
amen / E despues de lo susodicho en la dicha çiUdad / quatro dias de junio
del dicho año suso- / dicho el dicho senor liçençiado Tejada oydor / susodicho
para la dicha ynformaçion mando / Paresçer Ante sy A juan de Contreras /
ynt(r)erpret(r)e de esta Real aUdiençia del / qual fue Resçibido juramento en
forma de / derecho y el lo hizo e a la confusion E Conclu-

[fol. 5v]
Syon del dicHo juramento Dixo si juro / e amen / E despues de lo susodicho
en seys dias / del dicho mes de junio del dicho año / de myll e quinientos E
quarenta E quatro / años el dicho señor liçençiado tejada oydor / susodicho
Para la dicha ynformaçion mando / Paresçer Ante si A Rodrigo Ximon

Vecino de / la dicha çiUdad de mexico del qual fue Res- / Çibido juramento
En forma de derecho y el lo / hizo e a la Confusion E conclusion del dicho /
juramento diXo sy juro E Amen / E despues de lo susodicho en la dicha
çiUdad de / mexico siete dias del dicho mes e año / Susodicho el dicho Señor
liçençiado Tejada / oydor susodicho mando Paresçer Ante si / a cristobal de
escobar Vecino de la dicha çiUdad de / meXico del qual fue Resçibido juramento en for- / ma de derecho y el lo hizo e a la Confusion E con- / clusion
del dicho juramento dixo si juro e amen / e prometio de decir verdad / E
despues de lo susodicho en la dicha ÇiUdad / de meXico nueve dias del dicho
mes de / junio del dicho año el dicho senor liçençiado / tejada oydor susodicho
mando paresçer / ante sy A juan troyano que posa *en* Casa de / v

[fol. 6r]

819

bartolome de ezija artillero Vecino de la dicha / çiUdad de mexico del qual Fue
Resçibido / juramento en forma de derecho y el lo hizo / e a la Confusion E
Conclusion del dicho juramento / dixo si juro e amen / E despues de lo
susodicho en la dicha çiUdad / de mexico Veynte e çinco dias del dicho / mes
e año susodicho El dicho señor liçençiado / tejada oydor susodicho Para la
dicha ynforma- / Çion mando paresçer Ante sy A Rodrigo de frias / estante
en la dicha çiUdad que posa En las Ca- / sas de doña francisca muger que fue
de francisco flo- / rez del qual fue Resçibido juramento en for- / ma de derecho
y el lo hizo e a la Confision E conclu- / sion del dicho juramento dixo si juro
e amen / E despues de lo susodicho en la çiUdad de / guadalajara de esta nueva
galizia de la / nueva esPaña A doce dias del mes de / agosto de myll e
quinientos E quarenta E quatro / Años el dicho señor liçenciado tejada oydor
/ susodicho para la dicha ynformaçion mando / Paresçer Ante si a melchior
perez Vecino de la / dicha çiUdad del qual Fue Resçibido juram(i)ento / en
forma de derecho y el lo hizo e a la confision

[fol. 6v]

E conclusion del dicho juramento Dixo sy / juro e amen e prometio de decir
verdad testigos / cristobal de ocanete[48] e juan de çaldiVar

Chapter 4

The First de Oficio Witnesses, Francisca de Hozes and Alonso Sánchez

A Woman and Her Husband

On May 24, 1544 licenciado Tejada summoned Francisca de Hozes and her husband Alonso Sánchez to appear before him in the case. They had been among sixty or more disgruntled members of the expedition who had wanted to stay in Tierra Nueva even after Quivira proved to be a chimera. Vázquez de Coronado had threatened severe punishment if the group of would-be settlers did not abandon their petitions to stay in the north and instead return to Mexico City with the rest of the expedition, minus the priests who were intent on remaining to minister to the native peoples and over whom the captain general exercised little if any control. The couple probably remained vocally critical of the expedition's leader after their return to Mexico City and it is remotely possible that they complained in writing to the king.

The two were early settlers of Mexico City, having come from Spain in 1522 with at least some of their children. Suggestively, they were natives of Ciudad Real, home of Alonso de Estrada, eventually Vázquez de Coronado's father-in-law, who brought his family to Nueva España one year later to take up office as the royal treasurer.[1] At the time of their marriage Francisca brought a dowry of 100 pesos, not at all grand. Before coming to the New

World, Alonso had served the crown during the Comunero Revolt and in Italy, where it is conceivable he knew Juan Troyano, another witness in the 1544 pesquisa. Prior to the expedition, Sánchez worked as a shoemaker in Mexico City, with little financial success. At the time of the muster of the expedition at Compostela in February 1540, several witnesses testified to recognizing Sánchez as a vecino of Mexico City who had worked as a shoemaker, peddler, and merchant and was much in debt. It was said that it was indebtedness that led the couple, likely in their 40s, to expend what they had to take a chance on Tierra Nueva.[2]

Accompanying them to the north was a son old enough to be listed among the men-at-arms. Sánchez and Hozes had at least five other children and maybe as many as seven others.[3] They remained in Mexico City while their parents and brother pursued opportunities in the distant north. The story published by Herbert Bolton that Francisca gave birth to a child during the expedition is apocryphal, arising apparently from one of the many errors in Pedro de Requena's copy of the 1544 investigation record.[4]

Despite their reported poverty, Sánchez, Hozes, and their son took with them seven horses and two or more coats of mail, in addition to native arms and armor, considerably more than the average member of the expedition. In fact, this was a large enough remuda of horses that it was matched or exceeded by only four individuals who were not captains of companies, and even some of the captains had fewer horses.[5] This suggests that the reports of poverty of Alonso Sánchez and Francisca Hozes were somewhat exaggerated.

After their return to Mexico City with the expedition, they fared somewhat better than before, financially. Alonso died by 1553, leaving an estate of 1,521 pesos, 4 *tomines*, consisting in part of 7 *solares* or house lots and one half a *caballería* or farm in Puebla, 2 solares in Mexico City, and 2 black slaves. At the time of his death, Sánchez was owed a substantial sum of 250 pesos by an interpreter for the audiencia. The family's improved economic state indicates that the testimony the husband and wife gave in 1544 did not hurt them. They remained connected with several members of the expedition in Mexico City, including Melchior Pérez, one of the other de oficio witnesses in the 1544 investigation, who consistently defended the actions of the expedition's leader.[6]

Since Francisca de Hozes was the first witness called in the pesquisa, she was asked only very broad questions and a relatively small number of those, only eight. Despite Herbert Bolton's characterization of her as "talkative" and "sharp-tongued,"[7] Francisca actually had very little to say in her testimony and volunteered little information beyond what she was asked. Hers is, after her husband's, the second shortest testimony of the fourteen de oficio witnesses in the case. And Alonso's testimony is only marginally shorter. She provided very weak, hearsay testimony except when talking about treatment of the Spaniards who wanted to stay in Tierra Nueva. The only real accusation she made against Vázquez de Coronado concerned his heavy-handed treatment of those Spaniards. She even made one direct statement excusing Vázquez de Coronado in the death of El Turco by saying that he always defended the guide. She provided Tejada little that would have been new to him. Like her husband, she was absent from many of the events investigated, being always with the main body of the expedition and thus missing the capture of Cíbola, the death of El Turco, and the uprising at San Gerónimo.

Like his wife, Alonso Sánchez made mention of the burning and stabbing of captive Indians by expedition members, which became a subject about which several of the subsequent witnesses were questioned. But he placed no blame for the killings. He was also the first to specifically mention requisition of clothing and food from the Pueblos as a cause of the uprising in 1540–1541. The only specific individuals he singled out as culpable in any of the incidents about which he was questioned were Martín de Estepa, Diego de Alcaraz, and, weakly, Pedro de Tovar. Just as his wife did, he said that Vázquez de Coronado always defended El Turco and refused repeatedly to believe that he had done anything deserving capital punishment.

In sum, the testimony of Francisca de Hozes and Alonso Sánchez, though the least exculpatory of all the testimony in regard to Vázquez de Coronado and the expedition as whole, can hardly be regarded as powerful eyewitness indictments. In sixteenth-century Spanish legal proceedings hearsay evidence carried more weight than it is accorded in modern American jurisprudence. Nevertheless, the Hozes and Sánchez testimony was very lightweight, almost devoid of accusations against individuals and references to particular informants. Nor did either of them claim firsthand knowledge of any of the events being scrutinized by Tejada, except their own harsh treatment by the captain general when they persisted in wanting to settle Tierra Nueva. Their anger on that one point is understandable, since they, like most participants in the expedition had personally staked a great deal on its outcome.

Though neither Hozes nor Sánchez provided eyewitness testimony damaging personally to the captain general, they confirmed that members of the expedition, mostly unnamed, had frequently engaged in brutal and abusive acts against native peoples. According to Sánchez, dogs had been set on many Indians, including Bigotes and the cacique from Cicuique. Both husband and wife blamed the uprisings in Tiguex and Corazones on the expedition's extortion and thievery of clothing and food and seizure and rape of native women. Hozes and her husband both told of the seemingly gratuitous burning of pueblos and their residents, even after fighting had ended. Despite their unwillingness or inability to implicate Vázquez de Coronado in these brutal deeds, they made blanket accusations against the expedition as a whole. Additionally, Sánchez testified that a footman named Martín de Estepa committed brutality and set dogs on Indians. This allegation was not explored further by Tejada during the investigation.

FIGURE 7.
Dog set on Indian captive, after *Proceso de residencia contra Pedro de Alvarado*, ed.
José Fernando Ramírez, 1847

A TRANSLATION
OF THE TESTIMONY

First de Oficio Witness (Francisca de Hozes)[8]

[6v cont'd] Francisca de Hozes, wife of Alonso Sánchez, a citizen of the city of Mexico, accepted as a witness for this investigation, having given her oath in the presence of lord licenciado Tejada and having promised to tell the truth, was asked the following questions.

{1} She was asked whether she knows Francisco Vázquez de Coronado, don Diego de Guevara, don Tristán de Arellano, don García López de Cárdenas, the councilman of Sevilla Diego López , Hernando de Alvarado, and the other captains who went to reconnoiter and subjugate the province of Cíbola, Cicuique, and Tiguex and whether she was present during the subjugation and reconnaissance. She answered that she knows all of those mentioned in this question, by appearance, voice, and conversation that she has had with them for about the last five years. She was present during the subjugation and reconnaissance of all that land, [7r] from when they entered it until they returned to this city of Mexico. Except that she was not at the occupation of Cíbola because she and her husband, along with other captains and individuals, remained behind for a little while, and when they arrived the pueblo was occupied and at peace.

{2} Since she states and declares that she was present during the expedition of subjugation and exploration of those provinces and Tierra Nueva from the beginning until its return, [the witness] was asked what cruelties she witnessed and knows that Francisco Vázquez and the other captains committed, either on their own or by his order, in those provinces and against the Indians native there, especially in Tiguex and Cicuique. How and in what manner did the death of the Indian who guided them, called Turco, transpire? Also, how did it come about that dogs were set on the Indian known as Bigotes and on the cacique and interpreter from Cicuique? And for what cause and reason did Francisco Vázquez order them to be killed and set upon by dogs? Furthermore, what damage ensued from having committed those cruelties, or ordering them to be committed?

She replied that what she knows about what she is asked is that when Francisco Vázquez [7v] sent Hernando de Alvarado to make a reconnaissance, he returned to the camp and brought with him an Indian whom they called El Turco. He told about a good land and great wealth. Also, he said that the cacique and other persons from Cicuique said the same and knew it to be so because they had gone with him to that land and had brought back and still possessed a gold bracelet and other valuable jewelry. When that was known Francisco Vázquez sent [someone] to summon the cacique from Cicuique, which was at peace. He also summoned the Indian called Bigotes, who was in that same province. Because they did not corroborate what El Turco was saying and did not say what he said about the bracelet and jewelry and did not surrender them to Francisco Vázquez and other captains whom she does not remember, they set dogs on the cacique and Bigotes by [the general's] order.

After those two had healed and recovered their health, they spoke with and informed others from the province of Cicuique, and those from Tiguex, where the camp was situated. [8r] They told about the brutality and outrages that had been committed. Because their wives, daughters, and other things that the Indians had in their houses were taken by force and against their will, the people of the provinces of Cicuique and Tiguex rose up and killed Spaniards and all the horses they found in the countryside, as well as mules, and beasts of burden that carried their provisions.

She knows and saw that after the pueblos had been subjugated and occupied Francisco Vázquez ordered them burned and they were burned, as were many Indians who were tied to posts; and they set dogs on others. All of this was after the pueblos had been overpowered and entered, as she has said and testified. Before dogs were set on the cacique and the Indian Bigotes the provinces of Cicuique and Tiguex had offered peace without any conquest or war whatsoever. They welcomed the Spaniards into their pueblos and gave and provided them what they had. It was said and held to be [8v] true that they would not have risen up and revolted and the harm to Spaniards, the burnings, deaths, and injuries, would not have ensued, if it were not for that setting on of dogs and greed for the bracelet and jewelry.

{3} Because she answered as she did, she was asked whether she witnessed Francisco Vázquez order dogs set on those Indians and whether she was present. The witness answered that she knows what she said and declared because she was in the camp where all this occurred and Francisco Vázquez was there, too. But the witness did not see Francisco Vázquez give the order, although she believes and holds it as certain that he did so. Because the general saw to it that his captains and troops were obedient and subject to his command, they would not have done what she has stated without his order and consent, particularly since at that time Francisco Vázquez was in the camp where this happened.

{4} [Francisca de Hozes] was then asked whether she remembers which individuals were [9r] the ones who set dogs on the cacique and the Indian Bigotes. She replied that she does not know and does not remember, but she does know that all of the captains mentioned in the first question were in the camp where that took place.

{5} She was asked who killed the Indian called Turco, who ordered him killed, and for what reason. She stated that she did not know more than what she had heard, namely, that all of the aforenamed captains appealed to Francisco Vázquez that they might kill him because of the lies and falsehoods he had told them. And because of the troubles he had caused them by taking them by many roundabout ways and indirect roads. But Francisco Vázquez refused and blocked his execution until [at last] he told them to do what they wanted with him. So, then they hung him from a tree. The witness was not present and does not know more about it than by hearsay and what was public and common knowledge in the camp.

{6} [The witness] was then asked whether she had heard the captain or other person who hung the [9v] Indian called Turco mentioned by name. She replied that she did not know the name, but she does know that don Tristán de Arellano was not present at the killing because he had remained as general with the people who stayed behind.

{7} [Francisca de Hozes] was asked what other cruelty, mistreatment, or burnings she knew or had heard that Francisco Vázquez and his captains committed during the expedition, either against the Indians native to that land or against the Spaniards who traveled in the company. She said that she does not remember more than she has stated and testified except that he mistreated many Spaniards who wanted to stay in that land with fray Juan de Padilla. He confined them and threatened them with the gallows because they wanted to stay. Those who wanted to remain behind amounted to more than sixty persons, among whom were the witness and her husband. [The general] threatened that he would hang them if they stayed behind or talked any more about staying. This is what she knows.

[10r] {8} She was asked whether she knows that when Captain Francisco Vázquez and the other people with him passed through the valley of Corazones it was at peace and its people came out peacefully and provided necessary provisions. And afterwards did they rise up because of outrages and cruelty that were committed against them by the captains and men who remained there? Furthermore, who were the persons who perpetrated those cruelties and caused the people of the valley to rise up in arms, abandon it, and kill many Spaniards?

She answered that she knows and saw that when they passed through the valley and proceeded on the conquest and reconnaissance the Indians and towns of the valley came out in peace and gave them supplies from the food they had. But afterwards, when they returned, this witness and other persons with don García López de Cárdenas found the town and valley at war. She heard that they had risen up, killed many Spaniards and horses, and fled. The cause of this, she heard, was brutality and outrages committed by a [man named] Alcaraz, [10v] who had been left there as captain by Francisco Vázquez. He, together with other people among those who stayed with him, had seized women and children and committed other outrages and brutality against the Indians. She knows that the Indians killed Alcaraz and many other Spaniards and would have killed don García López de Cárdenas and those who went with him, if they had not turned back and gotten reinforcements from another captain who was coming close behind.

According to the oath she swore, she said that this is what she knows concerning this case and nothing further. She did not sign because she said she did not know how. As soon as she had finished speaking her statement was read to the witness and she confirmed it. The lord judge licenciado Tejada signed.

Second de Oficio Witness (Alonso Sánchez)

Alonso Sánchez, accepted as a witness for this investigation, having given his oath in the form prescribed by law and having promised to tell the truth, was asked the following questions.

{1} He was asked whether he knows Francisco Vázquez de Coronado, don Diego de [11r] Guevara, don Pedro de Tovar, don Tristán de Arellano, don García López de Cárdenas, Diego López (a councilman of Sevilla), Hernando de Alvarado, and the other captains who went to reconnoiter and subjugate the province of Cíbola, Cicuique, Tiguex, and Quivira and whether he was present during the subjugation and reconnaissance. He answered that he knows all of those mentioned in this question, by appearance, voice, and conversation that he has had with them for about the last five years. He was present during the subjugation and reconnaissance of all that land until the great barranca that is in the province of Quivira and Axa, from when they entered Tierra Nueva until they returned to this city of Mexico. Except that he was not at the occupation of Cíbola because he and his wife, along with other captains and people, remained behind and when they arrived at Cíbola the pueblo was occupied and at peace.

[11v] *{2}* Because he said that he was present during the reconnaissance and subjugation of these provinces and Tierra Nueva, [the witness] was asked what brutality and outrages he knew of, had seen, or heard tell of that Francisco Vázquez or the other captains committed, on their own or by his order, in those provinces and against the Indians native there. What pueblos and how many did he burn and lay waste in the province of Cicuique and Tiguex and what Indians did he burn and set dogs on? Why and in what manner did the death of the Indian called Turco who was guiding them come to pass? For

what reason were dogs set on the Indian called Bigotes and on the interpreter and the cacique of Cicuique?

[The witness] stated that what he knows about what he is asked is that the provinces of Cicuique, Tiguex, Brava, and Chia all offered peace and thoroughly welcomed the Spaniards, giving them the food they needed from what they had and clearing and vacating a pueblo for their quarters. All of the residents went to other [pueblos]. When the company was settled in this manner in the pueblo [12r] Hernando de Alvarado arrived after an *entrada* and reconnaissance he had made. With him he brought five Indians who were called El Turco, Ysopete, Bigotes, the cacique, and the interpreter from Cicuique.

The Indian called Turco said and revealed that he was from a land far from where they were lodged which was wealthy and very fruitful. He also said that the cacique and interpreter had gone to that land and had brought back a gold bracelet and other valuable and costly jewelry. Because the cacique and Bigotes denied what the Indian called Turco was saying they abused them and set dogs on them in front of the door of Francisco Vázquez's quarters. The witness did not see this, although he was in that pueblo. But he did hear about it and it was public and common knowledge that it was done by Francisco Vázquez's order. He heard that said and believes it because [the general] kept the people so obedient and subject to his command, that [the witness] believes and is certain that if he did not order it, no one would have dared do such a thing.

[Sánchez] knows that after the setting on of dogs [12v] the cacique and Bigotes went away and the interpreter fled and inspired the pueblo of Cicuique and its province to rise up. He believes and is certain that both that province and the province of Tiguex rose up in arms after the setting on of dogs because of the brutality and ill-treatment committed against the cacique and Bigotes. And another reason was the procurement of clothing and poultry against the will [of the Pueblos], which he knows because before that they had always been at peace and this was said as public and common knowledge.

{3} [The witness] was asked how many pueblos were burned and laid waste after that uprising and rebellion, how many Indians of those provinces they burned and set dogs on, and what other brutal acts they committed against them. He answered that some pueblos were taken by force and that they burned and laid waste both this group and another nine or ten of those that rebelled. This witness saw several posts at which he knew some Indians, who had been captured in those pueblos during war, had been tied and burned. He knows and saw in one pueblo they surrounded for two months that, after its occupation, the Indians who had been captured alive were stabbed and lanced and dogs were set on many others. [13r] What the pueblo was called he does not remember.

He recalls and remembers that one of those who committed these brutal acts and set dogs on the Indians was a footman named Martín de Estepa. Further, he knows and saw that the dogs that were set on the Indians belonged to don Pedro de Tovar. It seems to him that don Pedro was present on one occasion when his dogs were unleashed against Indians, but he does not remember this clearly. He does know that these acts were committed against Indians in the pueblo they had only partially occupied and subdued because it had many strong plazas such that, although one was overrun, the others would not sue for peace.

{4} [Sánchez] was asked for what reason they killed the Indian known as Turco, who ordered him killed, who did the killing, and why. The witness replied that he did not see Turco killed, but he had heard that the councilman of Sevilla Diego López, who was serving as [13v] maestre de campo because of the illness and absence of don García López de Cárdenas, ordered him killed. Also, that one Francisco Martín, a butcher, did the killing by choking him. Regarding Martín, he heard that he had killed Turco by order of Diego López because he had deceived the company and led it by many roundabout ways. And also because he was a deceiver and troublemaker.

{5} He was then asked whether Francisco Vázquez was present when they killed Turco. He replied that, on the contrary, he heard that the general was absent, that Turco's death grieved him, and that he always defended Turco against all those who said that he should be killed because he was a deceiver.

{6} Asked where Diego López and Francisco Martín are, [the witness] replied that he had heard that they are in Culiacán.

{*7*} He was asked further whether he knows or has heard about the brutality that was committed in the valleys of Corazones, who committed it, and who caused the [people of] that valley to rise up in arms and kill the Spaniards who died there. He said that [14r] when they went on the reconnaissance of that land all the towns of that valley came out in peace and provided corn and other food that they had. They rose up in arms and rebelled because of the cruelty and outrages committed by a [man named] Alcaraz, who had been left there as captain by Francisco Vázquez, and because they seized women and girls. This happened specifically in the town and province called Señora and in the valley of Comulpa. And they killed many Spaniards.

{*8*} [The witness] was asked how he knows what he stated and testified in response to the previous question, where Alcaraz is, and what became of him. [Sánchez] replied that he did not see what he has declared and stated in regard to the previous question. However, he has heard it said as very public and common knowledge. Also, on the way back he saw that those towns and provinces had erupted in war, and he learned that the Indians there had killed Alcaraz and many other men-at-arms, from among those who had remained in those provinces.

{*9*} He was asked what other brutality and outrages were committed by [14v] Francisco Vázquez, some of the captains, or other individuals, against either Indians or Spaniards. He stated that he does not know whether Francisco Vázquez committed other brutal acts and outrages beyond what he has said and declared except that when the witness, his wife and son, and another sixty persons wanted to stay in that land with fray Juan de Padilla, the general insulted them and abused them verbally, threatening that he would hang them. Others he put in shackles. This is why the land was abandoned.

Under the oath he has sworn, he said that this is what he knows and what occurred in this case; and he knows nothing more. He signed his name. Then, just after he finished testifying, he went back and read what he had said and certified it. And the lord judge affixed his signature.

Alonso Sánchez

A TRANSCRIPT
OF THE TESTIMONY

[fol. 6v cont'd]⁹

{T*estig*o}

La di*c*Ha Fran*cis*ca de hoçes muger del di*c*ho al*ons*o / Sanchez Vezino de mexico t*est*igo Resçibido / Para la di*c*ha ynformaçion la qual *h*abien- / do jurado ante *e*l di*c*ho señor liçençiado / tejada oydor E *h*abiendo prometido de decir / *ver*dad se le hizieron las preguntas syg*uiente*s / Fue preg*unta*da si conosçe A fran*cis*co Vazquez de / Coronado e a don di*eg*o de gueVara E A don / Tristan de arellano e a don g*arc*ia lopez de / Cardenas E A diego lopez veyntiquatro / de seVilla y a hernando de alVarado E / A los otros Capitanes q*ue* fueron a la conquis- / ta e descubrimiento de la proVinçia de çibola / çicuyque y teguex e si se hallo presente en el di*c*ho / desCubrimi*ent*o e conquista dixo q*ue* Conosçe A / todos los contenidos En esta pregunta por / Vista habla E ConVersaçion que con ellos / ha tenido E de çinco Años A esta p*art*e poco / mas o menos e se hallo presente A la conquis- / ta E descubrimi*ent*o de toda la di*c*ha Tierra / vi

[fol. 7r]

820

DesDe que entraron En ella HasTa q*ue* / VolVieron A esta çiUdad de mexico Eçe(b)*p*to q*ue* / no se hallo En la toma de çibola porq*ue* esta / T*est*igo y su marido Con otros Capitanes y per- / Sonas Se quedaron Un poco atras y quan- / do llegaron estaba tomado El p*ueb*lo E de / Paz / Fue preg*unta*da pues dize y aclara que se *h*allo / en el desqubrimi*ent*o E Conquista de las di*c*has / proVinçias e tierra nueva desde el prin- / Çipio hasta la Vuelta que crueldades Vio e sabe / q*ue* hiziese*n* el di*c*ho fran*cis*co Vazquez E los otros / Capitanes Por sy o por su m*anda*do en las di*c*has pro- / Vinçias y en los yndios naturales de *e*llas / especialmente En tiguex E çicuyaque y / Como y de que manera Pasa la muerte del / yndio q*ue* llamaban turco que los guiaba / y el Aperreami*ent*o que hizieron en el y el yn- / dio que dizian bigotes y en el Caçique E / naguatato de çicuyque e Por que causa / e Razon los mando matar e aperrear / el dicho francisco Vazquez y que fueron los da- / nos que se siguieron de haber hecho y mandado / hazer las crueldades dichas dixo que lo que / sabe çerCa de lo que le es preguntado es que

[fol. 7v]

hAvienDo el dicho francisco Vazquez ynViado A / desCubrir al dicho hernando de alvarado el / dicho hernando de alvarado VolVio al Real / y truxo Consigo Un yndio que llamaban / El turco el qual dio nuevas de buena / tierra y de grandes Riquezas e que el / Caçique e otras personas de çicuyque / sabian lo mismo porque hAbian ydo con el / a la dicha Tierra E habian traydo E tenian / Un braçalete de oro e otras joyas RiCas / y que esto Sabido ynVio el dicho francisco Vazquez / a llamar al Caçique de çicuyque que estaba de / paz en Cuya proVinçia estaban e ansi- / mysmo al yndio que llaman bigotes que como / no concertaban Con lo que el dicho turco / dezia ni declaraban lo del dicho bra- / Çalete e joyas ni las daban el dicho / Francisco Vazquez y otros Capitanes de / que no Tiene memoria Por su mandado / aperrearon a los dichos caçique e bigotes / los quales desPues de haber Sanado E / convaleçido hablaban e ComuniCa- / ban con los otros yndios de la dicha pro- / Vinçia de çicuyque e Con los de tiguex / donde a la Sazon el Canpo e rresidia / vii

[fol. 8r]

821

E Como les dieron notiçia de las crueldades / e malostratamyentos que les habian hecho / y Porque les tomaban Por fuerça y / contra su voluntad las mugeres e hijas / y las otras cosas que tenyan en sus caSas / Se alçaron las dichas proVinçias de çicuyque / y tiguex E les mataron a los esPañoles to- / dos los Caballos que en el Canpo hallaron / e asimismo las (h)azemilas e bes- / tias de Car- / ga en que lleVaban sus bastimyentos e / que sabe e vio que desPues de entrados / e conquistadoS los dichos pueblos el dicho / Francisco Vazquez los mando quemar y que- / mo y ansimismo quemo muchos yndios / atados a Unos Palos E Aperreo a o- / tros y que esto fue desPues Como tiene

/ dicho y declarado que los hobieron entrado / e conquistado Porque antes que aperre- / asen al dicho caçique e yndio(s) bigotes las / dichas proVinçias de çicuyque e tiguex se / habian dado de paz syn conquista ni gue- / rra alguna y aCogian en sus pueblos a los dichos / esPañoles y les daban y proVeyan de / lo que tenyan E que se dezia e tenia(n)

[fol. 8v]
por Çierto que no se alçaran ny Rebe- / laran ni se siguieran los dichos daños / y quemas y muertes y heridas de esPa- / noles Salvo Por el dicho aper- reamyento / y co(b)diçias que se TuVo del dicho braçalete / y joyas / Fue Pre- guntada Como sabe lo / que dicho e declarado Tiene e si Vio / que el dicho Francisco Vazquez mandase / aperrear a los dichos y si se hallo presen- / te dixo que sabe lo que dicho e decla- / Rado tiene Porque esta testigo Se hallo / en el Canpo donde todo lo susodicho / aCaesçio e que se hallo presente el dicho / Francisco Vazquez pero que este testigo no Vio / que el dicho francisco Vazquez lo mandase pero que / cree e tiene por Çierto Segun tenia / su(b)je(c)tos e obidientes su gente e Capi- / tanes que no Se haria cosa de lo que / Tiene dicho e declarado syn su mandado / e Consentimiento porque el dicho francisco / Vazquez a la Sazon Estaba en el Real / donde lo susodicho aCaesçio / Fue preguntada sy tiene memoria / PartiCularmente quienes fueron / viii

[fol. 9r]
822
los que aperrearon los dichos caçique / e yndio bigotes dixo que no lo Sabe ni / Tiene memoria pero que estaban en el Real / donde lo susodicho aCaesçio todos los / capitanes Contenidos en la primera pre- / Gunta / Fue pregun- tada quien mato o man- / do matar al yndio llamado turCo / y por que causa Dixo que no lo sabe / mas de que oyo dezir que todos / los Capitanes de susononbrados yn- / portunaban al dicho francisco Vazquez que lo / matasen Por las mintiras y burlas / que les habia Fecho y trabajos que les / habia hecho Pasar trayendolos y lleVan- / do(s)los Por muchos Rodeos e diVersos / Caminos E que el dicho(s) Francisco Vazquez lo / Re(h)usaba e defendia hasta

tanto q*ue* / les dixo q*ue* hiziesen de *e*l lo que quixesen e que / e(s)*n*tonçes lo
ahorcaron de Un arbol E / que *e*sta t*e*s*ti*go no se hallo presente ni sabe / lo que
tiene d*i*cho mas de por oydas E / ser pu*bli*co e noTorio en el Canpo / Fue preguntada sy oyo nonbrar el Capi- / tan o persona que llevo ahorcar al

[fol. 9v]

d*i*cho yndio llamado turco dixo que no / lo Sabe e que sabe que no se hallo /
en la d*i*cha muerte don tristan de are- / llano Porque quedo por General / con
la Gente que quedaba AtraSS / Fue preguntada que otras cruelda- / des
quemas o malostratamyentos sa- / be o *h*a oydo d*e*c*ir* que *h*ayan (f)*h*echo en
la / d*i*cha jornada el d*i*cho Fran*ci*sco Vazquez y / sus Capitanes ansi A los
yndyos natu- / rales de la Tierra Como a esPañoles / que andaban en el
Canpo dixo que no / Sabe mas ni se aquerda de lo que d*i*cho / e declarado
Tiene Ece(b)*p*to que maltra- / to a muchos esPanoles que se querian / quedar
en la tierra con fray juan / de padilla Poniendolos en Carçeles E / amenazandolos Con la horca Porque / Se querian quedar que serian mas de / sesenta
*h*onbres y que entre los que se / querian quedar era*n* esta t*e*s*ti*go y su ma- /
Rido a los quales Amenazo que los A- / horCaria si se le quedaban o habla-
/ ban mas En quedarse y que *e*sto es lo q*ue* / Sabe / ix

[fol. 10r]

823

Fue preguntaDa si sabe que el valle / de los coracones quando el Capitan /
Fran*ci*sco Vazquez y la otra Gente q*ue* Con el / Paso estava y salio de paz y les
dieron / el bastimento nesçesario y q*ue* d*e*spues / Se alço por malostratamyentos y cruel- / dades que en ellos hizieron la gente / y Capitanes
que en el quedaro*n* y que / Personas fueron los que hizieron las / d*i*chas crueldades y fueron causa q*ue* *e*l d*i*cho / Valle se Alçase y despoblase y murie- /
sen muchos esPañoles dixo que sabe e / Vio q*ue* quando Pasaron Por el d*i*cho
/ Valle e yban a la d*i*cha conquista e des- / qubrimyento los yndios e pueblos
del / d*i*cho Valle les Salieron de paz y les die- / Ron los bastimentos que
tenyan e q*ue* / VolViendo desPues Este t*e*s*ti*go e otras per- / sonas con don
Gar*çi*a lopez de Cardenas / hallaron de G*u*erra el d*i*cho pu*eb*lo e valle e / oyo

dezir que se *h*abian alçado y levan- / Tado y muerto muchos esPañoles y Ca-
/ ballos y q*ue* la causa d*e e*sto *h*Abia sydo las / crueldades y malosTratamyentos
que / les hizo Un alCaraz que *e*l d*i*cho fran*ci*sco Vazq*ue*z

[fol. 10v]
*h*Abia deXado alli Por Capitan / el qual les tomaba las mugeres e hijas / y les
hazia otros desafueros y ma- / lostratamy*ent*os juntamente con alg*un*as / Personas de los q*ue* Con el quedaro*n* al / qual sabe que mataron los d*i*chos yn- /
dios e a otros muchos esPanoles e / mataron al d*i*cho don g*a*r*ci*a lopez / y los
q*ue* Con el yban sino VolViera*n* a- / Tras e *h*obieran soCorro con otro / Capitan que çerca venya e que esto / es lo que sabe d*e e*ste Caso y no otra cosa /
Para el juramento que tiene (f)*h*echo / y no lo Firmo Porq*ue* dixo que no sa-
/ bia Fue le leydo este su d*i*cho a este t*esti*go / luego Como lo aCabo de *decir*
e Ratificose / en el(l) y firmolo el d*i*cho señor oydor el / licençiado Tejada

{T*esti*go}
El d*i*cho alonso Sanchez t*esti*go Resçibido / Para la d*i*cha ynformaçion el q*ua*l
*h*a- / biendo jurado en forma de d*e*r*ech*o e p*r*ometio / de d*e*cir *ver*dad e se le
hizieron las Preg*un*tas / siguientes / Fue Preguntado sy conosçe a francisco /
Vazquez de Coronado e a don diego de / x

[fol. 11r]
824
Guevara E A Don peDro De toVar / e a don tristan de arellano e a don /
G*a*r*ci*a lopez de Cardenas e a diego lopez / veyntiquatro de sevilla y a hernando / de alVarado e a los otros Capitanes / q*ue* Fueron a la conquista *e* d*es*-
Cubrimi*ent*o de / la proVinçia de Çibola çicuyque y / Tiguex e quiVira e si se
hallo presen- / te en el d*i*cho d*es*Cubrimi*ent*o E conquista / dixo q*ue* Conosçe
a todos los conteni- / dos en esta preg*un*ta por Vista habla / e conVersaçion
q*ue* Con ellos ha tenido / de Çinco Años a esta p*a*rte Poco mas / o menos E
se hallo presente a la con- / quista e d*es*Cubrimi*ent*o de toda la d*i*cha / Tierra
hasta la barranca grande q*ue e*S / en la proVinçia de quiVira e de axa / desde
que entraron en la d*i*cha Tierra / nueva *h*asta q*ue* VolVieron a esta çiUdad /

de meXico Eçe(b)*p*to que no se hallo / en la toma de çibola Porque *e*ste *tes-*
*tig*o / y su muger con otros Capitanes y / gente Se quedaron atras e quando /
llegaron a Çibola estaba tomado El / pu*eblo* e de Paz

[fol. 11v]
Fue Preguntado Pues dize que se hallo / en el descubrimiento e conquista de
las / d*ic*has pro Vinçias e tierra nueva que / crueldades e malostratamyentos /
Vio e oyo e sabe que hiziese el d*ic*ho / Fran*c*is*c*o Vazquez o los otros Capitanes / Por sy o Por su mandado en las d*ic*has / ProVinçias y en los yndios na-
/ Turales de *e*llas y que pueblos y (que) *cuantos* / (mas) quemo y asolo en la
d*ic*ha proVinçia / de çicuyque e tiguex e que tantos / yndios quemo e aperreo
y Como y / de que manera PaSa la muerte del / yndio que llamaban turCo
que los / Guiaba y por que causa aperrearon el / yndyo que dezian bigotes y
el Caçiq*ue* / y naguatato de çicuyq*ue* dixo q*ue* lo q*ue* / Sabe çerca de lo que le
es preguntado / es que las proVinçias de çicuyque e ti- / guex e braVa e chia
se dieron todas de / Paz e hizieron muy buen aCogemyento a / los esPañoles
dandoles los mantenimi*ent*os / nesçesarios E de lo que tenyan e les / dexaron
Para su Aposento desen- / baraçado Un pu*eblo* y Se paso Toda la gente / a
otros E q*ue* estando d*e e*sta manera vino / xi

[fol. 12r]
825
Hernando de alvarado al d*ic*ho pueblo / de una entrada e desqubrimiento q*ue*
/ *h*abia ido a hazer y truxo consigo / Çinco yndyos que se llamava*n* el turco E
/ ysopete e bigotes e el Caçique e nagua- / tato de çicuyq*ue* y el d*ic*ho yndio
llamado / TurCo dixo e publico ser de Una tierra / lexos de donde estaban
aposentados / e que (h)era Tierra RiCa e muy Viçiosa / y q*ue e*l d*ic*ho Caçique
y naguatato *h*abian / ydo a la d*ic*ha su tierra e *h*abian traydo / Un braçalete de
oro e otras joyas / RiCas e de Valor E Como el d*ic*ho (ç)caçique / y el d*ic*ho
bigotes negaron lo que *e*l d*ic*ho yn- / dio llamado Turco dezia los aperrea- /
Ron y maltrataron delante d*e* la puer- / ta del Aposento del d*ic*ho fran*c*is*c*o
Vazqu*ez* / y que *e*sto este *t*estig*o* no lo Vio aUnq*ue e*Staba / en el d*ic*ho pu*eblo*
pero que lo oyo y fue Pu*bl*i*c*o / y noT*o*rio y que cree e oyo dezir q*ue* / Fue por

mandado del dicho Francisco Vazquez / Porque tenia Tan sujeta e obidiente /
toda la gente que cree e tiene Por çierto / que si el no lo mandara nadie osara
hazer / tal Cosa e que supo que despues de aperre-

[fol. 12v]
ados el dicho Caçique e bigotes Se fue / e huyo el dicho naguatato e hizo alçar
el / pueblo de çicuyque e su proVinçia E que / cree e tiene por çierto que asy
la dicha pro- / Vinçia Como la de tiguex que alço desPues / del dicho aperreamyento fue Por la / dicha crueldad y maltratamyento que se / hizo en el
dicho Caçique e bigotes e por el / Recogimiento que Contra su voluntad les
hazian / de Ropa e aves Porque antes syenpre / habian estado de Paz e asy se
dezia / por muy publico e noTorio / Fue preguntado que tantos pueblos / Se
(^alçaron) quemaron e asolaron / desPues de la dicha Rebilion e levanta- /
myento e que tantos yndios de las dichas / ProVinçias quemaron E Aperrearon / e que otras crueldades les hizieron / dixo que algunos pueblos Se
tomaron por / Fuerça e que ansi este como otros nueve / o diez de los Rebelados los quemaron / e asolaron E que este testigo vio unos palos / en que supo
que se habian Atado y quema- / do çiertos yndios de los que en la dicha /
Guerra y pueblos Se tomaron e que sabe / e vio que en Un pueblo que no se
aquerda / {Va testado donde dizia alçaron no vala} / xii

[fol. 13r]
826
como se llamaba sobre el qual esTuVie- / Ron dos meses desPues de entrado
Vio / que los yndios que se tomaban ViVos / los alançeaban y aCuchillaban y
otroSS / muchos aperreaban y que se aquerda / y tiene memoria que uno de
los que / hazian las dichas crueldades y aperrea- / ban los dichos yndios (h)era
un soldado que / se llamaba martin de estepa e que / Sabe e vio que los perros
con que se / aperreaban (h)eran de don pedro de to- / Var e que le Paresçe
que se hallo una Vez / presente don pedro de toVar quando (h)e- / chaban sus
perros A los dichos yndios pero / que no Tiene bien memoria sy es ansi / e
que esto se hazia en los yndios que / en el dicho pueblo se yban tomando e
conquistan- / do porque tienen muchas plazas fuertes / por manera que

aunq*ue* Ganaban la / Una no se daban las otras / Fue preguntado por que causa mataro*n* / al yndio que llamaban Turco E / quien le mando matar E mato e Por / que causa dixo que *e*ste t*e*s*t*i*g*o no le vio ma- / tar p*er*o que oyo d*e*c*i*r q*u*e diego lopez ve- / yntiquatro de seVilla que yba por

[fol. 13v]

maese de Canpo por enfermeDaD E / ausençia de don g*arc*i*a* lopez de cardenas / le mando matar E q*u*e le mato e hago Un / Fran*ci*sco m*ar*t*y*n Cortador de Carne al / qual d*i*cho fran*ci*sco m*ar*t*y*n le oyo d*e*c*i*r que *e*l / lo *h*abia muerto por mandado del / d*i*cho diego lopez e que lo *h*abian muer- / to porque llevaba el real enga- / nado y por diversos Rodeos y porq*u*e / (h)era un ynViador[10] y alborotador / Fue preguntado sy el d*i*cho fran*ci*sco Vazq*ue*z / Se hallo presente quando lo mata- / Ron dixo que *e*ste t*e*s*t*i*g*o no lo sabe an- / tes oyo dezir que *e*staba ausente e / que le *h*abia pesado e que syenpre lo / *h*abia defendido de todos los q*u*e lo ma- / tasen Porq*u*e (h)era enganador / Fue preguntado donde estan los d*i*chos / diego lopez e fran*ci*sco m*ar*t*y*n dixo que / ha oydo dezir que estan en quliacan / Fue pregu*n*tado sy sabe o oyo dezir de las / crueldades que se hizieron en los Va- / ll(e)es de los coraçones y quienes las hi- / zieron y quien fue causa que se(s) alça- / se el d*i*cho Valle e muriesen los esPa- / ñoles que alli murieron dixo que / xiii

[fol. 14r]

827

quando yban en el descubrimyento / de la d*i*cha tierra todos los pu*eb*l*o*s del / d*i*cho valle Salieron de paz y les diero*n* / mayz e de l*o*s otros mantenimy*en*t*o*s q*u*e / tenian e que a Causa de las crueldades e / malostratamy*en*t*o*s q*u*e les hizo un alCaraz / que alli dexo el d*i*cho Fran*ci*sco Vazquez por / Capitan e Porque les tomaban las / hijas e mugeres Se levantaron y Re- / belaron esP*eci*al el pu*eb*l*o* E proVinçia / que dizen de Señora y el valle de Co- / mulpa e mataron muchos esPañoles / Fue preguntado como Sabe lo q*u*e d*i*cho / y declarado Tiene en la pregunta an- / tes d*e *e*sta e donde esta E que se hizo el / d*i*cho alCaraz dixo que lo q*u*e d*i*cho e decla- / Rado Tiene en la pregunta antes d*e* *e*sta / no lo Vio Pero que lo oyo d*e*c*i*r por muy / pu*b*l*i*co e noTorio e porque a la Vuelta Vio / levantados E de guerra los dichos pueblos E / ProVinçias e supo que los dichos yndios hA- / bian muerto al dicho alCaraz y a otros / muchos soldados de los que quedaron en las / dichas proVinçias / Fue preguntado que otras crueldades / e maloStratamyentos hAya (f)hecho El

[fol. 14v]

dicho Francisco Vazquez o algunos de los / Capitanes o otras personas Parti- / Culares asy a los dichos yndios como a es- / Pañoles dixo que no sabe que el dicho francisco / Vazquez haya (f)hecho otras cruelda- / des e malostratamyentos mas de lo / que dicho e declarado tiene Eçe(b)pto que qui- / Riendo se quedar Este testigo y su muger E hijo / e otras Sesenta personas en la dicha tierra / con fray juan de padilla los afrento y / maltrato de palabra Amenazandolos que / los (h)ahorcarian e a otros (h)echaban prisio- / nes y esta fue la causa Porque se des- / manparo la Tierra e que esto es lo que / Sabe y pasa de este Caso y no otra cosa para / el juramento que tiene (f)hecho y firmo- / lo de su nonbre fue le tornado a leer / este su dicho luego como lo aCabo de decir / y Ratificose en el e Senalolo el dicho señor / oydor *Alonso Sanchez*

Chapter 5

Juan Gómez de Paradinas, the Third de Oficio Witness

A Tailor, Alguacil, and Billeting Officer

Two days after Francisca de Hozes and Alonso Sánchez testified, Juan Gómez de Paradinas was summoned to answer Tejada's questions. In his late teens to around twenty when the expedition to Tierra Nueva left Compostela, Gómez was accompanied by his wife María Maldonado. She was remembered years later as having tirelessly nursed the sick and wounded of the expedition, and her service figured heavily in the award of a small grant to Gómez in 1560. During the expedition Gómez, a tailor by trade, served as *alguacil mayor* or chief constable and billeting officer.[1] He was a horseman in Diego Gutiérrez de la Caballería's company, Gutiérrez being either an uncle or cousin of Beatriz de Estrada, Vázquez de Coronado's wife. Gómez took with him 5 horses, a coat of chain mail, a helmet, and native arms and armor, again very much more than the typical expedition member.[2]

His service in the Gutiérrez company points to a link with the Vázquez de Coronado-Estrada family. That possibility is further strengthened by his place of origin, the town of Paradinas under the jurisdiction of Salamanca, the seat of the Vázquez de Coronado family. In addition, Gómez stated that he had left for Cíbola in 1538, which, if true, would mean that he was among those who made part of the reconnaissance with fray Marcos de Niza and would probably make him a member of either Vázquez de Coronado's or Mendoza's entourage assigned to accompany the friar, at least as far as Culiacán, if not farther. When the full-fledged expedition got underway in 1540 he was always in the vanguard, again associating him closely with the captain general.

When he departed for Cíbola he left a house behind him in Mexico City, to which he apparently returned in 1542. Just over a month before he testified in the pesquisa of 1544, Juan Gómez, described as a *cortador* or cloth cutter, was granted one and a half solares in Mexico City by the cabildo.[3] He must have been a vecino of the city by then and certainly was called so by 1544. In the late 1540s he was said to be unfit to work because of a fall he had suffered.[4] As six of his former expeditionary companions testified in 1560, Gómez had outfitted himself very well for the journey to Tierra Nueva and as a result had spent a great deal of money. Even eighteen years after the expedition's return he was still impoverished and in debt because of it. It was not until long after the expedition that he received compensation for his expenditures, being characterized in the late 1540s as "a settler without Indians [in encomienda]."[5] In 1560 the viceroy and audiencia recommended that he be given either a *corregimiento* or a caballería.

His family had been associated with the earliest Spanish conquest of Nueva Galicia, his father Pedro Gómez de Paradinas having accompanied Nuño Beltrán de Guzmán in his entrada in 1530. And Pedro Gómez died there.

For years after the expedition to Tierra Nueva, Juan Gómez de Paradinas remained in contact with other participants, especially those hailing from the province of Salamanca such as Gaspar de Salamanca and Pedro de Ledesma, the latter also a witness in the pesquisa of 1544.[6] Gómez de Paradinas was still living in Mexico City as late as 1591, when he testified for fellow expedition member Francisco de Santillana.[7]

Gómez's testimony during Tejada's pesquisa was mostly hearsay and conjecture, but like all of the remaining de oficio witnesses he made several statements justifying the Spaniards' actions, explicitly referring to those of Vázquez de Coronado. Nevertheless, by presuming that the captain general gave permission for the burning of Indians at Pueblo del Arenal, he made an indirect and perhaps inadvertent accusation against him. Although he thought violent actions of the expedition justifiable, Gómez de Paradinas also provided information on the scope of those acts. For example, he reported that 17 or 20 pueblos were burned and dismantled, that up to 150 Indian prisoners were tied to stakes and burned, and that the nose and hand of at least one native man were cut off to inspire terror among his friends and relatives.

A TRANSLATION
OF THE TESTIMONY

Third de Oficio Witness (Juan de Paradinas)[8]

[14v cont'd] Juan de Paradinas, a tailor and vecino of the city of Mexico, accepted as a witness for this investigation, having given his oath in the form prescribed by law and having promised to tell the truth, was asked the following questions by the lord judge.

[15r] {1} He was asked whether he knows Francisco Vázquez de Coronado, don Diego de Guevara, don Tristán de Arellano, don García López de Cárdenas, Diego López (a councilman of Sevilla), Hernando de Alvarado, Barrionuevo, Zaldívar, and the other captains who went to reconnoiter and subjugate the province of Cíbola, Tiguex, Cicuique, and Quivira and whether he was present during the subjugation and reconnaissance. He answered that he knows all of those named, by appearance, voice, and conversation that he has had with them for about the last five years and more. He was present during the subjugation and reconnaissance of those provinces from the beginning until they returned to this city of Mexico. And for some of the time he served as alguacil and billeting officer for the company.

{2} [The witness] was asked whether the provinces of Cicuique and Tiguex offered peace as soon as the company arrived, whether they welcomed [the Spaniards] into their houses and pueblos, and whether they provided the food they needed from what they had. He answered that it is true that those provinces did not offer resistance, but as soon as the company arrived they came out in peace, [15v] offered obedience to His Majesty, welcomed them into their houses and pueblos, and supplied the necessary provisions and whatever they had.

{3} [Paradinas] was then asked whether while these pueblos and provinces were at peace Hernando de Alvarado, who had gone on a reconnaissance, brought with him to the camp where the company was quartered the cacique of Cicuique, the Indian they called Turco, others they called Bigotes and Xabe, and an interpreter from those provinces. The witness stated that it is true that he learned that Hernando de Alvarado brought as prisoners the cacique, also called Bigotes, and the Indians called Turco, Xabe, and Ysopete. There were no others that the witness knew and saw that he brought to the camp. He saw that Alvarado delivered these [Indians] to the maestre de campo don García López de Cárdenas, who held them as prisoners under guard.

{4} He was asked whether he understood or heard that the Indian called Turco said that he was from a very wealthy, fertile, and abundant land, that the cacique, [16r] Xabe, and Ysopete had gone there, and that they had brought back a gold bracelet and other costly jewelry. He replied that it is true that he heard what he is asked about said and asserted by the Indian called Turco himself. He indicated that in his land there were large canoes and also valuable objects of gold and silver. And he indicated how they were accustomed to find the metals and wash them.

{5} [Next Paradinas] was asked whether he had witnessed and knew that because Bigotes, Xabe, and Ysopete denied what was said by the Indian called Turco, disagreed with what he asserted, and maintained that they did not have the bracelet and jewelry, they set dogs on them. [The witness] said that he heard as very public and common knowledge (and thus it was true) that it was because of their disagreement and because they did not surrender the bracelets and jewelry that dogs were set on them. But the witness did not see this.

{6} He was asked who unleashed the dogs on those Indians and who ordered it done. The witness declared that because he had gone with a another captain named Ovando [16v] to make an entrada he does not know. And he says that he does not know whether Francisco Vázquez was present at the time. But he heard and believes that Alvarado unleashed the dogs.

{7} [The witness] was asked whether he saw and knows that after the setting on of dogs the pueblos and provinces of Cicuique and Tiguex rose up and rebelled because of the brutality and outrages committed against the cacique called Bigotes and against Xebe and Ysopete. He answered that after the unleashing of dogs the cacique called Bigotes was freed and he went away to his pueblos. Then they rose up in arms and rebelled; and he believes that it was because of the aforesaid ill-treatment.

With regard to the Indians of Tiguex, he believes and is certain that they rose up because persons from the company went to their houses and, against their will, seized and carried off hides and *mantas*. One night the Indians along the Río de Tiguex killed fifty or sixty horses and mules that were wandering in the countryside. They put them in their dwellings and plazas and shot them with arrows. They also killed some Indian allies who had gone to find the stock. The company made war on them because of this uprising and rebellion and because they were never willing to return to peace, even though Francisco [17r] Vázquez delivered the requerimiento to them many times, on various days through various captains.

Thus, the Indians along the Río de Tiguex were captured and subjugated by force. But not those of Cicuique, because of the strength of their pueblo and because the Indians successfully defended themselves, so that the company could not defeat them and occupy the pueblo. During the siege of the Tiguex pueblos and the imposition of peace twelve or fifteen Spaniards died and [the Indians] wounded more than sixty.

{8} [Paradinas] was asked how many pueblos were captured and occupied by force and how many were burned and laid waste. He replied that only two pueblos were occupied by force and they were the ones where [the Indians] defended and fortified themselves. They abandoned the other pueblos and took refuge in those two. The company burned and laid waste a total of seventeen or twenty pueblos, including those two and the others, so that the Indians could not return and fortify them.

{9} He was asked what brutality was inflicted on the Indians when the pueblos had been captured and occupied. By whose order was it committed and [17v] how many Indians did they burn and set dogs on? [The witness] stated that the company lanced and stabbed a number of people and they burned as many as a hundred and fifty Indians, whom they burned alive, tied to posts. And they set dogs on some, but those were few.

Francisco Vázquez was not at the place where the burning was done because he was at another pueblo. However, these men were present: don García López de Cárdenas and Pablos de Melgosa, captain of the footmen; the councilman Diego López; don Diego de Guevara; Barrionuevo; don Rodrigo Maldonado; and Zaldívar. The burning was done by order of don García López, who was maestre de campo. And [the witness] believes that it was not done without orders from Francisco Vázquez, who was the general, but he does not know that for certain. He does believe it, however, because Francisco Vázquez was in a pueblo very near the one where the burning was done and the general kept the captains and [18r] all the people of the army so obedient and subject to his command that no one would dare disobey and do anything without his order and permission.

{*10*} [The witness] was asked who killed the Indian they called Turco, by whose order it was done, and why. And what sort of death was inflicted on him, and was Francisco Vázquez de Coronado present? The witness answered that he himself had not been there, but he had heard and it was well known and common knowledge that they strangled him, using a garrote, because he was a deceiver and led the company with lies by many roundabout ways and because he counselled the people of the towns [of Quivira] to rise up in arms and kill the Spaniards, telling them that they were already tired and worn out and the horses were weak. Furthermore, he heard that Francisco Vázquez, the councilman of Sevilla Diego López, Zaldívar, and other captains were present at Turco's killing, which was carried out on the general's order.

{*11*} [Paradinas] was asked what other cruelty he is aware of and saw or heard that Francisco Vázquez [18v] or the other captains committed during the expedition, either against the natives of those provinces or against the Spaniards who went in his army. [In response] he stated that he does not know more than what he has stated and testified except that when they returned through the valley of Corazones [the Indians] had risen up and killed all the Spaniards who had stayed behind in that valley. Two Indians killed a horse belonging to don Tristán de Arellano with poison and they would have killed him, too, if he had not been reinforced. Don Tristán

ordered that one hand and the nose of [an Indian] who had been taken prisoner be cut off and then sent him to the rest who had risen in arms, in order
to put fear in them. [This was] because they kept following and shooting
arrows at the army that were poisoned with a strong and virulent herb, which
no one who was wounded survived. Within twelve hours they died bloated
and raving. He knows also that when they passed through that valley don
Tristán tortured a Spaniard, whose name he does not remember, because it
was said by don Tristán's Blacks that he [19r] had stolen some mats.

Under the oath he swore he said that he knows this about what he is
asked and nothing else. And he signed his name. As soon as he finished
speaking, his statement was read to him and he confirmed it. The lord judge
signed.

Juan de Paradinas

A TRANSCRIPT
OF THE TESTIMONY

[fol. 14v cont'd][9]

{*testigo*}

El di*c*ho juan de paradinas sastre ve*cin*o de / mexico te*st*igo Resçibido Para la di*c*ha yn- / forma*c*ion el qual *h*abiendo jurado en / forma de de*rec*ho e *h*abiendo prometido de *decir* / ve*r*dad el di*c*ho señor oydor le hizo las / Preguntas syguientes / xiiii

[fol. 15r]

828

Fue preg*unta*do sy conosçe A Fran*ci*sco Vazquez / de Coronado e a don diego de guevara / e a don tristan de arellano e a don ga*rci*a / lopez de Cardenas y a di*e*go lopez Veynti- / quatro de seVilla e a hernando de alvara- / do e a barrionuevo e a saldiVar e a los o- / Tros Capitanes que fueron a la conquis- / ta e descubrimi*ent*o de las proVinçias de çibo- / la tiguex çicuyq*ue* y quiVira e si se hallo / presente en el di*c*ho descubrimi*ent*o e conquista / dixo q*ue* Conoçe a todos los de susononbrados / Por vista habla trato e conversa*c*ion Q*ue* / con ellos ha Tenido de çinco años y mas / Tienpo A esta parte E q*ue* se hallo presente / en el descubrimi*ent*o e conquista de las di*c*has / proVinçias desde el prinçipio *h*asta q*ue* / VolVieron a esta çiUdad e fue alguazil / e aposentador del (h)exerçito Çierto / tienpo / Fue preg*unta*do sy las proVinçias de çicuyque / y tiguex si se dieron luego q*ue* a ellas / llegaron de paz e los aCogieron en / sus pueblos e Casas e les dieron de lo que / tenyan e los mantenimi*ent*os nesçesarios / dixo que *es* ve*r*dad que las di*c*has proVinçias / luego que a ellas llegaron sin se poner / en Resistençia alguna Salieron de paz

[fol. 15v]

E diero*n* la obidiençia A su maG*esta*d e los / aCogieron en sus pueblos y caSas y les die- / Ron el bastimento nesçesario y de lo q*ue* elloS / tenyan / Fue

preguntado sy estando Asy de paz los / dichos pueblos e ProVinçias hernando
de / alvarado que habia ydo a çierto desCubri- / myento truxo Consigo al Real
donde / estaban Aposentados al caçique de / Çicuyque e al yndio que llamaban turco / e a otro que llamaban bigotes e a / otro que se llamaba xabe e a
un nagua- / tato de las dichas proVinçias dixo que eS / verdad que este testigo
supo Como el dicho / hernando de alvarado truxo presos / a los dichos caçique
que Por otro nombre / Se llamaba bigotes e al yndio lla- / mado turco e a xabe
e a ysope- / te que no Truxo mas que este testigo viese / ni supiese E que vio
que a estos loS / entregaron A don garcia lopez maestre / de Canpo el qual los
tenya Presos y / en guarda / Fue preguntado sy vio o oyo dezir que el / dicho
yndio llamado turco dezia que / (h)era de Una Tierra muy RiCa fer- / til e
abundosa e que el dicho Caçique / xv

[fol. 16r]
829
E xabe E ysopete habian ydo A ella e / habian traydo un braçalete de oro E
o- / tras joyas Ricas dixo que es verdad / que oyo decir al mismo yndio llama-
/ do turco e afirmar los que le es preguntado / y senalar que en la dicha su tierra
havia / Grandes Canoas e otras Riquezas / de oro e plata e de Como lo cogian
e la- / Vaban / Fue preguntado si sabe e vio que a Causa / que el dicho bigotes xabe e ysopete nega- / ban lo que el dicho yndio llamado Turco de- / zia
e discordaban de lo que el afir- / maba e que no Tenya el dicho braçalete / e
joyas l(e)os aperrearon dixo que oyo dezir / Por muy publico y noTorio y fue
asy ver- / dad que por la dicha causa e discordançia / e porque no daban los
dichos braçaletes e / joyas los Aperrearon pero que este testigo / no lo Vio /
Fue preguntado quien aperreo e mando A- / Perrear a los dichos yndios dixo
que / no lo sabe ni si se hallo presente / Francisco Vazquez de Coronado pero
que oyo / decir E cree que los aperrearon el dicho / alVarado Porque este testigo habia ydo con o- / tro Capitan que se llamaba oVando a

[fol. 16v]
hazer Una entrada / Fue preguntado desPues del dicho ape- / Reamyento si
sabe e Vio que los dichos / pueblos e proVinçias de Çicuyque e ti- / guex Se

alçaron E Rebelaron Por / las dichas crueldades e malostratamyentos / que hizieron a los dichos Caçique llama- / do bigotes Xebe e ysopete dixo que / Sabe que despues del dicho Aperreamiento se sol- / to el dicho caçique llamado bigotes y / se fue A sus pueblos y que luego se alça- / Ron y Rebelaron y que cree que fue / Por los dichos malostratamyentos y que / los de tiguex cree e tiene Por çierto / que se alçaron Porque yvan a sus / casas y Contra su voluntad les toma- / ban y trayan los queros y mantas / que tenyan y les mataron los yn- / dios del Rio de tiguex una noche / Çincuenta o sesenta Caballos E aze- / mylas que andaban en el Canpo me- / tiendolas en sus casas E patios e fle- / chandolas e ansimismo A çiertos yn- / dios Amigos que las fueron a buscar / y sobre la dicha Rebelion e alçamiento les / dieron guerra Porque jamas qui- / sieron VolVer de paz aUnque el dicho francisco / xvi

[fol. 17r]

830

Vazquez les hizo muchos e diVersos / Requerimyentos en diVersos dias E con / diVersos Capitanes e ansi los toma- / Ron e conquistaron Por fuerça A / los del dicho Rio de tiguex porque los de / Çiquyque se les defendieron e no los pu- / dieron entrar ni ganar Por la for- / taleza del pueblo e que en la Paçifica- / Çion E çerco de los dichos pueblos murieron / doze o quinze españoles y hirieron / mas de sesenta / Fue preguntado quantos pueblos fue- / Ron loS que tomaron y entraron / Por fuerça y quantos fueron los que / quemaron y asolaron dixo que so- / los doSS Fueron los que se entra- / Ron por fuerça que son los que se de- / Fendieron e hizieron fuertes porque / los demas los desmanpararon e aCogie- / Ron a estos dos pueblos e que ansi estos / como los demas que serian hasta diez E / siete o veynte pueblos los quemaron E A- / Solaron Porque no se pudiesen tor- / nar a hazer fuertes en ellos / Fue preguntado entrados los dichos / pueblos e ganados que crueldades hizieron / en ellos y por Cuyo mandado y que

[fol. 17v]

Tantos yndios quemaron y ape- / Rearon dixo que alançearon y pa- / saron A Cuchillo Cantidad de gente / e que quemaron hasta çiento e çinquenta /

yndios poco mas o menos e q*ue* los / quemaban ViVos Atados a unos / Palos
e que se Aperrearon Alg*un*os / q*ue* Fueron Pocos e que donde Se hizo la /
di*c*ha quema no se hallo el di*c*ho fran*c*i*s*co Vazqu*ez* / Porque *e*staba en otro
pu*eblo* pero q*ue* / se hallaron presentes do(s)*n* g*a*r*c*i*a* lopez / de Cardenas y
pablos de melgoça Capi- / tan de la gente de pie e di*e*go lopez Veyn- / tiquatro
e don diego de guevara e ba- / rrionuevo e don R*o*dr*i*g*o* maldonado / E saldiVar e que la di*c*ha quema se / hizo por mandado del di*c*ho don garç*i*a lo- /
Pez que (h)era maestre de Canpo e q*ue* / cree que no lo hizo syn mandado del
/ di*c*ho Fran*c*i*s*co Vazquez que (h)era general / Pero que no lo Sabe de çierta
çiença / Pero q*ue* lo cree porque estaba el di*c*ho / fran*c*i*s*co Vazquez en otro
pu*eblo* muy cerca / de donde Se hizo la di*c*ha quema e por- / que tenya Tan
sujeta su gente e obi- / dientes los Capitanes e gente de / xvii

[fol. 18r]
831
todo su Exerçito que nadie se / osaba desmandar a hazer cosa al- / Guna syn
su liçençia e mandado / Fue preguntado quien mato al yndio / que llamaban
Turco o por Cuyo man- / dado o por que causa e q*ue* genero de / muerte le
dieren e si se hallo presente / Francisco Vazquez de Coronado dixo q*ue* *e*ste /
*te*st*i*go no se hallo presente pero que oyo / dezir e fue muy pu*b*li*c*o e noT*o*rio
q*ue* lo *h*abian / ahogado e dado un garrote Porq*ue* (h)era / un ynbaydor e traya
enganado el / Canpo con diversos Rodeos e aun por- / q*ue* daba Aviso a los
pu*eblo*s Para q*ue* se al- / Çasen y matasen a los esPanoles dizien- / do q*ue* andaban ya Cansados e fatiga- / dos e trayan flacos los Caballos e oyo / dezir que
se hallaron presentes a la / di*c*ha muerte y donde le mataron el / di*c*ho Fran-
*c*i*s*co Vazquez e diego lopez Veynte- / y quatro de seVilla e çaldivar E / otros
Capitanes e que la di*c*ha muerte / Se hizo por mandado del di*c*ho General /
Fue preg*un*ta*d*o q*ue* otras crueldades sabe / Vio *o* oyo dezir que *h*oViese
(f)*h*echo / en la di*c*ha jornada el di*c*ho fran*c*i*s*co Vazquez

[fol. 18v]
o alguno de los otros Capitan*es* / asi a los naturales de las di*c*has pro- / Vinçias
Como a los esPañoles q*ue* yban / en su Exerçito dixo que no sabe / mas de lo

que d*i*cho e declarado tiene / eçe(b)*p*to que viniendo de Vuelta En el valle / de los Coraçones por dos yndios mata- / ron con yerba a don tristan El Ca- / ballo e le *h*obieran A el muerto sino fuera / Socorrido porq*ue* *e*staban alçados e *h*abian / muerto A todos los esPañoles que en el / Valle *h*abian quedado Preso el uno / de *e*llos el d*i*cho don tristan le mando / cortar la mano E nar- izes y lo ynVio / d*e* *e*sta manera a los demas q*ue* *e*staban / alçados por los ate- moriçar e / Porque todavia Vinyan siguiendo / e flechando El Exerçito con yerba / tan braVa e pestifera que no escapa- / ba nadie de quantos herian e mo- / Rian *h*inchados e Rabiando dentro / de doze *h*oras e que ansimismo sabe / que *e*l d*i*cho don tristan dio tormento / a un esPañol de Cuyo nonbre no / tiene memoria en el d*i*cho Valle quan- / do yban porq*ue* dezia q*ue* le *h*abia / xviii

[fol. 19r]

832

Hurtado çiertas petacas y esTo por / d*i*cho de los negros del d*i*cho don tristan e / que *e*sto Sabe Çerca de lo que le *es* preg*u*nt*a*do / y no otra cosa para el jura- m*e*nto q*ue* hizo / y firmolo de su nonbre Fue le leydo / este su d*i*cho luego Como lo aCabo de d*ecir* y / Ratificose en el e Señalolo el d*i*cho / señor oydor ju*an* de paladinas

Chapter 6

Domingo Martín, the Fourth de Oficio Witness

A Veteran of the Conquest of Mexico

After the very short testimonies of the first three witnesses, Domingo Martín's declaration on May 31 was one of the longest. He gave lengthy, detailed, matter-of-fact accounts of the incidents about which he was asked. All the witnesses seem to have been very relaxed and comfortable in the presence of licenciado Tejada and his assistants. Little of the testimony seems reluctantly given and rarely does anyone appear to try to evade an answer. For no one was this truer than for Domingo Martín. His statements make it seem as though he was in a formal but friendly atmosphere. Since what he had to say was almost uniformly supportive of the actions of Vázquez de Coronado and the rest of his company, this easygoing air bespeaks a lack of hostility to the captain general on the part of the judge. Unlike his counterpart, the visitador general Tello de Sandoval, Tejada clearly was no blood-thirsty interrogator.

The lack of confrontation between judge and witnesses in the pesquisa is made even more significant by the fact that Tejada selected and summoned the witnesses and that so many of them, like Martín, were close associates of Vázquez de Coronado. As he replied to the first of Tejada's questions, "during

the reconnaissance and subjugation he was always in the company of and personally with Francisco Vázquez." Martín's position on the muster roll of the
expedition shows him as not in any of the companies led by captains, but
instead directly under the captain general.[1] He was a native of Las Brozas in
Extremadura, Spain, born there about 1502 or 1503.[2] This was the alleged
home town of Marina Gutiérrez de la Caballería, Vázquez de Coronado's
mother-in-law, and in the jurisdiction of Cáceres, where his father-in-law
Alonso de Estrada had served as *corregidor*. Martín also had business dealings
with Hernando Pérez de Bocanegra, who linked his family tightly to Vázquez
de Coronado's through marriage of three of his sons to daughters of the
former captain general.[3] It is possible that Martín participated in the expedition because of his connection with the Vázquez de Coronado-Estrada
family.

Domingo Martín was a longtime resident of the New World. He had
been in Cuba as early as 1517, sailed with Juan de Grijalva, and participated
in the conquest of Tenochtitlán under Hernán Cortés.[4] He was also one of the
conquerors of Pánuco, where he was granted the pueblo of Yagualicán in
encomienda. For at least three years he collected tribute of gold, slaves,
clothing, household servants, and provisions. When he returned to Spain to
get his wife and children, Nuño de Guzmán stripped him of his encomienda,
even though he had express permission to be temporarily absent. That permission had been conceded by Alonso de Estrada, then acting as lieutenant
governor of Nueva España, another reason for a positive connection with the
Vázquez de Coronado-Estrada family.[5] Martín's connections with Lorenzo
de Tejada may have been even stronger; he testified in the oidor's defense
during his visita conducted in 1546 by Tello de Sandoval.[6] Nevertheless, he
was never successful in recovering the encomienda.

His wife died upon reaching the New World and by 1535 Martín remar-
ried. Then, in October 1537 he was granted a solar in Mexico City.[7] He left
his second wife behind in the viceregal capital when he joined the expedition
to Tierra Nueva. As part of his plans for benefiting from the expedition, he
and fellow expedition member (and also a witness in the 1544 pesquisa)
Cristóbal de Escobar formed a company and purchased livestock to take

along for sale.⁸ Martín was another individual of higher than average status in the expedition, to judge by the four horses he brought along.⁹

During his testimony before Tejada on the last day of May 1544, Martín consistently maintained that Vázquez de Coronado had behaved properly, even in ordering El Turco killed. In this respect, his testimony is in line with that of the rest of the witnesses, offering no criticism of the captain general and placing blame principally on dead men, especially Diego de Alcaraz. In general, he said he saw no brutality or outrages committed against Indians at all, and the violence done to them they brought on themselves by refusing repeatedly to submit to the dominion of the king. Consistently an apologist for the expedition, Martín nevertheless revealed that it had burned ten Tiguex pueblos and had cut off the hands of many Indians to put fear in others.

A TRANSLATION
OF THE TESTIMONY

Fourth de Oficio Witness (Domingo Martín)[10]

[19r cont'd] Domingo Martín, a citizen of the city of Mexico, presented and accepted as a witness for this investigation, having given his oath in the form prescribed by law and having promised to tell the truth about what he might be asked, was questioned as follows.

{*1*} He was asked whether he knows Francisco Vázquez de Coronado, don Diego de Guevara, don Tristán de Arellano, don García López de Cárdenas, the councilman of Sevilla Diego López , don Rodrigo Maldonado, Hernando de Alvarado, Barrionuevo, Zaldívar, and the other captains who went to reconnoiter and subjugate the provinces of Cíbola, Tiguex, Cicuique, and Quivira and [19v] whether he was present during the subjugation and exploration. He answered that he knows all of those referred to in the question, by appearance, voice, and conversation that he has had with them for about the last six years, and some of them for much longer than that. He was present during the subjugation and reconnaissance from the beginning when they entered [Tierra Nueva] until they returned to this city. And during the reconnaissance and subjugation he was always in the company of and personally with Francisco Vázquez, who was general of the army.

{*2*} [The witness] was asked whether, when the army was on its way and entered the valleys of Corazones and Señora to make the reconnaissance, [the people of] those valleys and the other towns and provinces of that region came out in peace and rendered obedience to his majesty without offering resistance. Did they provide the necessary food and other things they had to the people and the army? And did they welcome them into their houses and towns? He answered that it is true that in the valley of Corazones and in the valley of Señora, as well as in the province of Fuyas[11] [20r] and all the other provinces that they found until they reached Cíbola, the natives came out in peace, without the least resistance, and offered obedience to His Majesty and to the general in his royal name. They welcomed the people of the company into their houses and towns and provided necessary foodstuffs to the extent possible. This was especially true in the province of Señora, where they furnished supplies abundantly and loaded the horses and mules with them. The Spaniards did, however, obtain some things by trade.

{3} [Martín] was [then] asked which captains and people the general left in those provinces, especially in the valley of Señora, and for what purpose, inasmuch as the people there were and remained at peace. He replied that when Francisco Vázquez's company passed through those towns, valleys, and provinces no one remained behind in them. But the general left an order for don Tristán de Arellano, who had remained in Culiacán with most of the company, [to the effect] that he should proceed deliberately and take quarters in those valleys and towns, until he sent [20v] orders to do otherwise.

When don Tristán had arrived at those towns Francisco Vázquez sent a [man named] Melchor Díaz back from Cíbola in order that he would establish himself in those towns and provinces with a certain contingent of the people and from there make a reconnaissance to the Mar del Sur. Then don Tristán, with the rest of the people, would depart and travel on to Cíbola, where Francisco Vázquez was. When Melchor Díaz had arrived at the valley of Corazones and Señora, he went to explore toward the Mar del Sur with the people he deemed suitable. And he left in his place, as *alcalde mayor*, a [man named] Alcaraz, who had been a citizen of Culiacán.

{4} [The witness] was asked what brutality and outrages Alcaraz or the people who remained in those valleys committed against the native Indians, because of which they rose up in arms and killed the Spaniards and other people who had stayed there. He replied that he had not seen this, but he had heard it said publicly that [the Indians] had taken up arms because Alcaraz and the Spaniards [21r] asked for food and some Indian women to serve them, but not because of other outrages they had committed against [the Indians].

{5} [Martín] was [then] asked whether he knew or had heard that [the Indians] had risen up and killed the Spaniards because they had taken women and girls by force. And had Francisco Vázquez punished them, excused what they did, or held it to be permissible? He answered that he did not know more than that he had heard from some persons that [the Indians] had risen up for the reasons expressed in the question. He does know that [this situation] weighed on Francisco Vázquez, and [the witness] heard him swear that he would have to hang everyone whom he learned had committed any rapes in those valleys. Regarding Alcaraz, the Indians of those provinces and towns killed him and many Spaniards.

{6} He was asked whether the [people of the] province of Cíbola came out to Francisco Vázquez in peace and what brutality and noteworthy out-rages he committed against them. Or did he take them by force even though [21v] they offered no resistance, and what efforts did he make in order that they might offer peace? [Martín] replied that when he had come within three leagues of Cíbola, two or three Indians from that province and principal pueblo came to [the general]. And he spoke to them by means of signs, so that they would understand that they did not come to do them harm. And he told them that they should tell the people of the pueblo to offer peace.

So these Indians went away and then the general sent the maestre de campo don García López de Cárdenas in advance to reconnoiter and learn what was there. When they had established a bivouac in a woodland and night had fallen [the Indians][12] struck him and his troops, shooting arrows at them and letting loose some horses. When this was known to Francisco Vázquez, he had all the people moved. And he sent don García López ahead with fray Juan de Padilla, fray Marcos de Niza, and a scribe named Hernando Bermejo to summon the Indians to come in peace and to offer obedience to his majesty. Leaving the rest of the people behind so as not to provoke the Indians, the general himself soon came [22r] after the advance group and joined with the clerics to deliver the requerimiento.

When he saw that the summons did not succeed and the Indians were shooting arrows at them, [the general] ordered that they be attacked. He forced them back until they were shut up in the pueblo, where they fortified themselves and threw up barricades. They injured the general severely and don García López and other individuals and killed a number of horses. Then [the

Spaniards] demanded again that they submit and said that they would not harm them. [The Indians] came down [from their roofs] and left the pueblo.

{7} [The witness] was asked whether [the Spaniards] killed any of the native Indians or committed other brutality or outrages against them after they had offered peace. Who committed them and at whose order? He responded [by saying] that after [the Indians] had submitted no injury was done to them. Rather, all was comfort and kind treatment. [The general] had a public announcement made that no one was [22v] to harm [the Indians] nor should they take anything against their will, under pain of certain punishment. [The witness] knows and saw that the general punished several Nahua Indians because they had taken some things without the natives' permission. With this favorable treatment [the Indians] soon returned to occupy their houses and pueblos and to deal with the Spaniards.

{8} [Martín] was asked whether the [Indians of the] provinces of Tiguex, Cicuique, Brava, and Chia offered peace to the general and obedience to His Majesty without offering any resistance and defending themselves. He stated that it is true that all of those provinces offered peace and obedience to His Majesty and to the general in his royal name, without putting up any resistance whatever. And they left the first pueblo in the Tiguex province vacant, so that [the Spaniards] could have better quarters. The Indians moved to other neighboring pueblos. Furthermore, they supplied corn, flour, and some poultry,[13] as well as some [23r] clothing and hides that they had.

{9} He was asked whether [the Spaniards] seized a cacique of Cicuique they called Bigotes and others called Ysopete, Turco, and Xabe, even though those pueblos were at peace. Because the Indian called Turco gave an account of a wealthy land and said that the cacique and Ysopete had brought some gold bracelets and other valuable jewelry from there and because Bigotes and Ysopete did not confirm what the Indian called Turco said, but denied knowing about that land and having such bracelets and jewelry, did they set dogs on them? Speak and state whether the general ordered the dogs unleashed against them and whether he was present! Otherwise, who set the dogs on them?

[The witness] replied that what he knows is that he heard it publicly and widely said that Hernando de Alvarado had the dogs set upon them because Bigotes and the cacique denied what the Indian called Turco said. [23v] The witness saw that one of [the Indians] had a dog bite on one thigh. And afterwards he saw him healthy. He believes and is certain that this was done by order of the general. No one would dare do such a thing without his order and consent, if the general were in the pueblo where what has been said occurred (and he was), and he kept the people so obedient and subject to his order that even in minor things of little importance no one would dare disobey him or do such a thing without his permission and order.

{*10*} [Martín] was [then] asked what other cruelty, outrages, and lawlessness were committed by the general or by others at his command against those natives and pueblos before they rose up. He replied that he knows nothing more than that the Spaniards asked the Indians for food that was necessary because they did not have any.

{*11*} He was [then] asked whether the Indians and [24r] natives of the provinces of Tiguex, Cicuique, and Brava rose up in arms and rebelled because of dogs having been set on the cacique and Bigotes. He answered that he does not know more than that he had heard it said openly in the camp. And soon, within ten or twelve days, [the Indians] rose up and killed many horses and beasts of burden, so that [the general] had to besiege and fight against them in order to bring them to peace. There was a pueblo to which [the Spaniards] laid siege where they fought for about a month and a half. In that siege [the Indians] killed seven Spaniards and wounded more than another seventy or eighty.

{*12*} [The witness] was asked whether after the uprising and before [the Spaniards] battled against and occupied the pueblos the general had summoned them to offer peace and to render obedience to his majesty again. And did he tell them that [the Spaniards] would do them no harm and would not mistreat them? He stated that he saw the general send don García López de Cárdenas with a group of men to summon [24 v] the [people of the] first pueblo that rose up to offer peace or else he would make war on them and execute justice on them. He had also heard it said that none of those Indians were willing to come to peace until they killed and burned everyone except the women and children, none of whom were touched. [The Spaniards] had killed and burned the rest of them in the pueblo.

Before making war against them, [the general] had assembled the officials, clerics, and captains who came in the company, in order to consult with them as to whether he should make war against [the Indians] or whether they should let them be and move on forward. This witness saw that everyone agreed that he should make war on them and not leave any place in revolt, since [the Spaniards] had to travel beyond.

{13} [Martín] was [then] asked how many of the rebellious pueblos were burned and how many Indians from the pueblos that were overrun during the war were seized and set upon by dogs. And were all of the pueblos that were burned and laid waste in this province [25r] taken by force and did they offer resistance or did [the Spaniards] occupy them when they were empty and deserted? He replied that ten pueblos of the Tiguex province were burned and destroyed. Only two of them were entered by force, they being the one occupied by don García López mentioned earlier and the other one laid siege to by Francisco Vázquez. [The Indians] abandoned the rest.

The pueblo laid siege to and occupied by Francisco Vázquez was burned [with][14] a great many Indians inside their houses because [the Spaniards] could not subdue them and get them out without setting fire to the pueblo. And the Indians were doing significant injury [to the Spaniards] from their houses. But concerning those [Indians] captured alive, [the witness] did not see that any were burned, except a few as punishment. And to put fear in the rest, [the Spaniards] cut off their hands. He does not know who did this nor by whose order it was done. Further, he did not see that [25v] dogs were unleashed against any [of the Indians].

{14} Because he says that only two pueblos offered resistance and were fortified, he was asked why [the Spaniards] burned the remaining empty pueblos that neither offered resistance nor did any damage [to the Spaniards] by war. He answered that they were burned as firewood and [to produce] charcoal and to put fear in the rest of the pueblos and provinces that had risen up in arms. Also he heard that at the pueblo Francisco Vázquez subdued he had sent [persons] to summon [the Indians] with kind words to offer peace. [The Indians] came down and said to don García López, who had gone to deliver the requerimiento, that they were sorry for what they had done, that he should enter [the pueblo], and that they would deliver a peace agreement to him. When he had dismounted they embraced him and wanted to take him into the pueblo to kill him. And they would have done so, if he had not been helped by his companions.

{*15*} [The witness] was [then] asked why [the Spaniards] killed the Indian called Turco, [26r] who did the killing, by whose order it was done, and whether the general was present. He replied that the general was angry with the Indian called Turco because nothing he had said had turned out to be true and he had led [the Spaniards] deceptively by many roundabout ways so often as to put the camp and all the people in danger of being lost. One afternoon in Quivira at a town called Tabas [Martín] saw the Indian called El Turco taken from the tent of Hernando de Alvarado and led to that of Juan de Zaldívar and the councilman Diego López. He heard it publicly and widely said that in the night they garrotted and buried him. [The witness] never saw or heard about him again. He does not know on whose order this was done, but he believes and is certain that it was by Francisco Vázquez's order because [26v] he was present in the camp where this occurred. And furthermore, as he has said, all the people and captains were so obedient and mindful of his commands that no one would have dared to do such a thing without his permission and order.

{*16*} He was [then] asked to state and declare what other outrages and brutality Francisco Vázquez committed either against the natives of those provinces or against the Spaniards. He said that he does not know and did not see that outrages or brutality were committed against anyone beyond what he has already stated and declared. On the contrary, he saw that in Quivira [the general] traded with the Indians and bought food and the other necessary things.

By the oath that he swore, he said that this is what he knows and nothing further. And he signed his name. [27r] When he was read his statement as soon as he had finished making it, he confirmed it and signed his name.

Domingo Martín

A TRANSCRIPT
OF THE TESTIMONY

[fol. 19r cont'd][15]

{T*estigo*}

El d*i*cho domingo martin v*ezi*no de la / ÇiUdad de mexico t*esti*go presentado / y Rescibido para la d*i*cha ynformaçion / el q*ual* *h*aViendo jurado en
forma de / d*erec*ho e prometiendo de d*ecir* v*er*dad de / lo que le fuere preguntado Se le hizie- / Ron las pregu*n*tas syguient*es* / Fue preg*unta*do sy
conosçe A Fran*ci*sco Vazq*uez* / de coronado e a don diego de guevara / e a
don tristan de arellano e don / G*a*r*ci*a lopez de Cardenas e di*e*go lopez Ve- /
ynte y quatro de seVilla e don R*o*d*ri*go / maldonado e a hernando de alVa- /
Rado e a barrionuevo e çaldiVar / e a otros Capitanes q*ue* fueron a la / conquista e desqubrimi*ento* de la*s* proVinçias / de Çibola e tiguex çiquyq*ue* e
quiVira

[fol. 19v]

E que si se hallo presente al d*i*cho / desqubrimi*ento* e conquista dixo q*ue*
Conosçe / a todoS los contenidos En esta pregu*n*ta / Por Vista habla trato E
Conversacion / q*ue* Con ellos ha tenido de seys Años A / esta p*ar*te Poco mas
o menos algu*n*os / de *e*llos de mucho antes y que se hallo / en el d*i*cho
desqubrimy*ento* E conquista deSde / el prinçipio y entrada hasta que Vol- /
Vieron a esta çiUdad e que sienpre se / hallo en las d*i*chas conquistas e desCu-
/ brimyentos en la Conpañia E Con la misma / persona del d*i*cho fran*ci*sco
Vazquez ge- / neral que (h)era del d*i*cho Exerçito / Fue preguntado el Valle
de los Cora- / Çones E señora e los otros pueblos / e ProVinçias A estos
ComarCanos sy / quando yban y entraron a hazer el d*i*cho / d*e*sCubrimi*ento*
si les Salieron de Paz / E dieron la obidiençia A su mag*es*tad syn / se poner
en Resistençia y al Exer- / Çito e gente la Comida nesçesaria / e de lo que
ellos tenyan e los aCogie- / Ron en sus pu*eblo*s y Casas dixo que *es* / v*er*dad

que ansi los del Valle de los / Coraçones Como los del Valle de / Señora y de la proVinçia de fuyas / xix

[fol. 20r]

833

Y toDas las demas que hallaron / hasta llegar a Çibola les Salieron de / Paz y syn Resistençia alguna die- / Ron la obediençia a su magestad / e al dicho general en su Real nonbre / e los aCogieron en sus Casas e pueblos / y les dieron las Comida nesçesaria confor- / me A su posibilidad esPecial en la proVinçia / de señora donde los proVyeron largo de / bastimentos y Cargaron de ellos sus CaballoS / e azemylas aunque algunos Se habian / Por Rescate que los esPañoles les / daban / Fue preguntado que Capitanes e gente / dexo el dicho françisco Vazquez en las / dichas proVinçias esPecial en el dicho Valle / de señora y Para que Efecto pues / estaban y quedaban de Paz dixo / que al tiempo que por los pueblos / Valles e proVinçias PaSaron ninguna / Gente quedo en ellos Pero que dexo / mandado A don tristan de arella- / no que quedaba(n) en quliacan Con la / mayor parte del Canpo que se viniese / Poco a poco y se aposentase en los dichos / Valles y pueblos hasta que le ynViase

[fol. 20v]

A manDar otra coSSa E que habien- / do llegado el dicho don tristan a loS / dichos valles el dicho francisco Vazquez / Torno a ynViar desde Çibola a un / melchior diaz Para que Residiese / en los dichos pueblos E proVinçias Con cierta / parte de gente Para que de alli desCubri- / ese la mar del sur e que el dicho don tris- / tan con la demas Gente que traya Cami- / nase e se fuese A Çibola donde el dicho / Françisco Vazquez estaba y llegado / el dicho melchior diaz al dicho valle / de loS Coraçones y señora Con la dicha / Gente que le paresçio fue A descu- / brir la mar del sur y dexo en su lu- / Gar y por alcalde mayor a un alCa- / Raz Vecino que (h)era de quliacan / Fue preguntado que crueldades y ma- / lostratamientos hizo el dicho alCaraz / o las personas que en los dichos Valles ha- / bian quedado a los yndios natura- / les Porque se alçaron y mataron / los esPañoles y gente que en ellos / habia quedado dixo

q*ue* *e*ste t*e*st*i*go no lo Vio / p*er*o q*ue* oyo dezyr publicamente que / Porque el
d*i*cho alCaraz y españoles / xx

[fol. 21r]
834
les piDian basTimentos y algunas / yndias para su serviço Se *h*abian alça- /
do e no Por otros malostratamy*en*tos / que les *h*obiesen (F)*h*echo / Fue pre-
g*un*tado si sabe o oyo que se *h*obiesen / levantado E muerto los d*i*chos esPa-
/ ñoles Porq*ue* les Tomaban Por fuerça / las mugeres E hijas e si lo Castigo /
el d*i*cho Fran*ci*sco Vazquez o lo desimulo / e *h*obo por bueno dixo q*ue* este t*es*-
t*i*go no / lo sabe mas de que oyo algunas perso- / nas que se *h*abian levantado
por / lo en esta preg*un*ta Contenido e que sabe / que le peso al d*i*cho fran*ci*sco
Vazquez E / le oyo jurar que *h*abia de ahorcar / a todos los q*ue* supiese que en
los d*i*chos / Valles E pu*eb*los *h*obiesen (f)*h*echo alguna de / las d*i*chas fuerças
e q*ue* al d*i*cho alCaraz / los yndios de las d*i*chas proVinçias e / pu*eb*los le
mataron E A muchos esPa- / ñoles / Fue preguntado sy la proVinçia de /
Çibola Salio de paz al d*i*cho fran*ci*sco / Vazquez y que crueldades y nota- / bles
malostratamyentos les hizo o / Si los tomo por fuerça ni poniendo-

[fol. 21v]
Se Ellos En ResisTençia E / q*ue* diligencias hizo para que se diesen / de paz
dixo que llegado a treSS le- / guas de çibola Vinieron a el dos o / tres yndios
de la d*i*cha proVinçia e pu*eb*lo / prinçipal y el d*i*cho Fran*ci*sco Vazquez les /
hablo por señas dandoles a entender / que no Venyan para hazerles mal / q*ue*
dixesen a los del pu*eb*lo que se diesen / de paz e asi los d*i*chos yndios Se fueron
/ y el d*i*cho General ynVio luego delante / a don Garç*i*a lopez de Cardenas
ma- / estre de Canpo Para q*ue* d*e*sCubrie- / se e supiese lo que *h*abia e *h*abi-
endo- / se aposentado y (f)*h*echo noche en un / monte los dieron (dieron) En
el y en / su Gente y los flecharon e hiziero*n* / Soltar algunos Caballos y sabido
/ Por Fran*ci*sco Vazquez hizo moVer to- / da la Gente e ynVio delante al /
d*i*cho don g*ar*c*i*a lopez e a fray juan / de padilla e a fray marcos de / niça e a
Un escr*i*vano q*ue* se llama her- / nando bermejo a les Requerir vinie- / sen de
paz y diesen la obidiençia A / su mag*estad* y el mismo General fue luego / xxi

[fol. 22r]

835

Tras de ellos e Se junto con los / dichos Religiosos a les hazer el dicho Re- / querimiento dexando la demas Gente / atraSS por no los alborotar e visto / que no aproVechaban los dichos Reque- / Rimiento e que los dichos yndios los / Flechaban mando Ronper en ellos / y los Retruxo hasta los meter / en el pueblo donde se enCasTillaron E / hizieron fuertes e hirieron mala- / mente al dicho General e al dicho don / Garcia lopez e a otras personas e / mataron Çiertos Caballos e luego les / Tornaron A Requerir Se diesen / e que no les harian daño alguno / e los dichos yndios Se baxaron e les / dexaron el pueblo / Fue preguntado sy desPues que se dieron / de paz mataron algunos de los / dichos yndios naturales o les hizieron / otras crueldades e malostratamientos / e quien lo hizo e Por Cuyo mandado / dixo que despues que se dieron nin- / Gun daño Se les hizo antes todo / Regalo e buen tratamyento e hizo / dar un pregon que nadie les hiziese

[fol. 22v]

Daño ni les tomase Contra su / Voluntad Cosa alguna so çiertas / Penas e sabe e vio que Castigo A çier- / tos yndios mexicanos Porque contra / Voluntad de los dichos naturales / les habian tomado çiertas Cosas e / que con este buen tratamiento Se torna- / Ron luego A poblar sus Casas y pueblos / y Contratar con los esPanoles / Fue preguntado Sy las proVinçias de ti- / guex y çiquyque y b(i)raVa e chia si se / dieron de paz al dicho general y la / obidiençia A su magestad syn se poner / en defensa ni Resistençia alguna / dixo que es verdad que todas las / dichas proVinçias Se dieron de paz / syn hazer Resistençia alguna E la / obidiençia A su magestad e al dicho general / en su Real nonbre e les dexaron / porque se pudiesen mejor aposentar / desenbaraçado el primero pueblo que / en la Provinçia de tiguex y los yn- / dios Se pasaron A otros pueblos / ComarCanos e les proveyeron de ma- / yz harina e algunas aVes E / [no number]

[fol. 23r]

836

de la Ropa E Cueros que ellos / tenian / Fue preguntado sy estando Asy / de

Paz los dichos Pueblos pren- / dieron al Caçique de çiquyque que / llamaban bigotes e a otro y- / sopete e al turCo e a Xabe e a / Causa que el dicho yndio llamado turco / daba Relacion de Una Tierra RiCa / e dezia que el dicho caçique E ysopete / habian traydo de la dicha Tierra Unos / braçaletes de oro e otras joyas / RiCas Porque los dichos bigotes e yso- / pete no concordaban con lo que el / dicho yndio llamado turCo dezia / e negaban saber de la dicha tierra / ni tener Tales braçaletes ni joyas / los Aperrearon diga e aclare sy loS / mando aperrear El dicho General / y si se hallo presente o quien loS / aperreo dixo que lo que este testigo / Sabe es que oyo decir por muy / Publico E noTorio que porque el dicho / bigotes e Caçique negaban lo que el dicho / yndio llamado Turco dezia hernando / de alvarado los habia (f)hecho aperrear

[fol. 23v]
E que este Testigo ViDo al uno / de ellos Una mordedura de perro / en un muslo de una pierna e que / despues le vio Sano e que cree / e tiene Por çierto que fue por mandado / del dicho General e que nadie osa- / Ra hazerlo syn su mandado / E Consentimiento Por estar / Como estaba el dicho General en el / Pueblo donde lo susodicho aCaesçio E / Porque tenya la Gente tan / obidiente E suje(c)ta que aun en / las Cosas muy pequeñas E de poCa / ynportançia nadie no se osaba / desmandar ni hazerla syn su / liçençia E mandado / Fue preguntado que otros malos- / tratamyentos E desafueros hizo / el dicho General o otros por su / mandado en los dichos naturales e / pueblos antes que se alçasen dixo / que no lo sabe mas de pedirles la / C(a)omida nesçesaria Porque los españo- / les no la tenyan / Fue preguntado si los dichos yndios / [no number]

[fol. 24r]
837
e naturales de las dichas proVinçias / de tiguex çiquyque e braVa Se alçaron / e Rebelaron Por el dicho Aperreamyento / que hizieron en los dichos Caçique e bigo- / tes dixo que no lo Sabe mas de haber- / lo oydo dezir publicamente en el / Real Porque luego de(n)sde a diez o / doze dias Se alçaron y les mataron /

muchos Caballos e bestias de Carga e / hobo nesçesydad de los tener çercadoS / y Conbatirlos Para Reduzirlos / de paz e que hobo pueblo que lo tuVieron / Çercado Conbatiendole mes y medio / Poco mas o menos en el qual çerco / les mataron siete esPañoles y les hi- / Rieron mas de otros Setenta o ochenta / Fue preguntado sy despues de alçados / antes que los Conbatiesen y Entra- / sen sy el dicho General les hizo Reque- / Rir que se diesen de paz E VolViesen / a dar la obidiençia A su magestad e que / no se les haria daño ni maltratamiento / dixo que este testigo vio que el dicho general / ynVio A don garcia lopez de Cardenas / con çierta parte de Gente a Requerir

[fol. 24v]
Al primero pueblo que se hAbia / alçado que se diesen de Paz e sino / que les diese Guerra e hiziesen / de ellos justiçia E que oyo dezir que / ninguno de los dichos yndios Se quiso / dar hasta que Todos murieron / e se quemaron Eçe(b)pto los niños E / mugeres que en estos no se toCo e que / los demas los habian muerto y que- / mado en el dicho pueblo y que antes / que se les hiziese Guerra hizo juntar / los ofiçiales E Religiosos e capita- / nes que Venyan En el Canpo para con- / sultar Con ellos sy les haria la / Guerra o los deXaria e pasaria A- / delante y este testigo vio Como Todos / Se Concordaron en que se les hizie- / se guerra e no dexasen Cosa levanta(n)da / Pues habian de pasar adelante / Fue preguntado que tantos pueblos de los Rebe- / lados Se quemaron e que tantos / yndios de los TomadoS en la dicha / Guerra Tomarian E aperrearon / e si todos los pueblos que quemaron / y Asolaron en la dicha proVinçia los / [no number]

[fol. 25r]
838
Tomaron por Fuerça E se pusieron / en Resistençia o si los entraran / estando yermos y desmanParados / dixo que se quemarian y asola- / Rian diez pueblos de la dicha proVinçia / de tiguex e que solamente los dos / Se entraron Por Fuerça que (h)eran / el que entro don garcia lopez que de suso / Se haze mynçion e otro a que puso / çerco Françisco Vazquez Porque los / demas los

desmanpararon E que en el / Pueblo que entro y sobre que tenya(n) / puesto çerco el dicho francisco Vazquez / Se quemo Gran copia de yndios / dentro de las Casas porque si no (h)era / pegandoles fuego no los Podian con- / quisTar ni sacar de ellas e desde / ellas les hazian notable daño los / dichos yndios pero que de los que se / Tomaron ViVos no Vio que se que- / mase alguno Eçe(b)pto que algunos de es- / Tos por Castigo e Por poner temor / a los demas les Cortaron las manos / e que no sabe quien lo hizo ni por / Cuyo mandado e que no Vio que

[fol. 25v]
Aperreasen Alguno / Fue preguntado Pues dize que en / solos doS pueblos hubo Resistençia / y se hizieron Fuertes que porque quema- / Ron los demas pueblos pues es- / taban desmanparados y en ellos / no habia Resistençia e de elloS / Se les hazia Guerra ni daño alguno / dixo que se quemaron Para le- / na y Carbon e Por poner Temor / a los demas pueblos e proVinçias / que estaban alçados e que oyo / que en el pueblo que Conquisto francisco Vazquez / habiendolos ynViado a Requerir / diesen de paz Con buenas palabras / hizieron apear al dicho don Garçia lo- / pez que los yba a rrequerir dizien- / do que ellos estaban ArrepentidoS / de lo que habian (f)hecho que entrase / y le darian Asyento de paz e que habien- / dose apeado Se abraçaron con el e / lo quisieron meter dentro del pueblo pa- / Ra lo ma(ta)Tar e que de (f)hecho lo hi- / zieran sino fuera Socorrido de sus / Conpañeros / Fue preguntado que por que causa / mataron al dicho yndio llamado turco / [no number]

[fol. 26r]
839
quien le mato e Por Cuyo mandado / e sy se hallo presente el dicho gene- / Ral dixo que el dicho General / estaba mal con el dicho yndio lla- / mado turco porque jamas habian / hallado verdad de quanto les ha- / bia dicho e que los habia llevado / enGanados Por diversos Rodeos / tanto que puso el Real e toda la gen- / te en Condiçion de perderse e que vio / que una Tarde estando en quiVira / en un pueblo que Se dize tabas saCar / al dicho yndio llamado el turco

de la / Tienda de hernando de alvarado E / llevarlo a la de juan de çaldiVar /
e el veyntiquatro diego lopez e que / oyo decir por publico e noTorio que aquella
/ noche le habian dado Un Garrote / e le habian enterrado E que nunca mas /
le vio ni se supo de el ni se sabe por / Cuyo mandado mas de que cree e / tiene
por çierto que fue por man- / dado del dicho francisco Vazquez por-

[fol. 26v]
que esTaba Presente en el Real / donde lo susodicho aCaesçio e por- / que
Como dicho Tiene toda la gente e Ca- / pitanes le estaban tan sujetos / e obidientes que nadie osara / hazerlo syn su liçencia e manda- / do / Fue preguntado diga e declare / que otros malostratamyen- / tos e crueldades haya
(f)hecho / el dicho Françisco Vazquez asy / en los naturales de las dichas /
ProVinçias Como A esPañoles / dixo que no lo Sabe ni vio que / A nadie
hiziese malostrata- / myentos ni crueldades mas / de lo que dicho e declarado
tiene / antes Vio que en quiVira Con- / praba e habia Por Rescates / de los
yndios la Comida y las otras / cosas nesçeSarias E que esto es / lo que sabe y
no otra cosa para / el juramento que tiene (f)hecho / y firmolo de su nonbre
fue / [no number]

[fol. 27r]
840
le leydo A esTe testigo esTe / su dicho luego como lo aCabo de / decir y Ratificose en el / domingo martin

Chapter 7

Juan de Contreras, the Fifth de Oficio Witness

The Head Groom

Juan de Contreras received a license to go to Nueva España in 1538 from his home in Lepe near Huelva in Andalucía, Spain.[1] By September 1539 he was a member of Viceroy Mendoza's personal guard, in which he served until leaving with the expedition to Tierra Nueva.[2] During the expedition he was "always personally with Francisco Vázquez, because he was his head groom. He always ate and lived in his house and slept at the entrance to his tent." He took with him a respectable number of three horses.[3] Upon returning to Mexico City, he worked as an interpreter for the audiencia, a position he continued to occupy as late as 1582.[4]

As might be expected because of his very close association with both the captain general and the viceroy, the only suggestions of wrongdoing he made during his testimony before Tejada in June 1544 did not touch either of those individuals. He even gave a completely sanitized account of the capture of Cíbola, from which all reference to fighting was expunged, an account at variance with every other known account of those events. He did, however, suggest that some culpability for mistreatment of native peoples rested with Juan de Villegas, García López de Cárdenas, and Tristán de Arellano. Despite that, the pervading tenor of his statements was that Vázquez de Coronado and his captains always behaved properly toward the natives of Tierra Nueva, even though he said that the captain general had ordered and was present at the unleashing of dogs against Bigotes and the cacique. Nor, according to Contreras, did Vázquez de Coronado punish Juan de Villegas for the rape he committed, although he was aware of it.

Although Contreras spoke as though any violence committed by the captain general's order was justified, he provided some of the most graphic eyewitness testimony of that violence, which may have eventually led to the fiscal's lodging of charges of cruelty against Vázquez de Coronado. He told, for instance, of the hands, noses, and tongues of Indians being cut off at San Gerónimo; of dogs being set on messengers from Cicuique and on three prisoners at Pueblo del Cerco; of Bigotes and the cacique being tortured three times; and of 13 Tiguex pueblos burned, as well as 15 Tiguex prisoners. That testimony certainly must have added to the weight of evidence against López de Cárdenas who claimed that Contreras, Juan Troyano, and Melchior Pérez were among his principal enemies, for which reason their testimony concerning his actions during the expedition should be disregarded.[5]

A TRANSLATION
OF THE TESTIMONY

Fifth de Oficio Witness (Juan de Contreras)⁶

[27r cont'd] Juan de Contreras, an interpreter for the Royal Audiencia and a vecino of the city of Mexico, accepted as a witness for this investigation, having given his oath in the form required by law, by God, Santa María, and a sign of the cross, promised to tell the truth. He was asked the following questions.

{1} He was asked whether he knows Francisco Vázquez de Coronado, don García López de Cárdenas, don Diego de Guevara, don Tristán de Arellano, Diego López (a councilman of Sevilla), don Rodrigo Maldonado, Hernando de Alvarado, Barrionuevo, Zaldívar, [27v] don Pedro de Tovar, and the other captains who went to reconnoiter and subjugate the tierra nueva of Cíbola, Tiguex, Cicuique, and Quivira and the other neighboring provinces. He answered that he knows all of those mentioned in the question, by appearance, voice, behavior, and conversation that he has had with them for about the last five years. He was present during the subjugation and reconnaissance of all those provinces from the beginning until they returned to this city. He was always personally with Francisco Vázquez, because he was his head groom. He always ate and lived in his house and slept at the entrance to his tent.

{2} [The witness] was asked whether the people of the valleys of Corazones, Señora, and Uraba and the other towns and provinces that there are between Culiacán and Cíbola came out to Francisco Vázquez in peace, without offering any resistance, [28r] and rendered obedience to his majesty. Did they provide the necessary food they had and could get to the general and the armed force?' And did they welcome them and accommodate them in their houses and towns? Or were they put on the defensive? He answered that all of those towns and provinces came out to Francisco Vázquez and those who went with him in peace, without taking up arms or offering resistance. They welcomed [the company] into their houses and towns and provided the foodstuffs that they had. And they rendered obedience to his majesty and to the general in his royal name.

{3} [Contreras] was asked whether the general or any of the captains who have been mentioned perpetrated any brutality or outrage against those towns or any of their natives. And if others committed [such acts], did [the general] punish them or excuse [what they did]? He replied that the general always treated [the Indians] well [28v] and so did the captains. If any individual from the army disobeyed, committing any outrage or taking corn or property from [the Indians], Francisco Vázquez imprisoned and punished that person. [The witness] said that he saw that for very slight infractions individuals were kept in shackles for two or three days' travel.

{4} He was [then] asked for what reason the natives of those provinces had risen up and killed the Spaniards who had remained there and whether Francisco Vázquez or any of the captains were responsible for that. And did the general punish those who overstepped what was permissible? He answered that according to rumor and what was said publicly, the cause of the uprising was the brutal acts committed by a [man named] Alcaraz, whom don Tristán de Arellano had left as captain. He cut off many Indians' hands, noses, and tongues and took [29r] women and girls by force and against their will, in order to have sex with them. Francisco Vázquez had no responsibility whatsoever for the uprising. The Indians themselves killed Alcaraz, and it was he who had committed those outrages and rapes. This is what he knows about what he is asked.

{5} [The witness] was asked what cruelty and outrages Francisco Vázquez or any of the captains committed in the province of Cíbola and whether the people there came out in peace or in war. He replied that when the company had come near Cíbola, [the general] sent [some of] the important men with fray Juan de Padilla and other clerics to deliver the requerimiento to the Indians. [They told the Indians that] they came in His Majesty's name to bring them into obedience to him and into knowledge of our holy

Catholic faith. And they said that if [the Indians] came out in peace and rendered obedience, they would be afforded kind treatment in all ways and they would be maintained [29v] in justice. Although this was said to them and they were made to understand by signs (because there was no interpreter) and though they were summoned many times, [the Indians] refused to comply. Instead, they began shooting arrows at the clerics and the other persons who went with them.

Seeing this and that they were making a defense and putting up resistance, Francisco Vázquez and those who went with him attacked them. They forced [the Indians] back until they were pushed into the pueblo, where they threw up barricades. [The clerics] again delivered the requerimiento and when that had been done [the Indians] offered peace and left the pueblo vacant with everything they had there. [The witness] did not see that they were cruelly treated in any way nor were outrages committed against any of them after they had surrendered. If [such things] had been done, this witness would have seen it and known about it. And it could not be otherwise if he were present for all of this (as he was). On the contrary, he saw that because of the fair treatment they were afforded, [30r] [the Indians] returned to reside in their houses and pueblo. Likewise, [the Indians] of the other neighboring pueblos who had left their houses returned to live there.

{6} [Contreras] was asked whether the [people of the] provinces of Tiguex, Cicuique, and Brava and the neighboring provinces put up resistance and took up arms or whether they came to offer peace to the general. He answered that all of those provinces came in peace and rendered obedience to His Majesty and to the general in his royal name, without putting up any resistance whatever. And they gave all of the necessary food to the Spaniards of the army, consistent with what they had and with what was possible. They welcomed [the Spaniards] into their houses and pueblos, vacating one pueblo, in which [the Spaniards] could establish quarters. [The Indians] moved to other pueblos.

{7} [The witness] was [then] asked why those pueblos and provinces [30v] rose up again. [To this] he replied that when Hernando de Alvarado went to reconnoiter the province of Cicuique (by order of Francisco Vázquez), he seized four of the people who came out in peace to render obedience. They were the cacique, the Indian called Bigotes, the one they called Turco, and another they called Ysopete. When that province sent messengers [asking that] the four Indians be given back and returned, because they had come out in peace and had offered no resistance whatsoever, Hernando de Alvarado unleashed dogs on the messengers, who were bitten badly.

After that had been done, the Indian called Turco provided information about a very wealthy land and said that the cacique had a gold bracelet and other valuable jewelry that he had brought from there. The cacique and Bigotes [31r] denied that and did not agree with what the Indian called Turco was saying. Because of that Hernando de Alvarado, with Francisco Vázquez present and by his order, set dogs on them three times. This witness saw that they were bitten and injured severely, as he was present when this occurred. Within a few days they regained their health and went to their pueblos. As soon as they left, the pueblos rose up in arms and [the witness] believes that it was because of the brutality, outrages, and setting on of dogs.

He knows and saw that at the same time the [people of the] Tiguex province rose up. He believes and is certain they did so because of the brutality and setting on of dogs which they learned had been perpetrated against [the Indians] from the province of Cicuique. It was widely known and publicly acknowledged that a [certain] Villegas, a brother of the Villegas who is *regidor* of the city of Mexico, went to a pueblo in the Tiguex province with other soldiers from [31v] don García López de Cárdenas's company and took a quantity of clothing, poultry, and mats without the natives' permission. He also seized an Indian woman with whom it was said he had sexual relations. This was said on the day it occurred. It was on the following day that the province rose up in arms. Although Francisco Vázquez was aware of what Villegas had done, [the witness] did not see nor does he know that [the general] punished him.

{8} [Contreras] was [then] asked how many pueblos in those provinces [the Spaniards] occupied by force and burned. He replied by saying that the uprising happened one night and that [the Indians] killed fifty or sixty horses and pack animals. Both because of this and because they took up arms and rebelled, [the Spaniards] made war on them and burned thirteen pueblos. But only three were defended and occupied by force. They rest that they burned they found empty and abandoned.

{*9*} [The witness] was asked why [the Spaniards] burned the others that offered no resistance and were abandoned since only three pueblos were defended and occupied [32r] by force. And who ordered them burned? He answered that they were burned by Francisco Vázquez's order, so that [the Indians] would not return and fortify them since they were strong pueblos.

{*10*} [Next] he was asked what cruelty and outrages were committed against the Indians who were captured alive in those pueblos. He stated that when Francisco Vázquez had laid siege to one pueblo in the Tiguex province he sent this witness with haste to don García López, who had laid siege to and was battling another pueblo. He was to tell don García not to execute some Indians who had left the pueblo and come to don García's camp to offer peace until the Indians called Turco and Ysopete arrived, so that they could witness the execution [32v] that was to be carried out. This was so that they would communicate it throughout Tierra Nueva and spread word of the execution to the natives and pueblos. When the witness had delivered the message to García López he saw a group of Indians leave the besieged pueblo and come to the Spaniards' camp in peace and without any weapons like men in distress who were begging for mercy. There were three or four of them. And [the witness] saw don García López order them put in his tent, where there were twenty others who, they said, had come to the camp and surrendered to the Spaniards in the same way that the four had (as he has stated).

When the Indians called Turco and Ysopete had come to don García López's camp, [the witness] saw that don García ordered that fifteen [33r] of the Indians who had come to the camp and offered peace, in the way he described, be taken from the tent. He ordered them tied one each to posts and that dry willow canes be placed around them with which to burn them. When the Indians who remained in the tent saw this, they began to defend themselves with poles that were there and stakes they pulled up, because they expected [the Spaniards] to do to them what they were doing to their companions. There, inside the tent, [the Spaniards] lanced and put to the sword everyone who was there and defending themselves, in such a way that none of them survived. [The witness] saw that when this had been done, they set fire to the others, who were still tied to posts, and burned them all alive. He believes and is sure that the execution and burning were done by order of Francisco Vázquez. Because he kept the captains and [other] people obedient and subject to his orders, [33v] no one would have dared to carry out the execution without his command. Furthermore, if this had been done before he ordered it, he would not have sent this witness to tell the maestre de campo not to execute the Indians until Turco and Ysopete arrived, so that they could spread the word about what they saw.

{11} [The witness] was asked whether he saw any other Indians who were taken alive during the siege burned or set upon by dogs. He replied that in the camp where Francisco Vázquez was [the Spaniards] captured three Indians and put them in the tent where [the general] was. [The Spaniards] told him that those Indians had fled from the besieged pueblo the night before and that he should decide what he would order done with them. And he ordered [the Spaniards] to set dogs on [the Indians]. The witness saw them unleash the dogs and kill the Indians. He saw that these individuals were present at the setting on of dogs: don Pedro de [34r] Tovar, don García López de Cárdenas, don Diego de Guevara, Hernando de Alvarado, and don Alonso Manrique. He also saw that many other Indians were burned within their houses because [the Spaniards] could not overcome them without setting fire nor were the Indians willing to submit.

{12} [Contreras] was [then] asked whether [the Spaniards] burned any pueblos or set dogs on any Indians in the province of Cicuique. He answered that no pueblo in that province was burned since [the Spaniards] could not overrun them because the province was strong. Nor were dogs set on Indians other than the cacique and Bigotes, as he has stated.

{13} He was asked how and by what means the death of the Indian called Turco happened and came about, who killed him, for what reason, and by whose order. [In response] he said that when Francisco Vázquez was in the province of Quivira, [34v] the councilman of Sevilla Diego López, Zaldívar, and Gómez Suárez repeatedly urged Francisco Vázquez to kill the Indian called Turco because he had led [the Spaniards] deceitfully and with his lies had caused them to suffer many hardships. Francisco Vázquez refused, asking what honor was to be gained by killing the Indian. But one night Francisco Vázquez called this witness and told him to go to Diego López and Zaldívar and tell them that if they thought the hour had come to kill the Indian called Turco, then they should do it secretly and in such a way that there would be no cries and it would not be heard in the camp.

So this witness went to the tent of [those captains] and told them what Francisco Vázquez had ordered. Then he saw them take the Indian called Turco from the tent where he was prisoner and they told him [35r] that he had lied and misled them and they asked him where the gold and wealth was that he had told them about in Tiguex. The Indian responded by saying that the towns where the gold and riches were still lay ahead. And he said that he had led them to Quivira in order to get his wife, who was there, and take her with him to the wealthy land. Without waiting for further talk or counter arguments, a soldier whom they said was Pérez (whom the witness does not know about nor where he is), by order of Diego López and Zaldívar, who were present, put a cord around the Indian's neck from behind and tightened it with a stick. That strangled him, and then they buried him next to the tent. When this witness went [to them] they had already dug the grave where they buried him.

{*14*} [Contreras] was [then] asked what other brutality [35v] and outrages he saw Francisco Vázquez and the other captains commit. He answered that he knows no more than that when don Tristán de Arellano was returning from the reconnaissance with the vanguard, as he came through the valley called Señora, he went in pursuit of two Indians who were fleeing. One of them, seeing himself pursued, entered a little hut, from where he shot an arrow that hit don Tristán's horse. The horse soon died because the arrow had been poisoned with herbs. When don Tristán saw that the horse had died, he lanced and killed the Indian. [The witness] knows that at that time that valley and province were at war and had risen in arms. And the Indians there had killed Alcaraz, who had been left as captain, and many other Spaniards.

He said that this is the truth [36r] and what he knows about what he is asked, according to the oath that he swore. And he signed his name. As soon as he had finished speaking his statement was read to him and he confirmed it. The lord judge affixed his sign.

Juan de Contreras

A TRANSCRIPT
OF THE TESTIMONY

[fol. 27r cont'd]⁷

{T*estigo*}

El d*i*cho Juan de contreras ynt(r)er– / pret(r)e d*e e*sta Real aUdienç*i*a / V*ecin*o de *e*sta çiUdad de mexico t*e*st*i*go Res– / çibido Para la d*i*cha ynformaç*i*on el / qual *h*abiendo jurado en forma de / d*e*rec*h*o por dios e Por Santa Ma– / Ria e por una Señal de cruz / el q*u*al prometio de declarar ver– / dad e se le hizieron las preguntas / syguientes / Fue preg*u*nta*d*o si conosçe A franc*i*sco / Vazq*u*ez de coronado e a don g*a*rc*i*a / lopez de Cardenas e a don d*i*ego / de guevara e a don tristan de / arellano e a diego lopez veynti– / quatro de seVilla e a don R*o*dr*i*go / maldonado e a hernando de alva– / Rado e a barrionuevo e a çaldiVar

[fol. 27v]

E A Don peDro De toVar e / a los otros Capitanes q*ue* fuero*n* / a la conquista e d*e*sCubrimyento / de la tierra nueva de çibola ti– / guex çicuyque quiVira e otras / ProVinçias Comarcanas dixo / q*ue* Consçe A los Contenidos en la / pregunta(s) de çinco años y mas t*iem*po / a esta p*ar*te de vista habla trato / e conversaç*i*on q*ue* Con ellos ha te– / nydo y se hallo presente *en e*l / des-cubrim*ien*to E co*n*quista de todas / las d*i*chas proVinç*i*as desde el / prinç*i*pio hasta que VolVieron / A esTa çiUdad e sienpre con la / persona de Franc*i*sco Vazquez Porq*ue* (h)era su Caballerizo e Comia E / ViVia a la continua dentro de / su Casa y a la Puerta de su tienda / dormya / Fue preguntado el valle de los / Coraçones y de señora y Urava / y los otros pueblos y proVinç*i*as / que *h*ay des*de* qu(i)liacan hasta çibola sy / le salieron de Paz al d*i*cho franc*i*sco Vaz– / quez e dieron syn Resistenç*i*a / [no number]

[fol. 28r]

841

Alguna la obedienç*i*a A su / magestad e al d*i*cho general y (h)e– / XerÇito los

mantenimientos nesçe- / Sarios e de lo que ellos tenyan E / alCançaban e los
aCogian e alo- / Xaban en sus Casas y pueblos / o si se pusieron en
Resistençia dixo / que todos los dichos pueblos e pro- / Vinçias syn se poner
en armas ni / en Resistençia alguna salieron / de paz al dicho Françisco
Vazquez / e a loS que Con el yban e los aCogieron / en sus Casas y pueblos y
les dieron / de los mantenimientos que ellos teni- / an e la obidiençia A su
magestad y al / dicho Francisco Vazquez en su Real / nonbre / Fue preguntado sy el dicho general / o alguno de los dichos Capitanes / Hizo en los dichos
pueblos o en alguno / de los naturales de ellos alguna / crueldad o maltratamyento / o si otros lo hizieron lo castigo e / disimulo dixo que el dicho
General / les hizo syenpre muy buen tratamyento

[fol. 28v]
E ansimismo los dichos Capitanes / e que si alguno PartiCular del / Exerçito
Se desmandaba a les / hazer algun maltratamyento o / a tomarles sus mayzes
e hazien- / da el dicho Francisco Vazquez los Casti- / gaba e aprisionaba e vio
que / Por Eçesos muy liVianos los lle- / Vaba dos y tres jornadas con / grillos
/ Fue preguntado que Fue la causa / Por que los naturales de / las dichas proV-
inçias Se alçaron / y mataron a los esPañoles que / en ellas quedaron e si fue
en ello / Culpante el dicho francisco Vazquez o / alguno de los dichos capitanes e / si castigo a los que en ello Eçedieron / dixo que la causa del dicho
alçamiento / Fue Segun Publica Voz y fama / las crueldades que Un alCaraz
/ en ellos hizo que habia dexado / Por Capitan don tristan de a- / Rellano
Porque a muchos yn- / dios les corto las manos len- / guas y narizes y les
tomaba / [no number]

[fol. 29r]
842
por fuerça y contra su voluntad / las mugeres e hijas Para se (h)echar / con
ellas e que el dicho Francisco Vazquez / no TuVo Culpa alguna en el dicho /
alçamyento e que al dicho alCaraz / le mataron los mismos yndios A / quien
habia (f)hecho los dichos malos- / tratamyentos y Fuerças y que esto / es lo
que sabe çerca de lo que le es preguntado / Fue preguntado que crueldades y

/ maloStratamyentos hizo el / dicho francisco Vazquez o alguno de los / dichos
Capitanes en la proVinçia de / Çibola e si les Salieron de paz o de / Guerra
dixo que llegados çerCa / de Çibola el dicho francisco Vazquez en / nonbre de
su magestad les ynVio a Re- / querir con fray juan de padilla / e con otros
Religiosos E personas / prençiPales del Canpo que le venia / en nonbre de su
magestad a Reduzirlos A / su obidiençia y a que VinieSSen *en* /
Conosçimyento de nuestra Sant(e)a fee / Catolica que se diesen e saliesen /
de paz que el les haria Todo buen tra- / tamyento y los mantendria

[fol. 29v]
En jusTiçia e aunque esTo / les fue dicho e dado a entender / Por Señas a
Causa que no hAbia / ynterprete y Requerido muchas / Vezes jamas lo
quisieron hazer / Antes Començaron A flechar / a los Religiosos y a las otras
/ personas que Con ellos yban lo qual / Visto y que se ponyan en armas / y
deFensa ARemetio a ellos / el dicho Francisco Vazquez y los que / con el yban
y los Retruxeron / hasta los meter en el pueblo don- / de hizieron fuertes e
alli se les / Tornaron a hazer los dichos Reque- / Rimyentos los quales
(f)hechos se die- / ron de paz y dexaron libre el pueblo / con todo lo que en
el tenyan y no / Vio que desPues de dados Se hizie- / se crueldad ni maltratamiento a / alguno de ellos porque si se les hizie- / ra este testigo lo viera e
supiera e / no pudiera ser menos Por Se / hallar como se hallo presente / a
todo ello antes Vio que por / el buen tratamyento que les hazia / [no number]

[fol. 30r]
843
Se tornaron A poblar A sus Ca- / Sas y pueblo e ansimismo los de loS / otros
pueblos Comarcanos que an- / daban ausentados de sus Casas / Se tornaron
A poblar / Fue preguntado las proVinçias / de tiguex e Çicuyque braVa y las
o- / tras comarCanas y sy se pusieron / en armas y Resistençia o si se ve- /
nyeron a dar de paz al dicho gene- / Ral dixo que todas las dichas pro- /
Vinçias Vinieron de paz e dieron / a su magestad la obediençia y al dicho /
Francisco Vazquez en su Real nonbre / syn se poner En Resistençia Alguna /
e dieron a los esPañoles del dicho / Exerçito todos los mantenimientos /

nesçesarios Conforme a lo que ellos / Tenyan e a su posibilidad e los aCo- / gieron en sus casas y pueblos e les / desenbaraçaron un pueblo en que / Se aPosentasen y ellos se Pasa- / Ron a otros / Fue preguntado que fue la causa / que los dichos pueblos e proVinçias

[fol. 30v]
Se tornaron A alçar dixo / que quando hernando de alvarado / Fue A desqubrir por mandado del / dicho Francisco Vazquez la dicha proVinçia / de çiquyque de las personas que Salieron / de paz e a dar la obidiençia pren- / dio quatro de ellos que (h)eran El / Caçique y el yndio llamado bigotes / y el que llamaban turco e a otro que / llamaron ysopete y que habiendo / ynViado la dicha proVinçia mensaje- / Ros Para que les diesen y VolVie- / sen los dichos quatro yndios Pues / habian Salido de paz y no (f)hecho / Resistençia alguna el dicho hernando / de alvarado hecho A los dichos men- / Sajeros los perros y los mordie- / Ron malamente y que despues / de (f)hecho esto porque el yndio llama- / do turco daba nuevas de tierra / muy RiCa y dezia que el dicho Ca- / Çique tenia un braçalete de oro / E otras joyas de valor que habia / Traydo de la dicha Tierra y por- / que el dicho caçique E bigotes / [no number]

[fol. 31r]
844
lo negaban y no concordaban con / lo que el dicho yndio llamado Turco dezia / el dicho hernando de alvarado presente / el dicho Françisco Vazquez y Por su / mandado les (h)echo por treSS vezes / los perros los quales los mordieron / y lastimaron malamente lo qual / este testigo Vio y se hallo presente a ello / y que de(n)sde a pocos dias Sanaron / y se Fueron A sus pueblos e luego / que Fueron ydos Se alçaron e que cree / que Fue Por las dichas crueldades ape- / rreamyentos y malostratamyentos e / que en el mismo Tienpo Sabe e vio / que se alço la proVinçia de tigueX / e que ansimismo cree e tiene por / Çierto que se alçaron Por las cruelda- / des e aperreamientos que supie- / Ron hAber (F)hecho en los de la pro- / Vinçia de çiquyque y Porque fue publico / y

noTorio que un Villegas hermano / de Villegas Regidor de mexico fue a / un
pueblo de la proVinçia de tiguex con / otros soldados de la ConPania de

[fol. 31v]
don garcia lopez de cardenas e tomo / contra voluntad de los naturales / Cantidad de Ropa e Gallinas e peta- / tes e una yndia Con quien dezian que / Se
habia (h)echado Carnalmente e / que esto se dixo el dia que aCaesçio e / que
otro dia syguiente Se alço la / dicha proVinçia e que aunque lo supo el dicho
/ Francisco Vazquez no sabe ni Vio que / CasTigase al dicho villegas / Fue
preguntado que tantos pueblos / de las dichas proVinçias quemaron / y
entraron por Fuerça dixo / que hecho el dicho alçamyento Una no- / che les
mataron çinquenta o sesenta / Caballos y bestias de Carga y que / ansi Por
esto Como Por se haber / alçado y Rebelado les dieron / Guerra y quemaron
treze pueblos / y que solos los treSS de estos se en- / Traron Por Fuerça y se
de- / Fendieron y que los demas que / quemaron los hallaron (h)iermos / y
desmanParados / Fue PreGuntado que pues sola- / mente tres pueblos Se
entra- / [no number]

[fol. 32r]
845
ron Por Fuerça e Se defen- / dieron los demas que hallaron / desmamparados
e syn Resistençia / Por que los quemaron y quien los / mando quemar dixo
que se quema- / Ron por mandado del dicho francisco / Vazquez Porque no
se tornasen / a hazer fuertes En ellos Porque / (h)eran pueblos Fuertes / Fue
preguntado a los yndios que / Se tomaron ViVos en los dichos pue- / blos que
crueldades y malostratamyentos / les hizieron dixo que tenyendo / el dicho
Francisco Vazquez (c)ferc(ç)ado / en la proVinçia de Tiguex Un pueblo /
ynVio Por la posta a este testigo A de- / zir A don garcia lopez que tenia /
ÇerCado y conbatia otro pueblo que / de ciertos yndios que habian Salido /
del dicho pueblo e Se habian Venido al / Real del dicho don Garçia lopez a /
darse de paz que no hiziese de ellos / justiçia hasta tanto que llegasen / alli los
yndyos llamados turco E / ysopete Porque Viesen la justiçia

[fol. 32v]

que de aquellos se hazia e diesen / en su tierra nueva e notiçia / de ello a los pueblos E naturales e / que hAbiendo dicho este testigo al dicho don / Garçia lopez el dicho mensaje vio / que salieron del pueblo que estaba çerCa- / do çiertos yndios e Se vinieron / al Real de los esPañoles pa- / çificos e sin armas algunas a ma- / nera de honbres aFligidos e / que pidian miseriCordia los quales / Serian hasta tres o quatro e / Vio que el dicho don garcia lopez los / mando meter en su tienda donde / estaban otros Veynte que oyo / dezir que se hAbian Venido al / Real y entregado a los esPa- / noles de la misma manera que los / quatro que declarados tiene e / que Venidos al Real del dicho don / garçia lopez los yndios llamados / TurCo e ysopete Vio que el dicho don / Garçia lopez mando Sacar de la / dicha tienda hasta quinze yndios / [no number]

[fol. 33r]

846

de los que se hAbian dado De paz y ve- / nido al Real de la manera que / Tiene declarado a los mando atar / a sendos Palos y Poner alRede- / dor de ellos çiertos çarzos Secos de / minbres Para los quemar y que visto / esto los demas yndios que queda- / ban en la Tienda con Palos que / en ella hallaron y estacas que aRan- / caron Se Començaron a defender / creyendo que habian de hazer de ellos / lo que de los otros sus Conpaneros / e alli dentro de la dicha tienda los alan- / çearon y dieron de estocadas a todos / los que en ella Estaban y se defendi- / an por manera que nynguno de ellos / quedo ViVo y hecho esto vio que Pega- / Ron fuego a los otros que estaban A- / tados en los palos y los quemaron / ViVos a todos y que cree y tiene por / çierto que la dicha quema y justiçia Se hizo / Por mandado del dicho francisco Vazquez por- / que segun tenya sujetos e obidientes

[fol. 33v]

los Capitanes e Gente syn su man- / dado nadie osara hazer la dicha jus- / Tiçia e porque sino se lo hobieran / antes mandado no ynViara A este testigo A / dezir que no hiziese justiçia de los / dichos yndios hasta que(s) llegasen los

/ di*c*hos turco e ysopete Porque diesen nue- / vas de lo que *h*abian visto / Fue
pre*gunta*do sy vio quemar o aperrear / algunos otros yndios de los que *en* loS
/ di*c*hos çercos se Tomaron ViVos dixo que / en el Real donde estaba el di*c*ho
fran- / çisco Vazquez truxeron tres yndios y / los metieron en la tienda donde
/ estaba el di*c*ho Fran*cis*co Vazquez y le / dixeron que aquellos yndios *h*abian /
Salido huyendo del pueblo que tenyan / çercado otra noche antes q*ue* viese lo
/ que mandaba que se hiziese de *e*llos / el qual les mando que los ape- / rreasen
e ansi Vio q*ue* les (h)echaron / los perros y los mataron y que se / hallaron presentes al aPerrear / de los di*c*hos yndios don pedro de / [no number]

[fol. 34r]
847
ToVar e don garçi*a* lopez de Cardenas / e don diego de Guevara e hernando
/ de alVarado e don alonso manrrique / e que dentro de las Casas Se quemaro*n* / otros muchos yndios Porq*ue* no / los podian Ganar syn les pegar /
Fuego ni los di*c*hos yndios Se querian / dar / Fue preguntado sy de la proV-
inçia / de çiquyq*ue* quemaron algunos pu*eb*los / e yndios o los aperrearon dixo
que / ningun pu*eb*lo de la di*c*ha proVinçia Se / quemo porq*ue* Por su fortaleza
no / los pudieron entrar ni se Aperrearon / mas de los dos yndios Çacique e
bigotes / que declarado tiene / Fue preguntado como y de que manera / Pasa
y fue la muerte del yndio / llamado TurCo E quien le ma- / To e Por Cuyo
mandado E Causa / dixo q*ue* estando el di*c*ho françisco Vaz- / ques en la
proVinçia de quiVira

[fol. 34v]
Diego lopez Veyntiquatro de se- / Villa e ÇaldiVar e gomez xuarez / ynpor-
tunaron muchas vezes al di*c*ho / Françisco Vazquez que matase al / di*c*ho
yndio llamado TurCo Porque / los *h*abia traydo Engañados y con sus / mentiras (F)*h*echo Pasar muy Grand*e*s / trabajos E que *e*l di*c*ho Fran*cis*co Vazquez
/ Se Escusaba E dezia q*ue* que *h*onrrase / Ganaba en matar al di*c*ho yndio e
que / Una noche el di*c*ho françisco Vazquez / llamo a este te*s*tigo y le dixo que
fuese / a los di*c*hos diego lopez y çaldiVar e les / dixese que si les paresciese
que (h)era / *h*ora de matar al di*c*ho yndio llama- / do turco que lo hiziesen

Secreto y / de manera que no diesen Vozes ny / Se sintiese en el Real e que
ansi / Fue este testigo a la tienda de los Susodichos / e les dixo lo que el dicho
françisco / Vazquez le habia mandado e vio / que luego SaCaron al dicho
yndio / llamado Turco de donde Estaba / Preso y le dixeron que Como les /
[no number]

[fol. 35r]
848
hAbia mintiDo y traydo enga- / nados que donde Estaba el / oro E Riquezas
que les habia dicho / en tiguex e que el dicho yndio Respondio / que los
pueblos donde Estaba el / dicho oro e Riquezas estaban mas / adelante que
el los habia traydo / a quiVira por tomar y lleVar con- / sigo A su muger que
la Tenya alli / e que sin esperar a mas PlatiCas / ni desCargos un soldado que
se de- / zia perez que no sabe de el ny / donde esta por mandado de los di-
/ chos diego lopez E çaldiVar y estan- / do presentes le (h)echo Por detras /
Un Cordel a la Garganta y le / apreto con un garrote y le ahogo / y luego le
(^aho) enterraron junto / a la dicha Tienda e que quando este / testigo Fue
ya tenyan abierta la se- / pultura donde le enterraron / Fue preguntado que
otras cruel-

[fol. 35v]
DaDes y malostratamyentos / Vio que hiziesen el dicho Françisco / Vazquez
y los otros Capitanes / dixo que no lo Sabe mas de que / VolViendoSe del
dicho desCubrimiento / Viniendo Por el Valle que dizen de / Señora don
tristan Con el aVan- / Guarda Fue tras dos yndios / que yban huyendo y el
uno de ellos / como se Vido aCosado Se metio / en un Ranchuelo e de alli le
fle- / cho el Caballo El qual cayo luego / Por Ser la flecha yErbolada y el /
dicho don tristan Como Vi(d)o el Ca- / ballo muerto alançeo y mato / el
dicho yndio e que sabe que a la sa- / zon el dicho Valle e proVinçia es- / taba
de Guerra e alçada e habi- / an muerto los yndios de ella al / dicho AlCaraz
que habia quedado / Por Capitan e a otros muchos / esPañoles y que esta es
la verdad / [no number]

[fol. 36r]

849

Y lo que sabe de lo que le *es* pre- / Guntado Para el juramento q*ue* / hizo e firmolo de su nonbre fue / le leydo Este Su d*i*cho luego Como / lo aCabo de dezir e Ratifico- / se en el y senalolo el d*i*cho señor / oydor juan de contreras

Chapter 8

Rodrigo Ximón,
the Sixth de Oficio Witness

A Veteran of the Conquest of Nueva Galicia

Another native of the Spanish province of Huelva, Rodrigo Ximón was from Moguer and, with his father, was part of a force sent to Nueva España to aid Cortés. Later, in 1527, Alonso de Estrada, then governor, granted the towns of Cuatitanapa and Tenango in encomienda to Ximón as recompense for services in Nueva España. He went on the conquest of Nueva Galicia with Nuño de Guzmán in 1530, where he stayed more than ten years and received encomiendas. In 1534 his encomiendas in Nueva España were taken away and given to others. He never recovered them, although he brought suit in hopes of doing so. The fiscal in that case, as in the pesquisa of 1544, was Cristóbal de Benavente.[1] Ximón was in his early to middle 30s when he left Mexico City for Tierra Nueva. By 1544 he was a vecino of Mexico City and was said to have no encomiendas.[2] He had died by 1562.[3]

When Ximón testified during the pesquisa conducted by Tejada on June 6, he volunteered much additional information beyond simply answering the questions, as though he knew already what issues he was expected to address. This is the case with a number of witness, suggesting that they had detailed knowledge of precisely what the inquiry was about before they appeared as witnesses. The overall sense of his testimony, like that of so many others, is that the Spaniards were justified in what they did and that Vázquez de Coronado was always very solicitous of the welfare of the Indians. Still, he had little or no reluctance about telling of violence against the Indians ordered by the captain general, apparently because he was certain those actions were both reasonable and legal. Thus, he openly recounted the torture of Bigotes and the cacique, the burning of 20 to 30 Indian prisoners at Pueblo del Arenal, and the killing of most of another 80 to 100 at Pueblo del Cerco.

A TRANSLATION
OF THE TESTIMONY

Sixth de Oficio Witness (Rodrigo Ximón)[4]

[36r cont'd] Rodrigo Ximón, a citizen of the city of Mexico, presented and accepted as a witness for this investigation, having given his oath in legal form and having promised to tell the truth, was asked the following questions.

{1} He was asked whether he knows Francisco Vázquez de Coronado, don García López de Cárdenas, don Diego de Guevara, don Tristán de Arellano, [36v] don Rodrigo Maldonado, the councilman of Sevilla Diego López, don Pedro de Tovar, Hernando de Alvarado, Juan de Zaldívar, Barrionuevo, and the other captains who went to reconnoiter and subjugate the tierra nueva of Cíbola, Tiguex, Cicuique, Brava, and Quivira and the other neighboring provinces. He answered that he knows all of those mentioned in the question, by appearance, voice, behavior, and conversation that he has had with them for more than the last five years. He was present during the subjugation and reconnaissance of all those provinces from the beginning until they returned to this city of Mexico.

{2} The witness was asked whether the people of the valley of Corazones (the one they call Señora), [37r] Uraba, and the other towns and provinces that there are between Culiacán and Cíbola came out in peace, when [the Spaniards] passed through there, and rendered obedience to His Majesty. Did they provide food from what they had to the Spaniards, and did they welcome them into their houses and towns, without taking up arms or offering any resistance? He answered that it is true that the people of all those towns came out in peace. They made [the Spaniards] very welcome and gave the foodstuffs that they had. And they rendered obedience to His Majesty and to the general in his royal name. The witness did not see that any of them took up arms or offered resistance.

{3} [Ximón] was asked whether, when [the Spaniards] had arrived at

Cíbola, [the people] of that province offered peace or whether they offered resistance and went to war with the general and the army that went with him. Did [the Spaniards] summon them [37v] to come to peace and did they make them understand that they would not do [the Indians] any injury or ill-treatment. He replied that when Francisco Vázquez and those with him had come near Cíbola, the general sent fray Juan de Padilla and other clerics to the Indians, so that they would know of his arrival. [They were] to make [the Indians] aware that the general came in His Majesty's name to bring them into obedience to him and under his authority and also to bring them knowledge of our holy Catholic faith and that the general would not treat them badly. Although he made them understand these things by signs, [the Indians] refused to come out in peace. Instead, many warriors came forth and began shooting arrows at the clerics and Spaniards.

The general himself again proclaimed the requerimiento to them and made them understand that no injury whatsoever would be done to them. On the contrary, they would be treated well. Because the summons was not successful [38r] in bringing [the Indians] to peace and [since] they kept shooting arrows, he attacked them with the whole company. That forced them to retreat within the main pueblo, where they set up barricades and fortified themselves.

[The Indians] tried to kill the general because when he attempted to enter [the pueblo] they struck him with a stone slab that they threw from the upper story. [The Spaniards] again delivered the requerimiento, and because [the Indians] saw themselves hard pressed they surrendered. They left the pueblo to the Spaniards and moved to another one.

{4} [The witness] was asked whether after the surrender and occupation [the Spaniards] committed any brutality or outrages against [the Indians]. Did they lance, burn, or set dogs on any of them or take any of their children or wives by force? He replied that since [the Indians] submitted, [the Spaniards] let them go free, without injuring or mistreating them at all and without seizing any of their wives or daughters. They did, however, take possession of the food that [the Indians] [38v] left in the pueblo.

The next day all the people of the province of Cíbola came in peace to render obedience to his majesty. They were always treated well, and [the wit-

ness] does not know and did not see that any force was used or any injury
inflicted.

{5} [Next] he was asked whether [the people of] the provinces of Tiguex
and Cicuique offered peace and came to render obedience to His Majesty or
whether they offered resistance and took up arms. [Ximón] answered that
while Francisco Vázquez and the army were quartered at Cíbola, within a few
days of the pueblo's capture, messengers from the province of Cicuique came
in peace to offer obedience to His Majesty and to request support against
some pueblos with which they had [36v] differences and were at war. This
province of Cicuique is eighty leagues from the main pueblo of Cíbola. Francisco Vázquez sent Hernando de Alvarado and twenty-seven or thirty
horsemen with them. When they went and passed through the province of
Tiguex, all of the people came forth in peace and brought the general food
from what they had. They showed much affection and were pleased by the
coming of the Spaniards.

At the end of the journey on which they had been sent, Alvarado
returned bringing as prisoners the cacique of Cicuique, an Indian called Bigotes, an Indian they called Ysopete, and another they called Turco, the first
two being natives of Cicuique and Turco and Ysopete being natives of the
province of Quivira. It was commonly said that they had been brought as
guides and in order to learn about some gold bracelets and jewelry that Turco
said Bigotes and the Indian called the cacique had and had taken from [39v]
Turco and Ysopete and other companions of theirs when the cacique and his
people had captured them.

[The witness] saw them held as prisoners in chains for some time in Hernando de Alvarado's tent. And he knows that afterwards, by order of Francisco Vázquez, Alvarado set dogs on the Indian Bigotes. And they menaced
the Indian called the cacique with the dogs. This was done because they
denied having the gold bracelet and jewelry that the Indian called Turco said
they had and that the general asked them for and because they did not agree
with what the Indian Turco was saying. The witness did not see this, but he
heard it said widely and publicly throughout the camp.

Within a few days of this occurrence the province of Tiguex rose up, and during one night they killed approximately thirty or forty horses and pack animals [40r] that were wandering in the countryside. [Ximón] does not know whether the uprising resulted because of the outrage of unleashing dogs or for some other cause. [The people] of Cicuique did not rise in arms until, through kind words and good behavior, they got the Indians called Bigotes and the cacique back. But as soon as they had them and they had entered the pueblos, they all rose up.

{6} He was then asked which pueblos of the Tiguex province it was that rose in arms and were fortified. [In reply] he said that it was only three where all the people of the province gathered because they abandoned and left the rest deserted, which numbered as many as ten or twelve. [The Spaniards] occupied those three by force because they were not able to subdue and take possession of them in any other way. Since the houses were [so]⁵ strong, they could not capture them without setting fire to them. [40v] They tore down the rest of the pueblos on orders from Francisco Vázquez and other captains, so that [the Indians] would not return and fortify them. And they burned all the wood in them.

{7} [Ximón] was asked whether, in the pueblos that he says were fortified and [the Spaniards] took by force, any Indians from the besieged pueblos came out to offer peace to those who were besieging them. He answered that he has no memory about what he is asked. He knows, however, that some were captured alive, numbering fifty or sixty, and put in a tent. [The Spaniards] took twenty or thirty from the tent in order to tie them to posts and burn them. And they burned them alive. The others who remained behind, seeing what was being done to their companions, fortified themselves in the [41r] tent, where they defended themselves with poles and whatever they could lay hands on. [The Spaniards] killed them there, lancing and stabbing them, so that no one remained alive.

{8} Next he was asked who ordered that this execution be carried out and what captain was present at it. He stated that the maestre de campo don García López and Juan de Zaldívar, who were the captains in charge at that pueblo, took this action. He believes that Francisco Vázquez ordered it since he came there soon afterwards (whether that was before or after the battle he does not know) and because he kept the people obedient and subject to his command, so that no one would dare to have carried out the execution without his order. Also, he saw that before the execution was carried out don García López [41v] sent two or three messengers to Francisco Vázquez, so that he would be informed of what was to be done to those people. Speaking again with better memory, the witness said that when the execution had been carried out they ran into Francisco Vázquez, who was coming with some people from the pueblo he had under siege to the pueblo where the Indians had been executed and where don García López was in charge.

The witness also saw that at the pueblo besieged by Francisco Vázquez as many as eighty or a hundred Indians were captured alive from among those who had fled [from the pueblo] and others who had been dragged out by their hair and had been hiding in the rooms that had been taken. He saw that [the Spaniards] lanced, stabbed, and set dogs on [those Indians], so that very few survived, except [42r] the women and children, who were not injured at all while this was going on.

{9} [Ximón] was asked who killed the Indian called Turco, by whose order it was done, why and for what reason. He answered that he does not know who killed him nor who ordered him killed, but he has heard as something publicly and widely known that when [the Indian] was being held prisoner in his tent, the councilman of Sevilla Diego López and Juan de Zaldívar applied a garrote and strangled him. And then they buried him near the tent. He believes that this was done on orders from Francisco Vázquez and with his permission, since he was in the camp where they strangled him and because, as he has said, no one would have dared to do it without his permission and command. [As far as the reason for Turco's killing], the witness believes that it was done because it was found out and discovered that he had conspired with the Indians of the province of Quivira (where he was a native) to kill the Spaniards. [42v] And furthermore, he had led all the people deceitfully by many roundabout ways and had many times put them in danger of being lost, leading them through arid places that lacked water and other provisions and taking them away from settled areas. He was always misrepresenting things with many different lies.

{*10*} He was [then] asked for what reason [the people of] the valley of Corazones and Señora and the valley of Uraba rose up and killed the Spaniards who were there. [The witness] replied that he does not know more than having heard it said that it was because of the brutality committed against those Indians by the [man named] Alcaraz mentioned before.

{*11*} [Ximón] was [next] asked whether the general meted out any punishment against those [individuals] who perpetrated these outrages and caused the uprising. He answered that he does not know because those same Indians killed Alcaraz and the others who should have been found guilty.

{*12*} [Finally] he was asked what other brutality and outrages he knows that the [43r] general and the other captains committed against the natives of that province. He replied that he does not know of any; rather, he saw that they were all afforded good treatment and the general gave them what he had. And he punished those who exercised force against [the Indians] and caused any injury whatsoever.

He said that this is the truth and what he knows about this case, in accordance with the oath that he swore. And he signed his name. As soon as he finished speaking his statement was read to him and he confirmed it. The lord judge affixed his sign.

Rodrigo Ximón

A TRANSCRIPT
OF THE TESTIMONY

[fol. 36r cont'd]⁶

{*testigo*}

El d*i*cho Rodrigo Ximon / V*ecin*o de la çiUdad de meXico t*estigo* / presentado y Resçibido para la d*i*cha / ynformaçion el q*ual h*abiendo ju- / rado en
forma de derecho E / Prometio de dezir verdad / Se le hizieron las preguntas
/ siguientes / Fue preguntado sy Conosçe A / françisco Vazquez de Corona-
/ do e a don Garçi*a* lopez de Car- / denas e a don diego de Guevara / e a don
tristan de arellano e /

[fol. 36v]

A don Rodrigo maldona- / do e a diego lopez Veyntiquatro / de Sevilla e a
don pedro de to- / Var e a hernando de alvarado E / a juan de çaldivar e a barrionuevo / e a los otros CaPitanes q*ue* Fue- / Ron a la conquista e desCubri-
/ myento de la Tierra nueva de çi- / bola e tiguex E çicuyq*ue* E braVa / e
quiVira e otras proVinçias / ComarCanas dixo q*ue* Conosçe A / TodoS los
contenidos en la pre- / Gunta de Çinco Años y mas T*iem*po / a esta parte de
vista habla trato / e conVersaçion q*ue* Con ellos ha te- / nydo y Se hallo presente En el / desCubrimiento y conquista de to- / das las d*i*chas proVinçias
desde el / prinçipio hasta q*ue* VolVieron a esta / ÇiUdad de meXico / Fue preguntado el valle de los Co- / Raçones y el que dizen de se- / [no number]

[fol. 37r]

850

ñora e braVa y los otros pueblos / y proVinçias que *e*stan desde qulia- / can hasta
Çibola sy salieron de paz / quando Por ellos Pasaban E die- / Ron la obidiençia
A su mag*estad* e a los / esPañoles los mantenimyentos nes- / Çesarios e de lo
que ellos Tenyan e loS / aCogieron en sus Casas y pueblos sin / Se Poner en
armas ni Resistençia / alguna dixo que *es ve*rdad que todos / los d*i*chos pueblos

Vinieron de Paz y les / hizieron buen aCogymiento e les pro- / Veyeron de los mantenymientos que E- / llos Tenyan y la obidiençia A su / magestad e a fran*cis*co Vazquez en su / Real nonbre e que no Vio q*ue* alguno / de *e*llos se pusiese en armas ni Resis- / tençia / Fue preguntado sy llegados A çibola / los de la d*i*cha ProVinçia se dieron de / paz o si se pusieron de Guerra y / en Resistyn*cia a*l d*i*cho General y Exer- / Çito q*ue* Con el yba e si les Requiriero*n*

[fol. 37v]

Viniesen de Paz e dieron a enten- / der que no se les haria Agravio ni mal- / tratamyento alguno dixo que lle- / gado el d*i*cho fran*cis*co Vazquez y los q*ue* / con el yban çerCa de Çibola yn Vio A / Fray juan de Padilla e a otros Re- / ligiosos A los d*i*chos yndios a les ha- / zer saber su venida E a darles A / entender que yba en nonbre de / su mag*es*tad A Reduzirlos *a* su dominio / e obidiençia y en Conosçimi*ent*o de n*ues*tra / Santa fee catolica y que no se les ha- / Ria maltratamyento alguno e q*ue* / aunque lo d*i*cho se les dio a entender / Por Señas no quisieron venir de paz / mas antes Salio mucha Gente de / Guerra y Començaron A flechar / a los d*i*chos Religiosos y esPañoles / y el mismo General torno a ha- / zerles los d*i*chos Requerimyentos en / Perso*n*a e a darles a entender que / no se les haria daño ninguno syno / antes buen tratamyento E Como / ninguna CoSSa aProvecharon los d*i*chos / [no number]

[fol. 38r]

851

Requerimyentos Para los traer de / Paz y que todaVia los flechaban / aRemetio a ellos Con toda la Gente y / los hizo Retraer hasta dentro del / Pueblo prinçipal donde Se enCas- / tillaron E hizieron fuertes e *h*obie- / Ron de matar al d*i*cho General Por- / que queriendo *en*trar le dieron Con una / losa que le ARojaron de lo alto / E alli se les Tornaron a hazer los / mysmos Requerimientos E Como se / Vieron apretados se Rindieron y les / dexaron a los d*i*chos esPañoles el pueblo / y se pasaron A otro / Fue Preguntado sy desPues de entra- / dos y Rendidos si les hizieron algu*n*as / crueldades o malostratamyentoS a- / lançeando quemando o aPerreando al- / Gunos de *e*llos o tomandoles sus hijos / e mugeres dixo que como se Rindie- / ron los

deXaron Salir libremen- / te syn les hazer daño ni maltrata- / myento alguno
E sin les Tomar mugeres / ni hijas SalVo el bastimento q*ue* ellos

[fol. 38v]
Dexaron en el d*i*cho pueblo e lue- / go otro dia syguiente viniero*n* / Todos los
pueblos de la d*i*cha Pro- / Vinçia de çibola de paz e a dar la / obidiençia a su
mag*e*stad a los quales / Se les hizo syenpre todo buen tra- / tamyentó e no sabe
ni Vio que se / les hiziese fuerça ni Agravio al- / Guno / Fue preguntado las
proVinçia*s* de ti- / guex e Çiquyque sy se dieron de paz / e vinieron a dar la obidiençia a su / mag*e*stad o si se pusieron en armas e Re- / sistençia dixo que
*e*stando el d*i*cho fran- / çisco Vazquez y el Exerçito aposen- / tados en çibola
de(n)*s*de A pocos dias / que se *h*abia Ganado el d*i*cho pu*ebl*o Vinie- / Ron mensajeros de la proVinçia de / çicuyque que esta ochenta leguas poco / mas o menos
del pueblo prinçipal / de Çibola de paz e a dar la obidi- / ençia A su mag*e*stad
E a pedir soCorro / contra çiertos pueblos con quien tenian / [no number]

[fol. 39r]
852
Guerra E diferençia y el d*i*cho / Françisco Vazquez ynVio con ellos / a hernando de alvarado Con veynte E / siete o treynta *h*onbres de a Caballo / e
yendo e Pasando Por la proVinçia / de tiguex le Salieron todoS los pu*ebl*os /
de paz e le trayan Comida e de lo q*ue* / ellos tenyan mostrandoles mucho /
amor e que se holgaban Con la veni- / da de los esPanoles e a la Vuelta q*ue* *e*l
d*i*cho / alvarado VolVio de la jornada q*ue* / le ynViaron Truxo presos al
Caçique de / çicuyq*ue* e a un yndio llamado bigot*e*s / e al yndio q*ue* llamaron
ysopete E / a otro q*ue* le llamaron el turco los / doS naturales de la d*i*cha proV-
inçia de / Çicuyque y el turco e ysopete de la pr*o*- / Vinçia de quiVira e dezian
publicamente / que los *h*abian traydo Para guias e / Por Saber de unos
braçaletes e joyas / de oro que *e*l d*i*cho Turco dezia tener / el yndio llamado
Caçique E bigotes / e que se los *h*abia Tomado al d*i*cho

[fol. 39v]
turco e ysopete e a otros sus con- / paneros quando los prendieron los /

d*i*chos caçique y su gente y que los vio / asy presos çierto tiempo en Cade- / nas en la tienda del d*i*cho Hernando / de alvarado e que supo despues / que *e*l d*i*cho hernando de alvarado Por / mandado del d*i*cho Fran*cis*co Vazquez *h*abia / a(t)*p*erreado al d*i*cho yndio llamado bigo- / tes e al yndio llamado caçique le *h*a- / bian Açomado los perros Porque / negaban tener los braçaletes e jo- / yas de oro que *e*l d*i*cho General les / Pidia y el yndio llamado turco / dezia Tener E porque no Co(r)*n*forma- / ban Con lo que *e*l d*i*cho Turco yndio de- / zia Pero que *e*ste t*e*s*ti*go no lo Vio mas / de *h*aberlo oydo dezir Por muy pu*bli*co / e noTorio en todo el Real e que / de(n)*s*de A pocos dias que lo susod*i*cho / aCaesçio Se alço la proVinçia / de tiguex y les mataron en una / noche sobre treynta o quarenta / Caballos e bestias de Carga que / [no number]

[fol. 40r]

853

Andaban Por el Canpo e q*ue* / no sabe sy fue el alçamyento por / el d*i*cho maltratamyento de aperrea- / myento o por otra (^Causa) causa E que los / de çicuyque no se alçaron hasta que / por buenas Palabras y man*era*s *h*obie- / Ron los d*i*chos yndios llamados caçi- / que y bigotes e que luego que / los *h*obieron y entraron en (l)loS d*i*choss / pu*eblo*s Se alçaron todos / Fue Preguntado en la ProVinçia de / Tiguex que Pueblos Fueron los / q*ue* se alçaron e hizieron Fuertes / dixo que solos tres adonde Se Re- / cogio Toda la Gente de la pro- / Vinçia Porque los demas que / Serian hasta diez o doze los des- / manpararon y dexaron desiertos / Y que los d*i*chos tres los entra- / Ron Por Fuerça y quemaron / Porque de otra manera no los Po- / dieran *h*aber e conquistar Por- / que las Casas (h)eran fuertes que / sy no (h)era pegandoles fuego no / {va t*e*st*a*do do*nde* dizia causa no vala}

[fol. 40v]

las Podian Ganar e que los / demas pueblos los Asolaron / Por mandado del d*i*cho fran*cis*co Vazquez / y los otros (^T)Capitanes Porq*ue* / en ellos no se Tornasen a hazer / Fuertes e quemaron toda la / madera de *e*llos / Fue preguntado sy en los pueblos / que dize que se hizieron Fuertes / e Ganaron Por

Fuerça sy salie- / Ron algunos yndios de los que estaban / çercadoS a darse de Paz a los que / tenyan çercados dixo que no Tiene / memoria de lo que le es pregunta- / do Pero que sabe que se toma- / Ron ViVos algunos que serian / hasta çinquenta o sesenta / y los Pusieron En Una Tienda E / de alli Sacaron a quemar Ve- / ynte o treynta Atados en unos / Palos y los quemaron ViVos Y / como los otros que quedaban Vie- / Ron lo que hazian A sus conpa- / ñeros Se hizieron Fuertes en la / [no number]

[fol. 41r]

854

Tienda donde Se deFendian / con Palos e Con lo que pudieron / haber e alli los mataron a- / lançeandolos y a estoCadas que / ninguno de ellos quedo ViVo / Fue preguntado quien mando / hazer la dicha justiçia e que Ca- / Pitan Se hallo presente a ello / dixo que don Garcia lopez maestre / de Canpo e juan de çaldiVar la / hizieron que (h)eran los que estaban / Sobre el dicho Pueblo e que cree / Fue Por mandado del dicho francisco / Vazquez Porque luego Vino / alli e que no se determina / sy Fue antes de la quema / o desPues e Porque segun te- / nya su(b)jeta e obidiente la / Gente nadie oSara hacer- / lo syn su mandado e Porque / Vio que el dicho don garcia lopez an- / Tes que se hiziese la dicha justiCia

[fol. 41v]

ynVio al dicho Francisco Vazquez / dos o tres mensajeros a le / hazer Saber que se haria de a- / quella Gente torno A decir me- / jor aCordado que hecha la dicha jus- / Tiçia toParon al dicho Francisco Vaz- / quez que Venya Con çiertas per- / sonas del pueblo donde Tenia el çerco / al pueblo donde se hizo la dicha jus- / Tiçia e sobre que estaba el / dicho don Garcia lopez e que ansi- / mismo vio que desPues lo que / tenya çercado el dicho Françisco / Vazquez Se tomaron ViVos has- / ta ochenta o çien(t) yndios de / los que salian huyendo e otros / que saCaban de los Cabellos que / estaban (a)escondidos en los quar- / teles que yban Ganando e que / Todos Estos Vio que los alan- / Çearon e aCuchillaron E aperre- / aron Por manera que muy / Pocos quedaron ViVos Eçe(b)pto / [no number]

[fol. 42r]

855

las mugeres E niños que / en esto no se hazia daño ning*un*o / Fue preguntado quien mato / al yndio llamado turco o Por / Cuyo mandado y por que causa y Ra- / zon dixo que no Sabe quien / le mato ni mando matar mas / de *h*aber oydo Por muy Pu*bli*co E no- / torio que tenyendole preso y / en su tienda diego lopez Veynti- / quatro de se Villa e juan de çaldiVar / le dieron Un garrote y le Ahogaro*n* / y enterraron çerCa de la di*c*ha tienda / y que cree q*ue* Fue Por mandado / del di*c*ho Fran*cis*co Vazquez y con su li- / çençia Porque Se hallo En el Re- / al donde le ahogaron y porque / como di*c*ho Tiene nadie osara ha- / zerlo syn su liçençia y mandado e q*ue* / la causa a lo que cree fue Porq*ue* / Segun se supo y descubrio tenia / conçertado con los yndios de la pro- / Vinçia de quiVira donde el (h)era na- / Tural que matasen a los esPañol*es*

[fol. 42v]

E Porque *h*abia traydo / enganada toda la Gente Por / mucho Rodeo y puesto muchas Ve- / zes en peligro de se perder Por / lugares Secos e que careçian de / agua y de loS otros mantenimi*ento*s / y aPartandolos de los Poblados / Fing*i*endo sienpre muchas E diver- / sas mentiras / Fue preguntado que Fue la causa q*ue* *e*l / Valle de los Coraçones e de senora / e de braVa Se alçase*n* y matasen a los / esPañoles que alli *h*abia dixo q*ue* *e*ste t*e*st*i*go / no lo Sabe mas de *h*aber oydo d*e*cir / que las crueldades q*ue* en los di*c*hos / yndios hazia el di*c*ho alCaraz / Fue preg*un*ta*d*o sy hizo algun Castigo / el di*c*ho general en loS q*ue* Fueron / causa del di*c*ho alçami*ento* e malos- / tratamyentos dixo q*ue* no lo sabe por- / que al di*c*ho alCaraz le mataron los / mysmos yndios e a los otros q*ue* / dibieron ser Culpantes / Fue preguntado q*ue* otras crueldad*es* / y malostratamyentos Sabe que *e*l / [no number]

[fol. 43r]

856

Di*c*ho General e los otros Capitanes / *h*ayan (f)*h*echos en los naturales de la / di*c*ha ProVinçia dixo que no lo sabe / e que antes Vio que les hazia todo /

buen tratamiento e les daba de lo que te- / nya e Castigaba los que les hazian alguna / Fuerça e agravio y que esta es la verdad / y lo que sabe de este Caso Para el juramento / que tiene (F)hecho y lo firmo de su nonbre fue / le leydo este su dicho luego Como lo aCa- / bo de decir e Ratificose en el y senalolo / el dicho señor oydor Rodrigo Ximon

Chapter 9

*Cristóbal de Escobar,
the Seventh de Oficio Witness*

A Recent Arrival in the New World

When he immigrated to the New World in 1538, Cristóbal de Escobar brought his wife Isabel Ortiz and their household with him, including one black slave. On the same ship came fellow expedition member Alonso Álvarez, with whom he remained associated and who also testified during the 1544 investigation.[1] Escobar was a native of Aracena in the province of Huelva in Spain, though when he applied for a license to travel to the Indies he said he was from Sevilla.[2] He may have been as young as 16 to 18 when he arrived in Nueva España.[3]

On the expedition to Tierra Nueva he took with him one Spanish servant and two horses. In the course of the entrada, according to his own claims, he saved the lives of Mexican Indians, blacks, and Spaniards by bringing supplies to Cíbola across the *despoblado* or unsettled region from Corazones. He participated in an entrada of the valleys of Yuparo and Betuco in Sonora. And he also went in the party led by Melchor Díaz to the Mar del Sur, during which Díaz died. After that reconnaissance he went on to Tiguex and from then on served in the captain general's own company, being wounded several times. The shortage of European clothing among expedition members was so severe by 1542 that he returned to Nueva España dressed in hides. In spite of his service and expenditures, he maintained he was never compensated for his part in the expedition.[4] In the late 1540s Escobar was listed as one of the settlers of Mexico City who did not hold Indians in encomienda.[5] Nevertheless, in July 1551, he was granted a coat of arms by royal cédula that specifically referred to his participation in the expedition to Tierra Nueva.[6]

Whether as direct reward for his time in Tierra Nueva or not, he served in a series of *corregimientos* beginning in 1544, including ten years as *corregidor* of Xicotepeque or Xilotepeque, by personal appointment from the king.[7] As a result of his protests of insufficient salary in 1561, the audiencia awarded him assistance of 200 pesos. He also served as a *tasador* or assessor, reducing Indian tribute requirements as native populations in central Mexico plunged during the middle decades of the sixteenth century. According to chief scribe of the audiencia Antonio de Turcios in 1561, Escobar was by then one of the principal citizens of Mexico City.[8]

Although Escobar was said to be a vecino of Mexico City in 1544, the official conferral of that status did not happen until October 1546, and early the following year he was granted a solar on the street running from the Church of Santo Domingo to Santiago.[9] When he prepared a proof of his services in 1543, Domingo Martín and Alonso Álvarez were among those who testified on his behalf.[10] The following year they all testified at licenciado Tejada's request during the 1544 investigation.

When he replied to Tejada's questions on June 7, Escobar often stated that he had no personal knowledge of the point at issue, despite having been continuously in the service of the captain general. He consistently portrayed Vázquez de Coronado as concerned for the well-being of the Indians and offered much unsolicited detail, again as though aware of what others had been asked. For instance, without specifically being quizzed about responsibility for the uprising in Sonora, he said anyway that the general was not responsible. He also volunteered information about the lancing of Indians in López de Cárdenas's tent. And he offered one bit of testimony potentially damaging to Vázquez de Coronado, namely that the Spaniards, by the general's order, set dogs on more than 150 Indians. This assertion was never brought up again during the course of the investigation, which may indicate an unwillingness on the pesquisador's behalf to pursue energetically lines of investigation that might reflect discredit on the captain general. While rarely critical of the Vázquez de Coronado, Escobar conceded that the people of Tiguex and Cicuique took up arms against the expedition because of forced appropriation of their goods and torture of their leaders. At Corazones the trigger of violence was, in Escobar's view, the rape of women and thievery of food and clothing, all of which he, like the other witnesses, blamed solely on Diego de Alcaraz. Escobar's testimony comprises a familiar litany of murders, dismantling of Indian towns, and commandeering of food and clothing, all told of without regret.

A TRANSLATION
OF THE TESTIMONY

Seventh de Oficio Witness (Cristóbal de Escobar)[11]

[43r cont'd] Cristóbal de Escobar, accepted as a witness for this investigation, having given his oath in the form required by law, was asked the following questions under that obligation.

{*1*} He was asked whether he knows Francisco Vázquez de Coronado, don García López de Cárdenas, don Diego de Guevara, don Tristán de Arellano, don Rodrigo Maldonado, the councilman of Sevilla Diego López, don Pedro de Tovar, Hernando de Alvarado, Juan de Zaldívar, Barrionuevo, Pablos de Melgosa, and the other captains who went to reconnoiter and subjugate the tierra [43v] nueva of Cíbola, Tiguex, Cicuique, Brava, and Quivira and the other neighboring provinces. He answered that he knows all of those mentioned in the question, by appearance, voice, behavior, and conversation that he has had and continues to have with them for the last five years and more. He was present during the subjugation and reconnaissance of all those provinces from the beginning until they returned to this city of Mexico.

{*2*} The witness was asked whether [the people of] the provinces of Corazones, the valley of Señora, Fuya, and the others that there are between Culiacán and Cíbola came out in peace to offer obedience to His Majesty and to Francisco Vázquez in his royal name. Did they give and supply provisions and food that they had, and did they welcome [the Spaniards] into their houses and towns, without offering any resistance or making war? He answered that it is true that those valleys and all the other towns between Culiacán and Cíbola came out in peace and rendered obedience to His Majesty and to the general in his royal name. They gave supplies from the food and provisions they had and welcomed [the Spaniards] into their houses, demonstrating much affection and good will. And they made [the Spaniards] understand that they were pleased by their coming. The witness did not see that any of those towns and provinces took up arms or offered resistance at that time.

[44r] {3} He was [then] asked whether the general or any of the captains or any individual from the army exercised force or committed any cruelty, rape, or [other] offense against the natives of those towns and provinces. And did the general punish [such acts] or did he excuse them? [The witness] replied that he did not see nor did he know that when [the Spaniards] passed through there the general harmed those natives in any way. And if [such things] were done, the witness would have seen or learned of them. He could not have missed them since he went in the company with the general (as he did). If anyone disobeyed and took provisions or ears [of corn][12] against the will of the natives, the general punished them harshly, putting them in shackles and imposing other harsh penalties.

{4} [Escobar] was asked, since the Indians of the provinces of Corazones, Señora, and Fuya came out in peace and gave [the Spaniards] such good treatment and welcomed them, as he said, why was it that afterwards they rose up in arms and killed so many of the Spaniards who had remained in those provinces and that valley. He answered that he did not know more than what he had heard, which was that a [man named] Alcaraz, who had stayed in those provinces as captain, had been the cause of the uprising because of the brutality and outrages he perpetrated against those natives, taking their wives and daughters and their provisions. And he was not content with what the Indians provided to the Spaniards, which was two shares of the supplies they gathered. In regard to Alcaraz, he knows that those same Indians killed him along with other Spaniards who were in his company. The general was not responsible for any of this because he did not leave anyone as captain except a [man called] Melchor Díaz, who left those valleys to make a recon-naissance of the Mar [44v] del Sur.

{5} He was then asked whether the [people of the] province of Cíbola came out in peace or in war and whether [the Spaniards] had issued any summons to them and made them understand that they came in his majesty's name, in order that [the people of Cíbola] might render obedience to him. And did they tell the Indians that they were not going to do them any harm, but instead would give them the very best treatment and bring them to knowledge of our holy Catholic faith?

[Escobar] answered that when they had arrived near the province and pueblos of Cíbola, Francisco Vázquez sent fray Juan de Padilla and other clerics, a scribe, and other persons from the company to summon them and make them understand what was stated. The Indians were never willing to come in peace, but instead began to shoot arrows at the clerics and individuals who went with them. There were as many as three hundred or four hundred Indians, all fighting men. As [the witness] saw, the general ordered them to be attacked, and [the Spaniards] routed them and forced them into the first pueblo of that province. There they fortified and defended themselves. And they even wounded the general badly in the head with a stone slab that they threw from the upper story.

[The Spaniards] again issued the requerimiento there and made [the Indians] understand that the general would not do them any harm or commit any outrage against them. [45r] So, [the Indians] submitted and offered peace. They left the pueblo empty and clear, and [the Spaniards] let them go free, with their wives and children, without mistreating them in any way. Rather, the general gave them some of the things that he brought, so as to assure them further and make them understand that they could expect to be treated well. Because of this, on the following day all the rest of the people of the province came to offer peace, and they supplied critical provisions.

{6} [The witness] was asked whether in that province Francisco Vázquez or any of the captains committed brutality or significant outrages against the natives after they had come in peace, wounding and killing them or [seizing][13] their wives and daughters and goods against their will. He stated that he did not see nor did he know [45v] that the general, the captains, or any other person did such a thing. If they had committed [such acts], the witness would have seen it and learned about it, which he could not avoid because he was in that province while the company was there. Instead, he saw that the general gave them the best treatment and kept them largely at peace.

{7} He was [then] asked whether the provinces of Tiguex, Cicuique, and Brava offered peace or whether [the Spaniards] occupied them by force after they took up arms and offered resistance. He answered that when the general and the rest of the people were at Cíbola some messengers came from the province of Cicuique to offer peace and to tender their land to [the Spaniards]. Among them came the Indian called Bigotes and three or four others. They asked for support and assistance against certain neighboring pueblos with which they were at war. Considering their offer, Francisco [46r] Vázquez thanked them for it and received them in peace and as allies.

He dispatched with them Hernando de Alvarado as captain, with twenty-four horsemen and four arquebusiers, all of which the witness saw. And he heard that when [Alvarado] had reached that province and discovered the Río de Tiguex and the cattle [bison], coming back he brought with him as prisoners Bigotes and a brother of his who was a very important person in the province of Cicuique, whom afterwards the [Spaniards] called the cacique. In the same condition, he brought another Indian to whom [the Spaniards] gave the name Ysopete and also the Indian called Turco, who was said to be a slave of Bigotes. As such a slave, he had been given to Hernando de Alvarado, in order that he might guide [the captain] to the provinces and cattle [bison] which the general had ordered him to go and reconnoiter.

[The witness] saw that from those provinces Hernando de Alvarado sent [46v] the general the head of a cow [bison], several items of clothing, and some tanned hides, which the [people] of those provinces said that they presented to him as a gift. When he returned to the camp he brought Bigotes and the cacique as prisoners in chains.

{*8*} [Escobar] was asked what the reason was that [the Spaniards] set dogs on the cacique and Bigotes since they were such important persons and had come in peace to render obedience to His Majesty. And besides, they had guided Hernando de Alvarado and the rest of the people who went with him in the reconnaissance that he had gone to make. And they had supplied food and clothing and welcomed [the Spaniards] and treated them well in their lands. The witness replied that he had heard that they had set dogs on Bigotes because on the way back, as Alvarado returned to the Tiguex province, [47r] [the Indians of Cicuique] were not as forthcoming with presents as they had been on the trip out. Alvarado thought that Bigotes was the cause of this.

And they set dogs on the cacique because he would not turn over to Francisco Vázquez some gold bracelets and jewelry that the Indian called Turco said he had taken from him and his companions. Because he denied and did not agree with what El Turco was saying they unleashed the dogs, and they injured him severely on one leg and an arm.

{9} [The witness] was asked who set the dogs on the cacique and Bigotes, by whose order, and whether Francisco Vázquez was present. He answered that he did not see it, but it was common knowledge and widely held in the camp that Hernando de Alvarado ordered dogs unleashed on Bigotes and that dogs were set on the cacique by order of Francisco Vázquez. [Escobar] believes this and is certain of it [47v] because when they set the dogs on the cacique Francisco Vázquez was in the camp where it was done and, since he kept the captains and [other] people obedient and subject to his command, no one would have dared to do it without his permission and order.

{10} He was [then] asked whether, while the cacique and Bigotes were held prisoner, the [people] of the province of Cicuique sent to beg for their return, asking why, since they had come freely to offer peace and render obedience to His Majesty, had welcomed [the Spaniards] to their land, and had treated them well, their principales were held prisoner. And they said that [the Spaniards] had maintained the faithfulness and friendship that they had offered very poorly. The witness said that it is true that he heard said widely and in public what is referred to in the question. The general replied to them that they must first turn over the bracelets and jewelry. [48r] [To which] the messengers answered that first the Spaniards must return their leaders.

{11} [Next] he was asked whether, because those messengers asked for their leaders and insisted on this, [the Spaniards] unleashed dogs on them and they were bitten badly. And who ordered this? He answered that he did not see nor did he hear that any such thing was done to the messenger.

{12} [The witness] was asked what caused the provinces of Cicuique and Tiguex to rise up and rebel. He replied that the province of Cicuique did so because of the outrages that [the Spaniards] had committed against their principales. This must be so because as soon as [the Spaniards] released them and the natives saw them, they openly rose up in arms. From the time that [the Spaniards] were setting dogs on the cacique and Bigotes, however, [the Indians of Cicuique] stopped supporting the Spaniards and welcoming them into their pueblos. With regard to [the uprising] in Tiguex province, it was said publicly [48v] that it occurred because [the Spaniards] took provisions, clothing, and hides from their houses against their will.

{*13*} [Escobar] was asked which pueblos in the Tiguex province were fortified and were where the people gathered. He replied that all the pueblos of this province rebelled, but the people took refuge in only three. The rest they left empty.

{*14*} He was [then] asked since it was only three pueblos where the people took refuge, why did [the Spaniards] burn the rest, seeing that they were not defended at all nor did [the people] make war from them. He answered that they burned those pueblos in order to do injury to [the Indians], so that the others would be forewarned not to rebel, and so that [the Indians] would not return to fortify them.

{*15*} [The witness] was asked, regarding the three pueblos [49r] that rebelled and where the people took refuge and fortified themselves, whether they were burned and razed like the others and whether [the Spaniards] summoned them to offer peace. In reply he said that he saw that [the Spaniards] summoned the natives of the pueblos where they had taken refuge and thrown up barricades to come to peace many different times. And they told them that no injury would be done to them. But [the Indians] were never willing to come to peace, even though [the Spaniards] took some plazas from them and had burned them. [The Indians] were so stubborn and obstinate that they were not willing to come to peace until [the Spaniards] had burned most or all of their houses. This was in one of the pueblos, since the natives abandoned the other and went away. And in the third pueblo, seeing themselves hard pressed by the siege, [the Indians] sued for mercy.

The witness saw that [the Spaniards] gathered eighty or so of the Indians from that pueblo who offered peace [49v] in a tent. And they burned most of them alive. Because the others saw the brutality perpetrated on their companions, they rose up in don García López de Cárdenas's tent, where they were, and defended themselves with poles and arms that they found there. And [the Spaniards] lanced them and killed them with sword thrusts.

{16} He was asked whether [the Spaniards] set dogs on any other [Indians], in addition to those they burned. He answered that at the other pueblo taken by force, to which the general had laid siege, he saw [the Spaniards], by the general's order, set dogs on more than a hundred and fifty Indians who were taken alive. And that does not count many others who were lanced when they came out fleeing from the pueblo.

{17} [Escobar] was asked, regarding the burning of Indians that was done at the pueblo to which don García López de Cárdenas laid siege, whether it was done by the general's order. He said yes, because in the presence of the witness Francisco Vázquez ordered [50r] don García López to go to subdue that pueblo and the others that had risen up in arms and to put all [the Indians] to the knife. But whether or not he ordered them burned he does not know. He believes, however, that it would not have been done without the general's order since there was a distance of [only] half a league from one pueblo to the other and each hour messengers were sent between them. Furthermore, shortly before the burnings were carried out Francisco Vázquez sent the Indians called Turco and Ysopete to the camp of don García López in order to witness the punishment that was being administered to the Indians, so that they could spread word of it in their lands and in the rest of the pueblos through which [the Spaniards] might pass.

{18} He was [next] asked how many pueblos in the Tiguex province were burned and whether [the Spaniards] also burned the two pueblos that offered peace and were [50v] abandoned, of the three in which [the Indians] had fortified themselves. He answered that thirteen pueblos of that province were burned and that [the Spaniards] also burned the two pueblos about which he is asked.

{19} [Then] he was asked who the captain was who carried out the burning. He stated, regarding the three pueblos, that all of the captains and [other] people burned them. And Rodrigo Maldonado burned the rest by the general's order.

{*20*} [The witness] was asked who killed the Indian called Turco, who ordered it done, and for what reason. He replied that he was not present, but heard it widely and publicly said that a Francisco Martín, a butcher, strangled him on orders from the general and the councilman of Sevilla Diego López, who at that time was maestre de campo. It was done because he had incited the land and province of Quivira and because he had led the army deceitfully, tricking it with various lies and leading it through unpopulated [51r] areas where there was not any water or food and where it found itself in great danger and difficulty.

{*21*} [Escobar] was asked whether on returning from Quivira to Tiguex [the Spaniards] caused damage in that province or burned any pueblos. He answered that it is true that some of the same pueblos that [the Spaniards] had burned and laid waste to had been repaired and [the Spaniards] gutted them again, both to make use of the wood and to get the corn and [other] supplies [the Indians] had left buried there. Also the [people] of that province were still at war and were never willing to come to peace. Beyond that, the company had need of supplies and firewood since [the Spaniards] would have died of cold and hunger if it had not been for the supplies and wood that they got from the pueblos [the Indians] had repaired and rebuilt.

[51v] {*22*} He was asked what other brutality and outrages he saw Francisco Vázquez and the other captains commit against the natives during the return from those provinces and the journey to this city. He said that he neither saw nor knows that such things occurred.

He said that this is what he knows about what he is asked, and nothing further, in accordance with the oath he swore. And he signed his name. As soon as he finished making his statement he read and confirmed it. The lord judge affixed his sign.

Cristóbal de Escobar

A TRANSCRIPT
OF THE TESTIMONY

[fol. 43r cont'd]¹⁴

{T*estigo*}

El d*i*cho *cris*tobal d*e es*Cobar t*esti*go Resçibi- / do Para la d*i*cha ynformaçion
el q*ua*l / *h*abiendo jurado en forma de d*e*rec*h*o so Cargo / del q*ua*l se le hizieron
las pregu*n*tas syg*u*ientes / Fue preguntado sy conosçe A Fran*ci*sco / Vazquez
de Coronado e a don g*a*rc*i*a lopez / de Cardenas e a don di*e*go de guevara e a
/ don tristan de Arellano e a don R*o*drig*o* / maldonado e a diego lopez Veynte
y qua- / tro de sevilla e a don p*e*dr*o* de toVar e a her- / nando de alvarado e a
ju*a*n de çaldiVar / e a barrionuevo e a pablos de melgosa / e a los otros Capitanes q*ue* Fueron a la / conquista e desCubrimi*ent*o de la tierra

[fol. 43v]

nueva e de çibola e tiguex E çicuyq*ue* e bra- / Va e quiVira e otras p*ro*Vinçias
Comar- / canas dixo q*ue* Conosçe a todos los conte- / nidos en la pregunta
de çinco Años y mas / tienpo A esta p*ar*te de vista habla trato / e conVersaçion q*ue* Con ellos ha tenido e / tiene de çinco Anos y mas T*iem*po a esta /
Parte e que se hallo pres*ent*e en el desqu- / brimy*ent*o e conquista de todas las
d*i*chas pro - / vinçias desde el prinçipio hasta q*ue* VolVie- / ron a esta çiUdad
de mexico / Fue pregu*n*ta*d*o sy las proVinçias de los Coraçones va- / lle de
señora fuya E las otras que *e*stan / desde Culiacan hasta çibola sy les salier*on*
/ de paz e a dar la obidiençia A su mag*es*tad / e a fran*ci*sco Vazquez en su Real
nonbre e / les dieron e p*ro*veyeron de los bastimentos e / Comyda que ellos
tenian e los aCogieron / en sus pu*eblo*s y Casas sin se poner En ResiS- / tençia
ny hazer Guerra alg*un*a dixo q*ue* *e*s v*er*dad / q*ue* los d*i*chos Valles y todos los
otros pu*eblo*s q*ue* / *h*ay desde quliaCan hasta Çibola salieron de paz / e dieron
la obidiençia A su mag*es*tad e al d*i*cho gen*er*al en / su Real nonbre e les
p*ro*Veyeron de la Comida e bas- / timi*ent*os q*ue* ellos tenian e aCogieron en

sus Casas y pue*b*los / mostrandoles mucho Amor y buena voluntad e dando-
/ les a entender q*ue* les plazia con su venida e q*ue* no Vio / q*ue* alg*un*o de los
di*c*hos pue*b*los e p*ro*Vinçias por e(s)*n*tonçes Se pusiesen / en armas y en
Resistençia / [no number]

[fol. 44r]

857

Fue preg*unta*do si el di*c*ho gen*era*l o alg*un*o de los di*c*hos Capitanes / o personas
partiCular*es* del (h)exerçito les hiziesen / a los di*c*hos naturales de los di*c*hos
pue*b*los e p*ro*vinçias alg*un*a / Fuerça crueldad o desaguisado e si lo castigo el /
di*c*ho Gen*era*l o lo disimulo dixo q*ue* no Vio ni supo / q*ue* A los di*c*hos naturales
quando por alli pasaron se les / hiziese agravio alg*un*o porq*ue* si se les hiziera este
te*s*tig*o* lo / Viera e supiera e no pudiera ser m*e*nos Por yr como / yba en el Canpo
Con el di*c*ho General e si alguno / Se desmandaba a tomar algun bastimento o
ma- / Çorcas contra voluntad de los naturales el di*c*ho / Gen*era*l los Castigaba
asPeramente aprisionando- / los y dandoles otros castigos mas asPeros / Fue
preg*unta*do q*ue* pues los yndios de las di*c*has p*ro*Vinçias de / los coraçones e
señora E Fuya Salieron de paz / y les hizieron Tan buen tratami*ent*o e
aCogimi*ent*o como / di*c*ho e declarado tiene q*ue* fue la causa por q*ue* des- / pues
Se alçaron y mataron Gran p*ar*te de los es- / Pañoles que en las di*c*has p*ro*V-
inçias e valle *h*abia*n* / quedado dixo q*ue* este te*s*tig*o* no lo sabe mas de que / oyo
decir q*ue* Un alCaraz que *h*abia quedado por Ca- / Pitan en las di*c*has p*ro*Vinçias
*h*abia sido causa / q*ue* se alçasen por las crueldades e malostratami*ent*os / q*ue* en
los di*c*hos naturales hazia tomandoles sus / mugeres E hijas e sus bastimi*ent*os e
q*ue* no se Contenta- / ba Con que los di*c*hos yndios daban las dos p*ar*tes / a los
esPañoles de los bastimi*ent*os q*ue* cogian e q*ue* / a este di*c*ho alCaraz Sabe q*ue*
los mismos yndios / le mataron Con otros esPañoles q*ue* en su con- / Panya
estaban e q*ue* de *e*sto no fue Culpante el / di*c*ho Gen*era*l Porq*ue* *e*l no le dexo Por
Capitan salvo / Un melchior diaz q*ue* Fue A d*e*sCubrir la mar

[fol. 44v]

del sur desde los di*c*hos valles / v / Fue preg*unta*do la provinçia de çibola si les
salio de / Paz o de guerra e si les hizieron Requerimi*ent*os / algunos dandoles

A entender que yban / en nonbre de su mag*estad* para que les diesen la / obi-
dien*ç*ia E q*ue* no les Venyan a hazer daño / alguno mas antes a hazerles todo
buen / tratami*ento* e traerlos en Conos*ç*imi*ento* de n*ues*tra *santa* fe / Catolica
dixo que llegadoS *ç*erca de la d*i*cha / ProVin*ç*ia e p*ue*b*l*os de *e*lla el d*i*cho Fran-
*ci*sco Vazq*uez* / ynVio A fray ju*an* de padilla e a otros Re- / ligiosos e a Un
es*cri*vano e a otras personas / del Canpo a les Requerir e dar A enten- / der
lo q*ue* de suso Se haze min*ç*ion e q*ue* los / d*i*chos yndios jamas quisieron Venir
de paz / mas antes Comen*ç*aron a flechar A los d*i*chos Re- / ligiosos e personas que Con ellos yban / y que los d*i*chos yndios Serian hasta tre*ç*i- / entos
o quatro*ç*ientos todoS de guerra / e q*ue* Como esto Vio el d*i*cho General
man- / do ARemeter a ellos y los desbarataron / y metieron dentro del p*ue*b*l*o
prim*er*o de la d*i*cha / proVin*ç*ia donde se hizieron Fuertes e se de- / Fendieron
E aun hirieron malamente al d*i*cho / Gener*a*l en la cabeca Con Una losa q*ue*
/ le ARojaron de lo alto e alli se les / Tornaron a hazer los d*i*chos Requer-
imy*ento*s / y dar A entender que no se les harya / daño ni maltratamyento
alguno / [no number]

[fol. 45r]
858
[change of scribe and new bundle of paper]
E Ansi Se Rindieron e dieron de Paz / e les dexaron libre e desenbara*ç*ado el
/ d*i*cho Pueblo E a ellos los dexaron / yr libremente con sus mugeres e hijos /
Syn les hazer maltratamyento / alguno mas a*n*tes el d*i*cho General / les daba
Algunas cosas de las que / llevaba Para mas les asegurar e dar / A e*n*tender
que *h*abyan de ser byen / Tratados e con esto el dia Syguie*n*te / Todos los
demas Pueblos de la / d*i*cha ProVyn*ç*ia se vinyeron A / dar de Paz e los
ProVeyeron / del bastymento nes*ç*eSaryo / vi / Fue Pregunt*a*do Sy en la d*i*cha
ProVin- / *ç*ia el d*i*cho Fran*ci*sco Vazquez o al- / Gunos de los d*i*chos CAPitanes / hizieron en los naturales de *e*lla / algunas crueldades o notables / malostratamyentos desPues q*ue* / *h*obyeron Venydo de Paz hiriendo- / los o
matandolos Sus mu- / Geres e hijas o Sus hazienDas / contra su Voluntad
d*i*xo q*ue* / no vyo ny SuPo que cosa alguna / de lo que le es PreGuntado

[fol. 45v]

hiziesen el di*c*ho General ny CaPitanes / ny otra Persona alguna Porque / Sy lo hizieran *e*ste t*es*t*i*go lo / Viera e SuPiera e no Pudiera / Ser menos Por *e*star como estu- / Vo en la di*c*ha ProVinçia en tanto / que en ella *e*stuvo el CAmPo / mas a*n*tes vio que se les hazia / todo buen tratamyento y los ma*n*- / tenya en mucha Paz / Fue Pregunt*a*do las ProVinçias de ti- / guex çicuyque e braVa Sy se dieron / de Paz o Sy las entraron Por Fuer- / ça *h*Abyendose Puesto en ar- / mas e Resystençia d*i*xo que / *e*stando el di*c*ho Franc*i*sco Vazquez / e la(s) demas Gente en çibola vinye- / ron çiertos mensajeros de la / ProVinçia de qucuyque A dar- / Se de Paz e A ofresçerles su / Tierra *e*ntre los quales Venia*n* / el yndio (l)llamado bigotes e o- / Tros tres o quatro A Pedir / FaVor e ayuda contra çiertos / Pueblos vezinos con quyen / Tenyan guerra e Visto Su / ofresçimyento el di*c*ho Franc*i*sco / i

[fol. 46r]

859

Vazquez se lo AGradesçio E / los rresçibio de Paz e Por Amy- / Gos e les dio Por CAPitan A her- / nando de alVarado con Veynte e / quatro De a CAballo e quatro ar- / cabuzeros lo qual todo Vio *e*ste / t*es*t*i*go e oyo que llegado A la di*c*ha / ProVinçia e descubierto el rrio / de t*i*guex e las baCAs truxo / Consygo Presos A la Vuelta Al / di*c*ho bigotes e A otro hermano / Suyo que (h)era Persona muy / PrinÇiPal de la di*c*ha ProVinçia / de çicuyque al que desPues / llamaban CAçique e truxo / ansimismo A otro yndio que / le Pusyeron ysoPete e al / yndio llamado Turco que / dezian ser esclavo del di*c*ho / bigotes e Por tal su esclavo / Se lo *h*abia Dado al di*c*ho herna*n*do / de alVarado Para que le guia- / Se a las di*c*has ProVinçias e / VaCas que Por ma*n*dado del di*c*ho / General yba A descubryr / e Vio que el di*c*ho herna*n*do / de alVarado ynVio desde las

[fol. 46v]

di*c*has ProVinçias Al di*c*ho General / Una CAbeça de baCA e çiertas co- / sas de RoPa e cueros adobados / que los de las di*c*has ProVin- / çias dezian *h*Aberle dado en Pre- / Sente e que Vuelto Al real / TuVo Presos A los di*ch*os bigo- / tes e CAçique en CAdenas / Fue Pregunt*a*do que Fue la CAusa Por / que aPerrearon A los di*ch*os / caçique e bigotes Pues (h)eran / Personas Tan PrinçiPales e / *h*Abian venydo de Paz e a dar la / obediençia A su ma*G*estad / E *h*abyan Guyado al di*ch*o herna*n*do / de alVarado e a la(s) demas Gente / que con el yban en el descubrimye*n*- / To que Fue hazer e les *h*abian / ProVeydo de ma*n*tenymyentos / e rropa e (F)*h*echo buen acoximyento / e tratamyento en sus Tierras / d*i*xo que *e*ste t*e*stigo oyo / que los *h*abyan aPer- reaDo Al / bigotes Porque a la Vuelta / que VolVio el di*ch*o AlVarado / Por la ProVinçia de t*i*guex / ii

[fol. 47r]

860

no les *h*abian salido con tantos Pre- / Sentes como a la yda creyenDo / que el di*ch*o bigotes *h*Abia sido / causa de *e*llo e Al di*ch*o CAçique Por- / que no daba Al di*ch*o Françisco / Vazquez çiertos brazaletes E / joyas de oro que el di*ch*o yndio / llamado turco Dezia *h*aberle / tomado a el e a otros Sus conPa- / neros Porque lo negaba el di*ch*o CA- / çique e no concorDaba con lo que / el di*ch*o turco dezia lo APerre- / Aron e lastymaron malamenTe en / Una Pierna e (e)en Un braço / Fue Pregunt*a*do quyen les (F)echo / los Perros A los di*ch*os CAçique / e bigotes e Por cuyo mandado e / Sy se hallo Presente el di*ch*o / Francisco Vazquez d*i*xo que *e*ste / Testigo no lo vio Pero que Fue / muy Publico e notorio en el Re- / al que al bigotes le manDo / APerrear el di*ch*o hernando de / AlVarado e al CAçique el di*ch*o / Françisco Vazquez e que lo / cree Ansi e lo tiene Por çierto

[fol. 47v]

Porque quando APerrearon / Al di*ch*o CAçique estaba en el rreal / donde se hizo el di*ch*o Fran*ci*sco vazquez / e Segun(d) tenia su(b)jetos e obe- / dientes A los CAPitanes e Gente / nynguno osara hazerlo Syn su / liçençia e ma*n*dado / Fue Preguntado Sy tenyendo Pre- / Sos a los di*ch*os CAçique e big- otes / los de la di*ch*a ProVinçia de çicuy- / que los ynViaron A PeDir di- / ziendo que Pues se *h*abyan d*e* su / Voluntad venydo A dar de Paz / e la obe-

diençia A su magestad / e los *h*abyan acoxido en sus Tierras / e (f)*h*echo tan
buen tratamyento que / Por que CAusa les tenyan Presos / Sus PrinÇiPales e
les guardaba*n* / Tan mala Fee e amystad que / les *h*abian oFresçido dixo que
*e*s / *ver*dad que *e*ste t*e*stigo oyo / dezir Por muy Publico e notorio / lo que le
es Preguntado e q*ue* / el d*i*cho General les rresPonDia / que diesen Primero
los d*i*chos / braçaletes e joyas e los men- / iii

[fol. 48r]

861

Sajeros rresPonDian que les diesen / Primero sus PrinçiPales / x / Fue Preguntado Sy a los d*i*chos me*n*- / sajeros Porque Pedian Sus / PrinçiPales e
ynPortunaban / Sobre ello les (h)echaron los / Perros e los mordieron mala- /
mente e Por cuyo ma*n*dado dixo / que no vio ni oyo que a mensajero / Tal cosa
Se le hiziese / xi / Fue Pregunt*a*do que Fue la CAusa Por / que las d*i*chas ProV-
inçias de Çi- / cuyque e tiguex Se alçaron e / Rebelaron d*i*xo que la de çicuy-
/ que Fue Por el maltratamyento / que habian (f)*h*echo a los d*i*chos sus /
PrinçiPales Porque luego que / los Soltaron e los d*i*chos natu- / rales los Vieron
Se alçaron / A la clara Aunque desde el / TienPo que aPerrearon A los / d*i*chos
CAçique e bigotes se sus- / Trajeron de no les Favoresçer / ni acoxer A los
esPañoles *e*n sus / Pueblos e que lo de tiguex / Se dixo PubliCAmente

[fol. 48v]

que *h*abia Sydo Porque contra su / Voluntad les *h*abian SaCAdo el bas- /
Tymento e RoPa e cueros d*e* sus CAsas / xii / Fue Pregunt*a*do que Pueblos
Fueron / los que en la Provinçia de ti- / guex se hizieron Fuertes y a q*ue* / Se
Recogio la gente dixo que / Todos los Pueblos d*e* la d*i*cha / Provinçia Se rrebelaron Pero q*ue* / A Solos tres Se rrecoxio la / Gente e que a los demas los /
dexaron yermos e des*man*Para- / dos / Fue Pregunt*a*do que Pues solos tres /
Fueron donde Se rrecoxio la / Gente que los demas Por- / que los quemaron
Pues que / en ellos no *h*Abia deFensa Al- / Guna ni de *e*llos se les hazia Gue-
/ rra d*i*xo que los quemaron / Por hazerles daño e Porq*ue* / los demas se
esCArmentaSen / de no Se rrebelar e Porque / no se tornasen a hazer Fuertes
/ en ellos / xiii / Fue Pregunt*a*do los tres Pueblos / iiii

[fol. 49r]

862

que dyze *h*aberse (f)*h*echos Fuertes e Re- / belado e rrecoxido en ellos la gen-
/ Te Sy los quemaron e aSolaron / Como los demas E Sy les hi- / zieron
algunos Requyrimyentos / Para que Se diesen de Paz / dixo que vio que
muchas e d*i*- / VersAs Vezes rrequyrieron / A los naturales de los d*i*chos /
Pueblos que en ellos *e*staba*n* / Acoxidos y enCAstillados que se / dieSen de
Paz E que no les / Seria (f)*h*echo mal alguno e que / Jamas quysieron aunque
se les / Yban Ganando Algunas Plaças / e quema*n*doselas e que *e*stu- / Vieron
tan PurFyados e Pertina- / zes que jamas Se quysieron / dar hasta que les quemaron to- / das las CAsas o la mayor Parte / y esto Fue en uno de los d*i*chos
Pue- / blos Porque el otro lo desman- / Pararon los d*i*chos naturales / y se
Fueron y el otro vyendose / aPretado con el çerco Se / dieron A mysiricord*i*a
e vyo q*ue* / de los que d*e e*ste Pueblo se die-

[fol. 49v]

ron Recox*i*eron ochenta e tantos en / Una Tienda e quemaron ViVos la /
mayor P*a*rte de *e*llos e los demas como Vie- / ron la Crueldad que hazian En
/ Sus conPañeros Se alçaron *en* la / tienda de don garç*i*a loPez de CArde- /
nas donde eStaban e se deFendian / con Palos e con las Armas que en / ella
hallaron e ally los alançearon e / mataron A estoCAdas / xv / Fue Pregunt*a*do
Sy demas de los / que quemaron APerrearon A otros / Algunos Dixo que del
otro Pue- / blo que tomaron Por Fuerça don- / de Tuvo el çerco el General /
Vio que APerrearon Por su / ma*n*dado mas de çiento e çinquenta / Yndios
que tomaron ViVos syn / otros muchos que se alançearon / que salyan
huyendo del d*i*cho Pu*e*bl*o* / Fue Preguntado la quema de los / d*i*chos yndios
que Se hizo en el Pu*e*bl*o* / que tenia çerCAdo don garç*i*a lopez / de CArdenas
Sy se hizo Por / ma*n*dado del d*i*cho General dixo / que si Porque en Presençia
/ d*e e*sTe t*e*stigo ma*n*do Al d*i*cho / v

[fol. 50r]

863

D*o*n garç*i*a loPez que Fuese a conquystar / el d*i*cho Pueblo e los demas que /

*e*staban Alçados e que a todos los / matasen a cuchillo Pero que si / los mando quemar o no que no / lo sabe Pero que cree que no lo / haria Syn mandado del d*i*cho Ge- / neral Por *e*star como *e*staba / el un rreal del otro (E)*di*stançia de / media legua e Porque CAda *h*ora / del un rreal Al otro Se enViaba*n* / menSajeros e Porque Poco / a*n*tes que se hizieSe la / d*i*cha quema el d*i*cho Franç*i*sco / Vazquez ynVio Al rreal del d*i*cho / don garç*i*a loPez Al yndio llama- / do turco e a ysoPete Para que / Viesen la juSt*i*S*i*a que de los / d*i*chos yndios se hazia e diesen / noty*ç*ia de *e*llo en sus tierras / y en los demas Pueblos Por do*n*de / Pasasen / Fue Pregunt*a*do q*ue* tantos Pueblos / d*e* la d*i*cha P*ro*Vinç*i*a de tiguex / Serian los que quemaron e s*i* / quemaron Ansymismo los / dos que dize que se dio e desma*n*-

[fol. 50v]
Pararon de los tres En que se *h*Abian / (F)*h*echo Fuertes dixo que los Pueblos / que quemaron d*e* la d*i*cha ProVinç*i*a / Son treze E que ansymesmo que- / maron los dos que le son Pregunt*a*do / Fue Pregunt*a*do quyen (h)*e*ra el CAP- itan / que hazia la d*i*cha quema dixo que / los tres los quemaron toda la gen- / te e CAPitanes e que los demas / los quemo don Rodrigo maldona- / do Por ma*n*dado del d*i*cho General / Fue Pregunt*a*do quyen mato o mando ma- / tar Al yndio llamado turco e Por / que causa dixo que este t*e*st*i*go no se / (F)*h*allo Presente Pero que oyo / dezir Por Publico e notorio / que lo Ahogo un Franc*i*sco mar*t*yn / CArnyçero Por ma*n*dado del Ge- / neral y de diego loPez veynte / e quatro de sevilla que a la sa- / zon (h)*e*ra maestre De CAnPo Por- / que dezian que tenia movida / la tierra e P*ro*Vinç*i*a de qui- / Vyra e Porque *h*Abia traydo el / exerç*i*to *en*ganado con diversas / me*n*tyras llevandolo Por desPo- / (^x)vi

[fol. 51r]
864

blados donde no *h*Abia Agua ni mante- / nymyento Alguno donde se vio en grand*e*s / Peligros e trabajos / Fue Preguntado A la Vuelta que / Se VolVian de qu*i*Vira A tiguex / Sy hizieron Daño en la d*i*cha / ProVinç*i*a o algunas quemas / de Pueblos d*i*xo que es verdad / que los mysmos Pueblos que /

*h*Abian quemado e desbaratado / Algunos de los quales *e*staban / Ya ReFor-
mados tornaron A des- / truyrlos Ansy Para Se aPro- / vechar de la leña
Como Por sacar / el mayz e bastymento que *h*abian / dexado *en*terra(S)Do e
Porque / todavia los d*e* la d*i*cha ProVinçia / *e*staban de guerra e nunCA /
quysyeron venyr de Paz y Por / la nesçesidad que el CAnPo the- / nya de
bastymento e leña Porq*ue* / Peresçiera*n* de Frio e hambre / SalVo Por el bastymento e ma- / dera que se SaCAba de / los d*i*chos Pueblos que se *h*abian /
Tornado A ReFormar e ReydiFiCAr

[fol. 51v]

xxi / Fue Pregunt*a*do que otras Crueldad*e*s e / malostratamyentos Vio que en
la / Vuelta d*e* las d*i*chas ProVinçia*s* E / jornada a *e*sta ÇiUdad hiziese el / d*i*cho
Franc*i*sco vazquez e los otros / caPitanes en los naturales de / las d*i*chas ProV-
inçias dixo que no lo / Sabe ny vio que se hiziesen e q*ue* / esto es lo que Sabe
çercA de lo / que le es PreGunt*a*do e no otra / cosa Para el juramento que
hizo / e lo Fyrmo de Su nonbre Fue le tor- / nado A leer luego como lo
aCAbo de / dezir e RetiFycose en el e se- / ñalolo el d*i*cho Señor oydor
*cri*st*o*Val / d*e* escobar

Chapter 10

Juan Troyano,
the Eighth de Oficio Witness

A Professional Military Man

By a substantial margin, the lengthiest testimony given during the 1544 investigation, barring Vázquez de Coronado's, was that of Juan Troyano. According to fellow expedition member Rodrigo Maldonado, he was a *criado* or henchman of Antonio de Mendoza, and Troyano himself reported that he came to the New World in the viceroy's entourage in 1535. Further, the viceroy provided financial support to insure that Troyano could join the expedition to Tierra Nueva.[1] Among those who went on the expedition he was a rarity, a professional fighting man. Beginning in 1511, when he left his home in Medina de Rioseco in modern Castilla y León, Spain, at age 15 to the curses of his father, he had served as seaman and artilleryman, first in Italy and thereafter with Mendoza in Nueva España.[2]

Throughout the expedition to Tierra Nueva, Troyano served as an artilleryman in the company of the captain of artillery, Hernando de Alvarado. His companion-in-arms Rodrigo Maldonado reported that Troyano was in charge of six *versillos* (light, swivel-mounted, breech-loading guns which threw one- to two-inch shot).[3] During his 1544 testimony before Tejada, Troyano himself recalled one occasion on which he had been sent, with Juan Cordero, to pack half a dozen artillery pieces (*tiros de artillería*) from Cíbola to the expedition's winter quarters at Tiguex.

Troyano was among the vanguard of approximately 100 Europeans and "most of the [Indian] allies" who went ahead of the main body of the expedition from Culiacán to Cíbola.[4] Consequently, he was one of the relatively few European eyewitnesses to the storming of the "first pueblo" of Cíbola in July 1540 and to the arrival there of a diplomatic/trading party from Cicuique. Troyano was also among the small party who went to the towns of Tiguex and Cicuique and to the Great Plains shortly after the fall of Cíbola. He was, thus, one of the first members of the expedition to see bison and to hear about possible riches in the land of Quivira. Later, Troyano was present at the siege of Pueblo del Arenal commanded by García López de Cárdenas during the winter of 1540–1541, in the course of which several of the events took place for which the maestre de campo later was punished. López de Cárdenas claimed that Troyano, Juan Contreras, and Melchior Pérez were among his principal enemies, for which reason their testimony concerning his actions during the expedition should be disregarded.[5] Troyano had some knowledge of bridge building and, thus, undoubtedly was involved in the construction of a bridge that was built by the expedition in spring 1541. Juan Cordero claimed that the captain general and the captains never did anything without asking Troyano's opinion because of his long experience in matters of warfare.[6]

While in Tierra Nueva, Troyano made an alliance with a woman, who returned with him to Mexico in 1542.[7] Much later he pointed with pride to this "*compañera*" and boasted that no other such woman had returned with the expedition to Mexico City. At the same time, he extolled Tierra Nueva as "another new world as excellent as New Spain;" he claimed to have gone on all the explorations conducted there, lamented that a land of so many people had not been brought to the Catholic faith, and volunteered to go back under the leadership of Martín Cortés.[8]

After Troyano's return from Tierra Nueva in 1542, the viceroy conceded to him the sole right to build bergantines (shallow-draft, oared boats) with which to transport wood and stone to the island city of Mexico. Years later he claimed to have built at least one at a cost of 500 pesos.[9] Although, at the time of the 1544 investigation, Troyano was lodging with fellow artilleryman Pedro de Écija, by at least 1560 he was a vecino of Mexico City and maintained his own *casa poblada* or family seat there.[10]

He continued to serve the viceroys of Nueva España even after Mendoza's departure for Peru in 1551, filling various minor roles under viceroys Luis de Velasco, Gastón de Peralta, and Martín Enríquez de Almansa. Despite apparent frequent employment, Troyano complained of chronic poverty and sought compensation and preferment from the Spanish kings several times. Preferment apparently never came. His greatest service to a viceregal government, though, may have been his testimony during Tejada's 1544 investigation of the conduct of the expedition to Tierra Nueva. Certainly, that testimony helped to clear the former captain general Francisco Vázquez de Coronado and also to condemn Maestre de Campo García López de Cárdenas.

In 1563 Troyano was arrested and jailed, accused of fomenting rebellion in the estancias of San Juan Temamatlac, San José, San Gregorio, San Pablo Atlacalpa, San Marcos, San Mateo Zacamultelelco, San Andrés Yetla, and Santa María Atoyac, all places subject to Tlalmanalco in the province of Chalco southeast of Mexico City. These estancias had been settled by Indians who were newcomers to the area from Texcoco and Mexico City, who were bent on establishing their own separate *cabecera* or head town. Troyano employed workers from the eight disaffected estancias in hauling firewood and building walls and houses. As a result of their close association with Troyano, the immigrants designated him as their *procurador* or attorney and he filed many lawsuits on their behalf, which kept the province in turmoil. Over the next nine years, Troyano was in jail at least three times on the same charge. From prison he sent lengthy, vague, and repetitious letters to the viceroy and the king, warning of deep divisions within the Spanish population of Nueva España and railing against the mendicant religious orders and the royal officials. He repeatedly asked for a private audience with the king.[11] Although we have no written record of such a meeting, one may well have occurred, since in 1574 a Juan Troyano, vecino of Mexico City, and his son Bartolomé were granted license to return to Nueva España from Spain.[12]

During his June 9, 1544, testimony before Tejada, Troyano volunteered
extensive detail beyond what he was asked, including exculpatory information
about Vázquez de Coronado such as that he gave orders favorable to the
Indians of Corazones, had the requerimiento read three times at Cíbola, and
formally summoned the Indians of Tiguex before making war. But he also
said that Vázquez de Coronado ordered dogs set on Bigotes, though he was
not an eyewitness of the unleashing.   On the whole, Troyano presented
Vázquez de Coronado's actions as patient, reasonable, and moderate. He was
also first to say that López de Cárdenas had broken a solemn promise of
safety to the Indians of Pueblo del Arenal.

Troyano's testimony represents the clearest exposition of the attitudes
prevailing among the witnesses concerning treatment of natives of the Southwest by the expedition. These were also likely the dominant attitudes among
the expedition as a whole. Not unexpectedly for an artilleryman inured to the
savagery of battle, Troyano recounted in an offhand manner the slaughter of
hundreds of Indians as generally unavoidable and brought on the Indians by
themselves. He suggested, however, that there were instances of excess brutality and that those excesses provoked and stiffened native resistance against
the expedition and its plans for the people of Tierra Nueva. He portrayed the
actions of occasional individuals and the expedition as a unit as often alien-
ating native peoples. Throughout Troyano's testimony (and that of the other
witnesses), however, there is no hint of regret over the expedition's behavior,
and certainly no suggestion of remorse.

A TRANSLATION
OF THE TESTIMONY

Eighth de Oficio Witness (Juan Troyano)[13]

[51v cont'd] Juan Troyano, a resident of the city of Mexico, accepted as a witness for this investigation, having given his oath in legal form, was asked the following questions under that obligation.

{*1*} He was asked whether he knows Francisco Vázquez de Coronado, don García López de Cárdenas, don Diego de Guevara, don Tristán de [52r] Arellano, don Rodrigo Maldonado, Diego López (a councilman of Sevilla), don Pedro de Tovar, Hernando de Alvarado, Juan de Zaldívar, Barrionuevo, Pablos de Melgosa, and the other captains who went to reconnoiter and subjugate Tierra Nueva and Cíbola, Tiguex, Cicuique, Brava, Quivira, and the other neighboring provinces. He answered that he knows all of those mentioned in the question, by appearance, voice, behavior, and conversation that he has had with them for the last five years and more. He was present during the subjugation and reconnaissance of those provinces from the beginning until they returned to this city of Mexico.

{*2*} The witness was asked whether [the people of] the provinces of Corazones, the valleys of Señora and Fuya, and the others that there are between Culiacán and Cíbola came out in peace [52v] to offer obedience to His Majesty and to Francisco Vázquez in his royal name. Did they give and supply provisions and food that they had, and did they welcome [the Spaniards] into their houses and towns, without taking up arms or making war? He answered that it is true that those valleys and all the towns between Culiacán and Cíbola through which Francisco Vázquez went came out in peace and rendered obedience to His Majesty and to the general in his royal name. [The witness] did not see that the Indians either had provisions or gave them to the Spaniards. Nor did the Spaniards enter their settlements because Francisco Vázquez gave orders to them not to enter them and not to take anything.

{*3*} He was asked whether the general or any of the captains perpetrated any cruelty or outrage [53r] against the natives of those towns or any one of them. Also, he was asked whether, if others committed such acts, the general punished them or excused their behavior. In reply he said that the general and his captains always treated the Indians very well and that, in order to keep the Indians happy, the general sometimes gave them beads, glass baubles, small bells, knives, and other items. And if a Spaniard took anything from those Indians, the general reprimanded him in such a way that he strove to have the Indians treated very well.

{*4*} [Then] he was asked what the reason was that the natives of those provinces rose up and revolted and killed the Spaniards who stayed there and whether Francisco Vázquez or any of the captains was to blame for that result. And did he punish those who transgressed? He replied that, as was common knowledge and widely known, the cause of that uprising was the outrages and brutal acts committed by a [man named] Alcaraz. He was the captain [53v] who had been left in his place by Melchor Díaz, before [Díaz] died making a reconnaissance of the coast of the Mar del Sur. That Alcaraz, they said, took wives and daughters from Indians in order to have sexual relations with them. And he took the provisions that they had. Concerning these things, disagreements arose among the Spaniards and some of them went to Culiacán and others to the army of Francisco Vázquez.

The Indians, having seen the disagreement among the Spaniards and that some of them had left, revolted against Alcaraz. And they killed him and some of those who were with him. [The witness said] that Francisco Vázquez was not at all to blame for the revolt since he was not present and did not know of it.

{*5*} [The witness] was asked [next] what brutality and outrages Francisco Vázquez or any of [54r] the captains committed in the province of Cíbola and whether [the people there] came forth in peace or in war. He answered that when [the expedition] arrived near Cíbola Francisco Vázquez sent [a message] (in His Majesty's name) with some Indians who were natives of Cíbola and who, a day previously, had come voluntarily to the army, to summon the Indians who were in Cíbola. Through an Indian who was a native of the province of Señora, Francisco Vázquez told the three Indians to go to Cíbola and tell the leaders that he was coming on behalf of His Majesty to bring them to his obedience and so that they might know God. And they were to tell [the leaders] not be fearful because he would not do them any harm. And he gave them some of the trade goods he had, so that they would be content. Those Indians departed and did not return.

The following day, the general sent fray Juan de Padilla and other clerics and individuals [54v] from the company to talk to the Indians and to exhort them to submit peacefully and tell them that he would treat them well and that he would uphold justice. Although this was said to them and the requerimiento was read and made understandable by an Indian from the province of Señora who, they said, knew the language, the Indians of Cíbola never were willing to come in peace. On the contrary, they started to throw dirt, marking lines on the ground and making it understood that the clerics were not to pass beyond. And they began to shoot arrows at the Spaniards and clerics. Having seen that, the general and the Spaniards attacked [the Indians] and killed some of them by lancing as they withdrew to the pueblo. And there they again fortified themselves.

And once more, through the interpreter, the general delivered the requerimiento. [The Indians] were not inclined to come to peace. So Francisco Vázquez and other Spaniards [55r] began to talk with the Indians and approached them in order to enter the pueblo. And when [the Indians of Cíbola] saw them near at hand they hurled a stone slab from a roof, which struck Francisco Vázquez and knocked him down. The other Spaniards lifted him up and carried him to the camp.

Thereupon, he ordered that [the Spaniards] bombard them with artillery. They commenced to do so and killed some of [the Indians]. Then by means of signs and through the interpreter [the Indians] submitted and the Spaniards entered the pueblo. This was possible because all of the Indians withdrew, leaving the town deserted, but full of provisions, which were plentiful. [The witness said] that after the surrender of the pueblo he neither saw nor knew of mistreatment or brutality inflicted on any Indians. Nor was any committed because, if it had been, this witness would have seen or learned about it. And it could not be otherwise because he was present during all of the events he recounted.

On the contrary, he saw that Francisco Vázquez treated [the Indians] well and gave them articles of trade [55v] that he carried. And the Indians brought him a gift of hares and rabbits and other things, which he distributed among the captains. Francisco Vázquez demanded the return of an Indian from Petatlán, whom the Indians [of Cíbola] had captured at the time they killed a Black whom fray Marcos had sent. And they brought him. He was called Bartolomé and knew the Nahuatl language. Through him and the other interpreter [the Spaniards] talked with [the Indians of Cíbola].

{6} [The witness] was [then] asked whether the provinces of Tiguex, Cicuique, Brava, and the others in that region took up arms and offered resistance or whether they came out to offer peace to the general. He replied that [the people of] all those provinces came in peace and rendered obedience to His Majesty and to Francisco Vázquez in his royal name, without offering any resistance. Rather, the [Indians] of Cicuique, knowing that the Spaniards had taken Cíbola, came there, which is seventy leagues from Cicuique. [56r] They said that they were coming to be allies of [the Spaniards] and to offer peace. And the Indians gave the Spaniards of the army some of the provisions they had, as well as mantas and other things. Further, they welcomed the Spaniards into their houses and pueblos and vacated a pueblo in which [the Spaniards] could spend the winter. Thus, the Spaniards occupied that pueblo for a winter. The Indians went off to other pueblos in the area.

{7} He was then asked why those same pueblos and provinces reversed themselves and rose up in arms. And [he was also asked] how the Indians called the cacique, Bigotes, Turco, and Ysopete were taken captive. [In answer] he said that, as he had testified in regard to the previous question, when the army was in Cíbola, [Indians] came from Cicuique to offer peace to the general. Subsequently, the general dispatched Hernando de Alvarado and twenty-three other men, among whom [56v] was this witness, to examine the land and the settlements that were there. And so they made a reconnaissance. [The people there] offered peace [all the way] to Cicuique, giving [the Spaniards] everything they needed.

Then Hernando de Alvarado said that he wanted to explore on beyond and asked Bigotes to go with him to show him the land. [Bigotes] said that he was tired and that he could not go farther, but that he would provide a brother of his. Thus, he brought an Indian whom they called Turco and another called Zamarilla, who would show the land. One day while they were making their reconnaissance, the Indian called Turco said, by means of signs and in the Nahuatl language (which he knew slightly), that he was not familiar with the land towards the direction [they were then going], but that he would lead in another direction, towards which he pointed. He would lead them there because in that direction there were very large settlements and also gold, silver, and painted pictures.[14] And [further], he indicated the way in which the natives of that place obtained gold and silver.

Because Hernando de Alvarado [57r] was required in his instructions to proceed in the direction he was then going and not in that other direction, and also because he had completed the term [of his commission], he returned to Cicuique. And while they were on the way back the Indian called Turco said that [the Spaniards] should not tell Bigotes what he had said because they would kill him, since the land he had told of was Quivira and the people there were friends of Bigotes. When he was back at Cicuique the Indian Turco fled. Hernando de Alvarado made a search for him, but he did not turn up.

Then Hernando de Alvarado said that he would assist the [people] of Cicuique in defeating a province called Nanapagua, with which they were at war. The [people] of Cicuique assembled three hundred men for that purpose. Among them went the cacique, Bigotes, and El Turco. When they had marched two days' journey toward that province, El Turco did not make an appearance. Hernando de Alvarado asked Bigotes to force El Turco to come to him. Because [the Indians of Cicuique] did not bring him, Alvarado [57v] seized the cacique and Bigotes. He had collars with chains attached put around their necks and he said that he was holding them thus until El Turco came. [The two Indians then] sent for El Turco, and both El Turco and Ysopete came.

When they had come, Hernando de Alvarado and fray Juan de Padilla met with the four Indians and told all the other [Indians] that they should return to their country [Cicuique]. Then they told Bigotes, the cacique, and Ysopete that El Turco had said that he knew of a land called Quivira where there were gold, silver, painted cloths, and other things and that Bigotes and the others had a gold bracelet and other things that they had brought from there. [Then] Hernando de Alvarado and fray Juan de Padilla told them that they should state whether that was true and should turn over the jewelry. Then they would release them. But Bigotes and Cacique said that El Turco was lying, while El Turco and Ysopete maintained that what El Turco had stated was true. It was over this that Hernando de Alvarado took all four Indians prisoner [58r] in chains, until he got them to the camp where Francisco Vázquez was.

[The witness] said that they met in Tiguex, and Hernando de Alvarado told Francisco Vázquez that he was bringing those Indian as prisoners and the reason why [he was doing so]. And [this witness said] that he was present during all that he has told of.

[Further, Troyano] said that, since Francisco Vázquez saw that some Indians said one thing and the others another, he ordered them to set dogs on Bigotes in order that he might testify to the truth of what El Turco and Ysopete were saying. And thus, [the witness] saw that some dogs of don Pedro de Tovar were set on Bigotes, and they bit him on the leg and an arm. This happened within the camp outside the pueblo, there being present many captains and men whose names he does not recall. Francisco Vázquez, though, was not there.

Don Pedro de Tovar called off the dogs and took the Indian Bigotes before Francisco Vázquez, in order [58v] that he might tell the truth. He admitted to having at Cicuique a gold bracelet, a dog, an earthenware flask,[15] and other jewelry. And he said that an Indian principal called Querecho had these things in his possession. Because the Indians of Cicuique went about half ready to revolt and were hostile, in order to calm them, after a certain time [the Spaniards] sent Bigotes there. He never returned.

[In addition, the witness said] that when the army went to Quivira, because they had to go by way of Cicuique, they sent the cacique there, so that he could bring the pueblo to peace and ask the people there to furnish provisions. And so [the cacique] went. But when the Spaniards arrived [the Indians] refused to welcome them or furnish provisions.

{8} [The witness] was [next] asked to state whether the Indians of Cicuique and Tiguex rose up and revolted because dogs were set on Bigotes and he was otherwise mistreated. He answered that after the imprisonment and unleashing of dogs [against Bigotes][16] the Indians rose up [against the Spaniards]. He heard it said, [however], and it was [59r] common knowledge in the camp that they had risen in revolt because the [Spaniards'] horses were eating their planted fields and because the Christians occupied their houses and demanded mantas and other things from them. And also, it was said, because a brother of the Villegas who is regidor of the city of Mexico had taken an Indian woman by force to have sexual relations with her.

{9} [The witness] was asked whether it came to Francisco Vázquez's notice that the brother of Villegas had seized the Indian woman and whether he punished him for that. He said that he does not know because when the above-mentioned event occurred he had returned to Cíbola for some artillery pieces. When he returned [to Tiguex] he heard what was said above.

{10} [Troyano then] was asked how many pueblos of those provinces [the Spaniards] burned and entered by force. He said that the uprising he had mentioned came about when the Indians killed more than forty horses and pack animals one night . Both because of this and because they had rebelled, [the Spaniards] waged war against [the Indians]. [59v] They burned and destroyed thirteen pueblos. They occupied only two by force and those because [the Indians] fortified themselves in them and defended themselves. The other pueblos that [the Spaniards] burned they found empty and abandoned. And [the witness said] that before [the Spaniards] waged war against those two [pueblos] Francisco Vázquez summoned [the people] to come to peace and, thus, he would forgive what they had done. The Indians, though, never consented to peace. Therefore, [the Spaniards] burned the [pueblos].

And the [pueblos] that they found abandoned were burned so that [the Indians] would not fortify themselves in them.

{11} He was [then] asked who ordered those towns to be burned, inasmuch as no resistance was offered there. He replied that he heard it said that Francisco Vázquez had ordered the burning of three pueblos that were at the foot of a range of mountains. Concerning the others he does not know who ordered the burning, but they were burned so that [the Indians] would not fortify themselves there, as he has already said, and also so that other [Indians] could not supply themselves with provisions from those pueblos, since they had refused to come to peace.

[60r] {12} [The witness] was asked, concerning the Indians who were captured alive in those towns, what cruelty and outrages were committed against them. [In answer] he said that when don García López de Cárdenas had besieged the first pueblo, Pueblo del Cerco, the witness saw one day that, by bombarding it, [the Spaniards] reached the flat roofs and began to set fire to the pueblo. When the Indians saw that they were sorely pressed, some of them made a cross, displayed it through the windows, and declared that they would come out in peace. In this way sixty Indians came out. As they came [the Spaniards] put them in the tent of don García López. And they killed others.

When [the Spaniards] saw that no more [Indians] were coming out, they took the Indians who were in the tent and brought some posts that were in the camp. Setting the posts in the ground, they began tying some of [the Indians] to posts in order to burn them. Then [the Indians] who remained in the tent rose up in the tent itself [against the Spaniards]. Therefore, the Christians [60v] killed some of them by lancing and stabbing them and the rest they burned alive tied to the posts. [The witness said] that it appeared to him that those [Indians] whom they burned numbered between forty and fifty.

[The witness also said] he saw that before the burning El Turco and Ysopete were brought from the camp where Francisco Vázquez was, in order that they might witness the burning. He does not know who brought them nor by whose order it was done. He said that García López, as maestre de campo, was the one who ordered the stakes set up and the Indians burned.

None [of the Indians] remained alive. He does not know whether Francisco Vázquez ordered [García López to do what he did] or not.

{13} [Troyano] was asked whether he knew that all the captains and troops were very obedient to Francisco Vázquez and subject to his command and that no one would have dared to carry out those burnings and to unleash the dogs without his permission and command. He replied that he knows that everyone was very obedient [61r] to Francisco Vázquez. And he believes that no one in the army would dare do anything without his permission and command.

{14} He was asked to state whether he saw or knew that [the Spaniards] had set dogs on or burned any other Indians, in addition to those about whom he has already testified, either in the pueblo that don García López besieged or the one that Francisco Vázquez laid siege to. He replied by saying that at the pueblo where don García López was he saw no more than what he has already testified. And at the pueblo where Francisco Vázquez was, he saw that they burned Indian men, women, and children and all that was inside the houses, in order to capture those houses. But he did not see [the Spaniards] harm anyone after the houses had been captured. He neither heard nor knew of any such thing, although he was present when that pueblo was taken.

{15} [The witness] was [then] asked whether [the Spaniards] burned any towns or set dogs on Indians in the province of Cicuique. [61v] He answered that he did not see any town burned there; nor was any burned. Neither did he see dogs unleashed against any Indian, except Bigotes, as he has already said.

{16} He was [further] asked to state and declare how and in what way the death of the Indian called Turco came about and transpired, who killed him, when, for what reason, and by whose order. He replied that Turco and Ysopete went as guides from Cicuique to Quivira. [Turco] kept [the Spaniards] lost for more than three months. And afterwards he confessed that he had been leading them deceitfully by roundabout ways, so that they might die of hunger.

After [the Spaniards] had arrived at Quivira, Ysopete gave evidence that El Turco was telling [the Indians of Quivira] not to bring the Christians or their horses anything to eat, because then they would die. Ysopete said that to this witness and to others who knew how to speak his language somewhat. And he knew some of the Nahuatl language. Because of what Ysopete said, Francisco Vázquez, in the presence of this witness, ordered [62r] Juan de Zaldívar to apply a garrote to kill El Turco. Thus it was done and Turco was garrotted. This witness did not see who garrotted him, although he had heard it said that Francisco Martín had done it.

{17} The witness was asked what other brutality and outrages he saw or knew that Francisco Vázquez or the other captains committed. He answered that he knows of no more than what he has already stated.

{18} He was [then] asked in what way don García López de Cárdenas and Diego López (the councilman), who were in command at the first besieged pueblo, seized the Indians, whom he said they took, and whether they did so while [the Indians] were assured of safety. He answered that when the Spaniards had reached and secured the roofs, they slept there that night. The next day the Indians of the pueblo, seeing themselves sorely pressed [62v] and still being weary and hurt from the battle of the day before, communicated by signs to the [two] captains and [other] Spaniards that if they were assured of safety, they would offer peace. In turn, the captains and other Spaniards replied by means of signs that, if they were to come forth and offer peace, no harm or hurt would be done to anyone.

And [the Spaniards] displayed the cross in assurance of peace and security. With this guarantee and assurance, between sixty and seventy Indians came out from the pueblo, one by one and two by two, without weapons and without any protection. They were going to be put among the Spaniards and they were. But don García López ordered that they be gathered together and put in his tent. Right away he sent messengers to Francisco Vázquez, who was in the camp one or two leagues from there, to tell him what had transpired. [63r] Soon thereafter Francisco Vázquez [came][17] and spoke with don García López. And when he had talked with him, he returned immediately to the camp. The witness thinks that the meeting and conversation concerned the administration of justice to the Indians who had come to peace under the assurance of safety. He is certain that this was so because Francisco Vázquez said so to the Indians called Turco and Ysopete, whom [the Spaniards] had brought to don García López's camp, so that they might witness justice done. They watched the punishment inflicted on [the Indians] who had rebelled, and Francisco Vázquez returned to his camp very soon.

Don García López, who at that time was maestre de campo, ordered that some posts be set in the ground and that some Indians be bound to them two at a time until fifty Indians had been so secured. These were from the group that had come from the pueblo in peace and had been placed in the tent under assurance of safety. Then [the Spaniards] set fire to them and burned all of them alive. The rest of the Indians, who had remained in the tent, when they saw that [the Spaniards] were [63v] taking their comrades out and tying them to posts, were fearful and suspicious that what had been done to their comrades [would] thereafter [be done to them]. They rose up and fortified themselves in the tent and defended themselves with poles and stakes that they took from the tent. Then [the Spaniards] killed all of them by lancing and stabbing.

The witness said that [the Indians] of the other pueblo to which [the Spaniards] had laid siege knew and saw the cruelty with which [the Spaniards] had treated [the Indians] of the [first] pueblo and that [the Spaniards] had not kept the promise of safety they had given. As a result, they never were willing to yield and come forth in peace, although they were summoned repeatedly by Francisco Vázquez. [The Indians] said that [the Spaniards] were dishonest people and did not respect the truth. They said that although [the Spaniards] might give their word and guarantee, they would not hold to it, just as they had failed to do with their comrades and neighbors.

{*19*} [Troyano] was asked [further] what Indians were burned and set upon by dogs from among those taken alive at the pueblo to which Francisco Vázquez had laid siege. He answered that he knows no [64r] more than that within the pueblo [besieged by Francisco Vázquez][18] many Indians were burned because [the Spaniards] could not capture them nor were [the Indians] willing to offer peace until [the Spaniards] set fire to their houses.

{*20*} [The witness] was asked what other brutality and outrages he saw that the general and captains committed against the natives. He said [in reply] that, beyond and in addition to what he had already said and testified, he saw that at the first pueblo besieged, where don García López was in command, some Indians of that town came out one morning without weapons. [The Spaniards] allowed them to approach the distance of a crossbow shot. Although they could have taken them alive without any risk, two or three horsemen came up behind them and lanced them.

He said that this is what he knows about what he is asked, in accordance with the oath that he swore. The witness signed his name. As soon as he finished speaking his statement was read to him and he confirmed it. And the lord judge signed.

Juan Troyano

A TRANSCRIPTION
OF THE TESTIMONY

[fol. 51v cont'd]¹⁹

{T*estigo*}

El d*i*cho Juan troyano *e*stante en esta / Ç*i*Udad de mex*i*co t*e*stigo rresçibido / Para (en) la d*i*cha ynFormaçion / el q*ua*l *h*abyendo jurado en Forma / de d*e*rec*h*o So CArgo del qual Se le / hizieron las Pregunt*a*s sigu*ient*es / Fue Pregunt*a*do Sy conosçe A Fran*ci*sco / Vazquez de coronado e a don Garçi*a* / loPez de CArdenas e a don Diego de / GueVara e a don tristan de are- / vii

[fol. 52r]

865

llano E a don Rodrigo maldonado e a / dyego loPez Veynte e quatro de / Sevylla e a don Pedro de Tovar / e a herna*n*do de AlVarado e a / Juan de çaldivar e a barrionuevo / e a Pablos de melGoSA e a los / otros CaPitanes que Fueron en la / Conquista e descubrimyento de la / tierra nueVa e çibola e Tiguex / e çiquyque e braVa e quiVyra / e otras ProVinçias comarCAnas / dixo que conosçe A todos los con- / Thenydos en la Pregunta de çinco / Años e mas TienPo A *e*sta / P*a*rte de vista e habla trato e con- / v*e*rsaçion que con ellos *h*a / Tenydo e que Se hallo Pre- / Sente en el descubrimyento e / conquysta de las d*i*chas ProVinçias / desde *e*l PrinçiPio (f)*h*asta que / VolVieron A *e*sta ÇiUdad / de mexico / Fue Pregunt*a*do Sy las ProVinçias / de los coraçones e valles de / Señora Fuya e las otras que / Sean desde culyaCan hasta / Çibola Sy les salieron de Paz

[fol. 52v]

A dar la obediençia A su magestad e / a Fran*ci*sco Vazquez en su Real non- / bre e les dieron e Proveyeron de / los bastymentos e comyda que ellos / tenyan e los acoxieron en sus Pue- / blos e CAsas Syn se Poner en rre- / Sistençia ny hazer guerra Alguna / dixo que es verdad que los / d*i*chos valles e todos los

otros Pue- / blos que *h*ay desde qulyaCan *h*asta / Çibola Por donde Fue el
di*ch*o Fran*cis*co / vazquez Salieron de Paz e dye- / ron la obediençia A su
mag*e*stad / e al di*ch*o General *en* su rreal non- / bre e no Vido *e*ste *te*s*t*igo que
los / di*ch*os yndios tuviesen ny diesen / bastymento A los esPañoles ny los /
esPañoles *en*traban en los Po- / blados Porque el di*ch*o Fran*cis*co Vaz- / quez
ma*n*daba a los esPañoles / que no *en*trasen en los Poblados / ny les tomasen
cosa alguna / Fue Pregunt*a*do sy el di*ch*o General o / Alguno de los di*ch*os
CAPitanes / hizo en los di*ch*os Pueblos o al- / Guno de *e*llos A los naturales
/ alguna Crueldad o maltra- / viii

[fol. 53r]

866

Tamyento o si otros lo hizieron los / castigo o dysymulo dixo que el di*ch*o /
General e Sus cAPitanes A los / di*ch*os yndios SyenPre les hi- / zieron buen
tratamyento y el di*ch*o / General Por co*n*tentar A los / di*ch*os yndios les daba
algunas / Vezes Cuentas e viDrios e caxCA- / beles e cuchillos y otras cosas
e si / Algun(d) esPañol tomaba algo A los / di*ch*os yndios el di*ch*o General Se
lo / RePrenDia de manera que / Procuraba que los di*ch*os yndios / Fuesen
muy bien tratados / Preguntado q*ue* Fue la CAusa Por que / los naturales de
las di*ch*as Pro- / vynçias Se alçaron e rrebela- / ron e mataron A los espa- /
noles que en ellas quedaron e / si f*u*e en ello CulPante el di*ch*o / Fran*cis*co
vazquez o alguno de los / di*ch*os (P)CaPitanes e si CAstigo A los / que en ello
eçedieron dixo que / Segun(d) Fue Pu*bli*co e notorio la CAu- / sa del di*ch*o
alCAmyento Fue los / malostratamyentos e cruelda- / des que un AlCaraz
cAPitan

[fol. 53v]

en ellos hizo que *h*abia dexado *en* su / lugar melchior Diaz Antes que mu- /
riese yendo en el descubrimyento d*e* la / costa de la mar del sur e que el di*ch*o
/ Alcaraz dezia que tomaba A los / di*ch*os yndios Sus mugeres e / hijas Para
(h)echarse con ellas / e los bastymentos que tenyan e / Sobre *e*stas cosas entre
los / di*ch*os *e*sPañoles hubo d*i*Ferençias / y Unos se Fueron a culyacan e / otros
al exerçito del di*ch*o Fran*cis*co / Vazquez e los yndios como *h*abyan / visto las

diFerençias entre los es- / Pañoles e como algunos Se *h*abian / Ydo Se Rebelaron los d*i*chos / yndios contra el d*i*cho alCAraz e / le mataron a el y a algunos
de los / que con el *e*staban e que el / d*i*cho Fran*ci*sco vazquez no tuvo Cul- /
Pa nynguna en la d*i*cha Rebelion / Por *e*star Ausente e no saberlo / Fue Pregunt*a*do que crueldades e / malostratamyentos hizo el d*i*cho / Fran*ci*sco
Vazquez o algunos de los / ix

[fol. 54r]
867
d*i*chos CAPitanes en la ProVinçia de / Çibola o si les Salieron de / Paz o de
guerra d*i*xo que lle- / Gados çerCA de Çibola el d*i*cho Fran*ci*sco / vazquez *en*
nonbre d*e* su maGestad / les ynvio a rrequerir A los yn- / dios q*ue e*staban en
çibola con Unos / yndios naturales de Çibola que / Un dia Antes se *h*abian
venydo de / Su voluntad al exerÇito y el / d*i*cho Fran*ci*sco vazquez con Un
yndio / natural de la ProVinçia de señora / les d*i*xo A los d*i*chos tres yndios /
Fuesen a çibola e dixesen A los / PrincyPales como el Venya Por / Su
mag*e*stad y a rreduçirlos *en* / Su obediençia e a que conos- / çiesen A dios y
no tuViesen myedo / que no les Seria (f)*h*echo daño / nynguno e les dio del
rresCAte / que llevaba Para que Fuesen / Contentos e los d*i*chos yndios /
Fueron e no VolVieron e otro / dia siguyente el d*i*cho General yn- / Vio a Fray
juan de Padylla e / a otros Religiosos e Person*a*S

[fol. 54v]
del CAnPo A hablar A los d*i*chos ynDios / y a rrequeryrles que se diesen de
/ Paz e que el les (f)*h*aria buen Trata- / myento y les mante(r)nya justiçia y /
Aunque esto les Fue d*i*cho e rreque- / rido e dado a entender con Un yn- /
dio de la ProVinçia de señora que / dezian que sabia la lengua nunCA / los
d*i*chos yndios de Çibola quisieron / Venyr de Paz E antes començaron A /
(h)echar tierra e haziendo Rayas / en el suelo Dando a entender que / no
Pasasen Adelante e enPeçaron / a flechar A los esPañoles e Re- / lygiosos lo
qual Visto el d*i*cho Ge- / neral e *e*sPañoles ARemetie- / ron a ellos e mataron
Algunos / Alanzeandolos hasta que los / Retruxeron al Pueblo e ally / Se
tornaron a hazer Fuertes / e alli el d*i*cho General Por / la d*i*cha lenGua les

torno A hazer / los dichos Requyrimyentos los / quales no se querian Dar de
/ Paz y entonzes el dicho Francisco / Vazquez y otros esPañoles / x

[fol. 55r]

868

enPeçaron A hablar con los yndios e (h)alle- / Gandose A ellos Por entrar en
el Pueblo / e los yndios como los vieron junto de(n)sde una / AÇotea tiraron
una losa y dieron Al / dicho Francisco Vazquez e lo derroCAron / y los otros
esPañoles le tomaron / en Peso e lo VolVieron al CanPo y en- / tonzes mando
que les diesen ba- / teria con el artilleria e se les enPe- / ço A dar e mataron
Algunos de ellos / y entonzes Por señas e Por la dicha / lengua se Dieron e los
esPañoles entra- / ron en el Pueblo Porque los yn- / dios Se salieron todos de
el e lo de- / xaron desenbaraçado con los basti- / mentos que en el habia que
(h)eran mu- / chos e que desPues de dado el dicho / Pueblo ny vido ny suPo
que Fuese / (f)hecho maltratamyento ny crueldad / A nyngunos yndios ny se
hizieron / Porque si se hizieran este testigo / lo Viera e SuPiera e no Pudiera
/ ver menos Por estar Presente a todo lo / Susodicho Antes vydo que el dicho
/ Francisco Vazquez les trataba bien / e les daba del rresCAte que

[fol. 55v]

llevaba e los dichos yndios le truxeron / A el un Presente de liebres e conexos
e / otras C(A)oças que rrePartio entre / los dichos CAPitanes e les Pidio el
dicho / Francisco vazquez A los dichos ynDios un / yndyo de Petatlan que
habyan / tomado quando mataron Un negro que / ynvio fray marcos los quales
lo tru- / xeron e se llamaba bartolome que / Sabia la lengua mexiCana y Por
/ Su lengua e la del otro nagua- / Tato hablaban con ellos / Fue Preguntado
las ProVinçias de / Tiguex e çicuyque brava e las otras / ComarCas Sy se
Pusyeron en Armas / o en rresistençia o si se vinyeron A / dar de Paz Al dicho
General dixo / que toDas las dichas proVinçias Vinie- / ron de Paz e dieron
A su magestad / la obediençia e al dicho Francisco Vazquez / en Su rreal
nonbre Syn se Poner / en rresistençia Alguna Antes los / de çicuyque como
SuPieron que / los esPañoles habian Ganado A / Çibola Vinyeron A çibola
que / esta Setenta leguas de Çicuyque / xi

[fol. 56r]

869

E Dixeron como ellos venian A ser / Sus amygos e darse de Paz e die- / ron
A los eSPañoles del dicho / exerçito de los mantenymyentos / que ellos trayan
e mantas e otras / Cosas e los acogieron en sus CAsAs / E Pueblos e desenbaraçaron / Un Pueblo en que los esPañoles / YnVernasen e Ansy estuVieron
/ en el dicho Pueblo un ynVierno e / los dichos yndios Se Pasaron A / otros
de la rreDonda / Fue Preguntado que Fue la Causa que / los dichos Pueblos
E ProVinçias / Se tornaron A alçar e de que ma- / nera Prendieron Al yndio
lla- / mado Caçique Al otro bigotes e / Al otro turco e al otro ysoPete / dixo
que quanto tiene declarado / en la Pregunta Antes De esta que / estando el
exerçito en Çibola vy- / nyeron de çiquyque A darse de / Paz Al general
entonzes el dicho / General ynVio A hernando de / AlVarado e a otros veynte
e / Tres honbres entre los quales

[fol. 56v]

yba este testigo Para Ver la tierra e / las Poblaçiones que habia en ella e / Ansy
fueron descubriendo que dan- / do todos de Paz hasta llegar A / Çicuyque
dandoles todo lo que / habian menester y entonzes el dicho / hernando de
alVarado dixo que que- / ria descubryr Adelante e Pidio / A (^S) bigotes que
Fuese con el Para / mostrarle la tierra el qual Dixo / que estaba CAnsado e
que no PoDia / yr Adelante pero que le daria / Un hermano Suyo e truxo Al
/ yndio que llamaron Turco e a otro / yndio que llamaron çamarylla / Para que
mosTrasen la tierra / e yendo desCubrienDo un (y) Dya / el dicho yndio llamado Turco / dixo Por Señas y en lengua me- / xiCAna que sabia un Poco
que el / no sabia la Tierra hazia aquella / Parte que lo lleVasen hazia otra / que
el señalo Porque habia muy / Grandes Poblaçiones y oro e / Plata y lienços e
señalaba de la / manera que saCAban el oro y la / Plata e como hernando de
alVarado / xii

[fol. 57r]

870

en Su ynstruçion de yr A la Parte / que yba y no A la otra se VolVio A /

çiquyque cumPlido Su termino e / quando se volVia el dicho yndio / llamado
Turco dixo que no Dixe- / Sen a bigotes lo que el habia dicho / Porque lo
matarian Porque / la Tierra que el dezia (h)era qui- / Vira y (h)eran Amygos
de bigotes y es- / tando en çicquyque el dicho yn- / dio turco se Fue y el dicho
hernan- / do de alVarado lo hizo busCar y no / Paresçio y entonzes el dicho
her- / nando de alVarado dixo que queria / Ayudar A los de çicuyque A ga-
/ nar a Una ProVinçia que se lla- / maba nanaPagua con quyen tenya / Guerra
e los de çiquyque jun- / Taron tresyentos honbres Para / ello y entre ellos yba
el CAçique / e bigotes y el turco e AnDando dos / Jornadas hazia la dicha
ProVinÇia / el Turco no Paresçia el dicho / hernando de alVarado Pidio Al /
bigotes que hiziese Venyr Al / Turco e Porque no lo trayan

[fol. 57v]
PrenDio Al CAçique e bigotes / e les hecho sus colleras e CAdenas / Al
Pesquezo e dixo que los habia / detener hasta que el Turco vi- / nyese los
quales ynViaron Por el / Turco e Vinyeron el turco e yso- / Pete e Venydos el
hernando de Al- / Varado e Fray juan de Padilla se / Juntaron con los dichos
quatro yn- / dios e A todos los otros dixeron / que se VolViesen A Su tierra
e les / dixeron Al bigotes e CAçique e / {//} / ysoPete como el turco dezia que
sabia / Una tierra que se llamaba qui- / (Vi)Vira donde habia oro e Plata e /
lyençqos e otras cosas e que el bigo- / Tes e los otros tenyan Un braça- / lete
de oro e otras cosas que de / Alla habyan traydo e que dixesen / Sy (h)era
Aquello Verdad e diesen / las Joyas e los soltarian e el bi- / Gotes e el CAçique
dixeron que / mentya el turco y el turco e yso- / Pete aFirmaron ser Verdad lo
/ que el turco tenya declarado y / Sobre esto el dicho hernando de / AlVarado
truxo Presos en la / xiii

[fol. 58r]
871
CAdena A los dichos quatro yndios / (f)hasta traerlos al rreal donde esta- / ba
el dicho Francisco vazquez Se / Juntaron en tiguex y el dicho her- / nando de
alVarado dixo Al dicho Francisco / Vazquez como traya Aquellos / yndios
Presos y la CAusa Por que / Porque A todo lo que dicho tiene se / (f)hallo este

T*esti*go P*r*esente e como el / d*i*cho Fran*ci*sco Vazquez vi(d)o que los / Unos
yndios dezian uno y los / otros otro ma*n*do que aPe- / rreasen a bygotes Para
que / declaraSe la verdad de lo que el / Turco e ysoPete dezian y ansy / Vi(d)o
que dentro del CAnPo Fuera / del Pueblo *e*stando Presentes / muchos CAP-
itanes e gente que / no Tiene memoria de Sus non- / bres con unos Perros de
don PeDro / de toVar le APerrearon Al d*i*cho / bigotes e le mordio en la
Pierna / y en el braço no *e*stuVo Presente / el d*i*cho Fran*ci*sco Vazquez y el
d*i*cho don / Pedro de ToVar quito el Perro / e truxo Al yndio bigotes ante / el
d*i*cho Fran*ci*sco Vazquez Para

[fol. 58v]
que dixese la verdad el qual conFeso / *h*aber en çiquique un braçalete de oro
/ e Un Perro e Un barril e otras joyas / e que lo tenya en su PoDer un yndio
/ Prin*ç*iPal que se llamaba querecho / e de(n)*s*de a çierto tienPo Porque / los
yndios de çicuyque Andaban me- / dio leVantados e de Guerra Para / que los
aPaçificase yn Viaron / A bigotes e nunCA mas volVio y qua*n*- / do el exerçito
yba Para quyVira / Porque *h*abian de Pasar Por çicui- / que yn Viaron Al
CAçique Para / que Tuviese a los del d*i*cho Pu*eb*lo / de Paz e les hiziese dar
basti- / mento e Ansi se Fue e qua*n*- / do los esPañoles llegaron no les /
quysieron acoxer ny dar bastymentos / Fue Pregunt*a*do que declarase si / los
yndios de çicuyque e tiguex / Sy se (h)alzaron e rrebelaron Por / los malosTratamyentos e aPerrea- / myentos que hizieron a biGotes dixo / que
desPues de aPerreamyento / e Prision se alçaron los d*i*chos / Yndios e que oyo
dezir e Fue / xiii

[fol. 59r]
872
Publico en el CAnPo que se *h*abyan / Alçado Porque los caballos comya*n* /
las SemenTeras e Porque los / *cri*s*t*ianos les tomaban Sus CAsas / e les Pedian
mantas e otras cosas / Se *h*abyan Alçado e Porque un (herna*n*do) *hermano* /
de villegas R*e*gid*o*r de mexico dezian / que *h*abia tomado una yndia Por /
Fuerça Para (h)echarse con ella / Fue Pregunt*a*do si llego A notisia del / d*i*cho
Fran*ci*sco Vazquez *h*aber tomado el / (f)*h*ermano de villegas la yndia e si / lo

CAstigo Por ello dixo que no lo / Sabe Porque quando Paso / lo Susodicho habian Vuelto A / Çibola Por Unos tiros de artille- / ria y quando VolVio oyo lo suso- / dicho / Fue Preguntado que tantos Pueblos / de las dichas Provinçias que- / maron e entraron Por Fuerça / dixo que hecho el dicho alçamyento / Como dicho Tiene los dichos yndios / en Una noche mataron mas de / quarenta CAballos e bestias de / carga e ansy Por esto como Por / haberse rrebelado les dieron Guerra

[fol. 59v]

y quemaron e ASolaron treze Pueblos / e Solamente doS entraron Por Fuerça / Porque habian (f)hecho Fuertes en ellos / e se deFendieron e que los que de- / mas quemaron los hallaron yer- / mos e desmanParados e que antes / que a los dos se diese Guerra el / dicho Francisco Vazquez rrequyrio / que se diesen de Paz e les Per- / donarian lo que habian (f)hecho e / nunCA los dichos yndios quysieron / e Por esto los quemaron e los que / (f)hallaron desmanParados Fue Por- / que en ellos no se hiziesen Fuertes / Fue Preguntado quyen mando quemar / los dichos Pueblos Pues en ellos no / habia rresystençia dixo que oyo / dezir que habia mandado el dicho / Francisco Vazquez quemar tres Pue- / blos que estaban al Pie de una sie- / Ra e los otros no Sabe quyen / lo mando e que se quemaron Por- / que en ellos no se hiziesen Fuertes / Como dicho tiene y Porque de ellos / no Se Proveyesen los otros / de bastimento Pues no habyan / querido Venyr de Paz / xv

[fol. 60r]

873

Fue Preguntado que a los yndios que / en los dichos Pueblos se tomaron Vi- / Vos que crueldades e malosTrata- / myentos les hizieron dixo que Vi(d)o / Como Al TienPo que el dicho don / garçia loPez de CArdenas tenya / cer- Cado el Primero Pueblo del / çerCo dandole bateria les Ganaron / Un dya a los dichos yndios las açuteas / y enPeçaron A Poner Fuego Al / Pueblo e como los yndios vieron / que los APretaban Algunos / Por las Ventanas (f)hazian Una / Cruz e dezian que Saldrian / de Paz e de esta manera Sal- / drian Sesenta yndios e como / Salian los metyan en la tien- / da de don garçia loPez e otros

/ mataban e quando Vieron que no / Salian mas tomaron los yndios / que en
la tienda estaban y / los Sacaron A Unos Palos q*ue* / *e*staban en el canPo hin-
CAdos e en- / Pezaron A atar Algunos de *e*llos / Para quemarlos y entonzes /
los que *e*staban en la Tienda Se / Alzaron (con) *en* ella e los *cristi*anos

[fol. 60v]
mataron Algunos de *e*llos Alanzadas / y esToCadas e los demas quemaron /
VyVos en los d*i*chos Palos que le / Pareze que serian los que quema- / ron
hasta quarenta o Çinquenta / Personas e que vydo como Antes / que la d*i*cha
quema se hiziese / truxeron del rreal donde estaba / el d*i*cho Franc*is*co vazquez
al turco / e a ysoPete Para que Viesen / la quema no Sabe quyen los / truxo
ny Por cuyo ma*n*dado e q*ue* / don garç*i*a loPez Fue el que manDo / como
maestre de CAnPo Poner los / d*i*chos Palos e quemar los yndios / que no
quedo nynguno ViVo no / Sabe Sy a el se lo manDo el / d*i*cho Franc*is*co
vazquez o no / Pregunt*a*do Sy sabe(n) que todos los CA- / Pitanes e gente
estaban muy su(b)- / Jetos e obed*i*entes Al d*i*cho Franc*is*co / Vazquez e que
nynguno no osara / (f)*h*azer las d*i*chas quemas e aPe- / Reamyentos sin Su
lyçençia / e ma*n*dado d*i*xo que Sabe / que todos le estaban muy obedien- / xvi

[fol. 61r]
874
tes e que cree que naDie en el / d*i*cho exerçito no osara hazer cosa / nynguna
Syn su liçençia e man- / dado / Fue Pregunt*a*do que declare si Vio o / SuPo
que se *h*oViesen APe- / rreado o quemado Algunos otros / Yndios demas de
los que Tiene / declarado (e) *a*sy en el Pueblo que / tiene d*i*cho que tuvo çer-
CAdo el / d*i*cho don garç*i*a loPez como el que tu- / Vo Franc*is*co vazquez dixo
que en el / de don Garç*i*a loPez no Vi(d)o mas / de lo que tiene declarado y
en el / de Franc*is*co Vazquez Vi(d)o como den- / Tro D*e* las CAsas Por
Ganarlas que- / maban los yndios e yndias e nyños / e lo que Estaba dentro
Pero / no vydo que desPues de Ga- / nado A nadie hiziese daño ny tal / SuPo
ny oyo aunque se (f)*h*allo / P*r*esente quando se gano el d*i*cho / Pueblo / Fue
Pregunt*a*do Sy en la ProVin- / çia de çicuyque quemaron Al- / Gunos
Pueblos e yndios e

[fol. 61v]

los APerrearon dixo que no vy(d)o / que nyngun(d) Pueblo Se quemaSe / ny se quemo ny se aPerreo nyngun(d) / yndio Syno Fue el bigotes como / tiene dicho / {ytem} / Fue Preguntado que declare como e de / que manera Paso e Fue la muer- / te del yndio llamado Turco y / quyen le mato e quanDo e Por que / causa e Por cuyo mandado dixo / que el dicho Turco e ysoPete yban / Por guias de(n)sde çiquyque Para / quyVira e les truxo mas de tres / meses Perdidos e desPues de- / claro como el los habia traydo en- / Gañados Por rrodeos Porque / muriesen de hanbre y Porque des- / Pues de llegado A quyVira / YsoPete declaro como el Turco / dezia que no truxesen de comer / A los cristianos ny a los CAballos Por- / que muriesen e ysoPete lo / declaro a este testigo e A otros / Porque sabian hablar Algunos / en su lengua y el en mexicana e / Por esto mando Francisco vaz- / quez estando este testigo pre- sente / xvii

[fol. 62r]

875

A Juan de çaldiVar que hiziese dar / Un garrote Para matar Al dicho / Turco e ansy Fue e se le dio el ga- / rrote no vy(d)o quyen se le dio mas / de oyr dezir que Francisco martyn / Se lo habia dado / Fue Preguntado que otras cruelda- / des e malostratamyentos Vio e / SuPo que el dicho Francisco vaz- / quez hiziese o los otros CAPi- / tanes dixo que no Sabe mas / de lo que declarado Tiene / Fue Preguntado los yndios que / dize que se Prendieron Por / don garçia loPez de CArdenas e diego / loPez Veynte e quatro en el Pueblo / del Primero çerco Sobre el qual / estaban los dichos Garçia loPez / e veynte e quatro Sy los Pren- / dieron Sobre seguro e de que / manera dixo que como hobieron / Gañado las açuteas los esPañoles / durmyeron en ellas Aquella no- / che e que el dia siguyente los / Yndios del dicho Pueblo como / Se habyan visto APretados

[fol. 62v]

y habian quedado cansados e mal- / tratados del conbate del dia de an- / tes hizieron Señas a los dichos / CAPitanes e esPañoles que / Sy los Aseguraban

Se da- / rian de Paz e los dichos CAPi- / tanes e esPañoles los tornaron / A
rresPonder Por señas que / Saliesen e se(s) diesen de PaZ / e que les ASeguraban que no / les Seria (f)*hecho* mal ny daño Alguno / mostranDoles en
Señal de Paz / e Seguridad la cruz e con A- / quella conFyança e seguridad /
Salieron del dicho Pueblo *hasta* / SesSenta o Setenta yndios / Syn armas e sin
deFensa Al- / Guna uno A uno e dos A dos e se / Yban A meter e metyan
entre / los esPañoles y el dicho don garçia loPez / los mando rrecoxer e meter
/ *en* su tyenda e hizo mensaje- / ros luego de lo que Pasaba / Al dicho Fran-
*cis*co Vazquez que *es*ta- / ba de ally una o dos leguas en el / Real e el dicho
Francisco Vazquez / xviii

[fol. 63r]

876

Vino Luego e hablo con el dicho don garçia / loPez e hablando Se VolVio
luego / e que cree que la habla e Vistas / Fue sobre la just*ici*a que se *h*abia de
/ (f)*h*azer Sobre los dichos yndios q*ue* / Se *h*abian dado Sobre Seguro / e que
ansy lo tiene Por çierto Por- / que el dicho Francisco Vazquez dixo / A los
yndios llamados turco e yso- / Pete que *h*abian traydo al dicho / rreal de dicho
don Garçia loPez a ver / la dicha just*ici*a que myrasen la / Justicia que se hazia
de aquellos / que se *h*abian rrebelado e Por- / que luego que se VolVio el dicho
/ Francisco Vazquez a Su rreal / el dicho don Garçia loPez que a la / Sazon
(h)era maestre de canPo / ma*n*do *h*yncar çiertos Palos e atar / en ellos de dos
en dos *h*asta çinq*uen*ta / Yndios de los que *h*abian salydo / de Paz e sobre
seguro que estaban / Recoxidos en la dicha Tienda A los / quales Pegaron
Fuego e los que- / maron a todos ViVos e que los de- / mas yndios que
quedaron en la / Tienda como Vieron que saCAban

[fol. 63v]

A Sus ConPañeros e los Ataban A los / Palos the(n)*m*yendo e soSPechando
lo / que desPues se hizo de sus conPa- / neros Se alçaron e hizieron Fuer- /
tes en la Tienda deFendiendose con / Palos e con estaCAs que saCAron / de
la tienDa e alli los mataron / todos alanz*e*adas y estoCAdas e q*ue* / Sabido e
Visto los del otro Pu*eb*lo / Sobre que se Puso çerco la cruel- / dad Con que

_h_abyan tratado a los del / d_i_cho Pueblo e que no les _h_abyan guar- / dado el seguro que les _h_abyan / dado jamas Se quysieron Ren- / dyr ny salir de Paz Aunque mu- / chas Vezes Fueron Requeridos Por / el d_i_cho Fran_cis_co vazquez diziendo- / les que (h)eran Gente mentyrosa / E que no guardaban verdad / E que aunque les diesen Palabra / e Seguro no lo guardarian como / no la _h_abyan guardado a sus conPañe- / ros e vezinos / Fue Pregunt_a_do que yndios se que- / maron e aPerrearon de los que / Se tomaron ViVos en el Pueblo / Sobre que tenya çerco el d_i_cho Fran_cis_co / vazquez dixo que no lo sabe / xix

[fol. 64r]

877

mas de que dentro del Pueblo Se / quemaron muchos Porque no los / Pudieron tomar ny ellos Se / quysieron dar Syn Pegar Fuego / A las Casas / Fue Pregunt_a_do que otras cruelda- / des e malostratamyentos Vio / que el d_i_cho General o CaPitanes / hiziesen en los d_i_chos naturales / d_i_xo que demas e allende De lo / que d_i_cho e declarado tiene Vio q_ue_ / en el Pueblo del Primero çerco / Sobre que _e_staba el d_i_cho don g_ar_cia / loPez Se salieron una maña- / na çiertos yndios del d_i_cho Pueblo / Syn armas e los dexaban Ale- / xarse un trecho quanto un tiro de / ballesta y PuDiendolos tomar / ViVos e Syn rriesgo alguno sa- / lyan dos o tres de CAballo tras de _e_llos / e los Alanze- aban e que _e_sto es / lo que Sabe çerca de lo que le / es Pregunt_a_do Para el jura- mento / que hizo e fyrmolo d_e_ su nonbre / Fue le leydo _e_ste su d_i_cho luego como / lo aCabo de d_e_cir e RetiFicose en el / e firmolo el d_i_cho señor oydor / Juan Troyano

Chapter 11

Rodrigo de Frías, the Ninth de Oficio Witness

A Member of the Advance Guard

V ery little is known about Rodrigo de Frías and nothing after 1548, except that a person of that name was encomendero of Xolostotitlán, northeast of Guadalajara in 1570.[1] Frías was from the famous sixteenth-century center of ceramics manufacture Talavera de la Reina in the province of Toledo, Spain. In May 1536 he received license to travel to Nueva España at about age 19.[2] A little less than four years later he passed muster before the viceroy at Compostela, evidently, like Juan Troyano, in the company of Hernando de Alvarado. Judging from the three horses he took with him to Tierra Nueva, he was better supplied and perhaps of higher economic state than most of the expedition members.[3] Also like Juan Troyano, Frías was selected as a member of the advance guard that traveled with Vázquez de Coronado from Culiacán to Cíbola.

In June 1544, when he testified before Lorenzo de Tejada, he was residing in Mexico City, but had not been granted vecino status. He still maintained the same resident status as late as 1548.[4] Frías, the last of the witnesses questioned in Mexico City, like many of the others, volunteered unsolicited information that portrayed Vázquez de Coronado in a positive light.

For instance, he declared that the captain general had not allowed the Spaniards who went with him to lodge within the Indian towns they stopped at, in order to forestall potential friction and ill will. In further exoneration, he suggested that Vázquez de Coronado never heard about the rape of an Indian woman by one of his men. In addition to such exculpatory statements, Frías offered not the slightest hint of anything incriminating against the expedition leader. It should be remembered that Frías, like all the witnesses from Mexico City and Guadalajara whose testimony survives, was a de oficio witness, making the predominance, even profusion, of testimony favorable to the target of the pesquisa all the more remarkable.

Almost everything that Frías had to say to Tejada was hearsay evidence. He was present at almost none of the events he was asked about. He gave, nevertheless, perfunctory renditions of some of the same stories of rapes and commandeering of food and clothing told by other witnesses. He also reported as hearsay that when Hernando de Alvarado first visited the Tiguex pueblos all but two of them agreed to what they understood of the requerimiento. Those remaining two, though, had to be forced to submit. This is a possibility not raised elsewhere in known documents deriving from the expedition. The one bit of eyewitness evidence that Frías offered was that he saw the cacique from Cicuique threatened with hanging. Again, this is reported nowhere else.

FIGURE 8.
Indian captive threatened with hanging, after *Códice Azoyú*

A TRANSLATION
OF THE TESTIMONY

Ninth de Oficio Witness (Rodrigo de Frías)[5]

[64v] Rodrigo de Frías, accepted as a witness for this investigation, having given his oath in the form required by law and being questioned before the lord judge, was asked the following questions.

{1} He was asked whether he knows Francisco Vázquez de Coronado, don García López de Cárdenas, don Diego de Guevara, don Tristán de Arellano, don Rodrigo Maldonado, the councilman of Sevilla Diego López , don Pedro de Tovar, Hernando de Alvarado, Juan de Zaldívar, Barrionuevo, Pablos de Melgosa, and the other captains who went to explore and subjugate the tierra nueva of Cíbola, Tiguex, Cicuique, Brava, and Quivira and the other neighboring provinces. He answered that he knows all of those about whom he is asked, by appearance, voice, behavior, and conversation that he has had and continues to have with them for the last five years and more. He was present during the subjugation and reconnaissance of those provinces, with the exception of Quivira since he stayed with don Tristán de Arellano in the barranca on the plains (where most [65r] of the company remained). He went with Francisco Vázquez and his captains from the time they left the city of Mexico until they returned to it.

{2} [The witness] was asked whether the [people of the] provinces of Los Corazones, the valleys of Señora and Fuya, and the others that there are between Culiacán and Cíbola came out in peace to offer obedience to His Majesty and to Francisco Vázquez in his royal name. Did they give and supply provisions and food that they had, and did they welcome [the Spaniards] into their houses and towns, without offering resistance or making war? He answered that it is true that when Francisco Vázquez arrived at Culiacán, and so had all of the army, he announced that he would go in advance with horsemen to reconnoiter the land. And he left the rest of the people with don Tristán de Arellano, who went as his lieutenant. With a contingent of about sixty men, among whom was the witness, Francisco Vázquez [65v] departed from Culiacán bound for Cíbola.

And the witness saw that all those provinces and valleys about which he is asked and others through which they passed offered peace and rendered obedience to Francisco Vázquez in His Majesty's name. They supplied food and provisions from what they had, although in some places that was very little because they had nothing. And the Spaniards traded for some provisions. The Indians permitted and allowed the Spaniards to enter their towns, but Francisco Vázquez did not agree to having the Spaniards who went with him housed within the towns, but rather outside. Therefore, the general always had the camp in the countryside. No province or town came forth in war or offered resistance. Instead, as he has said, they all came out in peace.

{3} [The witness] was asked whether in those towns, or any one of them, the general or any of the captains committed [66r] any brutality or outrages against the natives of those provinces and whether, if others did so, did the general punish them or excuse [their actions]? [In reply] he said that he never saw nor was he aware that the Indians were treated badly. On the contrary, they were very well treated by the captains and the people who went with them. It was widely known that because a Spaniard had taken some ears of corn and the Indians had complained to Francisco Vázquez, he wanted to put the Spaniard to shame. (His name the witness does not know.) All along the route the Indians were treated very well.

{4} He was [then] asked to state what caused the Indians of those provinces to rise up in arms, rebel, and kill the Spaniards who stayed there. Was Francisco Vázquez or any of his captains responsible for that turn of events, and did the general punish those who transgressed? He replied that since he had passed through those provinces and gone in advance with Francisco Vázquez, as he has said, [66v] he did not know more about what caused the uprising than what he had heard in the camp at Tiguex. That was that the Indians of the provinces of Fuya and Señora had rebelled because of the outrages committed by a [man named] Alcaraz, who had been left there as captain by don Tristán de Arellano, and other Spaniards. Further, he had heard it said that they had rebelled because [the Spaniards] took provisions against their will, entered their towns, and seized their wives. [The witness] did not hear whether the women were taken to serve [the Spaniards] or so that they could have sexual relations with them. When the Indians rebelled they killed Alcaraz and some Spaniards. Francisco Vázquez had no responsibility for this because, as he has said, the general was in Tiguex at that time. And [the witness] believes that he did not leave Alcaraz as captain.

{5} Frías was asked what cruelty and outrages Francisco Vázquez or any of the captains committed in the province of Cíbola [67r] and whether [the people there] came out in peace or in war. He answered that when they arrived in the province of Cíbola Francisco Vázquez went in advance with a large part of the company, leaving Juan Gallego with some troops in the rear guard. The witness was not present when the Indians [made] war. [So he does not know] more about it than what he heard said and was common knowledge and widely held in the camp, which was that Francisco Vázquez had summoned them to offer peace and had told them that he would not do them any harm. But the Indians refused to do so. Instead, they came out in war, shooting arrows at the Spaniards and their horses. And they struck Francisco Vázquez on the head with a stone. Then the Spaniards attacked and occupied the pueblo, so that when the witness and the others in the rear guard arrived, the Indians were already coming forth in peace and half had surrendered.

[The witness] saw some Indians dead in the countryside. And soon all the Indians had offered peace and left the pueblo, [67v] leaving behind the provisions that were there. The Spaniards were quartered in the pueblo and consumed the provisions that they found. He saw that after seizure of the pueblo no outrage was committed against the Indians, but rather they were afforded thoroughly benevolent treatment, both by Francisco Vázquez and by the rest, as is well-known.

{6} [The witness] was [then] asked whether the [people of the] provinces of Tiguex, Cicuique, Brava, and the others in that region took up arms and offered resistance or whether they came out to offer peace and to render obedience to His Majesty and to Francisco Vázquez in his royal name, without offering any resistance whatsoever. He answered that when [the Spaniards] were in Cíbola the general sent Hernando de Alvarado with about twenty horsemen to reconnoiter the Río de Tiguex and the other provinces referred to in the question, about which they had heard. Within a few days Alvarado sent to inform [68r] Francisco Vázquez that all the [people of the] Río de Tiguex, Cicuique, and Brava had come out to him in peace, with the exception of two pueblos where they came forth in war and which he had pacified.

As a result, Francisco Vázquez went to Tiguex with the whole army. All along the route [the Indians] came out in peace and rendered obedience to His Majesty, supplied the provisions that they had for the journey, and welcomed [the Spaniards] into their pueblos. Along the Río de Tiguex the Indians vacated one pueblo, where the Spaniards might be quartered. Francisco Vázquez and everyone with him, the whole army and his captains, remained there. The Indians went to other neighboring pueblos.

{7} He was [then] asked what caused those Indians to rebel and rise up in arms, and how it was that [the Spaniards] seized the Indians called the cacique, Bigotes, Turco, and Ysopete. [In reply] he stated that when Hernando de [68v] Alvarado left to explore the provinces he has mentioned and had made the reconnaissance and returned to Tiguex (where the company was), he brought with him the Indians called the cacique, Bigotes, Turco, and Ysopete. Alvarado told this witness that he had taken those Indians [with him] as guides and that the one called Turco had said that in his own land, called Quivira, there were much gold and silver and other things. He had also said that Bigotes and the cacique had a gold bracelet and other jewelry in Cicuique.

Afterwards the witness heard it said publicly in the camp, by whom he does not recall, that dogs had been set on Bigotes and the cacique, so that they might tell whether what El Turco had said was true and so that they would turn over the bracelet and jewelry. But the witness was not present except to see afterwards that Bigotes was not well and had an arm and a leg crippled. It was after this that the Indians of Tiguex rebelled and rose in war against the Spaniards. [69r] Seeing that the province had rebelled, Francisco Vázquez set the cacique and Bigotes free, in order that [the Indians] might be soothed and pacified. The cacique and Bigotes never came back and the province remained at war.

{8} [Frías] was asked to state whether those Indians rebelled because of the outrages committed by the Spaniards against Bigotes and the cacique and because they had unleashed dogs against them. He answered that he does not know any more than that one night those Indians, apparently, killed and wounded more than twenty-five [horses]. They rose in war without the Spaniards having perpetrated any outrage other than what he has already stated and what he heard. Namely, that dogs had been set on the cacique and Bigotes and that a Spaniard in don García López's company had seized an Indian woman in a pueblo and had sexual relations with her, or tried to do so. [Frías] does not know that Francisco Vázquez learned of the event so that he might administer punishment, but he did not witness any punishment.

{9} He was asked how many pueblos [69v] in those provinces [the Spaniards] took, occupied by force, and burned after they rebelled. He replied that three pueblos were taken by force. One was called Pueblo de la Cruz, another was called Pueblo de la Alameda, and the last was called Pueblo del Cerco. After having taken possession they burned the wood from the pueblos and demolished some houses. [The Spaniards] found another three or four pueblos abandoned, and the people had fled. They burned the wood from them also and tore down some houses.

After the [people of the] pueblos had risen up in arms and before [the Spaniards] made war against the three pueblos that were [subsequently] entered by force, Francisco Vázquez summoned them to come to peace in their languages by means of interpreters and with signs. But [the Indians] were never willing to do so and, therefore, they had to be taken by force, as he has said.

{10} [The witness] was [next] asked why [the Spaniards] burned those pueblos, and who ordered them burned. He replied that he does not know who ordered the burning, but the three [pueblos] were burned because they

[70r] had rebelled, fought, and killed horses. The others were burned in order that the Indians would not fortify themselves in them and also because [the Spaniards] needed wood to burn, since there is little firewood and the land is cold.

{11} [Frías] was asked what brutalities and outrages [the Spaniards] committed against the Indians who were taken by force from those pueblos or who offered peace. [In answer] he stated that he had heard it said that some who were captured during the siege were burned and set upon by dogs, and also had their hands cut off. He does not know who ordered those things done, who did them, nor how they were done. He also does not know how many Indians [were affected] and how they were captured. That is because he was not present, but remained in don Pedro de Tovar's camp, which was three leagues from the camp at Pueblo del Cerco, where the aforesaid was done.

{12} He was asked whether he knows that the captains and [other] people were very obedient to Francisco Vázquez and that no one would have dared to carry out the burnings and unleashing of dogs [70v] without his permission and command. He replied that he knows that all the captains and [other] people were very obedient to him and subject to his command. And he believes and is certain that no one would have committed the burnings and unleashing of dogs, which he has mentioned and that he heard were carried out, without the general's order and permission.

{13} He was [then] asked to state whether he was aware or saw that Indians other than those about whom he has spoken were hung, burned, or set upon by dogs. He answered that he does not know of any because he was not present at the pueblos that were captured and burned by Francisco Vázquez and don García López until after they had been destroyed. When Hernando de Alvarado brought the Indian called the cacique [from] Cicuique [the witness] saw that Alvarado erected a gallows. So that [the cacique] would confirm what El Turco was saying, Alvarado terrified him, saying that he would have to hang [the cacique] unless he told the truth. And [the Spaniards] brought dogs to unleash against him. The witness, however, did not see him set upon nor was he present.

[71r] {14} [Frías] was asked whether in the province of Cicuique [the Spaniards] burned any pueblos or Indians or set dogs on [any Indians]. He replied that [he knows] no more than that when don Tristán de Arellano was there waiting for Francisco Vázquez to come from Quivira, [the Spaniards] were eating and laying waste to the cornfields in that province because the people there were at war and had rebelled.

{15} [The witness] was asked when, how, and in what way the death of the Indian called Turco occurred, who killed him, by whose order it was done, and for what reason. [In reply] he stated that he had heard it said that Turco was garrotted by order of the councilman Diego López, who was maestre de campo, or by Francisco Vázquez's order. He does not know who applied the garrote, when it was done, nor for what reason, except that he has heard that they killed Turco because he lied in the guidance he gave them.

{16} He was asked to state whether Francisco Vázquez, his captains, or the people who went with him committed any other outrages [71v] against those Indians beyond what he has already told. He answered that he knows no more than he has stated, which is the truth, in accordance with the oath that he swore. The witness signed his name. And the lord judge affixed his sign. As soon as he finished speaking his statement was read to him and he confirmed it.

Rodrigo de Frías

A TRANSCRIPT
OF THE TESTIMONY

[fol. 64v]⁶
{T*estigo*}
El d*i*cho R*odrig*o de Frias testigo rresÇibido / Para la d*i*cha ynformaçion e
siendo / el qual *h*abiendo jurado en forma de derecho / e Siendo Pregunt*a*do
a*n*te el d*i*cho señor / oydor S*e* le hizieron las Preguntas s*iguiente*s / Fue Pregunt*a*do Si conosçe A Françisco / Vazquez de coronado e a don Garçi*a* lo- /
Pez de CArdenas e a don diego de gue- / Vara e a don tristan de Arellano /
e a don Rodrigo maldonado e a diego / loPez veynte e quatro de sevilla / e a
don Pedro de toVar e a herna*n*do / de alVarado e a juan de Çaldivar e a / barrionuevo e a Pablos de melgoSA / E a otros CAPitanes que Fueron / en el
descubrimyento e conquista / de la Tierra nueva Çibola e tiguex / e çicuyque
E braVa e quyVira e otras / ProVinçias comarCAnas dixo / que conosçe A
todos los que le es / Pregunt*a*do de çinco Años a *e*sta / Parte e mas TienPo
Por vista / habla trato e conversaçion que / con ellos *h*A tenydo e que se /
(f)*h*allo Pr*e*sente en el descubrimi*ent*o / e conquista de las d*i*chas ProVinçias
/ eÇe(b)*p*to a quyVira que se quedo con don / tristan de arellano en la barranca / de los llanos donde quedo la mayor / xx

[fol. 65r]
[begins second half of bundle]
878
Parte del rreal e que salio con el d*i*cho / Franc*is*co Vazquez e sus caPitanes
de(n)*s*- / de que salieron de mexico hasta que / VolVieron A el / Fue Pregunt*a*do si las ProVinçias de los / Coraçones e Valles de señora Fuya / e las
otras que *e*stan desde cu- / liaCan hasta çibola si les salieron / de Paz A dar la
obediençia A Su / mag*e*stad e a Franc*is*co Vazquez *en* su / rreal nonbre e les
Dieron e Pro- / Veyeron de los bastimentos e comida / que ellos tenyan e los
acoxieron / En sus Pueblos e casas sin les / Poner *en* rresistençia ni les fazer /

Guerra Alguna dixo que es verdad / que quando el d*i*cho Fran*ci*sco Vazquez / llego a Culiacan e lleGo todo el exer- / çito junto e alli el d*i*cho Fran*ci*sco vazquez / d*i*xo que el queria yr delanTe / desCubriendo tierra con gente de / Caballo e dexo toda la demas gente / a don tristan de Arellano que / Yba Por su Tenyente y el d*i*cho Fran*ci*sco Vaz- / quez con obra de sesenta honbres / de a Caballo Poco mas o menos / *en*tre los quales yba *e*ste T*e*st*i*go

[fol. 65v]

Salieron de CuliaCAn hasta llegar A çi- / bola y este t*e*st*i*go vi(d)o como Todas las d*i*chas / ProVinçias e Valles que le es Pregun- / tado e otros Pueblos Por dond*e* / Pasaron todos se dieron de Paz / e dieron la obediençia Al d*i*cho Fran*ci*sco / Vazquez en nonbre d*e* su mag*e*stad / e les daban comyda e basti- mentos / de los que ellos tenyan Aunque en / algunas Partes (h)eran muy Poca / Porque no la tenyan e algunos / bastymentos rresCAtaban los / esPañoles e que los d*i*chos yn- / dios daban lugar e consentymiento / que los d*i*chos EsPañoles *en*trasen / en Sus Pueblos e que el d*i*cho Fran*ci*sco / Vazquez no consentya que los d*i*chos / EsPañoles que con el yban se a- / Posentasen dentro de los Pue- / blos Syno Fuera de *e*llos y Por eso / A la contynua tenian Su rreal / en el canPo e que nynguna ProVin- / çia ny Pueblo salio de guerra ni se / Puso a rresystirse sino todas / Como dicho tiene salieron de Paz / Fue Preguntado sy el d*i*cho General o al- / Gunos de los d*i*chos CAPitanes / hizo en los d*i*chos Pueblos o en / [no number]

[fol. 66r]

879

Alguno de *e*llos A los naturales de las / d*i*chas Provinçias algunas Crueldad*e*s o / malostratamientos e si otros lo hi- / zieron Sy los castigo o disimulo / d*i*xo que nunCA vi(d)o ny suPo que / A los d*i*chos yndios les Fuese hecho / mal- tratamiento alguno antes de los / CaPitanes e genTe que con ellos y- / ban (h)eran muy bien tratados e que / Fue notorio que Porque un esPanol / *h*Abia tomado unos (h)elotes de mayz / e los yndios Se *h*abian quexado / Al d*i*cho Fran*ci*sco Vazquez quiso aFren- / Tar Al esPañol que no Sabe como / se llamaba e en todo el Camyno Fueron / los d*i*chos yndios muy bien tratados /

Preguntado que declare que Fue la CAusa / Por que los yndios naturales de /
las di*ch*as P*ro*Vinçias se alçaron e rre- / belaron e mataron A los esPañoles /
que en ellas quedaron e sy Fue / en ello CulPante el di*ch*o Fran*cis*co / Vazquez
o alguno de los di*ch*os Sus / caPitanes e si CAstigo a los que en / ello
(h)ezedieron dixo q*ue* como este / te*s*tigo Paso Por ellos como di*ch*o tiene /
con el di*ch*o Fran*cis*co Vazquez Adelante

[fol. 66v]
no SuPo la Causa Por que se *h*abian Alçado / mas de que oyo Dezir *e*stando
el / rreal en tiguex como los di*ch*os yndios / d*e* las di*ch*as ProVinçias de Fuya
e señora / se *h*abian rrebelado Por los malostra- / tamyentos que les *h*Abian
(F)*h*e*ch*o un / AlCaraz que *h*abia(n) dexado Alli Por / caPitan don tristan de
arellano E / otros esPañoles e que oyo dezir / que se *h*abian rrebelado Porque
les / Tomaban los bastimentos contra su / Voluntad y les *en*traban en los Pue-
/ blos e les tomaban las mugeres no oyo / dezir Sy (h)era Por servirse de *e*llas
/ e Para (h)echarse con ellas Carnalme*n*te / e que al tienPo que los di*ch*os yn-
/ dios se *h*abian rrebelado *h*abian muer- / to Al di*ch*o alCaraz e a Algunos
esPa- / ñoles e que a esto no TuVo culPa / el di*ch*o Fran*cis*co Vazquez Porque
/ Como di*ch*o tiene *en* Aquella sazon / *e*staba en tiguex y el no dexo / Por
CAPitan A alcaraz a lo que cree / Fue Pregunt*a*do que crueldades e / malostratamientos hizo el di*ch*o Fran*cis*co / Vazquez o alguno de los di*ch*os CaPi-
/ Tanes en la ProVinçia de Çibola / [no number]

[fol. 67r]
880
o si les Salieron De Paz o de guerra / d*i*xo que al tienPo que llegaron / a la
di*ch*a P*ro*Vinçia el di*ch*o Fran*cis*co Vaz- / quez con mucha Parte del rreal / Se
adelanto e quedo juan Galle- / Go con çierta gente en la rretaguar- / d*i*a e no
Se hallo Presente qua*n*- / do los yndios de guerra mas de *h*aber / oydo dezir
e Fue Publico e noT*orio* / en el CAnPo como el di*ch*o Fran*cis*co Vaz- / quez
les *h*abia rrequerido que / Se diesen de Paz e que el no les / (f)*h*aria daño nynguno e que los / Yndios no *h*Abyan querido an- / tes *h*abian salido de guerra

e Fle- / chando esPañoles e CAballos y / que *h*abyan dado con una Piedra en / la CAbeza Al d*i*cho Franc*is*co Vazquez e / que entonzes *h*Abian acome- / tido a los esPañoles e entraron en / el Pueblo de manera que qua*n*- / do *e*ste test*i*go e los otros de la rre- / Taguard*i*a llegaron ya los / yndios salyan de Paz y estaban / medio rrendidos e vi(d)o algunos / yndios muertos en el CAnPo / e luego los d*i*chos yndios Se dieron / Todos de Paz e dexaron el P*u*eb*l*o

[fol. 67v]
Con los bas*T*imentos que en el *h*abia*n* e los / EsPañoles Se aPoSentaron en / el d*i*cho Pueblo Gastando de los basti- / mentos que (f)*h*allaban e que vi(d)o que / desPues de tomado el d*i*cho Pueblo no / Fue hecho nyngun(d) maltratamyento / A los d*i*chos yndios Antes todo buen / tratamyento ansy Por el d*i*cho Franc*is*co / Vazquez como Por los demas como / es notorio / Fue Preguntado las ProVinçias de / tiguex e çicuyque brava e las o- / tras Comarcas Sy se Pusyeron en / Armas e rresistençia (o rresistençia) / o si vinyeron A darse de Paz e dieron / la obediençia A su maGestad e Al / d*i*cho Franc*is*co Vazquez *en* su rreal non- / bre Syn Se Poner en rresisten- / çia alguna dixo que al tienPo / q*ue e*Staban en çibola el d*i*cho Franc*is*co / Vazquez enVio a hernan*d*o de / AlVarado con veynte honbres de / A Caballo Poco mas o menos A / descubrir el rrio de tiguex y / las demas ProVinçias conthenidas / *en* la Pregunta de que tenyan rrela- / çion e de(n)*s*de a Çiertos dias el d*i*cho / hernan*d*o de alVarado ynVyo a dezir / [no number]

[fol. 68r]
881
Al d*i*cho Franc*is*co Vazquez como todo el rrio de / Tiguex e çicuyq*ue* e brava le *h*abia saly- / do de Paz eÇe(b)*p*to dos Pueblos que le / Salieron de guerra los quales / el tenya PaçiFiCAdos e ansy el d*i*cho / Franc*is*co Vazquez con todo el exerçito / Fue a tiguex e en todo el Camyno le / Salieron de Paz e le daban la / obediençia Por su mag*e*stad e les / daban Por el CAmino de los basti- / mentos que ellos Tenyan e los aco- / xian en los Pueblos y en el rrio / de Tiguex los d*i*chos yndios de- / Senbarazaron un Pueblo donde / los EsPañoles

Se aPosentasen los / quales con todo el exerçito estuvo / alli el dicho Francisco
Vazquez e sus / CaPitanes con todo el exerçito e / los dichos yndios se Fueron
A otros / Pueblos ComarCAnos / Fue Preguntado que declare que Fue / la
CAusa Por que los dichos yndios / Se Rebe(be)laron e alçaron e / de que
manera PrenDieron A los / yndios llamados caçique e bi- / Gotes e turco e a
ysoPete dixo / que quanDo el dicho hernando de

[fol. 68v]
AlVarado Salio A descubryr las Pro- / Vinçias que Tiene declaradas e las des-
/ cubrio e VolVio A tiguex donde esta- / ba el CanPo truxo conSigo a los yn-
/ dios que llamaban CAÇique e bigotes / e turco e ysoPete e el dicho fernando
/ de alVarado dixo A este Testigo que / traya aquellos yndios Por guias / e que
el que Se llamaba turco / dezya que en su tierra hAbia mucho / oro e Plata e
otras cosas que se / llamaba quiVira e que bigotes e el / caçique tenyan Un
brazalete de / oro e otras joyas en çicuyque / e desPues oyo dezir PubliCA- /
mente en el rreal no se aCuerda A quyen / Como el dicho bigotes e al
CAçique habyan / APerreado Porque declarasen si / (h)era Verdad lo que el
turco dezia / e Para que Truxesen el dicho bra- / zalete e joyas Pero este testigo no / Se hallo Presente mas de haber / Visto al dicho bigotes malo e liaDo
/ Una Pierna e Un braço e desPues / de esto los dichos yndios de tiguex / Se
Rebelaron e alçaron de gue- / Ra contra los esPañoles e que / [no number]

[fol. 69r]
882
el dicho Francisco Vazquez como Vi(d)o que la dicha / ProVinçia se habia
Rebelado Solto A los / dichos CAçique e bigotes Para que los hA- / blasen e
PaçiFiCAsen e nunCA mas VolVie- / ron Sino todavia de guerra / Fue Preguntado que declare si los dichos / Yndios Se rrebelaron Por los ma- /
lostratamyentos que habian (f)hecho los / esPañoles A los dichos bigotes e
CAçique / E Por haberlos APerreado dixo / que no lo Sabe mas de que una /
noche los dichos yndios mataron e / hyrieron mas de Veynte e çinco A lo /
que le Paresçe e Se levanta- / ron de guerra Syn hAber hecho los / dichos

esPañoles nyngun maltrata- / myento Syno Fue lo que di*c*ho tiene / que oyo dezir de *h*aber APerreado / Al CAçique e bigotes e que Un es- / Pañol de la conPañya de don garçi*a* / loPez oyo dezir que *h*abia toma*D*o / Una yndia en el Pueblo e se *h*abia / (h)echado con ella carnalmente / o queridose (h)echar no sabe que el / di*c*ho Fran*cis*co Vazquez lo *h*obiese sa- / bydo Para CAsti-garlo ny lo vy(d)o CAs- / Tigar / Fue Pregunt*a*do que Tantos Pueblos

[fol. 69v]

de las di*c*has ProVinçias *en*traron e tomaron Por / Fuerça d*es*Pues de alçados y quemaron / dixo que se tomaron tres Pueblos Por / Fuerça que el Uno Se llamaba el / Pueblo de la cruz y el otro de la / Alameda y el otro el del çerco e / d*es*Pues de tomados quemaron la / madera de *e*llos e derroCAron Algunas / casas e que otros tres o quatro / Pueblos hallaron desPoblados e / que se habian huydo la gente los / quales Ansymesmo derroCA- / ban algunas casas e quemaron la / madera de *e*llos e que d*es*Pues de / Alzados los di*c*hos Pueblos antes / que se diese guerra A los di*c*hos tres / Pueblos que *en*traron Por Fuerça / el di*c*ho Fran*c*isco Vazquez Por sus len- / guas e ynterP*r*et(r)es e Por seña*s* les / Requyrieron que se Diesen los qua- / les nunCa quysieron e ansi Por Fuerça / se *h*obieron de tomar como di*c*ho tiene / Fue Pregunt*a*do que Fue la CAusa Por / que quemaron los di*c*hos Pueblos / e quyen los mando quemar dixo / que no sabe quyen los ma*n*do que- / mar y que los que quemaron / Fueron Porque se rresistieron / [no number]

[fol. 70r]

883

los tres e los *h*Abian muerto los caballos e / Rebeladose e los otros Porque en ellos / los yndios no se hiziesen Fuert*e*s e Por- / que la madera la *h*Abyan menest*er* P*a*ra / quemar Porque *h*ay Poca leña e la tierra / es Fria / {ojo} / Fue Pregunt*a*do que a los yndios que / de los di*c*hos (^yndios) Pueblos Se / tomaron ViVos o ellos Se dieron de P*a*z / que crueldades e malostrata- / myentos les hizieron dixo que / oyo dezir que algunos que *h*abyan / Tomado en el çerco los *h*Abyan que- / mado e aPerreado e cortado manos / no Sabe

quien lo ma*n*do ny quyen / lo hizo ny de que manera Fue ny qua*n*- / tos
Fueron los yndios ny de que ma- / nera Se tomaron Porque *e*ste t*e*st*i*go /
quedo en el rreal con don Pedro de / Tovar e no se hallo P*r*esente que / *e*staria
tres leguas el rreal del / di*c*ho Pueblo del çerco donde se / hizo lo Susodi*c*ho /
Fue Pregunt*a*do si sabe que los di*c*hos CA- / Pitanes e gente estaban muy
obe- / dientes Al di*c*ho Fran*cis*co Vazquez e / que nynguno osara hazer las /
di*c*has quemas e aPerreamyentos

[fol. 70v]
Sin Su liçençia e ma*n*dado d*i*xo que sabe / que todos los CAPitanes e gente
le *e*sta- / ban muy obedient*es* e Su(b)JJetos e que cree / e tiene Por çierto que
syn su lyçençia / e ma*n*dado nynguno hiziera los di*c*hos A- / Perreamyentos
e quemas que tiene / di*c*ho e que oyo dezir que se *h*Abia (f)*h*e*c*ho / Fue Pregunt*a*do que declare si sabe o / Vio que se *h*obiesen APerreado o / quemado
o ahorcado algunos otros / Yndios demas de los que tiene / declarados d*i*xo
que no lo Sabe / Porque no se hallo Presente a los / Pueblos que tomaron e
quema- / ron Fran*cis*co Vazquez e don Gar*Ç*i*a* lop*ez* / hasta desPues de
*h*aberlos Destruy- / do e que Vi(d)o como al tienPo que / fernan*d*o de
alVarado lleVo a Çicuyq*ue* / Al yndio llamado CAçique vy(d)o / como hernan*d*o de alVarado hizo una / horca y Para que declarase lo que el / Turco
dezia lo amedrentaba di- / ziendo que lo *h*abia de Ahorcar Sino / declaraba
la *ver*dad e trayendo los / Perros Para aPerrearlos Pero / *e*ste t*e*st*i*go no lo
Vi(d)o APerrear / ny Se hallo Presente a ello / [no number]

[fol. 71r]
884
Fue Pregunt*a*do Sy en la ProVinçia de çicuyq*ue* / Sy quemaron Algunos
Pueblos / o yndios o los aPerrearon dixo q*ue* / no mas de que *e*stando alli don
tristan / *e*sPerando a Fran*cis*co vazquez que Ve- / nya de quyVira comyan en
la di*c*ha Pro- / Vynçia los mayzales e los destru- / Yan Porque *e*staban de
guerra / que se *h*abyan rrebelado / Fue Pregunt*a*do que declare como e de /
que manera Pasa la muerte del / yndio llamado turco e quyen le / mato e Por

cuyo ma*n*dado e Por que / causa e quando dixo que oyo d*ecir* / que le *h*Abian
dado un garrote Por / ma*n*dado de diego loPez veynte e qua- / tro que (h)era
maestre de CanPo / o de Fran*cis*co Vazquez no sabe quyen / le dio el Garrote
ny Por que CAus*a* / ny quando mas de *h*aber oydo dezir / que le *h*abyan
muerto Porque les *h*abia / mentydo en la guia que les *h*abia (f)*h*echo / Fue Pregunt*a*do que declare sy el / d*i*cho Fran*cis*co Vazquez o sus CAPita- / nes e
gente que con el yba hizie- / ron otros Algunos malostrata-

[fol. 71v]
myentos a los d*i*chos yndios demas de los / que tiene declarado d*i*xo que no
sAbe / mas de lo que tyene declarado lo q*ua*l / es la *ver*dad Para el juramento
que / fizo e Fyrmolo d*e* su nonbre e seña- / lolo el d*i*cho Señor oydor fue l*e*
leydo *e*ste / Su d*i*cho luego como lo aCabo de d*e*zir / e RetiFycose en el
R*odr*ig*o* de F(y)rias

Chapter 12

Melchior Pérez,
the Tenth de Oficio Witness

Son of the Previous Governor

Having regained sufficient health to travel, licenciado Tejada made
the overland journey to Guadalajara in Governor Francisco
Vázquez de Coronado's province of Nueva Galicia. There, on
August 12, 1544, he called as the first witness in the continuation of his investigation of the expedition's treatment of Indians Melchior Pérez, son of
Vázquez de Coronado's predecessor in the governorship, Diego Pérez de la
Torre.[1] Pérez de la Torre, after having served less than two years as governor,
had died before Vázquez de Coronado arrived to replace him and conduct his
residencia late in 1538. The new governor and juez de residencia initially
announced that he would conduct the administrative review as ordered, thus
putting the goods of Pérez de la Torre's heirs at jeopardy. He subsequently
decided, however, to bring no charges, a turn of events for which Melchior
Pérez must have been grateful.[2]

The younger Pérez had come to Nueva España in 1529 at about age 15
from his home town of Torremejía near Mérida in Spain.[3] He married at least
twice, first to an Indian woman, with whom he had three daughters, and then
in the early 1550s to Juana de Cáceres, daughter of a first conqueror of Nueva

España who had arrived with Pánfilo de Narváez.[4] His household included not only his wife and children, but also at least three brothers and two sisters.[5] One of his daughters, Catalina Mejía, during the 1540s became the wife of fellow expedition member and fellow witness in the 1544 investigation Pedro de Ledesma.[6] Pérez and Ledesma are mentioned together in numerous documents of the period. Both of them, for example, testified on behalf of Juan de Zaldívar in 1566. Ledesma may even have lived in Pérez's household. At least, he also changed city of residence at the same time Pérez did.[7] Pérez was encomendero of Cuyupuztlán, west of Guadalajara, from the 1530s until he gave the encomienda as dowry to his daughter Catalina in her marriage to Ledesma.[8]

Said to be a vecino of the city of Guadalajara in 1544 and still in 1551, Pérez shifted his place of citizenship several times in later years.[9] In 1552, he said he was a vecino of Compostela.[10] In 1563, however, he was a vecino of Mexico City.[11] And just three years later he was a vecino of Colima.[12]

With his future son-in-law, Pérez went to Tierra Nueva in the company of Captain Juan de Zaldívar, also a witness in the 1544 investigation.[13] During the expedition he served as *alguacil mayor* or chief constable and *aposentador* or billeting officer for the whole force. He claimed to have spent more than 3,000 pesos because of the expedition, and he took a thousand hogs and sheep along, whether as a speculative investment for anticipated sale to other expedition members or as part of the financing of the expedition that would earn him a share of the proceeds is not known. Certainly though, he was one of the most well-to-do members of the expedition, a fact further underscored by the seven or eight horses and two *ladino* Blacks he also took with him. Years later he stated that on his return from Tierra Nueva he was in debt for more than 500 pesos.[14]

When questioned by Tejada in August 1544, Pérez was another witness who offered long, detailed information beyond what he was asked, as though he knew what he was going to be asked about. He suggested that Vázquez de Coronado was kept in the dark about the rape and robberies at Indian towns. He was the first witness to be grilled about López de Cárdenas and his possible culpability in the matter of brutality committed against Indians. It is as though the main target of the investigation had by now shifted decisively to the maestre de campo. Later, because of such testimony as that given by Pérez in 1544, López de Cárdenas claimed that Pérez, Juan de Contreras, and Juan Troyano were among his principal enemies.[15]

Like many of the other witnesses in the pesquisa of 1544, Pérez provided details about familiar events not recorded (and thus not confirmable) elsewhere. He identified himself as an eyewitness to López de Cárdenas's guarantee of safety to more than 80 Indians at Pueblo del Arenal, a pledge which he also later saw betrayed. Pérez also said that he witnessed the killing, maiming, and setting of dogs on 30 residents of Pueblo del Cerco, where Vázquez de Coronado was in charge. Furthermore, he claimed to have been present at the battle of Cíbola and to have seen many Cíbolans killed in that fighting. If there is an indictment in his testimony, however, it is against the maestre de campo and perhaps a more general one against the expedition at large. In this latter respect it is representative of the sum of testimony taken during the investigation. Brutal acts are recounted with apparent unconcern and without the placing of blame or responsibility, unless it be a collective responsibility.

A TRANSLATION
OF THE TESTIMONY

Tenth de Oficio Witness (Melchior Pérez)[16]

[71v cont'd] Melchior Pérez, a vecino of the city of Guadalajara, accepted as a witness for this investigation, having given his oath in legal form before the lord judge, was asked the following questions.

{*1*} He was asked whether he knows Francisco Vázquez de Coronado, don García López de Cárdenas, don Diego de Guevara, don Tristán de Arellano, don Rodrigo Maldonado, Diego López (a councilman of Sevilla), don Pedro de Tovar, Juan de Zaldívar, Hernando de Alvarado, Barrionuevo, Pablos de Melgosa, and the other captains who went to reconnoiter and subjugate the tierra nueva of Cíbola, Tiguex, Cicuique, Brava, and Quivira and the other [72r] neighboring provinces. He answered that he has known all of those about whom he is asked, by appearance, voice, behavior, and conversation for the last five years [and more].[17] He was present during the subjugation and exploration of some of the provinces about which he is asked.

{*2*} [The witness] was asked whether the [people of the] provinces of Los Corazones, the valleys of Señora and Fuya, and the others that there are between Culiacán and Cíbola came out in peace to offer obedience to His Majesty and to Francisco Vázquez in his royal name. Did they give and supply provisions and food that they had, and did they welcome [the Spaniards] into their houses and towns, without offering any resistance or making war? He answered that it is true that [the people of] all those valleys and the other towns from Culiacán to Cíbola through which Francisco Vázquez went came out in peace and rendered obedience to His Majesty and to the general in his royal name. [Further,] all of the towns gave [the Spaniards] [72v] food from what they had, welcomed [the Spaniards] fully, and accommodated them in their towns and houses (in which the Spaniards lodged).

{3} [The witness] was asked whether in those towns or any one of them the general or any of the captains committed any brutality or outrages against the natives and whether, if anyone [else][18] did so, did Francisco Vázquez punish them [or][19] excuse [their actions]? [In reply] he stated that he did not know or hear that the general, his captains, or any other person perpetrated outrages against the Indians. On the contrary, [the Spaniards] treated them very well.

{4} He was [then] asked to state what caused the natives of those provinces to rise up in arms, rebel, and kill the Spaniards who stayed there. Was Francisco Vázquez or any of the captains responsible for that [turn of events], and did the general punish those who transgressed? He replied [73r] that it was common knowledge and widely held in the army that the reason that those Indians rebelled was that a [man named] Alcaraz, who was a captain, committed many outrages against them, taking provisions against their will and seizing their wives and daughters in order to have sexual relations with them. For this reason they rose up, rebelled, and killed Alcaraz and other Spaniards. The witness does not know that either Francisco Vázquez or the other captains who went on the reconnaissance bear responsibility or guilt for this.

{5} [The witness] was asked what cruelty and outrages Francisco Vázquez or any of the captains committed in the province of Cíbola and whether [the people there] came out in peace or in war. He answered that when they arrived near Cíbola Francisco Vázquez went to the pueblo with the scribe Hernando Bermejo, two friars, and two other captains, among whom was the witness. Through an Indian who knew the language they delivered the requerimiento to the people of Cíbola, summoning them to offer [73v] peace and telling them that no harm would be done to them, but rather thoroughly benevolent treatment and justice. And they were told that they would be given knowledge of our lord Jesus Christ and the manner in which they would be saved. Although they were told this many times and made to understand it through their interpreters, those Indians were never willing to submit or come out in peace. On the contrary, they took up stones and arrows and began to launch them at the general, the friars, and those who went with them to deliver the requerimiento.

When Francisco Vázquez saw that, he ordered his captains to attack and enter the pueblo of Cíbola. Being thus at war, the Spaniards attacked [the Indians], killing whomever they found in front of them. In this way they stormed up to the pueblo. Some of the Indians gathered in the pueblo in order to fortify themselves. At that point Francisco Vázquez and the friars again summoned the Indians to submit, but they [74r] refused to do so. Rather, the witness saw that from a flat roof they threw a stone slab and struck Francisco Vázquez. And they knocked him to the ground, stunned. Then the Spaniards began to fire the artillery, which killed many Indians, as did lance thrusts. When the Indians saw that [the Spaniards] were driving them back and carrying them off defeated, they submitted and left the pueblo and the provisions. And [the Spaniards] did not do any further harm to the Indians. Instead, the general, the captains, and the [other] people all treated them very well.

{6} [Pérez] was [then] asked whether he knows that when the general and the army were in the pueblo of Cíbola a principal from Cicuique (to whom afterwards they gave the name Bigotes) came with half a dozen Indians to render obedience to His Majesty and to the general in his royal name and to offer themselves as allies. Were [Spaniards] sent and did they go to the province of Cicuique, where they were [74v] welcomed, and did [the Indians] feed them and give them what they had? He answered that he is aware of what is referred to in the question. He saw that in a short time the general sent Hernando de Alvarado with twenty horsemen (among whom was the witness) to accompany Bigotes and the other Indians.

Bigotes guided them through the pueblos and provinces and he went ahead, making sure that the Indians of those pueblos came out in peace with clothing and provisions and welcomed [the Spaniards] very well. In particular, he knows and saw that Bigotes assured that the people of Brava came out in peace. It was a large settlement which seemed to the witness to contain more than thirty thousand persons. They welcomed and quartered [the Spaniards] inside. The Spaniards entered, but they left and took up quarters outside, in order not to trouble or stir up [the Indians].

When Hernando de Alvarado wanted [75r] to pursue the reconnaissance in the direction the general had ordered, the Indian called Bigotes advised him and told him not to go beyond that place because it was unpopulated, though it was settled in the direction he would lead. Alvarado did not want to do that, telling him that he had to guide them in the direction the general had ordered. Seeing this, the principal begged Alvarado to go first to see his land, since it would not be a detour and the people there would welcome [the Spaniards] and treat them well. [The witness] saw that they went to that province and entered the main pueblo, which was called Cicuique. There [the Spaniards] were thoroughly welcomed, and the people provided them clothing that they had. [The Spaniards] took up quarters outside the pueblo.

When Hernando de Alvarado wanted to continue on his course in the direction the general had ordered, the [75v] Indian called Bigotes asked him for permission to stay behind in his house because he was worn out and had been guiding [the Spaniards] for forty or fifty days. [Pérez] knows that the permission was granted and that [Bigotes] provided Alvarado with three or four Indians who would guide him in the direction he wanted to go. To one of them [the Spaniards] gave the name Turco and to another the name Ysopete. They guided [the Spaniards] along the edge of a river for a distance of eighty leagues.

When the Indian called Turco was asked if he knew of any wealthy land he told Alvarado that a number of days' journey from where he was there was a land which, by clear and obvious signs, he portrayed and showed as being very wealthy in gold and silver. And also as bountiful and productive of all things. He said and made it understood that the principal called Bigotes was aware of and knew about that land and that he possessed a bracelet and other jewelry that had been brought from [76r] there.

When they returned to Cicuique Hernando de Alvarado found a way to get the Indian called Bigotes out of the pueblo and to take him along to show the general. When they had gotten away from the pueblo one or two days' journey, the Indian called Turco fled. Thinking that he had fled through the connivance of Bigotes (so that [the Spaniards] would not bring to light or learn [more] about the matter of the jewelry), Alvarado put Bigotes in a collar with a chain and told him the he would not be released until he turned Turco over. And he said that it had been because of Bigotes's warning and machinations that Turco had fled. Bigotes denied this and, excusing himself, he asked Alvarado to release one of the Indians who had come with him from his pueblo and whom they had also shackled when Bigotes was seized. That [Indian] would then go in search of Turco. So [the Spaniards] released one or two [Indians] and they went to look for Turco, [76v] whom they brought back with them. In addition, other Indians came, who begged Hernando de Alvarado to release Bigotes to them, since they were his allies, had thoroughly welcomed [the Spaniards], and had provided them what they had.

Alvarado was not willing to do that, but traveled with Bigotes towards the province of Tiguex, where the general was. On the way, he asked Bigotes to show him the jewelry, to tell him from what country it had been brought, and to tell him about that place. And he said that he wanted only to see the jewelry and would return it immediately. But Bigotes answered that he did not have the jewelry, did not know about such a land, and that Turco had lied to Alvarado about everything. Confronted by Turco and Ysopete, he said the same. And Turco said that he had told the truth. At other times when he was angry and saw that [the Spaniards] paid more attention to El Turco than to him, Bigotes made them understand that Turco [77r] did not tell the truth in anything.

{7} [The witness] was asked whether he knows that, because Bigotes did not confirm what El Turco said about his knowing about such a land and possessing that jewelry, after they had come to where the general was Hernando de Alvarado set dogs on Bigotes, by the general's order. And did they unleash the dogs, and did they bite him very severely? He replied that when they had arrived where the general was, Alvarado lodged with Bigotes and the other [Indians] he had brought as prisoners in the camp where the general was quartered, which was next to the Río de Tiguex. And Alvarado unleashed a dog against Bigotes in order that he might tell about the [wealthy] land and the jewelry. The witness did not see this because he was quartered at another part[20] of the river. But what is stated was common knowledge and widely held in both camps. Afterwards he saw [77v] the wounds and bites that the dog had inflicted. And Bigotes had bound the wounds on his arms and legs with some bandages. [Pérez] does not know whether this was done by the general's order or whether he knew about it.

{*8*} He was [next] asked whether he knows that because of the mistreatment and setting on of dogs, because Alvarado had taken the Indian called Bigotes and the others who came with him prisoners and had put them in collars, and because he had refused to release them, the province of Cicuique rose up in arms and rebelled. [In reply] he said that it is true that for the reasons stated in the question those provinces rose up and rebelled. And [the Indians] did not welcome [the Spaniards] there anymore, nor did they supply provisions.

{*9*} [Pérez] was asked whether he knows that likewise the province of Tiguex, which had rendered obedience and come to offer peace, rebelled because of the brutality and outrages committed by the general and the other captains and because a [man named] Villegas (brother of the councilman of that name) [78r] seized an Indian woman in a pueblo of that province and, by force and against her will, had sexual relations with her. And was it also because [other] people entered the pueblos against [the Indians'] will and took hides, mantas, clothing, and other things they had from them? [The witness] answered that he is not aware nor did he see that the general, his captains, or the [other] people committed outrages against those Indians. On the contrary, he ordered and directed that they be well treated. But he did hear it said that they rose up in arms because of what is related in the question concerning the Indian woman raped by Villegas and because [the Spaniards] entered the houses [of the Indians] and seized and took from what they had there.

{*10*} He was [then] asked whether he knew that the rape of the Indian woman and the robberies and ill-treatment came to the general's notice and that he punished the offenders. He stated that he does not know, but he heard it said that the captains and [other] people tried to keep the general from finding out about the rape and thievery because [78v] they believed that he would hang Villegas and punish the rest.

{*11*} [The witness] was asked whether he knows that, although the province of Tiguex rose in arms, the Indians gathered and fortified themselves in only two pueblos, and those were the pueblo to which Francisco Vázquez laid siege and the other one besieged by don García López. And was this because the Indians abandoned the rest of the pueblos, some of them going to the one the general laid siege to and the rest taking shelter in the mountains? He replied that he knows what is related in the question.

{*12*} Since he says that those [other] pueblos were abandoned and defenseless, he was asked for what reason [the Spaniards] destroyed and burned them, by whose order it was done, and how many pueblos were burned and laid waste. [In answer] he said that it was twelve or thirteen pueblos that were destroyed and burned. They were within a distance of three leagues adjacent to the river, six on one side of the river and the others [79r] on the other. By the general's order don Diego de Guevara, with a number of men-at-arms, had gone to travel through the land. [The witness], having gone along, saw one of the pueblos where don Diego de Guevara went burn, but he does not know whether he burned it. Nor does he know by whose order it was done, except that he heard it said by a number of persons (whose names he does not remember) that men-at-arms burned and laid waste the rest of the pueblos because of their need for firewood. He does not know whether the general ordered any of this done.

{*13*} [Pérez] was asked whether he knows that the general, at the pueblo he besieged, and don García López, at the other one he laid siege to, summoned the people who were inside to come to peace and told them that they would be pardoned and would be treated well, before assailing and occupying the pueblos. He answered that before the pueblos were attacked and occupied, the general [79v] and don García López, who was maestre de campo at that time, summoned the Indians of those pueblos to offer peace and told them they would be pardoned and well treated. [The Indians, though,] were never willing to come to peace. So [the Spaniards] made war and fought them.

{*14*} He was [then] asked whether he knows that at the pueblo besieged by don García López de Cárdenas, when [the Spaniards] had attacked it and gained the flat roofs, the Indians of the pueblo made signs that they were willing to offer peace, if they were given a guarantee for their lives and that they would not be mistreated. [Further,] did don García López promise, making the sign of the cross, that if they submitted, their lives would be guaranteed and they would not be harmed? [Pérez] replied that he knows what is related in the question because he saw it and was present. Suspecting that [don García] would not keep his word, he said to don García, "Lord, do not show them the cross [80r] unless you expect to fulfill [your promise]." Then García López replied [to the witness] that he had made the [sign of the cross] incorrectly.

{15} [Pérez] was asked whether he knows and saw that, under the promise and agreement that had been made and with the showing of the cross, some of the Indians, believing that [the maestre de campo] would keep his promise, came out of the pueblo where they were, without arms, towards the Spaniards, who then took them and placed them in a tent. And when the rest [of the Indians] saw them [being taken] as prisoners, did they withdraw to their houses and did the Spaniards, under orders from don García López, enter the pueblo and bring out about eighty of them, whom they put in the tent with the first group? He answered that he is aware of what is related in the question because he saw it and was there.

{16} [Next,] the witness was asked whether, after holding [the Indians] in the tent, don García López ordered that some posts be set in the ground, that [the Indians] be tied to them, and that they be burned alive. Did [the Spaniards] take them out and burn them? And, when [those who remained] in the [80v] tent saw their companions being burned and that [the Spaniards] did not keep their word, did they rise up in arms in the tent, and did [the Spaniards] lance and kill them there? He stated that he knows what is related in the question because he saw it and was present. The burning and killing was done by order of don García López, who was then maestre de campo and the captain in charge of that siege.

{17} He was asked who the other captains were who were there and carried out the burning and killing, either by their own authority or under orders from don García López. He replied that Juan de Zaldívar, don Rodrigo Maldonado, the councilman Diego López, and Pablos del Melgosa were present as captains and men who commanded [companies]. All of these individuals were present during the burning and killing, which were done by order of the maestre de campo don García López.

{*18*} [Pérez] was [then] asked whether, when these burnings and killings [81r] of the Indians in the tent were carried out, the pueblo had been captured and pacified. He answered that the entire pueblo had been captured and pacified when what is related in the question occurred.

{*19*} He was asked [next] whether he knew that don García López conducted the burning and lanced the Indians who were in the tent by order of the general, since the general had been notified by messengers that the maestre de campo sent and that the Indians were not burned and lanced until the messengers returned with the general's reply. He said he does not know. But what he remembers is that it seemed to him that the messengers were not sent until after the burning and killing had been carried out, although he does not know what the messengers were sent to say. He did hear it said, however, that they were to tell the general that the burning and killing had been done and to see whether he wanted don García to move on to other pueblos near there that were still at war.

{*20*} [The witness] was asked why [81v] [the Spaniards] killed the Indian called Turco, who did the killing, and by whose order it was done. He replied that he had heard it said by Captain Juan de Zaldívar that, under orders from the maestre de campo Diego López, he had garrotted El Turco because he had led the company deceitfully, put the whole army in danger, [exposed it to many difficulties],[21] and had lied in everything he said. And [furthermore], he had made a pact with [the Indians] of Quivira, telling them that because the horses were weak and worn out, [the Spaniards] would not be able to do them any harm with the horses, so that one night they would set upon the Spaniards.

{*21*} He was asked whether General don Francisco Vázquez de Coronado was present at that time in the camp where they killed Turco. He answered that he does not know because he himself was not there. But he heard it said that the general was present and he believes it because he saw the general go with the [other] people and the maestre de campo on the journey to Quivira.

{*22*} [Pérez] was asked whether he knows that during the expedition Francisco Vázquez [82r] committed any other cruelty or significant outrages and whether at the pueblo he laid siege to he set dogs on many people who had been captured during the siege. He stated that he knows and saw that at the pueblo besieged by Francisco Vázquez he ordered about thirty Indians to be killed, set upon by dogs, and have their hands cut off. These were from among those who had been taken by force during the siege. [The Spaniards] did no harm to the rest, who came out to submit. He saw, however, that those who fled were lanced. He does not know nor did he see during the expedition that Francisco Vázquez committed any other outrages.

He said that this is the truth, in accordance with the oath that he swore. As soon as he finished speaking his statement was read to him and he confirmed it. The lord judge signed.

Licenciado Tejada
Melchior Pérez

A TRANSCRIPT
OF THE TESTIMONY

[fol. 71v cont'd][22]
{T*estigo*}
El d*ich*o melchior Perez Vezino de la / d*ich*a ÇiUdad de guadalaxara te*stig*o
/ Res̗çibido Para la d*ich*a ynForma- / çion el qual *h*abyendo jurado en Forma
/ de d*erech*o a*n*te el d*ich*o Señor oydor / Se le hizieron las Preguntas s*iguiente*s
/ Fue Pregunt*a*do Sy conosçe a Fran*cis*co Vaz- / quez de Coronado e a don
g*ar*cia loPez / de Cardenas e a don diego de guevara / e a don tristan de arellano e a don / R*odrig*o maldonado e a diego loPez Veynte / e quatro de seVylla
e a don Pedro / de toVar e a juan de çaldivar e a / hernan*n*do de alVarado e a
barrionueVo / e a Pablos de melgosa e a los otros / cAPitanes que Fueron a la
con- / q*u*ysta e descubrimyento de la t*ie*rra / nueVa de Çibola e tiguex (a) *e*
çicuyque / e brava e quyVira e a otras Pro- / [no number]

[fol. 72r]
885
Vinçias ComarCAnas Dixo que conosçe / A todos los conthenidos en la Pregunta / de Çinco Años a *e*sta P*ar*te de Vista e ha- / bla e Trato e conversaçion
e que se / (f)*h*allo Pr*e*sente A la conquista e desCu- / brimyento de algunas
d*e* las d*ich*a*s* Pro- / Vinçias que le *h*an sydo Preguntadas / Fue Pregunt*a*do Sy
las ProVinçias de / los coraçones e Valles de señora Fuya / e las otras que *e*stan
desde cu- / lyaCan hasta Çibola (e) *si* les salieron de / Paz A dar la obediençia
A su mag*estad* / e a Fran*cis*co vazquez *en* su rreal nonbre / e les dieron e
ProVeyeron de los / bastymentos e comyda que ellos te- / nyan e los Acoxieron *en* sus Pue- / blos e CAsAs Syn se Poner en / Resistençia ny (f)*h*azer
guerra Al- / Guna dixo que es v*er*dad que / Todos los d*ich*os (^P) valles e
todos / los d*ich*os Pueblos que estan desde / CuliaCan hasta çibola Por donde
Fue / el d*ich*o Fran*cis*co Vazquez Sa- / lyeron de Paz e dieron la obe- / diençia

a Su mag*e*stad e al d*i*cho / General *en* Su rreal nonbre e todos / los d*i*chos
Pueblos les Daban

[fol. 72v]

d*e* la Comyda que ellos tenyan e los ha- / zian buenos acoximyentos e los aco-
/ xian *en* sus Pueblos e CAsas en q*ue* / los esPañoles Posasen / Fue Preguntado sy el d*i*cho General o Al- / Gunos de los d*i*chos CaPitanes hizo / *en* los
d*i*chos Pueblos o alguno de *e*llos / A los naturales Algunos malos- /
tratamyentos e crueldades e Si / Algunos lo hizieron Sy(n) les Cas- / Tigar
(e) *o* deSymulo el d*i*cho Franc*is*co / Vazquez d*i*xo que no suPo ny oyo / que el
d*i*cho General ny sus CaPi- / tanes ny otra Persona Alguna / (f)*h*iziese malostratamyentos a los / d*i*chos Yndios ant*e*s los trataVan / muy byen / Fue Preguntado que declare que / Fue la Causa Por que los natura- / les d*e* las d*i*chas
ProVinçias se / Alzaron e rreVelaron e ma- / Taron a los esPañoles que / en
ellas quedaron e si Fue / en ello CulPante el d*i*cho Franc*is*co / Vazquez o
alguno de sus CaPi- / Tanes o si (^hezedio) CAstigo / A(l) los que en ello
(h)ezedieron d*i*xo / [no number]

[fol. 73r]

886

que P*ubli*co e notorio Fue en el exerçito / que Porque los d*i*chos yndios se
*h*abya*n* / rrebelado *h*Abia Sydo Porq*ue* / Un alCaraz que (h)*e*ra CAPitan les
ha- / zia muchos malosTratamyentos to- / ma*n*doles Contra su Voluntad los
/ basTymentos e las mugeres e hijas / Para (h)echarse con ellas e Por esta /
CAUsa se *h*abyan Alçado e rrebelado / e muryo el d*i*cho AlCAraz e otros
esPa- / noles e *e*ste t*e*stigo no Supo CArgo / ny CulPa que el d*i*cho Franc*is*co
Vazquez / ny los otros CAPitanes que yban / en el desCubrimyento / Fue
Preguntado que crueldades e / malostratamyentos hizo el d*i*cho
Franc*is*co / Vazquez o algunos d*e* sus CAPita- / nes en la P*ro*Vinçia de çibola
o Si les / Salieron de Paz o de guerra dixo / que llegados junto A Çibola el /
d*i*cho Franc*is*co Vazquez con herna*n*do ber- / mejo esc*ri*vano e doS Frayles e
otros / doS CaPitanes y este t*e*stigo con ellos / llegaron A çibola e Por un
yndio / que Sabia la lengua Requyrieron / A los de Çibola que se diesen de

[fol. 73v]

Paz e que no les harian mal nynguno sino / Todo buen tratamyento e jusTiçia e / les daria*n* a conosçer A n*uest*ro Señor / Jesu *cristo* e la (h)orden como se *h*abian de / SalVar e aunque esto les dixe- / ron e dieron A e*n*tender muchas / Vezes Por sus ynTerP*r*et(r)es jamas / los d*i*chos yndios Se quysieron / dar ny Salyr de Paz a*n*tes to- / maron Piedras e Flechas y enPe- / zaron a tyrar al d*i*cho General e / Frayles e a los que con ellos *h*abian / Ydo Para hazerles el d*i*cho Re- / quyrimyento lo q*ual* visto Por el / d*i*cho Franc*is*co vazquez ma*n*do a sus / CaPitanes que ronPiesen e / e*n*trasen en los d*i*chos Pueblos de / Çibola e ansy de guerra los d*i*chos / EsPañoles los rronPieron ma- / Tando quantos hallaron delante / e ansy l(e)*os* (h)entraron hasta el Pue- / blo e los yndios Se Recoxie- / ron algunos de *e*llos en el Pue- / blo Para hazerse Fuertes e ally / el d*i*cho Franc*is*co Vazquez e los Frayles / los tornaron A rrequerir que / Se diesen e los d*i*chos yndios / [no number]

[fol. 74r]

887

no lo quisieron (f)*h*azer Antes Vi(d)o como / de Un açotea tiraron Una losa e dieron / al d*i*cho Franc*is*co Vazquez e lo derroca- / ron aturDido en el suelo y entonçes / con el Artilleria e*n*Pezaron A tirar e / mataron muchos de los d*i*chos Yndios / Con el artilleria y alançadas e qua*n*- / do los yndios Vieron que ansi los / Paraban e los llevaban de Vençida / Se dieron e dexaron el Pueblo / con los bastymentos e no hizieron / mas daño A los d*i*chos yndios nynguno / Antes DesPues Ansy el general / Como los caPitanes e gente los Trata- / ban muy bien / Fue Pregunta*d*o Sy Sabe que estando / el d*i*cho gen- eral y exerçito en el d*i*cho / Pueblo De Çibola Vinieron un Prin- / ÇiPal de çicuyque que des*pues* le Pu- / Sieron nonbre bigotes con meDia / Dozena de yndios A dar la obeDien- / çia A Su magestad e al d*i*cho Ge- / neral *en* su rreal nonbre e a oFre- / çerles Por amygos e que ynVia- / Sen o Fuesen A la d*i*cha ProVin- / çia de çicuyque e que les harian

[fol. 74v]

acoximyento e les Darian de comer / e de lo que ellos tenyan dixo que / Sabe

lo contenido en la Pregunta / e que Vio que el dicho General ynVio / luego
con el dicho bigotes e los demas / Yndios a hernando de alVarado con /
Veynte de a Cavallo entre los / quales Fue este testigo e que el / dicho bigotes
los yba guiando Por / los Pueblos e ProVinÇias / e Se adelantaba e hazia salir
de / Paz e con bastymentos e rroPa / A los yndios de los tales Pue- / blos e
les (f)hazia todo buen acoxi- / myento en esPecial Sabe e Vio / que les hizo
Salir de Paz el / Pueblo de brava PoblaÇion gran- / de que al Paresçer de este
testigo / hAbria en el sobre treynta myll / Personas e los acoxieron e a- /
PoSentaron Dentro y entrados / los esPañoles Se Salieron los / dichos
esPañoles e Se aPosen- / Taron Fuera Por no Darles Pesa- / dumbre ny
alborotarlos e que- / riendo el dicho hernando de al- / [no number]

[fol. 75r]
888
VaraDo (^descub) Proseguir el Descu- / brimyento Por el rrunbo que el dicho
/ General le habia mandado el dicho / Yndio llamado bigotes le aViso e / Dixo
que no Fuese Por aquel Para- / Je Porque (h)era desPoblado sino Por / donde
el le guiase que (h)era PoblaDo / y el dicho hernando de alVarado no lo /
quyso (f)hazer DizienDo que habia / de guyar Por donde el general / habia
mandado e visto esto el dicho / Yndio PrinçiPal le rrogo que / Fuese Primero
A Ver Su tierra / Pues no se Rodeaba nada e que / Alli se les harya todo buen
acoxi- / myento e Tratamyento e Ansi / Vio que Fueron A la dicha ProVinçia
/ e entraron en el Pueblo PrinçiPal / que se llama çicuyque donde / Se les hizo
buen acoGimyento e / les ProVeyeron de la rroPa que / ellos tenyan e se
aPosentaron / Fuera del Pueblo e querien- / do el dicho hernando de alVarado
Pro- / seguir Su derrota Por la via que / el dicho General le habia mandado el

[fol. 75v]
dicho Yndio llamaDo bigotes le dixo que / le diese liçençia Para quedarse en
su / CaSa Porque Venia ya CAnsado que habia / quarenta o çinquenta dias
que los / Venya guianDo e Ansy sabe que se / quedo e dio Al dicho hernando
de al- / Varado tres o quatro ynDios que / lo Guiasen Por donDe el queria yr
/ Al Uno de los quales le Pusyeron / Por nonbre Turco e al otro yso- / Pete

los quales los guiaron Por / la Vera de Un rrio esPaçio de / ochenta leguas e yendo Pregun- / Tando al dicho ynDio llamaDo / Turco Si sabia de alguna Tierra / Ryc(o)a le dixo que çiertas jornaDas / De alli habya una tierra que Por / Señas muy claras e eVydentes / dezia e mosTraba ser muy RiCa / de oro e Plata e abundante e / Fertil de todas las cosas e dixo e / dio A entenDer que el dicho Prin- / ÇiPal llamaDo bigotes sabia e / Tenya notiçia de la dicha tierra / e que tenya un brazalete e otras / Joyas que se habian traydo de la / [no number]

[fol. 76r]

889

dicha Tierra e Vueltos a çiCuyque tuVo / manera el dicho hernando de alVa- / rado de saCar del dicho Pueblo Al / dicho yndio bigotes y llevarle con- / Sygo para le mostrar Al / General e saCAdo del dicho pueblo / de(n)sde a una (e) o dos jornadas se / huyo del rreal el dicho ynDio / llamaDo Turco e creyendo que / Por ynDustria del dicho bigotes se / hAbia huydo Porque no Se / SuPiese ni desCubriese los / de las dichas joyas (h)echo una collera / Con una CAdena Al dicho bigotes Di- / ziendole que no le habia de soltar / hasta que truxese Al Turco Di- / ziendo que Por su aViso e ynDus- / tria Se habia huydo e desculPan- / dose el dicho bigotes e neganDolo dixo / que soltase uno De los yndios que / con el Venya de su Pueblo que ansi- / mesmo los habia APrisionado / quando Prendio al dicho bigotes e / que aque(e)llo (h)yria a busCAr / e ansi Soltaron uno o dos de ellos / e aquellos lo Fueron A busCar

[fol. 76v]

e lo traxeron con los quales ansimes- / mo vinieron otros yndios los quales / Rogaron Al dicho Fernando de alVarado / que Pues ellos (h)eran sus Amygos / e les habian (f)hecho buen acogimyento / e dado de lo que tenian que lo sol- / taSen al dicho bigotes e jamas lo / quyso (f)hazer e yenDo e CAmynan- / do con el (f)hazia la ProVinçia de / tiguex Donde el dicho General esta- / ba le dixo que le mostrase las / dichas joyas e le dixese de que tierras / las habyan traydo e les DieSe / notiçia de ella e que no queria sino / Verlas e que luego Se las / VolVeria y el dicho bigotes dixo que / ny el tenya tales joyas ny sabia /

de tal tie*rr*a e que el yndio lla- / mado Turco le *h*abia mentido en todo / e
Careado con el turco y ysoPete / Dixo lo mismo que el d*i*cho turco / Y que el
turco *h*abia d*i*cho *ver*dad e / otras Vezes qua*n*do estaba / (h)enojado e veya que
hazian / mas caso del turco que de *el* / daba a entender que el turco / [no
number]

[fol. 77r]
890
(que el turco) no Dezia verdad *en* todo / Fue Pregunt*a*do si sabe que Porque
el / d*i*cho bigotes no conFormaba con lo / que el d*i*cho Turco Dezia de *s*aber
tal / Tierra e *h*aber tales joyas d*es*Pues / de *h*aber llegaDo el d*i*cho General
*es*ta- / ba el d*i*cho herna*n*do de alVarado Por / ma*n*dado del d*i*cho General
aPerrea- / ron Al d*i*cho yndio llamado bigotes / e le (h)echaron los Perros e lo
mor- / dieron muy mal Dixo que syendo / llegados Adonde el d*i*cho Gene- /
ral *es*taba e *h*abiendose aPosen- / tado el d*i*cho herna*n*do de alVarado / Con
el d*i*cho bigotes e con los demas / que llevaba Presos en el / Real do*n*de el general *es*taba APosen- / tado que *es* junto al Rio de tiguex / el d*i*cho herna*n*do
de alVarado (h)echo / Un Perro Al d*i*cho bigotes Para que / declaraSe lo d*e* la
d*i*cha Tierra e jo- / Yas e que *es*te t*es*t*i*go no lo Vio / Porq*ue e*Staba APosen-
ta*d*o de la / otra P*ar*te del rrio Pero que / lo d*i*cho Fue Pu*bli*co e notorio en
entran- / bos Reales e que desPues Vio

[fol. 77v]
las heriDas e mordeduras que el d*i*cho Perro / *h*Abia dado e tenya AtaDas
las heriDas / Con unas VenDas en las Piernas e bra- / ços e que no Sabe sy
Fue Por / ma*n*dado del general o lo SuPo / Fue Pregunt*a*do Sy sabe que a
CAusa / del d*i*cho aPerreamyento e maltra- / Tamyento y Por *h*aber traydo
Pre- / Sos y en colleras Al d*i*cho YnDio / llamaDo bigotes e a los demas /
que con el venyan e Por no los *h*aber / queriDo soltar la d*i*cha ProVinçia / de
çiquyque se alço e rrebelo Dixo / que es *ver*dad que Por las Causas / en la
Pregunta co*n*thenidas se alÇo / e Rebelo la d*i*cha ProVinçia e no *l*os /
quysieron mas acoxer en ella / ny darles bastimentos / Fue Preguntado si

Sabe que la Pro- / Vinçia de tiguex que ansymismo / hAbia dado la obediençia e Venydo / A dar de Paz se rrevelo Por / las crueldades e malostratamientos que / el dicho General e los demas CaPi- / Tanes hizieron e
Porque Por Fuer- / ça e contra su Voluntad un villegas / hermano del
Regidor villegas / [no number]

[fol. 78r]

891

dentro De Un Pueblo de la dicha Provinçia / Tomo una yndia e Por Fuerça e
contra / Su voluntad Se (h)echo con ella e Por- / que contra Su voluntad la
gente / les entraba en los Pueblos e les to- / maban los Cueros mantas e rroPa
e / otras Cosas que tenian dixo este / Testigo no sabe ny Vio que el dicho
Gene- / ral ny sus CaPitanes ny gente hizie- / Sen maltratamiento A los
dichos yndios / antes lo Pro(y)Veian e mandaban / que Fuesen muy bien
tratados Pero / que oyo dezir que se alçaron Por / lo que la Pregunta dize de
la ynDia / que tomo el dicho villegas y Porque / les entraban en las Casas e les
Sa- / Caban e tomaban lo que en ellas / Tenyan / Fue Preguntado Sy sabe que
la dicha / Fuerça de la yndia e rrobos e / malostratamientos vinyeron A /
notiçia del dicho general e castigo los / delinquentes Dixo que no lo / Sabe
antes oyo Dezir que / Procuraba la gente e CAPitanes / que no SuPiese el
general de la / dicha Fuerça e rrobos Porque

[fol. 78v]

Creyan que le ahorCara e CAstigara A los demas / Fue Preguntado Sy sabe
que aunque / la dicha ProVinçia de Tiguex se / Alço Solos dos Pueblos
Fueron los que / Se hizieron Fuertes e adonde se / Acoxio la gente que Fueron
los Sobre / que se Puso çerco Francisco vazquez e / Al otro don garçia loPez
Porque los / demas los desmanPararon e algunos / de ellos se Fueron Al uno
de los dichos / Pueblos adonde el general tenia / Puesto çerco e la demas
Gente / Se acoxio A la sierra Dixo que / Sabe la Pregunta como en ella se contiene / Fue Preguntado que Pues Dize que / los dichos Pueblos queDaron
Des- / manParados e Sin deFensa que / Por que rrazon los asolaron / e que-

maron e Por cuyo ma*n*dado / e que tantos (h)eran los Pueblos / que asolaron
e quemaron Dixo / que los Pueblos que se asolaron / e quemaron Fueron
Doze o treze / que *e*staban en *di*stançia de tres / leguas junto Al rrio los seys
d*e* la / Una P*ar*te del rrio e los otros / [no number]

[fol. 79r]
892
D*e* la otra e que don Diego de guevara con / Çiertos Soldados Fue Por ma*n*-
dado / del general *h*abyan ydo a correr / la Tierra e *h*Abyendo ydo Vio Ar- /
der uno de los Pueblos donde / Andaba el d*i*cho don diego de gueVara / Pero
que no sabe Sy el lo que- / mo ny Por cuyo ma*n*dado mas de / *h*Aber oydo
Dezir A Çiertas Per- / Sonas que no Tiene memoria / d*e* sus nonbres e que
los demas / Pueblos los asolaron e quemaro*n* / los Soldados Por la
nesÇeSidad q*ue* / Tenyan de la lena ny sabe si lo uno / ny lo otro lo ma*n*do el
general / Fue Pregunt*a*do Sy sabe que el d*i*cho ge- / neral en el Pueblo Sobre
q*ue* / Puso çerco y el d*i*cho don garç*i*a loPez / en el otro do*n*de ansimesmo
PuSo çerco / Requyrieron Antes que los con- / batiesen e entrasen A la gente
/ que dentro *e*staban que se / diesen de Paz e que serian Per- / donados e byen
tratados dixo que / Vyo que antes que se conbatieSen / y entrasen los d*i*chos
General

[fol. 79v]
Y don garç*i*a loPez maesTre de cAnPo / que a la sazon (h)era rrequirieron / A
los yndios de los d*i*chos Pueblos / que se diesen de Paz e que los / perDonarian
e serian bien trataDos / e jamas quysieron Venir de P*a*Z / e ansy se les dio la
guerra e conb*a*te / Fue Pregunt*a*do si Sabe que en el / Pueblo Sobre que Puso
çerco / don garç*i*a loPez de CArdenas *h*AbyenDo- / lo conbatydo e GanaDo
las açoteas / los yndios del d*i*cho Pueblo hizie- / ron señas que se querian dar
/ de Paz Sy les aseguraban las / Vydas e que no serian maltra- / Tados e el d*i*cho
don García loPez / Se lo Prometyo (f)*h*azienDo la cruz / que si se daban que
les asegu- / raban las vydas e que no les ha- / rian mal dixo que sabe la Pre- /
Gunta como en ella se contiene / Porque lo Vio e se hallo P*r*esente / e que *e*ste

testigo SoSPechanDo / que no les habia de guardar la / Palabra dixo Al dicho don garÇia lo- / Pez señor no les hagays la cruz / [no number]

[fol. 80r]

893

Sino lo habeys de cunPlyr y que enton- / zes le rresPonDio que la hazia mal (f)hecha / Fue Preguntado si sabe e vio que algunos / de los dichos yndios Debaxo de la / dicha ConFyança e Palabra e cruz que / les habia sydo (f)hecha creyendo que guar- / dara lo Prometydo salieron del dicho / Pueblo donde estaban (f)hazia los espa- / noles Sin Armas e luego Fueron / tomados e Puestos en una TienDa / e como los demas Vieron llevar A- / quellos en son de Presos se Re- / truxeron A sus Casas e los españoles / entraron Por mandado del dicho don / garçia loPez e saCAron hasta ochenta / de ellos e los Pusyeron en la dicha / Tienda con los Primeros dixo / que sabe la Pregunta como en ella / Se contiene Porque lo vio e se / (f)hallo Presente / Fue Pre- guntado Sy despues de te- / nerloS en la dicha TienDa el dicho don garcia / loPez mando hinCAr unos Palos e / atarlos a ellos e quemarlos ViVos / e ansy los SaCaron e quemaron ViVos / e los demas que quedaban en la

[fol. 80v]

Tienda Viendo que quemaban A los / ConPañeros e no les Guardaban la / Palabra Se alzaron en la dicha tien- / da e alli los alanzearon e mataron / dixo que sabe la Pregunta como en / ella se Contiene Porque lo vio e se / (f)hallo Presente e que la dicha quema / e muerte se hizo Por mandado del / dicho don garçia loPez maestre de CAnPo / que a la sazon (h)era el CAPitan Prin- / ÇiPal del dicho çerco / Fue Preguntado que otros CAPitanes / Se hallaron (e)en el dicho çerco e Si / hizieron la dicha quema e muertes / Por Su Voluntad o mandado del dicho / don garcia loPez dixo que Se halla- / ron en el dicho çerco juan de çaldi- / Var e don rrodrigo maldonaDo e die- / Go lopez veynte e quatro e Pablos / de melgosa CaPitanes e honbres / que tenyan cargo de gente e que / Se hallaron todos los susodichos / en la dicha quema e muertes e que / Fue Por mandado del dicho don garcia / loPez maestre de CAnPo /

Fue Preguntado Si quando se hizo la / dicha quema e muertos los dichos / [no number]

[fol. 81r]

894

yndyos en la dicha Tienda Sy estaba / Ganado e PaÇiFyco el dicho Pueblo Dixo / que todo el dicho Pueblo estaba ga- / nado e PaçiFyco quando lo conthenido / en la dicha Pregunta se hizo / Fue Preguntado Sy sabe que el dicho don / Garçia loPez hizo la dicha quema / e alançeo los que estaban en la dicha / Tienda Por mandado del general / Porque se lo hizo saber Por men- / sajeros que le ynVio e hasta que / VolVieron con la rresPuesta no se / quemaron los dichos yndios ny se / Alançearon Dixo que no lo sabe / Antes a lo que se quiere aCorDar / le Pareze que desPues de hA- / berSe hecho la dicha quema e muer- / tes le enVio los dichos menSajeros Pero / que no Sabe que es lo que / les enViaba A dezir con ellos mas / de que oyo dezir que el enViaba A / dezir que aquello estaba / (f)hecho que viese Sy queria que Pa- / Sase adelante A otros Pueblos / que eStaban de guerra ally çercA / Fue Preguntado que Fue la CAusa Por

[fol. 81v]

que mataron Al ynDio llamaDo / Turco e quyen le mato e Por cuyo man- / dado dixo que este Testigo oyo dezir / A juan de çaldivar CAPitan que habia / dado un garrote Al dicho turco Por man - / dado de diego loPez y maestre de CAn- / Po Porque hAbia lleVaDo enGanaDo / e Puesto en mucho Peligro todo el / exerçito y mentyo en todo quan(d)to / hAbia dicho e Porque tenya hecho / Pacto con los de quyVira que dieSen / Una noche en los esPañoles / que ya con los CAballos no les Po- / Dian (f)hazer dano Por estar Flacos / e FatyGados / Fue Preguntado Sy en el rreal / donde mataron al dicho Turco si a la Sa- / zon se hallo Presente Francisco Vazquez / de coronado general dixo que / este testigo no lo sabe Por no ha- / llarse Presente Pero que oyo decir / que se habia hallado Presente e que / lo cree Porque le vio yr con la Gen- / te e maestre de CanPo la dicha jornada / de quyVira / Fue Preguntado si sabe que en la dicha / jornada el dicho Francisco Vazquez / [no number]

[fol. 82r]

895

(F)*h*aya hecho otras Algunas Crueldad*es* / e notables malostratamyentos e / que en el Pueblo Sobre que / Tenya el çerco aPerreo grand CAnty- / dad de Gente que se *h*abia toma*D*o / Por Fuerça en el d*i*cho çerco Dixo que / Sabe e Vio que el d*i*cho Fran*cis*co Vaz- / quez en el Pueblo que tenya el / çerco ma*n*do aPerrear e cortar ma- / nos e matar hasta treynta yn*D*ios / Poco mas o menos de los que Se / Tomaron Por Fuerça en el d*i*cho / çerco e los demas que se salieron / A darse no les hizieron daño Pe- / ro a los que Se salian huyen*D*o / Vio que los alançeaban e que / no sabe ny Vio que en la d*i*cha jornada / el d*i*cho Fran*cis*co Vazquez hiziese / otros algunos malostratamy*ent*os / e que *e*sta es la *ver*dad Para el jura- / mento que hizo e luego le Fue leydo / a este d*i*cho t*es*tigo *e*ste su d*i*cho luego como / lo aCabo de d*e*cir e RetiFycose en el / e Fyrmolo el d*i*cho Senor oydor mel- / chior Perez el liÇen*cia*do tejada

Chapter 13

Pedro de Ledesma, the Eleventh de Oficio Witness

A Member of Vázquez de Coronado's Household

Anative of Zamora in the jurisdiction of Vázquez de Coronado's hometown of Salamanca, the eleven- or twelve-year-old Pedro de Ledesma knew the future captain general at least seven years before they both sailed for Nueva España in the company of Viceroy Antonio de Mendoza in 1535.[1] From the time of their embarkation for the New World, Ledesma served in Vázquez de Coronado's household, accompanying him to Nueva Galicia to take up the governorship in 1538. He was still serving the former governor and captain general in 1545.[2] As a member of Vázquez de Coronado's household, Ledesma was included in the advance party that went ahead of the main body of the expedition to Tierra Nueva from Culiacán to Cíbola. His status as a henchman of the captain general is apparent in the five horses he took with him on the expedition.[3]

Following disbanding of the expedition, Ledesma remained in service to Vázquez de Coronado, in which capacity he was when questioned by Tejada in Guadalajara in August 1544. When Vázquez de Coronado was stripped of his governorship as a result of the residencia conducted by Tejada simultaneously with the investigation into treatment of Indians, Ledesma returned to Mexico City with his patron. He was resident there until at least 1547.[4] By 1552, though, he had returned to Nueva Galicia and was a vecino and deputy treasurer at Compostela.[5] It was evidently during this interval that he became the son-in-law of Melchor Pérez, marrying his daughter Catalina Mejía, who brought with her as dowry the encomienda of the pueblo of Cuyupuztlán, southwest of Guadalajara.[6]

In 1560, Ledesma identified himself as a vecino of Guadalajara and said that he had much contact with fellow witness during the 1544 investigation Juan Gómez de Paradinas and his wife María Maldonado.[7] Five years later, now about 50, he was a regidor or city councilman in the Guadalajara cabildo.[8] But in 1566, he and his father-in-law were both said to be vecinos of Colima.[9]

As a witness before oidor Tejada, Ledesma, like so many other de oficio witnesses, made long unsolicited statements, the gist of which was that

FIGURE 9.
Pueblo del Arenal, burning victim striking out at Spaniards, montage of images from the *Lienzo de Tlaxcala*

Vázquez de Coronado had done everything properly on the expedition, reading the requerimiento at Cíbola, for instance, and ordering the sieges of the Rio Grande pueblos made with as little harm as possible to the Indians. Like the other witnesses and probably most members of sixteenth-century Spanish expeditions of conquest in general, Ledesma expressed surprise and outrage that the native peoples did not immediately capitulate and eagerly become royal subjects. And he explained the warfare between Pueblos and the expedition during the winter of 1540–1541 as occasioned by the anger of the Pueblos over being asked for clothing to keep many members of the expedition from freezing, an anger Ledesma implied was illegitimate. In Ledesma's view, none of the Spaniards, except for Diego de Alcaraz at San Gerónimo, had anything to regret or to be held accountable for with regard to treatment of the Indians, a pervasive position among all the witnesses. He testified, though, as an eyewitness, to the lancing of up to 40 natives of Cíbola and to the burning of captives at Pueblo del Arenal, despite a guarantee of safety from the maestre de campo.

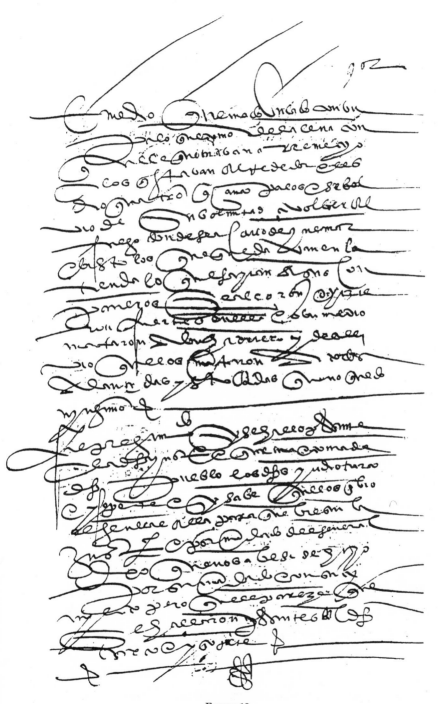

FIGURE 10.
Facsimile of Palo de la leña or firebrand, AGI, Justicia, 267, N.3, fol. 89r

A TRANSLATION
OF THE TESTIMONY

Eleventh de Oficio Witness (Pedro de Ledesma)[10]

[82r cont'd] After the aforesaid in the city of Guadalajara, the lord [82v] judge licenciado Tejada ordered Pedro de Ledesma, a native of Zamora and a resident of the city of Guadalajara, to appear before him, and he received his oath in the form prescribed by law, by God, Santa María, and the sign of the cross. Having promised to tell the truth under this obligation, he was asked the following questions.

{1} He was asked whether he knows Francisco Vázquez de Coronado, don García López de Cárdenas, don Tristán de Arellano, Diego López (a councilman of Sevilla), don Diego de Guevara, don Pedro de Tovar, Hernando de Alvarado, Juan de Zaldívar, Pablos de Melgosa, Velasco de Barrionuevo, and the other captains who went to explore and subjugate the tierra nueva of Tiguex, Cíbola, and the other provinces. He answered that he has known all of those about whom he is asked because the witness went with them from Culiacán to Cíbola and Quivira. And he participated in the subjugation and reconnaissance of those provinces [83r] until the expedition returned.

{2} [The witness] was asked whether he saw that from Culiacán to Cíbola [the people of] all the towns and provinces through which [the Spaniards] passed came out in peace and rendered obedience to His Majesty and gave the army the food that they had. He answered that he knows what is related in the question because he saw it, except that he does not know that they supplied provisions, since they did not have them. Instead, the general gave them trade goods from among those he had brought, so that they would not be offended and so that the people who remained behind, which was most of the company, would find themselves welcome there.

{3} He was [then] asked whether the general, captains, or Spaniards who went in the army committed any brutality or outrages against the natives of any of the towns they passed through. And if the general learned of [such occurrences], did he punish [the offenders] or excuse [their behavior]? He answered that he had no knowledge that the general or any of the captains or men perpetrated outrages. On the contrary, he knows [83v] that they were very prudent, giving [the Indians] presents and benevolent treatment, so that he saw that not a single man complained. And, as he has said, he saw that they gave [the Indians] trade goods and trinkets that they carried, because of which they remained very satisfied.

{*4*} Since he says that during the journey no outrages were committed in those towns, he was asked for what reason the [people of the] valley of Señora and its environs rose up in arms. He replied that he knows no more than what he has heard said publicly, [namely,] that the uprising occurred because of outrages committed by a [man named] Alcaraz, whom Melchor Díaz left in that town as his lieutenant and whom the Indians killed, along with other Spaniards.

{*5*} [Next] he was asked whether, in the capture of Cíbola, Francisco Vázquez or any of the Spaniards or captains perpetrated brutalities or significant outrages against the natives of that province. [In reply] he said that what happened in regard to what is asked in the question is this. When they had gotten to within three leagues [84r] of Cíbola, about thirty Indians came with food to the general and the roughly a hundred horsemen and footmen who were with him, among whom was the witness. The Indians wandered about looking over the army like men who had come to see what people were in the camp and how they were organized. When [the Spaniards] arrived at where they expected to sleep, they discovered that all those Indians had left.

The general ordered the maestre de campo don García López to go reconnoiter and see whether there was any hazardous passage ahead. He went with about twenty horsemen and brought word of a dangerous passage where there were some boulders. The general ordered him to go back and secure the passage and to sleep there. The men were to be vigilant, so that they would not be taken unawares. And if anything happened to them, they were to let the general know immediately. When he had returned and taken possession of the passage and a fourth of the first watch had passed, [the Indians] fell upon don García López and the men he had with him. When [the men] had mounted, they attacked [the Indians], who, according to what they said, [84v] numbered as many as a hundred men, and routed them.

When the general had learned what had occurred, the whole company moved toward Cíbola once daybreak had arrived. Having come within a crossbow's shot of Cíbola, [the witness] saw as many as four hundred fighting men come forth with bows and arrows and small clubs. They were made to understand, with signs and through an interpreter [the Spaniards] had brought from the valley of Corazones, that they were not coming to do them any harm, but rather to be their friends, to protect them from whoever might want to do them injury, and to teach them so that they would come to know God.

The Indians refused to listen to this or to come in peace. This must be true since [Francisco Vázquez] delivered the requerimiento to them two or three times in the presence of a scribe and with the clerics who had gone there, but the Indians drew lines [in front of him], indicating that the army should not cross them, threw dirt in the air, struck one of the scribe's horses with an arrow, and gave fray Daniel an arrow wound. Seeing this, the general attacked them with the whole force, and they lanced up to forty men. When they had reached the [85r] pueblo, the general ordered that [those Indians] who had not been able to get in not be pursued or harmed and, likewise, that those who were fleeing not be chased, but be allowed to go in peace.

After [the Indians] had taken shelter, they again delivered the requerimiento. Seeing that it was to no avail, the general ordered that the pueblo be attacked. Since he was first to [try to] enter, [the Indians] struck the general down with a great many rocks they threw at him from above. And they might have killed him, if several captains had not thrown themselves over him. He was brought out wounded in the nose and one leg and bruised all over, and he remained unconscious for more than three hours. When [the Spaniards] began attacking the pueblo the Indians let themselves down from the other sides. Once the general returned to his senses and was told that [the Indians] were leaving the pueblo, he ordered that they be allowed to go without doing them any injury. When they had gone, [the Spaniards] entered the pueblo and found a great store of provisions.

Within a few days both the Indians [85v] who had fled from that pueblo and [those from] the other seven pueblos came in peace, bringing the general gifts from the things they had. Francisco Vázquez welcomed them in a kindly way and gave them items from among the trade goods that he had brought. Always thereafter all the pueblos of this province were at peace, the witness does not know whether from fear of the punishment they had been given or because of the benevolent treatment the general had afforded them.

{6} [The witness] was asked whether he knows that while the general and his force were in Cíbola Indian leaders from the province of Cicuique came to render obedience and offer themselves to the general as allies. And did those from the province of Tiguex do the same? He stated that he knew and saw that as many as twenty Indians came to render obedience and to offer themselves as allies. Among them came a principal, said to be from Cicuique, to whom [the Spaniards] gave the name Bigotes, and another one they called the cacique. [86r] The general received them, gave them trade goods that he had brought, and thanked them for coming. And he sent Hernando de Alvarado and twenty horsemen to return with them to see their pueblos and to reconnoiter the land.

[Pedro de Ledesma] heard that Alvarado had gone and that Bigotes made sure that the people of all the pueblos came forth in peace and provided food, hides, and clothing. [Further,] he heard it said that Bigotes remained at Cicuique, but that he furnished two Indians to guide [the Spaniards] on the route and in the direction they wanted to take. To one of these Indians [the Spaniards] gave the name Turco and to the other the name Ysopete. Bigotes said they were his slaves. It was said that the one was from Quivira and the other from Arahe.

While traveling, the Indian called Turco told [the Spaniards] that he knew of a land, thirty days' travel distant, that was wealthy in gold and silver and was well supplied with all things. And he said that he had brought from there a certain bracelet and other things, which the Indian called Bigotes had taken from him. On returning from the reconnaissance, Alvarado [86v] brought Bigotes, Turco, and Ysopete with him to Tiguex, where the general had established quarters. The witness heard it said that because Bigotes did not confirm what El Turco was saying and denied having the bracelet and jewelry, [the Spaniards] set dogs on him. And afterwards, the witness saw that he had been bitten on one leg. It was common knowledge and widely held that the dogs had done that.

{7} He was [then] asked who had unleashed the dogs and by whose order it was done. He answered that he heard it said that don García López and don Pedro de Tovar had unleashed the dogs.

{8} [The witness] was asked for what reason the provinces of Cicuique and Tiguex reversed themselves and rose up in arms. Was it because dogs were set on Bigotes and because of other cruelty and outrages that [the Spaniards] committed against the Indians? [In answer] he said that many of the people of the company were without clothing and, because it was the month of December, were suffering the cold badly. In order to remedy that, the general ordered don García López to go to the pueblos and ask for [87r] some clothing. [The maestre de campo] brought ninety or a hundred articles of clothing, with which those who were lacking clothes were aided. The next day they woke to find thirty or forty horses that had been wandering in the countryside shot with arrows. And [the Indians] had clubbed and killed four or five Nahua Indians. The entire province of Tiguex had risen up and rebelled, and all the people had gathered in two pueblos. [Pedro de Ledesma] thinks that they were motivated to rebel because of the clothing that the general ordered to be gathered from those pueblos. He said that, likewise, the pueblo of Cicuique and the other pueblos of that province rebelled not to make war, but so that they would not have to provide provisions or anything else.

{9} He was [then] asked whether he thinks or knows that the people of the province of Cicuique rose in arms because Bigotes and the cacique had been taken prisoner and dogs had been set on them. He answered that he does not know.

{*10*} Since two pueblos of the province of Tiguex [87v] were fortified and defended, he was asked why [the Spaniards] burned the other twelve that remained abandoned. He replied that only nine were burned, and that was done on the general's order to admonish those Indians farther on, as well as to punish the people of those pueblos who had barricaded themselves in the other two. [He also said] that the pueblos had not been completely burned, but only partially because, although [the Spaniards] wanted to burn them, they could not do it, since they would not burn.

{*11*} [Pedro de Ledesma] was asked whether, before attacking the two pueblos that had taken up arms, [the Spaniards] summoned them to come to peace. And what brutality and significant outrages, burnings and unleashing of dogs, did [the Spaniards] commit against those Indians? He answered that what he knows is that they were summoned to offer peace three times and were told that they would be pardoned and afforded benevolent treatment. Yet they were never willing to do so, but rather tried to kill don García López and [88r] the other messengers who went to deliver the requerimiento. In view of this, [the Spaniards] went into combat. The witness did not see that [at] the siege where Francisco Vázquez was any brutality was committed. Nor does he know that any Indian was burned or set upon by dogs.

The general ordered the witness to get up and be off early to the camp where don García López was, to tell him not to lift the siege until he had taken the pueblo, which was to be done with as little harm to the Indians as he could manage. When the pueblo had been taken, the camp was to remain, but the maestre de campo was to leave in order to meet the general at Pueblo de la Alameda, which was between their two camps. Having arrived at the camp where don García López was, the witness saw that the pueblo was burning and that the Spaniards were already inside some of the houses. Held as prisoners in a tent were as many as thirty Indians who had been captured inside the pueblo.

When [the witness] had delivered the message he had gone for [88v] and wanted to return, don García López told him to wait until he saw the end, which he did. He saw that four or five Indians who were in one house made a sign of peace to don García López and indicated that they wanted to submit. The maestre de campo replied that it was good that they should come out. Thus, the four Indians came out through a window. One of them threw a manta around don García, which among them is a sign of peace. But the maestre de campo ordered them seized and put in the tent with the others who were there. Without further resistance, the Spaniards occupied the pueblo and houses and brought out other Indians and put them in the tent.

Within a short while [Pedro de Ledesma] saw [the Spaniards] bring twenty or twenty-four Indians [from the tent] and tie them to some posts, where they burned them alive. The rope that bound the hands of one of those being burned was consumed by the fire. [89r] Burned on one side, he took up a stick from among the firewood with which they were burning him and attacked [the Spaniards] who were around him, giving them four or five blows. Then he freely returned to the fire, where he finished burning. When [the Indians] who remained in the tent saw what was being done to their companions, they rose up and fortified themselves there. By some means they even killed a muleteer. There [the witness] saw [the Spaniards] kill all [the Indians] [in the tent] with thrusts from lances and swords. None of them remained alive.

{12} He was [then] asked whether the Indians Turco and Ysopete were present for this administration of justice, the burning, and the capture of the pueblo. Does he know that they were sent there by the general in order to witness the punishment? And was the punishment carried out by the general's order? He replied that he does not know whether this was done by the general's order and with his consent, but it seems to him that El Turco and Ysopete were present.

[89v] {13} [The witness] was asked whether the Indian called Turco was killed and by whom and under whose order it was done. He stated that [the Spaniards] killed that Indian on orders from Francisco Vázquez because he had led them deceitfully and had often placed the whole company in situations where it might have been lost. Turco himself acknowledged that he had led them by many roundabout ways, so that they might die. Also the general had information that Turco had advised [the Indians] of Quivira not to provide corn for the horses and to kill [the Spaniards].

{*14*} [Finally,] he was asked what other cruelty and outrages Francisco Vázquez or any of the captains or men committed and whether he excused [such behavior] if he learned about it. He replied that he did not see Francisco Vázquez or the captains or men commit any outrages.

He said that this is what he knows concerning what he [90r] is asked, in accordance with the oath that he swore. The witness signed his name. He read again what he had said as soon as he had finished speaking and he confirmed it. The lord judge licenciado Tejada signed.

Pedro de Ledesma

A TRANSCRIPT
OF THE TESTIMONY

[fol. 82r cont'd][11]

E desPues de lo susodicho en la dicha ÇiU- / dad de guadalajara el dicho señor

[fol. 82v]

liçençiado tejada Juez Susodicho Para la / dicha ynformaçion manDo Paresçer / Ante si a Pedro de ledesma natural de / çamora estante en eSta ÇiUdad de gua- / dalajara del qual Fue rresçibido / Juramento Por Dios e Por sanTa ma- / ria e Por una Senal de cruz en / Forma de derecho So CArgo del qual / hAbyendo PromeTido de decir verdad / Se le hizieron las Preguntas syguyentes / Fue Preguntado Sy conosçe A Francisco / Vazquez de Coronado e a don garcia / loPez de Cardenas e a Don tristan de / Arellano e a Diego loPez Veynte e / quatro de Sevylla e a don Diego de / GueVara e a don Pedro de toVar e a hernando / de alVarado e a juan de Çaldivar e / A Pablos de mel- gosa e a VelasCo de / barrionuevo e a los otros CaPita- / nes que Fueron a la conquista e des- / Cubrimiento de la tierra nueva de tiguex e / Çibola e las otras ProVinçias dixo / que conosçe A Todos los que le es / Preguntado Porque este testigo / Fue con ellos desde CuliaCan hasta / Çibola e quyVira e anDuVo en el / desCubrimiento e conquista de ello / [no number]

[fol. 83r]

896

Hasta que VolVieron / Fue Preguntado Sy vio que desde Cu- / lyaCan hasta Çibola todos los Pueblos / e ProVinçias Por donde Pasaron sa- / lyeron de Paz e dieron la obediençia / A su magestad e al exerçito los man- / thenymyentos que ellos te- / nyan dixo que sabe la PregunTa / Como en ella Se contiene Porque / lo Vio eçe(b)pto que no sabe que diesen / bastymentos Porque no los tenyan / Antes el general les (f)hazia dar de / los ResCates que llevava e Por- / que no quedasen esCandaliçados / e hallaSen la gente que Atras que- / daba

que (h)era la mayor P*a*rte en ellos / buen acoximyento / Fue PregunTado Sy
Por los d*i*chos / Pueblos el d*i*cho General CAPitan / y esPañoles que *e*n el
exerçito / Yban hiziesen A algunos de los / naturales algunas crueldad*e*s / o
malostratamyentos e sy sabye*n*- / dolo el d*i*cho General Sy lo CAs- / Tigo e
desymulo Dixo que no s*A*be / que el d*i*cho General ny algunos d*e* los / CaP-
itanes e gente hiziesen nyng*u*n(d) / maltratamyento a*n*tes sabe

[fol. 83v]
que yban tan rrecAtados en hazer- / les todo rregalo e buen tratamyento /
que no Vio que honbre se quexaSe / e Vio que como d*i*cho tiene les Daban /
de los Rescates e buxerias que(e) / lleVaban Con que queDaban muy con-
te*n*tos / Fue Pregunt*a*do Pues Dize que en el / d*i*cho Viaje no se les hizo mal-
trata- / myento en los d*i*chos Pueblos que / Fue la Causa que el Valle de
señora / e otros comarCAnos se Rebelaron / d*i*xo que no lo sabe mas De
*h*aber / oydo dezir PubliCamente q*ue* / Por malostratamyentos que / les hizo
un alCaraz que dexo Por / Tenyente en el d*i*cho Pueblo mel- / chior Diaz al
qual mataron los / mesmos yndios Con otros *e*spañoles / Fue Pregunt*a*do Sy
en la toma de / Çibola el d*i*cho Franc*i*sco Vazquez o Al- / Gunos de los
*e*spañoles o Ca- / Pitanes hizieron Alguna cru- / eldad o notable mal-
tratamye*n*to / a los naturales de la d*i*cha P*r*oVinçia / d*i*xo que lo que PaSsA
ÇerCa / de lo Conthenido en esta Pregunta / es que lleGados A treS leguas
/ [no number]

[fol. 84r]
897
D*e* Çibola Vinyeron Al d*i*cho General con el q*ua*l / Yba *e*ste t*e*st*i*go e hasta
Çien(t) honbres de / Caballo e de Pie (f)*h*asta treynta yndios / Con comyda
que anDuvieron myranDo el / exerçito como honbres que Venyan A / Ver
que gente (h)era la qual Venya / en el rreal y que orden trayan e lle- / Gados
adonde *h*abyan de dormyr halla- / ron que se *h*Abian ydo Todos los / d*i*chos
ynDios y el d*i*cho General manDo / A don garçi*a* loPez maesTre de CAnpo
/ que Fuese A descubrir e a Ver sy *h*abia / Algun(d) Paso Peligroso el q*ua*l Fue
/ Con hasta Veynte honbres de Caballo / e dio Relaçion de Un Paso Peli-

groSo / que *h*abya en Unas Peñas y el d*i*cho Gene- / ral le ma*n*do que lo
VolViese a tomar / el d*i*cho Paso e durmyese *e*n el e se / VelaSen Porque no
los tomasen / d*es*Cuydados e que sy algo le aCAes- / ÇieSe Se lo hiziese luego
saber / e *h*abyendo Vuelto e tomado el d*i*cho / PaSo Rindiendo el quarto d*e*
la / Prim*er*a dieron en el d*i*cho don garÇi*a* / loPez e gente que consygo tenya
/ e *h*abyendo CAbalgado arremetyo / A ellos que segun(d) dezian

[fol. 84v]
Serian has*T*a çien honbres e los deSba- / rato e hecho saberlo susçedydo Al
ge- / neral Camyno todo el Real en Amanes- / çiendo hazia Çibola e lleganDo çerCA / de Çibola A un tiro de ballesta Vio q*ue* / Salyeron hasta
quatro çientos honbres / de guerra Con arCos e flechas e sus ma- / çetas e
*h*abyendoles DaDo A entenDer / Por señas e Por lengua que lle- / Vaban del
Valle de los coraçones / que no yban a hazerles daño sino A / Ser sus Amygos
e anPararlos de / quyen mal les quysieSe hazer / y a enseñarlos A que
conosçiesen / A dios los d*i*chos yndios no lo quysieron / oyr ny Venyr de Paz
Puesto que Por / doS o tres Vezes Se les rrequerio / Por a*n*te es*cri*vano e Por
los Reli- / Giosos que alli yban antes los d*i*chos / Yndios hazian Rayas Para
que / no Pasasen de alli el exerçito e (h)e- / chaban tierra en Alto e flecharon
/ Un Caballo del es*cri*vano e dieron un / Flechazo a un Fray danyel e Visto
este / el general con todo el exerçito Ron- / Pio en ellos e alanzearon hasta /
quarenta honbres e llegados Al / [no number]

[fol. 85r]
898
Pueblo el general ma*n*do que no se siguie- / Sen ny hizieSen mal A los que
no / *h*Abian PoDido *en*trar e a los que hu- / Yesen que no *los s*iguiesen e los
dexa- / Sen yr en Paz e desPues que / Se *h*obieron acoxido se les tornaron /
A hazer los mesmos Requyrimi*ento*s / e visto que no AProVechaba el / d*i*cho
General mando que se conbatieSe / el Pueblo e como Fue el Primero q*ue* /
*en*tro con gran coPia de PieDras que / de lo alto le (h)echaron le deRibaron
/ e le *h*obieron muerto Syno se (h)echa- / ran Sobre çiertos CAPita*nes* que /
lo saCaron herido en las narizes e en una / Pierna e magullado toda la CArne

/ e estuVo Syn sentydo mas de tres / *h*oras e como començaron a conba- / Tyr
el Pueblo los yndios se desCol- / Garon Por otra Parte e *h*abyendole dado /
Rela*ç*ion que los yndios Se yban / Porque ya *h*abia Vuelto en su / ACuerdo
ma*n*do que los dexasen yr / Sin les hazer daño alguno e (h)idos / Se entro el
Pueblo donde se hallo / Gran(d) coPia de bastymento e de(n)*s*de / A Pocos
dias ansi los yndios del

[fol. 85v]
d*i*cho Pueblo que se *h*abian huido como los / otros Syete Pueblos Vinyeron
de / Paz e truxeron PreSentes d*e* las / Cosas que ellos tenyan Al general / el
qual les hizo buen acogimyento / e les dio de los rreSCates que lle- / Vaba e
que syen*p*re Todos los / Pueblos de la d*i*cha ProVin*ç*ia estu- / Vieron de Paz
no sabe Si Por / temor de Castigo que se les *h*Abia / (f)*h*ecbo o Por el buen
tratamy*ent*o que se les / (F)*h*azia / Fue Pregunt*a*do Sy sabe que *e*stan- / do el
d*i*cho General y exer*ç*ito *en* / *Ç*ibola Vinyeron ynDios Prin*Ç*ip*a*l*e*s / de la
P*ro*Vin*Ç*ia de *ç*icuyque / A dar la obedien*ç*ia e oFre*ç*erse / Por amygos Al
d*i*cho General e ans*i*- / mesmo los yndios de la ProVin- / *ç*ia de tiguex dixo
que sabe e / Vio que Vinyeron hasta veynte yn- / dios A dar la d*i*cha obedi-
en*Ç*ia e a / ofre*ç*er(e)Se Por amygos e que entre / ellos Venya un yndio
Prin*ç*iPal / que dezian s*er* de *ç*ycuyque que / Pusyeron nonbre bigotes e a otro
/ que llamaban el CA*ç*ique e *h*abyendo- / i

[fol. 86r]
899
Los R*es*Ç*ibido e dado de los ResCates q*ue* / llevaba e aGrades*ç*ido Su venyda
/ YnVio con ellos a Ver sus Pueblos / e d*es*Cubrir la tierra A hern*an*do / de
alVarado con veynte de a CAballo / el q*ual* oyo que *h*Abia ydo e que el / d*i*cho
bigotes les (f)*h*azia salir todos los / Pueblos de Paz e darles comyda / Cueros
e RoPa e oyo dezir que / el d*i*cho bigotes Se q*u*edo en *ç*iqui- / que e les Dio
Para que los Guia- / Sen el Camino e derrota que que- / rian llevar A dos
yndios que / Al uno Pusyeron Turco e al otro / ysoPete que el bigotes Dezia
ser / Sus esClavos e que el uno dezian que / (h)era de quyVira y el otro de
arahe / e que en el CAmyno les Dixo el d*i*cho / Yndio llamado turco dezia

q*ue* / Sabia una tierra jornada de / Treynta dias RicA de oro e de / Plata e abundosa de todas las / Cosas e que *h*abia traydo de *e*lla / Çierto brazalete e otras cosas las / quales le *h*Abia tomado el d*i*cho / Yndio llamado bigotes e que / VolVyendo del d*i*cho desCubrimyento

[fol. 86v]
lleVo consigo A Tiguex Donde ya *e*sta- / ba APoSent*a*do el general al d*i*cho / bigotes e Turco e ysoPete e Porque / el d*i*cho *b*igotes no concordaba con lo q*ue* / dezia el d*i*cho turco e negaba tener los / d*i*chos (P) brazalete y joyas oyo d*e*cir / que le *h*abian APerreado y este / t*e*stigo le vio DesPues morDido en una / Pierna e Fue Pu*b*lico e notorio que / le *h*Abian (f)*echado l*os Perros / Fue Pregunt*a*do quyen e Por cuyo ma*n*- / dado le *h*abian (h)echado los d*i*chos Pe- / rros dixo que oyo d*e*cir que don g*a*rc*i*a / loPez e don P*edr*o de tovar Se los / *h*Abian (h)echado / Fue Pregunt*a*do que Fue la Causa Por / que la d*i*cha ProVinçia de çicuy- / que e tiguex se torno a Rebelar Sy / Fue Por aPerrear Al d*i*cho bigotes e Por / otras Crueldades e malostrata- / myentos que les *h*obiesen (f)*h*echo d*i*xo q*ue* / *e*stando la mucha Parte d*e* la gente / del rreal desnuda e PaDeçiendo / mucho Frio Por ser en el mes de / dizienbre Para rre- mediarse el / General ma*n*do a don Garç*i*a loPez / que Fuese a los Pueblos A Pedyr Al- / ii

[fol. 87r]
900
Guna RoPa el qual truxo hasta (^Veynt) nove*n*- / ta o çien Pyeças con que se rremedia- / ron los que estaban desnudos E / que otro dia Amanesçieron flecha- / dos treynta o quarenta CAballos / que andaban en el CAnPo e muertos / e AP*e*rreados quatro o çinco yn- / dios mexicanos e alzada e Rebela- / da toda(s) la ProVinçia de Tiguex e / Recoxidos todos en doS Pueblos e / que cree que se moVieron a hazer / la d*i*cha rrebelion Por la rroPa / que el general ma*n*do rrecoxer / de los d*i*chos Pueblos e que el Pu*e*b*l*o / de çiquyque Ansymesmo Se / Rebelo e los otros Pueblos / de la d*i*cha Pr*o*Vinçia no Para darles / Guerra Syno Para no darles basti- / mento ny otra cosa alguna / Fue Pregunt*a*do si cree o sabe que los / de la d*i*cha Pr*o*Vinçia de

çiCuyque / Se alzaron Por *h*aber Preso e aPe- / Reado al d*i*cho bigotes e
CAçique / d*i*xo que no lo sabe / Fue Pregunt*a*do que Pues doS Pueblos / d*e*
la d*i*cha ProVinçia de TigueX se

[fol. 87v]
Hizieron Fuertes y en deFensa que Porq*ue* / quemaron otros doze que
quedaron / desma*n*Parados d*i*xo que no Se que- / maron sino nueVe e que
aquellos los / quemaron Por ma*n*dado de gove*r*nador / Franc*i*sco Vazquez que
(h)era general / Porque los de adelante esCarme*n*- / tasen e Por CAstigar a
los de los d*i*chos / Pueblos que se *h*Abian enCAstilla- / do en los otros dos e
que no se que- / maron del Todo salvo Parte Porq*ue* / Aunque los querian
quemar no Po- / dian ny querian arder / Fue Pregunt*a*do si antes que se con-
batie- / Sen los dos Pueblos que estaban / Alzados Sy los Requyrieron que /
Se diesen de Paz y que cruelda- / des e notables malostratamyentos / e
quemas e aPerreamyentos que hi- / zieron A los d*i*chos yndios d*i*xo que / lo
que Sabe es que Por tres Vezes / Fueron Requeridos que se diese*n* / de Paz e
que los Perdonarian / e harian todo buen tratamyento / e Jamas quysieron
a*n*tes Procuraron / de matar a don garç*i*a loPez e A / iii

[fol. 88r]
901
los otros mensajeros que les Fueron / A rrequerir e Visto *e*sto les dieron / Conbate e que no Vio el çerco donde / el d*i*cho Franc*i*sco vazquez estaba que Se /
hiziese Crueldad Alguna ny se aPerre- / Ase ny quemase nyngun(d) yndio e
qu*e* / Vio que el d*i*cho Franc*i*sco Vazquez ma*n*do / A este t*e*stigo que madru-
gaSe e amanes- / ÇieSe en el rreal donde el d*i*cho garç*i*a / loPez estaba e le
dixese que no alçaSe / el çerco h(i)*a*sta tomar el Pueblo e / que Fuese con el
menos daño que / Pudiese de los yndios e que / Tomadose estuviese quedo el
rreal / e el Saliese A Verse con el A el Pue- / b*l*o de la *a*lameda que *e*staba entre
los / doS Reales e llegado *e*ste t*e*stigo / Al Real donde don garç*i*a lo- / Pez *e*staba
Vio que el Pueblo (h)ar- / dia e que los eSPañoles *e*sta- / ban ya dentro en
algunas Casas / e dentro en una tienda tenyan Pre- / sos hasta treynta yndios
de los qu*e* / *h*Abyan tomado dentro del Pueblo / e *h*abyendo d*i*cho a lo que yba

[fol. 88v]

e queriendose VolVer el dicho Don garçia / loPez le dixo que esPerase hasta /
Ver el Fyn el qual lo hizo ansi e Vio que / quatro o çinco yndios que estaban
en una / casa hizieron seña de Paz al dicho don garçia / loPez e que Se querian
Dar y el dicho / don garçia loPez dixo que byen que / Saliesen e que Ansy
salieron los / quatro yndios Por una ventana / e habyendoles (h)echado el uno
de ellos / Al dicho don garçia loPez Una manTa / ençima que entre ellos es
señal de Paz / Y el dicho don garçia loPez los mando tomar / Y meter en la
dicha Tienda con los / demas que en ella estaban / e syn hazer mas Resistençia
los espa- / noles entraron en el dicho Pueblo / e Casas e saCAron otra
CAntydad de / Yndios E los metieron en la dicha / Tienda e de(n)sde a Poco
Vio que / Sacaron (f)hasta Veynte o Veyn- / te e quatro yndios e los ata- / ron
A Unos Palos e los quema- / ron ViVos e Vio que uno de los que / quemaban
Se le quemo la Cuerda / con que tenya atadas las manos / iiii

[fol. 89r]

902

E medio quemado Un lado con un / Palo que tomo de la leña con / que le
quemaban arremetyo / A los que eStaban Alrededor e les / dio quatro o çinco
Palos e se Vol- / Vio de Su voluntad a VolVer Al / Fuego donde se aCavo de
quemar / e Visto los que quedaban en la / Tienda lo que (f)hazian A sus Con-
/ Pañeros Se alçaron e hizie- / ron Fuertes en ella e a un medio / mataron A
Un (h)arriero y de alli / Vio que los mataron A todos / A lançadas y esto-
CAdas que no quedo / nynguno / Fue Preguntado Sy se hallo Presente / A
la dicha justiçia e quema e toma de / dicho Pueblo los dichos yndios turco / e
ySoPete e Sy sabe que los enVio / el general alla Para que Viesen la / Justiçia
e Por mandado del general / Dixo que no sabe si se hizo / Por su mandado e
consenty- / myento Pero que le Pareze que / Se hallaron Presentes El dicho /
Turco e ysoPete

[fol. 89v]

Fue Preguntado quyen mato Al ynDyo / llamado turco e Por cuyo mandado
e / Sy le mato dixo que el dicho / Yndio le mataron Por mandado / del dicho

Francisco Vazquez Por- / que los *h*abia llevado *e*ngañados / e Puso muchas *veces en* condiçion todo el / Real de PerderSe y el mesmo / ConFeso que los *h*abia llevado Por / muchos Rodeos Porque se PerDieSe / Y Porque el d*i*cho General tuVo / Ynform*aci*on que tenya Tratado / Con los de quyVi(^Vi)ra que los ma- / tasen e que no diesen mayz P*ara* / los Caballos / Fue Preguntado que otras cruel- / dades e malostratamyentos hizo / el d*i*cho Franc*i*sco Vazquez o algunos / de los CAPitanes e gente e q*ue* / Sabyendolo disimulo d(e)*i*xo / que no vy(d)o que el d*i*cho Franc*i*sco / Vazquez ny los CAPitanes y / gen(erales)*te* hiziesen nyngunos / malostratamyentos e que *e*sto / es lo que sabe ÇerCA de lo que le / v

[fol. 90r]

903

*e*s Pregunt*a*do Para el Juramento que / (F)*h*yzo e Fyrmolo de su nonbre e Fue le / Tornado a leer *e*sta su d*i*cha luego / Como lo aCavo De d*e*cir e RetiFycose / en el e Fyrmolo el d*i*cho Señor oydor / el l*i*Çenc*ia*do tejada P*edr*o de ledesma

Chapter 14

Juan de Zaldívar,
the Twelfth de Oficio Witness

A Captain

Juan de Zaldívar was a member of the powerful Oñate-Zaldívar clan and nephew of Vázquez de Coronado's lieutenant governor in Nueva Galicia, Cristóbal de Oñate.[1] The lieutenant governor later became son-in-law to Viceroy Mendoza. Like the other Zaldívars and Oñates, Juan was a Basque, perhaps a native of Vitoria in Spain.[2]

According to his own statement, Zaldívar had gone to Nueva Galicia in 1533.[3] When Vázquez de Coronado arrived there as governor in 1538, he appointed new regidores for Guadalajara, including Zaldívar.[4] He continued in the post of *alcalde ordinario* until at least 1565.[5] In the following year three of his fellow regidores supported his claims of merit as he sought to secure license from the king to lead a conquest in the Philippines. At the time he was very wealthy and, with his wife doña Marina de Mendoza and their eight children, maintained one of most important households in the province, in his own estimation. He was encomendero of the pueblo of Cuistlán northeast of Guadalajara, and owned mines, grain fields, farms, slaves, estancias, and caballerías.[6] The title of adelantado that he sought was not forthcoming, and he died around 1570 without having mounted the ambitious expedition to the Far East.[7]

On the heels of the return of fray Marcos de Niza from Tierra Nueva in late summer 1539, Zaldívar and Melchor Díaz were dispatched northward with a company of men to verify the friar's report. After delivering a discouraging account of that reconnaissance to Vázquez de Coronado, Zaldívar journeyed south to apprise the viceroy of the same disappointing news in Colima. Mendoza then sent orders to the captain general with Zaldívar to the effect that the main body of the expedition should not move forward until a small party had been able to reach Cíbola and learn whether it lived up to Marcos's descriptions. Though he hurried back northward by ship, Zaldívar arrived in Culiacán too late to relay the viceroy's message, since Vázquez de Coronado had already gone ahead.

The captain general had left instructions that Zaldívar was to be assigned a company of horsemen as a captain, if he wanted to join the expedition. Zaldívar chose to assume the office of captain and was present for the remainder of the expedition. In his company went fellow witness in the 1544 investigation Melchior Pérez, who, years later, testified to Zaldívar's worthiness for royal preferment. While in Tierra Nueva, Zaldívar was present at the siege of Pueblo del Arenal, though because of a severe wound he did not see Indians tied to stakes and burned after the fighting. He also went to Quivira and testified that he heard El Turco confess to having willfully misled the expedition and having conspired to kill the captain general and his men.

According to his son's estimate, Zaldívar returned from Tierra Nueva in debt for 5,000 to 6,000 pesos because of expenditures incurred in going on the expedition.[8] Within days of returning from Tierra Nueva he assembled a fighting force and went with Vázquez de Coronado to put down an uprising of the Tecoxquines near Compostela. He also participated in a number of other punitive expeditions against the Indians of Nueva Galicia, both before and after the journey to Tierra Nueva.[9]

As a witness before licenciado Tejada in Guadalajara August 22, 1544, he gave very brief answers, all to the effect that the Spaniards were completely justified in doing what they did in Tierra Nueva. This might be expected from the only one of Vázquez de Coronado's ten captains to be questioned by the pesquisador. Zaldívar volunteered a minimum of additional information (to show that he was not present at the burning of Indians, for instance), and made many statements serving to exonerate Vázquez de Coronado. He offered damaging testimony about López de Cárdenas, to the effect that the maestre de campo had ordered Indians burned and that he himself had seen the remains of the victims. He testified further that at Pueblo del Cerco Tiguex prisoners had been set upon by dogs, and their hands had been cut off by order of the captain general. On the whole, though, Zaldívar side-stepped most issues in the questions he was asked while portraying an expedition conducted according to accepted standards. What brutality Zaldívar acknowledged as committed by the expedition he explained as the normal outcome of warfare.

FIGURE 11.
Cutting off the hands of an Indian captive, after the *Florentine Codex*

A TRANSLATION
OF THE TESTIMONY

Twelfth de Oficio Witness (Juan de Zaldívar)[10]

[90r cont'd] After the aforesaid in the city of Guadalajara on the twenty-second day of the month of August in the year one thousand five hundred and forty-four, the lord judge licenciado Tejada had Juan de Zaldívar, a citizen of the city of Guadalajara, appear [before him] for this investigation, and he received his oath in legal form. By God [and] Santa María, and making a sign of the cross, he promised to tell and state the truth. Under this obligation he was asked the following questions.

{*1*} He was asked whether he knows Francisco Vázquez de Coronado, don García López de Cárdenas, [90v] don Tristán de Arellano, the councilman of Sevilla Diego López , don Diego de Guevara, don Pedro de Tovar, Hernando de Alvarado, Pablos de Melgosa, Velasco de Barrionuevo, and the other captains who went to explore and subjugate the tierra nueva of Tiguex, Cíbola, and the other provinces. He answered that he knows all of those about whom he is asked because the witness went on that expedition as a captain from the time they left this province until they returned here. And he participated in the subjugation and reconnaissance of [all of][11] that land together with the general and those captains who went there.

{*2*} [The witness] was asked whether he saw that from Culiacán to Cíbola [the people of] all the territory they went through and all the towns and provinces they passed came out in peace and rendered obedience to His Majesty and to his captains in his royal name. And did they give the army and the people [91r] the food they had and that the people needed? He answered that he knows that [the people of] all of the towns and provinces between Culiacán and Cíbola came out in peace and rendered obedience to His Majesty and to his captains in his royal name. That is because the witness, as captain with sixteen horsemen, scouted the land ahead until Chichitequecale, which is about seventy leagues before Cíbola. When he had scouted to there and obtained information about what was ahead, he returned to Colima (which is in this province of Nueva España and under the jurisdiction of Mexico City), where the viceroy of Nueva España was. By his order, the witness went to give him a report of what he had seen and what he had been told about what was ahead. He told the viceroy that he had not passed beyond Chichitequecale because it was very cold and they had been told that because of deep snow he and his men could not get through.

[91v] Since Francisco Vázquez and the army were already going forward across the uninhabited land between Culiacán and Compostela, the viceroy ordered the witness to deliver some letters to the general. In the letters he wrote that the army was not to continue on. Instead, the general was first to send a captain to reconnoiter as far as Cíbola and to learn what it was. Therefore the witness went to Compostela, since the viceroy told him to go by sea, in order to get to Culiacán more quickly. He embarked on a ship, and when he arrived at Culiacán Francisco Vázquez had already gone ahead eight days before with about eighty men. The witness saw that he could not succeed in delivering the letters since the general was eight days ahead of him.

He found his own company there and orders from the general to take the men who were in his command and proceed with the army, which was commanded by don Tristán de Arellano as general. They were to go as far as Cíbola, [92r] where Francisco Vázquez would be. So, the witness went with the army and saw that all the people and provinces came out in peace. They did not, however, supply provisions, since until they reached Corazones each person carried what he needed. And there they bought supplies [for the trip] to Cíbola. He does not know whether the other captains received provisions along the way, but the witness did not and he did not see others get any. All of them were on the lookout, so that no one would do injury to the natives or steal supplies or other things.

{3} He was asked whether the general, captains, or Spaniards who went in the army committed any brutality or outrages against natives of the towns through which they passed. And if the general was aware that any of them did so, did he punish them? He stated in answer that he knows that the general and his [92v] captains and men treated the natives of the land very well and did not permit anyone to hurt them. If any Indian complained about a Spaniard or an ally (even when it was without cause), they reprimanded and punished him, so that the natives would see that [the Spaniards] were not harming them and did not want them to be harmed. When the Indians gave anything voluntarily, [the Spaniards] paid them for it.

{4} Since he says that during the journey outrages were not committed in those towns, what caused the [people of the] valley of Señora and others in the vicinity to rebel and rise up in arms? [In reply] he said that when don Tristán de Arellano, this witness, the other captains, and the army departed from the valley of Corazones and Señora, don Tristán left a number of Spaniards there. And he left Melchor Díaz as their captain. Afterwards, when the witness was in Tiguex, he heard it said that Díaz had died and had [93r] left a [man named] Alcaraz in charge. He heard that the Indians had rebelled because Alcaraz had committed some outrages or permitted others to commit them, but the witness does not know what the outrages were.

{5} He was asked [next] whether, during the capture of Cíbola, Francisco Vázquez or any of the Spaniards or captains committed any brutality or significant outrages against the natives of that province. He answered that he does not know because when he and the other captains arrived at Cíbola, it was already at peace and the Spaniards and General Francisco Vázquez were inside. He heard it said that the Indians of Cíbola had come out in war and that [the Spaniards] had several clashes with them before they were subdued.

{6} [Zaldívar] was [then] asked whether he knows that while the general and the army were in [93v] Cíbola Indian principales came from the province of Cicuique to render obedience to His Majesty and to offer themselves as allies. And did the Indians of the province of Tiguex do likewise? He replied, regarding what is referred to in the question, that he heard it said publicly when he arrived at Cíbola. Because he and his men had not gotten to Cíbola when those Indians came, he did not see it.

{7} He was asked who brought the Indian called Turco and Ysopete, Bigotes, and the cacique from Cicuique to Tiguex as prisoners. He replied that when he arrived at Cíbola he was told that Hernando de Alvarado had gone to reconnoiter and see the land that was there with a number of men and some Indians who had come from Cicuique. The army with Francisco Vázquez traveled in two units to Tiguex. When they had arrived there, Alvarado came, [94r] bringing with him an Indian whom [the Spaniards] called Turco. Alvarado let it be known that the Indian he brought with him said that there was much gold and silver in Quivira, and houses of mortared cut stone and very good land. He also said that there was gold at Cicuique, which was the pueblo that Bigotes was from.

As a consequence, Alvarado went to Cicuique, by the general's order, to learn whether what El Turco said was true. When he returned he brought a string of gold [beads] like pieces of an ingot. And he brought Bigotes and the cacique as prisoners. [The witness] heard it said publicly (though he does not remember by whom, unless it was by Bigotes) that Hernando de Alvarado had set a dog on Bigotes and that the dog had bitten him in the thigh. And [Bigotes] showed him the bite.

{8} [The witness] was [then] asked to say why they had set the dog on Bigotes and by whose order it was done. He answered that [94v] [he had heard it said that][12] it was done because Bigotes would not tell and confirm what El Turco was saying about there being gold in his land, but he does not know who ordered it.

{9} [Zaldívar] was asked for what reason [the Indians in] the provinces of Tiguex and Cicuique reversed themselves and rebelled. Was it because of the dog being set on Bigotes or because of other cruelty and outrages that [the Spaniards] had committed against them? He said that he knew of no reason why the Indians of Tiguex and Cicuique rose up in arms, unless it was because [the Spaniards] asked them for the gold that was in their land, but from what the witness knows, no outrages were committed against them whatsoever. Rather he knows that, before they rose up, [the Spaniards] had entered by the Indians' permission and consent.

{10} He was asked to state whether [95r] Bigotes had already been set upon by dogs and the cacique, Turco, and Ysopete had been held as prisoners, when the Indians of Cicuique and Tiguex rose up in arms. He answered that it is true that the pueblos of Tiguex and Cicuique rose up and rebelled after he heard that Bigotes had been bitten, and Cicuique had rebelled after [the Spaniards] released the cacique and Bigotes .

{*11*} [The witness] was asked why, since only two pueblos in that province rebelled and fortified and defended themselves, [the Spaniards] burned another twelve that [the Indians] had left abandoned. He replied that he does not remember that more than one of the deserted pueblos was burned. He thinks that don Rodrigo Maldonado burned it because in it [the Spaniards] found many horses shot with arrows and eaten. [95v] The rest they dismantled because of the need they had for firewood, since it was winter, the snow was very deep, and the mountains were far away. Besides, they did not dare to go to the mountains for fear of their enemies and the deep snow.

{*12*} He was asked, regarding the pueblos [the Spaniards] burned and laid waste, whether it was done on orders from Francisco Vázquez. He said that he does not know, but he thinks that each of them was torn down to provide insurance against the cold, which was extreme, especially for people without clothing, [as][13] everyone in the camp usually was.

{*13*} [Zaldívar] was asked whether [the Spaniards] had summoned [the Indians] to offer peace and told them that they would be pardoned, before they attacked the two pueblos that had risen up and where the people were gathered and had fortified themselves. He said that he knows that before they joined combat, [96r] he saw the general send [individuals] to them to deliver the requerimiento and to tell [the Indians] that if they came in peace, he would pardon their rebellion and uprising. Further, he knows that [the Indians] were never willing to do so.

{*14*} He was [then] asked what brutality and outrages, burnings and unleashing of dogs against Indians, he saw committed during the siege and capture of the [two][14] pueblos. And were they done with the permission and by the order of Francisco Vázquez? He answered that he went, at Francisco Vázquez's command, with don García López to one of the two pueblos to lay siege to it. Because [the Indians there] refused to come to peace, although they were summoned many times, [the Spaniards] made war and, using ladders, reached the flat roofs. When the witness entered one of the rooms to help don Lope de Urrea and another soldier, whom [the Indians] had surrounded and were trying to kill, he received three arrow wounds, [96v] one on the nose and two others in the temple and on his head. Because of this he was gravely wounded and very ill after the battle concluded. When they had captured the pueblo he withdrew to a building outside of it and next to his tent. Therefore he could not see whether any brutality was committed afterwards nor by whose order it might have been done. While they were offering battle he did not see that any brutality was committed, other than that they fought with each other. He knows that more than [seventy]¹⁵ Spaniards [and their]¹⁶ allies came out of the fight wounded.

{15} [The witness] was asked whether he knows or saw or heard it said that the Indians who had fortified themselves and retreated to some houses after the pueblo was occupied made signs to don García López to the effect that they would offer peace, if [the Spaniards] assured them that they would not be harmed and that their [97r] lives would be spared. Did don García López promise that and, with that assurance, did eighty or a hundred of them come out of the pueblo in peace and unarmed, this being outside the pueblo where the maestre de campo don García López had his camp? He answered that he knows and saw nothing of what is referred to in the question because, as he has said and declared, since he was so ill and sorely wounded, when the battle was over [the Spaniards] got him to take shelter in the house and he remained inside.

{16} [Next] he was asked whether he knows that, the next day, eighty or a hundred of the Indians who came out to don García López in peace or who were brought out of their houses after the pueblo had been captured were put in don García López's tent. [In answer] he said that he neither knows nor saw what is referred to in the question. But he heard that a number of Indians who were captured and brought out of the houses [97v] were put in García López's tent.

{17} He was asked [further] whether [he knows]¹⁷ that as many as forty of those Indians were taken from the tent and tied to some posts. And did [the Spaniards] burn them alive? He replied that he does not know that they were taken out and burned. He had heard his companions say, however, that, by order of don García López (who was there), and next to his tent, a number of the Indians who were in the tent were taken out, and [the Spaniards] tied them to some posts, and they were burned (he does not remember whether [it was said they were][18] alive or dead). Within a month or so, when the witness had gotten out of bed and returned to health, he saw burned human bones at the place where the burning had been done. In the witness's opinion these were from six persons.

{18} [Then] he was asked whether he knows that [the Spaniards] lanced and killed the Indians who remained in the tent and who ordered them killed. He answered that he does not know and did not see what is referred to in the question. But he heard it said that the Indians had risen up [98r] and that some had been lanced in the tent. Others were taken out of the tent, let loose, and then lanced. He thinks that this was done by order of don García López, since, as maestre de campo, everyone obeyed him, and he was present.

{19} [Zaldívar] was asked whether he knows that, before he administered this punishment, don García sent [messengers] to notify Francisco Vázquez de Coronado of it and that the general ordered that what was done be done. So that they would see the burning and punishment carried out and would spread the word throughout their land about the extreme measures [the Spaniards] employed, did Francisco Vázquez order the Indian called Turco and the one called Ysopete to be sent to where the burning would occur? And were they present to see the burning done and justice administered? He stated that he does not know what is referred to in the question.

{20} He was asked whether he knows that at the pueblo besieged by Francisco Vázquez de Coronado, after [98v] it had been overrun and occupied, many Indians were burned, set upon by dogs, and lanced. And did these include Indians who had been pulled from their houses after the capture and occupation and those who had come out of the pueblo unarmed because of the hunger and thirst they were suffering? The witness said that he did not see this, but has heard it said that some Indians were set upon by dogs and had their hands cut off. And these were from among those who had been captured by force.

{*21*} He was asked what other cruelty and outrages he may have seen committed by the general, captains, and other Spaniards during the expedition. He answered that he is not aware of [such things]. On the contrary, he knows that during the entire expedition Francisco Vázquez was always watchful and very vigilant to be sure that the natives of that province not be harmed or subjected to any brutality or outrage whatsoever. [Further,] he harshly punished those who committed such acts.

{*22*} [The witness] was [then] asked who killed the Indian called Turco and for what [99r] justification and reason. He answered that the maestre de campo Diego López killed him by order of Francisco Vázquez because it was learned that Turco had conspired with [the Indians] of Quivira, showing them the horses that were good for battle and those that were weak, so that they could kill the good ones, in order to kill the Spaniards. And also because El Turco caused the company to be lost, led it by long and time-consuming roundabout ways, put it in many situations where it could be lost, and led [the Spaniards] deceitfully from one place to another, so that they would die and perish from hunger. In the presence of this witness, the Indian Turco himself acknowledged this, through the translation of Ysopete and by clear signs. By these he said and made it understood that he had been held as a slave at Cicuique, and in order to go to his land, he had told the lies he had and had led the company [by roundabout ways][19] into so much danger. And he had done it also because Bigotes and the cacique of Cicuique had directed him to lead [the Spaniards] by way of a place where they would not have water or food, so that everyone would die.

He said that this is the truth and what he knows concerning this case, [99v] in accordance with the oath that he swore. He read again what he had said as soon as he had finished speaking and he confirmed it. And he signed his name. Licenciado Tejada [signed].[20]

Juan de Zaldívar

A TRANSCRIPT
OF THE TESTIMONY

[fol. 90r cont'd][21]

E desPues de lo susodicho en la dicha / ÇiUdad de guadalajara Veynte e / dos dias del mes de agosto del dicho / Ano de myll e quynyentos e quaren- / Ta e quatro años el dicho señor / liÇenciado tejada oydor Para ynFor- / maçion de lo susodicho (f)hyzo Pa- / resçer a Juan de Çaldivar Vezino / de la ÇiUdad de guadalajara / del qual Fue rresçibido juramento / en forma de derecho Por dios e Por / Santa maria e Por una se- / ñal de la cruz Prometyo de decir / e aclarar verdad so CArgo del qual / se le hizieron las Preguntas siguientes / Fue Preguntado Sy conosçe A / Francisco Vazquez de Coronado e a don / Garçia loPez de Cardenas e a

[fol. 90v]

Don trisTan de arellano e a diego / loPez veynte e quatro De sevylla / e a don diego de GueVara e a don / Pedro de tovar e a Fernando de al- / varado e a Pablos de melgosa e a / VelasCo de barrionueVo e a los / otros CaPitanes que Fueron A la / Conquista e desCubrimyento / de la tierra nueva de tiguex e / Çibola e las otras ProVinçias dixo / que conosçe A todos los que le es / Preguntado Porque este testigo / Fue Por CAPitan en la dicha jornada / desde que salieron de esta ProVin- / çia e VolVieron a ella conquisTan- / do e desCubriendo la dicha Tierra / juntamente con los dichos CaPita- / nes e general e que a ella Fueron / Fue Preguntado Sy Vio que de(e)sde / quliaCan hasta çibola toda la tierra / Por donde (^v)Fueron e Pueblos e / ProVinçias que Pasaron si / salieron de Paz e dyeron (^que) / la obediençia a su magestad / e a sus CaPitanes en su rreal / nonbre e al exerçito e gente / vi

[fol. 91r]

904

los mantenymientos que ellos tenyan e / hAbian menester dixo que sabe que

todos los / Pueblos e ProVinçias que *hay* desde / CuliaCan hasta Çibola
Salieron de Paz / e dieron la obediençia A Su / magestad e a Su*s* CAPitanes
en Su rreal / nonbre Porque *e*ste t*e*stigo como CaPitan / con dyez e seys honbres d*e* a CAballo / corrio la Tierra hasta llegar a chichi- / tequecale que *e*s
Sesenta leguas / Poco mas o menos *antes* çibola e quando / *e*ste t*e*stigo *h*obo
corrido hasta alli e / Tenydo notiçia de lo que *h*abia Adelan- / te VolVio a
colyma que es en esta / ProVinçia de la nueva eSPaña e / de la gov*er*naçion
de mexico donde / *e*staba el visorrey d*e e*sta nueva / esPaña Por cuyo ma*n*dado
*e*ste / T*e*stigo *h*abia ydo a darle Relaçion de lo / que *h*abia visto e de lo que
*h*Abia*n* / di*c*ho que adelante *h*abia e que / *e*ste t*e*stigo no Paso adelante Por /
los grandes F(y)rios que hazia e / Porque Fueron ynFormados / que *h*abia
grandes nyeVes e que / no Podian Pasar Y entonZes

[fol. 91v]

el di*c*ho Visorrey ma*n*do a *e*ste t*e*stigo Por- / que Franc*i*sco Vazquez y el
exerçito / yban adelanTe Por el desPoblado / de CuliaCAn e conPosTela que
lle- / Vase al di*c*ho General unas CArtas / en las quales d*i*xo que le escribia /
que no PaSAse el exerçito Syno / que ynViase Algun(d) CaPitan q*ue* /
Primero desCubriese A çibola e Su- / Piese lo que (h)era e ansy *e*ste t*e*stigo /
Fue a co*n*Postela Porque le d*i*xo el di*c*ho / Visorrey que Fuese Por la mar / Por
yr mas breve hasta culyaCAn / e *e*ste t*e*stigo se enbarco en un naVyo e /
quando llego a CuliaCAn ya el di*c*ho / Franc*i*sco Vazquez Con hasta ochenTa
/ *h*onbres yba Adelante ocho Dias / e como *e*ste t*e*stigo vi(d)o que no le / Pudo
alCAnçar Por llevarle ocho / dias de delantera e Porque *h*allo / Alli su con-
Pania e ma*n*do el general / que tomase la gente que llevaba / *en* Su conPania
e Fuese con el exer- / çito e que llevaSen Por general / A don tristan de arellano hasta / Tanto que llegasen A çibola A- / vii

[fol. 92r]

905

Donde *e*sTuviesen e Ansi Fue con el exer- / çito *e*ste t*e*stigo e Vy(d)o *c*omo toda
la / Gente e ProVinçias Salyan de / Paz Pero no les daban basTyme*n*- / tos
Porque CAda uno lleVaba / lo que *h*abia menest*er* hasta los / Corazones e ally

tomaron basTi- / mentos hasta Çibola no sabe *e*ste / t*e*stigo Sy Por el CAmyno
Alguno / de los otros CaPitanes lo rres- / Çibian Pero este T*estig*o no lo rresçi-
/ byo ny lo vi(d)o rresçebir A otros Por- / que todos llevaban muy gran Vixi-
/ lançia que nadie hiziese daño A / los naturales ny les tomaSe basti- / mentos
ny otras cosas / Fue Pregunt*a*do Sy Por los d*i*chos / Pueblos donde Fueron el
d*i*cho / General e CAPitanes e esPaño- / les que en el exerçito yban hi- / ziesen
A alguno de los naturales / Algunos malostratamyentos o cruel- / dades e que
si SuPo de algunos / de *e*llos el d*i*cho general Sy los / CAsTigo (^si sabe) dixo
que sabe / que el d*i*cho General e sus Ca-

[fol. 92v]
Pitanes Y gente trataban muy bien / A los nat*u*rales de la tierra e no con- /
Sentyan que nadie les hiziese / {ojo} / (^Guerra) daño e que si Algun(d) yndio
/ Se quexaba de algun(d) *e*sPañol / o amygo aunque Fuese Syn CAusa lo /
RePre*h*endian e Castigaban Por- / que Viesen los naturales que no / les
hazian daño ny querian que / Se les hiziese*n* e si daban Algo / d*e* Su Voluntad
se les PaGaba / Fue Pregunt*a*do Pues Dize que en el d*i*cho / Viaje no Se les
hizo maltrata- / my*e*nto en los d*i*chos Pueblos que Fue / la CaUsa Por que el
Valle de Señora / e otros comarCAnos Se Rebela- / ron e Alzaron d*i*xo que
al tienPo q*ue* / don tristan de Arellano e *e*ste / t*e*stigo e los otros CaP(P)itanes
e / *e*xerçito que Salieron del / Vall*e* de señora e corazones dexo / el d*i*cho don
tristan en ellos a çiertos / *e*sPañoles e Por CAPitan de *e*llos A / melchior diaz
e de*s*(F)Pues *e*stando / *en* tiguex oyo d*e*zir como el d*i*cho mel- / chior diaz
*h*abia muerto e que *h*abia que- / (^x) viii

[fol. 93r]
906
Dado Por el Un aLcaraz el qual oyo d*e*cir / (^e) que Porque *h*abia (f)*h*echo
algunos ma- / lostratamyentos o conSentydo / que otros los hiziesen Se /
*h*Abian Rebelado los d*i*chos yndios / no sabe *e*ste t*e*stigo que Fueron los / malostratamyentos / Fue Pregunt*a*do Sy en la toma de / Çibola el d*i*cho Franc*is*co
vazquez o Al- / Guno de los eSPañoles o CaPi- / Tanes hizieron Algunas
cruel- / dades o notables malosTratamy*en*tos / A los naturales d*e* la d*i*cha

ProVinçia / Dixo que no lo sabe Porque quando / este testigo e otros CaPitanes lle- / Garon a Çibola ya esTaba de Paz / e dentro de ella los dichos
esPañoles / Y el dicho General Francisco Vazquez / E que oyo decir que los
yn- / dios de Çibola les habian salydo / de guerra e que habian hAbydo /
çiertos Recuentros con ellos hasta / que los habia Sujetado / Fue Preguntado
Sy sabe que estando / el dicho General y exerçito En

[fol. 93v]
Çibola Vinyeron yndios PrinçiPales de la / ProVinçia de çiCuyque A dar la /
obediençia A su magestad e a oFre- / ÇerSe Por amygos e ansymesmo los /
Yndios de la ProVinçia de tiguex / dixo que lo en la Pregunta Conthe- / nydo
este testigo oyo decir PubliCa- / mente quando llego a çibola Por- / que
quando los dichos yndios Vi- / nyeron este testigo Con Su gente / no habia
llegado E Por eso no lo / Vy(d)o / Fue Preguntado que quyen Truxo A /
tyguex Preso Al yndio llamado / turco e ysoPete e CAçique e bigo- / tes de
çicuyque dixo que quando / este testigo llego A Çibola le dixeron / Como hernando de alVarado con çierta / gente yba con unos yndios que / hAbyan
venido de çicuyque A des- / Cubryr e Ver la tierra que (h)era y el / exerçito e
con el (el) dicho Francisco Vaz- / quez Fueron en dos Partes A ti- / guex e llegados A tiguex Vyno / el dicho hernando de alVarado el qual / ix

[fol. 94r]
907
Traya conSyGo un yndio que le llama- / ban turco el qual dixo que aque(e)l
/ yndio que consiGo traya dezia que / en quyVira hAbia oro e Plata en /
Gran(d) CAntydad e CAsas de CAl y / CAnto e la Tyerra muy buena e que
/ en çiCuyque hAbia oro que (h)era el / Pueblo donde bigotes (h)era natural
/ E ansy el dicho hernando de alVarado Por / mandado del General Fue A
çicuyque / A saber Sy (h)era verdad lo que / turco dezia el qual Fue e quando
Vol- / Vio traya un hilo de oro como a rriel / en Pedaços e a bigotes e al
CAçique / Presos E oyo decir Publicamente no / Se aCuerda a quyen mas de
al bigo- / tes que el hernando de alVarado / le habia (h)echado un Perro e le
habia mor- / Dydo un muslo e le mostro la / {ytem} / mordedura / Fue Pre-

guntado que / declare que Fue la Causa Por / que (h)echaron el Perro Al dicho / bigotes Por Cuyo mandado / e Por que dixo que oyo

[fol. 94v]

Dezir que Porque el Dicho bigotes no que- / ria decir ny declarar lo que turco dezia / del oro que habia en Su tierra / Pero que no sabe Por cuyo / mandado / Fue Preguntado que Fue la CAusa Por / que en la dicha ProVinçia de Ti- / guex Se torno A rrebelar / e la de çicuyque Sy Fue Por APe- / Rear Al dicho bigotes o Por otras cruel- / dades y malosTratamyentos que / les hoVieron (f)hecho dixo que no sabe / CAusa nynguna Por que los dichos yn- / dios de Tiguex e çiCuyque se / Alzasen Syno Fue Porque / Pedyan el oro que en Su tyerra hAbia / Pero que no les Fueron hechos / A lo que este Testigo sabe mal-ostra- / tamyentos Algunos antes sabe que / de su ProPia voluntad de los yn- / dios e de su conSentymiento An- / tes que se Alzasen hAbyan en- / Trado los esPañoles / Fue Preguntado que declare si quan- / x

[fol. 95r]

908

Do los dichos Yndios de çiquyque e ti- / guex se alÇAron Sy hAbian APe- / Reado a bigotes e tenyan Preso Al / caçique e al turco e ysoPete dixo / que es verdad que el dicho Pueblo / de Tiguex e çiCuyque Se alça- / ron e rrebelaron desPues que / oyo que habian mordido A bigotes / e habia çiquique Rebelado desPues / que Soltaron Al CAçique e a bi- / gotes / Fue Preguntado Pues dos Pueblos / de la dicha ProVinçia solamenTe / Se Rebelaron e hizieron Fuer- / tes e se Pusyeron en deFensA que / Por que quemaron otros doze / que dexaron desmanParados dixo / que no Tyene memoria que / se haya quemado mas de Un / Pueblo de los que dexaron de- / Syertos e que cree que le / quemo don rroDrigo maldonado / Porque en aquel Pueblo ha- / llaron muchos de los CAballos / flechados e comydos e que los

[fol. 95v]

demas los deshizieron Por la nes- / ÇeSidad que tenyan de la leña Por- / que (h)era ynVierno y nyeVes (h)eran muy / Grandes y la sierra estaba lexos / e

no osaban yr alla Por temor d*e* / los (h)enemygos e de las Grand*es* nyeves /
Fue Pregunt*a*do Sy los d*i*chos Pue- / blos que quemaron e d*e*sbara- / taron Sy
Fue Por ma*n*dado del / d*i*cho Fran*ci*sco Vazquez dixo que no lo / sabe Syno
que cree que CAda / Uno lo hazia Por guaresçerSe / el F(y)r*io* que (h)era eçe-
Sivo *e*sPeÇial / A gente que *e*staba desnuda comu*n*- / me*n*Te los *e*staban
todos los del / Real / Fue Pregunt*a*do si a*n*tes que se / Conbatiese*n* los d*i*chos
doS Pue- / blos q*ue* *e*Staban alçados y en que / *e*staba la gente rrecogida e
(F)*h*echos / Fuertes Sy les Requirie- / ron que se diesen de Paz / e que Seryan
Perdonados dixo / que sabe que a*n*tes que se / d*i*ese el Conbate el general / xi

[fol. 96r]
909
Vio que les *en*Vio A Requerir q*ue* / VinyeSen de Paz e que les Per- / Donaria
la d*i*cha Rebel(aç)ion e al- / çamyento e sabe que jamas lo / quySieron
(ff)*hace*r / Fue Pregunt*a*do que crueldad*es* e m*a*los- / Tratamyentos quemas
aPerr*e*a- / myentos de yndios Vio que Se hiziesen / en el çerco y toma de los
d*i*chos Pu*e*b*l*os / e si Se hizieron Por ma*n*dado e / Consentymy*en*to del d*i*cho
Fran*ci*sco Vaz- / quez Dixo que *e*ste T*e*st*i*go Por / ma*n*dado del d*i*cho Fran-
*ci*sco Vazquez / Fue con don garç*i*a loPez a uno de los / D*i*chos doS pueblos
A Poner sobre e*l* / el Çerco e como no quysieron Ve- / nyr de Paz aUnque
muchas / Vezes Fueron Requerydos le*s* / Dieron conbate e con esCAlas les /
Ganaron las aÇoteas y entra- / do *e*ste t*e*stigo en un aPosento / A socorrer A
don loPe de URea / e a otro soldado que los tenyan / çerCAdos y Para
matarlos die- / ron a *e*ste t*e*st*i*go tres Flecha-

[fol. 96v]
Zos Uno en la nariz e otros dos en la / Syen e en la CAbeza e Fue nesçesa- /
rio Por *e*star tan malo e Peligro- / Samente herido desPues de ACa- / bado
el Conbate e *h*aber tomado el / Pueblo Retraerse a una CAsa que / *e*staba
Fuera del Pueblo junto / a su tienda d*e* *e*ste t*e*st*i*go e Ansy no / Pudo ver Sy
d*e*sPues Se hiziero*n* / Algunas crueldades ny quyen las / ma*n*do (F)*h*azer
Porque *en* Tanto que el / Conbate dieron no Vio que se hizie- / Se crueldad
alguna mas de que / Peleaban los unos con los otros e / sabe que del d*i*cho

Conbate Salie- / ron heridos mas de Se(s)*t*enta / *es*Pañoles amygos / Fue Pregunt*a*do Sy Sabe e vio o oyo / D*ecir* que los yndios que se *h*abyan (f)*h*echo /
Fuertes e rretraydo en algunas / CaSAs desPues de *h*aber *en*trado / en el
Pueblo e hizieron Señas / Al d*i*cho don garç*i*a loPez que se / darian de Paz Si
les Aseguraban / que no les harian daño y las / xii

[fol. 97r]

910

Vydas y el d*i*cho don garç*i*a loPez se lo Pro- / metyo e con esta Confyança
salieron / de Paz e Syn Armas ochenta o / çiento de *e*llos Fuera del Pueblo A-
/ donde el d*i*cho don garç*i*a loPez maestre / de CanPo tenya el rreal d*i*xo que
no / Sabe ny Vio ny oyo cossa Alguna / de lo *en e*Sta Pregunta Co*n*tenydo
Por- / que como d*i*cho e declarado tiene / ACabado el conbate Por *e*star / tan
malo e Peligrosamente he- / rido le hizieron que se RecoxieSe / e *es*Tuviese
quedo den Tro de *l*a / d*i*cha Casa / Fue Pregunt*a*do si sabe que de los yn- /
Dios que salieron de Paz Al d*i*cho / don garç*i*a loPez o de los que saCA- / ron
d*e* sus Casas desPues de *h*aber- / Se tomado el Pueblo otro Dia / Syguyente
Se metieron *en* la / Ti*en*da de don Garç*i*a loPez *h*asta / ochenta o çien yndios
dixo que / no sabe ny Vio lo Co*n*thenydo en la Pre- / Gunta mas de *h*aber
oydo que çier- / ta CAntydad de yndios que Se / Tomaron e SaCAron de las
Casas

[fol. 97v]

e Pusieron en la tienda de don garÇia lopez / Fue Pregunt*a*do Sy d*e* la d*i*cha
tienDa sacaron / hasta quarenta de los d*i*chos yndios e los / Ataron A unos
Palos e los quemaron ViVos / D*i*xo que no Sabe que los sacasen / e quemasen
mas de que oyo dezir A / Sus ConPañeros que Por ma*n*dado / del d*i*cho don
garç*i*a loPez y *e*stando el Pre- / Sente e junto A su Tienda Se *h*abian /
SaCAdo çiertos yndios de los que en ella / *es*Taban E los *h*abian a Tado A
Unos / Palos e quemado no se aCuerda / Sy dezian ViVos o muertos e que
de(n)*s*- / de a un mes Poco mas o menos que / *e*ste t*e*stigo Se levanto e con-
Valeçio / Vy(d)o en el lugar donde se *h*abia (F)*h*echo / la quema huesos de
honbres que- / mados que A*l* Paresçer d*e* *e*ste t*e*stigo / serian de Seys Personas

/ Fue Pregunt*a*do Sy los yndios que / quedaron en la tienda sy ansimis- / mo Sabe que los Alanzearon e ma- / taron dentro d*e* la d*i*cha Tienda e Por / Cuyo ma*n*dado los mataron dixo que no / Sabe ny vio lo Co*n*thenido en la Pre- / Gunta mas de *h*aber oydo d*ecir* que / los d*i*chos yndios Se *h*abian Alçado / xiii

[fol. 98r]

911

(co)*e*n la Tienda e que alli *h*Abian Alan- / çeado Algunos y otros *h*abian SaCAdo d*e* la / Tienda e los Soltaban e alançea- / ban e que cree que se hizo Por / ma*n*dado del d*i*cho don garçi*a* loPez Por- / que (h)era maesTre de CanPo A quyen / todos obedesçian y estaban P*r*esent*e*s / Fue Pregunt*a*do Sy sabe que el d*i*cho don / Garçi*a* loPez antes que hiziese / la d*i*cha just*ici*a lo envio a hazer / Saber Al d*i*cho Franc*i*sco vazquez de / Coronado y el d*i*cho Franc*i*sco Vazquez / ma*n*do que Se hiziese como Se / hizo e Para que lo viesen hazer / e Poder dar Relaçion *en*tre Su / Tierra de la Crueldad que con Aque- / llos se (h)usaba ynVio Adonde la / Just*ici*a se hizo al yndio llamado / Turco e al yndio llamado yso- / Pete los quales se hallaron Pre- / Sentes a Ver hazer la d*i*cha quema / e just*ici*a d*i*xo que no sabe lo con- / Tenydo en la PregunTa / F(y)ue Pregunt*a*do Sy sabe que en (e)el / Pueblo *sobre* que TuVo el çerco Franc*i*sco / Vazquez de Coronado d*es*Pues de

[fol. 98v]

*en*trado e Ganado el Pueblo quema- / ron APerrearon e alanzearon mu- / cha Cantydad de yndios de los que d*es*pues / de *en*trado e ganado Sacaron de / las Casas e de los que se salyan sin / Armas del Pueblo Por la sed e / (F)*h*anbre que PaDeszian *en* el Pue- / blo dixo que *e*ste t*es*tigo no lo Vio mas / de *h*aber oydo d*ecir* que se *h*Abian APe- / Reado algunos yndios e Cortado ma- / nos A *e*sTos de los que se *h*abyan To- / mado Por Fuerça / Fue Pregunt*a*do que otras Crueldad*e*s / e malostratamyentos viese que Se / *h*obieSen (F)*h*e*c*ho Por el d*i*cho General CA- / Pitan*e*s e otros esPañoles en la / d*i*cha jornada dixo que no lo sabe Ant*e*s / sabe que el d*i*cho Franc*i*sco Vazquez *en* Toda / la jornada Tuvo SienPre gran(d) / Cuydado e Vigilançia que los natu- / rales de la d*i*cha P*r*oVinçia no Se les / hiziese daño crueldad ny maltrata- / myento

Alguno Antes los CasTigaba / ASPeramente / Fue Preguntado quyen mato
Al dicho / Yndio llamado Turco e Por que / xiiii

[fol. 99r]

912

CaUsa e Razon Dixo que diego loPez ma- / estre de canPo lo mato Por mandado del / dicho Francisco Vazquez Porque se aVeriguo / el dicho Yndio turco
Avisar a los de / quyVira mostrandoles los Caballos / que eStaban buenos Para
Pelear e / los que eSTaban flaCos Para que mata- / Sen los buenos Para matar
los / esPañoles e Porque el dicho Turco / truxo Perdido el CAnPo Por largos
/ e grandes Rodeos y en mucha Con- / DiÇion de Perderse trayendolos /
enGañados de Una Parte A otra / Para que Peresçiesen e mu- / rieSen de
hanbre e que en Presençia / de este testigo lo conFeso el dicho ynDio / Turco
Por lengua de ySoPete / e señas claras que de ello dio y dy- / Ziendo que le
tenya en çicuyque / Por esClavo e que Por venyr A su / Tierra hAbia dicho las
mentiras / que dixo e traydo el CAnPo el tanto / PelyGro e Porque bigotes e
el / caçique de çiCuyque le habian / mandado que los guyaSe Por Parte /
donde no hubiese aguada ny Comyda Porque / Todos Peresçiesen e que esta
es la / verdad e lo que sabe de este CASo

[fol. 99v]

Para el Juramento que hizo Fue le tor- / nado a leer este su dicho luego como
lo aCabo / de decir e RetiFicose en el juan de ÇaldyVar / el liçenciado Tejada

Chapter 15

The Nominal Target of the Investigation, Francisco Vázquez de Coronado

Investor and Captain General

Francisco Vázquez de Coronado was about 29 years old when, in January 1540, Viceroy Mendoza formally designated him captain general of the expedition about to depart for Tierra Nueva.[1] By virtue of an investment of more than 50,000 pesos, Vázquez de Coronado and his wife Beatriz de Estrada were among the principal financial backers of the privately-funded expedition, the remaining two being Pedro de Alvarado and Viceroy Mendoza, himself, each of whom also invested at least 50,000 pesos.[2] The investors certainly expected huge financial rewards from the Tierra Nueva venture, at least equal to those amassed by the conquerors of Peru. An indication of their expectations is that at the distribution of Atahualpa's treasure at Cajamarca in Peru in 1532 the individual receiving the largest share, Francisco Pizarro, was allotted 57,220 pesos. Yet each of the three parties underwriting the expedition to Tierra Nueva *invested* about that much.[3]

In November 1540, while the expedition was taking up quarters along the Rio Grande, the third principal supporter and shareholder of the expedition was added, by virtue of a royally mandated contract between Pedro de Alvarado and the viceroy. The terms of the contract are complex, but the import of them is that the expedition to Tierra Nueva was to be considered as one element of a much larger and more ambitious program of exploration and conquest to the west and north of Nueva España, in which the viceroy and Alvarado, the governor of Guatemala, were to share expenses and profits.[4] Thus, the expedition that is usually coupled with Vázquez de Coronado's name was a joint venture, with the viceroy first among three equal investors. It was the viceroy after all who had received license to mount the expedition,[5] and there is some evidence that he at first intended to lead it himself.[6]

Vázquez de Coronado had come to Nueva España with the viceroy in 1535, and since then Mendoza had consistently favored and advanced his young henchman.[7] The year 1537 was pivotal in Vázquez de Coronado's career. First, he married Beatriz de Estrada, daughter of the former royal treasurer in Nueva España, Alonso de Estrada, and Marina Gutiérrez de la Caballería. Importantly, one of the consequences of the marriage was Vázquez de Coronado's receipt as dowry of one fourth of the encomienda of Tlapa, the third richest encomienda in Nueva España, which provided financial leverage he lacked as the second son of Juan Vázquez de Coronado, *comendador* of Cubillas and former corregidor of Granada.[8]

Also in 1537, he was tapped by Viceroy Mendoza to investigate and mete out punishment for an uprising of black slaves and Indians at the mines of Amatepeque southwest of Mexico City. A group of Blacks confessed to fomenting the uprising and were drawn and quartered in punishment. Mendoza was more than satisfied with Vázquez de Coronado's discharge of the assignment and wrote as much to the king.[9] Furthermore, Vázquez de Coronado was sent as *juez visitador* or inspecting judge to investigate reported mistreatment of Indians working in the mines at Sultepec in the same general area as Amatepeque.[10]

The career of Mendoza's young protege advanced rapidly in 1538. In June he and his brother-in-law Juan Alonso de Sosa were both made regidores of the cabildo of Mexico City, an office Vázquez de Coronado continued to occupy until within three months of his death in September 1554, at about age 43.[11] The most momentous change in his standing within the viceroyalty came in November of 1538, when the viceroy designated him governor and juez de residencia or residencia judge of Nueva Galicia on the northwest fringe of Spain's dominion in North America.[12] As governor, he undertook a search for the rumored gold mines of Topira, suppressed uprisings among several recently subjugated Indian communities, investigated charges of abuse of Indians,[13] and launched fray Marcos de Niza and Esteban de Dorantes on their reconnaissance of the northern mysteries before being charged with the captaincy general of the expedition to Tierra Nueva.

The reasons behind Mendoza's patronage and support of Francisco Vázquez de Coronado are shadowy. It is highly likely that the service of Juan Vázquez de Coronado, the captain general's father, as corregidor in Granada in 1515 and 1516 and as *prefecto* or chief administrator there established or cemented a relationship of rapport and reciprocal support with the Mendoza family, especially Luis Hurtado de Mendoza, conde de Tendilla and marqués de Mondéjar, the future viceroy of Nueva España's older brother, who was captain general in Granada from 1512 until 1564, and perhaps with Antonio de Mendoza himself.[14] Throughout Mendoza's tenure in Nueva España, the viceroy and Vázquez de Coronado remained very close, a fact clear to the younger man's fellow regidores. It was Vázquez de Coronado they sent, for example, to visit Mendoza when in 1549 he was ill and away from Mexico City in Huastepec.[15] In October of the following year, as the newly named second viceroy of Nueva España Luis de Velasco approached Mexico City from Veracruz, Vázquez de Coronado pled with the other members of the cabildo to petition the king to permit Mendoza to remain as viceroy, in consideration of his poor health. The proposal was rejected unanimously as a challenge to royal authority,[16] and Mendoza was transferred to Peru, where he died within months. Whatever the underlying *vínculos* or ties between the viceroy and Vázquez de Coronado, an intricate web of social relations bound them and their associates. Juan Alonso de Sosa, Vázquez de Coronado's brother-in-law, was a close friend of Mendoza, while Hernán Pérez de Bocanegra, several times Vázquez de Coronado's *consuegro* or father-in-law of his children was one of the viceroy's business partners.[17]

In his capacity as leader of the expedition of reconnaissance to Tierra Nueva and one of the principal investors in it, Vázquez de Coronado tenaciously pursued rumors of wealth in the north, as was attested by nearly all the witnesses in the 1544 investigation. This despite having optimism dashed even before reaching Cíbola when, as related by de parte witness Captain Diego López, Juan de Zaldívar and Melchior Díaz failed to confirm fray Marcos's reports during an extended scouting trip as far north as Chichilticale. Vázquez de Coronado repeatedly dispatched exploring parties to various points and himself led the whole expedition to the Rio Grande Valley and the Great Plains in vain search for precious metals. Only after enduring two severe winters and learning of massive uprisings of indigenous peoples behind him in Sonora and Nueva Galicia did he call the enterprise off and return south.[18] Certainly, it was not for lack of effort on the captain general's part that the kind of wealth that had been anticipated was not found and that, therefore, many members of the expedition lost their investments and were a long time in extricating themselves from debt; some never did.

Vázquez de Coronado himself was heavily in debt on his return from Tierra Nueva. At his own expense he had taken many henchmen, servants, black slaves, and beasts of burden.[19] In 1544 he was still 10,000 pesos in debt and had been forced to sell property in an effort to raise funds for repayment. Furthermore, because of two serious head injuries suffered during the course of the expedition, his physical and mental capacity seemed to be reduced, at least for a time. Nevertheless, within days of returning to Nueva Galicia he led a force of settlers to put down an uprising of Tecoxquines near Compostela. In this operation he relied on his captain Juan de Zaldívar to raise a contingent from Guadalajara.[20]

Less than two years later the administrative performance of Vázquez de Coronado was scrutinized during two investigations. As the result of the residencia conducted by Lorenzo de Tejada at the same time as the pesquisa into the expedition's treatment of Indians, Vázquez de Coronado was removed from the governorship of Nueva Galicia and fined. Additionally, he was stripped of several encomiendas. After lengthy appeals, the fines were reduced and the encomiendas returned, but the process consumed much of Vázquez de Coronado's remaining life. Half a century after his death, a grandson, Francisco Pacheco de Córdova y Bocanegra, made formal application for a title of marqués or conde, partly on the basis of his grandfather's service in Tierra Nueva.[21] In 1617, Pacheco de Córdova y Bocanegra was made first marqués de Villamayor de las Inviernas, a title still held by descendants in Spain today.[22]

The written instructions Mendoza gave the young captain general in 1540 concerning treatment of the native peoples the expedition to Tierra Nueva was sure to meet simply referred to standard instructions given to all "persons who go to reconnoiter and bring to peace new lands and provinces."[23] Doubtless, Mendoza meant Vázquez de Coronado to adhere to the same directive he gave Hernando de Alarcón a year and a half later, namely that he was to make sure that the people with him did not harm the Indians, nor take anything from them against their will, nor enter their homes without permission.[24] In response to a question formulated by Vázquez de Coronado and his attorney Pedro Ruiz de Haro, the de parte witnesses, from whom testimony was taken in Culiacán province in early 1545, confirmed that ". . . four days' journey beyond the city of Compostela the general made decrees and issued ordinances very much in favor of the natives and had them publicly proclaimed. Among those...there [was] one according to which no man of war was to enter an Indian's house or take anything or burn a house without permission from his captain, under penalty of death." Specifically, Captain don Pedro de Tovar replied that ". . . some proclamations were made. Among them were one to the effect that the Indians were to be treated very benevolently and [another] to the effect that no abuse was to be inflicted on them." Based on such evidence, the king in his definitive decision in the case found that Vázquez de Coronado "was especially careful to order that all the natives of the lands through which [the army] traveled be treated very benevolently, under severe penalties. He also ordered that nothing belonging to the natives be taken from them against their will and without paying for it and that no other mistreatment be perpetrated against them."

By all reports, the captain general was also conscientious about formally summoning native peoples to voluntarily capitulate and become subjects of the king before waging war against those who chose not to do so. The reading of the summons or requerimiento in Spanish was usually accompanied by interpretation in indigenous languages or through manual signs. Although a futile and absurdly arrogant act, the reading of the requerimiento was required by law. Since it was, Vázquez de Coronado routinely saw that it was done, sometimes even in the midst of attack by the Indians to whom it was being read. In this, as in most other things, it can safely be said that the captain general "played by the book," making sure that what was mandated by the king and viceroy was performed. It is equally true that at least some of his captains kept him ignorant of actions that might not adhere to the letter of the law and, furthermore, Vázquez de Coronado himself clearly avoided enquiring too deeply or energetically into cases of potential legal infraction.

Given his literal, if minimal, adherence to the directives, proclamations, and commands of the king and viceroy regarding treatment of Indians, it is understandable that Vázquez de Coronado's replies to Tejada's questions on September 2, 1544, seem self-assured. His answers are very detailed and lengthy, often to the effect that things did not happen as stated in the questions or that he did not know about what was asked or did not remember. But on many matters of substance he maintained that his actions and those of his subordinates were justified. He insisted that, without exception, Indians rejected the formal summons and attacked the Spaniards without provocation, thus bringing war on themselves. He explained the fighting at Cíbola as a result of the belligerence of the native people and the expedition's hunger. He claimed always to have read the requerimiento three times before launching an attack and to have pardoned Indians after fighting was over. In his account, he always consulted the religious members of the expedition when there was any question of violating royal edicts regarding the Indians. In the sequel, the friars supported waging war, and it was fray Juan de Padilla, for instance, who called for and conducted the interrogation of Bigotes, during which dogs were set on him. According to Vázquez de Coronado, the killing of El Turco was fully justified because he was trying to kill the Spaniards. Absent from the captain general's account of events during the expedition are references to any acts of cruelty or abuse. In this, his testimony is in marked contrast to those of the other witnesses. Implied is either faulty memory, outright obfuscation, or a captain general largely removed from daily conduct of the expedition he led.

Thus, the former captain general was shocked and dismayed when his friend licenciado Cristóbal de Benavente, fiscal for the Royal Audiencia of Nueva España, lodged formal charges against him based on Tejada's investigation. As Vázquez de Coronado himself lamented, Benavente could just as well not have filed a complaint. And, indeed, the surviving testimony fails utterly to provide firsthand evidence of the captain general's direct responsibility for the acts of brutality with which Benavente charged him. Vázquez de Coronado appealed to Benavente on the basis of friendship not to file charges, but the fiscal replied that he had a higher duty than friendship. In retrospect, three years later, Vázquez de Coronado readily admitted that Benavente was a diligent and honorable person.[25] Thus, it was not until the audiencia rendered its decision in the case in February 1546 that Vázquez de Coronado obtained the result he felt Benavente could have rightly effected without further proceedings.

The possibility of his having suffered long-term disability as a result of the injuries received in Tierra Nueva has been exaggerated.[26] His death in 1554, rather than being a direct consequence of his Tierra Nueva injuries, is more likely to have been the result of communicable disease. Many regidores were ill that year.[27] On June 1, because of lack of a quorum, Vázquez de Coronado and Alonso de Villanueva were called to the *ayuntamiento* to fill out the requisite number of members. Both men were dead by November, as was Juan Alonso de Sosa, Vázquez de Coronado's brother-in-law and also a regidor.[28] Furthermore, on the day Vázquez de Coronado's death was announced at a meeting of the cabildo, no fewer than five other regidores were listed as ill.[29]

A TRANSLATION
OF THE TESTIMONY

[99v cont'd][30]
Sworn Statement of the Governor, Francisco Vázquez de Coronado

After the aforesaid in the city of Guadalajara on the third day of the month of September in the year one thousand five hundred and forty-four, licenciado Tejada, lord judge of the Royal Audiencia of Nueva España, visitador, and judge of the residencia for Nueva Galicia, ordered Francisco Vázquez de Coronado, former governor of this province, to appear before him, and he received his oath in legal form, by God, Santa María, and a representation of the holy cross, on which he placed his right hand. He promised to tell and declare the truth about everything he might know and be asked. Under that obligation, he was asked the following questions.

{1} The accused was asked whether he had been named general of the entire army for subjugation and reconnaissance of the tierra nueva of Cíbola. [100r] [What][31] captains, maestre de campo, and alférez went in the army, and who appointed them? He answered that the viceroy of Nueva España named the accused as general of all the people and the army that was to go and did go to explore and subdue Tierra Nueva and the province of Cíbola and the rest of the provinces that were found. Likewise, the viceroy named the alcaide Lope de Samaniego as maestre de campo and don Pedro de Tovar as *alférez mayor*. In consultation with the viceroy, the accused named the rest of the captains who departed from the city of Compostela. The captains of the horsemen were don Rodrigo Maldonado, don Diego de Guevara, don Tristán de Arellano, don García López de Cárdenas, and the councilman of Sevilla Diego López. He also assigned companies of horsemen to the maestre de campo and the alférez mayor. He named Hernando de Alvarado captain of artillery and Pablos de Melgosa captain of the footmen. [100v] Because of the death of the alcaide Lope de Samaniego, the accused named don García

López de Cárdenas as maestre de campo in his place. When he consulted the viceroy, it seemed to him that the positions had been well filled.

Having arrived in the town of San Miguel in the province of Culiacán, the accused thought that it would be very trying to travel with the entire force, since he had information that there was a shortage of provisions. Therefore, he took the maestre de campo don García López and about eighty horsemen with him to go in advance and reconnoiter, seeing what was there. In the town of San Miguel he left the rest of the force, don Tristán de Arellano as his lieutenant, and Velasco de Barrionuevo as maestre de campo, with instructions as to how they were to proceed. He also left an order that if Juan de Zaldívar (who had come from the province of Cíbola and had gone to inform the viceroy of what he had seen in that land) chose to serve His Majesty further in the expedition, they were to form a company for him [101r] by taking a number of men from each of the other companies. This company would then be assigned [to Zaldívar] as captain, which he designated him.

With this arrangement and instruction, the accused departed with the horsemen he mentioned and Pablos de Melgosa with some footmen. When he arrived at Cíbola and saw that it was not what had been said, he ordered Melchor Díaz to return to the valley of Corazones, where he was to remain, settle, and try to bring the natives into obedience to His Majesty and to knowledge of God our Lord. Taking with him some horsemen from among those that had remained with don Tristán, he left that place quiet and at peace and went to reconnoiter the Mar del Sur, in conformance with instructions he carried. The accused also named Díaz as alcalde mayor of the town he was ordered to found [in the valley of Corazones].

{2} He was [next] asked whether the [people of the] towns and provinces through which the accused [101v] and the rest of the force passed, between San Miguel and the province of Cíbola, came out in peace, rendered obedience to His Majesty, supplied the provisions that they had, and welcomed everyone warmly. Or did they come forth in war? He replied that all of the towns there are between Culiacán and the province of Cíbola, through which the accused passed, came out in peace and welcomed him very warmly. Where they had provisions, they provided them. This was because the accused had some individuals from the army go ahead carrying a cross as a sign of peace. And they were to assure [the natives] that the general would do them no harm. Further, the accused gave [the natives] items of trade and things that the viceroy had provided for this purpose. With these they were very satisfied.

{*3*} He was asked whether he had committed any brutality, injuries, or outrages against the persons or property of the Indians of the valley of Corazones and Señora and the other towns through which [the Spaniards] passed. [102r] And did he punish those who did, or did he excuse them? He answered that he does not know that any individual in the army perpetrated any brutality, outrages, or injury against the natives of those towns or their property. This is because the accused took the army to task and disciplined it such that no one dared to disobey or go counter to his orders. And if any of the Indians who went as servants for the army entered any sown land, [the Spaniards] punished them severely in the presence of the natives. Because of a public announcement he had made, no one, neither Spaniard nor Indian, dared to enter the houses of the natives, and the army always took up quarters outside the town[s],[32] in order to avoid the injury that fighting men are accustomed to do.

{*4*} [Vázquez de Coronado] was asked whether, when he had arrived at Cíbola, the [people of the] province came forth in peace or offered resistance. And did he deliver the requerimiento to them in conformance with what [102v] His Majesty orders? [In reply] he said that when he had arrived near Cíbola, he ordered don Pedro de Tovar and Melchor Díaz to bring him an Indian from among those who were walking near a lake, in order to get information and an interpreter from them. And they were not to harm any of them. [Tovar and Díaz] brought two or three [Indians]. Through an interpreter that he had brought from the valley of Corazones, the accused made them understand that he came in His Majesty's name, in order to bring them under his dominion and to bring them to knowledge of God (so that they would be Christians). And he let them know that, if they chose to come in peace and render obedience to His Majesty, no harm would be done to them or their property. He sent two Nahua Indians away with them carrying a cross in their hands as a sign of peace.

When the accused had gotten three leagues from Cíbola, he found there the Nahuas that he had sent, and they told him that the pueblo and province were at war and were not willing to come to peace. He [then] ordered don García López to go with twenty or [103r] thirty horsemen to examine a passage among some boulders that appeared to be rugged and where the company could be hurt by the natives. They were to prepare themselves and sleep at the top of the pass. And they were to inform him of what transpired. Don García López went and established quarters in the pass. When a quarter of the second watch was over, Indians struck and shot some horses with arrows. They would have done more harm except that don García was on the alert. When the accused had been informed of this and it was daylight, he travelled with the force until he joined don García.

When they had arrived near Cíbola (within sight of it), Vázquez de Coronado saw many smoke signals that were being sent from one place and another and some Indians [outfitted] in a manner for war, who were sounding a conch trumpet. He sent don García López, fray Luis, and the scribe Hernando Bermejo with some horsemen to deliver the requerimiento that His Majesty orders. And they went forward to do [103v] so. The accused decided to be there [himself] and, taking some horsemen and trade goods that he carried, he left marching orders for the army and joined don García López and the clerics. [Then] three hundred Indians with bows and arrows and round shields approached close to where the accused and the others were. Although they were summoned three times to offer peace and made to understand, through the interpreter who had been sent to speak with them and went to them, they were never willing to come in peace nor to render obedience to His Majesty. Nor did they stop shooting arrows. Seeing that they were wounding the horses and had given fray Luis an arrow wound, the accused ordered [the Spaniards] to attack [the Indians]. And they turned their backs [and fled] until they got inside the pueblo, where they fortified themselves.

The accused ordered that they again be summoned to offer peace, it being certified to them that [the Spaniards] would do them no harm and they would be well treated. [104r] Seeing that they refused to do so and that they still were shooting arrows from the upper floor and, mainly, that the army was suffering from hunger, [Vázquez de Coronado] ordered that an attack be made. When he was trying to enter by means of an alleyway in the pueblo [the Indians] struck him down twice with many stones they were hurling from above. They knocked him from the ladder by which he sought to mount to the flat roofs. There he was snatched from death by don García López and [some] men-at-arms, with three wounds in the face, an arrow wound in one leg, and bruises all over his body. They put him in a tent, where he was unconscious a great while. When he had come back to his senses, they came to tell him that the pueblo had been captured and many provisions were found inside. The accused and the other men-at-arms entered the pueblo and took possession of it.

{5} He was [then] asked whether, after the pueblo had been entered and occupied, the accused or any of the captains or men-at-arms [104v] committed any cruelty or outrages or caused any deaths of Indians whom they found inside. He answered, "No." Rather, he ordered that everyone be treated benevolently, especially the women and children, regarding which, he ordered that they not be touched, under serious penalties. Some of the *principales* having been called, he made them understand, through an interpreter, that they had done wrong in not coming to peace and rendering obedience, as he had sent to tell them and to summon them. But because they now chose to render obedience, he was pardoning them. And if any of them wanted to remain [in the pueblo] with their wives and children, they would receive thoroughly benevolent treatment, and [the Spaniards] would leave their property and houses alone and would nurse the wounded.

[The *principales*] answered that they knew they had done wrong and that they wanted to go to the pueblo of Mazaque, so that from there they would come to render obedience, with [the people from] all the neighboring pueblos, [105r] since in the pueblo that had been captured, there had been people from all those pueblos. The next day or within two days, the principal from Mazaque and those from the other pueblos came with a gift of deer and bison hides, yucca fiber mantas, some turquoise, and some bows and arrows. The accused gave them trade goods that he carried, with which they returned very satisfied, after having rendered obedience to His Majesty and saying that they wanted to serve [the king] and be Christians.

{6} [Next, the accused] was asked whether, while he resided in the pueblo of Cíbola, Indian leaders from the province of the pueblo of Cicuique came to render obedience to his majesty and to offer themselves to the general as allies, entreating the Spaniards to go to see their pueblo. And among those who came were there three principales, one called the cacique and another called [Xabe].[33] [He said] that, while he was in the pueblo of Cíbola, he saw [105v] three or four Indians come from the pueblo of Cicuique. To one of them he gave the name Bigotes, but he does not remember what they called the others nor whether [the Indians] called the cacique and Xabe came among them.

They told [the general] that they had learned that foreign people had come to their land, brave men who hurt those who defended themselves and gave benevolent treatment to those who submitted. They said that they came in order to know [these men] and to have them as friends. The accused thanked them and told them that he came in His Majesty's name to bring them to his obedience and so that they might know God and be Christians. If they did so, they would be treated well and would be [the Spaniards'] allies. Afterwards he ordered them to be given accommodations, afforded benevolent treatment, and given some trade goods.

Within two or three days he told them that he wanted to send Captain [106r] Hernando de Alvarado with horsemen, in order to make his arrival and the reason His Majesty had sent him known to [their] provinces and the neighboring pueblos. Also, he wanted Alvarado to reconnoiter what was farther on. The Indians were happy about this and said that he might go to their pueblo and that there [the Spaniards] would be afforded a fine welcome and the people would give them provisions and guides. So he knows that Hernando de Alvarado went with twenty horsemen and that [the Indians] from the pueblo of Cicuique afforded them a very fine welcome. Along the way they made sure that [the people of] all the other pueblos came out in peace and brought [the Spaniards] food and provisions. Because [the Spaniards] wanted to go farther on, the people of Cicuique provided them with two Indians as guides, to whom [the Spaniards] gave the names Turco and Ysopete.

{7} He was asked whether, after they had gone on beyond Cicuique, Captain Hernando de Alvarado returned there and was afforded a [106v] warm welcome, and did they give him a number of hides, mantas, and other things as gifts? And did Alvarado send the gifts to the accused where he was in Cíbola? He replied that he knows that Captain Hernando de Alvarado and the men he took with him returned by way of Cicuique, where he was given [very][34] fine treatment, [reception],[35] and welcome. He does not know whether it was from that pueblo or from Yuraba that Alvarado sent some hides and mantas to him at Cíbola. He heard it said that those things had been given to him and [Alvarado] had sent them to him on his outward-bound trip, rather than on his return.

{8} [The accused] was asked whether he knows that Captain Hernando de Alvarado took the principal called Bigotes and the Indian they called the cacique by trickery from the pueblo of Cicuique, by saying that he needed him to show him and guide him to a number of pueblos. [Vázquez de Coronado] answered that he saw that Alvarado brought with him the [107r] Indians called Bigotes and the cacique, as well as Turco and Ysopete. He told the general that [the Indians] from Cicuique remained loyal, except that it had seemed to him that the Indian called Bigotes was found to be in a foul state and had been somewhat deceitful in what he had revealed.

{9} He was [next] asked whether he knows that, when Hernando de Alvarado took the cacique and Bigotes away from Cicuique, he put them both in shackles and collars and brought them that way. Did he put them [in the camp][36] where the accused was because the Indian called Bigotes refused to give him a gold bracelet, which the Indian called Turco said he had, along with other jewelry, and because he refused to reveal where he had gotten them or tell about the wealthy land that El Turco was talking about? And did he tell the accused that it was for this reason that he had shackles and collars put on them?

He answered that Alvarado told him that he had put Bigotes in [107v] shackles and [collars][37] because he thought that he had wanted to make the Indian called Turco flee and, if [Bigotes] were to return [to Cicuique], the land would rise up in arms. And [the accused] remembers that Alvarado did keep [Bigotes] in shackles, and he saw [Bigotes] in them in the camp where he was. At the time, Alvarado did not tell him that he had put the shackles on for the reasons mentioned in the question, but rather, for the reason that the accused has said and declared.

He remembers that it was the same night the witness arrived in Tiguex and the pueblo of Coofer, where quarters were established, that the Indian called Turco came with Hernando de Alvarado to see [him]. Among the things that he said was that in the pueblo of Cicuique there were a bracelet and other items of gold that he had brought from Quivira. The Indian called Bigotes had ordered them hidden. If [the general] allowed him to return [there] without Bigotes, he would bring the jewelry.

[108r] {10} [Vázquez de Coronado] was asked whether, in order to learn what is referred to in the previous question, he ordered dogs unleashed against the Indian called Bigotes, so that he would speak and tell about the gold bracelet and jewelry. How many times did they set dogs on [Bigotes] and who did it? He replied that fray Juan de Padilla told the accused that it was very important to His Majesty's service that the wealthy land that El Turco told of be learned about with certainty and that this could be learned from Bigotes. And fray Juan said that El Turco was saying that Bigotes had the gold bracelet and jewelry. The accused answered that as a man who had spoken more with [Bigotes] (since he had gone with Hernando de Alvarado), fray Juan would understand him better than [the general] did. And he told fray Juan that he might take [Bigotes] and try to learn the truth from him. Fray Juan answered that Alvarado understood [the Indian] better than he did and that he wanted both of them to try to learn the truth.

[The accused said][38] that it should be done that way. Father fray Juan told [Vázquez de Coronado] that they had interrogated [108v] [Bigotes] and he denied everything. Within a few days, seeing Bigotes with one arm tied [in a bandage], [the accused] asked what had happened to that Indian, and they told him that a dog had bitten him. [Long] afterwards, when they had come to this province [Nueva Galicia], he learned that since [Bigotes] denied what don Pedro de Tovar asked him and because he refused to confess, don Pedro told him to tell the truth or else "that dog that was wandering loose would bite him." Seeing that he chose not to confess, don Pedro called the dog and it bit [Bigotes].

{*11*} He was [then] asked whether Hernando de Alvarado's tent and the place where the dogs were set on the Indian called Bigotes were in the same camp and pueblo where the accused was lodged, and near his quarters. He answered that Alvarado's quarters were near his own. But he heard it said that they had not unleashed the dog against [Bigotes] in those quarters; rather, they had taken him away from the camp to ask [109r] him what the accused has stated and said.

{*12*} [Further,] the accused was asked whether he also saw that the Indian called Bigotes had been bitten on the legs and whether any person informed him, on the very night or day that it happened, that dogs had been set on Bigotes because he was not willing to confirm what the Indian called Turco was saying. He replied that, as he has said, he does not remember knowing that they had set dogs on Bigotes [while] he was in that camp or [even] in that province. And he saw no other wound [on Bigotes] than the one on his arm or leg.

{*13*} [Vázquez de Coronado] was asked whether he knows that a number of Indians were sent from the pueblo of Cicuique to him to ask for the Indian called Bigotes and the others from that pueblo that he held prisoner. Did they tell him that [the Spaniards] were repaying them poorly for their friendship and the kind treatment [the Indians] had afforded them and the friendship and obedience they had offered? And did he ever consent to what they asked? [In reply] he said [109v] that such [a delegation] was never sent to make a petition. On the contrary, after the aforesaid had happened, Bigotes and the cacique told him that they and the people of their pueblo were enemies of the people of Tiguex. The pueblo of Cicuique had a serious shortage of land, while the province of Tiguex had an abundance. They asked the general to give them a pueblo there, which they could settle with their people. And they said that they were coming to help in the war.

{14} He was asked [next] whether the [people of the] province and pueblos of Tiguex came to offer peace to the accused and obedience to him in His Majesty's name. Did they welcome the Spaniards and the army into their land and pueblos and give them hides, mantas, poultry, and the rest of the necessary provisions? And did they afford them friendly treatment in every way? He answered that, when Hernando de Alvarado and fray Juan de Padilla [went] through that province with the rest of the Spaniards they took with them, the [people of the] pueblos there came out in peace and provided them corn, poultry, [110r] mantas, and hides from what they had, in exchange for trade goods that he says Alvarado and fray Juan gave them. [The Indians] afforded them a friendly welcome in every way, without giving any hint of war and without offering resistance.

Fray Juan wrote to the accused in Cíbola (where he was) that on the banks of the river in that province there were very good pastures and that it seemed to him that [the general] ought to come to establish a camp in that place. He sent don García López and some [Indian] allies, with Indians from Cíbola, to establish the camp and erect shelter where fray Juan suggested. The Indians of the pueblo of Coofor, seeing that don García López wanted to build houses, told him not to build them. They would leave their pueblo vacant for him and move to others nearby, where their friends and relatives were. Therefore, they vacated the pueblo and [the Spaniards] took up quarters in it.

{15} [The accused] was asked whether he ordered [110v] some persons to go to the pueblos of that province to gather hides and mantas, with which to clothe the people, poultry to feed them, and some feather robes. Who were the persons he gave that order to and, in accordance with his order, did they gather the necessary mantas, hides, robes, poultry, provisions, and corn from those pueblos and bring them to the pueblo where [the Spaniards] were quartered? He answered that a number of Spaniards, men-at-arms, and Indian allies complained to the accused that they did not have clothing and were dying of cold. And they asked that he order some clothing to be gathered from the neighboring pueblos, with which they might cover and protect themselves from the cold. Seeing the need that existed, [Vázquez de Coronado] ordered don García López to take trade goods and with them try to purchase, from the pueblo of Chia, some robes, hides, and mantas with which to clothe and save the people.

Thus, the accused knows that they went and brought a number of mantas, hides, and robes, though not as many [111r] as the people needed because [the Indians] would not give that many. The clothing obtained with the trade goods that they carried was distributed among the people who had the greatest need. The items of trade were among those that the viceroy had directed them to carry for the purpose of trading with the Indians.

{*16*} He was [then] asked whether he knows or saw that this gathering of clothing, poultry, and provisions caused resentment. And were items taken from the Indians' houses without their consent? He stated that he knows no such thing. On the contrary, he was told that they were provided by the Indians of their own free will, in exchange for the trade goods. And he believes that was the case, since don García López is a Christian and a gentleman.

{*17*} [Vázquez de Coronado] was asked whether he knew that a man-at-arms of his army, one Villegas, when he went to gather the clothing, hides, robes, and provisions, seized an Indian woman by force and had sexual relations with her against her will. Does he know that, because of this and because [the Spaniards] took clothing from their houses against their will, [the natives] [111v] were very offended and disagreeable? Did this come to [the accused's] notice and did he administer punishment for it? He replied that he had not been aware of any such thing, since whenever he learned of things like that, he would administer punishment for them, in keeping with a public announcement that he had issued. [Only] when he arrived in this province [Nueva Galicia], did he hear it said that Villegas had sexual relations with an Indian woman and the rest that is referred to in the question. He said that he does not know that it [occurred].

{*18*} [Next,] he was asked whether he knows that, because of the confinement of the Indian called Bigotes and the unleashing of dogs against him, because of the rape committed by Villegas, and because [the Spaniards] took clothing and provisions from those pueblos against the natives' will, both the pueblo of Cicuique and the province of Tiguex rose up in arms and rebelled. And was it said publicly that it was for those reasons and because of other cruelty and outrages that they rose up and rebelled? [Vázquez de Coronado] replied that, as he has stated and testified, he was never aware of what is referred to in the question. Nor does he believe that this was the cause of the uprising, [112r] because, after the gathering of clothing, [the Indians] from the pueblo of Chia came to the camp and talked with the accused. And they brought him poultry and other supplies and offered him assistance. Likewise, he knows that the [people of the] pueblo of Cicuique did not rise up because of confinement of Bigotes or for the other reasons stated in the question, since after all that had occurred and the province of Tiguex had rebelled, the accused went to the pueblo of Cicuique to ask [the Indians there] for help, taking Bigotes and the cacique with him. They welcomed him into their pueblo and gave him friendly treatment in every way. He entered the pueblo with only Lope de Urrea and fray Juan de Padilla, although he did not stay in the pueblo to sleep. [The Indians of Cicuique] were not willing to do him the favor that he asked, excusing themselves, saying that everyone was then in their planted fields, but if the accused still ordered them all to leave, they would do it. Since he saw that they would not offer assistance [112v] willingly, he did not try to press them further about it. Instead, he told them that he was grateful [for their offer] that when he needed help, it would be provided.

{*19*} Since the [people of the] pueblo of Cicuique and the province of Tiguex came voluntarily to render obedience and offer themselves as allies and, as he has said, no outrage was committed against them, he was asked what caused the natives to rise up in arms and rebel. The witness replied that he did not know more about the cause than that, being at peace and without [the Spaniards] having given the Indians any reason that the accused knows of, they rebelled. [The Spaniards] woke up one morning [to find] about thirty-five horses that had been abroad in the countryside and two Nahuas, who had been guarding them, dead and shot with arrows.

{*20*} [Vázquez de Coronado] was [then] asked in how many pueblos of Tiguex Province the people gathered and fortified themselves. And how many pueblos did they leave [113r] abandoned and empty? He replied that the people gathered and fortified themselves in only two pueblos and left the other nine or ten that were in that province abandoned and empty.

{*21*} [The accused] was asked why, since [the Indians] left those ten pueblos empty and without defense, [the Spaniards] burned them and tore them down. Was it done by the accused's order or did he know who did it and ordered it done? He answered that he himself did not order those pueblos burned and torn down nor does he know which particular captain may have burned and destroyed them. But he believes that, because of the great cold that there was and because the camp was in the open country far from the mountains, the soldiers would have burned them and the wood to save themselves. He does not know whether they demolished the walls or destroyed those pueblos completely.

{*22*} [Next,] he was asked whether [he] ordered don Rodrigo Maldonado to burn and tear down the first of those pueblos, or one [113v] of them. [The accused] replied that he ordered don Rodrigo Maldonado to go to one of the pueblos that was abandoned, the one that was said to be the strongest, and to remove all of the supplies that were in it. He does not remember whether he ordered [Maldonado] to burn or demolish it. If it was so ordered, it would have been so that the Indians who had left that pueblo and others would not return and fortify themselves. When [the accused] was in the camp he saw smoke rising from those pueblos. He asked what it was and they told him that one of the pueblos was burning. He never knew which captain burned it or ordered it burned.

{*23*} He was asked how far from the abandoned pueblos that were burned and torn down was the camp that he had near one of the pueblos that the Indians had fortified? He replied that some pueblos were half a league from the camp; others were one, [114r] two, and three leagues.

{*24*} [The accused] was asked whether he summoned [the Indians] to offer peace and told them that [the Spaniards] would pardon them and would do them no injury, before laying siege to the two pueblos and attacking them. [Vázquez de Coronado] said that when he saw the rebellion of those Indians, he called the clerics fray Juan de Padilla and fray Antonio de Castilblanco and the royal officials to his quarters. When they discussed what should be done, fray Juan de Padilla said that, according to them, it was not right to kill anyone. [But] he approved and pronounced as justifiable what the general might do. Fray Antonio responded in the same way. It seemed to everyone that they ought to make war on [the Indians]. With this agreement, the accused sent the councilman of Sevilla Diego López to Pueblo del Arenal to explain to [the Indians] the wrong they had done. And he was to tell them that, if the uprising had occurred because of [114v] any injury or outrage committed by any man-at-arms, they should declare it and in their presence justice would be done. If they again rendered obedience to His Majesty, [the general] would pardon them. He sent don Rodrigo Maldonado on the same mission to the pueblo of Moha, which was the other one that was barricaded. In both [pueblos the Indians] sought to kill [the emissaries] by trickery.

Seeing that [the Indians] were rebels and that to go on, leaving that [land] at war behind them, was dangerous, [the general] laid siege to the pueblos and attacked them, with great danger to the army. This is evident since during the first attack at the pueblo besieged by don García López, more than forty Spaniards and Indian allies were wounded. And at the pueblo besieged by the accused, called Noha, many men-at-arms were wounded, and they killed Captain Francisco de Ovando and four or five men-at-arms. In the end, although the siege was long and wearisome, the pueblos were restored [to obedience] and pacified.

{*25*} [Vázquez de Coronado] was asked how many [115r] Indians were set upon by dogs and burned at the pueblo that he besieged. By whose order was this done, and did it come to the notice of the accused? He replied that he himself did not order any Indian burned or set upon by dogs nor does he know that any such thing was done. But he did learn that, while he was ill in his tent, [the Spaniards] had let loose some Indians who had been captured in war and had been taken as prisoners from that pueblo, and a dog ran after them and bit them, though they did not die. He knows that no one unleashed dogs on [the Indians]. When they were captured, he ordered them released, so that they could go where they wanted.

{*26*} [The accused] was asked whether he saw or was aware that Indians who left the pueblo because of thirst or hunger, without arms and without offering resistance, were lanced and dogs were let loose to track them down so that they could be lanced. He replied that he knows nothing about what [115v] is referred to in the question. Those who left the pueblo and came into the control of the accused were afforded thoroughly benevolent treatment. He ordered them to return to the pueblo to tell the others that if they surrendered, they would be pardoned.

{*27*} He was [then] asked whether he knows that, at Pueblo del Arenal which was besieged by don García López de Cárdenas, when [the Spaniards] had made an attack and gained some of the flat roofs, those who remained to be subdued made signs to don García López. By these signs did they indicate that if their lives were guaranteed, they would offer peace? Did don García promise that by means of signs and assure them? And because of this, did as many as eighty persons leave the pueblo without any arms, and did don García order them gathered together in his tent in the camp? The accused answered that he heard that, when an attack was being made, a number of Indians came forth from the pueblo, without arms and in peace, and that [116r] don García López ordered them gathered together and put in his tent.

{*28*} [Then] he was asked whether don García López had made him aware that those Indians were put together in the tent and asked him to review what [the maestre de campo] had ordered done with them. Did the accused send a directive to him with his head groom Contreras to burn all [of the Indians], but to put off administration of the punishment until the Indians called Turco and Ysopete arrived to see it done? And was this so that they would spread the word in their land about the punishment that was meted out to those who rebelled? He replied that he denies what is referred to in the question. Further, he says that what occurred is that don García López sent to tell the accused that the pueblo was occupied, but a number of houses still remained to be taken, along with the Indian men and women in them. And he wanted to find out whether the general wanted him to go on to make war on the rest of those who had rebelled. [Francisco Vázquez] sent a reply that he was not to relinquish control of the [116v] pueblo until he could leave it fully pacified. In addition, the accused answered that he would go to examine the situation at that pueblo. When he went, they would meet at Pueblo de la Alameda.

{*29*} [The accused] was [then] asked whether he was aware or whether it came to his notice that don García López ordered forty or fifty of the Indians he had gathered in the tent to be burned alive, tied to some posts, and that they were burned. He answered that he was never aware that, in the vicinity of the besieged pueblo, don García López ordered any Indians burned. And he does not remember that any such thing came to his notice.

{*30*} [Vázquez de Coronado] was asked whether he was aware that don García López and the men-at-arms, by his orders, lanced and killed with sword thrusts another thirty or forty Indians who were in the tent. In reply he said that he heard that some of the Indians [117r] who were in the tent had risen up in arms, fortified themselves, and had died.

{*31*} He was asked [next] whether the Indians Turco and Ysopete were present and in the camp where don García López was at the time the burning was carried out and the Indians in the tent were lanced. And did the accused send them to that camp? He stated that he has no memory of anything referred to in the question.

{*32*} [The accused] was asked whether he ordered the Indian called Turco to be killed, who did the killing, and for what reason it was done. And was he present in the camp where Turco was garroted? The accused replied that he had gone to the province of Quivira with a contingent of his men and had taken with him the Indians [117v] called Turco and Ysopete. Finding themselves short of corn in the last town of that province (where the accused was), the general asked why [the people there] would not provide corn. They answered that the Indian called Turco had told them not to supply corn, since if they did not give corn, the horses would soon die. And he had told them to keep an eye on particular horses that were the best, in order to kill them. [Further, he had told them that] once those horses were dead they would soon kill the Christians.

When this was known to [the accused], he ordered the maestre de campo Diego López to administer justice, once he had investigated what has been said. He also ordered him to ask El Turco why [he][39] had entered into that conspiracy and why he had led [the Spaniards] deceitfully so as to become lost. When he learned from the maestre de campo that Turco was trying to kill them, he had [Turco] killed in the camp [118r] where the witness was.

He stated that this is the truth and what he knows concerning this case, in accordance with the oath he swore. As soon as he finished speaking, he was read his testimony and sworn statement. And he confirmed it. The lord judge signed.

Francisco Vázquez de Coronado
licenciado Tejada

A TRANSCRIPT
OF THE TESTIMONY ·

[fol. 99v cont'd][40]
ConFysion del gover*nad*or / Fran*cis*co Vazquez

E D*es*Pues de lo susod*i*cho *en* la d*i*cha / ÇiUdad de guadalajara tres dias / del
mes de Se*p*tienbre de myll e / quiny*ent*os e quarenta e quatro años el / d*i*cho
Señor liçen*ci*ado tejada oydor del / Audiencia Real de la nueva esPaña / ViSy-
tador e Juez de rresydençia d*e* la / nueVa galyçia ma*n*do Paresçer Ante / Sy a
Fran*cis*co vazquez de Coronado gover- / nador que Fue de *es*ta d*i*cha ProV-
inÇia / del qual Fue rreçibido juramenTo / Por dios e Por santa maria e Por
Una / señal de cruz en que Puso Su / mano derecha en Forma de d*erec*ho el /
q*ua*l Prometyo de d*ecir* e aclarar la / *ver*dad de Todo lo que SuPiese e / le
Fuese Preguntado So CArgo del / q*ua*l se le hizieron las Preguntas siguy*ente*s
/ Fue Pregunt*a*do sy Para el descubrimyento / e conquista de la tierra nueVa
de / Çibola Fue nonbrado *e*ste conFesante / vx

[fol. 100r]
913
Por general de todo el exerçito e sus Ca- / Pitanes ma*e*stre de CanPo AlFe- /
rez Fueron en el d*i*cho exercito e quyen / los nonbro d*i*xo que el Visorrey d*e*
*e*sta / nueVa esPaña nonbro A este conFesan- / te Por general de toda la gente
y exer- / çito que *h*Abia de yr e Fue al descubri- / myento e conquista d*e* la
tierra nueVa / E provinçia de Çibola e de lo demas q*ue* / Se desCubriese e
Ansymesmo el / d*i*cho visorrey nonbro Por maesTre de can- / Po al all*c*ayde
loPe de samanyego e Por / AlFerez mayor A don Pedro de Tovar / e que los
demas CaPitanes que / Salieron d*e* la ÇiUdad de conPos- / Tela los nonbro
*e*ste conFeSante / Con Paresçer del d*i*cho visoRey que / Fueron don Rodrigo
maldonado don / diego de guevara don tristan de are- / llano e don gar*ci*a
loPez de CArdenas / diego loPez Veynte e quatro de Se- / Vylla CAPitanes

de gente de a CAballo / E ansymismo Se les dio conPanya / de gente de a
CAballo A los d*i*chos maestre / de CanPo e AlFerez mayor e hern*a*ndo / de
alVarado Por CAPitan de Artilleria / e Pablos de melgosa de la ynFanteria

[fol. 100v]
y Por muerte del all*ca*ide loPe de sama- / nyego *e*ste conFesante nonbro *e*n su
lu- / Gar Por maesTre de canPo A don garç*i*a / loPez de Cardenas e consul-
tado con el / Visorrey le Paresçio que *e*sTaba / bien Proveydo e llegado A la
villa de / San(t) myguel que es en la ProVin- / çia de CuliaCan Paresçiendole
a este / ConFeSante que (h)era Grande yncon- / Vynyente CAmynar con
todo el exer- / cito Por la notiçia que Se tenia / de falta de basTymentos tomo
consigo / hasta ochenta de a Caballo Poco mas / o menos e al d*i*cho don
Garç*i*a loPez / ma*e*stre de cAnpo Para AdelanTar- / se e descubryr e ver lo
que *h*abia e con el / Restante de todo el exerçito dexo en / la d*i*cha villa de
san(t) myGuel Por su / thenyente A don tristan de arella- / no con ynstruyçion de es que *h*abia de / (F)*h*azer e Por maestre de CanPo A velasCo / de
barrionueVo e dexo ma*n*dado que / Sy juan de çaldivar que Venya d*e* la / d*i*cha
P*r*oVinçia de Çibola q*ue* (h)era Pasado / A dar Relaçion Al Visorrey de lo q*ue*
/ *h*Abia visto en la Tierra quysiese Vol- / Ver a Servir A su mag*e*stad en la
d*i*cha / xvi

[fol. 101r]
914
Jornada SaCAndo de CAda conPañya / çierta CAntydad de gente Se hizie*S*e
/ Una ConPañya e Se entregase como / A CAPitan que le dexaVa nonbrado /
e con *e*ste conçierto e ynstruyçion se / Partio *e*ste conFesante con la gente / de
Caballo que declarado Tiene e / Con algunos de Pie y Pablos de mel- / Gosa
con ellos e llegado A Çibola e / Visto que no (h)era lo que se dezia / ma*n*do
volVer A melchior Diaz Al / Valle de los corazones donde le / ma*n*do q*ue* *e*Stu-
viese e Poblase e Procu- / raSe de Reduzir A los naturales / A la obediençia de
Su mag*e*stad / e al conosçimyento de dios n*ue*st*r*o / Señor e tomado Consygo
alguna / Gente de a CAballo de la que que- / daba A don tristan dexado A- /
quello Asentado e PaçiFyco Fue / Por aquella Parte en desCubrimy*e*nto / de la

mar del sur conForme a una / ynstruiçion que llevaba e ansimes- / mo le nonbro Por allcalde mayor de la / Vylla que ally se mando Asentar / Fue Preguntado Sy los Pueblos e / ProVinçias por donde Passo este con-

[fol. 101v]

Fesante y el demas exerçito desde la / Villa de san(t) myGuel (f)hasta la Pro- / Vinçia de Çibola Si le salieron de / Paz e dieron la obediençia A su / magestad e de los bastymentos que / thenian (F)hazienDoles Todo buen Aco- / gimyento o Salian de guerra Dixo / que Todos los Pueblos que hay desde / la dicha villa de CuliaCan hasta la Pro- / Vinçia de çibola Por donde este con- / fesante Paso le Salieron de Paz / e les hazian todo buen Acoximyento / e donde alCAnçaban basTimento se lo / daban Porque este conFeSante / hazia que Se Adelantasen algunas / Personas del exerçito e llevaSen / Una cruz en señal de Paz e Para / que los asegurase que no les se- / ria (f)hecho daño Alguno y este conFeSan- / te les daba de los rresCates e coSas / que el visorrey les dio Para / este (h)eFecto con que quedaban muy / Contentos / Fue Preguntado si a los dichos yndios del / Valle de los corazones e señora / e de los otros Pueblos Por donde Pa- / Saron se les hizo algunas cruel- / xvii

[fol. 102r]

915

Dades AGravios o malostratamientos / en sus Personas e haziendas e Si CAs- / tigo A los que lo hizieron e Sy deSi- / mulo con ellos dixo que no Sabe que / Persona alguna del dicho exercito hi- / ziese Crueldad maltratamyento ny daño / Alguno A los naturales de los dichos Pue- / blos ny en Sus (F)haziendas Porque / este conFesante llevaba tan CAsti- / Gado e correGido el exerçito que naDie / oSaba desmandarSe ny deSobedeçerle / e Si algunos yndios de los que yban / en serVycio del exerçito entraban en Al- / Guna Sementera los CAstigaban / AsPeramente en PreSençia de los / naturales e Por el PreGon que hizo / dar naDie ny esPañol ny yndio oSa- / ba entrar en las Casas de los natu- / rales y el exerçito se aPosenTaba / SienPre Fuera del Pueblo Por / (h)eVitar el daño que la gente de / guerra suele (F)hazer / Fue

Preguntado Sy llegado / A Çibola la ProVinçia le salio e / Vyno de Paz (e) *o*
si se Puso en rre- / Sistençia e si les hizo los rre- / quyrimy*ento*s conForme a
lo que

[fol. 102v]
Su mag*e*Stad ma*n*da D*i*xo que llega- / dos çerca de çibola ma*n*do A don
Pedro de / toVar e melchior Diaz que le Truxesen / Algun(d) yndio de Unos
que andaban / çerCA de una laguna e que no les / hizieSe*n* mal Para se
ynFormar e tomar / lengua de *e*llos los quales truxeron / d*o*S o tres de *e*llos y
*e*ste conFeSante / Por una lengua que llevaba del / Valle de los corazones les
daba / A entender que el en nonbre d*e* su / mag*e*stad yba a Ponerlos debaxo
de / Su domynio y A traerlos en conos- / Çimyento de Dios e que Fuesen
*cristi*a- / nos e que nynGun(d) daño se les ha- / ria en sus Personas e
hazienDas / e queriendo Venyr de Paz e dar la obe- / diençia a su mag*e*stad
con los quales / YnVio dos yndios mexicanos con / Una cruz en la mano *en*
Senal de / Paz e llegado *e*ste conFesante / A tres leguas de Çibola Adonde /
(F)*h*allo los mexicanos que *h*abya enVia- / do e le Dixeron que el Pueblo e /
ProVinçia *e*staba*n* de guerra e / no querian venyr de Paz ma*n*do / A don
garçi*a* loPez que con Veynte o / xviii

[fol. 103r]
916
Treynta de A Caballo Fuesen A Ver un / Paso que Paresçia asPero en unas /
Peñas Por do*nde* Podrya rresçibir el / exerçito Daño de los naturales / e que
lo Aderezase e durmyese / ençima de *e*l e le avisase de lo que / Su(b)çediese e
*h*abyendo ydo el d*i*cho / don garçia loPez e aPoSentadose / en el d*i*cho Paso
quando querria Ren- / dyr el quarto de la modorra naturales / dieron en el e
le Flecharon Algunos / CAballos e le hisieran mas daño / SalVo que *e*staba
sobre aviso y *e*ste / ConFeSante como se le (F)*h*izo saber ya / que Fue de dya
CAmyno con el exer- / Çito hasta se junTar con el d*i*cho don / garçi*a* loPez
e llegado a visto / de Çibola e çerCA de *e*lla Vio muchas / A*h*umadas que se
hazian A unas P*a*rtes / e a otras e algunos yndios A ma- / nera d*e* *e*star de

guerra y que toCAban / Una bozina ynVio Al dicho don garcia / loPez e a
Fray luys con Algunos de / A Caballo e a hernando bermejo / escrivano a les
hazer los Requy- / rimyentos que su magestad / manda e adelantados A hazer

[fol. 103v]
lo dicho este conFesante Acordo de hallar- / Se Presente e tomados Algunos
de a Caballo / e de los ResCates que llevaba dexado / mandado que el exerçito
And(i)uViese / se junto con el dicho don garçia loPeZ / y Religiosos llegaron
çerCa de don- / de este conFesante y los demas / estaban trezientos yndios
con arco / Flecha e rroDela e aUnque Por tres / Vezes se les Requyrio Se die-
/ Sen de Paz e se les Dio A en- / Tender Por la dicha lenGua / A lo que yba
e les hAbia enviado / A decir jamas quysieron Venyr de / Paz ny dar la obediençia A su / magestad ny ÇeSar de los Flechar e / Visto que los herian los
CAba- / llos e que habyan dado Un Flechazo / Al dicho fray luys mando
rronPer / en ellos los quales VolVieron las / esPaldas hasta Se meter en el
Pueblo / donde Se hizieron Fuertes y este / ConFesante mando tornar A rre-
/ querir que se diesen de / Paz e ÇerteFycandoseles que / nyngun(d) daño les
harian e que / Serian byen tratados e / xix

[fol. 104r]
917
Visto que no quysieron e que / todaVya los Flecharon de lo alto e / PrinÇi-
Palmente que el exerçito / Padesçia de hanbre mando se diese / Conbate y
entrando este conFeSan- / te Por un CAllejon del dicho Pueblo / Con la
mucha Piedra que de alto / le arrojaron le derroCAron doSS / Vezes de Una
esCala Por donde quySo / Subir A los teRados donde / le SaCAron Por
muerto el dicho don / Garçia loPez e soldados con tres / heridas en el rrostro
e Un Flechazo / en Una Pierna e magullado todo / el CuerPo e le meTieron
en Una / Tienda donde estuVo gran Rato / Sin aCuerdo e vuelto en si le vi-
/ nyeron a dezir que el Pueblo / (h)era Ganado e se hallaba en el / mucho
basTymento e este conFe- / Sante e los demas soldados / entraron en el dicho
Pueblo e se a- / Poderaron de el / Fue Preguntado Sy este conFeSante / o
alguno de los CAPitanes o / Soldados desPues de Ga-

[fol. 104v]

nado e *en*Trado el Pueblo hiziera Alguna / Crueldad muertes o mal-osTratamy*ento*s / *en* los yndios que se hallaron dentro / d*i*xo que no a*n*tes ma*n*do que todos / FueSe muy bien tratados esPeÇial- / me*n*te las muGeres e nyños en las / quales ma*n*do So Graves Penas / que no toCAsen e ma*n*-dados lla- / mar Algunos PrinçiPales les dio / A e*n*tender Por la lengua que *h*abyan / (F)*h*e*c*ho mal en no Venyr de Paz e dar / la obediençia Como Se les / *h*Abia yn Viado A d*e(s)*zir e Reque- / rido Pero que les Perdonaba / que-rienDo dar la obediençia / e que sy algunos q*uy*siesen que- / dar con Sus mugeres e hijos / Se les haria todo buen Tratami*ento* / e les d*e*xarian libres Sus ha- / ziendas e Casas e Se Curarian los / heridos los quales rresPon- / dieron que ellos conosçian *h*aber / (h)errado e se querian yr Al Pue*b*l*o* / de maçaque Para que desde / Alli con los demas Pueblos comar- / canos Venir A dar la obediençia / xx

[fol. 105r]

918

Porque De todos Aquellos Pueblos / *h*Abia gente en el d*i*cho Pueblo que / Se *h*abya Ganado e luego otro Dia / desde A dos dias Vinyeron el Prin- / çiPal de maçaque e los de los otros / Pueblos con Presente de cueros de / Venados e baCas e mantas de *h*enequen / e algunas turquesas y algunos ar- / cos e Fle-chas y *e*ste conFeSante / les dio de los rresCates que lle- / Vaba con que ellos VolVieron muy / Contentos d*e*sPues de *h*Aber dado la / obediençia A su mag*e*stad e d*i*cho q*ue* / querian s*er*Vir e s*er* *cristi*anos / Fue Preguntad*o* Sy *e*stando en el / d*i*cho Pu*eb*l*o* de Çibola vinyeron ynDios / PrinÇiPales d*e* la ProVinçia del / Pu*eb*l*o* de çicuyque A dar la obe- / Di*e*nçia A su mag*e*stad e a oFreçerSe- / les al d*i*cho General Por amyGos Ro- / Gando que Fuesen A Ver su / Pueblo y entre los susod*i*chos / Vinyeron tres yndios PrinÇipa- / les el uno llamado el CAçique y el / otro xacobe e Vio *e*stando en el / d*i*cho Pueblo de Çibola vinyeron

[fol. 105v]

Tres o quatro yndios del Pueblo de / ÇiCuyque que el uno Puso nonbre /

bygotes e que los otros no Tiene / memoria Como se llamaban / ny Si vinyeron
*en*tre ellos los que Se lla- / maban CAçique e jabe e le dixeron / Como ellos
*h*Abian Sabido que / *h*Abia venydo a Su tierra Gente / *e*straña valyentes honbres que / A los que Se deFenDian les / (F)*h*azian daño e a los q*ue* Se les /
daban buen tratamiento que *e*llos / Venyan Por conosçerlos e tenerlos / Por
amygos e *e*ste Co*n*Fesante / Se lo Agradesçio e les Dixo / que venya en nonbre
d*e* su mag*e*st*ad* / a los rreDuzir en su obedienÇia / e Para q*ue* conosçiesen A
dios e Fue- / Sen *cristi*anos que lo hizyesen ansi / e que Serian de *e*llos byen /
Tratados e los te(r)n*d*ryan Por amygos / e d*e*sPues de *h*Aberles mandado /
APoSentar e (f)*h*echo buen tratami*en*to / e dado algunos ResCates de(n)*s*de /
a doS o tres Dias les dixo que / queria yn Viar Al CaPitan her- / xxi

[fol. 106r]
[begins second half of bundle]
919
na*n*do de al Varado Con gente de CAballo / A (F)*h*azer Saber Su Venyda e a
lo / que su magestad le envyaba A las / *Pro*Vinçias e Pueblos comarCAnos /
A d*e*sCubrir lo que *h*abia mas Ade- / lante e los d*i*chos yndios se holGa- / ron
de *e*llo e dixeron que Se / Fuesen Por Su Pueblo e que ally / les harian todo
buen acogimyento e / les darian bastymentos e guias e / AnSi Sabe que el
d*i*cho herna*n*do de / Al Varado Fue con Veynte de a CAba- / llo e suPo que
los del d*i*cho Pueblo / de çiCuyque les hizieron en Su / Pueblo todo buen
acogimyento / e Por el Camy*n*o (F)*h*azian Salir de / Paz todos los otros
Pueblos / e Traerles bastimentos e comy- / da e les Dieron queriendo PaSAr
/ Adelante Por guias doSS yndios q*ue* / Pusyeron Por nonbres el Turco / e
YsoPete / Fue Pregunt*ad*o sy d*e*sPues de *h*aber / Pasado Adelante de çicuyqu*e*
/ el d*i*cho CaPitan herna*n*do de al Va- / rado Vol Vio al Pueblo de çicuyqu*e* /
donde Asymesmo le hizieron

[fol. 106v]
Buen acoximyento donde le Dieron de / PreSente çiertos cueros e mantas e /
otras cosas e las en Vio A *e*ste conFe- / Sante A Çibola donde *e*staba dixo que
/ Sabe que el d*i*cho CAPitan Fer- / na*n*do de al Varado con la gente que /

llevaba volVio Por çicuyque / donde Se le hizo buen tratamyento e /
Acogimyento e no Sabe si des- / de el dicho Pueblo o de yuraba yn- / Vio a
este conFesante al Pueblo / de Çibola donde estaba(^n) Algunos / cueros e
mantas e que oyo dezir / que se los habian dado y el los / habia ynViado no
a la Vuelta Sino A la yda / Fue Preguntado Sy sabe que del / Pueblo de
çicuyque SaCo en- / Ganosamente Al dicho CaPitan Fer- / nando de
AlVarado Al dicho yndio Prin- / ÇiPal llamado bigotes e al yndio / que llamaron CAçique que diziendo / que tenia nesçesidad de el Para / le enSeñar e
guiar Por çiertos Pue- / blos dixo que este conFesante vio / que el dicho CaP-
itan Fernando de al- / Varado traxo consyGo A los dichos / [no number]

[fol. 107r]

920

YnDios llamados bigotes e CAçique e / a los yndios llamados turco e ysoPete
/ e le dixo que los de çicuyque / quedaban muy buenos Syno que / le habia
Paresçido que el yndio lla- / mado bigotes le habia hallado de mala / Suerte e
algo Avieso en las muestras / Fue Preguntado Sy sabe que habyendo el / dicho
hernando de alVarado SaCAdo / de çiquyque a los dichos CAçique e /
bygotes les (h)echo Prisiones e sen- / das Colleras e de esta manera los / Truxo
e metyo donde este Con- / FeSante estaba A Causa que el / dicho yndio llamaDo bigotes no que- / ria Darle Un brazalete de oro / que el ynDio llamaDo Turco / dezia Tener con otras joyas / e Porque no queria conFesar / de
donde las habia traydo ny la / Tierra RicA que el dicho turCo de- / zia e Ansy
le dixo A este con- / FeSante que Por aquella CAusa / les hAbia (h)echado
las Prisiones e / Colleras dixo que hernando / de alVarado Dixo a este Con-
FeSante / que habia (h)echado las dichas

[fol. 107v]

PriSiones o otras Al dicho ynDio / llamado bigotes Porque sintyo(o) / en el
que le quiso (f)hazer huyr / el ynDio llamado turco e que si se / VolViera le
alçara la tierra / e que se ACuerda que el dicho Al- / Varado le Tenya en Prisiones / y este conFeSante le vio con ellas / en el rreal donde estuvo e que / Por
entonzes no le dixo que / le habia (h)echado Prisiones Por las / cauSas que la

PregunTa dize sino / Por las que este conFeSante tyene / dicho e declarado e que la misma / noche A lo que se aCuerda este / testigo llego A tiguex Al Pueblo / de cooFer donde estaba (f)hecho el aPosento / el dicho yndio llamado turco Vyno / Con hernando de alVarado a Ver / a este conFesante e entre otras co- / sas que dixo Fue que en el Pueblo / de çiCuyque hAbia Un braÇale- / te e otras Piezas de oro que el / hAbia traydo de quyVira e que las / hAbia mandado (a)esconder el dicho / yndio llamaDo bigotes e que sy / le dexaba VolVer syn el dicho bigotes / que las tra(h)eria / [no number]

[fol. 108r]

921

Fue Preguntado Si este conFesante mando sabido / lo conthenido en la Pre- gunta Antes De esta A- / Perrear Al dicho Yndio llamado bigotes / Para que dixeSe e declarase lo del / braÇalete e joyas de oro e quantas / Vezes le (h)echaron los Perros e quyen / Se los (h)echo Dixo que Fray juan / de Padilla Dixo A este confesante / que ynPortaba mucho Al servycio de / Su magestad que Se suPiese la / çertenydad de la Tierra RiCA de que / daba noTiçia el turco e que esto Se / Podria saber de bigotes el qual / dezia el turco que tenia el dicho / brazalete e Joyas de oro e que este / ConFesante le rresponDio que el / Como honbre que lo habia conversado / mas Por haber (h)ido con el dicho hernando / De alVarado le entenderia mejor / que el lo tomase e Procurase de / Saber de el la verdad e el dicho / Fray Juan De Padilla le rresPon- / Dio que hernando de alVarado le / entendia mejor que si queria que / Anbos lo Procu- rarian de saber / que Fuese ansi e que el PaDre Fray / Juan dixo que le habian ynterro-

[fol. 108v]

Gado e que toDo lo habia negado e que / de(n)sde algunos Dias vyendole que / Traydo Atado Un braÇo Pregunto que / que habia habido aquel yndio e alli le / Dixeron que le hAbia morDiDo un Perro / e desPues SuPo venydo A esta / ProVinçia que como negaba lo que le / Preguntaban don PeDro de toVar / Porque no lo queria conFeSar le / hAbia dicho que dixeSe la verdad / Syno que le morDeria Aque(e)l / Perro que andaba Suelto e Visto / Como no lo

quiso conFesar *h*Abia / llamaDo el Perro e le *h*abia morDiDo / Fue Pregun-
t*a*do si la Tienda de her- / nando de alvarado e lugar donde / (h)ec*h*aron los
Perros al d*i*cho ynDio / llamaDo bigotes (h)era en el mes- / mo rreal e Pueblo
donde *e*ste con- / Fesante *e*staba aPosent*a*do e çerca / de Su aPosento dixo que
el aPo- / Sento del d*i*cho hernan*d*o de alVa- / rado (h)era çerCA del aPosento
d*e* *e*ste / ConFesante e que oyo Dezir que / no le *h*abian (h)echado el Perro
en el / d*i*cho aPoSento sino que le *h*abian SA- / Cado Fuera Al canPo a Pre-
gunTar- / [no number]

[fol. 109r]
922
Le Lo que d*i*cho e declarado Tiene / Fue Preguntado Sy ansimismo *e*ste /
ConFeSante Vio mordido en las Pier- / nas Al d*i*cho yndio llamado bigotes
/ e Si l(l)e dixo Alguna Persona luego / Aquella noche o dya que acaesçio /
que *h*abian (h)echado los Perros Al / d*i*cho bigotes Porque no queria / Con-
Fesar lo que el d*i*cho yndyo / llamado Turco dezia Dixo que / no Se aCuerda
*h*aber sabido en el / d*i*cho rreal ny(n) en la d*i*cha ProVinÇia / Como declarado
tiene que *h*obiesen / APerreado Al d*i*cho yndio llama- / do bigotes ny *h*aberle
visto otra heriDa / mas de la Del braço o de la Pierna / Fue Pregunt*a*do Sy
sabe que del d*i*cho / Pueblo de çicuyque ynVia- / ron Çiertos yndios A *e*ste
con- / Fesante A Pedyrle el d*i*cho ynDio / llamado bigotes e los demas que /
Tenya Presos del d*i*cho Pueblo dy- / ziendo que les Pagaban mal el / buen
tratamyento que les *h*abia / (f)*h*ec*h*o e amystad e obed*i*ençia que *h*A- / bian
oFresçido e que jamas con- / Syntyo que se le dyesen dixo

[fol. 109v]
que nunCA tal enviaron A PeDir Antes / los d*i*chos bigotes e CAçique
d*e*sPues de / Pasado lo Susod*i*cho le dixeron que / ellos e los de Su Pueblo
(h)eran (h)e- / nemygos de los de tiguex y que / tenyan gran(d) Falta de tierras
de que / AbunDaban(ban) las ProVinçias de / Tyguex que les Diese Alli un
Pue- / blo Para que le Poblase*n* d*e* su / Gente e que le ven*d*ryan A ayudar /
en la guerra / Fue Pregunt*a*do Sy la ProVinçia e Pue- / blos de Tiguex Sy se
vinyeron A / dar de Paz A *e*ste ConFeSante e la / obed*i*ençia *en* nonbre d*e* Su

magestad / e acoxieron A los esPañoles y exer- / ciTo en Su tierra e Pueblos e
les / dieron cueros mantas Aves e / los demas bastymentos nesçesa- / rios e
(f)haziendoles todo buen tra- / Tamyento Dixo que venyendo her- / nando
de alVarado e el dicho Fray juan / de Padilla Por la dicha ProVinçia / Con los
demas esPañoles que / Consygo hAbian llevado los Pueblos / de ella le
Salieron de Paz e / les Proveyeron de mayz Gallinas / [no number]

[fol. 110r]
923
mantas e Cueros e de lo que ellos te- / nyan Por ResCates que dize que les
dieron / el dicho hernando de alvarado e Fray juan / de Padilla e les hizieron
todo buen / Acogimyento Syn mosTrarse de / Guerra ny hazer rresistençia
alguna / e que Fray juan de Padilla le escri- / bio A çibola donde este con-
Fesan- / te estaba que rribera del Rio de / Aquella Provinçia hAbia muy bue-
/ nos Pastos que le Paresçia se debia / Venir A asenTar rreal en aquel / Sytio
e hAbyendo ynviado A / don garcia loPez con yndios de Çibola / e amyGos
Para Asentarse el / Real e (f)hazerSe rrancho donde el / dicho Fray juan dezia
los yndios / del Pueblo de CooFor vyendo que / el dicho don Garçia loPez
queria / (F)hazer CAsas le dixeron que no las / (F)hyziese que ellos le dexarian
vaçio / Aquel(l) Pueblo E Se Pasarian / A otroS çercanos Donde estaban /
Sus Amygos e Parientes e / que ansy lo dexaron Vaçio e Se / APosentaron en
el dicho Pueblo / Fue Preguntado Sy mando este conFesante

[fol. 110v]
e a que Personas que Fuesen A los Pue- / blos de la dicha ProVinçia A
rrecoxer / cueros e mantas Para Vestyr la gente / E gallynas Para Darles de
comer / e algunos Pellones de Pluma / e ansi Por su mandado Recoxieron /
de los dichos Pueblos e traxeron Al / Pueblo donde estaban APosentados / las
dichas mantas Cueros e Pellones / e aves e basTymento e mayz neçesa- / rio
Dixo que çiertos esPañoles sol- / dados e yndios amygos se queXaron / A este
conFesante que eStaban DeSnu- / dos e morian de Frios que mandase / que
de los Pueblos comarCAnos / Se rrecoxiese Alguna rroPa / Con que se
cubriesen e guaresçiesen / del F(y)rio e Vista la nesçesidad / que habia este

conFesante mando / A don garçia loPez que tomase rres- / cate e con ellos Procurase de rres- / CAtar del Pueblo de chia Algunos Pe- / llones Cueros e mantas Para / vestyr e (^e) Remediar la gente e que / Ansi sabe que Fueron e truxe- / ron çiertas manTas Cueros e / Pellones no tanta CAntydad / [no number]

[fol. 111r]

924

Como la gente hAbia menester Porque / no Se la dieron e Se rrePartyo entre / la gente que mas nesçesidad te- / nyan la qual RoPa hobieron Por los / ResCates que llevaron que son de / los que el visorrey mando llevar / Para (h)eFecto de rresCatar Con los yn- / Dios / Fue Preguntado Si sabe o oyo que el / dicho Recogimyento de la rroPa / Aves e bastymentos Se hizo con / Vexaçion e Sacandolo de las / casas contra voluntad de los yndios / Dixo que no sabe tal cosa antes le / Fue dicho que lo dieron los ynDios A / trueque de los dichos ResCAtes de Su / voluntad e Ansy lo cree Por ser el / dicho don garçia loPez cristiano e Caballero / Fue Preguntado Sy suPo Ansymismo / que yendo A Recoxer la dicha / RoPa cueros Pellones e bastymento / Un villegas Soldado del dicho / exerçito tomo Por Fuerça una yn- / dia e se (h)echo con ella carnalmente / Contra Su voluntad de que los / naturales ansy de esto como de / hAberles tomado de sus CASAs / contra Su voluntad la dicha RoPa

[fol. 111v]

quedaron muy desSabriDos e esCanda- / lizados e Si le vino A su noTiçia / e lo CAstigo Dixo que nunCA tal suPo / Porque Si lo SuPiera lo CAsti- / gara conforme A Un Pregon que / tenya dado e que venydo A esta Pro- / Vinçia oyo Dezir que el dicho ville- / gas Se habia (h)echado con la dicha yn- / dya e lo demas en la Pregunta conthe- / nydo que no lo Sabe / Fue Preguntado Si sabe que ansi Por / la Prision e aPerreamyento del / dicho yndio llamado bigotes como / Por la Fuerça Cometyda Por el dicho / Villegas e haber SACado la dicha Ro- / Pa e basTymentos de los Pueblos con- / tra Voluntad de los naturales se / Alzaron e rrebelaron Ansy el dicho / Pueblo de çiquyque como la ProVin- / çia de tiguex E que Ansy se dixo / PubliCA-

mente que Por las Causas / dichas e otras crueldades e malos- / Tratamyentos
Se alzaron e rre- / belaron dixo que como dicho e decla- / rado Tiene nunCA
suPo lo conthe- / nydo en la Pregunta ny cree que Por / las dichas Causas no
se alçaron Por- / [no number]

[fol. 112r]

925

que los del dicho Pueblo de chia desPues del / Recogimyento de la dicha RoPa
vinyeron / Al Real e Se ComunyCAron con este con- / Fesante e le Truxeron
Gallynas / E otras cosas de ProVision e le ofres- / çieron Ayuda e que
ansymesmo / Sabe que los del Pueblo de çiqui- / que no Se alzaron Por la
dicha Pry- / Syon ny Por lo que la Pregunta dize / Porque desPues de haber
Pasado / Todo lo Susodicho e habersele rre- / belado la ProVinçia de Tiguex
/ este conFesante Fue al Pueblo de / Çicuyque e llevo Consygo A los dichos /
bigotes e a Caçique A les PeDir Ayu- / da e le acogieron dentro de su Pue- /
blo e le hizieron todo buen Trata- / myento e que entro solo con don loPe /
de (h)urrea e fray juan de Padilla / Aunque no quedo a Dormyr / en el Pueblo
e que no le quysie- / ron dar el Favor que PeDia esCu- / Sandosele que
estaban todos en / Sus sementeras e que Si toda- / Via les mandaba que lo
dexasen / todo que lo harian e como Vio que / no Se le ofresçian de buena

[fol. 112v]

Voluntad no proCuro de APretarles / mas en ello Antes les dixo que / Se lo
agradesçio que quando Fuese / menester Se lo daria / Fue Preguntado Pues el
dicho Pueblo / de çiquique e ProVinçia de ti- / guex de su voluntad Vinyeron
A / dar la obediençia e A ofreçer- / Se Por Amygos y como dicho Tiene no /
Se les hizo nyngun(d) maltrata- / myento que Fue la CAusa Por / que se
alzaron e rrebelaron los na- / Turales dixo que este testigo no sabe / la Causa
mas de que estando de Paz / Syn les haber dado oCasion que / este ConFesante SePa se Re- / belaron e Amanesçieron Una ma- / ñana muertos e
Flechados hasta treyn- / ta e çinco CAballos Poco mas o me- / nos de los que
andaban en el CAnPo / e doS mexiCAnos que los guardaVan / Fue Preguntado en que tantos Pue- / blos de la ProVinça de tiguex / se Recoxio la gente

e se hizieron / Fuertes e que tantos Fueron los / Pueblos que deXaron deSS- / [no number]

[fol. 113r]

926

ma*n*Parados e yermos Dixo que la gen- / Te Se rrecoxio e hizo Fuerte*s* en Solos / doS pueblos e que otros nueVe o diez / que *h*abia en la di*c*ha Provinçia de- / xaron deSSma*n*Parados e yermos / Fue Pregunt*a*do que Pues los di*c*hoS *diez* Pue- / blos quedaron yermos e sin de- / FenSa Por que CAusa los quemaron / e deRibaron e si Fue Por ma*n*dado / d*e e*ste conFesante o suPo quyen lo / *h*Abia (f)*h*e*c*ho o ma*n*dado (f)*h*azer d*i*xo que / *e*ste confesante no ma*n*do quemar / ny deRibar los di*c*hos Pueblos ny / Sabe Particularmen*T*e que / CAPitan los quemase o deRi- / base Pero que cree que Por el / Gran(d) Frio que (f)*h*azia Por *e*star / lexos los montes e *e*star el rreal / {ojo} / en el CAnpo los Soldados Para se Re- / medyar los quemarian e (^quen) la made- / ra e que no Sabe sy derroCA- / ron las Paredes ny Sy destruye- / ron del todos los di*c*hos Pueblos / Fue Pregunt*a*do Sy *e*ste conFeSante Si / ma*n*do a don rrodrigo maldonado q*ue* / quemase e deRibase el Pri- / mero de los di*c*hos Pueblos o Uno

[fol. 113v]

de *e*llos dixo que *e*ste conFeSante mando / A don rroDrigo maldonado que FueSe A / Uno de los di*c*hos Pueblos que *h*Abian / quedado deSSmanParados que dezian / *ser* el mas Fuerte e SaCAse*n* de *e*l todo / el basTymento que en el *h*obieSe e / que no tiene memoria Sy le ma*n*- / do que lo quemase o deRoCAse / E Sy Se lo manDo Seria Porque / no se tornasen A (F)*h*azer Fuertes los / yndios que de aquel(l) e De otros Pue- / blos se *h*abyan Salydo e que *e*stando / en el rreal vio Salir humo en los / di*c*hos Pueblos e Pregunta*n*do que / (h)era Aquello le dixeron que se / quemaba uno de los di*c*hos Pue- / blos e que nunCA SuPo que / (que) CAPitan lo *h*abia quemado ny / ma*n*dado quemar / Fue Pregunt*a*do el Real d*e e*ste / ConFeSante que tenya Sobre uno / de los Pueblos donde *e*staban / los yndios hechos Fuertes que tan / lexos *e*staba de los di*c*hos Pueblos / desma*n*Parados que se quemaron /

e deRibaron d*i*xo que unos *e*sta- / ban A media legua e otros a una /
[no number]

[fol. 114r]
927

e doS e tres del d*i*cho Real / Fue Pregunt*a*do antes que Pusiese / çerco Sobre
los d*i*chos Pueblos y / los conbatiese Sy los rrequi- / rio que se diesen de Paz
e que / los Perdonarian e no les harian / daño nynguno dixo que *e*ste conFe-
/ Sante vista la rreVelion de los / d*i*chos Yndios llamo A su aPosen- / to A los
Religiosos Fray Juan de / Padilla e a Fray antonyo de CAstil- / blanco e a los
oFyçiales d*e* su mag*e*stad / e ComunyCados Sobre lo que se de- / bia de
(f)*h*azer el d*i*cho Fray Juan de / Padylla d*i*xo que a ellos no les (h)era / lyçito
matar a naDie que el APro- / baba e daba Por bueno lo que el / General
hiziese e lo mismo rres- / Pondio el d*i*cho Fray antonyo e to- / dos les Paresçio
que Se les / debia de (F)*h*azer guerra e ansi acor- / dado *e*ste ConFeSante
ynVio Al / Pueblo que se dize del arenal / A Diego loPez veynte e quatro /
de SeVylla Para que les / D*i*xeSe lo mal que lo *h*Abian (f)*h*echo e q*ue* / Sy
*h*abia sydo el alçamyento Por

[fol. 114v]
Algun(d) AGravio o ma*l*Tratamiento que / Algun(d) soldado les *h*obiese
(F)*h*echo que lo d*i*- / xesen que en su Presençia les (f)*h*aria / Just*i*c*i*a E que
VolViesen A dar la / obediençia a Su mag*e*stad e los Per- / donarian E
ansimismo ynvio A / don RoDrigo maldonado al Pueblo de / moha que
(h)era el otro enCAstillado / Y entranbos los quysieron enGa- / nosamente
matar e Visto que *e*staban / Rebeldes e que dexando aquello / de guerra e a
las esPaldas (h)era Peli- / Groso Pasar Adelante Se les PuSo / çerco e Se les
dieron conbate con *h*arto / Peligro del exercito Porque en el / Primero conbate del Pueblo / Sobre que Puso çerco don g*a*rc*i*a lo- / Pez le hirieron mas
de quarenta / *e*sPañoles e yndios Amygos e en el / en que *e*ste ConFesante
Puso / çerco que se llama noha (l)*s*e hirieron / muchos Soldados e le mataron
/ A Franc*i*sco de oVando CAPitan e otros / quatro o çinco soldados e al Fyn

Aun- / que el Uno çerco Fue largo e Proli- / xo Se tornaron e PaçiFiCAron / Fue Preguntado (e)en el Pueblo do*nde e*ste / ConFesante tuVo el çerCo q*ue* tantos / [no number]

[fol. 115r]

928

Yndios Se aPerrearon e quema- / ron (o) *e* Por cuyo ma*n*dado Se hizo e / Sy vino A notiçia d*e e*ste conFe- / Sante Dixo que *e*ste conFeSante / no ma*n*do quemar ny aPerrear yn- / Dio alguno ny sabe que tal cosa se / *h*obieSe (f)*h*echo mas de que SuPo *e*s- / Tando en Su tienda enFermo / Se *h*abian Soltado unos yndios / del d*i*cho Pueblo que *e*staban / Presos e Se *h*abian Tomado en la / Guerra e Fue un Perro tras / de *e*llos e los mordio Pero ny / murieron ny Sabe que naDie les / (F)echase los Perros y traydos / los ma*n*do soltar Para que / Se Fuesen do*nde* quySiesen / Fue Preguntado Sy Vio o suPo q*ue* / de los yndios que se salyan / del d*i*cho Pueblo Por nesçe- / Sydad de Sed o de hanbre / e Syn (f)armas e syn hazer Re- / Systençia los Alançeaban / o (h)echaban los Perros Para los / AlCançar y montearlos dixo que / no Sabe cosa alguna de lo en la

[fol. 115v]

Pregunta Co*n*thenido e que los que / Se salieron e vinyeron A Poder d*e e*ste / ConFeSante les hizo todo buen trata- / myento e les mando que los VolVie- / Sen Al Pueblo Para que dixesen / A los otros que Se diesen e que / Serian Per- donados / Fue Preguntado Sy sabe que en el Pue- / blo del Arenal Sobre que te- / nya çerco don Garçi*a* loPez de CAr- / denas *h*Abyendoles dado conbate e / Ganado P*ar*te de las açoteas los que / quedaban Por conquistar hizieron / Señas al d*i*cho don Garçi*a* loPeZ / que Sy les aseguraban las vydas / Se darian de Paz y el d*i*cho don g*ar*ci*a* / loPez Por señas Se lo Prometyo e / Aseguro E ansy salieron del / d*i*cho Pueblo (f)*h*asta ochenta Personas / Sin armas nyn- Gunas y el d*i*cho don / Garçi*a* loPez mando Recoxer / en el rreal en s(y)u tienda d*i*xo / que *e*ste conFesante oyo que / dandole (^V) conbate Çiertos yn- / dios *h*abian Salido del d*i*cho Pue- / blo Syn armas e de Paz y que / [no number]

[fol. 116r]

929

eL dicho don Garçia loPez los mando meter / Y rrecoxer en Su tyenda / Fue
Preguntado Sy el dicho don Garcia lo- / Pez hizo saber A este ConFesante /
que venyan rrecoxidos los dichos / Yndios en la dicha Tienda que viese / lo que
mandaba (F)hazer de ellos y este / ConFeSante le envio A dezir con / Contreras Su CAballerizo que los / quemase A todos e que diFyrieSe / la Justicia
hasta que llegasen a ver- / la (F)hazer los yndios llamados turco e / YsoPete
Porque diesen en su / Tierra RelaÇion de la justicia / que Se hazia contra los
que Se Re- / belaban dixo que nyega lo con- / thenydo en la Pregunta e que
lo que / Pasa es que el dicho don garçia lo- / Pez ynvio A dezir A este con- /
FeSante que aquel Pueblo / estaba entrado e que todavia esta- / ban çiertas
CASAs Por Ganar e yn- / dios e yndias en ellas que vie- / Se sy queria que
Pasase A- / delante A (F)hazer Guerra A los / demas Rebelados e que enVio
/ A dezir que no alÇaSe mano del

[fol. 116v]

(que no AlCAse mano del) dicho Pueblo hasta / lo dexar del Todo PaçiFico
E que este / confesante le ResPondio que el / Yria a ver el estado en que estaba
/ el dicho Pueblo e yendo se en- / Contrarian en el Pueblo de la Ala- / meda
/ Fue Preguntado Sy suPo o Vino A su / notiçia que el dicho don Garçia
loPeZ / de los yndios que el tenya rrecoxidos / en la dicha tienda mando
quemar / e quemo ViVos atados A unos / Palos hasta quarenta o çinquenta /
de ellos Dixo que nunCa SuPo / que el dicho don Garçia loPez hobie- / Se
quemado Sobre el dicho çerco / Yndios algunos ny tal vyno a su / notiçia que
este ConFesante se A- / Cuerde / Fue Preguntado Sy suPo que el dicho / don
Garçia loPez Alançeo e mato / A estoCAdas y los soldados Por / Su mandado otros treynta / o quarenta yndios que estaban / en la tienda dixo que oyo
decir / que los yndios (que los yndios) / [no number]

[fol. 117r]

930

que esTaban en la dicha Tienda se habian / Alçado e (f)hecho Fuertes hAbyan muerto / Algunos de *e*llos / Fue Pregunt*a*do Sy al tienPo que / Se hizo la d*i*cha quema e alan- / çearon en la d*i*cha Tienda los / d*i*chos yndios Sy se hallaron en el / Real donde *e*sTaba el d*i*cho don G*ar*ci*a* / loPez e acaesçio lo Susod*i*cho Se / (F)*h*allaron Presentes los d*i*chos yndios / Turco e ysoPete e si los ynVio / *e*ste conFeSante Al d*i*cho Real / Dixo que no tiene memoria de coSSA / Alguna de lo que en esta Pre- / Gunta Se contiene / Fue Pregunt*a*do el yndio llamado / Turco Sy le ma*n*do matar *e*ste / conFeSante e Por que CAusa e quyen / Fue el que le mato e Si Se hallo / *e*ste conFesante delante o en / el Real donde le Dieron garroTe / d*i*xo que *h*abyendo *e*ste conFeSante / Ydo a la ProVinçia de quyVira / con çierta P*ar*te de Gente e *h*abyendo / llevado consygo A los d*i*chos yn-

[fol. 117v]
Dios llamados Turco e ysoPete en el / Postrero Pueblo d*e* la d*i*cha ProVinÇia / donde *e*ste conFesante *e*sTuVo / Vyendo que les Faltaba el mayZ / Pregunto que (h)era la CAusa / Por que no les ProVeyan / y le ResPondieron que Por- / que el d*i*cho yndio llamado turco / les *h*abia d*i*cho que no les Diesen mayZ / e que no Dandolo Se moririan lue- / Go los Caballos e que tuViesen ojo / en çiertos Caballos que (h)eran los / mejores Para matarlos que aque- / llos muertos luego matarian los / *cristi*anos e Sabido *e*sTo ma*n*do / A diego loPez maestre de CAnPo / que *h*abyda ynformaçion de lo Suso- / d*i*cho hiziese jus-*ti*ci*a* E ansymismo / le ma*n*do que Preguntase al / Turco que Por que CAuSa *h*Abyan / conçertado Aquello e Por que / los Trayan enGañados e Perdidos / e que Sabydo Por el d*i*cho ma*e*sTre / de CanPo como el d*i*cho yndio lla- / mado turco les Trataba la muerte / lo hizo matar lo q*ual* en el CAnPo / [no number]

[fol. 118r]
931
Dond*e* *e*ste t*e*stigo *e*staba e que / *e*sta es la *ver*dad E lo que *en* *e*ste CASSo / Sabe Para el juramento que / (F)*h*yzo Fue le leydo Su d*i*cho e confision / luego Como lo ACabo de de*(s)*zir e / RetiFycose en el e (A)Firmolo el d*i*cho / Señor oydor Fran*cis*co Vazquez / de coronado El liÇen*cia*do tejada

Chapter 16

Alonso Álvarez,
the Fourteenth de Oficio Witness

The Standard Bearer

D uring the expedition to Tierra Nueva Alonso Álvarez de Valle
served as *paje de guión* or standard bearer for Vázquez de Coronado
and was a member of the captain general's household until the
siege of the Tiguex pueblos during the winter of 1540–1541. Why he did not
continue as standard bearer is unknown, but he was not quartered even in the
same camp with Vázquez de Coronado during the expedition's second winter
in Tiguex.[1] Whether there were hard feelings between the captain general and
Álvarez over this separation can only be guessed. The standard bearer's junior
status as a dependent of Vázquez de Coronado at the time the expedition set
off in February 1540 is attested by the fact that he took no horses with him.[2]
A native of Villanueva de Barcarrota in Badajoz in Spain,[3] he was in his
middle teens at the time[4] and had arrived in Nueva España in 1537 or 1538
on the same ship that brought Cristóbal de Escobar, another of the de oficio
witnesses called by Tejada in 1544. Less than a year before the Tejada investigation, Álvarez and another fellow witness, Domingo Martín, had testified
on behalf of Escobar in a formal statement of his service to the king.[5]

Álvarez returned to Mexico City with the expedition, but then backtracked to Nueva Galicia sometime between November 1543 and September 1544, being questioned there, in Guadalajara, by Tejada on September 5, 1544, the final witness called by the oidor. In 1576, when he testified on behalf of two other expedition members, Alonso Rodríguez and Juan Rodríguez Parra, he was a vecino of San Sebastián[6] in the Copala district of what had been part of Nueva Galicia and had recently been annexed to Nueva Vizcaya.

During his brief testimony before licenciado Tejada, Álvarez made few excuses for Vázquez de Coronado, though one is left with no feeling of outrage or accusation. On many points he contradicted the testimony of the captain general and portrayed him as fully aware of violence against Indians and having condoned or even ordered it. Álvarez, for example, told matter-of-factly that the captain general ordered that Tiguex Indians whose hands and noses had been cut off after their capture be conducted to their pueblos, so that the people there might see what punishment had been inflicted on them. And he stated that he believed Vázquez de Coronado ordered the burning of Indians at Pueblo del Arenal and the killing of others by dogs at Pueblo del Cerco. Furthermore, he claimed to have been present when the captain general ordered Rodrigo Maldonado to burn and dismantle Tiguex pueblos. Álvarez was most voluble in expressing his opinions about the causes of the uprising in Tiguex, among which he put the gathering of clothing for the men-at-arms, which was done very clumsily and against the will of the natives, and the rape of an Indian woman by Juan de Villegas, brother of Pedro de Villegas, who served with Vázquez de Coronado as regidor of the cabildo of Mexico City. Álvarez's testimony is some of the most damaging to the former captain general and damning of the expedition as a whole. It was evidently dismissed or overlooked by the audiencia in reaching its decision in the case.

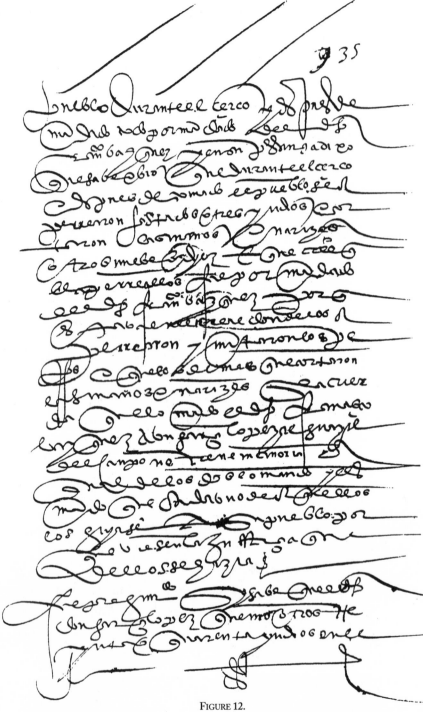

FIGURE 12.

Facsimile of Cortaron manos e narizes or they cut off hands and noses, AGI, Justicia, 267, N.3, fol. 122r

A TRANSLATION
OF THE TESTIMONY

Final de Oficio Witness (Alonso Álvarez)⁷

[118r cont'd] After the aforesaid in the city of Guadalajara on the fifth day of the month of September in the year one thousand five hundred and forty-four, the lord licenciado Tejada ordered Alonso Álvarez, a vecino of this city, to appear before him for this investigation, and he received his oath in the form required by law. He promised to tell and state the truth and was asked the following questions.

{*1*} He was asked whether he knows Francisco Vázquez de Coronado, Hernando [118v] de Alvarado, and don García López de Cárdenas, and whether he knows about the provinces of Cíbola, Tiguex, and Cicuique and the exploration and conquest that were carried out in that land. He answered that he knows those referred to in the question and knows about those provinces and the reconnaissance and conquest carried out there. That is because the witness served as Francisco Vázquez de Coronado's page and in his household from the city of Mexico until the siege of the pueblos in the province of Tiguex.

{*2*} [The witness] was asked whether he knows that, when the first pueblo of the province of Cíbola had been captured and occupied and Francisco Vázquez (who was the general) was in that pueblo, Indians came from the pueblo of Cicuique and the province of Tiguex to offer themselves to him as allies and to render obedience to His Majesty. Does he know that [119r] all [the people of] those pueblos and provinces welcomed the army and the Spaniards into their pueblos in peace? And did they supply provisions and other necessary things? He replied that it is true that he knows what is referred to in the question, since he saw that seven or eight Indians came from the pueblo and province of Cicuique. Among those who came were two principales, to one of whom [the Spaniards] gave the name Bigotes and to the other, the cacique. He remembers that Bigotes was one of those who came, but he does not remember whether the cacique came then or afterwards.

{3} He was [then] asked whether he knows that Francisco Vázquez sent Hernando de Alvarado and a number of horsemen with the Indians from [Cicuique],[8] in order to see their pueblo and reconnoiter what there was beyond. [119v] Does he know that, when they had gone, Alvarado returned with Bigotes and the cacique as prisoners in collars? And did he bring before Francisco Vázquez de Coronado two Indians known as El Turco and Ysopete, also as prisoners? He replied that what is referred to in the question is true, except that he does not remember whether, when Alvarado arrived before Francisco Vázquez, [the Indians were] brought [as] prisoners or not. He does know, however, that afterwards they were chained and imprisoned in collars by the general's order.

{4} [Álvarez] was asked whether he knows that Francisco Vázquez ordered dogs to be set on Bigotes because he denied having a gold bracelet and other valuable jewelry, which the Indian called Turco said he had. Did he do this so that Bigotes would speak and tell about what he was asked? And did they, in fact, unleash the dogs, and did they bite him cruelly? He answered that he knows that [the Spaniards] set dogs [120r] on the Indian called Bigotes and that he was badly maimed by bites on the legs and, he seems to remember, on one arm. It took many days for him to heal. He believes and is certain that this was done by order of Francisco Vázquez, or by his wish and consent.

This is because the witness saw Francisco Vázquez leave his quarters and go to those of Hernando de Alvarado. Within a short while it was known and said that they had set dogs on that Indian. Further, the witness saw Bigotes brought from where the dogs had been unleashed, and he was placed in Alvarado's lodging. From there [the Spaniards] took him the next day, or many days later, to the lodging of Francisco Vázquez, where they fed him. And Francisco Vázquez saw him. It seems to the witness that the general then ordered a surgeon called Ramos to treat [Bigotes]. The witness also saw that, even though [120v] [Bigotes] had been set upon by dogs and bitten, [the Spaniards] always kept him in collar and chain. Francisco Vázquez said that it distressed him to see [Bigotes] injured and ill-treated. Nevertheless, it had occurred on the general's order and by his wish and consent, since no one would have dared to unleash dogs [against Bigotes]. This is because the general held the army and the captains so subject to his command that no one would dare to arrange or carry out such a thing without his order and permission.

{5} [The witness] was asked why the pueblos of Cicuique and the province of Tiguex rose up in arms. He stated that he believes that it was because of the confinement of and unleashing of dogs against the Indians called the cacique and Bigotes. He also heard it said that [the Spaniards] had set a bitch on the cacique because he had fled from them. In addition, the uprising occurred because the general sent [individuals] to the pueblos of the province of Tiguex to gather clothing for [121r] the men-at-arms, and it was done very clumsily and against the will of the natives. Another reason for the uprising was that a man-at-arms [named] Villegas seized an Indian woman and had sexual relations with her by force. All of this was spoken of publicly. As soon as the collection of clothing had been carried out, the rape they said was committed against the Indian woman had occurred, and dogs had been unleashed against the aforesaid Indians, the pueblos rose up. As he remembers, first the people of Tiguex rose up in arms and then, within a few days, the people of Cicuique.

{6} Álvarez was asked whether he knows that the Indians of Tiguex who revolted fortified themselves and gathered in only two pueblos. And did the rest, which totalled as many as eight or nine, remain abandoned and deserted? He answered that it is true and happened as stated in the question, [121v] since he saw it. Also, [the Indians] left their provisions in the pueblos.

{7} He was asked [next] whether he knows that, by Francisco Vázquez de Coronado's order, the captains and men-at-arms of the army burned and laid waste to all the pueblos that were abandoned. [In answer] he said that he knows and saw that, by order of the general, don Rodrigo Maldonado burned two of those pueblos and tore down parts of the others, in order to supply firewood to the camp. The witness was present when the order was given and saw the pueblos burned and torn down.

{8} [The witness] was asked whether he knows that, at the pueblo besieged by Francisco Vázquez in the province of Tiguex, many Indians were set upon by dogs and [the Spaniards] cut off their hands and noses. [Did these include] both those who had been taken by force and those who had left the [122r] pueblo during the siege? And was this done by the general's order and in his presence after the whole pueblo had been captured? He replied that he knows and saw that, during the siege and after the pueblo's capture, two or three Indians were set upon by dogs and another nine or ten had their hands and noses cut off. He believes that the unleashing of dogs was carried out under the general's order, since Francisco Vázquez was in the camp where [the Indians] were set upon and killed by dogs. In regard to the others who had their hands and noses cut off, he remembers that Francisco Vázquez ordered don García López or the alguacil of the camp (he does not remember which of the two) to do it. [Further,] he ordered them to conduct each of those [Indians] to his pueblo, so that [the people there] might see what punishment had been inflicted on them.

{9} Álvarez was asked whether he knows that don García López burned another thirty or forty Indians in the [122v] camp at the other pueblo that he besieged. And was this done by the general's order or was he aware of it and had it come to his notice? He answered that he did not see the burning done, but it is public knowledge and widely held (and he believes it) that Francisco Vázquez ordered it. This is because one day before [the Indians] were burned the witness saw a messenger come to Francisco Vázquez from don García López de Cárdenas, and the general sent him another messenger, though he does not remember [whether][9] it was his head groom Contreras.

Soon he heard it said in the camp that the messenger had come from don García so that the general would know that he had a number of Indians in his tent and to ask whether he should burn them or how he should punish them. The next day it was known and said publicly that don García López had burned them. Because of what [123r] he has said, the witness believes and is certain that the maestre de campo would not have burned them unless it was by order and consent of the general. This must be since, as he has said, everyone was so subject to his order and obedient that nothing happened without the responsible party informing him of it.

{*10*} He was asked whether he knows that the general sent the Indians called Turco and Ysopete from his camp to that of don García López before he carried out the burning. And did he send them so that they would witness the punishment [the Spaniards] inflicted on [the Indians]? He stated that he does not remember, but he knows that, when the dogs were unleashed and the hands and noses of those Indians captured during the siege where Francisco Vázquez was were cut off, they brought the Indians Turco and Ysopete to see the punishment administered. This was so that they would spread the word through their lands about the punishment that was inflicted on those who rebelled. He believes this was done by the general's order, since [123v] [the two Indians] were taken from near his tent.

He said that this is the truth and what he knows concerning this case, in accordance with the oath he swore. He signed his name. [And the lord judge signed.][10]

Alonso Álvarez
licenciado Tejada

A TRANSCRIPT
OF THE TESTIMONY

[fol. 118r cont'd]⁷

E desPues de lo Susodicho en la dicha / çiUdad de Guadalajara Çinco / dias
del mes de Septienbre del / dicho año de myll e quynyentos e / quarenta e
quatro años (^Para) / {S} / (^la d) el dicho Señor liçençiado Te- / Jada Para la
dicha ynformaçion / mando Paresçer Ante sy a alon- / So AlVarez Vezino de
la dicha / ÇiUdad del qual Fue rresçibido / Juramento en Forma de derecho el
qual / Prometyo de decir e aclarar la / verdad e Se le hizieron las Pre- / Guntas
siguyentes / Fue Preguntado Sy conosçe A Francisco / Vazquez de coronado
e a hernando

[fol. 118v]

De AlVarado e a don Garçia loPez de CAr- / denas e Si tiene notiçia de las
Pro- / Vinçias de çibola e tiguex e çicuyque / e desCubrymyento e conquista
que / en la dicha Tierra se hizo Dixo que / Conosçe A los en la Pregunta con-
/ thenidos e Tiene noTiÇia de las / dichas ProVinçias desCubrimyento / E
conquista que en ellas Se / (F)hyzo Porque este testigo desde / la ÇiUdad de
mexico hasta el çerco / de los Pueblos de la ProVinçia de / Tiguex SerVio de
Paje y en su CASSA / Al dicho Francisco vazquez de coronado / Fue Preguntado Sy sabe que habyendo / Tomado y entrado Por Fuerça / el Primero
pueblo de la ProVinçia de / Çibola estando en el Primero Pue- / blo Vinyeron
Al dicho Francisco Vaz- / quez General que (h)era yn- / dios del dicho Pueblo
de çicuyque / E ProVinçia de Tyguex A / Se le oFresçer Por / AmyGos e dar
la obediençia / A Su magestad e Sy sabe que / [no number]

[fol. 119r]

932

todos Los dichos Pueblos e ProVinçias / los ResÇibieron en sus Pueblos / A
los esPañoles y exerçito / de Paz e les ProVeyeron de / basTymentos e de las

otras / Cosas nesçesarias dixo que es *ver-* / dad que sabe lo en la Pregunta /
Conthenido Porque lo Vio e vio / que de la dicha ProVinçia e Pue- / blo de
çicuyque vinyeron (F)hasTa / Syete o ocho yndios entre los / quales Vinyeron
dos Prin- / ÇiPales que al uno Pusyeron / Por nonbre bigotes e al otro el /
CAçique e que el bigotes se aCuer- / da que es el uno de los que / Vinyeron
AUnque del CAçique / no Se aCuerda byen Sy Vyno / entonzes o desPues /
Fue Preguntado Sy sabe que con los / dichos yndios del (CAçi)*cicuique* ynVio
/ el dicho Francisco Vazquez a hernando / de alVarado con çierta gente de /
CAballo Para que Viese su / Pueblo e desCubriese mas / Adelante lo que
habia e que

[fol. 119v]

Ansy (h)idos Sabe que a la Vuelta / VolVio consygo el dicho bigotes e al CA-
/ çique Presos en colleras e que / Ansimesmo Traya A dos yndios / que Se
llamaba el uno el Turco / Y el otro ysoPete e los Truxo de esta / manera ante
el dicho Francisco Vazquez / de Coronado dixo que es verdad / lo que la Pregunta dize eÇe(b)pto que / no tiene memoria Sy quando llego / el dicho hernando de alVarado ante el / dicho Francisco Vazquez trayan Pri- / Syones o
no Pero sabe que / Por mandado del dicho Francisco Vazquez / Se las
(h)echaron luego Prisiones / que Fueron collera e CAdena / Fue Preguntado
Sy sabe que A CaUsa / que el dicho bigotes negaba tener un / braÇalete de
oro e otras joyas / RiCas que el yndio llamado / Turco dezia tener el dicho
bigotes / Porque lo dixese e conFeSase / el dicho Francisco vazquez mando /
APerrear al dicho bigotes e de / (f)hecho le (h)echaron los Perros e le / mordio
bravamenTe dixo que / este testigo Sabe que aPerrearon / [no number]

[fol. 120r]

933

Al dicho yndio llamado bigotes e de las / mordeduras quedo mal lisiado en las
/ Piernas y A lo que se quyere acor- / dar en el braço e que esTuVo mu- / chos
dias en Sanar e que cree e / Tiene Por çierto que Fue Por / mandado del dicho
Francisco vazquez / o de Su voluntad e consenty- / myento Porque este Testigo / Vio al dicho Françisco Vazquez / Salir de Su Posada e yr A la / de her-

nando de AlVarado e de(n)s- / de A Poco se SuPo e dixo que / hAbian APerreado al dicho yndyo / Y este testigo le Vio traer del lu- / Gar donde le
hAbyan aPerrea- / do e le metieron en CASSA de her- / nando de AlVarado
e de ally / le truxeron otro dia e otros mu- / chos a CASa del dicho Francisco
Vazquez / donde le daban de Comer e lo Veya / el dicho Francisco Vazquez e
que le / Pareze que el dicho Francisco Vaz- / quez mando luego A un çirujano
/ que Se dize Ramos que le / CuraSe E que SyenPre aun-

[fol. 120v]
que esTaba morDydo e aPerreado le tra- / Yan con la Collera e cadena e el dicho
/ Francisco Vazquez dezia que le PeSAba / de verle herido e tan maltratado / e
que Sino Fuera Por (^el dicho) man- / dado del dicho Francisco vazquez o / Por
su (mandado) voluntad e conSentymyento / nynguna PerSona le oSara (h)echar
/ los Perros Porque tenya tan su- / Jetos los CaPitanes y exerçito que / nadye se
osara moVer ny (f)hazer / tal cosa Syn su mandado e liçençia / Fue Preguntado
Por que se levan- / Taron los dichos Pueblos de / çicuyque e ProVinçia de tyguex
/ dixo que cree que Fue Por las / Prisiones e aPerreamyento que / (F)echaron e
hizieron A los / dichos Yndios llamados CAçi- / que e bygotes Por tanbyen oyo
/ dezir que habyan (F)echado una / Perra Al dicho CAçique Porque / Se les
(h)iba huyendo e Porque / el general habya enviado A los / Pueblos de la dicha
ProVinçia / de tyguex A Recoxer RoPa Para / [no number]

[fol. 121r]
934
Los Soldados e la hAbian Recoxido / muy en desGraçia e contra Su / voluntad de los naturales e / Porque un Villegas Soldado / hAbya tomado una
yndia e (h)echado- / Se con ella Por Fuerça todo / lo qual Se dezia Publi-
CAmente / Porque luego que Se hizo / el dicho Recogimyento de RoPa / e
Fuerça que dezian haberSe / (F)hecho a la dicha yndia y aPerrea- / do A los
dichos Yndios e que / Se aCuerda que Primero se / Alzaron los de tiguex e /
de(n)sde a Pocos dias los de / çicuyque / Fue Preguntado Sy sabe que los /
yndios de la dicha ProVinçia de / Tiguex que Se Rebelaron / Se hizieron

Fuertes e se rre- / Coxieron en solos dos Pueblos e que / los demas que serian hasta o- / cho o nueve quedaban desman- / Parados e deSyertos dixo / que es verdad que Pasa de la ma- / nera que en la PregunTa

[fol. 121v]
Se ConTyene Porque este testigo lo / Vio e que dexaron en ellos los / baSty-mentos / Fue Preguntado Si sabe que todos los / dichos Pueblos que quedaron / desmamParados los quemaron e / desbarataron los CAPitanes e sol- / dados del exerçito Por mandado / del dicho Francisco Vazquez de coronado / Dixo que Sabe e Vio que don / Rodrigo maldonado Por mandado del / dicho Fran-cisco Vazquez de coronado / quemo dos de los dichos Pue- / blos e deSbarato Parte de los otros / Para Proveer de leña el CAnPo por- / que este testigo se hallo Presente / quando se lo mando e Vio quemados e / desbaratados los dichos Pueblos / Fue Preguntado Sy sabe que en el / Pueblo que tuVo çer-CAdo el / dicho Françisco Vazquez de la / ProVinçia de Tiguex Se aPe- / Rearon e cortaron manos e na- / rizes A muchos yndios Ansi / de los que toma(ta)ron Por Fuerça / Como de los que se salyan del / [no number]

[fol. 122r]
935
Pueblo Durante el çerco y desPues de / (mandado) *ganado* todo Por mandado del dicho / Francisco Vazquez y en su Presençia dixo / que sabe e Vio que durante el çerco / e desPues de tomado del Pueblo se A- / Perrearon (F)hasta dos o tres yndios e cor- / Taron las manos e narizes / *de* otros nueVe o dyez E que cree que / el aPerrearlos Fue Por mandado / del dicho Francisco vazquez Porque / esTaba en el rreal donde los A- / Perrearon y mataron los Pe- / Ros e que los demas que cortaron / laS manos e narizes Se acuer- / da que lo mando el dicho Françisco / vazquez A (un) *don* garçia loPez o alguazil / del CanPo no Tiene memoria A / qual de los dos lo mando y les / mando que CAda uno de Aquellos / los guyase A Su Pueblo Por- / que viesen la Justicia que / de ellos se hazia / Fue Preguntado Sy sabe que el dicho / don garçia loPez quemo otro tre- / Ynta o quarenta yndios en el

[fol. 122v]
Real del otro Pueblo Sobre / que tenya Puesto çerco / Y si Fue Por mandado
del / dicho Francisco VazqueZ o lo SuPo e / Vyno A Su notiçia dixo que / este
testigo no vio (F)hazer la dicha / quema Pero es Publico e / notorio e cree que
Fue Por / mandado del dicho Françisco / Vazquez Porque Un dia An- / Tes
que los quemasen vio que / Vyno un mensajero de don garçia / loPez de CArdenas Al dicho Francisco / Vazquez y el dicho Françisco VaZ- / quez le torno
A ynViar otro / menSajero que no Tiene memo- / ria s(e)i (h)era contreras
Su CA- / ballerizo e que luego oyo decir / en el CAnPo que (h)era Para /
(F)hazerle saber que tenya çiertos / Yndios en su tyenda Sy que- / ria que los
quemase o que / Justicia haria de ellos e que otro / dia Se suPo e dixo Pub-
liCA- / mente que el dicho don garÇia loPeZ / los habia quemado e Por lo
que / [no number]

[fol. 123r]
936
dicho Tiene cree que tiene Por Çierto que no / los quemara Syno Fuera Por
man- / dado e Consentymyento del dicho Ge- / neral Porque como dicho tyene
le / esTaban todos tan Su(b)jetos e obe- / Dyentes que nynguna cosa se hazia
/ Syn darle Por ello Parte / {ytem} / Fue Preguntado que el dicho General yn-
/ vio de Su rreal a el del dicho don / Garçia loPez antes que se hi- / zieSe la
dicha quema A los yn- / dios llamado Turco e ysoPete / Para que vyesen la justicia que / de ellos se hazia dixo que no tiene / memoria mas que sabe que quan-
/ do Se aPerrearon e los cortaron las / manos e narizes A los que tomaron / en
el çerco donde estaba el dicho Francisco / Vazquez llevaron a Ver (f)hazer la /
dicha justicia a los dichos yndyos / Turco e ysoPete Para que / DyeSen noTiçia
en sus Tierras / de la juSTiçia que se hazia / Contra los que se rrebelaban / e
que cree que Fue Por mandado / del dicho Francisco vazquez Por-

[fol. 123v]
que los llevaron desde ÇerCA de Su / Tyenda e que esta es la verdad e lo que
/ de este caso sabe Para el juramenTo que / (F)hyzo e Fyrmolo de su nonbre
Alonso Al- / Varez el liÇenciado tejada

Chapter 17

The Fiscal's Accusations against Vázquez de Coronado

The Fiscal Cristóbal de Benavente

Within two weeks of completion of testimony at Guadalajara, licenciado Tejada ordered Vázquez de Coronado to present himself to the president and oidores of the audiencia in Mexico City before 50 days elapsed. In February 1545 Tejada committed the former captain general to house arrest and one month later delivered a transcript of the testimony he had taken from the fourteen de oficio witnesses to the audiencia's fiscal or prosecutor, licenciado Cristóbal de Benavente, for his determination as to whether charges would be lodged against Vázquez de Coronado or any of the other expedition members.

A native of Benavente in the jurisdiction of Zamora, born there about 1505,[1] the fiscal was, thus, a distant neighbor of Vázquez de Coronado and a fellow *Castellano.* The two were friends in Nueva España before Tejada's investigation and evidently returned to cordiality afterwards. At least, Vázquez de Coronado testified on Benavente's behalf during the latter's residencia in 1547. The future fiscal was in Nueva España by at least 1529, when he was serving as an escribano in the city of Antequera.[2] Sometime after 1535 he became the second fiscal of the audiencia of Nueva España, replacing his father-in-law

Antonio Ruiz. Prior to becoming fiscal, Benavente had been an attorney for the audiencia and had done legal work for Vázquez de Coronado in a private capacity. He was specifically targeted for investigation by the visitador general Tello de Sandoval in 1546, during the visita secreta he conducted regarding the performance of all royal officials in the viceroyalty of Nueva España. Nine of the 61 questions of Tello's interrogatorio dealt with Benavente. The ninety-third witness in the case was Lorenzo de Tejada, who called the fiscal's integrity into question in one case in which he had private dealings with an individual whom he was proceeding against in an official capacity.[3] When Benavente had testified concerning the work of Viceroy Mendoza in 1545, he spoke in a very positive way about the viceroy's separation of his private and public business and in general about Mendoza's tenure in office.[4]

By 1548, the fiscal had acquired by grant at least two house lots in Mexico City.[5] After more than 10 years of service as fiscal, Benavente resigned his post and returned to his hometown in Spain in 1550.[6]

By Vázquez de Coronado's own account, Benavente was extremely honest and conscientious in his work as fiscal, going so far as to divest himself of property so as to avoid conflict of interest. Despite their friendship, he refused a plea from Vázquez de Coronado to render a decision that no charges were warranted by the evidence Tejada had taken.[7] Certainly the evidence was weak with regard to the captain general's direct personal responsibility in brutality against Indians of Tierra Nueva. Spanish legal tradition of the period, however, held that generally a superior was accountable for the actions of his subordinates.[8] Such being the case, Benavente had little choice but to bring charges against his friend because, even by sixteenth-century Spanish standards, repeated inhumane acts had been perpetrated against various indigenous peoples of the Greater Southwest by members of the expedition to Tierra Nueva.

Specifically, Benavente charged the former captain general with six instances of criminal malfeasance and negligence:

1) that Vázquez de Coronado wantonly ordered the execution of Indians at Chiametla;

2) that Vázquez de Coronado had failed to leave a competent and law-abiding subordinate in his stead at San Gerónimo;

3) that Vázquez de Coronado had, without legitimate provocation, waged war against the Indians of Cíbola;

4) that Vázquez de Coronado precipitated an uprising of the people of Tiguex by illegally setting dogs on Bigotes and the cacique;

5) that Vázquez de Coronado ordered the execution of El Turco without reason and in secret; and

6) that Vázquez de Coronado failed to settle Tierra Nueva and forcibly blocked others from doing so.

It is worthy of note that with regard to the first accusation, concerning execution of natives of Chiametla, Tejada received no testimony and never raised the issue with the witnesses in the pesquisa. The hanging and quartering of Indians there was done in retaliation for the killing of Lope de Samaniego, first maestre de campo of the expedition.[9]

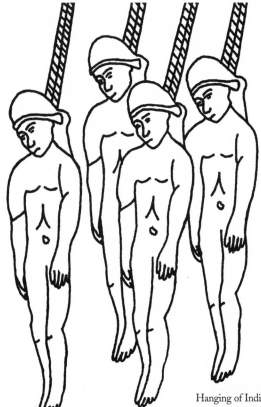

FIGURE 13.
Hanging of Indian captives, montage of images
from the *Lienzo de Tlaxcala*

A TRANSLATION
OF THE DOCUMENTARY RECORD

Order that He Appear in the City of Mexico within Fifty Days[10]

[123v cont'd] In the city of Guadalajara in Nueva Galicia on the sixteenth day of the month of September in the year one thousand five hundred and forty-four, the lord licenciado Tejada, judge of the Royal Audiencia of Nueva España, visitador and residencia judge for Nueva Galicia, having reviewed this record of the investigation and the sworn statement made by Francisco Vázquez, announced that he was ordering and did order that Francisco Vázquez de Coronado be notified that within the first fifty days following his notification by this instrument he is to present himself in person in the city of Mexico before the lords president and judges of the Royal Audiencia. Once he has done so, he is to take as his prison whatever place they indicate to him. He is not to dare to fail to comply with this order under penalty of two thousand gold pesos [124r] [to be paid] to the council and their majesties' treasury. Thus, he ordered it done by this document.

licenciado Tejada

Notification

On this day, I gave notice and read the aforesaid document to Francisco Vázquez de Coronado in person. He stated that he heard it. Witnesses: bachiller Sebastián Gutiérrez and don Pedro de Toro.

Pedro de Requena, scribe

Vázquez de Coronado Ordered to House Arrest[11]

[104r]. . . Having reviewed the record of investigation, the lord licenciado Tejada ordered that Francisco Vázquez de Coronado go to the city of Mexico

within the succeeding fifty days. Afterwards, in the city of Mexico on the twenty-sixth day of the month of February in the year of one thousand five hundred and forty-five, the aforesaid licenciado Tejada delivered a ruling by which he ordered that Francisco Vázquez de Coronado, under penalty of one thousand pesos, was to take his house as his prison in the city of Mexico. He was notified of this ruling and remained imprisoned. Likewise, he had an order issued that Hernando de Alvarado[12] was to come in person to this audiencia within thirty days.

The legal proceeding against the above-mentioned [individuals] is and remains in this situation as of the eleventh of March in the year one thousand five hundred and forty-five.

Delivery of the Report to the Fiscal[13]

[124r cont'd] The report of the investigation was delivered to licenciado Benavente, fiscal for His Majesty in this royal audiencia, so that he might review it and lodge what charges are appropriate. On the twenty-first day of March in the year one thousand five hundred and forty-five, he made his decision and filed the following accusation.

Accusation

I, licenciado Benavente, His Majesty's fiscal, file criminal charges against Francisco Vázquez de Coronado, governor of Nueva Galicia in Nueva España. To lay out the case in this complaint that has observed the legal formalities required, I say that the governor was named by His Majesty's audiencia and his most distinguished viceroy as captain general of Tierra Nueva and the province of Cíbola. He was given royal decrees and instructions for reconnoitering, pacifying, and settling the places he would find in those provinces toward the west. He was also instructed in the method with which he would have to make war against those people, compel their obedience, and bring them to knowledge of our holy Catholic faith and under the control [124v] and dominion of His Majesty. More than two hundred horsemen and many other footmen, well armed and provisioned in order to carry out the journey, went with the general.

Contrary to what was imposed on him by the decrees and instructions, in this journey, Francisco Vázquez and his captains and lieutenants, by his order, committed and perpetrated the following offenses:

First, in the province of Chiametla, without any legitimate cause, since the Indians were at peace, he seized eight Indian men and women, more or less, and had some of them quartered and others hung.

Further, when he established a town of Spaniards in the valley of Corazones, he should have left there a trustworthy and prudent person to administer justice and pacify the province. But he did not do so. Because of the mischief and outrages committed against the Indians and natives of the province by the person and persons he left there, all of its people rose up in arms and killed many Spaniards. The town was abandoned and the people of the region rose up because the general had been remiss in not leaving a person competent to govern the people and the town.

Further, when he arrived in Cíbola the people of the principal town came forth in peace and provided food and needed supplies to the people whom the general took with him. Without legitimate reason the general and his captains waged war against them and burned the pueblo, in which they killed many people. On account of this, much of the province rose up and rebelled.

[125r] Further, when the general went onward with his company sixty or seventy leagues, he reached the province of Tiguex, which was heavily settled and had much food and many structures built like those in Spain. The people came forth in peace, rendered obedience to His Majesty, and fed everyone in the army corn, poultry, and other foodstuffs. When they were at peace and without legitimate cause the general and his captains, by his order, set dogs on the leaders of that pueblo and its neighbors. The dogs were unleashed so they would bite the Indians and they did so. Because of this, the leaders and people of those pueblos rebelled and rose up in arms. In waging war again, the Spaniards destroyed and burned many pueblos. In others the Indians fortified themselves, as they do in that province. Though they had been at peace,

they returned to war and are so to this day. In response, the Indians killed many Spaniards and everyone was on the verge of being lost.

Further, pursuing his course onward, the general reached the province of Quivira. He took with him as interpreter and guide an Indian known as El Turco. He discovered that the province was very wealthy, heavily settled, and productive of food. [The people] came out in peace and provided foodstuffs for all of the people the general took with him. Without reason, he ordered the guide called Turco killed. This punishment should have been public, rather than secret as it was.

[Further,] these provinces were heavily settled, very productive of food, with plentiful livestock (consisting of wild cattle) and many other foodstuffs. Although he could have settled there, not only did he not do so, but he also blocked and restrained some Spaniards who wanted to settle the province, so that they would not settle it and would leave the aroused provinces deserted, abandoned, and at war. He had consumed and used up all the equipment, trade goods, munitions, and arms that had been provided to him for such a war. In this General Francisco Vázquez and his captains committed serious offenses.

Having completed the aforesaid report of the investigation, I ask your grace to order that proceedings be instituted against Francisco Vázquez and against his captains or any of them who appear to be responsible. And, when they are found guilty, to order that they and their property be seized, so that their offenses will not go unpunished. In this case the full force of justice should be applied, which is what I ask, with costs. I present the investigation record, prepared at your grace's request.

licenciado Cristóbal de Benavente

A TRANSCRIPT
OF THE DOCUMENTARY RECORD

[fol. 123v cont'd][14]

{manda *A* el q*ue* / dentro de / 50 dias se / Presente en / me*X*ico}

En la ÇiUdad de guadalaJara de la nue- / Va galyçia Diez e seys dias del / mes
de Se*p*tienbre de myll e quy*nient*os / e quarenta e quatro años el señor / liÇen-
*cia*do tejada oydor de la audiençia / Real de la nueva *es*Paña Visitador / e juez
de Resydençia de la nueVa / Galyçia *h*Abiendo Visto *e*sta / Ynformaçion e
conFysion (f)*he*cho Por / el d*i*cho Franc*i*sco vazquez dixo que ma*n*- / daba e
ma*n*do que le notiFyque al / d*i*cho Franc*i*sco Vazquez de coronado que /
dentro de çinquenta Dias Pri- / meros syguyentes desPues que / *e*ste aUto le
Fuere notiFyCAdo Se / P*re*SSente Personalmente en la ÇiUdad de / mex*i*co
a*n*te los Señores P*re*SSydente *e* / oydores de la *a*udiençia rreal e Pre- / Sen-
t*a*do tenga Por carçel la que / ellos le señalasen e no sea osado / de la que-
bra*n*Tar en manera alg*un*a / So Pena de doS myll Pesos de oro / [no number]

[fol. 124r]

937

(PeSos de oro) Para la CAmara e Fisco / d*e* sus magestades e ansy lo mando
/ Asentar Por aUto el *h*içençiado Tejada

{not*ificaci*on}

*e*ste dia ley e notiFyque el aUto de / SusoConthenido Al d*i*cho Franc*i*sco Vaz-
/ quez de coronado en su Persona el / q*ua*l d*i*xo que lo oyo t*e*stigos el ba- /
chiller sebastian Gutyerrez e don P*edr*o / de toro Pedro de Requena esc*ri*vano

[fol. 104r][15]

[. . .]

E Vista la d*i*cha ynformaçion por el d*i*cho señor lis*encia*do teJada / mando Al dicho francisco Vazquez de Coronado que (^tuViese) / (^En) fuese A la dicha ÇiUdad de mexico dentro de Çin- / quenta dias primeros syguyentes y desPues *en* la / dicha ÇiUdad de mexico Veynte E seys dias del mes / de febrero de myll E quynientos E quarenta e (^quatro) / (e) Çinco Años el dicho señor lisenciado tejada pronunçio / Un AUto por el qual mando Al dicho francisco Vazquez / de Coronado que so pena de (^myll) myll pesos[16] tuViese / *en* la dicha ÇiUdad de mexico su casa por carçel el qual / AUto se le noti-Fico y queda Encarçelado y asy- / mysmo mando dar su mandamyento para que Fernando de al- / Varado (^tuVo) Vinyese perSonalmente en esta AUdiencia / dentro de treynta dias y en este estado esta y queda / el dicho pleyto contra los suSodichos en honze de março / del dicho Año de myll E quynientos E quarenta y (^quatro) / Çinco Años. . . .

[fol. 124r cont'd][17]
{darse la / inFormacion / al Fiscal}

la qual dicha ynformaçion Fue *en*tregada Al lisenciado / benavente Fiscal Por su magestad en *e*sta rreal audiencia / Para que la vieSe y PusieSe la acuSaçion que conVinyeSe / el qual Pareze que en veynte e Uno de março / de myll e quinientos e quarenta e çinco años Puso / la aCuSaçion siguyente / muy mag-nifico señor

{acusa- / çion}

el liÇenciado benavente Fiscal Por su magestad aCuSo criminal- / mente A Francisco Vazquez de coronado governador / de galiçia d*e* la nueva españa e contando el cAso en *e*sta aCusa- / çion Pr(o)esuPuesta las solemnydades que de derecho en *e*sta CAso / Se Requyere digo que habiendo sido nonbrado Por el audiencia d*e* su / magestad e Por su yllustrisimo visorrey Por CAPitan gen-eral d*e* la tierra nueVa e / ProVinçia de çibola e habiendole sido dado Reales ProVisiones e ynstru- / çiones Para deSCubrir e PaçiFicar e Poblar lo que deSCu- / briese d*e* las dichas ProVinçias hazia el Ponyente e la (h)orden / que

*h*abia de tener de Fazerles la guerra e ReduÇirles / e traerlos A conosçimi*ent*o
de n*uest*ra s*an*ta Fee CatolyCa y al dominyo

[fol. 124v]

e SuJeçion d*e* su m*a*g*estad* e Por ella mas de doz*ient*os honbres de A Caballo
Poco / mas o m*en*os y otra mucha Gente de Pie bien armada e P*ro*Veyda / Para
efe*c*tuar el di*c*ho viaje el di*c*ho Fran*cis*co Vazquez Veniendo contra / lo q*ue* le
Fue cometydo Por las di*c*has P*ro*Visiones e *i*nstruçiones en *e*l di*c*ho / Viaje hizo
e PerPetro el y Por su m*an*dad*o* sus CaPitanes e te(y)ni*ent*es los / delitos sigu-
i*ent*es / {y*tem*} / Primeram*ent*e en la P*ro*Vinçia de chiametla sin CauSa q*ue*
legitima fuese *e*sta*n*do los / yndios de Paz tomo ocho yndios e yndias Poco mas
o menos / y a los unos quarteo y a los otroS Ahorco / {y*tem*} / Yten *h*abiendo
Poblado una Villa de *es*Panoles en el Valle de los / Coraçones y diviendo dexar
en ella Persona de Recaudo / Y de Confiança para q*ue* administrase justiçia y
Paçificase / la di*c*ha provinçia por no lo *h*aber hecho y por las malas obras y tra-
/ tamy*ent*os que la persona y personas que alli dexo hizieron a los / di*c*hos
Yndios E naturales de la di*c*ha proVinçia toda Ella Se Re- / belo y mataron
muchos espanoles y la villa se despoblo y / la gente de la di*c*ha Comarca Se alço
por *h*aberse ydo el di*c*ho ge- / neral Remiso en no dexar persona sufiçiente para
/ Governar la di*c*ha villa y gente / Yten llegando e llego a la proVinçia de
Çibola la gente / de la Cabeçera le salio de paz a el y a la gente q*ue* Consigo /
llevaba dandoles Comida y mantenimi*ent*os nesçesarios sin / causa q*ue*
legitima fuese el di*c*ho general y sus Capitanes les hizie- / Ron la Guerra y les
quemaron el p*ueb*lo Adonde mataron / mucha gente de donde mucha p*ar*te de
la provinçia se rebelo y alço / Yten yendo el di*c*ho gene*r*al Con su gente adelante sesenta o / setenta leguas llegado a la provinçia de tiguex y estando / muy
poblada de gente y Comida y muchos Edefiçios al modo de / *es*Pana hechos
le salieron de paz y dieron la obidiençia a su / m*a*g*estad* y dandoles mucha
Comida de mayz y aVes y otros / mantenimi*ent*os Para todo el di*c*ho EXerçito
y estando de paz / sin *h*aber causa ligitima el di*c*ho General y sus Capitanes por
su / m*an*da*d*o Aperrearo*n* los caçiques del di*c*ho p*ueb*lo y de loS comarcanos A
el (h)echan- / doles los perros que los mordiesen los quales les mordieron de /
Cuya causa los di*c*hos Caçiqu*es* y gente de los di*c*hos p*ueb*los se Rebelaron / y

alçaron y para tornarlos A hazer g*u*erra de nuevo destruye- / Ron muchos de los d*i*chos pu*eb*l*o*s y quemaron y en otros se hizieron / Fuertes por manera que la d*i*cha p*ro*vinçia estando de paz se VolVio / de guerra y lo Esta el dia de *h*oy y sobre *e*llo murieron mu(n)chos esPaño- / les y esTuVieron todos A punto de se perder / [no number]

[fol. 125r]

938

Yten El d*i*cho general prosiguiendo su Camino mas adelante llego a la / Provinçia de quiVira y llevando por lenGua y guia a Un yndyo que se / dezia el turco *h*Abiendo desqubierto la d*i*cha proVinçia que (h)era muy RiCa / y poblada y abundante de Comida y saliendole de paz y dandole manteni- / mi*ent*os para toda la gente q*ue* llevaba Consigo le mando matar a la d*i*cha / guia que se dezia el turco sin *h*aber causa y a que la *h*obiera *h*Abia / de ser el Castigo publico y no secreto Como se hizo / Yten siendo las d*i*chas proVinçias muy pobladas y abundosas / de Comida y de muchos ganados de VaCas sal-Vaginas y de otros / muchos mantenimi*ent*os y podiendo poblar las d*i*chas proVinçias no / solamente no lo hizo mas A alg*un*os esPañoles q*ue* querian poblar la d*i*cha / proVinçia Se le estorbar y ynpidio que no poblasen y dexasen des- / *m*anparada*s* y despoblada*s* las d*i*chas proVinçias alborotadas y de / guerra *h*Abiendo Consumido y gastado todoSS los adereços / Rescates y muniçiones y armas que le fueron dados para la / d*i*cha guerra en lo qual el d*i*cho General Franc*is*co Vazquez y sus / Capitanes Cometieron delito y delitos graves

a V*uest*ra m*erce*d pido que *h*abiendo ynformaçion de lo sobred*i*cho mande / proçeder y proçeda Contra el d*i*cho Franc*is*co Vazquez y Contra los / d*i*chos sus Capitanes y Contra qualquier de *e*llos q*ue* Culpados pares- / Çieren Condenandoles en ellas mandando las (h)exeCutar / en sus personas E bienes porq*ue* los delitos no queden sin cas- / tigo haziendome En el Caso entero Cumplimi*ent*o de justiçia el q*ua*l / pido con Costas y hago presentaçion de la ynformaçion / en el Caso tomada por V*uest*ra m*erce*d Y El liçençiado Crist*ob*al de ben*avent*e

Chapter 18

The Maestre de Campo Held Responsible

The Penalty Paid by García López de Cárdenas

T en days before fiscal Benavente filed charges against Vázquez de Coronado for mistreatment of Indians in Tierra Nueva, licenciado Tejada issued an opinion that the maestre de campo of the expedition, García López de Cárdenas, was culpable for some of that mistreatment. Therefore, Tejada ordered that a copy of the pesquisa record be prepared and sent to the Council of the Indies in Spain, so that proceedings could be instituted against López de Cárdenas, if the Council saw fit. Prosecution of the former maestre de campo could not be carried out by the audiencia in Mexico City because López de Cárdenas, now known as Ramírez de Cárdenas,[1] had returned to his home in Madrid to take possession of the entail held by his older brother who had died while the expedition had been in Tierra Nueva.[2]

López de Cárdenas had received a license to travel to the Indies in May 1535, Peru his planned destination.[3] It is possible that he crossed to the New World in the same fleet that carried Viceroy Mendoza and Vázquez de Coronado, but spent a year in Cuba and Santa Marta before making his way to Nueva España. There the viceroy was delivered a royal cédula directing him to favor López de Cárdenas with an official position "because he has served us in Spain, Italy, and other places."[4] According to López de Cárdenas himself, he was in Oaxaca for three years at Mendoza's behest, settling disputes between Indians and Spaniards.[5] Then, in 1538, he was appointed alguacil mayor of the audiencia.[6]

Sometime after Vázquez de Coronado had begun preparations for the expedition to Tierra Nueva, the viceroy ordered López de Cárdenas to join him as captain of a company of horsemen.[7] His high status within the expedition is evident in the 12 horses, many servants, muleteer, and black slaves he took with him, as well as in his position as captain.[8] Only a few days into the expedition's northward journey, Lope de Samaniego, who had been designated maestre de campo by the viceroy, was killed while attempting to obtain provisions from Indians at Chiametla.[9] Feeling certain that the viceroy's approval would be forthcoming, as indeed it was, Vázquez de Coronado appointed López de Cárdenas as maestre de campo in Samaniego's place. He was not anxious to occupy the office and was said to have been burdened by it when he acquiesced to the captain general's nomination.[10] Nevertheless, he served as maestre de campo for more than a year, until he broke or dislocated his arm badly in May 1541 while the expedition was on the Southern Great Plains. He was therefore present at the battle of Cíbola/Hawikkuh, oversaw occupation of the Tiguex pueblo Coofor as winter quarters for the expedition, commanded the siege of Pueblo del Arenal, and was in charge of at least some of the requisitioning and purchase of clothing from Pueblo Indians during the winter of 1540–1541, all events involving alleged misdeeds toward indigenous people.

After the end of the Tierra Nueva expedition, López de Cárdenas had little time to enjoy his increased wealth and status before, on January 7, 1546, licenciado Juan de Villalobos, fiscal of the Council of the Indies, after a review of Tejada's investigation record sent from Mexico City, ordered him imprisoned and lodged formal complaints against him. He was charged with rapes, robbery, burnings, unleashing dogs, and other brutality committed against the natives of Tierra Nueva. The fiscal asserted that the people of Tiguex had risen up in self defense because of the maestre de campo's actions and that he had broken his solemn oath of security by burning Indians who surrendered at Pueblo del Arenal.[11]

For several months, while the fiscal's investigation got under way, Ramírez de Cárdenas was confined to the Torre de Homenaje in the town of Pinto south of Madrid.[12] There, his sworn statement was taken in February 1546. In this statement the former maestre de campo presented himself and the other Spaniards as long-suffering and slow to anger in contrast to the Indians of Tierra Nueva who, in his view, were hot-tempered and precipitate in their actions. For instance, he claimed that the nearly three-month-long Tiguex War was triggered by the rape of one woman and the theft of only one manta. At the same time, he maintained that the expedition purchased clothing from the Tiguex and admitted that it also took some by force, though only because Indian and black members of the expedition had died of cold for lack of proper clothing. Ramírez de Cárdenas all but ignored the pivotal question of Indians of Arenal being tied to stakes and burned alive at his command after having been promised security, referring instead to the pueblo being set afire during battle and denying acquaintance with Melchior Pérez.[13] Pérez, in his de oficio testimony in 1544, had sworn that he had warned the maestre de campo that he was breaking his sacred word by burning prisoners at Arenal. Four years later in appealing the decision of his guilt by the Council of the Indies, Ramírez de Cárdenas, through his attorney Sebastián Rodríguez, not only admitted knowing Pérez, but claimed that his testimony should be dismissed because he, Juan de Contreras, and Juan Troyano were among the principal enemies of the former maestre de campo.[14]

As early as one week after giving his sworn statement, Ramírez de Cárdenas initiated a series of legal maneuvers aimed at lessening the discomfort of his imprisonment, if not ending it altogether. Over and over again he adduced family illness, pressing personal business, and the aggravation of his own expedition-related infirmity as reasons to be allowed to travel to various places in Spain and finally to leave the torre in exchange for house arrest. He was eventually successful in these pleas, so that he seems to have served only about three months imprisonment at Pinto, being released to house arrest April 2, 1546.[15]

It took nearly three years for the fiscal and Ramírez de Cárdenas to secure testimony, both of them sending requests to Mexico City and Guadalajara, as well as locations in Spain, for that purpose.[16] Then, on December 20, 1549, the Council reached its verdict, holding the former maestre de campo accountable on all the charges levelled by fiscal Villalobos.[17] After being notified of the verdict and the sentence, a fine of 800 ducats and 30 months of service to the king at Orán in North Africa at his own expense, Ramírez de Cárdenas, through his lawyer Rodríguez, appealed both. Fiscal Villalobos died in 1550, but his interim successor doctor Verástegui argued to uphold both the Council's decision and the penalty imposed. The Council, acting in 1551 as an appellate court, confirmed its original finding of culpability, but reduced the sentence to 12 months of service on the frontier of Navarra, plus a 200-ducat fine and banishment from the Indies for 10 years.[18] Still not satisfied, Ramírez de Cárdenas and his attorney immediately appealed directly to the king, saying that service in Navarra would be extremely detrimental to the health of the former maestre de campo. Before the end of the year, the king issued a cédula authorizing a change in venue of service to Granada. The conde de Tendilla, brother of the newly transferred viceroy of Peru Antonio de Mendoza and a distant relative of Ramírez de Cárdenas through marriage, was ordered, as captain general of Granada, to designate a post for his kinsman within his jurisdiction.[19] Thus it was that Ramírez de Cárdenas fulfilled his obligation to serve the king in Vélez Málaga on the Mediterranean coast,[20] the only individual found guilty and punished for brutality committed against the Indians of Tierra Nueva. Even that punishment was largely symbolic, both the fine and service requirement having been drastically tempered.[21]

A TRANSLATION
OF THE DOCUMENTARY RECORD

[104v][22]

This Record of Investigation Is Forwarded
to the Council of the Indies because
don García López de Cárdenas Is Accused[23]

In the city of Mexico on the eleventh day of the month of March in the
year one thousand five hundred and forty-five, the lord licenciado Tejada,
judge of the Royal Audiencia of Nueva España and [residencia] judge (as said
above), has reviewed the enclosed record of investigation of Francisco
Vázquez de Coronado, former captain general of the army that went to reconnoiter and subjugate the tierra nueva of Cíbola, and the other captains
who went with him.

Investigation was made into the burnings, setting on of dogs, and other
brutality and outrages they committed against the natives of Tierra Nueva.
As a result, blame was fixed on don García López de Cárdenas, maestre de
campo of the army. He is absent from Nueva España and cannot be taken
into custody so that he may be punished and penalized in conformance with
the law. It is said that he is in the kingdoms of Castile. Therefore [licenciado
Tejada] directed that a copy be made of the entire investigation record and
that His Majesty's commission be included with it. So that justice can be
done, the lord licenciado directed that it be sent to His Majesty and the lords
of his Royal Council of the Indies, in order that they may review it and determine what will be suitable concerning don García López. Thus he proclaimed and ordered that it be recorded in a directive.

licenciado Tejada

I, Pedro de Requena, Their Majesties' scribe and scribe of the Royal
Audiencia of Nueva España, was present with the lord licenciado at what is

stated. I had this investigation record written out on a hundred and four sheets. Written in a place on each one of them is my customary rubric. And the corrections are certified.

[105r] Therefore, in testimony of the truth I affixed here my sign, made in this way.

Pedro de Requena, scribe

{This is a duplicate of another document that was submitted. Therefore it was not returned. It has been reviewed.}

A TRANSCRIPT
OF THE DOCUMENTARY RECORD

[fol 104v]²⁴

{por q*ue* resulta / culpado d*o*n / Garcia enVio / al conseJo esta / informaçion}

En la çiudad de mexico A HonZe dias d*e*L mes de março / de myll E quy*nien*tos E quarenta E çinco Años Vista por el / señor lis*encia*do Tejada oydor del Audiençia Real de la nueVa / españa E Juez suSod*i*cho la ynfor-maçion de susocontenyda / (F)*h*echa contra el d*i*cho fran*ci*sco Vazquez de coronado Capitan / General del exerçito q*ue* fue en el descubrimy*ent*o y con-quysta / de la ti*e*rra nueVa de Çibola E los otros capitanes q*ue* Con el / Fueron sobre las quemas ApeReamy*ent*os E otras cruel- / dades E malostratamy*ent*os que Hizieron A los naturales / de la d*i*cha ti*e*rra nueVa E q*ue* por ella Resulta Culpa / contra don Garçia lopez de Cardenas maestre de Canpo / del d*i*cho eXerçito el qual esta AUSente de esta / nueVa españa E no puede ser *h*Abido p*a*ra ser penado / E casTiGado conforme A JusTiçia el qual diz*en* q*ue* / esta *en* los Reynos de Castilla por tanto que man- / daba E mando que se saque Un traslado de toda la d*i*cha / Ynformaçion ynserta *en e*lla la comysyon de su maG*esta*d / q*ue* p*a*ra ello el d*i*cho señor liçençiado tiene lo qual se ynVie / A su mag*esta*d y a los señores del su Real conseJo De / Yndias p*a*ra que ellos lo Vean y proVean en lo que / toca Al d*i*cho don Garçia lopez lo que Fueron serVido / E Asy lo pronunçio E mando Asintar por aUto / El liçençiado teJada

E Yo pedro de Requena es*crib*ano de sus mag*esta*de*s* / E de la d*i*cha Real Audiençia de *e*sta nueVa es- / paña preSente Fuy A lo q*ue* d*i*cho es con el d*i*cho señor / lis*encia*do y esta ynformaçion (F)*h*ize escribir en estas / çiento E quatro hojas es*cri*ptas con esta en Cada Una / de las quales Va en la Una parte my Rubrica A- / cosTumbrada y salVadas las enmyendas / [no number]

[fol. 105r]

105

Por ende *en* tesTimonio de Verdad (F)*h*ize Aquy / este my sygno (a)tal /
Pedro de / R*e*quena esc*r*yv*a*no

{esta es dupp*lica*da de otra pr*o*visy*o*n *pr*e*sent*a*da / y por eso no se Cobro Vista}

Chapter 19

Defense Offered by Vázquez de Coronado

Francisco Pilo and the Beginning of Testimony in the Province of Culiacán

On August 2, 1544, within a day or two of the arrival of Lorenzo de Tejada in Guadalajara and almost a full week before he would make the *pregón* or public proclamation of his commission to investigate the treatment of Indians by the expedition to Tierra Nueva and to conduct the residencia of Francisco Vázquez de Coronado as governor of Nueva Galicia,[1] the governor himself was busy putting in motion his defense. On that day, he granted a power of attorney to Francisco Pilo, a resident of Culiacán, for the purpose of having testimony taken on his behalf in that northern outpost. Perhaps on that same day, Vázquez de Coronado and his attorney Pedro Ruiz de Haro formulated an interrogatorio to be used in securing such testimony in Culiacán and elsewhere and gave a copy of it to Pilo.

The prompt initiation of steps in a specific line of defense and the formulation of an interrogatorio responding to the questions Tejada had put to witnesses in Mexico City strongly suggest a meeting or conference between the juez pesquisador (or someone close to him) and the principal target of his investigation almost immediately upon the judge's arrival in Guadalajara. At least, in some way Vázquez de Coronado was alerted to both the seriousness and substance of the charges he was facing and took immediate action, a full ten days before Tejada called his first Guadalajara witness in the case, Melchior Pérez, and a month before the former captain general himself was questioned by the judge.

As has already been seen, Tejada completed his examination of witnesses in the case on September 5. Precisely four months later, Francisco Pilo presented both power of attorney and interrogatorio before Pedro Hernández, the *alcalde* or judge and administrator at the mines of Nuestra Señora de los Remedios in the province of Culiacán and asked that the alcalde examine the witnesses he would bring forward.

Review of Vázquez de Coronado's interrogatorio provides insight into the strategy of his counterarguments in the case. Because, like interrogatorio questions in general, most of the questions provided to Pilo were framed to elicit a responses of "yes, that is correct; I saw that happen," they outlined an argument that was thought would be effective in proving that the former captain general did not himself commit outrages against the indigenous people of Tierra Nueva or permit such acts to be committed. It needs to be kept in mind that the interrogatorio was both formulated and employed months before fiscal Benavente formally filed charges against the former captain general. The thrust of the questions was that Vázquez de Coronado had always done what the laws, cédulas, and instructions enjoined and the representatives of the Church advised, regarding humane treatment of Indians. He had, for instance, published ordinances for the expedition intended to safeguard the lives and property of native peoples. Indians were always given the opportunity to submit to the king of Spain voluntarily. The concurrence of the priests and royal officials was always obtained before war was waged. The Indians were informed that Vázquez de Coronado would punish those who mistreated them. The expedition never made slaves of Indians and always paid for the food and clothing it received from them. Despite this care and concern, the indigenous inhabitants of Tierra Nueva, according to the interrogatorio, often were unwilling to render obedience to the king or attempted to abrogate their submission. Furthermore, the Indians killed horses and native allies and tried to kill the Spaniards by trickery. In the case of the guide El Turco, he was punished as befitted a traitor, which he was found to be by standard legal procedures. Beyond that, nothing worthwhile was found in Tierra Nueva, even though conscientious efforts were made to locate a place to settle. So the captain general brought the expedition home because the people were dying and suffering. This was very similar to the picture presented by the de oficio witnesses in the case.

Little-Known Lorenzo Álvarez

After accepting the interrogatorio and power of attorney, the alcalde, citing other pressing business that would keep him from the task, delegated the responsibility for taking testimony at the mines of Nuestra Señora de los Remedios to Hernando Gómez de la Peña, a scribe of the court and also former member of the expedition to Tierra Nueva. Two days after having been appointed, Gómez de la Peña took and recorded the statements of Pilo's first de parte or defense witness, Lorenzo Álvarez. Almost everything known about Álvarez comes from this testimony in January 1545. He was about 25 years old when the expedition to Tierra Nueva began and took with him only two horses and a few items of native arms and armor, indicative of his relatively low economic status, about the same as de oficio witness Cristóbal de Escobar, who is separated from him on the January 1540 muster roll by only one individual.[2] It is possible that the two were friends or companions at the time, since proximity on personnel rosters of that era often indicated close social or even family connection. In any case, Álvarez and Escobar, in their respective testimonies, seem to have shared a view that Vázquez de Coronado had been very mindful of the welfare of the natives of Tierra Nueva. Álvarez, in particular, was uniformly supportive of the former captain general and did not refer to outrages committed against the people of Tierra Nueva. He attested to the seemly internal behavior of the expedition, but had little to say about its external relations, which were the focus of the investigation. Likewise, the questions he and all the de parte witnesses were asked aimed at peripheral issues and did not attack the fiscal's accusations directly.

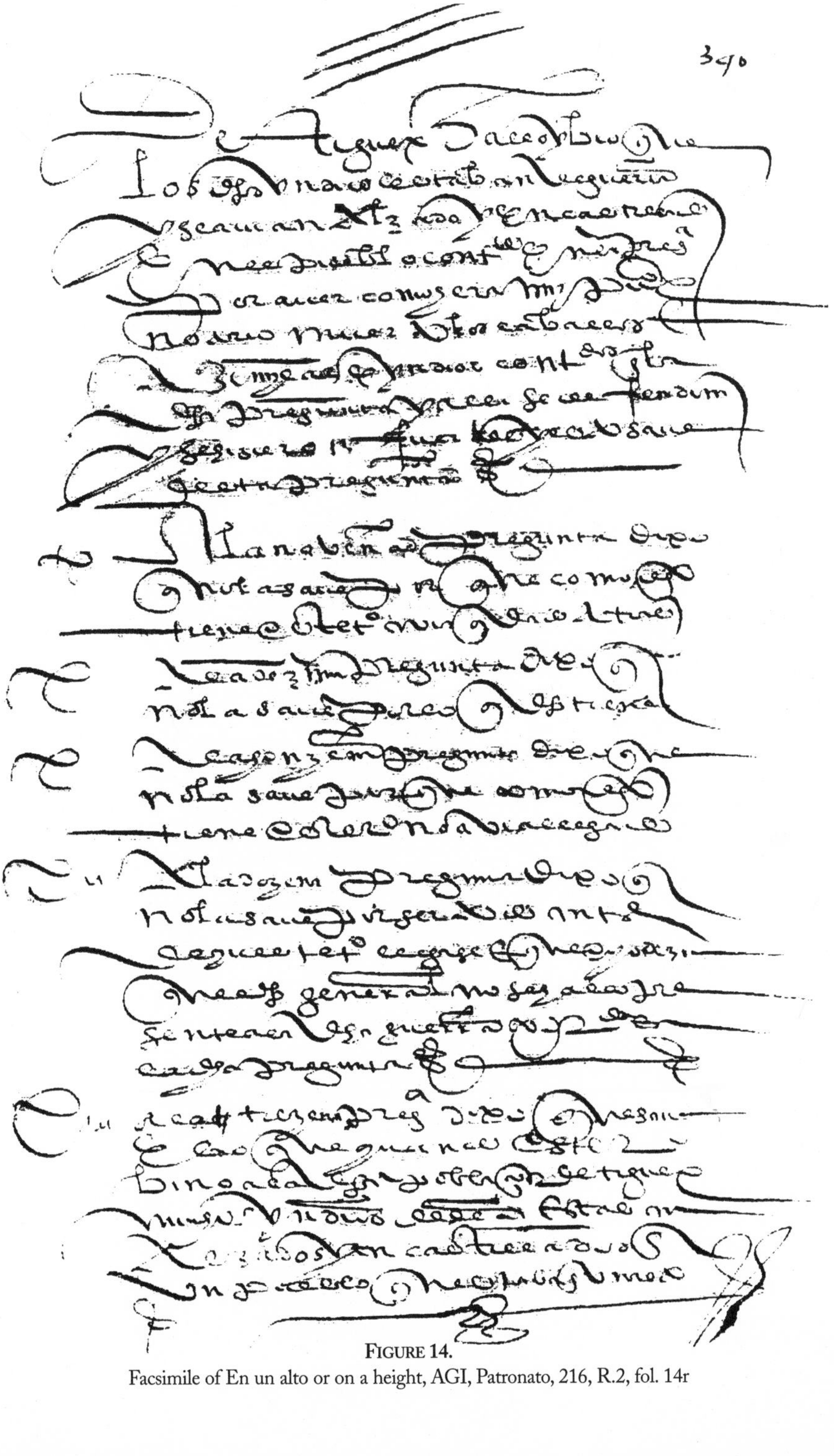

FIGURE 14.
Facsimile of En un alto or on a height, AGI, Patronato, 216, R.2, fol. 14r

A TRANSLATION
OF THE DOCUMENTARY RECORD

*Inquiry on the Part of Francisco Vázquez de Coronado, 1545*³

[1v] At the mines of Nuestra Señora de los Remedios in the province of Culiacán, in Nueva Galicia, Nueva España, on the fifth day of the month of January in the year of the birth of our savior Jesus Christ one thousand five hundred and forty-five, Francisco Pilo, a resident of these mines, appeared before the very noble lord, His Majesty's alcalde here, Pedro Hernández, and in my presence as scribe and that of the witnesses listed below. In the name of Francisco Vázquez de Coronado and with his power of attorney, he presented a petition and an interrogatory, the substance of which is as follows, the one following the other:

Very noble lord,

I, Francisco Pilo, in the name of the governor Francisco Vázquez de Coronado and by virtue of the power of attorney I hold from him, state before the present scribe that it is fitting and within the rights of my party that an affidavit of evidence (record it in perpetuity) be prepared in this province. I ask and petition that your grace receive and examine the witnesses that I will present in this case in accordance [2r] with the questions of the interrogatory that I lay before you. And that what the witnesses say and declare be signed, sealed, and secured by the present scribe. Further, I ask that you order that this be done in a public manner and in such a way that the scribe may certify it, so that everything can be submitted in keeping with the rights of my party. And he is to insert in all of this his written authority and the judicial degree under which he proceeds. In the necessary form I apply to your grace's very noble office. I, Francisco Pilo, ask for justice.

Power of Attorney to Francisco Pilo[4]

[35r] . . . Know all those who may see this document that, in the city of Guadalajara in the province of [Nueva] Galicia, I, Francisco Vázquez de Coronado, governor and captain general for His Majesty of the aforesaid province in Nueva España and resident there, concede and [35v] make it known by this instrument that I give and grant my full power of attorney to you, Francisco Pilo, without restriction, fully, and as completely as I [myself] have and possess it, in the fullest and best way in which I can and should give and grant it, according to what can and should be protected by law. This is so that, whether you are [personally] present or absent, you can and would present evidence, one, two, or more times, before the justices of the villa of San Miguel and of the province of Culiacán in [Nueva] Galicia, in Nueva España, or before any other justices of His Majesty whatsoever in whatever other places, in all of the lawsuits, legal cases, and affairs that I have or expect to have, either civil or criminal, whether active or [yet] to be initiated, against whatever persons or initiated by whatever persons against me, in whatever form, both in filing suits and in making defense. [36r] [This can be done] both to record them legally in perpetuity and in any other form.

[This is also granted] so that in any case or matter whatsoever affecting me you [can and would] present any document, instrument, interrogatory, or other [piece of writing] whatsoever or any other witnesses. And so that [you can and would] ask [that the justices] receive them, take their oaths, and make a clean copy of their statements and depositions, which is to be sealed and secured. Those justices are to insert in the copy [the] authorization and judicial decree and send it to me.

[This is also granted so that] you [can and would] present [the copy] in my behalf and in my name wherever it is appropriate within my rights. [And so that you can and would] execute all of the case records and written documents concerning the case, and anything else necessary that is associated with or pertinent to it whatsoever. [And further,] so that you can and would appear before Their Majesties and before any of their alcaldes, judges, or justices whatsoever, both in the villa of San Miguel and in whatever other places and locales, in regard to what has been previously mentioned or any other matter relating to my legal actions. [36v] [And so that you can and would] submit and execute before them or any one of them all of the suits, petitions, injunctions, objections, subpoenas, and summonses; [so that you can and would] file suits, lodge defenses, deny accusations, admit wrongdoing, and request and take testimony. [And so that you can and would] make any oath on my soul whatsoever, against both slander and censure. [And further, so that you can and would] request the other parties to do these things and see that they do them. [And also so that you can and would] acquire and [make] extract[s from] any documents whatsoever that concern and pertain to me, which are in the possession of any scribe or person, both in those provinces and in any others. [And so that you can and would] present documents, instruments, evidence, and any other type of proof. [Also, so you can and would] request announcement and appearance of my witnesses and challenge the opposing witnesses and refute [their testimony] with statements and persons and reconcile and conclude arguments.

[And so that you can and would] ask for and hear a decision or decisions, either provisional [37r] or definitive, and either consent to them or, on the contrary, appeal them, petitioning and requesting an appeal there and wherever it rightly ought to be done, depending on how things proceed. [And so that you can and would] see to all the other matters and both judicial and extra-judicial proceedings that are appropriate and necessary to enter into, given [my] status (as they say).

I myself have done and will do what is presently possible, even should you require another special power of attorney or directive from me or my personal presence. So that you could designate and substitute one, two, or more agents in my name and in your stead and revoke [those appointments] and designate other new agents, this power of attorney remains with you as principal agent. It is as complete and full a power of attorney as I [myself] have and possess for [the purposes] stated. And for each of the [substitute agents it constitutes] another such [power of attorney] equally as complete, [with] all the [associated] rights. Also, I give and grant it to you, the aforesaid Francisco Pilo [37v] and to your surrogates with all of its elements, additions, concomitants, and adjuncts. Further, I relieve you [of responsibility and blame] in the customary manner prescribed by law. So that this may be taken as a firm [commitment], I pledge my chattel and real property, both what I have [now] and what I will have [in the future] and my profits and proceeds.

The document was executed in this city of Guadalajara. It is the last [document] of the second day of the month of August in the year of the birth of our savior Jesus Christ one thousand five hundred and forty-four.

Witnesses who were present at what is stated: Juan Sánchez de Ozar, Juan de Villareal, and Juan de Pereda, residents of the aforesaid city. The grantor signed his name in the [scribe's] register for this document.

Francisco Vázquez de Coronado

[2r cont'd] The witnesses who are and will be presented on behalf of Francisco Vázquez de Coronado, governor of the province of Nueva Galicia and captain general of the armed force [that went to] the lands that fray Marcos de Niza said he had discovered, are to be asked the following questions:

{1} First they are to be asked whether they know Francisco Vázquez Coronado, the captain general who went to reconnoiter the lands that fray Marcos said he had discovered and the rest.

{2} Item: [they are to be asked] whether they know that when the aforesaid general went in search of the lands [2v] fray Marcos de Niza said he had discovered, he always kept his army in check and well managed. Did he refuse to allow or permit any man-of-war to blaspheme against God, Our Lord, and his blessed mother? Did he punish those living in concubinage and those who gambled to excess? And did he punish licentiousness and disturbances, as is apparent from the decrees, ordinances, and proclamations that he made and ordered announced in this regard? The witnesses are to testify where, how, and in what way [this was done].

{3} Item: [they are to be asked] whether they know, saw, or have heard it said that the aforesaid fray Marcos de Niza said that he had discovered the province of Cíbola, in which there are seven towns, the kingdom of Aqucui and Totonqueade, and the rest that the friar said he had discovered.

{4} Item: [they are to be asked] whether they know, etc., that the aforesaid captain general Francisco Vázquez de Coronado was very solicitous of the natives of all the lands through which he passed in Tierra Nueva and while searching for it. Did he see to it both that no harm was done to the persons of those natives and that nothing was taken from them, nothing they had either in their houses or in their fields in the countryside?

[3r] {5} Item: [they are to be asked] whether they know that four days' journey beyond the city of Compostela the general made decrees and issued ordinances very much in favor of the natives and had them publicly proclaimed. Among those was there one according to which no man-of-war was to enter an Indian's house or take anything or burn a house without permission from his captain, under penalty of death?

{6} Item: [they are to be asked] whether they know that the war waged by the aforesaid general and his army during the entrada and reconnaissance was fully justified, the Indians having prompted it. First, before waging the wars, was the requerimiento read to the Indians once, twice, and three times, in conformance with the law, telling them that they were to submit and be placed under the yoke and royal dominion of His Majesty? Were they assured that if they did that, they would be treated benevolently and kept in peace and justice? And was this [procedure] held to specifically in the provinces of Cíbola and Tiguex? They are to say what they know.

{7} Item: [they are to be asked] whether they know, etc., that [at first] when the army was lodged in the province [3v] of Tiguex [the Indians] were at peace. When they came to see the aforesaid captain general and bring him food items, did he give them trade goods and treat them with a full measure of love like vassals of His Majesty? And did he make them understand through interpreters that if any soldier or other person of the army mistreated them in any way or committed rape or stole anything of theirs, they were to come to the general and he would give them satisfaction and bring to justice those who had committed any thievery or done them any wrong?

{8} Item: [they are to be asked] whether they know, have seen, or have heard it said that while they were at peace, without being provoked, the native Indians of the province of Tiguex rose up in arms and killed thirty-some horses and mules that were abroad in the countryside grazing and killed two Nahua Indians. And afterwards did the natives take refuge and fortify themselves in a pueblo called del Arenal.

{9} Item: [they are to be asked] whether they know, etc. that when the uprising [4r] and death of the aforesaid Indians and horses came to the general's knowledge, he notified the preaching priests who were in the army at the time and the officials in charge of His Majesty's royal treasury and asked their opinion about what was proper to do in that case. They are to say what they know.

{10} Item: they are to be asked whether they know, etc., that during the aforesaid council the general, priests, and officials decided and agreed that it was just to make war against the Indians of that province and punish them because they had risen up and rebelled against serving His Majesty, even though their rebellion had not been provoked.

{11} Item: they are to be asked whether they know that after it was decided to make war on the natives of Tiguex, before launching that war the general ordered the councilman of Sevilla Diego López, a captain of horsemen, to go from the army to Pueblo del Arenal, [4v] where the rebellious natives had taken refuge and fortified themselves, and read them the requerimiento on behalf of His Majesty and the general in his royal name. Was he to tell them that they should come into obedience to His Majesty and that if any soldier or soldiers had given them cause to rise up and rebel or had done them injury, they should tell him? Were they to be told that if they said they were willing to be placed in the service of the holy emperor and majesty don Carlos, king of Spain, etc., our lord, the general would bring to justice those who had provoked the rebellion?

{12} Item: they are to be asked whether they know that the aforesaid Diego López told the Indians who had risen up and rebelled and made them understand what is referred to in the previous question. Did they reply that they were not familiar with his majesty nor did they want to be his subjects or serve him or any other Christian? While they were talking did they begin shooting arrows [5r] at Diego López and the Spaniards who went with him, thus making such serious provocation that there was no way war could be avoided? And when this happened the general was not present, correct?

{13} Item: [they are to be asked] whether they know that after war was made on Pueblo del Arenal, the Indians who left there went to a pueblo called Mocha. Did they and all the rest of the Indians of that province take refuge there, since it was a strong pueblo? And did they fortify themselves, resolving to persist in the treachery and rebellion they had started?

{14} Item: they are to be asked whether they know that once the aforesaid captain general knew that all the Indians of the province of Tiguex had risen up and taken refuge in Pueblo de Mocha, he sent don Rodrigo Maldonado, a captain of horsemen in the army, to deliver the requerimiento [5v] to those Indians. Did he tell them what is included in the eleventh question, just as Captain Diego López had told it to them? Did the Indians who had rebelled and taken refuge say in reply that they were not familiar with his majesty and did not want to serve him or have him as their lord? Did they tell don Rodrigo that he should dismount and come inside with them, all for the purpose of killing him? And did [the Indians] who were on the flat roofs start shooting arrows because he refused to do so, since he had no orders to that effect?

{15} Item: [they are to be asked] whether they know that after the general learned that the Indians refused to submit and place themselves in obedience to and service of His Majesty, he had the requerimiento read to them again by don García López de Cárdenas, maestre de campo of the army, so that [what he did] would be further justified and in order to carry out what His Majesty ordered in his instructions. Did the general order López to say the same words to the Indians that he had sent Captain Diego López to Pueblo del Arenal to deliver?

Did Maestre de Campo don García López [6r] go to Pueblo de Macha and tell [the Indians] what is referred to in the eleventh question, which preceded this one? Was there an Indian called Jumena who had been with the army in the pueblo of Coofor and who was the principal instigator of the uprising and did he tell don García López de Cárdenas, on behalf of all the Indians, "We know that you are well loved by the lady [the holy virgin] and we believe that you are telling us the truth. But to reassure us further, dismount from that horse and leave your sword and lance behind. We will come down from here and embrace you and we will be good friends."

Did the aforesaid don García López tell a soldier who was with him to tell the rest of the soldiers to draw a little closer, so that they could come to his aid? Was this because he had decided to do what the Indians asked, although he saw clearly that they wanted to kill him? Did he do this so that the general would not say that it was his fault that he had failed to place that province in the service and [6v] vassalage of His Majesty?

As a result, did the maestre de campo dismount from his horse and leave his sword and lance. And thereupon did the Indian Jumena and three others from among those who were on the flat roofs descend and come to embrace don García López? Further, when they put their arms around him, did they draw out some small clubs and strike don García on the head? Did they then wrestle with him in order to drag him inside [the pueblo] and kill him?

Would they have succeeded, if don García had not defended himself with a dagger that he still had and if the men he had as his guard had not come to his rescue? And, after he had been rescued, was the aforesaid don García López found to have suffered many blows to his body and a serious arrow wound in a foot?

{16} Item: they are to be asked whether they know that never, neither during battle nor outside of it, did the captain general consent to any cruelty to or excessive punishment of the Indians [of that province].

[7r] {17} Item: they are to be asked whether they know that neither the general nor [any other] person in the aforesaid army ever made slaves of Indians, male or female. Were there some Indians who were captured in war and were servants of the camp? And when the army wanted to return to Nueva España did the general order that a public announcement be made to the effect that, under severe penalties, no one was to keep any Indian, male or female, boy or girl? Further, the general did not permit Indians to be taken from those lands to these, even though some Indians said that of their own free will they wanted to come, correct?

{18} Item: they are to be asked whether they know or saw that when

[any] Indians of that land brought the general a present of hides or mantas, which is what there is in that land, he ordered that they be given trade items, such as beads, knives, hawksbells, and other things, [in exchange] for what they had brought.

{19} Item: they are to be asked whether they know [7v] that the general never consented to having corn or other things taken from the natives of that region, even though the army was in much need of food, clothing, and other items. Was the lack of food such that one Luis de Quejada, alférez of Juan de Zaldívar's company, paid forty pesos de minas for two slave's rations⁵ of corn and that Pedro de Ledesma, being in the lodgings of the general, purchased twenty-five skins⁶ of shelled corn and corn on the cob, one half of which cost a hundred gold pesos de minas.

{20} Item: they are to be asked whether they know or saw that the afore-said general and all of those who went with him suffered great hardships and excessive want, both from hunger and [for lack of] clothing with which to cover their bodies.

{21} Item: [they are to be asked] whether they know that the general spent a great sum of gold pesos [8r] without pursuing any other interest than His Majesty's service and the increase of His Majesty's royal patrimony. And did they hear this said on many occasions?

{22} Item: they are to be asked whether the Indian to whom the name El Turco was given and who told about Quivira tried to kill the general and those who went with him, while in Quivira. When the general became aware that El Turco was attempting to kill him and the others, did he order the maestre de campo called? Did he tell the maestre de campo to inquire and make investigation into what was happening in this case? And once he had seen [the results], was he to administer justice and what would be found to be in accordance with the law?

{23} Item: they are to be asked whether they know, saw, and have heard it said that the general and the aforesaid armed force went to Cíbola and the other places to which the most illustrious lord viceroy of Nueva España ordered them to go in His Majesty's name. And did they find there none of the wealth and magnificence that were proclaimed in the report? Instead, did they find in Cíbola seven small pueblos [8v] with stone houses having three or four levels of flat roofs in which there was a people lacking wealth, order, and understanding? Did they find that the kingdom called Acus was a single strong mesa called Acuco and that the kingdom of Totonqueates was a hot spring without inhabitants?

{24} Item: they are to be asked whether they know and saw that when the general saw that in the kingdom of Cíbola and the others that had been reported there was nothing that would increase the royal patrimony, he sent don Pedro de Tovar with horsemen in one direction in search of a province of which he had word, called Trosayán. Did he send the maestre de campo of the force don García López de Cárdenas in search of the Mar del Sur? And did he send Hernando de Alvarado in another direction, following the route to the east, and Captain Francisco de Ovando in another direction? Did they all have instructions as to what they were to do in those places; [9r] did he charge them especially and with affection to treat benevolently the natives of the areas through which they would pass and where they would reside?

{25} Item: they are to be asked whether they know that the captains and scouts traversed and reconnoitered a great extent of land and returned without finding or hearing about people to whom the Holy Gospel could be preached or [lands] where Christian doctrine could be sowed and which would serve to increase the royal patrimony. Was the only exception two Indians whom Captain Hernando de Alvarado brought, who told about the province of Quevira and the Guaches? Did the general and the army go in search of that province of Quivira, and after having traveled two hundred and fifty leagues through a wilderness was he told that he had been deceived and that the land and people toward which he traveled and about which he had been told and assured did not exist, nor did one part in a thousand [of what he had been told]? Having seen that this was so, in order not to place the army in a situation where it might perish, did the general decide [9v] to send it [back] to Tiguex to wait there? Did the general travel to Quivira with thirty-five horsemen, along which route there was a huge wilderness, causing them to suffer greatly from hunger and thirst? When he arrived at Quivira and saw that the people were few and settlement sparse and of little use in increasing the royal patrimony, did he return to Tiguex by another route, so he could reconnoiter further, and thus nothing would remain undone in the service of His Majesty.

{26} Item: they are to be asked whether they know that after the aforesaid, in the province of Tiguex, the horses were dying and the soldiers were falling sick. Did some of the people die from lack of both medicines and a physician to administer them? Was there no priest who could hear the confessions of the sick or say mass? Was food running out, and was there nowhere [more] could be gotten? And did the general take great care in ministering to the sick and leaving from there with those he had [brought]?

{27} Item: [they are to be asked] whether they know that the general saw [10r] that he had gone to that place and had taken the army there and to the other places to which he was ordered to take it in His Majesty's name and that a great amount of territory had been reconnoitered by him and [his] captains, more than fray Marcos said he had reconnoitered, in none of which had they seen, talked with, or had reports of civilized people among whom it would be possible to increase His Majesty's royal patrimony. As has been said in the questions before this, were the horses and soldiers dying, and was the whole army in danger of being lost because of the unproductiveness of the land and shortage of medicine, foodstuffs, and clothing with which to cover their bodies? And when he became aware of this, did the general agree to take the army and lead it to Nueva España, from where it had departed?

{28} Item: [they are to be asked] whether they know, etc., that during the siege of the pueblo of Cíbola the general came away sorely afflicted with four wounds in the face and one foot. Did everyone think that because of them he would not survive? And was he in a very bad way [10v] and on the point of death for a long while because of this? Likewise, during the siege he laid to Pueblo de Mocha was he incapacitated and were his legs useless because of swelling and bruises and because of failure to recover from the arrow wound? Furthermore, at the pueblo of Coofor did he have a very serious disorder from which it was thought he would die, and did he say [even so] that he was content with his malady since it was suffered in His Majesty's service? They are to say, etc.

{29} Item: [they are to be asked] whether they know that the general went on this conquest without any other interest than to serve His Majesty. Because of it was he compelled to expend a great sum of gold pesos and was he indebted for more than ten thousand gold pesos de minas, which debt he still has to extinguish? As a result, has he been forced to sell both chattel and real property, but still has not been able to finish paying the debt? And are his funds depleted because of the entrada he made?

{30} Item: [they are to be asked] whether they know, etc., that all of the above is public knowledge, widely and commonly known. The witnesses are to state and declare what they know concerning this [case].

[11r] Item: When this petition and interrogatory had been presented in the manner related and when the lord alcalde reviewed them, he stated that he held them and was holding them as [properly] presented. Inasmuch as the request was not frivolous, he ordered that the aforesaid Francisco Pilo bring and present the witnesses he intends to use in the name [of Francisco Vázquez de Coronado]. [He stated further] that he had ruled that the witnesses were to be examined according to the interrogatory presented and that justice was to be done in all things.

Item: Thereafter, the lord alcalde said that because he was occupied with other business and other suits and cases in keeping with His Majesty's service and execution of royal justice, he charged and was charging me, the aforesaid scribe, with receiving the testimony and statements of the witnesses to be presented in this case by Francisco Pilo. For this he gave me a commission in the required form and signed it. Witnesses: García de Villarreal and Diego Herrera, residents at these mines.

Item: After the aforesaid in this villa on the seventh day of the month of January in the same year, Francisco Pilo appeared in the name [of Francisco Vázquez de Coronado] and presented as witness Lorenzo [11v] Álvarez, a resident of this province. His oath was taken in the form required by law: by God, by Santa María, by the words of the four holy evangelists (wherever they are most fully written), and by a representation of the cross (on which he roughly placed his right hand). [He swore], as a good and loyal Christian, to speak the truth about what he may be asked and may know about this case, in which he is presented as a witness. And he asked that God help him in this corporeal world and in the other spiritual world, if he spoke the truth. If he did the contrary, God should stringently and dearly hold him accountable as a bad Christian, knowing that he has sworn in vain by His holy name. At the conclusion of the oath he said, "Yes, I swear, amen. What I state and declare is the following."

Item: Afterwards at these mines on the twelfth day of the month of March in the same year, Francisco Pilo appeared in the name [of Francisco Vázquez de Coronado] and presented as witnesses Diego López [12r] (a councilman of Sevilla), Luis de Figueredo, and don Pedro de Tovar, [all of whom are] residents of this province. Oaths were taken and received in the form required by law from all and each one of them. What each one stated and declared is the following.

First de Parte Witness (Lorenzo Álvarez)

The aforesaid Lorenzo Álvarez, a resident at the mines of Nuestra Señora de Esperanza and a witness presented by Francisco Pilo in the name of Francisco Vázquez de Coronado, having sworn his oath in the form required by law and being questioned in accordance with the substance of the aforesaid interrogatory, stated and declared the following.

{1} To the first question he stated that he has known the Francisco Vázquez de Coronado referred to in the question for seven or eight years.

{personal matters} Being questioned about personal matters according to the questions prescribed by law, he said that he is about thirty years old, that he is not a relative of Francisco Vázquez de Coronado, and that none of the other questions on personal matters applies to him.

[12v] {2} To the second question he stated that he knows that when he

went in search of the land referred to in the question, Francisco Vázquez de Coronado did so with his army very well governed and controlled. He did not permit anyone to swear profanely, blaspheme, or live in concubinage. Further, he did not allow anyone to gamble in public, and some people did so in hiding, so that the alguacil would not see them gambling and tell the general. This was because Vázquez de Coronado ordered that it be publicly proclaimed that [the people] were not to swear, blaspheme, or live in concubinage or licentiously. He ordered the proclamation made two days' march beyond where the expedition began its journey. For this reason the army was well governed and controlled, without licentiousness or blasphemy or other vices, which is publicly known and widely held. This is what he knows concerning the question.

{3} To the third question he replied that it was publicly said and widely known that this was so, among the people of the expedition and many others, too.

[13r] {4} To the fourth question he replied that he knows what is referred to there. Asked how he knows it, the witness answered that it is because he was one of those who went on the expedition, and he observed that always and wherever the general passed he would not permit brutality against any native of that land; nor did he consent to any [other] Spaniard harming even one native. [Further,] the witness believes and holds it as certain that if the general had become aware that any man-at-arms had committed brutality against a native, he would have punished him for it. Contrary [to what the question states], the witness saw that the general gave the natives some trade goods and other things and that he stole nothing of theirs. This is what he knows concerning the question.

{5} To the fifth question he said [in reply] that he knows that two days' journey from the city of Compostela the governor ordered a decree and ordinances publicly proclaimed. These directives ordered so many things that the witness does not remember them all. Regarding what was ordered and announced, he refers to the decrees [themselves], which were executed before the scribe. This is what he knows concerning the question.

[13v] {6} To the sixth question the witness answered that because he had

remained behind, he was not present when the requerimiento was read to the Indians referred to. But it is public knowledge and very widely held that before war was waged in any place, many exhortations were made in the presence of friars who went on the expedition. Furthermore, [Álvarez] heard it said that the natives were given all the assurances referred to in the question. It is public knowledge and widely held that those Indians were never willing to accept the pledges. Instead, they made threats and shot arrows, for which reason [the Spaniards] were forced to wage war. This is what he knows concerning the question.

{7} To the seventh question the witness replied that when he arrived at the pueblo referred to in the question, he found that the land was in rebellion and at war, for which reason he did not see what is mentioned in the question, but he heard it said with assurance. He knows this about it.

{8} To the eighth question [Álvarez] responded that when he came to the aforesaid province [14r] of Tiguex, he saw and found that the Indians were at war, having risen up and taken refuge in the pueblo specified in the question. As was common knowledge, [the people of Tiguex] had killed the Indians and mules referred to in the question, had set up fortifications, and were making a stand [in the pueblo]. This is what he knows concerning the question.

{9} To the ninth question the witness answered that he does not know because, as he has said, he remained behind.

{10} To the tenth question he responded by saying he does not know for the reason he has [already] stated.

{11} To the eleventh question the witness replied that he does not know because, as he has said, he had not [yet] arrived.

{12} To the twelfth question he said he does not know because this all happened before he arrived. But he heard it said that the general was not present during the battle referred to in the question.

{13} To the thirteenth question [the witness] said that he knows and saw that when he arrived at the settlement of Tiguex many of the Indians there had risen up and taken refuge in a pueblo situated on a height [14v] which, afterwards, was called Pueblo del Cerco. There they had fortified themselves and made a stand for a number of days. This is what he knows concerning the question.

{14} To the fourteenth question [Álvarez] replied that he knows that Captain don Rodrigo Maldonado went to the pueblo referred to there. He heard it said that [the captain] went in order to bring the Indians to peace. And he knows nothing else concerning what is stated in the question.

{15} To the fifteenth question [the witness] answered that what he knows about it is that don García López went to the cited pueblo to bring it to peace. It was common knowledge and widely known that the Juan Eman referred to in the question told [López] that he should dismount and leave his weapons, helmet, and beaver because [the Indians] wanted to meet and talk with him, which would have happened [already] except that they were afraid of the others. After he had dismounted [the Indians] seized him and did violence to him, and they would have killed him, if it had not been for those who came to his aid. This is what the witness heard from some of those who [15r] went with don García López and from [the captain] himself. This is what he knows concerning the question.

{ 16} To the sixteenth question the witness responded [by saying] that he knows that in no place where they fought was brutality committed against the natives. [He says this] because at Pueblo del Cerco, which is where the Indians were at war, some native Indians were put to death [only] because they were rebels and also because they had killed many Spaniards and Indian [allies]. This is what he knows concerning the question.

{17} To the seventeenth question [Álvarez] answered that he knows that neither before nor during the war did the army make slaves, male or female. Likewise, he knows that when [the expedition] departed for Nueva España it was announced publicly that no one was to take any Indian, female or male, from that land. Rather, they were to be left in their native land, under pain of certain [15v] penalties. This is what he knows concerning the question.

{18} In response to the eighteenth question [the witness] said that he had heard what is referred to in the question.

{19} To the nineteenth question he replied that what he knows about it is that in the pueblo of Tiguex, where [the company's] quarters were, he was told by a soldier of the expedition, named Mayorga, that they gave him a sack of corn to help him pay Pedro de Ledesma for thirty sacks of corn which he owed him. Ledesma had paid a hundred pesos de minas for the corn, from which was deducted what Mayorga owed him. Further, the witness knows that nothing, neither corn nor anything else, was taken from peaceful Indians, only from those at war. This is what he knows concerning the question.

{20} To the twentieth question [Álvarez] replied that he knows what is referred to because, as he has said, being one of those who went in the armed force, he suffered the [hardships mentioned] and saw others suffer them.

[16r] {21} To the twenty-first question [the witness] answered that he knows that the general could not have avoided spending a large amount of money because of the campaign. Regarding the [exact] quantity, he knows nothing more than that the general took along many horses, mules, and servants, as well as many fine clothes for himself and his household. For all of this he could not have avoided spending a great sum of money, in the opinion of the witness, though how much it was he does not know.

{22} To the twenty-second question the witness said he does not know.

{23} To the twenty-third question [Álvarez] responded by saying that the general went to the province of Cíbola with the army and found there only seven pueblos in which the Indians of the province resided. The Indians had three- and four-story houses, but no wealth. [Again,] no wealth was found there. [He said that he knows] that the pueblo of Acuco was only the one pueblo situated on a strong promontory. [16v] He heard it said that what was called the kingdom of Acuco was [only] that pueblo and that [the place] known as Toton-queates was [only] a hot spring. These were things contained in [fray Marcos's] report. This is what he knows concerning the question and nothing more.

{24} To the twenty-fourth question the witness answered that what he knows about it is that he heard that it was common knowledge and widely held throughout the expeditionary company that the Pedro de Tovar referred to in the question went to the pueblos of Tusayán and don García López went in search of the Mar del Sur. Also, Hernando de Alvarado went to the pueblos of Tiguex, Cicarique, and Uraba and to the bison plains, and the Francisco de

Ovando referred to in the question went in another direction. The witness did not see this, but it was common knowledge and widely held throughout the army. [Álvarez] did not see it because when the announcement was made he was not present in the pueblo of Cíbola, from which the captains were sent to make reconnaissance. This is what he knows concerning the question.

{25} To the twenty-fifth question [17r] he responded by saying that what he knows about it is that he heard it said as something publicly known and widely held that the captains referred to went to reconnoiter those lands and where they traveled they never found any place to settle. Also, when Hernando de Alvarado returned from the plains referred to, and from Cicuique and Uraba, he brought two Indians with him. The one was given the name Turco and the other, Ysopete. They spoke and told about Quivira and the Guales, saying that it was a land heavily populated and very wealthy in gold and silver. And they said that the people there were very civilized and many other things. These [two] Indians guided the general and the army through the bison plains, where they traveled across a great expanse of unsettled land. In the opinion of the witness it amounted to about two hundred and fifty leagues.

Because certain things the Indians said would be found along the way were not found, it was concluded that everything [they said] was a lie and that they were leading the army deceptively. For that [17v] reason the general decided to go in search of the province of Quivira with up to forty men supplied with horses and food. And he ordered don Tristán de Arellano to take the rest of the company back to the province of Tiguex. [This was] so that those who were poorly supplied with food and the footmen would not perish and die.

Thus the army returned, and the general went [to Quivira] with those previously mentioned. Afterwards, the witness saw [the general and his company] return. They said that there were very few people and no food in the province of Quivira. If the [whole] army had gone there [the people] would have died from the hunger and thirst that the general and those who went with him said they had suffered. [That is] because they traveled through a large unsettled territory. Since the population of Quivira was small and the land unfruitful they returned. This is what he knows concerning the question.

{26} To the twenty-sixth question [Álvarez] replied that he knows that upon returning from the aforesaid [entrada to Quivira], while the army was overwintering [18r] in the province of Tiguex, some Spaniards fell ill and were dying because of the great cold and many hardships they endured and because they had few medicines and little clothing. And many horses died. Also, [he knows] that the food was running out, without anywhere to get more. Furthermore, mass was not being said in the camp; nor was there anyone to say it.

He also knows that when the general was healthy he went to visit the sick, some of whom he brought to his tent, so that they might have better care. And he had them tended to there. This is what he knows concerning the question.

{27} To the twenty-seventh question [the witness] answered that what he knows about it is that the aforesaid general traversed a great expanse of territory, either personally or by means of his captains. In all of those [lands] he did not find nor was he told about any place that, in the witness's opinion, could be settled and that would augment His Majesty's royal patrimony.

Further, as has been said, he knows that the people [18v] were sick and dying because of the scarcity of medicines and servants and the severe need the Spaniards were in. He saw that the general left [there] and returned with the army to Nueva España, from where he had led it. [Álvarez] believes and is certain that the general took the army and led it [here] because they did not find any place to settle, for the reasons mentioned in the question.

{28} To the twenty-eighth question he responded [by saying] that what he knows about it is that he heard it said publicly and as common knowledge throughout the army that the general came away wounded from Cíbola. And the people thought the Indians had killed him. [The witness] is aware that when he was in the siege in the province of Tiguex the general was hurt in one leg and, on returning from the province of Quivira, he was very unwell. This and nothing else is what he knows concerning the question.

{29} To the twenty-ninth question the witness replied that he answers the same as he has in the questions before this one. And he does not know the rest of what is included in the question.

[19r] {30} To the thirtieth question he answered that he says the same as he has to the previous questions. He says that what he has stated is the truth and what he knows about the case, in accordance with the oath he swore. And he signed it.

Lorenzo Álvarez

A TRANSCRIPT
OF THE DOCUMENTARY RECORD

[fol. 1v][7]

En las mynas de n*ues*tra señora de / los rremedios de la Provinçia de / culiacan De galizia de la nueVa esp*aña* / A çinco di*a*s del mes de (h)enero año /
del naÇimi*ento* de n*ues*tro salvador *jesu* / *Cris*to de myll e quy*nien*tos e
quarenta / e çinco años ante *el* muy noble s*eñor* / P*edr*o hernandez al*ca*lde En
estas / Di*c*has mynas Por su mag*es*t*a*d y *en* Pre- / sençia de my el es*cr*i*ban*o E
*testi*gos yuso escritos / Paresçio Presente Fran*cis*co Pilo / Estante En estas
di*c*has mynas / En nonbre de Fran*cis*co Vazq*uez* / De coronado y con su Poder
/ E Presento Una Peti*ci*on e un / Ynterrogatorio de Preguntas el / thenor de
lo qual uno en Pos de / otro Es este que se sigue

muy noble señor

Fran*cis*co Pilo *en* n*ombr*e del governador Fran*cis*co / Vazquez de coronado y
por Virtud / Del Poder que tengo de *el* ante *el* / Presente es*cr*i*ban*o digo que
a d*erec*ho / De my P*ar*te conviene hazer una / Probanç(c)a Ad PerPetuan Rey
/ memoria[8] En esta Provinçia a / V*uestra* m*erced* Pido y Suplico la mande /
Reçibir y esamynar los *testi*gos q*ue* / En este casso Presentare

[fol. 2r]
328
Por este ynterrogatorio de Pre- / Guntas de que ante v*uestra* m*erced* hago /
Presentaçion y lo q*ue* dixeren / E depusieren çerrado y sellado / y signado del
presente es*cr*i*ban*o y *en* / Publica Forma y en manera q*ue* / haga fee lo mande
dar Para lo / Presentar todo al d*erec*ho de my P*ar*te / convenga y (e)*in*ter-
Ponyendo En / todo ello Su autoridad y decreto / Judiçial Para lo qual y *en* lo
nezes*ari*o / El muy noble offi*ci*o de v*uestra* m*erced* ynploro / Pido just*ici*a
Fran*cis*co Pilo

[fol. 35r]⁹

[…]

SePan quantos esta *carta* vieren / como yo Francisco Vazquez de / coronado
governador y capitan / general En esta provinÇia / de galizia De la nueVa
España / Por su magestad Estante que ser y En es- / Ta ÇiUdad de
guadalaXara / de la dicha provinçia otorgo E

[fol. 35v]

conozco Por esta carta q*ue* doy e / otorgo todo my poder cunpl*i*do / libre
llenero bastante segun(d) / que lo yo he y tengo y segun(d) q*ue* / mejor y mas
cumplidamente lo / Puedo E debo dar E otorgar y / de derecho mas Puede e
deve / Valer A Vos Francisco Pilo q*ue* / Soys ausente bien Ansi como / sy
Fuesedes presente general- / mente para en todo mys pleitos / E caussas E
negoçios Çeviles / y crimynales moVidos e por / mover que yo *h*E y tengo y
es- / Pero *h*aver e thener E mover / contra todas e qualesqu*i*er / Perssonas E
las tales Per- / Sonas contra my En qual- / qui*er* manera Ansi En de- / mandando como En defendiendo / E Para que por my y *en* my nonbre / Podais
hazer E hagais Ante / las justiçias de la villa de san / myguel E de la Provinçia
de / culiacan de galizia de la / nueva españa e ante / otras qualesqu*i*er justi*Ç*i*as*
/ De su mage*s*tad de otras quales- / qu*i*er P*ar*tes Una e dos e mas pro-

[fol. 36r]

362

Banças Ansi ad Per- / Petuan rrey memorian / como En otra qualqu*i*er
manera / Para en qualqu*i*er casso / E cossa A my tocante y p*ar*a / Ello presentar qualesqu*i*er / Escritos escripturas de yn- / Terrogatorios E otras quales-
/ quier e qualesquyer t*e*st*i*gos / y pedir los rreçiban y los *ver* / Jurar e sus d*i*chos
y dePusiçiones / los Pedir sacados En linpio / y çerrados y sellados ynterPo-
/ nyendo En ello las tales just*i*c*i*as / Su autoridad E decreto judi*Ç*ial / me lo
Enviar e presentarlo / Por my y *en* my n*o*mbre Ado*n*de A my d*e*rec*h*o / convenga E hazer Sobre *e*llo todos / los aUtos E cosas A ello E / qualquiera cosa
de *e*llo anexa y / Pertenesçiente E nezesaria / E Para que ansi Sobre lo /

Susod*i*cho E Sobre otra qualqu*i*er / cosa A los d*i*chos mys Pleitos Podais /
Paresçer y parezcais ante / Sus magestades y ante sus / qualesqu*i*er al*ca*ldes
juezes / E Just*i*Çias Ansi de la d*i*cha Vi*ll*a

[fol. 36v]

De san myguel como de otras quales- / quier partes e lugares que sean / E
ante *e*llos e qualqu*i*er de *e*llos / Poner E hazer todas las demandas / Pedimy*en*tos rrequir*i*my*en*tos Pro- / Testaçiones ÇitaÇiones y *en*pla- /
Zamyentos y demandas e de- / Fender demandar negar y / conozer y t*e*sti-
m*on*yos Pedir E sacar / E para jurar *en* my anyma quales- / quier juramento
Asi de calu*m*nya / como de çensorio E pedir A las o- / tras partes los Hagan
E verlos / Hazer E para sacar E tomar *en* las / qualesqu*i*er escripturas ansi /
de las d*i*chas Provinçias como / otras qualesquier / A mi tocantes E
perteneçientes / De Poder de qualesqu*i*er / es*cri*banos e Perssonas q*u*e / las
tengan E para Presentar / es*critura*s y probanças y escritos E / Todo genero
de prueba E pedir / Publicaçion y aso(n)*m*ar mys t*e*sti*g*os / E los En contrario
tachar y con- / Tradezir *en* d*i*chos y En Personas / E condecir E çerrar
Razones / y pedir E oyr s*en*ten*c*ia e s*en*tencyas / Ansi ynterlocutorias

[fol. 37r]

363

como diFinitivas E de las Por my / consentir e de las En contrario / APelar y
suplicar E pedir / la Apelaçion Suplicaçion / Alli e do*nde* con d*e*re*c*ho se deba
segun / E dar que *e*n las siga e Hazer / todas las otras cosas e autos / judiçiales
y estrajudiÇiales / q*u*e A la calidad de lo q*u*e d*i*cho es / convengan E menester
se *h*an / de se hazer E yo mysmo Haria / E hazer Podria Presente / s(e)yendo
aunque P*ar*a ello / se rrequiera *h*aber otro / my mas EsPeçial poder E / mandado E presençia Personal / E para que *en* V*uest*ro lugar y *en* my n*on*b*r*e /
Podais hazer E sustituir / Un procurador e dos e mas e / Aquellos rreVocar E
otros / de nuevo hazer quedando / *en* Vos este poder de procurador / Prinzipal
e q*u*e tan cunpl*i*do / E bastante poder como yo he / y tengo para lo q*u*e d*i*cho
es e / Para cada cosa de *e*llo o- / Tro tal E tan cunpl*i*do E los d*e*re*c*hos / y
(h)asimysmo lo doy e otorgo / A vos el d*i*cho Fran*ci*sco Pilo

[fol. 37v]

E A los dichos Vuestros susti- / Tutos con todas sus ynÇidencias / e dependençias Anexidades E / conegidades E vos rrelievo segun(d) / Forma Acos-
tunbrada de derecho E / Para lo haber Por firme / obligo mys bienes muebles
E / Rayzes havidos e Por haver E / mys Frutos E rrentas (f)hecha / la carta En
esta dicha ÇiUdad / De guadalaXara postrero dos / del mes de agosto año de
nas- / Çimyento de nuestro salvador *jesu cristo* de / myll e quinientos e
quarenta e quatro / Años testigos que fueron Presentes / A lo que dicho es juan
ssanches De (h)ozar / y Juan de villarreal y juan de / Pereda Estantes En esta
/ dicha ÇiUdad y el dicho otorgante / lo Firmo de su nonbre en el rregistro /
de esta carta Francisco Vazquez de / coronado

[fol. 2r cont'd]

{ytem} / Por las preguntas siguientes / sean preguntados los testigos que son /
e Fueren presentados Por parte / De Francisco Vazquez de coronado Go- /
bernador de la Provinçia De la / nueVa galizia E capitan general / Del exerçito
De las tierras que / Fray marcos De nyca dixo haver / Descubierto / {i} /
Primeramente sean preguntados si conozen / al dicho Francisco Vazquez coronado Ca- / Pitan general que Fue A des- / cubrir las tierras que Fray marcos
/ Dixo haber descubierto y de lo demas / {ii} / Yten si saven que yendo el dicho
general / en demanda de las dichas tierras

[fol. 2v]

que el dicho fray marcos de nyca dixo / haber descubierto lleVo sienPre su /
Exerçito muy corregido y bien gobernado / no consintiendo ny dando lugar
que / nyngun soldado blasfemase contra / Dios nuestro señor y Su bendita
madre / y castigando los AmanÇeVados y los que / Xugaban juegos eçesivos
y escandalos / E rruidos segun(d) Parezera Por / los Edictos (h)ordenanças y
pregones / que sobre ello hizo y mando Prego- / nar digan los testigos A
donde como y de / que manera / {3} / Yten si saven Vieron oyeron dezir / que
el dicho fray marcos de nica / Dixo haver descubierto la Pro- / vinçia De
Çibola en que hay siete pue- / blos y el rreyno de aquCuy y de toton- / queade
y lo demas que el dicho Fray mar- / cos dixo haber descubierto / {4} / Yten si

saven E*tcetera* que *e*l d*i*cho ca*P*itan / general Franc*i*sco Vazqu*ez* de coronado tuVo / mucho cuydado de los naturales De / todas las tierras Por do*nde* Passo / de la d*i*cha tierra nueva y *en* demanda / de *e*lla Ansi En q*u*e no se le*s* hiziese / A los d*i*chos naturales algun daño En / Sus personas como En q*u*e no se les / tomase nada De lo que thenian / En sus casas ny *en* las sementeras / Del canpo do*nde* las *h*abian

[fol. 3r]
329
{5} / Yten si saven que el d*i*cho general / quatro jornadas delante de la / Ç*i*Udad de conPostela hizo e m*a*ndo / Pregonar (h)ed*i*ctos (h)ordenanças / muy *en* favor de los d*i*chos naturales *en*tre / las quales Fue una que nyngun(d) / Soldado Entrase en casa de yndyo / ny le tomase nada ny le quemase cassa / syn liçençia de su caPitan So / pena de muerte / {6} / Yten si saven que la guerra que / En la d*i*cha *en*trada y descubrimy*en*to / que *e*l d*i*cho general y su eXer*Ç*ito hizo / (y) Fue muy Justificada dando A / Ella los yndios con quyen se hizo / ocassion y pr*i*m*er*o que se hiziese la d*i*cha / guerra e guerras los d*i*chos yndios / Fueron rrequeridos Una e dos e tres / Vezes conForme a derecho diziendoles / que se diesen y pusiesen debaxo / Del yugo E domynyo R*e*al de su mag*e*st*a*d / Asegurandoles y haziendolo ansi / seran bien tratados E tenidos En / Paz E justiçia E se les Guardara / EsPezialmente En las / Provinçias De Çibola E tiguex / Digan lo que saven / {7} / Yten si saven E*tcetera* que *e*st*a*ndo el d*i*cho / EXerçito Aposentado *en* la pro-

[fol. 3v]
Vinçia de tiguex estaban de Paz / E quando Venian a ver al d*i*cho ge- / neral y le trayan Alguna cosa de comyda / el d*i*cho capitan general les daba / rrescates E los trataba con todo / Amor e como A Vasallos de su mag*e*st*a*d / y les hazia Entender Por yn- / terpr*e*t(r)es que si algun soldado / o otra persona del exer*Ç*ito / les hiziese Algun m*a*ltratamy*en*to o les / hiziese Fuerça o tomase Algo de / lo suyo Vinyesen Al d*i*cho general / que *e*llos desAgraviaria e haria / justiçia de los q*u*e algo les tomasen / E algun mal les hiziesen / {8} / Yten si saven Vieron y oyeron / Dezir que estando de paz los / d*i*chos yndios

De la Provinçia / De tigueX sin les dar ocassion / Alguna los d*i*chos naturales
se le- / Vantaron E mataron treynta E / Tanto caballos e aÇemylas que /
Andaban Al canpo Paçiendo / E mataron dos yndios mexicanos / E luego se
Encastillaron E hi- / Zieron Fuertes los d*i*chos naturales / E*n* un pueblo que
se dezia Del arenal / {9} / Yten si saven E*tcetera* si sabido Por el d*i*cho / general el d*i*cho levantamyento

[fol. 4r]
330
E muerte de los d*i*chos yndios E / caballos el d*i*cho general apunto *a* / los rre-
ligiosos de mysa q*ue* Al presente / *h*avia En el d*i*cho EXerçito y los o- /
Fiçiales que tenian cargo de la / rreal hazienda de su mag*esta*d y les pidio /
Parezer de lo que conVenya hazerse / Sobre *e*l caso digan lo que saven / {10}
/ Yten sean preguntados si saven E*tcetera* / q*ue en* la d*i*cha junta del d*i*cho general / E rreligiosos E offi*ci*ales se / Determyno e aCordo ser justo ha- /
Zerseles Guerra E castigar los / d*i*chos yndios de la d*i*cha ProvinÇia / Por
rrazon de se *h*aber levantado / E rrebelado contra el servi*ci*o / De su mag*esta*d
sin se les *h*aber dado / ocasion A su rrevelaçion / {11} / Yten sean Preguntdos
si saben / q*ue* despues de determynado / que se hiziese guerra A los d*i*chos /
naturales De tiguex antes / que se començase la d*i*cha guerra / el d*i*cho general mando A di*e*go lopez / Veynte e quatro de sevilla Ca- / Pitan de gente de
a caballo / que (qu)*d*el d*i*cho EXerçito Fuese al d*i*cho / Pueblo Del arenal

[fol. 4v]
Do*nde* los d*i*chos naturales estaban / Encastillados alÇados y he- / chos Fuertes
y les rrequiriesen / De parte De su mag*esta*d y del d*i*cho gener*a*l / En su rreal
nonbre Vinyesen / A dar la obidiençia A su mag*esta*d y / les dixese que *e*sta su
rrebelion / y levantamy*ento* les *h*abian dado causa / Alguna soldado o soldados
/ o les *h*abian hecho demasia lo dixesen / E que diziendolo quiriendose / Poner
En servidunbre De la / saCra mag*esta*d del Enperador don / carlos rrey e*tcetera*
de *es*Paña n*uest*ro señor / En presençia de los d*i*chos yndio*s* / haria justiçia de
los que *h*o- / biesen dado ocasion a la d*i*cha Revelion / {12} / Yten sean preguntados si saven / que *e*l d*i*cho capitan diego lopez / Dixo E les hizo *en*tender

/ lo cont*eni*do En la pre*gunt*a antes de *e*sta / A los d*i*chos yndios que ansi es- / Taban alzados E rrebelados / E le rresPondieron q*ue* no / conoçian A su mag*esta*d ny le querian / Estar su(b)jetos ny servyrle / A el ny a otro nyngun(d) *Cristi*ano / y estando los hablando comen- / caron los de flechar

[fol. 5r]

331

Al d*i*cho diego lopez e A los EsPañoles / que con el yban E dando los / d*i*chos yndios ocasion tan grave(s) / que no se pudo Escusar En / nynguna manera la guerra e ansi / se hizo no se hallando el d*i*cho ge- / neral Presente a ella / {13} / Yten si saven que desPues / De *h*aberse hecho la guerra al d*i*cho / Pueblo que se dize del arenal / los yndios que del d*i*cho pueblo / salieron se Fueron Al pueblo / que se dize De mocha e ally como En / Pueblo Fuerte se Encastillaron / como todos los demas que *h*abia / En *a*quella Provinçia E se / hizieron Fuertes con deter- / mynaçion De sustener la Re- / belion y trayçion q*ue h*abian començado / {14} / Yten sean Preguntados si saben / que sabido Por el d*i*cho caPitan / general que *e*staban todos los d*i*chos / yndios de la d*i*cha Provinçia De / Tiguex Alçados y encastillados / En el d*i*cho Pueblo de mocha / *en*Vio A don R*odrig*o maldonado caPitan / De gente De a caballo *e*n *e*l d*i*cho E- / Xerçito A que rrequiriese

[fol. 5v]

los d*i*chos yndios y les dixese lo cont*eni*do / En la (h)onzena Pregunta como / el d*i*cho capitan di*e*go loPez se lo *h*abia / d*i*cho e los d*i*chos yndios q*ue* Ansi esta- / ban encastillados E rrebelados / Dieron por rresPuesta q*ue* / no conoçian A su mag*esta*d ny le que- / rian servir ny tener Por señ*or* / E dixeron al d*i*cho don R*odrig*o que / se apease y *en*trase con ellos A / Fin de matarle e como no lo quyso / hazer Por no *h*aberse lo mandado le / començaron A flechar los que / Estaban enÇima de los AÇoteas / {15} / Yten si saven que despues de / *h*aber savido el d*i*cho capitan / general como no *h*abian querido / los d*i*chos yndios darse ny Ponerse / En obidiençia E servidunbre / De su mag*esta*d Para mas justi- / Ficaçion y cumplim*yent*o de lo que / Su mag*esta*d por su ynstruçion lo manda / los Volvio otra vez A rrequerir / Con don garÇia

lopez de cardenas / maestre de canPo del exerÇito / E le mando dixese A los
dichos / yndios las mysmas Palabras / que el le enVio A dezir Al pueblo / Del
arenal con el dicho capitan / Diego lopez y el dicho don Garcia lopez

[fol. 6r]
332
maestre de canpo Fue al dicho / Pueblo de macha E les dixo / todo lo contenido En las (h)onze Preguntas / Antes de esta E un yndio que / se dezia
jumena que estaba en el / Pueblo de coofor con el e- / XerÇito que Fue el
primer yn- / Ventor del dicho levantamyento / Dixo al dicho don garÇia lopez
de / cardenas En nombre de todos los yn- / Dios bien sabemos que la (h)ama
/ Te quiere bien e cre(h)emos que nos / Dizes Verdad E para mas A- / segu-
rarnos APeate de ese caballo / E deXa la esPada E la lanza / E baXaremos de
aqui A A- / braÇarte y seremos buenos amygos / y el dicho don garÇia lopez
dixo con / soldado que estaba con el / que dixese A los demas sol- / Dados
que se llegasen Un / Poco mas para que le / Socorriesen Porque de- / Ter-
minaba de hazer lo que / los yndios le Pedian aUnque / Veya claro que le
querian / matar Porque el general no / Dixese que Por su culPa / DeXava de
Poner aquella / ProvinÇia En serviÇio y

[fol. 6v]
servidunbre de su magestad e ansi el / dicho maestre de canpo se apeo / de su
caballo y dexo la lança / y espada y luego baxaron el / dicho yndyo jumena E
otros tres / yndios de los que estaban / En las açoteas E llegan / A abraçar al
dicho don garÇia lopez / E al tiempo que le abraçaron / sacaron Unas maçetas
E co- / mençaron A dar golpes sobre / la cabeça al dicho don garÇia lopez / E
asirse con el Para matarle / Dentro a matarle como lo hi- / Zieran si el dicho
don garçia lopez / no se defendiera con un puñal / que el (h)abia quedado y no
le / Socorriera la gente que thenia / En rresguarda y ansi desPues / De ser socor-
ridos el dicho don / garÇia lopez quedo con muchos gol- / Pes en el cuerpo E
con Un mal / FlechaÇo en el pie / {16} / Yten sean preguntados / sy saven que
el dicho capitan / general nunca consintio que / En la guerra ny Fuer(e)a de ella
/ se hiziese nynguna crueldad / ny castigo Demasiado A los dichos yndios

[fol. 7r]

333

{17} / Yten sean preguntados (y) si saven / que el dicho general ny otra Per- /
Sona del dicho Exerçito nunca / hizo esclaVos ny esclaVas / E que Algunos
yndios de los que / En las guerras se prendieron / que estaban Para serviÇio
del / canpo quando (e)el exerçito se / queria Volver a la nueVa españa / El
general mando pregonar so / grandes Penas que nadie / Traxese yndio ni yndia
muchacho / ny muchacha ny el consintio sacar / De aquellas tierras Para /
Traer a estas Aunque al- / gunos yndios dezian que de / Su propia Voluntad
se que- / rian Venir / {18} / Yten sean Preguntados si / saven e Vieron quando
los yn- / Dios de aquella tierra trayan / Al general Algun serviçio de / cueros
e mantas que es lo que / En aquellas Partes (h)abia / el general les mandaba
dar / Por lo que trayan rrescate / de quentas y cuchillos E / cascabeles y otras
cosas / {19} / Yten sean preguntados si saben

[fol. 7v]

como el dicho general nunca / consentia ni consintio tomar mayz / ny otras
cosas A los naturales / De aquell(o)as partes aunque / El Exerçito tenia mucha
neze- / sidad de comida E rroPa E de / otras cosas E la nezesidad / De comida
(h)era tanta que un / luys de quexada Alferez / De la conPañia de juan / de saldivar dio quarenta / Pesos de minas Por dos / Zele(s)mines de mayz E Pedro
de / ledesma con estar En la / Posada del general con- / Pro veynte y çinco
Pellexos[10] / De mayz E maçorca la / mytad Podria Por Çien(t) / Pesos De oro
de mynas / {20} / Yten sean Preguntados / Sy saven e vieron que el dicho / general E todos los que / con el Fueron Padeçian / grandes trabajos y exÇe- / sivas
nezesidades Ansi de / hanbre como de rropa con que / cubrir sus carnes / {21}
/ Yten si saven que el general / gasto mucha suma de pesos de oro

[fol. 8r]

334

syn pretender mas ynterese de / servir A Su magesttad y acrecentar / El pat-
rimonio rreal de su magestad / y ansi se lo oyeron dezir muchas / Vezes / {22}
/ Yten sean preguntados que el / yndio que por nonbre se llamo / El turco que

dio rrelaÇion de / quiVira trato de matar Al ge- / neral en quiVira e a los q*ue* / yban / con el E sabido Por el general / que *el* di*c*ho turco trataba la muerte / Al di*c*ho capitan general E a los de- / mas mando llamar Al maese de / canpo E le dixo que se ynfor- / mase E hiziese Pesquisa de lo / que En aquel caso Pasaba y vista / hiziese justiçia y lo que hallase Por d*e*re*c*ho / {23} / Yten sean Preguntados si saven / Vieron *e* oyeron dezir que *el* di*c*ho / general y el di*c*ho Exerçito Fue / A Çibola y a lo demas que *el* Yll*u*stri*s*imo / Señor visorrey de la nueVa españa / En n*omb*re de su mag*es*t*a*d mando yr e q*ue* / no se hallo nynguna de las Ri- / quezas E grandezas que se / Publicaron que (h)avian *en* la / rrel*a*cion mas de que se hallaron / En Çibola siete pueblos pe-

[fol. 8v]

queños de casas de Piedras / E de tres o quatro altos de / Terrados en q*ue* (h)abian gente Pobre / de rriquezas E de Poli(a)z*i*a y *en*ten- / Dimyento y el rreyno que se dixo / Acus (h)era Un solo Peñon Fuerte / que se dize Acuco y el rreyno de / Totonqueates (h)eran unas Fuen- / Tes de agua Caliente syn gente / {24} / Yten sean preguntados si saben *e* / Vieron que despues de (h)ab*er* / Visto el general que *en* lo de çibola / y *en* lo demas que tenia Rela-*c*ion / no (h)avia en q*ue* Acreçentar El / Patrimo*n*yo rreal De su mag*es*t*a*d *en*Vio / Por una banda A don P*ed*ro de / ToVar con gente de a caballo / En demanda de una Provinçia / de que tuVo notiçia que se dize / trocayan y *en*Vio En demanda de / la mar del sur A don garçia lopez / De cardenas maestre de canpo / Del di*c*ho ExerÇito y *en*Vio Por / otra banda la via del (e)este / A hernando de alVarado capitan / De la *a*rtilleria y *en*Vio Por o- / Tra banda Al caPitan Fran*c*isco / De oVando todos con ynstru- / Çiones de lo q*ue* (h)abian de hazer / En las quales Particular

[fol. 9r]

335

y aFe*c*tuosamente se les Encargaba / El buen tratamyento de los / naturales de aquellas Partes / Por do*nde* pasasen y EstuViesen / {25} / Yten sean pre-guntados si saven / que los di*c*hos caPitanes y / descubridores Anduvieron / y descubrieron cantidad de / Tierras E Volvieron sin hallar / ny tener notizia de

gentes do*nde* se / Pudiese Predicar el santo (h)e- / Vangelio y plantar la doc-
trina Cris*t*iana / y acreçentar Sobre el Patrimo*n*yo rr*e*al / sino Fueron dos
yndios que traxo / El d*i*cho capitan her*nan*do de alvarado / los quales dieron
notiçia de la / Provinçia De quevira E de los / guaches En demanda de la qual
/ d*i*cha provinçia de quiVira el d*i*cho / general Fue con el EXerçito y / desPues
de (h)aber camynado con el / EXerçito dozientas y çinquenta / leguas *en* un
disierto tuVo notiçia / De que yba *en*Gañado E que no (h)era / la tierra E
gentes A do*nde* yba lo que / le (h)abian d*i*cho y af*i*rmado ny de / myll partes
la una y visto esto / Por no Poner todo El EXerÇito / En condiçion *de perderse*
el general de-

[fol. 9v]
termyno de *en*Viar El EXerçito A / tiguex Para q*ue* Aguardase alli / y el d*i*cho
general con treynta e / çinco de a caballo Paso a quiVira / *en e*l qual camyno
*h*ubo grandes disiertas / E asi se Paso gran nezesidad sed / y hanbre y llegado
A quiVira y / Visto que la gente y poblaz*i*on / (h)era poca y de poco
AProvechamy*ento* / Para acreçentar El patrim*on*yo / rreal volvyo A tiguex Por
otro / camyno para Volver descubriendo / Porq*ue* no le quedase de hazer /
nada de lo Posible En serv*i*cio de su mag*e*s*t*tad / {(^X)26} / Yten sean preguntados si saven / que despues de lo susod*i*cho En / la d*i*cha Provinçia de
tiguex se / morian los caballos y adoleçian / los soldados y morian Algunos /
Ansi Por falta de me(l)d*e*çinas / como de medico que las Aplicase / y no *h*avia
saçerdote que con- / Fesase los Enfermos ny les / Dixese mysas y la comyda
se acabava / y no *h*avia donde se poder *h*aber / el d*i*cho general tenia mucho
cuydado / De curar los Enfermos y Par- / tir con ellos de lo que thenia / {27}
/ Yten si saven q*ue* visto Por el d*i*cho *gener*al

[fol. 10r]
336
q*ue h*avia ydo e llevado El d*i*cho / EXerçito A la parte o partes / Do*nde* En
nonbre de su mag*e*s*ta*d se le mando llevar / e que *h*avia descubierto Por si E /
Por capitanes mucha cantidad / de mas tierras de las q*ue e*l d*i*cho / Fray marcos

dixo *h*aber des- / cubierto y q*ue* no se *h*abia visto ha- / blado ni tenido notiçia de gentes / de poliçia do*nde* se pudiese A- / creçentar El patrimo*n*yo rreal / De su mage*sta*d e que como d*i*cho es En / las Preguntas antes de *e*sta / los caballos se morian y los sol- / Dados se morian y estaban en / Peligro de Perder todo el / EXerçito Por la esterelidad / De la tierra y Por la falta / De mediçinas mantenymientos / E rropas con que cubrir las / carnes el d*i*cho general Acordo / De traer el d*i*cho exerçito y lo traxo / A la nueVa esPaña donde lo *h*abia sacado / {28} / Yten si saven E*t*cetera que en el çerco / Del d*i*cho Pueblo de Çibola salio / el d*i*cho general herido de quatro he- / ridas En el rrostro y una Pierna / muy mala de que todos Pensaron / q*ue* no escaPara Por cuya caussa / estuVo mucho tienPo muy malo

[fol. 10v]
Y En Punto de Perder la Vida / y ansimysmo En el çerco q*ue* tuvo / Sobre *e*l pueblo de mocha estuvo / Enfermo E tuVo las Piernas / Para perder de *h*yn- chadas E gol- / Pes E de nunca tornar flechado / y ansimismo En(tre) el Pueblo / De coofor tuvo muy rreçia En- / Fermedad de que se creyo / Perdiera la vida y dezia / que se holgaba con el mal q*ue* thenia / Por Pasarse En servi*ci*o De / Su mage*sta*d digan lo E*t*cetera / {29} / Yten si saven que Fue a la d*i*cha / conquista sin ynterese nyngu*n*o / sino Por servir A su mage*sta*d donde el / Fue Forçado gastar mucha suma / De Pesos de oro E q*ue*do Adeudo / En mas can- tidad de diez myll / Pesos de oro de mynas que hasta / El dia de *h*oy tiene que pasar / Donde le *h*a sido ForÇado ven- / der sus bienes muebles E / rrayzes y aun con todo esto / no lo *h*a Podido Acabar de pagar / y esta gastado Por (^rra) Razon / De la d*i*cha *en*trada que asi hizo / {30} / Yten si saven E*t*cetera q*ue* todo lo suso / es pu*b*lico E not*o*rio E pu*bl*ica voz e fama / Digan E declaren lo que saven los / d*i*chos t*e*st*ig*os e lo qual Açerca de *e*sto saben

[fol. 11r]
337
{y*tem*} / E Ansi presentada la d*i*cha pet*ici*on / E ynterrogatorio En la manera / que d*i*cho es y por el d*i*cho señor alc*al*de / Visto dixo que lo *h*avia E *h*obo Por

/ Presentado e quanto no es ynper- / Tinente mando al dicho Francisco pilo trayga / E presente los testigos de que se entiende / AProvechar en el dicho nonbre que / Esta puesto de los mandar E- / Xaminar por el dicho ynterrogatorio / que presentado tiene y en todo / hazer justiçia

{ytem} / E luego el dicho señor alcalde dixo / que por quanto el Esta ocupado / En otros negoçios y casos y pleitos / cunplideros Al servicio de su magestad y a la / EXecuçion de la su justicia rreal / que cometia y cometio a my el dicho / escribano la rrese(s)pçion de dichos E de- / Pusiçiones de los testigos que / En este caso el dicho Francisco Pilo / Presentare E para ello me / Dio comysion en forma E lo firmo / Testigos garçia de villarreal E diego herrera / Estantes En las dichas mynas

{ytem} / E despues de lo Susodicho / En esta dicha villa siete dias / del dicho mes de (h)enero del dicho / Año Paresçio Presente el dicho / Francisco Pilo En el dicho nonbre / E Presento Por testigo a lorenÇo

[fol. 11v]
Alvarez Estante En esta Pro- / Vinçia del qual se tomo E Recibio / juramento En forma devida de / derecho Por dios E Por santa / maria E por las Palabras de / los santos quatro (h)evangelios / doquier que mas largamente / Estan escritos y Sobre Una / señal de la cruz En que as- / Pera(l)mente Puso Su / mano derecha que como bueno / E Fiel Cristiano themyendo a dios / Dira verdad del que le fuese / Preguntado y En este casso de / que es presentado Por testigo / Supiere y si la verdad dixere / Dios nuestro señor le ayude En este / mundo Al cuerPo y en el otro al / Anima lo contrario haziendo / El se lo demande mal y cara- / mente como mal Cristiano que / sabiend(as)o jura El santo nonbre / De dios En vano E a la con- / clusion del dicho juramento / dixo si juro y amen y lo que dixo / E depuso es lo syguiente / {ytem} / E despues de lo susodicho / En estas dichas mynas / Doze dias del mes de marÇo / del dicho año Paresçio presente / el dicho francisco Pilo en el dicho nombre y / Presento Por testigos A diego lopez

[fol. 12r]

338

Veynte e quatro de sevilla y a luis / de Figueredo y a don Pedro de / Tovar
Estantes En esta dicha pro- / Vinçia de los quales y de cada / Uno de ellos se
tomo E rreÇibio jura- / mento en forma debida de(r) derecho / y lo que cada
uno dixo E de- / Puso es lo siguiente

{Testigo}

El dicho lorenço alVarez / Estante En las mynas De / nuestra señora de buena
esperança / Testigo Presentado Por el dicho francisco / Pilo En nombre del
dicho Francisco / Vazquez de coronado habiendo / jurado En forma devida de
derecho / E siendo Preguntado Por el tenor / del dicho ynterrogatorio dixo /
E dePuso lo siguiente / {i} / A la primera pregunta dixo que / conoze al dicho
Francisco Vazquez / De coronado contenido en la pregunta / De siete u ocho
años a esta parte / {generales} / Fue preguntado Por las pre- / guntas generales
de la ley dixo / que es de (h)edad de treynta años poco / mas o menos e que
no es Pariente / de francisco vazquez de coronado / ny (e)inqu(ie)rren en el
nynguna de las / otras preguntas generales

[fol. 12v]

{ii} / A la segunda Pregunta dixo que / save que yendo En demanda de la /
tierra conthenida En la dicha pregunta / el dicho general Francisco Vazquez /
con su EXerçito muy bien corregido / E governado no dando lugar A que /
nyngunos jurasen ny rrenegasen ny / Fuesen amançeVados ny consin- /
Tiendo que fuera de su casa / jugasen y se escondian Algunas / Personas de
que el Alguazil / no los Viese Xugar Porque / no lo dixese al general Porque
/ Asi lo mando (a)Pregonar que / no Xugasen Fuera de su casa / y que no
jurasen ny rrenegasen / ny Fuesen AmançeVados ny / hobiese escandalos lo
qual / mando (A)pregonar dos jornadas / Adelante de donde comenÇo A /
seguir la jornada A cuya caussa / el dicho EXerçito fue bien coRegido / y governado sin escandalos ny / blasFemias ny otros Viçios E / que de ello es publico E notorio y es- / to save de esta pregunta / {iii} / A la tercera Pregunta dixo

q*ue* Asy / Fue publico E notorio Entre todas / las personas del canPo y / otras muchas

[fol. 13r]

339

{iiii} / A la quarta Pregunta dixo / que la save como En ella se conti*ene* / Pre-gunt*a*do como la save dixo que por- / que *e*ste t*e*st*i*g*o* Fue uno de los que / Fueron En la d*i*cha jornada y sienpre / Vio que por dondequiera que *e*l / d*i*cho general Pasaba no con- / sentia hazer maltratamyento nyn- / guno A ningun(d) natural de la tierra / ny consentir que se hiziese nyngun(d) / Daño nyngun(d) español A nyngun(d) / natural y cre(h)e y tiene Por (a) / çierto Este t*e*st*i*g*o* q*ue* si A su not*i*c*i*a / Vinyera que algun(d) Soldado / hizo mal-tratamyento *a* Algun(d) / natural que lo castigara por ello / y antes Vio este t*e*st*i*g*o* que *e*l d*i*cho / general daba A los naturales / Algun rrescate E otras cosas / q*ue* no tomarles de lo suyo nada / y esto save de *e*sta preg*un*t*a* / {V} / A la quinta Pregunta dixo / que save que a dos jornadas de / la ÇiUdad de conpostela el d*i*cho / governador m*an*do pregonar (h)ed*i*c*t*o / y (h)ordenanças que mandaba / Tantas cosas que *e*ste t*e*st*i*g*o* / no tiene memoria de todas ellas / que se rremyte A los (h)ed*i*c*t*os que / Sobre *e*llo se m*an*do E pregono que / Paso ante *e*l esc*ri*b*an*o y esto save de *e*sta preg*un*t*a*

[fol. 13v]

{vi} / A la sesta pregunta dixo que *e*ste t*e*st*i*g*o* / no se hallo Presente al t*iem*po de / los rrequerimy*en*tos que se hizieron / A los d*i*chos yndios Por *h*aberse este / T*e*st*i*g*o quedado atras mas de q*ue* / Es muy pu*b*l*i*co E notorio q*ue* Antes / que se (f)*h*iziese guerra En qual- / quier parte se les (F)*h*izo muchos / Requer-imyentos delante / De algunos frayles que / En la d*i*cha jornada yban y *h*a o- / ydo dezir que se les daba / todas las seguridades cont*eni*das / En la d*i*cha pre-gunta las quales / Es pu*b*l*i*co E notorio que nunca / quisieron los d*i*chos yndios aÇeptar / Antes hazian Amenaçado / E tiraban flechas A cuya / caussa se les Fue forÇado ha- / Zerles guerra y esto save / de *e*sta pregunta / {Vii} / A la se*p*tima Pregunta dixo q*ue* / quando este t*e*st*i*g*o* llego al d*i*cho pueblo / cont*eni*do En la d*i*cha pregunta y hallo / que la d*i*cha tierra estaba Alzada / y

de guerra A la qual caussa / este t*e*st*i*go no Vio En lo A el / cont*e*n*i*do mas de
lo oyr Por / muy çierto lo En ella cont*e*n*i*do / y esto save de *e*lla / {Viii} / A la
o*c*tava Preg*u*nt*a* dixo que / quando este t*e*st*i*go Vino A la d*i*cha ProV*i*nc*i*a

[fol. 14r]

340

De Tiguex Hallo y Vio que / Los d*i*chos yndios Estaban de guerra / y se
*h*avian Alzado y Encastillado / En el pueblo cont*e*n*i*do En la Preg*u*nt*a* / Por
*h*aver como (h)era muy Pu*b*l*i*co e / notorio muerto los caballos e / Azemylas
E yndios cont*e*n*i*dos *e*n la / d*i*cha Pregunta y alli se defendian / y se hizieron
Fuertes y esto save / De *e*sta pregunta / {ix} / A la novena Pregunta dixo / q*u*e
no la save Porque como d*i*cho / Tiene este t*e*st*i*go *h*avia q*u*edado Atras / {X} /
A la dezima Pregunta dixo q*u*e / no la save Por lo q*u*e d*i*cho tiene / {Xi} / A
la (h)onzena Pregunta dixo que / no la save Porque como d*i*cho / Tiene este
t*e*st*i*go no *h*abia llegado / {Xii} / A la dozena Pregunta dixo q*u*e / no la save
Por ser todo antes / de que *e*ste t*e*st*i*go llegase e que oyo dezir / que *e*l d*i*cho
general no se hallo pre- / sente a la d*i*cha guerra cont*e*n*i*do en / la d*i*cha pregunta / {Xiii} / A la(^s) trezena preg*u*nt*a* dixo que save / E Vio que quando
Este t*e*st*i*go / Vino a la d*i*cha Pobla*Ç*ion de tiguex / muchos yndios de *e*lla
estaban / Alzados y encastillados *e*n / Un pueblo que *e*staba *e*n un alto

[fol. 14v]

que despues se llamo / el pueblo del çerco Alli se / deFendieron y hizieron /
Fuertes muchos d*i*as y esto / save de *e*sta Pregunta / {Xiii*i*} / A la catorzena
Pregunta / Dixo que save que *e*l d*i*cho / capitan don R*o*dr*i*go Fue al d*i*cho /
Pueblo cont*e*n*i*do *e*n la preg*u*nt*a* / este t*e*st*i*go oyo dezir q*u*e yba A / Traerlos
de paz y no save / otra cosa de lo cont*e*n*i*do En / la pregunta / {Xv} / A la
quinzena preg*u*nt*a* dixo / que lo que de *e*lla save (h)es / que *e*l d*i*cho don garçia
lopez fue / al d*i*cho pueblo cont*e*n*i*do *e*n la d*i*cha / Pregunta A traerle de paz
/ e Fue pu*b*l*i*co E notorio q*u*e *e*l d*i*cho / juan eman le dixo que se A- / Pease
e quytase las armas / y Çelada y barbote Porq*u*e / le querian conozer y hablar
/ E que se Fuese solo Porq*u*e / se temyan de los demas E / que despues que
se apeo / los d*i*chos yndios le Asieron y le / maltrataron y sino Fuera / Por los

que le SoCorrieron / le mataran y ansi lo oyo dezir / este *testigo* A algunos de los q*ue*

[fol. 15r]

341

Fueron con el d*i*cho don G*arci*a lopez / y al mysmo y esto save de *e*sta pre-g*un*ta / {Xvi} / A la diez e seis Pregunta dixo / que *e*ste *testi*go no save que *en* nynguna / Parte no *h*abiendo guerra / se (f)*h*yziese maltratamyento A / nyngunos naturales Porq*ue* save / que En el d*i*cho çerco Adonde / Estaban los d*i*chos yndios / de guerra se mataron algunos / naturales (Porque save / que *en e*l d*i*cho çerco Adonde / Estaban los d*i*chos yndios de / guerra se mataron algunos) yn- / Dios por ser Ellos Reveldes / y *h*aber ellos tanbien muerto / muchos Españoles E yndios / y esto save de *e*sta Pregunta / {Xvii} / A las diez y siete preguntas / Dixo que save que nunca du- / rante la d*i*cha guerra ny antes / el d*i*cho EXerçito no se (f)*h*izo es- / clava ny escalvo y save asimysmo / que al tienpo de partirse / Para (a la a) la nueVa esPaña / El canpo se (a)Pregono que / nynguno traxese nyngun(d) yndio / ny yndia de aquella tierra / Syno que todos los dexasen / En su natural so çiertas

[fol. 15v]

Penas y esto save de *e*sta pregu*n*ta / {Xviii} / A las diez y ocho preguntas / Dixo que oyo dezir lo cont*eni*do / En la d*i*cha Pregunta / {XjX} / A las diez y nueve Preguntas / Dixo que lo que de *e*lla save es / que En el Pueblo de los A- / posentos de tiguex le dixo / a este *testi*go un soldado del canpo / que se d*i*ze mayorga que le diesen / Un costal de mayz para ayuda / A pagar a P*ed*ro de ledesma treyn- / Ta costales de mayz que le / Devia los quales el *h*abia / conprado y dado Por ellos çien(t) / Pesos de mynas y se los quyto / que se los devia el d*i*cho mayorga / Al d*i*cho ledesma por los d*i*chos / Treynta costales de mayz y / q*ue* no save que se contiese / Tomar a Yndio de PaZ / nynguna cosa Asi mayz como o- / tra cosa salvo A los de guerra / y esto save de *e*sta pre-g*un*ta / {Xx} / A las veynte Pregunt*a*s dixo q*ue* / la save como En ella se con-ti*en*e / Pregu*n*tado como lo save dixo que / Porque como d*i*cho tiene / este *testi*go Fue uno de los q*ue* fueron / *en* *e*l d*i*cho EXerçito e las Paso e / Vio pasar a otros

[fol. 16r]

342

{xxi} / A las veynte E una Preguntas / dixo que save que *e*l d*i*cho general / no pudo dexar de gastar muchos / Dineros En la d*i*cha guerra la can- / tidad de la qual este *testi*go no save / mas de que vio que *e*l d*i*cho general / lleVo muchos caballos Azemylas / criados E atavios de su persona / E casa En todo lo qual no pudo / Dexar de gastar mucha can- / Tidad de dineros A su pareçer / de *e*ste *testi*go pero que quantos Fue- / ron no lo save / {XXii} / A las veynte E dos Pregunt*a*s / Dixo que *e*ste *testi*go no la save / {Xxiii} / A las veynte E tres preguntas / dixo que save que *e*l d*i*cho general / con el d*i*cho EXerçito Fue a la d*i*cha / Provinçia de Çibola E hallo / En ella solamente siete pueblos / En los quales (n)*m*oraban los yn- / Dios de aquella Provinçia / y tenia*n* las casas de tres y / quatro altos y no tenian Ri- / quezes ny se hallo En ellos / nyn-gunas y que save q*ue* *e*l d*i*cho / pueblo de aquco (h)era un / Solo pueblo que *e*staba / *en* Un peñol Fuerte y que

[fol. 16v]

oyo dezir que por aquel dezian / que (h)era el rreyno De acuco / E ansimysmo oyo dezir que / Por una Fuente caliente lla- / man totonqueAtes e q*ue* aqu*e*lla / (h)era lo que *en* la rrelaÇion *h*a- / bia y esto save de *e*sta pregu*n*ta / E no otra cosa / {xxiiii} / A las veynte y quatro pregunt*a*s / Dixo que lo que de *e*lla sabe (h)es / que *e*ste *testi*go oyo dezir que Fue / muy Pu*b*lico E notorio En todo el d*i*cho / EXerçito que *e*l d*i*cho P*e*dro de toVar / Contenido *en* la d*i*cha Pregunta Fue / A los Pueblos de tuçayan y el d*i*cho / Don garç*i*a loPez En busca del mar / del sur e *e*l d*i*cho hern*an*do de al- / varado Fue a los Pueblos de tiguex / y çicarique y (h)uraba y a los llanos / De las Vacas y a otra p*ar*te el / d*i*cho Franc*i*sco de ovando cont*e*nido / En la Pregunta pero que *e*ste *testi*go / no lo Vi(d)o mas de ser Pu*b*lico E not*o*rio / En todo el d*i*cho Exerçito E / no lo vio porq*ue* Al presente pre- / gon este *testi*go no se hallo *en* *e*l d*i*cho / pueblo de

Çibola donde se / enViaron los dichos capitanes / En el dicho descubrimyento
/ y esto save de esta pregunta / {XXv} / A las veynte E Çinco preguntas

[fol. 17r]
343
DiXo que lo que de ella save es / que oyo dezir Por publico E notorio / que
los dichos capitanes fueron / En descubri(n)myento de las dichas / Tierras y en
lo que anduvieron / nunca hallaron cosa nynguna que / Fuese para poblar y
que save / que el dicho hernando de alvarado de / Vuelta de los dichos llanos
e çiquique / y (h)uraba traxo dos yndios consigo / que el uno se puso nonbre
/ Turco y el otro ysopete los quales / Dixeron e dieron notiçia de / quiVira y
los guales e dezian / que (h)era Una tierra muy poblada / y muy rrica de oro
y plata y la / gente de ella de mucha poliçia / y otras muchas cosas y estos /
dichos yndios guiaron el dicho E- / Xerçito y al dicho general Por / los dichos
llanos de las Vacas por / donde se anduvo Gran termino / de tierra despoblada
que / al parezer de este testigo serian / Dozientas E Çinquenta leguas / Poco
mas o menos E por / çiertas cosas que los dichos yn- / Dios dixeron que hal-
laria en el / camyno que no se hallaron se / coligio ser todo mentira y que /
llevaban los dichos yndios el dicho / EXerÇito Engañado por lo

[fol. 17v]
qual el dicho (^Exerçito) ^general de- / Termyno con los demas APer- /
Çebidos de caballos y comyda que / serian hasta quarenta honbres / se partio
en demanda de la dicha / Provinçia de quivira y el / demas canpo mando A
don tristan / De arellano lo tornase A la / dicha provinçia de tiguex e / Porque
los que no yban bien / Proveydos de comyda y los pe- / (h)ones no peresçiesen
y se / muriesen y ansi se volvio el / dicho Exerçito y el dicho general / Fue con
los que dicho es y despues / los Vio Volver este testigo y dixeron / la dicha Provinçia De quiVira ser / muy Poca gente y sin comyda y que / h(a)aber Passado
el dicho Exerçito / hallase muriera de hanbre y sed / lo qual dizen haber Passado / el dicho general y los que con el / yban Porque AnduVieron / mucha
tierra y desPoblada y / Por ser la dicha tierra y PoblaÇion / De quiVira poca

y de Poco pro- / Vecho se *h*abian Vuelto y esto save / De *e*sta pregunta /
{XXVi} / A las veynte e seis pregunt*a*s / Dixo que save que de vuelta / De lo
susod*i*cho cont*e*n*i*do ynvernando

[fol. 18r]

344

El d*i*cho EXerçito En la / d*i*cha provinçia de tiguex A causa / De los grandes
Frios E trabajos / que *h*abian passado y el poco Re- / medio E rroPa q*ue*
thenian E otras / cosas Adoleçian E morian Algunos / Españoles y murian
muchos / caballos y ansimysmo save / que la comyda se acabava y no *h*abia /
De donde la *h*Aber e q*ue* no se / Dezia mysa En el canPo ny / quien la dixese
y save que *e*l d*i*cho / general En el tienpo que es- / taba sano yba A Visitar los
*e*nfer- / mos y algunos Porque tu- / Viesen mejor rrecaudo lo traxo / A su
cassa y alli lo (f)*h*izo curar y esto / save de *e*sta pregunta / {XXvii} / A las
veynte e siete preguntas / Dixo que lo que de *e*lla save (h)es / que *e*l d*i*cho general Anduvo Por / sy e por sus capitanes mucha / cantidad de tierras En todas
/ las quales no se hallo ny tuVo / notiçia De nynguna tierra A- / Donde A su
parezer de *e*ste / T*e*st*i*go se pudiese Poblar ny el / Patrim*o*nyo rreal de su
mag*e*sta*d* / Fuese AcreÇentado y save / que como d*i*cho tiene la gente

[fol. 18v]

EnFermaba y moria A caussa / del Poco rrecaudo y serviçio y gran / nezesidad
que los d*i*chos EsPanoles / thenian E vio que *e*l d*i*cho general / se Fue E torno
con el d*i*cho Exerçito / A la nueVa españa donde lo saco / y cre(h)e E tiene
por çierto que lo saco / E truxo el d*i*cho EXerÇito por / no hallar P*a*rte donde
Poblasen / Por las caussas cont*e*n*i*dos / *e*n la d*i*cha Pregunta / {xxviii} / A las
veynte E ocho preguntas / Dixo que lo que de *e*lla save (h)es / que oyo dezir
por pu*b*lico E notorio / En todo el d*i*cho EXerÇito q*ue* *e*l d*i*cho / general salio
herido De Çibola / E q*ue* pensaron que le mataran / los yndios E que save
que qu*a*ndo / EstuVo *e*n *e*l (^E) çerco *e*n la Provinçia / De tiguex EstuVo malo
de / Una pierna y asi (h)era muy Pu*b*lico / y save Ansimysmo que de vuelta /
De la d*i*cha provinçia De quiVira / EstuVo muy malo y esto save de *e*sta / Pre-

gunta E no otra cosa / {XXjX} / A las veynte E nueve Preguntas / Dixo que
dize lo que dicho tiene / En las preguntas antes de esta / y lo demas En ella
Contenido / Este testigo no lo save

[fol. 19r]

345

{xxx} / A las treynta Preguntas dixo / que dize lo que dicho tiene En las / Preguntas antes de esta y que / lo que hA dicho es la verdad y lo que / save de este
casso para el juramento / que hizo e lo firmo lorenÇo alvarez

Chapter 20

Diego López,
the Second de Parte Witness

A Councilman of Sevilla and Veteran of the
Conquest of Nueva Galicia

After Lorenzo Álvarez testified, an interval of more than two months elapsed before Francisco Pilo presented his final three witnesses: Diego López, Luis de Figueredo, and Pedro de Tovar, all of whom gave answers in response to the interrogatorio on March 12, 1545.

Diego López, always referred to by his title as one of the 24 regidores or city councilmen of Sevilla in Spain,[1] mustered into the expedition to Tierra Nueva as a captain of horsemen. As was befitting his high status and relative wealth, he took seven horses with him.[2] If his statement before Gómez de la Peña was correct, he was about 25 years old when the expedition began. This would also mean that he was only in his mid teens when, as a participant in Nuño Beltrán de Guzmán's entrada into Nueva Galicia, he became one of the original settlers of Guadalajara in 1531.[3] He was, thus, one of the members of the expedition to Tierra Nueva with longest service in the Indies. That veteran status may have recommended his election to the post of maestre de campo of the expedition when, in early summer 1541, García López de Cárdenas was disabled by a broken arm. In Quivira later that summer the captain general assigned Diego López to investigate the reportedly traitorous acts of El Turco and to execute him. He had earlier been sent by Vázquez de Coronado to read the requerimiento at Pueblo del Arenal.

In 1539, a royal cédula directed Viceroy Mendoza to provide López with a corregimiento. Following the expedition, he took up residence in the province of Culiacán, where he became a vecino or citizen. In the late 1540s he was encomendero of the pueblo de Guachimeto and half of two others.[4] In the course of his residence in the New World, López returned to Spain at least twice. After the last sojourn in Spain he returned to Nueva España in 1555 with his wife doña Beatriz Grijalvo and a son.[5] Twelve years later, López having evidently died, 19 pueblos in the province of Culiacán once held by him in encomienda, were now held by his son Gonzalo.[6]

In his testimony in 1545 concerning treatment of Indians by the expedition to Tierra Nueva, López, like most other witnesses, both de oficio and de parte, judged the Spaniards' actions there to have been completely justified. In his view, all hostility had been provoked by the natives, and any punishment inflicted on them was deserved because they had killed many members of the expedition. He admitted that he himself, while acting as maestre de campo, had ordered the killing of El Turco, of which he gave a very brief account, attempting to justify his action. López insisted that no Indian servants had been taken by members of the expedition, a claim contradicted by several other witnesses who referred to the captain general's order that all such individuals had to be left in Tierra Nueva when the expedition returned to the south. The councilman of Sevilla revealed in his testimony that the fighting at Pueblo del Arenal had been savage, "without mercy." On the whole, López was righteously indignant and denied that abuse of any sort had been perpetrated against the indigenous peoples encountered by the expedition.

A TRANSLATION
OF THE TESTIMONY

Second de Parte Witness (Diego López)[7]

[19r cont'd] Diego López (councilman of Sevilla), a resident at the mines [of Nuestra Señora de los Remedios] and a witness presented on behalf of the aforesaid Francisco Vázquez, having sworn in legal form and being questioned in accordance with the substance of the interrogatory, testified and declared himself as follows.

{1} To the first question he answered that he has known the Francisco Vázquez mentioned in the question for seven years.

{personal matters} He was questioned on personal matters in accordance with the law and replied [by saying] that he is about thirty years old and is not a relative of the aforesaid Francisco Vázquez. None of the other questions on personal matters required by law applies to him.

{2} To the second question the witness replied that he knows what is referred to in the question just as it is stated there. Asked how he knows that, he said that it is because he [19v] was one of those who went in the aforesaid armed force and he saw that Francisco Vázquez kept the army very well governed and controlled. He did not permit blasphemy, living in concubinage, or excessive gambling. López knows that the general ordered these and other things proclaimed in the army {note}[8] two days' journey from the city of Compostela, while going in search of the lands referred to. In this regard, he believes that [the people] adhered to the decrees that the general ordered announced in this way.

{3} To the third question he stated that what is referred to in the question is very widely known and commonly held, although the witness never heard fray Marcos say it. This is what he knows about it.

{4} To the fourth question the witness answered that he knows it as stated in the question. Asked how he knows, he said that it is because he saw many soldiers in dire need of servants, both to bake their bread and to tend their horses. And further, he saw many of them ask Francisco Vázquez for native servants. So as not to annoy the natives, the general did not want them to furnish [servants]. [20r] Nor did he condone taking clothing from the natives, although the [people of the army] were in great need of it. Many [people] asked him for clothing because they lacked mantas, since they were no longer transporting much of the supplies they had been bringing [to the camp]. [López] also said that it was public knowledge and widely held that some hidalgos of the army were baking bread themselves because they did not have anyone to bake it for them.

{5} To the fifth question he replied that he knows what is referred to in it. Asked how he knows it, he said that it is because of what he has stated in the previous questions.

{6} To the sixth question [the witness] answered that what he knows about it is that all the battles in which the witness was and found himself were justified because the Indians attacked the army and provoked [war]. [López] knows this because he was present and saw that Tiguex feigned [peace] and that the natives were playacting when they submitted. He considered Francisco Vázquez de Coronado to be a man who was fearful of god and his conscience and was His Majesty's servant. He treated [20v] benevolently the natives of the provinces through which he traveled and did not allow any harm or injury to be done to them. For this reason he believes that [even] the battles at which the witness was not present were justified and were provoked by the natives. This is what he knows concerning the question.

{7} To the seventh question he responded [by saying] that he knows what is referred to in it. Asked how he knows, the witness said that it is because he was present in the aforesaid province of Tiguex {note} in a pueblo where the army was quartered, though he does not remember what it was called. Whenever [López] was present and natives came, he saw that the general spoke in a kindly way with them, treated them benevolently, and gave them some of the things that he had taken with him. And [Vázquez de Coronado] told them and made them understand, in the way he could, that if any soldier did them harm or hurt and they came to make a complaint, [the general] would punish that [person].

[21r] {8} To the eighth question he replied that he knows what is referred to in it. Asked how he knows, the witness said it is because, as he has said, since he was present at all this, he saw what is stated in the question.

{9} To the ninth question [López] answered that he knows what is included in it. Asked how he knows it, he said it is because he was present during the aforesaid council of the [clerics], His Majesty's officials, the captains, and other notable persons of the army. And he saw that the general solicited their opinions as to what ought to be done regarding the uprising of the Indians and the death of the horses.

{10} To the tenth question he responded by saying that he knows it as stated in the question. This is because, as he has said, the witness was present at the council and saw that everyone who was there jointly determined that war should be waged against the Indians of that province and that they should be punished, as is stated in the question. Further, López was one of those who voiced that opinion.

After it became known [21v] that the natives had killed one of the Indian allies, "whom we brought along," the general sent to have the witness called and told him what had happened. [Vázquez de Coronado] ordered him to take some companions and go round up all the horses that were wandering loose, which were many because of the lack of servants who would do it, since they were afraid that what had been done to the [one] Indian would be done to them.

[López] went to round them up and found the maestre de campo of the army don García López de Cárdenas, who had also gone out, and the horses, too. Tracking the horses together, they found that the natives had barricaded and fortified themselves in all the pueblos they passed, from which the Indians shrieked at them. They saw and found many of the horses dead inside the pueblos and returned with those that had not been killed. And they made a report of what had occurred to the general.

{11} To the eleventh question the witness said [22r] that what he knows about it is that the general Francisco Vázquez ordered him (who is the Diego López referred to in the question) to go to the cited Pueblo del Arenal and see whether the Indians of that pueblo were at war. If they were, he was to summon them to peace by the best way he could and make them understand what is referred to in the question. If they were not willing to [come to peace], he was to notify don García López de Cárdenas, maestre de campo of the army, who was at Pueblo del Almeneda, waiting for a response with people [from the company]. The [councilman of Sevilla] went to the aforesaid Pueblo del Arenal and found many dead horses there and the Indians fortified.

When the witness arrived [at Pueblo del Arenal] they shrieked at him and sang the songs of war they are accustomed to sing. By means of signs, he told them that they should be quiet and listen to him, but the Indians refused to. Nor was there an opportunity to talk to them because they gave [22v] a huge shout. He informed don García López de Cárdenas of this, sending a man-at-arms to speak [with him]. And the witness remained on guard at the pueblo with his companions until López de Cárdenas could come, since that is what he was ordered [to do]. This is what he knows concerning the question.

{12} To the twelfth question he replied that he says what he has said [in response] to the previous question, to which he refers. It is true that the general was not present at the aforesaid fighting, since he remained at the pueblo where the army was quartered.

{13} To the thirteenth question [López] answered that what he knows about it is that war was waged against the aforesaid pueblo and he was there. He does not know, however, whether those who escaped from there went to the pueblo referred to in the question. But he does know that another pueblo farther on from Pueblo del Arenal was fortified and had many people, including many from the aforesaid province. There [the Spaniards] were detained for many days [23r] because it was a strong pueblo. This is what he knows concerning the question.

{14} To the fourteenth question he replied that he does not remember about it because many days have passed [since then].

{15} To the fifteenth question [the witness] responded [by saying] that what he knows about it is that what is referred to in the question, [that is] what happened to Maestre de Campo don García López, was public knowledge and widely held. [The councilman of Sevilla] knows that López de Cárdenas was wounded in the foot and that he was wounded at the aforesaid pueblo. The witness went to look at the wound, since he was not present when the aforementioned [events] occurred in that pueblo. Nor does he know how the maestre de campo fared [thereafter].

{16} To the sixteenth question [Diego López] answered that what he knows about it is that the war that was waged against the cited pueblo and Pueblo del Arenal was without mercy. He does not know whether the fighting at Pueblo del Arenal was engaged in by the governor's order or not, because the witness was not present, but his maestre de campo [was]. At the other pueblo, where [the Indians] took refuge and which was fortified afterwards, the general was present. This is what he knows concerning the question.

[The witness] said further [23v] that it seems to him that [the Indians] deserved the full [measure of] punishment that was inflicted on them because they had killed many Spaniards [and] important persons in the army at those pueblos. Further, the pueblos were so strong that it would have been impossible to wage war without fire and without killing some [Indians], since they were "killing others of us Spaniards."

{17} To the seventeenth question [López] replied that he knows it as stated in the question. Asked how he knows, he said that it was because he was present when the public announcement was made and he heard the general say it on many occasions.

{18} To the eighteenth question he answered that the witness does not remember seeing the natives bring anything to the general. Nevertheless, he does know that if the Indians gave anything to the Spaniards, they were paid for it.

{19} To the nineteenth question he responded [by saying] that what he knows about it is that he often saw that there was very great need of provisions and that they were available in the province and provinces through which the aforesaid company passed. He also saw that [the general] often did not allow the Spaniards [24r] to take [such items] from the natives. At no time during peace was the witness aware of nor did he see clothing taken from any native; nor did he see any abuse being committed. About the rest of what is contained in the question he does not remember.

{20} To the twentieth question [López] replied that what he knows about it is that he saw many people in the army endure great want of food and clothing. And the general endured a full measure of travails and danger in many places because of lack of water. This is what he knows concerning the question.

{21} To the twenty-first question he stated that what he knows about it is that he saw that the general was very well equipped with everything necessary for the campaign and it is impossible that he did not spend a great deal of money. The [exact] sum of money the witness does not know. He believes that the general never pursued any other interest than to fulfill what had been entrusted to him. [That is] because after the day they met Melchor Díaz, the witness held no hope that they would come across anything [worthwhile] in that land. [24v] And it was because of the ruins encountered there and because it was publicly known and widely held that fray Marcos had not seen things previously that he had pretended to. This is what he knows concerning the question.

{22} To the twenty-second question he answered that what he knows about it is that it [was] public knowledge and widely held, when the company was in the *barranca* where the general left it when he went to Quivira, that the Indian called Turco had led the army deceptively, so that the horses would die and, afterwards, the Querechos and Teyvas would kill [the people]. Those are the Indians who dwell on those plains. From there onward the general never trusted El Turco or used his services.

Afterwards, in Quivira, as it seemed to those who went there with the general, [El Turco] refused to bring food to the people who went there and ordered that [the Quivirans] do likewise. Even though it was certain that they had not been provoked, [the people of] that land rose up in arms. Because of what had been done the general ordered the witness, who was [then] maestre de campo, to carry out justice, once he had found out what wrongs El Turco had committed [25r] and was continuing to commit. And he did it in that way. This is what he knows concerning the question.

{23} To the twenty-third question he stated that he knows it as stated in the question. Asked how he knows, he said that it is because he saw and experienced everything contained in the question.

{24} To the twenty-fourth question he responded by saying that everything referred to in it was public knowledge and widely known. However, the witness was not present because he was occupied with something else.

{25} To the twenty-fifth question [López] replied that he says what he has said [in response] to the previous question and, further, that he went with the general in search of the province of Quivira. He saw and experienced what the question mentions, as it is stated there, except that he does not know for certain that there was so much distance between the pueblo from which the general left and the place he left the expedition. This is what he knows about it.

{26} To the twenty-sixth question he answered that he knows what is stated in it, as it is stated there. Asked how he knows, he said that it is because he saw and experienced what is mentioned in the question.

{27} To the twenty-seventh question [the witness] replied [25v] that he knows what is contained in it. Asked how he knows, he said that it was because he was present during these events.

{28} To the twenty-eighth question he responded [by saying] that it [was] public knowledge and widely held in the army that the aforesaid general left the pueblo of Cíbola wounded. The witness, however, was not there. He also knows that at Pueblo del Cerco the general's legs were swollen, though he did not see the general. Afterwards, in the pueblo where the army was quartered, Vázquez de Coronado had a very severe disorder, from which he thought he would die. This is what he knows about it.

{29} To the twenty-ninth question [López] answered that he says what he said [in response] to the twenty-first question, to which he refers.

{30} To the thirtieth question he replied that he says what he has said [in response] to the previous questions. He states that what he has said is the truth and what he knows about this case, in accordance with the oath he swore. He affirms and ratifies it. And he signed.

Diego López

A TRANSCRIPT
OF THE TESTIMONY

[fol. 19r cont'd]⁹

{T*estigo*}

El d*i*cho diego lopez Veynte E / quatro de sevilla Estante En / las mynas *testigo* presentado por p*a*rte / del d*i*cho fran*ci*sco Vazq*uez h*Abiendo jur*a*do / En Forma de derecho y siendo / Preg*unta*do por el thenor del d*i*cho yn- / Terrogatorio dixo E deP*u*so lo sig*uien*te / {*i* } / A la Pri*mer*a pregunta dixo que / conoze al d*i*cho Fran*ci*sco Vazq*uez* En la / Pregunta cont*eni*do de siete Años / A esta parte / {*Generale*s} / Fue preg*unta*do Por las Pregunt*a*s / Generales de la ley y dixo que *e*s / de (h)edad de treynta años poco / mas o menos e q*ue* no es Pariente / del d*i*cho fran*ci*sco Vazquez ny encurren / *en e*l nynguna de las otras Pregunt*a*s / generales de la ley / {ii} / A la segunda pregunta dixo q*ue* / save lo cont*eni*do En la Pregunta / como En ella se *contien*e Preg*unta*do como / la save dixo que porque *e*ste t*esti*go

[fol. 19v]

Fue uno de los que fueron *en e*l d*i*cho / EXerçito y Vio que *e*l d*i*cho fran*ci*sco / vazquez llevo muy bien castigado / E corregido el d*i*cho EXerÇito no dando / lugar A blasfemyas ny amançe- / vados ny a juegos eçesivos y save / que los y otras cosas m*an*do (a)pre- / gonar En el d*i*cho EXerÇito A / {ojo} / Dos jornadas de la ÇiUdad De con- / Poste̜la yEndo E*n* demanda de las / d*i*chas tierras E de *e*llo cre(h)e / q*ue* tendran los (h)edi*c*tos el d*i*cho gen*er*al / que ansy m*an*do (a)pregonar / {iii} / A la terzera Pregunta dixo / que *e*s muy p*ub*lico E notorio lo *conteni*do / En la d*i*cha Pregunta aunque / este t*esti*go nunca lo oyo dezir / Al d*i*cho fray marcos y esto save de *e*lla / {iiii} / A la quarta pregunta dixo q*ue* / la save como En ella se conti*en*e / Preg*unta*do como la save dixo q*ue* por- / que *e*ste t*esti*go Vio muchos soldados thener / muy gran nezesidad de serviÇio / Ansi para que les (f)*h*iziesen / Pan como Para que les curasen / Sus caballos y Vio a muchos / Pedir servi*c*io de los nat-

urales / de la tierra al dicho francisco Vazquez / El qual Por no molestar / los
naturales no lo quiso dan

[fol. 20r]

346

ny consintio tomar a los dichos naturales / rropa aUnque tenian mucha neze-
/ sidad de ella y muchos que se la / Pedian que Por Falta de / Una manta dexaban de lleVar / mucho bastimento de lo que lleVaban / E que (h)era publico
E notorio que / Algunos hidalgos de exerçito / Por Falta de quien les hiziesen
/ Pan se lo hazian Ellos mesmos / {V} / A la quinta Pregunta dixo / que la
save como En ella Se contiene / Preguntado como la save diXo / que por lo
que tiene dicho En las / Preguntas Antes de esta / {Vi} / A la sesta Pregunta
dixo que lo / que de ella save (h)es que en las gue- / rras que Fue testigo y se
hallo en el dicho / EXerçito sienpre Fueron jus- / Tificados y dando A ellos
los yndios / A quien se hizo ocassion E que / lo save Porque este testigo se
hallo E / Vio que se (F)hizo tiguex E Vio / que los dichos naturales Dieron /
Para que se les (f)hiziese e que / Thenia Por honbre Al dicho francisco /
Vazquez De coronado themeroso / De dios E de su conçiençia y servidor / De
su magestad y que trataba

[fol. 20v]
Bien Los naturales de las Pro- / vinçias por donde yban y no / consintio que
se les hiziese daño / ny agravio nynguno y que por esto / cre(h)e que por las
demas guerras / Donde este testigo no se hallo ser / justificadas E darian la o-
/ casion los naturales y esto es / lo que save de esta Pregunta / {Vii} / A las
septima Pregunta dixo / que la save como En ella se contiene / Preguntado
como la save dixo que / Porque este testigo se hallo presente / En la dicha provinçia de tiguex / {ojo} / En un pueblo (^que se dize) de el / Donde estaba
aposentado / el dicho Exerçito Eçepto que este / Testigo no save como se
(l)llamo el dicho / pueblo E vio que el dicho general / cada vez que este testigo
se ha- / llaba Presente quando algunos na- / turales Venian el dicho general /
les hablava y trataba bien y les / Daba algunas Cosas de las que / llevaba y les
dezia que esto / se les(^os) daba A entender Por / manera que podia que si

algun sol- / Dado les (F)*h*iziesen mal o daño / se vinyesen A q*ue*Xar al qual / castigaria

[fol. 21r]

347

{viii} / A La o*c*tava pregunta dixo q*ue* / la save como En ella se contiene / Pre-
g*unta*do como la save dixo que / Porque *e*ste t*estig*o como d*ic*ho tiene se / hallo
A todo Presente Porque lo / Vio ser como la Pregunta dize / {iX} / A la
noVena Pregunta DiXo q*ue* / la save como En ella se contiene / Preg*unta*do
como la save dixo que por- / que *e*ste t*estig*o se hallo Al d*ic*ho Ayun- /
Tamyento de los d*ic*hos (E) ofi*ci*ales / de su mag*esta*d E capitanes y otros /
caballeros del d*ic*ho EXer*Ç*ito / E Vio que *e*l d*ic*ho general les / Pidio sus
parezeres de lo q*ue* / se deb*e*ria hazer Sobre *e*l d*ic*ho Al- / Zamyento de los
d*ic*hos yndios y / muerte de los d*ic*hos caballos / {X} / A la dezima Pregunta
dixo q*ue* / la save como En ella se contiene / Porque *e*ste t*estig*o como d*ic*ho
tiene / se hallo En el d*ic*ho ayuntamyento / E Vio que todos los que alli es- /
taban juntos determynaron / se les (F)*h*iziese guerra y Fuesen / castigados los
d*ic*hos yndios de la d*ic*ha / Provin*ç*ia segun(d) En la d*ic*ha / Pregunta se contiene y que *e*ste t*estig*o / Fue unos de los que dieron el d*ic*ho / Parezer porq*ue*
luego que se supo

[fol. 21v]

*h*Aber muerto Los d*ic*hos naturales / Un yndio de los Amygos que lle- /
Vabamos el d*ic*ho general *en*Vio / A llamar A este t*estig*o y le dixo lo q*ue* /
Pasava y le mando q*ue* tomase / çiertos conpañeros y Fuese y rrecogiese /
todos los caballos q*ue* Andaban / Sueltos que (h)eran muchos Por / la Falta
de servi*ç*io que p*ar*a / (^E)ellos *h*abia Porque temian / que harian de *e*llos lo
q*ue* de *e*l yndio / y este t*estig*o los fue A rrecoger y hallo / A don gar*Ç*i*a* lopez
de cardenas maese / De canpo del d*ic*ho EXer*ç*ito que / *h*Abia salido
Ansimysmo los / d*ic*hos caballos E yendo Anbos / En el rrastro de los d*ic*hos
/ caballos Por todos los pueblos / que pasaban hallaban los / naturales
Encastillados / y Fortale*Ç*ados y les daban / Grita E hallaban e(e) vieron /
muchos de los d*ic*hos Caballos / Dentro En los d*ic*hos pueblos / muertos y

Volvieron con los / demas Caballos q*ue* hallaron / que no *h*abian muerto y dieron / quenta de lo q*ue* pasaba Al / d*i*cho general / {Xi} / A la (H)onzena pregunta dyXo

[fol. 22r]

348

que lo que de *e*lla save (h)es / que *e*l d*i*cho general Fran*ci*sco Vazquez / m*a*ndo A este *testi*go que *e*s el d*i*cho di*e*go lopez / cont*eni*do En la d*i*cha pregunta que / Fuese al d*i*cho Pueblo del arenal / En ella cont*eni*do y Viese si los yndios / del d*i*cho Pueblo estaban de / Guerra E que si lo EstuViesen / Por la mejor via que pudiese / los llamase de paz y les diese A / Entender lo cont*eni*do En la d*i*cha / Pregunta y que si no quisiesen / Avisase de *e*llo A don G*arci*a lopez / de cardenas ma(h)ese de canPo / del d*i*cho EXer*ç*ito El qual estaba / con gente En el Pueblo del al- / meneda EsPerando la d*i*cha rres- / Puesta y que *e*ste (^d*i*cho) ^*testigo* Fue al d*i*cho / Pueblo del arenal y hallo / los d*i*chos yndios hechos Fuertes / En el d*i*cho Pueblo E muchos / caballos muertos En el y q*ue* / En llegando este *testi*go le dieron / grita y (f)*h*izieron otras armonyas / de guerra que *e*llos Suelen hazer / y que *e*ste *testi*go les dezia Por señas / que le *e*scuchasen y estuViesen / qui*e*tos y los d*i*chos yndios no qui- / sieron ny les daba lugar A ha- / blarles porque daban

[fol. 22v]

muy gran grita y que *e*ste *testi*go aviso de *e*sto / al d*i*cho don gar*çi*a lopez de cardenas / EnViandoselo A dezir con un soldado / y este *testi*go se quedo A guardar el d*i*cho / Pueblo con sus conPañeros / hasta que *e*l d*i*cho don gar*Çi*a lopez de / cardenas Vinyese porque asi le / Fue mandado y esto save de *e*sta pregu*n*ta / {Xii} / A la dozena Pregunta dixo q*ue* / Dize lo q*ue* d*i*cho tiene En la pregu*n*ta / antes de *e*sta a que se rrefyere / y que es Verdad que *e*l d*i*cho gen- eral / no se hallo Presente a la d*i*cha guerra / Porque se quedo En el pueblo / Donde *e*staba Aloxado el d*i*cho / EXer*ç*ito / {Xiii} / A la trezena Pregunta dixo / que lo que de *e*lla save (h)es que al / d*i*cho pueblo del arenal se hizo / la d*i*cha guerra y que *e*ste *testi*go se hallo / En ella y q*ue* no save si de los / que de alli Escaparon / se Fueron a hazerse el d*i*cho / Pueblo cont*eni*do *en* la d*i*cha pregunta / mas de que save que en un pueblo / que esta mas Adelante del dicho / Pueblo de arenal se hizo / Fuerte con mucha gente Con o- / tros muchos de la dicha Provinçia / que alli se detuVieron muchos dias

[fol. 23r]

349

Por ser el dicho pueblo Fuerte / y que esto save de esta pregunta / {Xiiii} / A la catorzena pregunta dixo que no / se acuerda de ella Por haver dias que paso / {Xv} / A la quinzena Pregunta dixo que lo / que de ella save es que fue publico e notorio / lo contenido En la dicha pregunta Aca(h)eçer / Al dicho ma(h)ese de canpo don Garcia lopez / y supo este testigo Estar herido el dicho / don garÇia lopez en el pie y le habian he- / rido en el dicho pueblo este testigo le fue a ver / de la dicha herida Porque este testigo / no se hallo Presente quando lo suso- / dicho aca(h)esçio En el dicho puebl(c)o ny sabe / A que yba el dicho don garÇia lopez / {Xvi} / A las diez y seis preguntas dixo / que lo que de ella save (h)es que / En la guerra que se les hizo / En el susodicho pueblo y En el / del arenal Fue a sangre y fuego / y que no save Si la que se hizo en el / Pueblo del arenal Fue por / mandado del dicho governador o no / Porque el no estaba presente / Sino Su maese de canpo E que / En el otro pueblo donde des- / Pues se hizieron fuertes y se en- / castillaron el dicho general se / hallo En ella y esto es lo que / save de esta Pregunta e que le

[fol. 23v]

Pareze a este testigo que mereçian / todo el castigo que se les (f)hizo / Porque en los dichos Pueblos mataron / muchos Españoles personas Prin- / zipales del dicho EXerçito y los / Pueblos (h)eran tan fuertes que / no se les podia hazer la guerra / sin fuego y sin matar A algunos / Pues ellos mataban A nosotros / los españoles / {Xvii} / A las diez y siete preguntas dixo / que la save como En ella se contiene / Preguntado como la save dixo que / Porque se hallo Presente quando / se pregonaba y se lo oyo muchas / Vezes dezir al dicho general / {Xviii} / A las diez y ocho preguntas dixo que / no se acuerda Ver tra(h)er nynguna / cosa al dicho general los naturales / mas de que este testigo save que si los yn- / Dios daban Algo A los dichos (naturales) españoles / se lo

paGasen / {Xjx} / A las diez y nueve Pregunt*a*s dixo / que lo que de *e*lla save
es que / muchas Vezes Vio q*ue h*Abian muy / gran nezesidad De bastimentos
/ y que los *h*avia En la Provinçia / e Provinçias Por donde Andaba / el di*c*ho
canpo E q*ue* muchas Vezes Vio / no consentir A los EsPañoles

[fol. 24r]

(^7)^9 350

q*ue* lo tomasen A los di*c*hos naturales / y que ningun tienPo durante / la Paz
SuPo este t*e*stig*o* ny Vi(d)o tomar / A ningun natural Ropa nyngu*n*a / ni haz-
erseles nyngun maltratamy*en*to / y que lo demas cont*en*ido En la di*c*ha / Pregunta este t*e*stig*o* no se Acuerda de *e*llo / {xx} / A las veynte preguntas dixo
que / lo que de *e*lla save es que vio q*ue* / muchas personas del di*c*ho EXer- /
Çito passaron mucha nezesidad / De comida E rropa el di*c*ho gen*er*al / Passo
harto travajo y En muchas / Partes hartos peligros por / Falta de aguas y esto
es lo q*ue* / save de *e*lla / {xxi} / A las veynte E una pregunt*a*s / dyXo que lo
que de *e*lla save es / que vio q*ue* el di*c*ho general Fue muy / bien adereÇado
de todo lo nezes*a*rio / Para la di*c*ha guerra E q*ue* no puede / ser q*ue* no gastaria muchos dineros / la cantidad de lo qual este t*e*stig*o* / no save y que cre(h)e
este t*e*stig*o* / que nunca el di*c*ho general / Pretendia mas ynterese de cunplir /
lo que le Fue Encomendado por- / que nunca este t*e*stig*o* tuvo es- / Peranza
desde el dia que se / *en*Contro melchor diaz de que En la / Tierra se *h*obiese
cosa nyngu*n*a

[fol. 24v]

y por las rruinas que de alla se dieron / y por lo que el di*c*ho canpo fue pu*b*-
*li*co / E notorio el di*c*ho fray marcos no / *h*Aber visto cosa de las q*ue* Antes /
se *h*abia hecho y esto save de *e*sta pregun*t*a / {Xxii} / A las veynte e dos Preguntas / Dixo que lo que de *e*lla save (h)es / que *e*s pu*b*lico E notorio q*ue e*l
di*c*ho yndio / llamado turco est*a*ndo En la ba- / rranca donde el di*c*ho general dexo / El canpo quando Fue a quivira / que *h*abian traydo El canpo En-
/ gañado por fyn que los caballos / se muriesen y despues los ma- / Tasen los
querechos E teyvas / que son los yndios q*ue h*Abitan / Por aquellos llanos y
que / desde alli nunca el di*c*ho gen*er*al / se sirVio ny fio El qual des- / Pues

En quivira A lo que / Pareçio A los que Alli yban / con el d*i*cho general el d*i*cho turco / Escusaba E mandaba(n) que no / Traxesen de comer Para los / q*ue* Alli yban y tenyendo q*ue* / no diese ocassion Aquella / tierra se leVantase y Por / las que *h*abia dado Al d*i*cho general m*a*ndo A / Este t*e*st*i*go que (h)era maese de / canpo que despues q*ue h*Abia / Visto los EXçesos que *e*l d*i*cho / Turco *h*Abia cometido / 1

[fol. 25r]

351

E cometia (F)*h*iziese justiçia E / Ansi la (f)*h*izo y esto save de *e*sta preg*u*nt*a* / {Xxiij} / A las veynte E tres Preguntas / dixo que la save como En ella / se contiene preg*u*nt*a*do como la save dixo / que porque vio y anduVo todo lo / cont*e*nido En la d*i*cha Pregunta / {Xxiiij} / A las veynte e quatro Preguntas / dixo que ansi fue Pu*b*lico E notorio todo / lo cont*e*nido En la d*i*cha pregunta pero / que *e*ste t*e*st*i*go no se hallo Presente / Por *h*aber quedado A otra cosa / {xxv} / A las Veynte e çinco Preguntas dixo / que dize lo que d*i*cho tiene En la pre- / gunta antes de *e*sta y que *e*ste t*e*st*i*go / Fue con el d*i*cho general En demanda / de la d*i*cha provinçia de quivira / y que Vio ser y passar como la / d*i*cha pregunta lo dize lo En *e*lla / cont*e*nido salVo q*ue* no save çierto / que tanto *h*Abria desde *e*l d*i*cho Pue- / blo donde Partio el d*i*cho general / hasta donde dexo el canPo y esto / save de *e*lla / {xxvi} / A las veynte e seis preguntas dixo / que la save como En ella se conti*e*ne / Preguntado como la save dixo que / Porque lo vio ser E passar como la / Pregunta lo dize / {Xxvij} / A la veynte e siete preguntas dixo

[fol. 25v]

que la save como En ella se contiene / preguntado como la save diXo q*ue* / Porque lo vio E se hallo pres*e*nte A ello / {xxviij} / A las veynte e ocho pre- / guntas dixo / que ansi es publico E notorio *en e*l / d*i*cho EXerçito que *e*l d*i*cho General salio / herido del d*i*cho pueblo de Çibola / Pero que *e*ste t*e*st*i*go no se hallo Presente / y que save que *en e*l d*i*cho Pueblo del / çerco el d*i*cho general tuVo *h*ynchadas / las piernas pero que *e*ste t*e*st*i*go no / le vio y que despues En el pueblo / donde el d*i*cho EXerçito estaba Apo- / sentado tuVo muy Reçia

Enfermedad / de que penso que muriera y esto / save de ella / {xxjx} / A las
veynte E nueve preguntas / Dixo que dize lo que dicho tiene En / la veynte E
una Pregunta a que se rremyte / {xxx} / A las treinta Preguntas Dixo que /
dize lo que dicho tiene En las Pre- / guntas antes de esta y que lo que / hA
dicho Es Verdad y lo que de este / caso save Para el juramento que hizo / y En
ello se afirma E rretifica / y lo firmo diego lopez

Chapter 21

Luis de Figueredo, the Third de Parte Witness

Sent to Sonora

U ntil the record of de parte testimony in Culiacán was located appended to AGI, Patronato 216, R. 2, in the Archivo General de Indias in Sevilla late in 1997 by Shirley Cushing Flint, not even the existence of an expedition member by the name of Luis de Figueredo was known. His name did not appear on the muster roll.[1] Nor is such a person mentioned in any of the other known documents associated with the Coronado expedition. Diligent search in the collections of the AGI has so far revealed no information about Figueredo beyond the tiny bit he provided in his 1545 testimony before Gómez de la Peña. At about 33 years of age in 1540, he was considerably older than the typical member of the expedition to Tierra Nueva. His settlement in the province of Culiacán following the expedition, combined with his age, suggest that he was a resident of Nueva Galicia prior to 1540. Although he was not a captain or other officer, he was a person of some confidence, having been sent with dispatches to Sonora during the winter of 1540–1541. This assignment also argues for his being an experienced frontiersman.

Because of his absence in Sonora, he did not witness many of the crucial events asked about in the interrogatorio. Thus, his replies were very sketchy, and he frequently answered simply that he did not know. Figueredo was the least informative of all the witnesses in the case, either de oficio or de parte. He insisted that he saw no cruelty committed against native peoples during the course of the expedition, a position clearly at odds with those of most other witnesses.

A TRANSLATION
OF THE TESTIMONY

Third de Parte Witness (Luis de Figueredo)[2]

[25v cont'd] The aforementioned Luis de Figueredo, a vecino of the villa of San Miguel and a witness presented on behalf of [26r] Francisco Vázquez, having sworn in the form required by law and being asked the questions of the aforesaid interrogatory, stated and declared the following.

{1} To the first question he replied that he knows the Francisco Vázquez de Coronado referred to by sight, speech, behavior, and conversation he has had with him for about six years.

{personal matters} Asked the questions concerning personal matters specified by law, he said that he is about thirty-eight years old and is not a relative of Francisco Vázquez. None of the other questions concerning personal matters applies to him.

{2} To the second question the witness answered that he knows what is referred to in it. Asked how he knows, he said that it is because he went on the expedition with Francisco Vázquez and witnessed the public announcement referred to in the question. And, further, he saw that it was adhered to, as related in the question.

{3} To the third question he responded [by saying] that he had heard it said that fray Marcos had discovered the land of Cíbola. He knows that in that land there are seven pueblos, as stated in the question.

[26v] {4} To the fourth question [Figueredo] replied that what he knows about it is that he saw that when the aforesaid Francisco Vázquez was traveling along the route to Tierra Nueva, he ordered that nothing belonging to the natives [of the lands] through which [the expedition] passed was [even] to be approached without their consent and nothing was to be taken from them without paying for it. This is what he knows concerning the question.

{5} To the fifth question [the witness] answered that he says what he has said [in response] to the previous questions. The rest of what is referred to in the question he does not remember, except that he saw [the directives] adhered to exactly as stated in the question.

{6} To the sixth question he stated that he says what he has said [in response] to the previous questions. Further, he was present during the war waged against the natives of Cíbola and saw that it was exactly as the question states. However, he was not present during the war in Tiguex. Nevertheless, he heard it said that way. This is what he knows concerning the question.

{7} To the seventh question [Figueredo] replied that he had [only] heard what is stated in the question said as something publicly known and widely held. [27r] [That is] because he was not present since, at that time, he had gone with some messages to the valley of Señora.

{8} To the seventh question the witness answered that he had [only] heard what is stated in the question said as something publicly known and widely held because, as he has said, he was not present.

{9} To the ninth question he responded that he does not know.

{10} To the tenth question he stated that he does not know.

{11} To the eleventh question the witness replied that he says what he has said [in response] to the previous questions, and the rest he does not know.

{12} To the twelfth question [Figueredo] answered that he does not know.

{13} To the thirteenth question he stated that he does not know.

{14} To the fourteenth question he replied that he does not know.

{15} To the fifteenth question he responded [by saying] that he had heard what is referred to in the question said as something publicly known and widely held throughout the army.

{16} To the sixteenth question [the witness] answered that since he had traveled in the army with the general [27v] he saw that [the general] never permitted any cruelty or abuse to be committed against any Indian, even though there was reason to. He knows this concerning the question.

{17} To the seventeenth question [Figueredo] replied that he knows and saw that [the general] announced publicly in the army what is referred to in the question, under serious penalties. But he does not know about the sentences referred to in the question.

{18} To the eighteenth question [the witness] responded [by saying] that from time to time he saw Indians given trade goods from among those referred to in the question. And [the Indians] brought some gifts.

{19} To the nineteenth question he answered that he does not know.

{20} To the twentieth question the witness replied that he knows what is referred to in it. Asked how he knows, he said that it is because he was one of those who endured [those things].

{21} To the twenty-first question [Figueredo] answered that what he knows about it is that the aforesaid Francisco Vázquez was well outfitted and equipped [28r] in keeping with his person and in conformance with the position he held. Because of this he could not have failed to spend a large sum of money, but the witness does not know [exactly] what [amount] he may have spent. Nor does he know more about what is referred to in the question.

{22} To the twenty-second question he responded [by saying] that he does not know.

{23} To the twenty-third question the witness replied that he knows it as stated in the question. Asked how he knows, he said that it is because he saw it all and was present, except at the hot springs. But he does know that this was publicly known and widely held.

{24} To the twenty-fourth question he said that what he knows about it is that he saw the captains referred to in the question depart in search of the lands mentioned. The rest he does not know.

{25} To the twenty-fifth question [Figueredo] answered that he knows that the aforesaid Hernando de Alvarado brought [with him] the Indians referred to in the question and that they told about Quivira [28v] and the Guaces. He saw that the general went in search of those places, passing through extensive plains. There, because of lack of food, the army that the general took endured great want. Further, he knows that in order that some [people] might not suffer, [Vázquez de Coronado] left most of the expedition on those plains in the barranca they tell about. From there he went with thirty men in search of Quivira and the expedition returned to Tiguex. After some days the general returned from there, but, so they said, not by the route he had followed in going. They said that in the province of Quivira and the Guaches there was nothing that was worth anything. He does not know the rest of what is referred to in the question.

{26} To the twenty-sixth question the witness replied that he knows that there was plenty of food in the province [of Tiguex], corn, beans, and meat (if they went to slaughter it, since they were near [the hunting grounds]). Also he knows that in the pueblos there were fowl to be purchased. He does not know that the horses were dying. [29r] Nor does he know that more than a few people were sick, which could not be otherwise wherever people are. The rest he does not know.

{27} To the twenty-seventh question [Figueredo] answered that even though there were no shirts or other articles of clothing, the army was assisted with extra local hides and mantas. He saw that the general led the army [back to Nueva España], but he does not know why he did that. [The people] turned around completely against their will, but he does not know for what purpose. The rest he does not know.

{28} To the twenty-eighth question he responded [by saying] that he knows that at the pueblo of Cíbola the general was incapacitated because of wounds the Indians inflicted on him. And afterwards, in Tiguex, he was so unwell because of a fall that it was thought he would die. The witness does not know about the rest of what is referred to in the question.

{29} To the twenty-ninth question he replied that he does not know.

[29v] {30} To the thirtieth question he answered that he says what he has said [in response] to the previous questions and that what he has stated is the truth and what he knows about the case. He affirmed and ratified [his testimony] and signed it.

Luis de Figueredo

A TRANSCRIPT
OF THE TESTIMONY

[fol. 25v cont'd]³

{T*estigo*}

El d*i*cho luis de Figueredo V*ezino* / De la villa de san myGuel / T*estig*o present*a*do por P*a*rte del d*i*cho / 2

[fol. 26r]

352

Fran*cis*co Vazquez *h*Abiendo jurado En / Forma devida de derecho e / syendo
preguntado Por las Pre- / guntas del d*i*cho ynterrogatorio dixo / e depuso lo
siguiente / {i} / A la primera pregunta dixo que / conoze al d*i*cho fran*cis*co
Vazq*uez* de / coronado cont*eni*do De vista E habla / Trato E conversaçion que
con el / *h*A tenido de seis años a esta parte / Poco mas o menos / {*Generales*}
/ Fue preg*unta*do por las preguntas generales / De la ley E dixo que *e*s de
(h)edad / De treynta E ocho años poco mas / o menos E q*ue* no Es Pariente
/ del d*i*cho fran*cis*co Vazq*uez* ny Encurren / En el nynguna de las otras pre- /
guntas generales / {ii} / A la segunda Pregunta dixo q*ue* / la save como En ella
Se contiene / Fue preg*unta*do como la save Dixo que / Porque *e*ste t*e*stigo Fue
*en e*l d*i*cho canpo / con el d*i*cho Francisco Vazq*uez* E vio (A)Pre- / gonar lo
cont*eni*do En la Pregunta / E guardarlo como En ella se *contien*e / {iii} / A la
terzera pregunta dixo que / oyo dezir que *e*l d*i*cho fray marcos / Descubrio la
d*i*cha tierra de Çibola / E que save que En ella *h*ay / syete pueblos como la
preg*unt*a dize

[fol. 26v]

{iiii} / A la quarta Pregunta dixo que / lo que de *e*lla save (h)es que *e*ste / T*es*-
*tig*o Vio que *en e*l d*i*cho camyno de la tierra / nue*V*a Andaba el d*i*cho Fran-
*cis*co Vazq*uez* / E mandava q*ue* no se llegase A / cosa nynguna de los naturales
/ Por do*nde* pasaba contra su voluntad / E q*ue* no les tomasen nada sin Pa- /

garselo y esto save de esta pregunta / {V} / A la quinta pregunta dixo que /
Dize lo que dicho tiene En las / Preguntas antes de esta y lo de- / mas contenido En esta Pregunta / no se Acuerda de ella mas de que / Vio que se
guardaba Asi como la / Pregunta lo dize / {vi} / A la sesta Pregunta dixo que
/ Dize lo que dicho tiene En las Pre- / guntas antes de esta y que este testigo /
se hallo En la guerra que se / hizo a los naturales de Çibola / y Vio que fue
ansi como la pregunta / lo dize Pero que En lo de tiguex / este testigo no se
hallo Presente / mas de que lo oyo dezir ansi / y esto save de esta pregunta /
{Vii} / A la septima Pregunta DiXo / que ha oydo dezir lo contenido En / la
pregunta por publico E notorio / 3

[fol. 27r]

353

Porque este testigo no se hallo presente / Porque havia Venido En este tiempo
/ con çiertos desPachos al valle / De señora / {viii} / A la octava Pregunta dixo
que / hA oydo dezir lo contenido Por publico E / notorio Porque como dicho
tiene / Este testigo no se hallo *presente* / {jX} / A la novena Pregunta Dixo /
que no la save / {X} / A la dezima pregunta dixo que no la save / {xj} / A la
(h)onzena Pregunta dixo que / Dize lo que dicho tiene En las / Preguntas
antes de esta y lo de- / mas contenido En esta Pregunta / Este testigo no lo
save / {Xii} / A la dozena Pregunta dixo / que no la save / {xiii} / A la trezena
Pregunta Dixo que / no la save / {Xiiii} / A la catorzena Pregunta Dixo / que
no la save / {Xv} / A la quinzena Pregunta dixo que / oyo dezir lo En ella contenido / por publico E notorio en todo el dicho ExerÇito / {Xvi} / A las diez
y seis preguntas dixo que / En quanto este testigo AnduVo / con el dicho general en el dicho ExerÇito

[fol. 27v]

que Vio que nunca consintio / que se hiziese nyngun maltra- / Tamyento ny
nynguna Crueldad / A ningun(d) yndio Aunque ho- / biese caussa Para ello
y esto / save de esta pregunta / {Xvii} / A las diez e siete preguntas / Dixo que
save E Vio que (a)pre- / gono lo contenido En la dicha / Pregunta En el dicho
ExerÇito / So graves penas E de condenas / En ella contenido este testigo no

lo save / {Xviii} / A las diez y ocho preguntas dixo que / Este te*sti*go Vio algunas Vezes dar / Algunos rrescates de lo cont*eni*do / En la pregunta A algunos yndyos / y que trayan algunos Presentes / {XjX} / A las diez E nueve Pregunt*as* / Dixo que no la save / {Xx} / A las veynte Pregunt*as* Dixo q*ue* / la save como En ella se contiene / Preg*unta*do como la save dixo que / Porque *e*ste te*sti*go Fue uno de los / que la passaron / {xxi} / A las veynte E una preguntas / dixo que lo que de *e*lla save (h)es / que *e*l d*ic*ho fran*ci*sco Vazquez Fue / bien aderezado y aPerÇeVido / 4

[fol. 28r]

354

como cunplia A Su Persona y / conforme Al cargo que lleVava / Por lo qual no Pudo DeXar / de gastar muchos dineros Pero / que *e*ste te*sti*go no save lo que se Po- / Dria gastar ni mas de lo cont*eni*do / En la pregunta / {xxii} / A las veynte e dos Preguntas / Dixo que no la save / {xxiii} / A las veynte E tres Pregunt*as* / DiXo que la save como En ella / se contiene Preg*unta*do como la save / Dixo que porque *e*ste te*sti*go lo Vi(d)o todo / y se hallo En ello salvo En las / Fuentes calientes mas de que *e*sto / Fue ansi Pu*bli*co E notorio / {xxiiii} / A las veynte e quatro Pregunt*as* / DiXo que lo que de *e*lla save (h)es / que *e*ste te*sti*go Vio salir los Capitanes / conthenidos En la d*ic*ha Pregunta / En demanda de las tierras E- / n ella conthenidas y lo demas Este / T*e*stigo no lo save / {Xxv} / A las veynte e çinco pregunt*as* dixo / que save que *e*l d*ic*ho her-*nan*do de alvarado / Truxo los d*ic*hos yndios cont*eni*dos / En la d*ic*ha pregunta los quales / Dieron rrelaÇion De quiVira

[fol. 28v]

y los guaces y Vio que *e*l d*ic*ho gen*er*al / Fue en demanda de *e*llos Por / Unos llanos grandes Adonde / Por Falta de comida el d*ic*ho / EXerçito que lleVava Paso / Gran nezesidad e que save que / A efe*c*to de q*ue* no padeçiesen alg*uno*s / DeXo la mayor parte del d*ic*ho canpo / En los d*ic*hos llanos En la ba- / rranca que dezian y de alli / El con treynta honbres Fue / En demanda de quivira y el / canpo se torno a tiguex y desde / *h*Aya çiertos dias el d*ic*ho fran-

*cis*co / Vazquez Volvio y no Por el camyno / q*ue h*Abian ydo segun dezian y dezian / que En la d*ic*ha provinçia de qui- / Vira y los guaches no (h)era cosa / que valiese nada y lo demas / Cont*eni*do En la Pregunta no la save / {XXvi} / A las Veynte e seis Preguntas / Dixo que save q*ue h*Abia harta / comida En la d*ic*ha provinçia de / mayz y frisoles y carne sy la / Fueran A matar Porque es- / Taban çerca de alli y que en / los Pueblos de los yndios se ha- / llavan Aves Por rresgate / E q*ue* no save q*ue* morian los Caballos / 5

[fol. 29r]

355

ny EnFermase la gente mas de / Algunos de *e*llos q*ue* no pueda ser / menos Ado*nde h*ay gente y lo demas este / T*estig*o no lo save / {Xxvii} / A las veynte e siete preguntas / Dixo que save que si no (h)era de / Alguna rroPa de camysas y o- / Tras cosas que de lo mas se / Remediava el d*ic*ho Exerçito / con mantas y cueros de la tierra / E que vio que *e*l d*ic*ho General / Traxo al d*ic*ho Exerçito Pero / no save a que Fin lo hizo y Vio q*ue* / Traxo y se Volvyeron hartos contra / Su voluntad Pero q*ue* no save a que / (h)efe*c*to y lo demas no lo save / {Xxviii} / A las veynte E ocho Preguntas / DiXo que save que *e*l d*ic*ho general / EstuVo En el pueblo De Çibola / malo de çiertas heridas que le dieron / los yndios E despues En tiguex / De Una cayda EstuVo muy mal / que se penso que muriera y / lo demas cont*eni*do En la Pregunta / Este t*estig*o no lo save / {XXjX} / A las Veynte E nueve preguntas / DiXo que no la save

[fol. 29v]

{xxx} / A las treynta preguntas dixo q*ue* / Dize lo que d*ic*ho tiene En las / Pre- guntas antes de *e*sta y que lo / que *h*a d*ic*ho es la Verdad y lo que del / caso save y En ello se afirma / E rretiFica y lo f*ir*mo luis de / Figueredo

Chapter 22

Pedro de Tovar, the Fourth de Parte Witness

Captain and Nephew to the Viceroy

At age 22 in 1540, don Pedro de Tovar was both a captain of horsemen and *alférez mayor* or chief standard bearer for the expedition to Tierra Nueva. Only Vázquez de Coronado and Lope de Samaniego, briefly the maestre de campo, took more horses with them than the 13 Tovar did.[1] In the documents dealing with the Coronado expedition only eight individuals of the 300-odd Europeans who participated are routinely accorded the title of the minor nobility, "don." Pedro de Tovar, the brother of don Sancho de Tovar of the house of Boca de Hulgamo, regidor of Sahagún, in the jurisdiction of León in Spain is one of those.[2] In addition to holding hidalgo status through his immediate family, Tovar was also a nephew of Viceroy Mendoza[3] and married to a daughter of the governor of Cuba, doña Francisca de Guzmán.[4]

A thirteen-year-old in 1531, he was one of first settlers of Guadalajara and a founder of Culiacán and participated in the conquest of Nueva Galicia under Nuño Beltrán de Guzmán,[5] making him an experienced frontiersman by the time of the expedition to Tierra Nueva. During the two and a half years the expedition was seeking wealthy places in the north, Tovar led a reconnaissance to the pueblos of Tusayán or Hopi. As the advance party led by Vázquez de Coronado approached Cíbola in July 1540, the captain general sent him and fellow witness in the mistreatment of Indians case Melchior Pérez to secure an interpreter from among a group of nearby Zunis. It was reportedly Tovar's dog that was unleashed against Bigotes, in the course of interrogation by don Pedro. He was also dispatched in April 1541 to the tiny encampment of San Gerónimo in Sonora in an effort to stem mutiny among the Spaniards Tristán de Arellano had left there a year earlier on orders from the captain general.

After the return of the expedition from Tierra Nueva in 1542, Tovar remained in the province of Culiacán until his death.[6] Tovar succeeded to the encomiendas of Diego de Alcaraz and Melchor Díaz, both of whom had died while on the expedition under Vázquez de Coronado. That of Alcaraz was reputedly one of the richest encomiendas in the province.[7] In 1549 he was appointed alcalde mayor of the whole of Nueva Galicia.[8] Tovar was encomendero of the pueblo of Anacatarimeto in the late 1540s[9] and later of Mocorito on the river of the same name in modern Sinaloa. His rights over Mocorito were reformalized by Francisco de Ibarra in 1566. Two years earlier he was alcalde mayor of Culiacán.[10]

Historians fray Antonio Tello in the seventeenth century and Matías de la Mota Padilla in the eighteenth both consulted documents written by Tovar which have disappeared since they wrote their regional histories. Many of the details that they were able to provide about the expedition to Tierra Nueva came from that source.[11] Only with the appearance now of Tovar's 1545 testimony at the mines of Nuestra Señora de los Remedios do we have a more direct, if very brief, account of events in Tierra Nueva by Tovar himself.

His statements on Vázquez de Coronado's behalf at that time were minimal, volunteering little information beyond what he was specifically asked. His answers, though, uniformly defended and supported the actions of the former captain general. If one were to credit Tovar's testimony, no violence against native peoples occurred during the entire expedition. As could be expected of a de parte witness and former captain on the expedition, Tovar's statements are thoroughly sanitized.

A TRANSLATION
OF THE TESTIMONY

Fourth de Parte Witness (Pedro de Tovar)[12]

[29v cont'd] The aforementioned don Pedro de Tovar, a vecino of the villa of San Miguel and a witness presented on behalf of Francisco Vázquez de Coronado, being asked the questions of the interrogatory, stated and declared the following.

{1} To the first question he answered that he knows the Francisco Vázquez de Coronado referred to in the question by sight, speech, and conversation he has had with him for the past nine years.

{personal matters} Being asked the questions concerning personal matter specified by law, he said that he is about twenty-seven years old and is not a relative of Francisco Vázquez. None of the other questions concerning personal matters applies to him or is relevant.

{2} To the second question [Tovar] replied that the general kept [30r] the army with which he was entrusted very well governed and controlled while in the land referred to in the question. In regard to the proclamations and ordinances, he refers to them [the documents], from which [what is asked] will be evident. This is what he knows concerning the question.

{3} To the third question the witness responded by saying that he heard many persons in Mexico City say what is referred to in the question, namely that fray Marcos said [what is stated there]. But, as he remembers it, he [himself] never heard fray Marcos say it. This is what he knows concerning the question.

{4} To the fourth question he answered that he knows what is referred to in the question to have been as stated there. He saw it transpire and occur as stated, since he went in the army and saw it. If it had been otherwise, he would have seen and been aware of it.

{5} To the fifth question, [Tovar] stated that he does not remember where the public announcement of what is referred to in the question was made, but he does remember that some proclamations were made. Among them were one to the effect that the Indians were to be treated very benevolently and [another] to the effect that no abuse was to be inflicted on them. [30v] As he has [already] said, he refers to the ordinances and proclamations [themselves].

{6} To the sixth question the witness replied that he was present during the war waged against the natives of Cíbola and saw that the exhortations mentioned in the question were made to the Indians. Also, he saw that during the [other] battles at which he was present the requerimiento was read. Effort was always made to be sure that war was just. This is what he knows concerning the question.

{7} To the seventh question he answered that he knows that what is mentioned in the question [came to pass] while there was peace. Asked how he knows, he said that it is because he was present in the aforesaid province of Tiguex at the time and saw that it was and transpired as stated in the question.

{8} To the eighth question [Tovar] responded by saying that while they were at peace, the natives of the province of Tiguex rose up and killed the horses and mules referred to in the question. He does not know why; nor were they provoked at all. [31r] He does not remember that they killed Indians, but he did hear it said that one Indian had been killed. However, he does not remember seeing that. In the province of Arenal [the Indians] took refuge in Pueblo Quemado and fortified themselves. This is what he knows concerning the question.

{9} To the ninth question he answered that he remembers what is referred to in it.

{10} Likewise to the tenth question he said that he remembers what is referred to in it.

{11} To the eleventh question he replied that he does not remember [anything] about it, except that he heard Diego López say it. The rest he does not know.

{12} To the twelfth question the witness answered that what he knows about it is that war was waged against the Indians in Pueblo del Arenal. And don García López and Captain Diego López [were the leaders who] waged it. He knows nothing else because he [31v] was not there. Nor was the general present during the battle at that pueblo. [Tovar] says that they both stayed in the pueblo where quarters were. This and nothing else is what he knows concerning the question.

{13} To the thirteenth question [Tovar] responded [by saying] that he knows that after war had been waged against the aforesaid pueblo, the natives of the province of Tiguex took refuge and fortified themselves in Pueblo del Cerco. It was said that they took refuge there, fortified themselves and sought to defend themselves. This is what he knows concerning the question.

{14} To the fourteenth question he answered that it was said that don Rodrigo went to Pueblo del Cerco while the aforesaid Indians were in revolt and had taken refuge there. Don Rodrigo [himself] told the witness that [he and his companions] had gone in peace to deliver the requerimiento. The witness knows that Maldonado returned, saying that the Indians refused to receive him in peace. Instead, before [he could read the requerimiento] they were shrieking at him. So he came back. This is what he knows concerning the question.

[32r] {15} To the fifteenth question he replied that he knows that, likewise, don García López went to Pueblo del Cerco to try to bring [the Indians] to peace. He heard don García and many others say that what is referred to in the question did occur with those Indians. And the witness saw the bruises and the helmet and the arrow wound in [don García's] foot. However, the witness did not go [to Pueblo del Cerco]; nor does he know more about what is referred to in the question.

{16} To the sixteenth question [Tovar] stated that he knows and saw that the general Francisco Vázquez would not allow any cruelty to be committed against the Indians. Nor was any committed that he saw. This is what he knows concerning the question.

{17} To the seventeenth question he answered that he does not know that anyone in the army, neither the general nor any other person, enslaved [any Indian]. And that was not done. Further, he heard it said that the public announcement referred to in the question was made.

{18} To the eighteenth question [the witness] responded [by saying] that he knows that when native Indians of those places came from time to time bringing something [32v] to the general, he ordered them given trade items that he had brought. And the witness saw them given [trade goods]. This is what he knows concerning the question.

{19} To the nineteenth question [Tovar] replied that what he knows about it is that the general never permitted anything to be taken from the Indians of that region. Nor did the witness see [such a thing occur]. He knows that they were at peace. But he does not know the rest of what is contained in the question.

{20} To the twentieth question he answered that he knows that the army endured hunger and great want of clothing [in] which to dress themselves. By and large everyone knows this.

{21} To the twenty-first question [the witness] stated that he knows that the general was very well outfitted and equipped with the things necessary for the expedition. In [acquiring these things] he could not have failed to spend a large amount of money. But the witness does not know [exactly] how much he spent.

{22} To the twenty-second question he replied that he does not know.

{23} To the twenty-third question [33r] he responded [by saying] that he knows that the general and the army went to Cíbola and other lands. Also, he knows that they found there none of the riches that were talked about. In the province of Cíbola they found nothing more than the seven pueblos referred to in the question, lacking wealth and civilization. Furthermore, he knows that the kingdom called Acus was a strong promontory known as Acuco, and he heard it said that the kingdom of Totonqueantes was [only] some hot springs, although he did not see them. This is what he knows concerning the question.

{24} To the twenty-fourth question [Tovar] answered that he knows that the aforesaid general sent the captains referred to in the question to the places mentioned in search of new lands and with the instructions referred to. He knows this because the witness was one of the captains who went; he is the don Pedro de Tovar, mentioned in the question, who went to the province of Tusayán.

[33v] {25} To the twenty-fifth question he replied that he knows that those captains returned without bringing word of a land in which it would have been possible to settle. In addition, he knows that the aforesaid Alvarado brought [with him] the Indians referred to in the question, who told about the land of Quivira and all the rest mentioned in the question. The witness also heard that said publicly and as something widely known in the camp and the army. However, he was not present [in the camp] and did not go to the province of Quivira because he went back, as the general ordered him to do, to the [camp] at Señora. When he returned from there he found that the general had already come back.

{26} To the twenty-sixth question [the witness] stated that what he knows about it is that while [the expedition] was in Tiguex some horses and Spaniards died. From what he does not know. He saw that the general was attentive to the sick, visited them, and did what he could. This and nothing else is what he knows concerning the question.

{27} To the twenty-seventh question [Tovar] answered that what he knows about it is [34r] that the general led the army to the place to which he was ordered to lead it in his majesty's name. He knows that [Vázquez de Coronado] reconnoitered more lands than those said to have been discovered by fray Marcos. Further, he knows that in all those lands he did not learn of any land better than what [the witness] has told about the provinces of Cíbola, Tusayán, and Quivira. Also, some people and horses died, and the [expedition] had great need of clothing, medicine, and everything else. [The general] returned and brought the people and the army back to Nueva España, from where he had led it. This is what he knows concerning the question.

{28} To the twenty-eighth question he replied that he knows that the general was wounded and incapacitated at the pueblo of Cíbola, also in Pueblo del Cerco, as the question states. He does not know the rest of what is referred to in the question.

{29} To the twenty-ninth question [Tovar] answered that he says what he said [in response] to the twenty-first question, [in response] to which he declared what he knows about this. The rest of what is referred to in the question he does not know.

[34v] {30} To the thirtieth question he responded by stating that he says what he has said in the previous questions and that what he has said is the truth and what he knows about the case. In accordance with the oath he swore, he states that the rest of what is referred to in it he does not know. He affirmed and ratified [his testimony] and signed it.

don Pedro de Tovar

{item} After what has been recorded, at the aforesaid mines on the twentieth day of the month of May in the year one thousand five hundred and forty-five, the aforementioned Francisco Pilo appeared before the lord alcalde and, in my presence as scribe and that of the witnesses listed below, petitioned and asked, in the name [of Francisco Vázquez de Coronado], that the lord alcalde order me, as scribe, to prepare one, two, or more copies of the evidence that has been gathered. I was to provide it to him, sealed and secured, written on unused [paper] and authenticated by me, the aforesaid public scribe, in the manner and form that would be valid in a legal action or anywhere else, so that it could be presented wherever it might be appropriate in accordance with his rights. And his authorization and decree were to be inserted [among the papers], in order that it might be proper [35r] and valid in a legal action or anywhere else. He is ready to pay me, the aforesaid scribe, the exact salary owed to me. He asked for justice.

{item} Promptly the lord alcalde ordered me, the aforesaid scribe, to prepare one, two, or as many copies of the evidence as Francisco Pilo wanted. And I gave them to him, in the name [of Francisco Vázquez de Coronado], in a public way and in a manner that would be valid, sealed, secured, and with my sign affixed.

On paying me the exact salary owed to me, he said that he was inserting and did insert [among the papers] his authorization and the judicial decree.

He affixed his sign, but because he does not know how to write, he did not sign.

Witnesses: García de Villareal and Juan Gutiérrez, residents at the aforesaid mines. . . .[13]

[37v cont'd] I, Hernando Gómez de la Peña, His Majesty's scribe and public notary in his court and in all his kingdoms and dominions and a scribe of the court at these mines, was present for all that was said and recorded from the aforesaid witnesses. By order [38r] of the lord alcalde I wrote down what transpired before me. Therefore I affixed here my sign, which is made this way. In testimony of the truth.

Fernando Gómez de la Peña
His Majesty's scribe

{item} This copy was corrected and reconciled with the original. Thus I, Juan Niñez de Zavaleta, secretary of the aforesaid commission, prepared it in the city of Mexico on the twenty-fourth day of the month of January one thousand five hundred and sixty-eight.

Witnesses who saw it reconciled and corrected: Cristóbal de Montoya, Juan de Avendaño, and Melchor Hurtado, citizens of this city.

Juan Niñez de Zavaleta

A TRANSCRIPT
OF THE TESTIMONY

[fol. 29v cont'd]¹⁴

{T*estig*o}

El d*ic*ho don P*edr*o de toVar v*ezin*o / de la villa de san myguel T*estig*o / Presentado Por parte del d*ic*ho / Fran*cis*co Vazq*uez* de coronado y / siendo Preguntado por las Pre- / guntas del ynterrogatorio(s) dixo / E dePuso lo
siguiente / {i} / A la Primera Pregunta dixo q*ue* / conoze al d*ic*ho Fran*cis*co
Vazquez / De coronado cont*en*ido *en* la d*ic*ha preg*unt*a / De vista e habla e
conversaÇion / que con el *h*a thenido de nueVe a*ñ*os / A esta parte / {*General*es} / Fue preg*unta*do por las Pregunt*a*s / generales de la ley dixo que *e*s /
de (h)edad de veynte e siete años / Poco mas o menos e q*ue* no le tocan / ny
es pariente del d*ic*ho Fran*cis*co Vazq*uez* / ny yncurren *en el* nynguna de las
otras / Preguntas generales de la ley / {ii} / A la segunda Pregunta dixo que /
save que *el* d*ic*ho general lleVaba / 6

[fol. 30r]

356

Bien corregido conçertado y / castigado el EXerçito q*ue* llevo / Encomendado
de la tierra con- / thenida *en* la pregunta y que en / quanto A los (h)edi*ct*os y
(h)ordenanças / que se rremyte A ellos que / Por ellos Parezera y esto / save
de *e*sta Pregunta / {iii} / A la terzera pregunta dixo q*ue* / oyo dezir En mexico
A muchas / Personas lo cont*en*ido En la / Pregunta que lo dezia el d*ic*ho /
Fray marcos mas que *e*ste t*estig*o / nunca se lo oyo dezir Al d*ic*ho / Fray marcos
que a este t*estig*o se le / Acuerde y esto save de *e*sta preg*unt*a / {iiii} / A la
quarta pregunta dixo que / save ser lo conthenido En la pre- / gunta como En
ella se declara E / Vio ser y passar como dize Porque / Este t*estig*o Fue *en el*
d*ic*ho EXerçito y / lo Vio E si otra cosa Fuera Este t*estig*o / lo Viera E Supiera
/ {v} / A la quinta Pregunta dixo que / no se AcuerdA donde se (A)Pre- /
gono lo que la d*ic*ha pregunta dize mas / De que se acuerda se (A)pregonaron

/ çiertos Edictos Entre los quales / Fueron de que se tratasen / muy bien los yndios E no se les diziese

[fol. 30v]

maltratamyento e que se rremyte / como dicho tiene A las dichas (h)orde- / nanças y Edictos / {vi} / A la sesta pregunta dixo que / Este testigo se hallo En la guerra que / se hizo a los naturales de Çibola / E vio que se les hizo los rre- / quirimyentos que en la pregunta / Dize e ansimysmo vio En las / guerras en que este testigo se hallo / se hizieron los dichos Requiri- / myentos e que sienPre se / Procuraba justificar la / guerra y esto save de esta pregunta / {vii} / A la sePtima pregunta dixo / que save que estando de paz / que la save como En ella se contiene / Preguntado como lo save dixo / que Porque este testigo se hallo / En aquel tienpo En la dicha / Provinçia De tiguex y lo / Vio(o) ser y pasar como la pregunta / lo dize / {viii} / A la octaVa Pregunta dixo que / save que estando De Paz los / dichos naturales de la dicha pro- / vinçia de tiguex no save este testigo / Porque ny les diesen oca- / Sion Alguna A ello se rrebelaron / 7

[fol. 31r]

357

E mataron los caballos / que la pregunta dize y aÇemylas / y no se acuerda si mataron yn- / Dios mas de que oyo dezir An- / simysmo que hAbian muerto un / yndio Pero que este testigo no se A- / cuerda de haber lo Visto E se en- / castillaron E hizieron fuertes / En la provinçia del arenal / que se llamaba el pueblo que- / mado y esto save de esta pregunta / {jX} / A la noVena pregunta dixo que / Este testigo se acuerda de lo contenido en la pregunta / {X} / A la dezima pregunta dixo que / Ansimysmo se Acuerda de lo / contenido en la dicha Pregunta / {Xj} / A la (h)onzena Pregunta diXo que / no se Acuerda de ello mas de que / se lo hA oydo dezir Al dicho diego lopez / E lo demas no lo save / {xii} / A las doze Preguntas dixo que lo / que de ella save (h)es que se les / Hizo guerra A los dichos yndios / que estaban en el dicho Pueblo del / Arenal e se la hizo don Garcia / lopez e diego lopez capitan y no save / otra cosa Porque este testigo

[fol. 31v]

no se hallo En ella ny el dicho general / TanPoco se hallo En la guerra / del dicho pueblo que se habian / quedado En el Pueblo de los a- / Posentos y esto save de esta / Pregunta E no otra cosa / {Xiii} / A las treze preguntas dixo que / save que despues de hecha / la guerra al dicho pueblo los / naturales de la dicha provinçia / se Encastillaron E hizieron / Fuertes En el Pueblo del / Çerco que dezian Alli se en- / castillaron E Procuraron ha- / Zer Fuertes E se defendieron / y esto save de esta pregunta / {Xiiii} / A las catorze preguntas dixo / que save que estando los dichos / yndios Asi alzados y encastillados / En el pueblo del çerco que dezian / el dicho don Rodrigo Fue alla y el dicho / Don rrodrigo le dixo A este testigo / que los habian ydo A rrequerir / con la paz y save que se Volvyo / De alla y dixo no haberle / querido rreÇibir de paz / los dichos yndios sino que Antes / le gritaban y ansi se volvyo / y esto save de esta pregunta / 8

[fol. 32r]

358

{Xv} / A las quinze preguntas dixo que / save que el dicho don garÇia lopez Fue / Ansimysmo al dicho pueblo del / çerco A los procurar tra(h)er de paz / E oyo dezir Al dicho don garÇia lopez / E a otros muchos hAberles A- / conteçido lo conthenido En la dicha / Pregunta con los dichos yndios E el / Vio los golpes que le habian dado / E la zelada y el Flechazo del / Pie pero que este testigo no fue (h)alla / ny save mas de lo contenido en la pregunta / {Xvi} / A las diez y seis preguntas Dixo que / save que el dicho general Francisco Vazquez / no consintio que este testigo Viese / que no se hiziese nynguna crueldad / nunca A los dichos yndios ny se hizo / que este testigo Viese y esto save de esta / Pregunta / {xvii} / A las diez y siete Preguntas dixo / que no save que el dicho ExerÇito por el dicho / general ny por otra PerSo(in)na alguna / se hiziese nyngun(d) esclaVo ny se hizo / e que oyo dezir que se habia dado el / Pregon contenido en la pregunta / {Xviii} / A las diez E ocho preguntas dixo que / save que quando Algunas Vezes / Venyan los yndios naturales / De aquellas Partes A traer alguna cosa

[fol. 32v]

Al dicho general E(e) les mandaba / Dar del rrescate que lleVava / y este testigo se lo Vio dar y esto save / de esta pregunta / {XjX} / A las diez y nueVe preguntas dixo / que lo que de ella save (h)es que el dicho / general nunca consintio que es- / te testigo Viese ny Supiese que se / les tomase cosa nynguna A los yn- / Dios de aquellas Partes e que / Estaban de paz e que lo / Demas contenido En la Pregunta / Este testigo no lo save / {XX} / A las Veynte Preguntas dixo que / save que el dicho EXerçito Passo / Hanbre E grandes nezesidades / de rropas que se vestir y / Esto saven todos En general / {xxj} / A las veynte E una Preguntas / DiXo que save que el dicho ge- / neral Fue bien AdereÇado / y aperÇeVido de las cosas ne- / zesarias Para la jornada en lo / qual no Pudo deXar de gastar / cantidad de dineros E que lo / que gastaria Este testigo / no lo save / {XXii} / A las veynte e dos Preguntas / DiXo que no la save / {xxiii} / a las veynte E tres preguntas

[fol. 33r]

359

DiXo que save que el dicho general / y EXerçito fue a Çibola y o- / Tras tierras e que save que no / se hallo En ninguna de ellas las / Riqueças que dezian nyngunas / mas de que se hallaron En la / dicha provinçia de Çibola los siete / Pueblos como se contiene / En la pregunta E pobres de / rriquezas E policia(z) e que Ansimysmo / save que el rreyno que dezian que / (h)era de acus Era el Penol / Fuerte que se dezia de acuco / E el de totonqueantes oyo / Dezir que (h)eran Unas fuentes / calientes Pero que este testigo / no las Vio y esto save de esta / Pregunta / {Xxiiii} / A las veynte e quatro Preguntas / DiXo que save que el dicho / general Envio A los capitanes / conthenidos En la dicha Pregunta A / las Partes que En ella Se contiene / En demanda de tierras nuevas / Con la ynstruçion contenido en la / Pregunta e lo save porque este / Testigo Fue (le) uno de los Capitanes / que Fueron que es el dicho don / Pedro de tovar contenido En la Pregunta / que Fue a la Provinçia de / Tuçayan

[fol. 33v]

{xxv} / A Las veynte E çinco preguntas / DiXo que save que se volvyeron / los dichos capitanes sin dar noticia / De tierra que fuese Para / Poder En ella Asentar E save / que el dicho alvarado Truxo los yn- / Dios contenidos En la Pregunta / que dieron notiçia de la tierra / De quivira y todo lo demas / contenido En la Pregunta e este testigo / lo oyo dezir Por Publico E notorio en el / dicho rreal E ExerÇito Pero que este testigo / no se hallo En ello ny fue a la dicha provincia / De quivira Porque torno atras / que le mando Volver el dicho general / A lo de señora e quando Vol- / vio de (h)alla ya hallo de vuelta / Al dicho general / {Xxvi} / a las veynte e seis Preguntas / DiXo que lo que de ella save es / que estando En la dicha Provinçia / De tiguex se morian Algunos / Caballos e algunos EsPañoles / Este testigo no save de que E vio / que el dicho general thenia cuydado / de los dichos Enfermos e los / Visitava E hazer lo que podia y / Esto save de esta pregunta E no o- / Tra cosa / {XXvii} / A las veynte e siete Preguntas / Dixo que lo que de ella save es

[fol. 34r]

360

que el dicho general lleVo el dicho / EXerçito a la parte donde En nombre / de su magestad se le mando llevar / E save que descubrio mas tierras / De las que dezian hAber des- / cubierto El dicho Fray marcos e que / En todas ellas no se thenia / notiçia de tierra mejor que lo que / Tiene dicho de la provinçia de Çibola / E tuçayan e quivira e que se / morian Algunos caballos e alguna / gente E thenia nezesidad grande / De rropa E de mediçinas E de todo / lo demas e que traxo e torno / la gente y EXerçito A la nueVa españa / Donde lo saco y esto save de esta / Pregunta / {Xxviii} / A las veynte e ocho Preguntas / DiXo que save que el dicho general / Estuvo herido E malo En el / Pueblo de Çibola y ansimysmo / En el pueblo del çerco como lo / Dize la pregunta E lo demas / En ella contenido no lo save / {xxjx} / A las Veynte e nueVe preguntas / DiXo que dize lo que dicho tiene / En las veynte E una preguntas / que Alli aclaro lo que de esto save E / lo demas en ella conthenido este / Testigo no lo save

[fol. 34v]

{xxx} / A las treynta preguntas dixo / que dize lo q*ue* d*i*cho tiene En las / Preguntas antes de *e*sta e que lo q*ue* / *h*A d*i*cho es la verdad e lo q*ue* de *e*ste / casso
save E lo demas En ella *conteni*do / este t*esti*go no lo save Para el juram*en*to /
que hizo y En ello se af*i*rmo / E rretifico y lo f*i*rmo don P*edr*o / De toVar

{y*tem*}

E despues de lo Susod*i*cho / En estas d*i*chas mynas veynte / d*i*as del mes de
mayo de *e*ste d*i*cho año / de myll e quy*nien*tos e quarenta e / çinco años ante
*e*l d*i*cho s*e*ñor al*c*alde / y *en* presençia de my el d*i*cho escri*b*ano / y de los t*e*s-
t*i*gos de yuso escritos pa- / recio presente El d*i*cho fran*ci*sco pilo / En el d*i*cho
n*ombr*e E dixo que / Pedia E pidio al d*i*cho s*e*ñor al*c*alde / mande a my el d*i*cho
escri*b*ano saque un tr*asl*ado / e dos e mas De la ProbanÇa / que hecha tiene
E se la de Çe- / Rada y sellada Escripta En / linpio E autoriçada de my el
d*i*cho / escri*b*ano pu*bli*co *en* forma *en* manera que / haga fe En juicio y fuera
de *e*l P*ar*a / lo presentar Ado*nde* A Su d*erec*ho / convenga En los quales /
ynterponga Su autoridad / y decreto judiÇial p*ar*a q*ue* valga

[fol. 35r]

361

E Haga fe *en* ju*i*cio y fuera de *e*l / que el *e*sta presto de paGar / A my el d*i*cho
escri*b*ano my justo e devido / salario E pidio justiÇia

{y*tem*}

E luego el d*i*cho señor al*c*alde m*an*do / a my el d*i*cho escri*b*ano saque un
tr*asl*ado / De la d*i*cha provança e dos e mas / los que *e*l d*i*cho Fran*ci*sco Pilo
quy- / siere y cerrados y sellados E / signados con my signo En pu*bli*ca forma
/ En manera que haga fee los de / Al d*i*cho Fran*ci*sco pilo *en e*l d*i*cho n*ombr*e
/ Pagandome Ante todas cosas / my justo E debido salario en los / quales dixo
q*ue* ynterponya / E ynterpuso su autoridad / E decreto judiçial E lo señalo /
E Por no saver escrivir no f*i*rmo / T*esti*gos garÇia de villarreal / E juan
gutierrez estantes E- / n estas d*i*chas mynas / [. . .]¹⁵

[fol. 37v cont'd]

E yo her*nan*do gomez de la peña / es*cri*b*an*o de su mag*esta*d e su not*ari*o Pu*b*-
*li*co En / la Su corte y *en* todos los Sus / Reynos y señorios es*cri*b*an*o del juz-
gado / de *e*stas d*i*chas mynas Fuy pres*en*te / A todo lo que d*i*cho es e vino con
/ los d*i*chos t*e*st*ig*os E de pedimy*en*to del d*i*cho / Fran*ci*sco pilo E de mandamyento

[fol. 38r]

364

del d*i*cho señor al*ca*lde lo susod*i*cho / Escrivi segun(d) q*ue* Ante mi passo y /
Por ende (f)*h*ize Aqui este myo / sygno que *e*s (a)tal *en* t*e*stim*on*io de *ve*rdad
/ Fernando gomez de la Peña / es*cri*b*an*o de su mag*esta*d

{*ytem*}

Fue corregido e conçertado este d*i*cho / Treslado con el oreginal de ende / Fue
sacado Por my Ju*an* nynez de / Çavaleta secret*ari*o de la d*i*cha comysion / En
la ÇiUdad de mexico veynte E / quatro d*i*as del m*e*s de (h)en*e*ro de myll / E
qu*i*ni*en*tos e ses*en*ta E ocho años siendo t*e*st*ig*os / a lo *ve*r corregir E conçertar
*Cri*st*o*val / De montoya E ju*an* de avendaño E / melchor hurtado *ve*z*in*os de
*e*sta d*i*cha ÇiUdad / ju*an* nynez de çaValeta

Chapter 23

Further Defense

Summary of Testimony in Mexico City

In addition to the record of de parte testimony already presented, there exists a short, incomplete summary of statements made by three other witnesses on Vázquez de Coronado's behalf. Such summaries were often prepared by scribes to save judges and attorneys the trouble of wading through complete testimony records. In this case, the full record is no longer known to exist, and all that remains of the testimony of Gaspar de Saldaña, García Rodríguez, and Rodrigo Maldonado is five folios of scribal summary. The interrogatorio used to examine these three witnesses in Mexico City,[1] consisted of questions very similar, though not identical, to those given to Francisco Pilo, although many of the questions used in Culiacán were omitted altogether. Thus, the total number of questions recorded in the Mexico City summary is 17, compared to 30 used at Culiacán. Of the 17 questions of the Mexico City interrogatorio 14 correspond to questions provided to Pilo. There were, however, three questions that did not appear in Pilo's interrogatorio: 12) whether Vázquez de Coronado was absent from the battle of Pueblo del Arenal, 14) whether the captain general had the requerimiento read before waging war on Pueblo del Cerco, and 17) whether Quivira was left at peace and crosses were set up there as signs of possession.

It is not known who acted as Vázquez de Coronado's agent in securing the testimony at Mexico City. It was certainly not Francisco Pilo. The former captain general could have and probably did grant his power of attorney to other persons in order to secure testimony from expedition members who, by 1544, were dispersed throughout the Western Hemisphere. Almost certainly, many more than seven de parte witnesses were examined in total. Places besides Culiacán and Mexico City to which Vázquez de Coronado's agents were dispatched to secure defense testimony would certainly have included Guadalajara, Compostela, Navidad, Acapulco, and Colima in western Nueva España, as well as Puebla de los Angeles, Antequera, and Veracruz in the east and south of the viceroyalty. Nevertheless, no record of examination of witnesses in these places is known to exist. The summary of testimony of the three Mexico City witnesses does not indicate when the testimony was taken, but given the former captain general's pressing need for rebuttal testimony and the relative ease of communication between Guadalajara and Mexico City, it was likely in late 1544 or early 1545.

The first witness presented in Mexico City on Vázquez de Coronado's behalf was García Rodríguez, a native of Alcázar de Consuegra in the jurisdiction of Ciudad Real, Spain, the hometown of the former captain general's father-in-law, Alonso de Estrada. Rodríguez had come to Nueva España at about age 16 less than two years before the expedition to Tierra Nueva was launched.[2] He arrived in the company of the royal *contador* or accountant Rodrigo Albornoz and served as a clerk in the *contaduría* or accountancy office under Albornoz for a considerable time. He mustered before Viceroy Mendoza at Compostela in February 1540 as a horseman in the company of don Diego de Guevara.[3] His exact social and economic status at the time of the expedition is unclear. During the muster he was listed as bringing only one horse with him, which would indicate a relatively humble status.[4] Nearly 40 years after the expedition, however, Rodríguez asserted that he had taken several horses and two servants with him. He also claimed to have spent a large sum of money because of the expedition and suffered from debt for a long while after his return to Mexico City before being able to repay it. According to Rodríguez, because of the expedition many mines were discovered and much territory settled.[5]

In the 1550s Viceroy Luis de Velasco appointed Rodríguez corregidor of the pueblo of Capulalcolulco, which is in modern Guerrero. He was apparently married and had at least one child. But, in 1557, he took vows as a priest and by 1578 had a benefice of the pueblos of Tasco and Tlamagazapa, southwest of Cuernavaca. He was proud of being fluent in Nahuatl, which allowed him to confess his parishioners, something that many other priests in Indian communities could not do.

During his testimony concerning the treatment of Indians in Tierra Nueva, Rodríguez's statements were usually very brief, limited to confirming what was asked in the questions. Exceptions were his emphatic assertions that Vázquez de Coronado had not known about the burning of Indians at Pueblo del Arenal until after it had happened, that El Turco had purposely led the expedition astray, and that nothing of value had been found in the north.

The second de parte witness examined in Mexico City was Gaspar de Saldaña. When he came to Nueva España from his native Guadalajara, Spain, in 1535 in company with Viceroy Mendoza, he was in his mid-teens.[6] From at least September 1537 until the departure of the expedition to Tierra Nueva, and again in 1543, Saldaña served as a member of Viceroy Mendoza's personal guard, making him a companion in arms of Juan de Contreras, a de oficio witness before licenciado Tejada, as well as of expedition members Velasco de Barrionuevo and Diego de Guevara.[7]

Like the summaries of García Rodríguez's answers to the interrogatorio presented by Vázquez de Coronado's agent, those of Saldaña were extremely succinct for the most part. When he supplied additional detail, though, it was frequently recorded as very strongly stated and uniformly in support of the former captain general. For instance, Saldaña claimed to have been an eyewitness to the burning of Indians at Pueblo del Arenal and swore that Vázquez de Coronado had not ordered that brutality. And he provided an ostensibly verbatim quote from El Turco, showing that he sought to kill the

Spaniards and their horses. In addition, he said, as other witnesses had, that for a long while the former captain general defended El Turco from his accusers in the army.

Judging from the summary of their testimony, both García Rodríguez and Saldaña became more voluble as the questioning progressed. This suggests that they warmed to the idea of defending Vázquez de Coronado or were progressively encouraged to be more forthcoming. It is also possible that the increasing expansiveness of their testimony is only a scribal artifact, resulting from the process of preparing an extract.

The last of the de parte witnesses for whom a record of testimony survives is Rodrigo Maldonado. He was one of the captains of horsemen in the expedition to Tierra Nueva and was implicated in or said to be present at several of the outrages committed against the indigenous peoples there. It is extremely unfortunate, therefore, that only tiny fragments of his statements exist even in summary. The only answer attributed to Maldonado is incomplete and also appears not to be germane to the question asked.

Don Rodrigo Maldonado, like Saldaña, was a native of Guadalajara in Spain and said to be brother-in-law to the duque del Infantado. His wife was Luisa de Aux, a daughter of Miguel Díaz de Aux, an early settler of Mexico City and well-to-do entrepreneur.[8] He arrived in Nueva España in 1535, probably in the viceroy's fleet. He was about 24 years old when he embarked on the expedition to Tierra Nueva,[9] taking with him five horses and an appreciable amount of European armor (a coat of mail, and a helmet and beaver), compared to the majority of expedition members.[10]

Early in the expedition, Maldonado was sent to the Mar del Sur to rendezvous with the ships of Hernando de Alarcón.[11] Thus, he was not present during the fighting at Cíbola. But he was in Tiguex while battles raged between the Pueblos and the expedition. Indeed, several witnesses during Tejada's 1544 investigation placed him at Pueblo del Arenal at the time Indian captives were burned. He and his company were said variously to have despoiled, demolished, or burned at least one of the abandoned Tiguex pueblos. And he was supposed to have made an unsuccessful attempt to convince the people of Moha/Pueblo del Cerco to capitulate without a fight. What details he shed on these and other incidents when questioned according to Vázquez de Coronado's interrogatorio are apparently lost.

Maldonado was an encomendero, having received as dowry in his marriage to Luisa de Aux, a one sixth interest in the tribute from Mextitlán, northeast of Mexico City.[12] One of the other encomenderos of Mextitlán was fellow expedition member Diego de Guevara.[13] In 1564, Maldonado and nine other vecinos of Mexico City, including in-laws of Vázquez de Coronado Bernaldino Pacheco de Bocanegra and Alonso Dávila Alvarado, pled by letter with the king for the allowance of perpetual encomiendas.[14]

A TRANSLATION
OF THE TESTIMONY SUMMARY

[1r] Report Extracted From the Affidavit Prepared On Behalf Of Francisco Vázquez de Coronado In Which Three Witnesses Are Certified On the Part of the Fiscal: Gaspar de Saldaña, García Rodríguez, and don Rodrigo Maldonado[15]

{2}[16] Item. Whether they know, etc., that going in search of the lands that fray Marcos de Niza said he had discovered, the aforesaid general kept his armed force well governed and very disciplined and controlled. Did he not countenance any blasphemy against God Our Lord or his blessed mother Our Lady? Did he order this proclaimed publicly and was it announced in the army so that it was public knowledge and widely held?

The three witnesses are aware of what is referred to in the question.

{3} Item. Whether they know, etc., that after traveling onward with the army from the city of Compostela the aforesaid Francisco Vázquez de Coronado issued and ordered proclaimed ordinances very beneficial to the natives of the lands to which he was going and went and through which the army passed.

The witnesses are familiar with what is referred to in the question.

{4} Item. Whether they know that Francisco Vázquez de Coronado, general of the aforesaid army, took great care that the natives of all the lands and provinces through which the army passed, both men and women, were treated very benevolently. Did he take care that no harm, cruelty, or abuse would be done to them and that nothing would be taken from their houses and estates without their being paid for it, since for this purpose the general took trade goods. Did this happen and occur and was this observed, as stated in the question, by the general and his lieutenants and the captain of the armed force. They are to state what they know about this.

{Witness} García Rodríguez stated that he knows what is referred to in the question. Asked how he knows it, he said it was because he saw every-thing and was present during this. What is referred to in the question is true and is public knowledge and widely held.

[1v] {Witness} The witness Gaspar de Saldaña declared that he knows what is referred to in the question. Asked how he knows it, he answered that it is because he saw everything and was present during all of it. Further, it was and is public knowledge and widely held.

{Witness} Don Rodrigo Maldonado stated that at the time when Fran-cisco Vázquez went on the aforesaid reconnaissance the witness saw that he took with him many henchmen, Blacks, horses, and mules and much [in the way of] arms. He went very well accoutered, because of which the wit-ness. . . .[17]

{5} Item. Whether they know, etc., that the warfare waged by the general and his armed force during the entrada and reconnaissance was justified because the Indians against whom it was waged provoked it. Before engaging in war were the Indians against whom battle was undertaken summoned to submit and place themselves under the dominion of His Majesty? Were they assured that if they did [as they were asked] they would be well treated and maintained in peace and justice and would be protected in this way with their persons and goods? And [were they told] that where [they chose not to do as they were asked] war would be waged against them and they would be pun-ished? Were they made to understand this by means of interpreters and trans-lators, particularly in the provinces of Cíbola and Tiguex?

{Witness} García Rodríguez replied that he knows what is referred to in the question. Asked how he knows it, he said that it is because he saw every-thing and was present during it. What is referred to in the question is true and is public knowledge and widely held.

{Witness} Gaspar de Saldaña stated that he knows that Francisco Vázquez de Coronado sent [persons] to summon the Indians at Cíbola to offer peace and come to the service of His Majesty. [He also knows] that the reading of the requerimiento went on so long that the Indians shot an arrow that struck one of the friars who were taken in the company. This he knows because he heard it said by credible persons who saw it and it was public knowledge and widely held [that it was] this way.

{6} Item. Whether they know, etc., that during the time they were at peace, those Indians who rendered obedience to his majesty and were at peace [2r] were treated benevolently. Did the general order that they were to be well treated like his majesty's vassals? Further, did he make some of the Indians understand that if any man-at-arms wronged them or took something from them and if they came to complain to the general, one of his lieutenants, or the maestre de campo, they would give them satisfaction?

{Witness} García Rodríguez stated that he is aware of what is referred to in the question. Asked how he knows it, he answered that it is because he saw it all and was present during it. What is referred to in the question is true and is publicly known and widely held.

{Witness} Gaspar de Saldaña declared that he knows what is referred to in the question. Asked how he knows it, he replied that it is because he saw it and was present during it. Furthermore, what is referred to in the question was and is publicly known and widely held.

{7} Item. Whether they know, etc., that while the native Indians of the province of Tiguex were at peace and without any abuse having been committed against them, they rose up and fortified themselves in one pueblo of the province. They also stole thirty-plus horses, mules, and beasts of burden that were wandering in the countryside and put them in a patio enclosed within Pueblo del Arenal. There they shot them with arrows and killed them. They sent the animals' tails to other pueblos to notify them of what has been stated, since they were at war. Also, they clubbed and wounded some of the Indian allies who were guarding the animals and killed some of them. When the natives had done this they fortified themselves in all the pueblos of the province of Tiguex. They are to state what they know about this.

{Witness} García Rodríguez replied that he knows what is referred to in the question. Asked how he knows it, he said that it is because he saw everything [happen] as it is stated in the question. Also, it was public knowledge and widely held.

{Witness} The witness Gaspar de Saldaña stated that he knows that the aforesaid Francisco Vázquez de Coronado sent don García López, the maestre de campo, to the Río de Tiguex to establish quarters, in order to pass the winter there. [López] wanted to build straw huts, [2v] but the winter was so harsh that it was not possible to maintain the people there. The maestre de campo asked the Indians to provide quarters for him in the pueblo where they were, after which the Indians left it.

The captain general was aware that without abuse having been perpetrated against any of the Indians, they killed the horses and mules that they held and were carrying the tails from there and showing them off. The Indians had closed the animals up in a patio of their [pueblo] and there they shot them with arrows. And [they shot] others in the countryside. Saldaña knows that they clubbed many Indian [allies] who were about in the countryside, fortified themselves, and took refuge in three pueblos in Tiguex province.

He knows what he knows because he saw it and also it was publicly known and widely held.

{8} Item. Whether they know, etc., that when the general became aware of the aforementioned uprising, the deaths of the horses and mules, and the wounding of the Indian allies who were guarding them, he asked to meet and did meet with His Majesty's officials and the priests who at the time were with the army. And did he ask their opinion as to what was proper to do about the rebellion? They are to state what they know.

{Witness} Gaspar de Saldaña stated that he is aware of what is referred to in the question. Asked how he knows it, he said that it is because he saw everything and saw [the general] secure the opinions of the clerics, His Majesty's officials, and [other] principal persons of the army.

{Witness} [What] don Rodrigo Maldonado [said] will be seen in the original.

{9} Item. Whether they know, etc., that in the opinion of the general, the priests, and His Majesty's officials it was determined that punishment of the rebels was just and that war was to be waged against them because they had risen up and rebelled against the service of his majesty, without being provoked. They are to say what they know.

{Witness} Gaspar de Saldaña declared that he knows what is referred to in the question. Asked how he knows it, he replied that it is because he saw everything and was present during it. Further, he saw that war was waged as stated in the question.

[3r] {10} Item. Whether they know that before the general ordered war to be waged against the Indians of the province of Tiguex and before war was waged against them, he sent [persons] to summon [them] one, two, and three times, and more to come and place [themselves] under the yoke and royal dominion of His Majesty, as they had been before. Did they tell [the Indians] this and that if they did [as they were asked], [the Spaniards] would do what they ought to, and they would be treated well? Otherwise, war would be waged against them and they would be punished. Were they made to understand all of this by means of interpreters and translators? They are to state what they know about this.

{Witness 1} The witness García Rodríguez stated that he knows what is referred to in the question. Asked how he knows it, he answered that it is because he saw it all and was present during it. Furthermore, what is referred to in the question was public knowledge and widely held.

{Witness} The witness Gaspar de Saldaña declared that he knows what is referred to in the question. Asked how he knows it, he answered that it is because he saw it and saw [those individuals] go to read the requerimiento, as the question states. Also, it is and was publicly known and widely held [that it happened] thus.

{11} Item. Whether they know, etc., that when [the Indians] had been summoned as stated, they refused to render obedience to His Majesty or to come to peace. Did they instead shoot arrows at those who were reading the requerimiento? Seeing that [the Indians] refused to render obedience to His Majesty and were stubborn in their rebellion, did Maestre de Campo don García López de Cárdenas (whom the general had directed and ordered to make the summons) make war and attack Pueblo del Arenal? They are to state what they know about this.

{Witness 1} García Rodríguez declared that he is aware of what is referred to in the question. Asked how he knows it, he said it is because he saw it and it happened just as stated in the question. Also, he was present during [this event] and it is publicly known and widely held.

{Witness} The witness Gaspar de Saldaña said that he heard it said just as referred to in the question. Further, he saw [the individuals] go to read the requerimiento to [the Indians], as it is stated in the question.

{12} Item. Whether they know, etc., that the general was not present at the combat and war that was waged against the Indians of that pueblo, since, if he had been present, [3v] the witnesses would have known it. And, if burning or punishment was inflicted on any Indian, did the aforementioned maestre de campo order it, as the person in charge of [administering] justice in the army? They are to state what they know.

{Witness} García Rodríguez replied that he knows what is referred to in the question. Asked how he knows it, he stated that it is because when don García López de Cárdenas waged war and administered certain punishments against the Indians of that pueblo, Francisco Vázquez de Coronado was not there. Furthermore, this witness knows that [the general] did not know this [had happened] until after justice had been administered against those who had been in rebellion. This happened thus.

{Witness 2} The witness Gaspar de Saldaña stated that he knows and saw that, when the fighting and burning referred to in the question were carried out, the general Francisco Vázquez de Coronado was not there. What was done was by order of the maestre de campo. [The witness] did not see the general order it. He believes completely and saw that the maestre de campo burned [the Indians] and waged the war. [That is was] thus is public knowledge and widely held.

{13} Item. Whether they know, etc., that most of the Indians of the province of Tiguex took refuge in Pueblo del Arenal and in another [pueblo] called [Pueblo] de Moha, where they fortified themselves. When this became known to the general, did he send [individuals] with don Rodrigo Maldonado (a captain of horsemen) and don García López de Cárdenas to summon [the Indians] to render obedience to his majesty? Although they were at peace and were read the requerimiento, did they never chose to render obedience and be at peace? Did they instead try by trickery to kill don

Rodrigo Maldonado and don García López? And did they wound don García? They are to say what they know.

{Witness 1} The witness García Rodríguez declared that he is aware of what is referred to in the question. Asked how he knows it, he answered that it is because he saw it and it happened just as stated in the question and referred to in it.

{Witness} Gaspar de Saldaña said that he knows and saw that the Indians took refuge in three pueblos. They were summoned to render obedience, but refused to do so. Instead, they tried by trickery to kill the maestre de campo when he went to summon [them]. The witness saw that he came [from there] wounded [4r] in one foot by an arrow. The rest referred to in the question was publicly known and widely held.

{14} Item. Whether they know, etc., that when the general saw that the Indians were in rebellion and refused to render obedience to his majesty, he laid siege to them and went again in peace to summon [them]. When he saw that they [again] refused to render obedience, did he attack the pueblo and capture it? They are to state what they know.

The witnesses know what is referred to in the question because they saw it and were present during it.

{15} Item. Whether they know, etc., that the general went with part of the armed force from the province of Tiguex to the province of Quivira. Because of the many wildernesses and the lack of water, food, and provisions, did the general and those who went with him endure much hardship and want; that is, because of the lengthy wilderness and unsettled areas, as was said. When the general had arrived in the province of Quivira, did he try to get the natives there to render obedience to His Majesty? Did they do so and because they had rendered [obedience], were the natives and their houses and estates treated well? They are to state what they know.

{Witness} The witness García Rodríguez said that what he knows about this is that Francisco Vázquez de Coronado departed from the province of Tiguex exactly as stated in the question. The witness went with him until more than half the route [had been covered]. From there [the general] left for the province of Quivira with certain horsemen, companions of his from the army. During the time the witness was with the [general] Rodríguez saw what is referred to in the question transpire. Afterwards he heard it said by those who went with the [general] that they had endured much more. The rest he heard said publicly by those who returned from there.

{Witness} The witness Gaspar de Saldaña stated that he is aware of what is referred to in the question. Asked how he knows it, he replied that it is because he saw everything and was with the general Francisco Vázquez de Coronado during all of the journey related in the question. He saw it [happen] thus.

[4v] {16} Item. Whether they know that an Indian called Turco, who told about the province of Quivira, tried several times to kill the general and those who went with him by guiding and leading the army through wilderness and unsettled areas far distant and away [from] the route to Quivira, all so that the general and the army would be lost and would die. [Did he do] the rest particularly in a town of the province of Quivira where he attempted, along with the native Indians of [the town], to kill the general and those who went with him? When the general became aware of this, did he order Maestre de Campo Diego López to investigate the case and, when he had made investigation and learned the truth, to administer justice in the case? Because, through the investigation, the maestre de campo found El Turco guilty, did he impose justice on him? They are to say what they know.

{Witness} The witness García Rodríguez stated that what he knows concerning the question is that in all the time they traveled, from the time they left the province of Tiguex until they arrived at a large barranca, he always heard it said by the Indian companions of the Indian [called] Turco that they were lost and that they were leading [the army] deceitfully. [This they knew] because that was not the correct route, which was very clear from the return [trip] that Francisco Vázquez made from the province of Quivira to the province of Tiguex. That is because [Rodríguez] heard that Francisco Vázquez came from the province of Quivira to that of Tiguex in thirty days by a good route with water and it took more than a hundred and thirty to go [the other way]. The rest he heard said by don Rodrigo Maldonado and Diego López, who went with him.

{Witness 1} The witness Gaspar de Saldaña responded by saying that he knows and saw that the Indian Turco led them lost and away from the route. [That is what] ended up being said and it was public knowledge and widely known [that it happened] thus among all [his] companions [in the army], namely, that El Turco had wanted to lead them lost by that route, so that they would not go to his land to subjugate his parents, relatives, and forebears. [That was] because it was a worthier thing for him to die, so that his relatives would not be subjects of the Christians.

Traveling in Quivira, at the first town of [the province Turco] saw the horses running and said that they must not [be allowed to] run, since they ate corn. A large horse belonging to [Hernando de] Alvarado went there, and an Indian commented about how large the horse was. El Turco said, "titley," which means "kill it." [5r] [He said that] because he thought that [if] the horses [were] dead, they could kill the Christians. The witness believes that everything El Turco did was [done] to kill and destroy them.

Concerning the death [of El Turco], the witness did not see it, but it was publicly known and widely held that the maestre de campo and [Juan de] Zaldívar and [Juan de] Torquemada killed him and were present at his death. It is true that what most annoyed everyone was the great partiality the general showed to Turco. If it were not for that, [the general's] companions would have killed him. [This must be true] since they had a saying among the Christians which held that the general supported El Turco.

This is what he knows concerning the question.

{17} Item. Whether they know, etc., that when the general wanted to leave the province of Quivira, its natives remained at peace and subjects under the dominion of Their Majesties. Were crosses left in the some of the towns, put there as a sign of possession of the land, which was taken in His Majesty's name. They are to state what they know.

{Witness} Gaspar de Saldaña said that he knows what is referred to in the question. Asked how he knows it, he answered that it is because he saw everything and was present during it, as stated in the question.

{18} Item. Whether they know, etc., that the general and the army went where the viceroy of Nueva España ordered in His Majesty's name. When he saw that there was nothing with which to increase His Majesty's royal patrimony because the land was barren and poor and had few people, did the general send captains with horsemen to various places to seek out and reconnoiter other lands and peoples where he might be better able to increase His Majesty's royal patrimony? Seeing that the captains and scouts neither found nor heard news of anything good, did they return to give a report to the general of the aforesaid? They are to state what they know.

{Witness} The witness García Rodríguez declared that he knows that Francisco Vázquez [himself] reached the province and barranca farther on from Tiguex, and before that [the captains] reached Cíbola, [5v] Tiguex, and other places in search of and looking to discover other lands which might be better. This witness went with some of the captains who went to reconnoiter, and never did he see or hear it said that [anyone] found another land better than the province of Cíbola. Everyone who went on reconnaissance returned to report about it to Francisco Vázquez de Coronado, general of the army.

{Witness} The witness Gaspar de Saldaña stated that he knows and saw that the general and those of [his] company went where they were ordered [to go] by the lord viceroy. When he was there in Cíbola, General Francisco Vázquez dispatched don Pedro de Tovar and, afterwards, don García López to proceed on beyond don Pedro. They thought they would perish from thirst because they found the land infelicitous and uninhabitable. This is what he heard from his companions. He knows also that [the general] sent Francisco de Ovando with men to another place and he sent Francisco Mondragón to another place, and Hernando de Alvarado to another. None of them found anything and returned to report to the general about what there was. Hernando de Alvarado learned news from El Turco and Yupo [who was] with him. [Saldaña] knows this concerning the question because he saw it.

[rubric]

In this affidavit will be found in the original the statements of the witnesses in the investigation summary, both those [who were] certified and those who were not certified.

Item. This is correctly extracted in what is of substance.

Santander [rubric]

A TRANSCRIPT
OF THE TESTIMONY SUMMARY

[fol. 1r]

Relaçion sacada de la probança (f)*he*cha Por parte de Fran*cis*co Vazquez / de coronado en la qual estan Ratificados tres te*sti*gos por p*ar*te de / el fiscal q*ue* son gasPar de saldaña y garçi*a* Rodriguez y don rr*odrig*o maldonado[18]

{ij} / Yten si saben *etcetera* que yendo el di*c*ho general en de- / manda De las tierras que *e*l di*c*ho fray marcos / De niça Dixo *h*A*ber* descubierto llevo / SienPre su ejerçito muy corregido castigado / bien gobernando no consin- tiendo ny dando / lugar que neng*un*o blasfemase contra dios / N*uest*ro senor ny su bendita madre n*ues*tra Señora / y lo m*an*do (A)Pregonar y se (a)pregono *en e*l / Di*c*ho exerçito Como fue pu*bl*ico e not*or*io / Los tres te*sti*gos saben la Preg*un*ta Como en ella se *contien*e / {iij} / Yten si saben *etcetera* que *e*l di*c*ho fran*cis*co Vazquez de / coronado desPues que (h)iba con el exerçito / ADe- lante de la dicha çiudad De conPostela / hiço e mando APregonar (h)orde- nanças / muy en faVor De los naturales de las tie- / Ras Ad*on*de (h)iba y fue por d*on*de Paso el di*c*ho exerçito / Los te*sti*gos saben lo en la Preg*un*ta *con- tenid*o / {iiij} / Yten si saben q*ue e*l dicho fran*cis*co Vazques De / coronado gen- eral del di*c*ho exerçito tuVo mu- / cho cuydado que todas Las tierras e Pro- / Vinçias Por d*on*de Paso el di*c*ho exerçito fuesen / muy bien tratados Los nat- urales de (h)ellas / Ansi honbres como mugeres e que no se / Les hiçiese ningun daño ni Crueldad ny mal- / Tratamyento ny se les tomase nenguna Cosa / De sus Casas e haçiendas sin se lo Pagar / Porque Para (h)ello lleVaba el di*c*ho gene- / Ral ResCates y esto fue e Paso e / se guardo como esta Pre- g*un*ta Lo Diçe Por el di*c*ho / general Por su lugartenyentes capita- / nes de el di*c*ho exerçito digan lo que Çerca de / Esto saben / {T*estig*o} / garçi*a* Rodriguez dixo q*ue* sabe la di*c*ha Preg*un*ta Como en ella se *contien*e / Pre- g*un*ta*d*o Como lo sabe dixo que porque lo Vi(d)o todo y se *h*allo / Presente A (h)ello y es *ver*dad e pu*bl*ico e not*or*io lo en la preg*un*ta *contenid*o

[fol. 1v]

{T*estig*o} / gasPar de saldaña dixo este t*estig*o q*ue* sabe la Preg*un*ta Como en ella se *contien*e / Preg*unta*do como lo sabe dixo que porque lo Vi(d)o todo e se *h*allo Pre- / Sente A todo (h)ello e fue y es ansi Pu*b*lico e notorio / {T*estig*o} / Don R*odrig*o maldonado dixo que en el d*ich*o tienPo q*ue* *e*l d*ich*o / Fran*cis*co Vazquez fue al d*ich*o Descubrimyento este t*estig*o vi(d)o que lle- / Vaba con el muchos Criados negros e Caballos e armas e açe- / mylas E (h)iba muy bien Adereçado a Cuya Causa este d*ich*o t*estig*o[19] / {V} / Yten si saben *etcetera* que en la guerra que / En la dicha entrada e desCubrimyento del / D*ich*o general e su eJerçito hizo fue Justificado / Dando los (h)indios a quyen se hiço oCasion y / Prim*er*o q*ue* se hiçiesen las d*ich*as guerras (e guerras) / Los (h)inDios A quyen se hiço la dicha guerra / Fueron Prim*er*o Requeridos una e dos e tres / Veçes que se Diesen e Pusiesen Debajo de el / Domynyo D*e* su mag*estad* segurandoles e haçiendo- / lo Ansi serian bien tratados y tenydos / en Paz y en Just*ici*a e que se les guardaria / Ansi (ansi) con sus Personas e bienes Don- / De no q*ue* se les haria guerra e serian Castigados / Lo qual se les Dio A entender Por lenguas / YnterP*r*et(r)es que los entendian esPeçial- / mente en la p*r*oVinçia De çibola e tiguex / {mark} / {t*estig*o} / g(^aspar*)*^*arcia* Ro*drig*uez dixo que sabe la Preg*un*ta Como en ella se contiene / Preg*unta*do Como lo sabe dixo que Porque lo Vi(d)o todo e se Hallo / Pre- sente A (h)ello y es *ver*dad Pu*b*lico e not*or*io lo *contenid*o en la / Preg*un*ta / {t*estig*o} / [illegible, crossed out marginal note] / gasPar de saldaña dixo que sabe q*ue* *e*l d*ich*o fran*cis*co Vazquez de / Coronado (h)enVio A rrequerir A los d*ich*os (h)indios en çibola / q*ue* se diesen de Paz e vinyesen al *ser*Viçio D*e* su mag*estad* E que los / Requyrio tanto que los d*ich*os yndios tiraron Un flechaço / Y dieron Con el A Un frayle de los que lleVaban en su / ConPanya E que *e*sto que lo sabe Porque lo oyo d*ecir* A / Personas de Credito que lo Vieron E ansi fue pu*b*lico e not*or*io / {Vj} / yten si saben *etcetera* que los (h)indios q*ue* dieron / La obidiençia A su mag*estad* que estuVieron de paz / Durante el tienPo que estuVieron De paz

[fol. 2r]

Se les hiço buenos tratamyentos y el d*ich*o general / mandaba que fuesen bien

tratados Como / Vasallos de su mag*estad* e a algunos de los d*i*chos / (h)indios
Dio A entender que si algun soldado / Les hyçiese mal o les tomase Alg*un*a
Cosa / se Vinyesen A quexar al d*i*cho general o A / Sus lugartenyentes o al
maese De / Canpo q*ue* (h)ellos los desagraViarian / {*testigo*} / ga(sPar)*rcia*
Rodriguez Dixo q*ue* sabe la d*i*cha Pregu*n*ta Como en ella se *contiene* / Preguntado Como la sabe dixo que Porque lo Vi(d)o todo y se / hallo Presente
A (h)ello y es la *v*erdad e pu*b*lico e not*o*rio lo *contenido* en la Pregu*n*ta / {*testigo*} / gasPar de saldaña Dixo q*ue* sabe la Pregu*n*ta como en ella se contiene
Pregu*n*tado / Como lo sabe Dixo que Porque lo Vi(d)o e se hallo Presente e
fue y / es pu*b*lico e not*o*rio todo lo *contenido* en la Pregu*n*ta / {Vij} / Yten si
saben *etcetera* que est*an*do de paz los dichos yndios / De la pr*o*Vinçia De
tiguex sin les *h*aber *h*echo neng*un*os / malostratamy*en*tos los d*i*chos naturales
se rrebelaron / e hiçieron fuertes en un Pueblo de la dicha Pro- / Vinçia e
tomaron treynta e tantos Caballos / mulas E açemylas que anDaban Al canPo
/ Y las metieron en Un Patio çercado Del Pue- / blo de el arenal e alli las
flecharon E / mataron e las Colas De las d*i*chas bestias Les / (h)enViaban A
otros Pueblos Para da- / rles notiçia De lo d*i*cho e Como estaban De guerra
/ E Ansimesmo Aporrearon e hirieron alg*un*os / (h)inDios Amigos De los
q*ue* guardaban las / d*i*chas bestias e murieron algunos de (h)ellos / Y *h*echo
esto los d*i*chos naturales se hiçieron fuer- / Tes en todos los d*i*chos Pueblos de
la d*i*cha pr*o*- / Vinçia de tiguex Digan lo q*ue* çerca de *e*sto / Saben / {*testigo*}
/ garç*i*a Rodriguez Dixo que la sabe como en ella se *contiene* Pregu*n*tado
como / Lo sabe Dixo que Porque lo Vi(d)o todo como se *contiene* en la Pregu*n*ta / E fue pu*b*lico e notorio / {*testigo*} / gasPar de saldaña Dixo q*ue* sabe
este *testigo* q*ue* *e*l d*i*cho Franc*i*sco Vazquez / De coronado enVio al rrio De
tiguex Al d*i*cho don garç*i*a Lopez / maese de canPo A que hiçiese Un
aPosento Para tener / Alli el ynVierno y que quiso haçer Ranchos de paJa

[fol. 2v]
E que el (h)inVierno hiço tan Reçio que no se Pudo a*h*y sustentar / la gente
e que *e*l D*i*cho maese De canPo Pidio A los d*i*chos (h)indios / le diesen
Aposento en el Pueblo Donde (h)ellos estaban e que / DesPues los (h)inDios
se salieron De el E que sin haçerles / nengun maltratamy*en*to A nenguno De

(h)ellos el d*i*cho Capi- / Tan general Supiese los d*i*chos (h)indios le mataron los Caballos / E Açemylas que tenyan e trayan Las coLas Por a*hy* mostran- / Dolas e los (h)ençerraron en Un Patio De su casa e alli los / Flecharon Y otros en el canPo e que sabe que A- / Porrearon Muchos (h)indios que andaban *en* *e*l Canpo / y *h*echo esto Vi(d)o q*ue* se hiçieron Fuertes Y se rrecoxeron / En tres Pueblos De la d*i*cha ProVinçia De tiguex e que *e*sto / que lo Sabe porque lo Vi(d)o e ansi fue Pu*b*lico e notorio / {Viii} / Yten si saben *etcetera* q*ue* sabido Por el d*i*cho ge- / Neral el d*i*cho leVantamyento e muertes De / los d*i*chos Caballos e mulas y heridas De / Los d*i*chos yndios Amygos que las guardaban / hizo Juntar e Junto los Religiosos De / mysa que de Presente *h*Abia COn el d*i*cho e- / xerçito y a los d*i*chos ofiçiales D*e* su mag*esta*d / y les pidio Pareçer de lo que conVenya A / haçer sobre la d*i*cha Rebelion digan / lo q*ue* saben / {*testigo*} / gasPar de salDaña Dixo que sabe la Preg*un*ta Como en ella / se contiene Preg*un*tado como lo sabe dixo que Porque lo Vi(d)o / ToDo e el Vi(d)o tomar el d*i*cho Pareçer Por los Religiosos / E Personas PrençiPales De el d*i*cho exerçito ofiçia- / les D*e* su mag*esta*d / {*testigo*} / don *R*odrig*o* maldonado se vera por el original / {jx} / Yten si saben *etcetera* que Por Pareçer de el / D*i*cho general Religiosos e ofiçiales / D*e* su mag*esta*d se Determyno ser Justo el Cas- / Tigo de los d*i*chos Rebelados e haçerseles / guerra Por Raçon de *h*aberseles le- / Vantado e Rebelado Contra el *ser*Viçio / D*e* su mag*esta*d syn les *h*aber dado A ello / oCasion Digan lo q*ue* saben / {*testigo*} / Gaspar De saldaña Dixo q*ue* sabe la Preg*un*ta Como en ella se *contiene* Preg*un*tado / (Preg*un*tado) Como lo sabe dixo que Porque lo Vi(d)o todo y se *h*Allo Presente / A (h)ello e Vi(d)o q*ue* se hiço la d*i*cha guerra como lo diçe la Preg*un*ta

[fol. 3r]

{x} / Yten si saben q*ue* *e*l d*i*cho general Antes q*ue* les hiçiese / guerra ny la mandase haçer A los d*i*chos (h)inDios de / la ProVinçia De tiguex les (h)enVio A rre- / querir Una e dos y tres Veces y mas q*ue* se Vi- / nyesen A Poner debajo de el yugo *y* domynyo / Real d*e* su mag*esta*d Como De antes estaban e (h)ansi / Diçiendoles que haçiendolo ansy harian Lo que / Debian y serian bien tratados donde no q*ue* se / Les haria gueRa e serian Castigados todo / lo qual les fue *h*echo Entender Por lenguas / ynterpr*e*tes digan lo q*ue* çerCa de esto saben / {j *testigo*} / garçi*a* Rodriguez Dixo este *testigo* que sabe la Preg*unta* como en ella se contiene / Preg*unta*do como lo sabe Dixo que Porque lo Vi(d)o este testigo e se hallo / Presente A (h)ello Fue Pu*bli*co e notorio lo *contenid*o en la Preg*unta* / {*testigo*} / Gaspar de (ledesma) *saldaña* dixo este d*ich*o *testigo* que sabe la Preg*unta* como en ella se *contien*e / Preg*unt*a*do Como lo sabe dixo que Porque lo Vi(d)o e los Vi(d)o (h)ir A / Requerir Como lo diçe la Preg*unta* e ansi fue y es pu*bli*co e not*or*io / {xj} / Yten si saben *etcetera* que *h*abiendoles Requerido / segun D*ich*o es no quysieron dar la obi- diençia / A su mag*estad* ny Venyr De Paz Antes tiraron / Flechas A los que les hiçian los d*ich*os Re- / querimyentos e Viendo el maese De CanPo Don / garçi*a* loPez De Cardenas A quyen el d*ich*o ge- / Neral cometio mandar haçer los d*ich*os rre- / querimy*ent*os e la guerra si no quysiesen dar La obi- / Diençia A su mag*estad* Viendolos pertinaçes(^des) en / su rrebelion les hiço la guerra e Conbatio el / D*ich*o Pueblo De el arenal digan lo que çerCa / De esto saben / {1 *testigo*} / garçi*a* Rodriguez Dixo que sabe la Preg*unta* Como en ella se contiene / Preguntado Como La sabe dixo que Porque lo Vi(d)o y Paso ansi / Como se COntiene en las Preguntas e se hallo Presente A / (h)ello y es pu*b-* *li*co e notorio / {*testigo*} / gasPar De salDaña Dixo este *testigo* que ansi lo oyo D*ecir* como se *contien*e en / la Preg*unta* mas de que Vi(d)o que Fueron a haçerle*s* Los d*ich*os Re- / querimy*ent*os Como se *contien*e en la Preg*unta* / {xij} / Yten si saben *etcetera* q*ue* *e*l d*ich*o general no se *h*Allo presente / En el conbate e guerra q*ue* se hiço A los (h)inDios / De el d*ich*o Pueblo Porque si se hallara(n) presente(^s)

[fol. 3v]

Los testigos Lo suPieran e si alguna quema o Castigo / De algun (h)indio se hiço el dicho maese De Canpo / Lo mando haçer Como Persona A Cuyo cargo esta- / ba la JustiÇia (^man) De el d*ich*o exerçito Digan *lo que saben* / {*testigo*} / garçi*a* Rodriguez dixo q*ue* sabe la preg*unt*a como en ella se contiene Preg*unta*do Como lo sabe dixo que Porque quando El d*ich*o don garçi*a* lo- / Pes De cardenas Dio la guerra e hizo çiertos Castigos a los (h)in- / dios d*el* d*ich*o Pueblo El d*ich*o franc*is*co Vazquez de coronado no se hallo en ello / ny este *testigo* sabe que el lo suPiese hasta desPues de *ser h*echa la / Just*ici*a de los

que Rebeldes *h*abian sydo y que es- / to Paso ansy / {ii t*estig*o} / gasPar de saldaña dixo este t*estig*o q*ue* sabe e Vi(d)o que al tienpo q*ue* se / hiço la dicha
guerra e quema q*ue* la Pregu*nt*a diçe el d*ic*ho general / Franci*sc*o Vazquez De
coronado no se hallo P*res*ente a (h)ello e lo q*ue* se / {ojo} / hizo Fue por m*an*-
*da*do del d*ic*ho maese de canPo E que no Vi(d)o q*ue* lo / mandase el general e
que bien Cree e Vi(d)o q*ue* *e*l d*ic*ho maese de Campo / los quemo e hiço la
guerra y asi es pu*b*lico e notorio / {xiij} / Yten si saben *etcetera* que toDos Los
mas De los d*ic*hos / (h)indios de la d*ic*ha ProVinçia De tiguex se rrecoxie- /
Ron *en el* d*ic*ho Pueblo De el arenal y en otro q*ue* se / Deçia De moha Donde
se hiçieron Fuertes / y sabido Por el d*ic*ho general les (h)enVio A / Requerir
Con Don R*odrig*o maldonado Capitan / De la g*ent*e De a Caballo e Con el
d*ic*ho Don garçia lopez / De Cardenas q*ue* Diesen la obidiençia A / Su
mag*estad* y estuViesen De Paz E aunq*ue* fueron / Requeridos nunCa lo
quysieron (^haçer) Dar la / obiDiençia y estar De paz Antes Procuraron / De
matar Con engaño A los d*ic*hos Don / R*odrig*o malDonado e Don garçia
loPez e hirie- / Ron al d*ic*ho Don garçia loPez Digan lo q*ue* saben / {j t*estig*o}
/ garçia RoDriguez dixo este t*estig*o q*ue* sabe la Pregu*nt*a como En ella se *con*-
*tien*e / Pregu*nt*ado como Lo sabe Dixo que Porque lo Vi(d)o e Paso / Ansi
como lo Diçe la Pregunta y en ella se *contien*e / {T*estig*o} / gasPar De salDaña
Dixo q*ue* sabe e Vi(d)o q*ue* los d*ic*hos yndios / Se Recoxeron en tres Pueblos e
q*ue* sabe que fueron Re- / queridos que se diesen De Paz E que no lo quysieron
haçer Antes / ProCuraron De matar Al d*ic*ho maese De CanPo Con engaño
/ quanDo les fue A rrequerir e Vi(d)o este t*estig*o q*ue* Vino herido

[fol. 4r]
En Un Pie De Un flechaço e lo Demas *contenid*o en la pregu*nt*a / Fue pu*b*-
*l*ico e notorio / {xiiij} / Yten si saben *etcetera* q*ue* Viendo el d*ic*ho General q*ue*
los / d*ic*hos (h)inDios estaban en su rrebelion e no que- / Riendo Dar la obidiençia A su mag*estad* el d*ic*ho gene- / Ral les Puso çerco y los torno A rrequerir / con la Paz e Viendo que no querian Dar la obi- / Diençia Conbatio
el d*ic*ho Pueblo y le tomo / Digan lo que saben / los t*estig*os saben la Pregu*nt*a
como en ella se *contien*e porque lo Vi(d)*er*on y se ha- / llaron Presentes A
(h)ello / {Xv} / Yten sy saben *etcetera* q*ue* Desde las Pro- / Vinçias De tiguex

el dicho general con parte / De el dicho exerçito fue a la ProVincia De / quyVira e Pasaron el dicho general e los que con / el (h)iban grandes trabajos e neçesiDaDes / Por los muchos Desiertos falta de agua Co- / myda mantenymiento Por largos Desiertos e des- / Poblados Como dicho es e llegado el dicho general / A la dicha ProVinçia De quyVira Procuro que / Los naturales de (h)ella Diesen la obidiençia A / Su magestad los quales la dieron E Por Raçon / De haber la daDo los dichos naturales fueron bien / tratados e sus casas e haçiendas Digan lo que / Saben / {Testigo} / garçia Rodriguez Dixo este testigo que lo que de (h)ella sabe es que francisco / (que francisco) Vazquez De coronado salio De la dicha ProVinçia De / Tiguex segun e como la Pregunta Lo Diçe y este testigo fue con el hasta mas / De la mytad De el camyno e desde alli se partio Con çiertos / Caballeros ConPañeros De el exerçito Para la Pro- / Vinçia De quyVira e que en el tienPo que este testigo fue con el / Vi(d)o que Pasaron toDo lo contenido en la Pregunta e desPues oyo decir A / los que Con el fueron que habian Pasado mucho mas E / que lo Demas Lo oyo decir publicamente A los que de / Alla Vinyeron / {testigo} / g(g)asPar De salDaña Dixo este dicho testigo que sabe la Pregunta Como en ella / Se contiene Preguntado Como lo sabe dixo que Porque lo Vi(d)o todo y / se hallo Presente Con el dicho General Francisco Vazquez de Coronado / En todo el dicho Viaje Como lo Diçe la Pregunta e ansi lo Vi(d)o

[fol. 4v]

{Xvj} / Yten si saben que Un yndio llamado turCo / que dio notiçia De la dicha ProVinçia De quyVira / trato algunas Veçes De matar al dicho general / E a los que con el (h)iban guiando e lleVando el dicho e- / Xerçito Por desiertos e desPoblaDos muy fuera / E APartado El Camyno De quyVira todo / Por que el dicho xeneral y exerçito se Perdiesen / e muriesen Demas De esto senalaDamente en / Un Pueblo De la dicha ProVinçia De quyVira don- / De trato Con los yndios naturales de (h)ella de / matar al dicho general e a los que Con el (h)iban e sa- / bido Por el dicho general mando al maese de / Canpo diego loPez que se ynFormase so- / bre el Caso e sabida E aVeriguaDa la verdad / hiciese en el caso Justiçia e Por hallarse culpado / el dicho turCo Por la dicha ynformaçion el / Dicho maese De canPo hiço Justiçia De el dicho

turco / Digan lo que saben / {testigo} / garçia Rodriguez Dixo que lo que sabe
de la Pregunta es que en todo el / TienPo que andaron Desde que salyeron
De la dicha ProVin- / Çia De tiguez hasta que llegaron A una barranÇa
grande / (grande) sienPre oyo decir este testigo A los ConPañeros yndios de /
dicho yndio turco que (h)iban Per(i)didos e que los lleVaban en- / Ganados
Porque aquel no (h)era el Camyno Derecho lo qual / Pareçio muy claro A la
Vuelta que el dicho francisco Vazquez hiço de / la dicha ProVinçia De
quy(rab)vira A la proVinçia De tiguex Porque oyo / Decir que Vino el dicho
Francisco vazquez DesDe la Dicha ProVinçia / De quy(rib)vira A la De
tiguex en treynta dias e Por buen Camyno / e con aguas e tardo en (Ve) (h)ir
mas De çiento y treynta e lo / Demas que Lo oyo Decir A Don Rodrigo mal-
Donado e al dicho / Diego LoPez que Fue con el / {i testigo} / gasPar de saldaña Dixo este testigo que sabe e Vi(d)o que el dicho (h)inDio tur(co)Co / los
lleVo Perdidos e Fuera del Camyno e que Vino A decir / E Fue ansi Publico
e notorio entre todos Los ConPañeros que el / Dicho turco los habia querido
lleVar por el Camyno Perdidos / E que no Fuesen A su tierra A soJuzgar sus
parientes / E Padres e PasaDos Porque mas valia que Pereçiese el / que no que
fuesen sus Parientes suJetos A los cristianos / y que yendo en quy(rib)vira en
el Primer Pueblo De quyVira les Vio / Correr los Caballos e Dixo el dicho
turco Como no han De correr que / Comen maiz e que (h)iba Alli Un caballo
granDe De alvarado / E que dixo Un (h)indio que que grande es este Caballo
/ E que el dicho turco dixo titley que quyere decir matarle

[fol. 5r]
{16} / Porque creya el dicho turco que muertes Los caballos los podian / matar
a los cristianos e que cree este dicho testigo que todo lo que haçia / El dicho
turco (h)era Por matarlos e destru(h)irlos E que en lo / De la muerte no lo
Vi(d)o este dicho testigo mas De que Fue publico e notorio / que el dicho
maese De canPo e çaldiVar e torquemaDa lo mataron / E Se hallaron en su
muerte e que es verdad que lo que / mas los (h)amoynaba a todos (h)era el
gran faVor que el dicho ge- / neral daba Al turco que si no Fuera Por el los
dichos Con- / Pañeros le mataran Porque se traya Un Refran / entre los cristianos que deçia que el general Sostenya Al / turco E que esto es lo que sabe

de esta Preg*un*ta / {xvij} / Yten sy saben *etcetera* que quando El d*i*cho general / Se quyso Partir de la d*i*cha ProVinçia de / quyVira quedaron los naturales de (h)ella de / Paz e suJetos debajo del d*i*cho Domynyo De sus / mag*es*tade*s* y en algunos de los d*i*chos Pueblos que- / Daron e se Pusieron Cruçes en señal De la / Posesion q*ue* se tomo De la d*i*cha tierra en *n*on- / bre de su mag*es*tad Digan lo q*ue* saben / {*testigo*} / Gaspar de saldaña dixo que sabe la d*i*cha Preg*un*ta Como en ella se *contiene* / Preg*un*tado Como lo sabe dixo que Porque lo Vi(d)o todo y se / hallo Presente A (h)ello Como se *contiene* en la Preg*un*ta / {xviij} / Yten si saben *etcetera* q*ue* *e*l d*i*cho general y exerçito / Fue Donde el d*i*cho Virrey De la nueVa esPaña / en nonbre D*e* su mag*es*tad mando e Visto que no / *h*Abia en q*ue* Acrecentar el patrim*on*yo / Real d*e* su mag*es*tad Por ser la tierra esteril y / Pobre e de Poca gente el d*i*cho general (h)enVio / Por div*er*sas p*ar*tes CaPitanes Con gente / De a caballo A busCar e descobrir / otras tierras e gentes Donde mejor se / Pudiese ACreçentar El Real / Patrim*on*yo D*e* su mag*es*tad e Visto q*ue* los d*i*chos / Capitanes e descobriDores no halla- / Ron ni tuVieron notiçia De neng*un*a cosa / buena VolVyeron A Dar Raçon Al / D*i*cho general De lo susod*i*cho Digan lo q*ue* / Saben / {*testigo*} / garç*i*a Rodriguez Dixo q*ue* sabe este *testigo* que el dicho Franc*is*co / Vazquez llego A la d*i*cha ProVinçia e barrança ADelante de / Tiguex e que antes que alla llegasen Ansi en Çibola Como

[fol. 5v]
en tiguex y en otras Partes en busca De Descobrir e buscar / Otras tierras que meJores Fuesen y este *testigo* fue con / Algunos De los caPitanes que (h)iban A Descobrir e nunCa / Vio ny oyo d*ecir* que *h*allase otra mejor tierra q*ue* la d*i*cha p*ro*Vinçia / De çibola e que todos los que (h)iban A descobrir Venyan / A Dar notiçia De (h)ella Al d*i*cho Franc*is*co vazquez de / coronado general del d*i*cho exerçito / {*testigo*} / gasPar de salDaña Dixo que este *testigo* sabe e Vi(d)o q*ue* *e*l d*i*cho / general e los De la conPanya Fueron Donde les Fue m*an*dado / Por el d*i*cho señor Visorrey E que *e*stando Alli en cibola / (h)enVio El d*i*cho general franc*is*co Vazquez A Don p*ed*ro De toVar / e DesPues A don garç*i*a loPez que Pasase ADelante / De don Pedro e que Pensaron Perderse De sed Porque ha- / llaron la tierra yn*h*abi(li)table e mala E

que esto q*ue* lo oyo d*ecir* / A los conPaneros e q*ue* sabe q*ue* (h)enVio A fran-
*cis*co De / oVando a otro cabo con gente e que (h)enVio A fran*cis*co / (^gor-
balan) mondragon Por otro cabo e a her*nan*do De alVarado / Por otro cabo e
que todos (h)ellos no *h*Allaron naDa e se / Volvyeron A dar quenta Al general De lo q*ue* habia / E q*ue* *e*l d*ic*ho (al*onso*) *Hernando* A*N*arado hallo la
noticia del turco e iUpo / Con (h)el e que *e*sto sabe De la preg*un*ta Porq*ue* lo
Vi(d)o / [rubrica] / [change of scribe] / En esta probança Se veran por el original los dichos de los *testigo*s de la Su- / maria informaçion ansi los ratificados
como los q*ue* no se Ratificaron / Yten esto esta bien sacada en lo Substancial
/ Santander [rubrica]

Chapter 24

A Final and Definitive Decision

The Captain General Exonerated

Without explaining their action in detail, on February 19, 1546, Viceroy Mendoza and the four oidores of the audiencia issued their judgment in the case of mistreatment of Indians in Tierra Nueva, at least as far as Francisco Vázquez de Coronado was concerned. In one short paragraph they announced that the fiscal had not substantiated his complaint, while the accused had disproved responsibility for all offenses with which he was charged. And they enjoined the fiscal from pursuing the case farther.

Fiscal Benavente did not appeal the audiencia's decision, an acknowledgement that the case for his original accusation had not been strong. Besides, Francisco Tello de Sandoval's visita of all of the royal officials of Nueva España, including the fiscal, was now in full swing. Benavente's decision not to appeal the exoneration of Vázquez de Coronado bespeaks a closing of ranks among the royal officials to present a united front in order to thwart the full-scale assault that Tello de Sandoval's visita was seen to be. Breaking ranks with the viceroy and oidores over the decision in the Vázquez de Coronado case would have been ill-advised, and the benefits of allowing the decision to go uncontested had positive results for Benavente himself. As a result of his decision not to mount an appeal, for example, Vázquez de Coronado was a friendly and supportive witness during the fiscal's own visita, which began that year and extended into 1547.[1]

With no appeal lodged, Vázquez de Coronado was free to forestall possible future pursuit of the case by requesting that a statement of final judgment be issued in the king's name. In due course, on December 20, 1547, the sought-after final judgment was forthcoming. It recapitulated the course of the legal proceedings in the case, summarized the fiscal's accusations and Vázquez de Coronado's defenses, included a copy of the audiencia's decision, painted a picture of the former captain general in the most glowing terms, and concluded by mandating that the audiencia's decision henceforth be fully and strictly adhered to in all courts of law. Not only did the statement pronounce Vázquez de Coronado not culpable on the issue of mistreatment of indigenous people of Tierra Nueva, but even judged him worthy of reward for his performance as captain general of the expedition.

The statement of final judgment was brought forward in 1553 in Vázquez de Coronado's successful effort to regain his status as encomendero of the towns Aguacatlán and Xala west of Guadalajara and the estancias of Mezquitlán to the north, and Guaxacatlán, Tepuzuacán, Amaxaque, Amatlán, and a second Mezquitlán to the west. And it served in 1605 as part of the proof of the worthiness of Francisco Pacheco de Córdova y Bocanegra, one of the grandsons of Francisco Vázquez de Coronado.[2] When, in 1617, Pacheco de Córdova y Bocanegra was made marqués de Villamayor de las Inviernas it was partly in belated reward for his grandfather's service commended so highly in the final judgment of 1547.

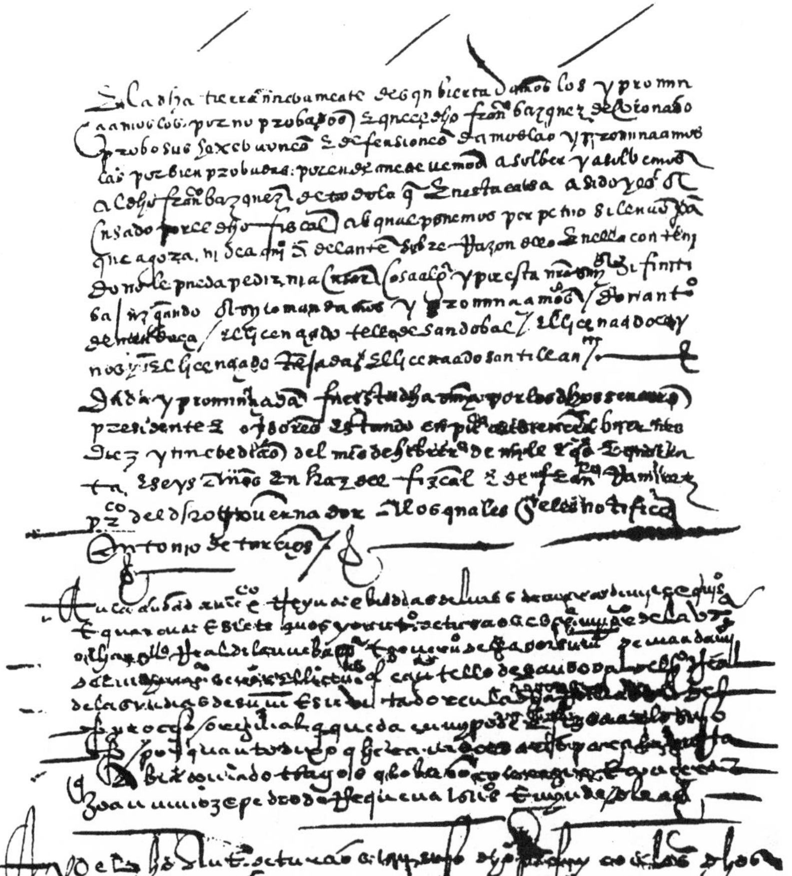

FIGURE 15.
Facsimile of Final page, AGI, Justicia, 267, N.3, fol. 125v

A TRANSLATION
OF THE DECISIONS

Decision of the Audiencia in the Case[3]

[125r cont'd] I was ordered to give a copy of the accusation to Francisco Vázquez, to which he responded with a number of justifications. On this account, he asked to be set free. The parties were received and a time limit was agreed upon. Within that time [the parties each] submitted affidavits. When the case was definitively closed, the lord licenciado Tejada sent the proceedings to the royal audiencia. When the lords president and judges of the audiencia had reviewed it, they announced and rendered a final decision in the case, the sum and substance of which is as follows.

In the criminal proceedings involving Cristóbal de Benavente (His Majesty's fiscal of the royal audiencia), as one party, and Francisco Vázquez de Coronado (formerly His Majesty's governor of the province of Nueva Galicia and formerly named and designated as captain general of the province of Cíbola and the newly discovered land) and his attorney on his behalf, as the other party, having considered the records and merits of the case, we find that the fiscal licenciado Benavente has not proven the indictment and charges he lodged against Francisco Vázquez de Coronado for offenses he claimed the general committed and perpetrated [125v] in that newly discovered land. We decide and proclaim that they were not proven. Francisco Vázquez de Coronado has proven his defenses and objections. We decide and proclaim that they have been thoroughly proven. Therefore, we must and do absolve Francisco Vázquez of everything he has been and is accused of in this case by the fiscal. And we impose permanent silence on the fiscal, so that neither now nor in the future may he make any petition or lodge any complaint regarding anything dealt with in this case and by our final judgment. Finding it thus, we order and proclaim it.

don Antonio de Mendoza
licenciado Tello de Sandoval
licenciado Ceynos
licenciado Tejada
licenciado Santillán

This decision was rendered and proclaimed by the lords president and judges in public court on Friday, the nineteenth day of the month of February in the year one thousand five hundred and forty-six, in the presence of the fiscal and Francisco Ramírez, attorney for the governor, to whom it was read.

Antonio de Turcios

In the city of Mexico on the thirty-first day of the month of March in the year one thousand five hundred and forty-seven, by order of the excellent lord licenciado Francisco Tello de Sandoval, of His Majesty's Royal Council of the Indies and his visiting judge of the royal audiencia, I, Antonio de Turcios, chief scribe of the Royal Audiencia and Chancery of Nueva España and its government for His Majesty, had the preceding copy prepared. The original remains in my possession. Licenciado Tello de Sandoval stated that it was necessary for the visita that he has conducted. The witnesses who saw it corrected and reconciled are Martín de Olid and the scribes Juan Muñoz and Pedro de Requena.

I, Antonio de Turcios, the aforesaid scribe, went with the witnesses to see the copy corrected and reconciled. Therefore, I affixed my sign, made in this way: {sign} It is the official sign.

Antonio de Turcios [rubric]

Definitive Decision of the King and Audiencia[4]

[5v] It appears that by virtue of our royal decree and order included above
and in fulfillment of it, our judge licenciado Tejada, in the presence of our
scribe Pedro de Requena, made and recorded an investigation by means of
witnesses regarding the matter mentioned in the order. This he did both in
the city of Mexico and in the city of Guadalajara in Nueva Galicia. Having
reviewed the investigation record and the sworn statement he took from
Francisco Vázquez de Coronado on this matter, the judge ordered [Vázquez
de Coronado] to appear in person in the audiencia of Mexico City before the
president and judges of that audiencia of ours, which has its seat there. When
[Vázquez de Coronado] had made his appearance he was ordered to take as
his prison that place which they indicated to him and not to defy this order
in any way under penalty of one thousand gold pesos de minas [to be paid]
to our council and treasury. It appears that this was communicated to Francisco Vázquez de Coronado.

In compliance with the order, thereafter he appeared in person at the
audiencia before our president and judges and [6r] was directed by our judge
licenciado Tejada to take his house as prison for the aforesaid reason and not
to leave it or contravene his order without his permission and command,
under the same penalty. And he ordered that the investigation record be given
to our fiscal licenciado Cristóbal de Benavente, who was to lodge before the
judge any accusation against Francisco Vázquez de Coronado that arose from
the investigation and that he might see was in our service. If, in the prosecution of justice on our behalf it [were] fitting that an accusation be lodged, he
was to hear and receive [Vázquez de Coronado's] rebuttals and transmit them
to our audiencia, as he was directed by us in our decree and order. It seems
that Francisco Vázquez de Coronado was informed of this.

Thereafter, on the twenty-first day of the month of March of last year,
one thousand five hundred and forty-five, in fulfillment of the aforesaid, our
fiscal appeared before our judge licenciado Tejada and stated, in a document
he laid before him, that he was lodging and did lodge criminal charges against

Francisco Vázquez de Coronado. Stating the case of the accusation, following the formalities of law, [6v] he said that Francisco Vázquez de Coronado was captain general of the newly discovered land and province of Cíbola, having been named such both by our viceroy and by our audiencia of Nueva España. He had been given our royal orders and instructions for reconnoitering, pacifying, and settling [those lands] he would find toward the west. And he was informed of the procedures he had to follow in waging war [against the natives] and in bringing and attracting them to knowledge of our holy Catholic faith and to our royal dominion and control. Further, for this he took an armed force of more than two hundred horsemen and many footmen well armed and supplied with what was necessary to carry out the journey.

The fiscal asserted that, in violation of the directives and injunctions included in our royal orders and instructions, in the course of that journey, both Francisco Vázquez de Coronado and his captains and lieutenants (by his order) had committed and perpetrated the following offenses:

First, in the province of Chiametla, without any justification or cause that was in the least legitimate and while its natives were at peace, he seized eight Indian men and women, [7r] more or less, and had some [of them] hung and the rest quartered.

Item: Having established a town of Spaniards in the valley of Corazones, he should have left there a person of circumspection and trust to administer justice and pacify the province. He did not do so, and because of the misdeeds and abuses committed by the person [or] persons he left there, all the natives of that province rebelled and killed many Spaniards. The town was deserted, and the people of the region have risen up because the captain general was remiss and did not leave a competent person to govern the town and its people.

Item: When the armed force and its personnel managed to reach the province of Cíbola, the natives of its principal town came out to them in peace, giving them food and necessary supplies. Without legitimate cause Francisco Vázquez and his captains made war, burned the pueblo, and killed many people. Because of this, a large part of the province and its people rebelled and rose up in arms.

Item: Proceeding on and going sixty or seventy leagues farther, the general arrived at the province of Tiguex, which is heavily populated and well furnished with supplies and buildings of the sort erected in Spain. Its natives came out to him [7v] in peace, rendered obedience to us, and provided to the people of the army a large quantity of corn, poultry, and other foodstuffs. When they were at peace and without having legitimate reason, the general and his captains (by his order) set dogs on the caciques of that pueblo and its district, unleashing the dogs so that they would bite [the caciques]. Because [the dogs] did bite them, the caciques and natives of those pueblos and provinces rose up and rebelled. [Vázquez de Coronado and his captains] again made war, destroying and burning many of the pueblos. In others, fortifications were made in the way they do in that province. Being at peace, they turned to war and are so now. For this reason the natives killed many Spaniards and the whole army was on the verge of perishing. In addition to that, [the general and his captains] killed many of the natives by fire and sword.

Item: Furthermore, when the general went farther on, continuing his journey and travels, he managed to [reach] the province of Quivira. And he took with him an Indian called El Turco as interpreter and guide. Although he discovered that the province was very wealthy, well-populated, and produced foodstuffs abundantly and, although its natives came out to him in peace, giving provisions to all the people of the army, he ordered that the guide be killed, without any reason or justification. [Even if] he should have done that, the punishment ought to have been carried out in public and not in secret, as it was.

Item: Although those provinces were well-populated and abundantly supplied with foodstuffs and numerous [8r] wild cattle and although he could have settled them, not only did he not do so, but he hindered and prevented some Spaniards who wanted to settle there. He did so, and they left those provinces abandoned and deserted, stirred up and at war. And he had used up and consumed all the fittings, trade goods, munitions, and arms provided to him for war.

In all these ways Francisco Vázquez de Coronado and his captains have perpetrated and committed serious offenses. Therefore the fiscal was requesting and did request that our judge [of the audiencia] (also our judge by commission, who had conducted the investigation of these matters) order that legal proceedings be instituted against them [as a group] and against any of them [individually] who seem[ed] responsible. And he requested that the judge institute such proceedings, sentencing those individuals to the heaviest and most serious penalties, both civil and criminal, provided by law in such a case, ordering that they be carried out against their persons and property. This was so that these offenses not go unpunished.

In addition to all this, he asked that justice be carried out [and that] costs [be assessed]. And he presented the investigation record.

When the aforementioned [investigation record] was received and accepted by our [audiencia] judge and judge by commission, he ordered that a copy of all of it be provided to Francisco Vázquez de Coronado and that at the first [session of] the audiencia he make his counter statements and assertions concerning it, stating before our judge his opinion and whether he concurred with the investigation.

[Vázquez de Coronado] presented before the judge written justifications which [8v] stated that the indictment against him was not proper because he had not committed any offense or done anything wrong or failed to do anything that was possible to do in fulfillment of our royal service. Furthermore, in the expedition he did everything that was possible (or would have been possible for any person) with complete willingness and loyalty in the service of ourselves and God Our Lord. This was true both in managing and governing the army and doing everything he had been enjoined and directed to do by our royal orders and instructions, as well as in exposing his person to the dangers of battle when that was necessary, in enduring hunger and hardships, and in doing what he should in all things.

Because of this, not only does he not deserve to be penalized, but his labors and good service are worthy of remuneration, which he was expecting from us when we were informed of the truth and the indictment was answered. He said that he ought to be released and set at liberty and exonerated for the following reasons.

[This is] because, for one thing, the accusation was not filed by the correct party nor against the guilty party. It was not filed within the time limit, and its form was erroneous and faulty. It failed to follow the method and formalities of law. Further, it was not accurate in its narration [of events]. And [Vázquez de Coronado] denied [the accusation] in exactly the same manner and form followed in it, [to wit]:

Regarding the first charge of the indictment, the gist of which was [9r] that when the natives of the province of Chiametla were at peace he had ordered a number of Indians hung and quartered without any reason, he said that the point cannot and should not be pursued against him. This is because in the residencia of the office he held as governor of that province, which was conducted by our order, charges were levelled concerning this [matter] and he was exonerated of them. The residencia having once been conducted and the period during which he had been compelled [to stand accountable] having passed and the residencia being completed, he is not obliged to go through it again. He asked that it be decided thus in regard to this charge.

In case he was required to respond [to the charge], and not otherwise, he stated that what really and in fact transpired with regard to what is referred to in the charge is that when he, Francisco Vázquez de Coronado, went in our royal name to govern the province of Nueva Galicia, the province of Chiametla was at war. And in the province of Culiacán were many towns that had risen up and rebelled. The cause of this had been an Indian named Ayapín who had been leading and persuading the natives of those towns to rise up and rebel. Seeing that it would be conducive to our service and that of [God] Our Lord to apply the necessary countermeasure in all haste, [Vázquez de Coronado] went personally to apply it. Passing through the province of Chiametla, he found that the natives there had risen up and rebelled. In order [9v] to pacify them and bring them to our holy Catholic faith and to our service and dominion, he dispatched some of the horsemen who had gone with him. One of those among them was the maestre de campo of the army Lope de Samaniego, who went with him to deliver the necessary requerimientos.

Since the natives came out in war against him and wounded many people, some of them were seized and imprisoned. Not only did he not harm [the prisoners] or order them harmed, but rather he had [them] treated benevolently. He had them given clothing and clothed them and had them spoken to through interpreters, saying to [the prisoners] that they should tell the Indians of that province that they would be brought to our holy Catholic faith and under our royal dominion. And the interpreters assured them that they would not suffer any mistreatment. The native [prisoners] went to tell and explain this message to the rest of the people of the province who were up in arms. Having delivered the requerimiento to [the prisoners], Lope de Samaniego and the others who went with him sent that message.

Not only were the natives unwilling to come to peace, but they came against [the Spaniards] in war and killed the maestre de campo and many other people and worked much harm. In order to continue the expedition, it was appropriate for [Vázquez de Coronado] to go in person (as he did). He pacified the province and administered justice to some of the Indians who were [10r] unconditionally guilty of what has been related. This [the Spaniards] did with much moderation and with the least injury that could be done. In this regard he did not commit any offense that he could be accused of.

With regard to the second charge in the indictment, he said that it should not be pursued against him because he was without responsibility for what he was accused of. [This is] because when he passed through the valley of Corazones, it was populated and he was told and was aware that there was a large number of Indians in its territory. With discussion, consultation, and agreement, it seemed conducive to bringing its natives to knowledge of our holy Catholic faith and under our royal dominion and conducive to establishment and preservation of the land, to establish a town of Spaniards there and to attract the natives to knowledge of God Our Lord and our holy Catholic faith and to maintain them in it. With that intention and the understanding that it was fitting, he ordered that a town be settled there and appointed Melchor Díaz as its captain and alcalde mayor. He [was] a very upright individual with high intelligence and understanding, a good Christian, competent and suitable for that office, and a man very experienced in matters of war, a prudent person very mindful of the conversion and welfare of the natives.

At the time that [Vázquez de Coronado] ordered this, Díaz did everything that was and seemed appropriate and useful. If afterwards [10v] the Indians rose up in arms, it was not by his fault. This is particularly true since at the time that the natives of the town were said to have risen up in arms and depopulated it, [Vázquez de Coronado] was absent and more than three hundred leagues farther in the interior of the land.

In the third charge he was accused as follows. When he arrived in the province of Cíbola, the people of the principal pueblo came out in peace and provided what was needed. Without cause, he made war on them and burned the pueblo, and many people died. For this reason many people of the province rose up in arms. Regarding this charge, he said that he was not at fault and that what really happened was that from the province of Culiacán he went in advance with part of the army. When he had arrived and established camp about three leagues from the province of Cíbola, without having given them any cause, its natives came in war against the maestre de campo of the army don García López, who was half a league ahead of the general, guarding a passage. [Vázquez de Coronado], who was to the west, ordered him to do so. And if he had not had the foresight to have it guarded, the army would have been severely hurt [since] the natives who were at war attacked them at night, shooting arrows at them and wounding some horses.

He denied that he had been aware of [the likelihood of attack], so that he could have taken preventive measures. He was traveling with his men and sent in advance some clerics and the maestre de campo (and a scribe with them), in order to deliver the requerimiento to the natives, telling them to come [11r] in peace and to render obedience to us. And telling them that if they did so, they would not experience ill-treatment. [Vázquez de Coronado] had gone ahead and joined the friars. By means of signs and the language of interpreters, they delivered the necessary requerimientos to them many times. [This was] in keeping with what we have decided and ordered in this regard.

While they were delivering the requerimientos the natives shot arrows and wounded many people and horses of the army. Among those they shot was fray Luis, one of the ecclesiastics who delivered the requerimientos. For this reason it was fitting to attack them in war. Which they did and captured the first pueblo. The general came out of the battle that was joined with three serious wounds in the face and other blows, wounds, and bruises. Even with all the abuse that he and the rest of the men suffered, he did not commit or allow to be committed any brutality against the native Indians. Neither were they set afire, as was said by the opposing party. Rather, [the Spaniards] treated them benevolently. And he ordered that they be treated thus. By attracting them through kind [treatment], the whole province came to peace and rendered obedience to us.

As to the fourth charge he was accused of, he said that likewise he was without guilt for what is referred to in it. [That is] because during the whole time that the natives were [11v] at peace and obedient to us they were well treated and aided until they agreed and arranged among themselves to rise up and rebel and put [that plan] into effect, taking up arms and rebelling. One night they shot forty or so horses, mules, and beasts of burden with arrows and killed some of the Indian allies that the general took with him. When they had risen in arms, rebelled, and fortified themselves in the pueblos, [Vázquez de Coronado] sent many times to have the requerimiento delivered, saying that they should return to peace and to obedience to us, assuring them and certifying to them that, if they did so, they would be forgiven and treated in a kindly manner. And, further, that no hurt or harm would be done to them. Otherwise, war would be waged against them with full severity. This they were made to understand thoroughly by means of the language of interpreters.

But the natives refused to come to peace and render obedience to us. Seeing their rebellion and with the considered advice and agreement of the clerics, our officials, and other persons, it was [deemed] appropriate to make war against them. And [the general] did that with the least amount of injury he could possibly do and without doing anything improper. Because of this he was not at fault in any way.

In regard to this charge and the rest he was accused of in the fifth particular of the indictment, he said that he ought to be set free and exonerated of what is referred to in it [12r]. [This is] because he was not guilty of anything related therein since the Indian called Turco, while guiding the army, led it deceptively with false words, saying that he knew a very wealthy and populous land and would guide [the Spaniards] to it. With these lies and deceits he led the army through unpopulated places, because of which all of its members were in great danger and suffered extreme want, hunger, and thirst. The Indian called Turco did this falsely and deceitfully, so that all the people of the army would die and perish from hunger and thirst.

When the lies, deceits, and untruths of that Indian became publicly known and he was asked for the truth, without any compulsion [Turco] admitted having led the army deceitfully by way of those places, so that the people would perish and die. This was well known. Further, it was ascertained and shown that this Indian told and persuaded the natives of the province of Quivira to kill the horses, pointing out to them the best ones. And he told them that when the horses were killed, they could easily kill the Spaniards, who were few in number.

When this had come to [the general's] attention and he saw that it would be well to apply a countermeasure in regard to this [situation], he ordered Diego López, who at the time was maestre de campo, to investigate fully what had taken place in this regard, [12v] in order to administer justice. It is well known that, having made investigation and inquiry and come to a conclusion, he, as maestre de campo, ordered that justice be carried out against that Indian. And it seemed to him that the punishment should be secret because he was a native of that province, as [indeed] he was. Also so that the rest of the natives would not rise up.

Although [Vázquez de Coronado] did not specifically order [Turco] killed, he did direct the maestre de campo to ascertain the truth, in order to administer justice. And after the deed, it seemed to him, judging by the report and record of investigation which had been conducted, that the maestre de campo had done what was fitting. [That is] because by his falsehood and deceit the Indian fully deserved the death that was meted out, both as his punishment and to avoid severe harm that could have occurred to the army.

Because he could not help but find the Indian deceitful and treacherous and because he was aware of the matters and details concerning [Turco] and the counsel he could have given the enemy, [Vázquez de Coronado] was not guilty of what was referred to in the fifth charge.

With regard to the remainder of what he was accused (namely, that although he found many populous lands productive of food, not only did he not have them settled but he would not have others do it who wanted to and because of this those lands were left and remained up in arms and at war), he said that he was not guilty of what was referred to in the charge.

The reason why [13r] he did not settle those provinces or have them settled was that they were not such as the opposing party said [they were], since he had no chance to maintain or sustain the people [of the army] there. Nor would it have benefitted or increased our royal patrimony, because some of those lands were too cold and infertile, while others had very few people and foodstuffs. In the region where the wild cattle were found, the lands were uninhabited and there were no people there except for some Indian hunters. In a space of three hundred leagues of unsettled land through which the general had traveled, not even three hundred men were found.

With the intention and desire to settle [the land] and to increase and augment our royal patrimony, seeing that in the entire distance that he traveled he found no land that had the [requisite] qualities and was suitable for settlement, [the general] sent captains with men through many and various regions with instructions that they locate lands that could be settled. They went, but did not find lands suitable to that purpose; nor did they hear of ones that were, notwithstanding having [13v] travelled more than five hundred leagues beyond Cíbola (which was the land that fray Marcos de Niza told about).

The army had to traverse that distance, travelling always through wilderness and unpopulated lands, most of which were infertile. Both [the general] and the rest of the people who went with him suffered many severe trials there, [including] hunger and thirst. If they had any foodstuffs, it was those that the people of the army carried on their shoulders. There was always such a great lack of food that he and the entire army consumed corn by ounces. They never found a land where it seemed to him possible to settle or sustain [themselves] or to increase our royal patrimony. This [is clear] since, to aid [him he took] to Quivira only about thirty-five or forty men, who suffered much want for lack of foodstuffs and particularly since no one ever asked him to settle there, saying that they wanted to. Nor were they disposed to do so.

Instead, he was always being asked the opposite. They said that since no land that could be settled had been found and the people of the army were dying, he ought to take the return route to Nueva España.

He saw that the army had traveled and wandered for a long time [14r] and he personally had journeyed a thousand leagues from the city of Mexico (from which he had departed), without counting the many additional leagues traveled by his captains, reconnoitering on his orders. And he saw that many horses had died and were dying every day and that the people of the army were falling ill without relief for either body or soul because they had neither physician nor priest, all of whom had returned. Further, he saw that the army was shrinking every day and would continue to do so. For these reasons he turned around: in order that the people not die and actually, in the course of the expedition, he had done everything that was possible, both in our service and that of God Our Lord.

He said that he was not guilty nor did he deserve punishment. On the contrary, he deserved to be recompensed and repaid for the great expenditures he had incurred and the serious troubles he had suffered in our service during the expedition. Despite them, the outcome and result he desired was not obtained, which was not because of him nor his fault.

Therefore, he made petition, asking that our fiscal be removed from the case, that his indictment be declared defective and erroneous, and that the petition against him be denied. Further, he asked, that it be declared that he did not perpetrate or commit any offense, that he be absolved and set free, and that he be acquitted of everything of which he was accused. In addition, he asked that it be stated that he was a good general [14v] and captain of ours and that, as such, he should be recompensed and rewarded for his services by being entrusted with offices and affairs pertaining to our royal service. Above all what he asked for was the fulfillment of justice, with costs.

In this regard, the legal action was summarized. When it had been reviewed by our oidor and judge by commission, he decided and decreed this in the decision. For this, in fact, he received evidence from the parties in a specified form and within a specified period. Within that period both parties prepared their affidavits and presented them before our oidor.

The affidavit prepared on behalf of Francisco Vázquez de Coronado showed (and it was confirmed by numerous witnesses) that our viceroy and president and oidores of our audiencia of Nueva España had selected and named him as captain general of the armed force that was sent, in our royal service, to the newly discovered lands of Cíbola to subdue and pacify them and for the safety and assistance of the natives and the ecclesiastics who went to work toward the conversion of the natives of those provinces, because Francisco Vázquez is a gentleman, an hidalgo, and a [15r] trustworthy and moral person. In him the qualities needed for similar duties came together. He had served us in other offices and duties and at the time was serving us as governor of Nueva Galicia.

For this expedition and journey he sold much of his goods and estate and indebted himself for a large amount of gold pesos, arms, horses, Blacks, pack mules, and other appurtenances necessary for it. And also for many henchmen whom he took with him well armed, mounted, and equipped for war. In all of this he had expended great sums of gold pesos. And he still remained obligated and indebted.

It was shown that at the time he acceded to this office, he was married and had his house and seat and his wife in the city of Mexico. And he also had very good estates and income from sales of produce.

Further, it was shown that during the entire time he held office he kept the army well regulated and in order, maintaining in it very excellent watchfulness, vigilance, and order for war. And he was always loved, revered, and held [in high regard], as well as obeyed, by the people of the army. Among other measures he took in that journey and subjugation was that he required and ordered especially that all the individuals of the army live like good Christians. He imposed very large penalties in order to prevent blasphemy against God Our Lord; Our Lady, his glorious mother; and the saints; as well as to prevent cohabitation [15v] and other public sins. He investigated them and ordered them investigated and found out [what had occurred], in order to punish and remedy them. And when anything was presented because of these public warnings and came to his notice, [Vázquez de Coronado] took the necessary corrective action.

He was especially careful to order that all the natives of the lands through which [the army] traveled be treated very benevolently, under severe penalties. He also ordered that nothing belonging to the natives be taken from them against their will and without paying for them and that no other mistreatment be perpetrated against them. He ordered and had proclaimed many very good ordinances, both about this and about other things concerning our service and that of God Our Lord and about the welfare of the army and of the natives. And those ordinances were adhered to. When it came to [the general's] attention that they had been broken, he punished those [who had offended], or ordered them punished.

It was shown that, if in the region of the valley of Corazones the natives of some places rose up and rebelled, it was not his fault or because of him. [That is] because at that time he was in a land far in the interior. Further, at all times the natives of the provinces through which he traveled were at peace, obedient, and subject to our royal control. And they were treated benevolently and aided by [Vázquez de Coronado] and by the captains and men of the army. Whenever any of [the natives] rebelled, the necessary requerimientos were delivered to them through the language of interpreters.

If punishment was carried out against Turco by the maestre de campo, it was because of many deceptions and acts of treachery he perpetrated and [16r] committed. Through these acts he placed the army in [a situation of] want and hunger, as a result of which all the people might have perished (as experience has shown). The punishment inflicted was conducive to our royal service and the welfare of the army.

If [Vázquez de Coronado] did not settle anywhere in those areas, lands, and provinces through which he travelled, it was because he did not find a land to settle and in which to support the people of the army. [That is] because some lands were unsettled by people and other were uninhabitable, being very cold and sterile, lacking foodstuffs, and being [otherwise] unsuitable for this purpose.

Nevertheless, with a desire to settle and to increase our royal patrimony, [Vázquez de Coronado] sent captains with men through many regions in order to locate some lands that could be settled. Also, he himself went beyond the province of Cíbola more than five hundred leagues, passing through more unsettled areas and uninhabitable lands. But no land [suitable for settlement] came to his notice.

Because the friars had returned, the army went on without a priest to whom the people could confess when they reached the dire straits of hunger and sickness. Since the army had neither ecclesiastic nor priest, many individuals died without confession and without protection because of a similar lack of [16v] doctors and medicines.

For these reasons it was necessary that the army return to Nueva España as it did, since it was certain that, having come to such straits, all its people would perish, having arrived at a state in which [the general] and all the rest were eating bread by the ounce.

Furthermore, Francisco Vázquez recorded that in the labors of war, vigilance, making expeditions, and other things of war, he had exposed himself to these troubles and those of the battles that occurred, putting himself in the lead. Because of this he was badly wounded and hurt many times. He always adhered to and fulfilled our royal instructions that contain our orders that the captains who go to reconnoiter and subdue regions in our Indies and new lands must adhere to. Likewise, he saw to it that the rest of the captains of the army abided by them, having the [instructions] read [out] for this purpose.

In none of the expeditions, conquests, or reconnaissances that were made in those provinces was any native made a prisoner or branded, even though they made war and refused to offer obedience to us after having been admonished to do so in conformance with our instructions and although some of them rebelled and committed serious offenses after having rendered obedience.

Furthermore, neither [Vázquez de Coronado] nor his captains that he sent for the purpose of locating lands and populated places ever found [suitable] places. And since then [17r] no information about such places has been received.

The natives rendered obedience to us and remained obedient.

Although it has been the custom in making reconnaissance for lands, both in Nueva España and in the islands and mainland [South America], to transport arms, artillery, munitions, and other necessary things on the backs of Indians, in this expedition Vázquez de Coronado never agreed to load the Indians with any of these things, since the artillery was carried by beasts of burden and the people of the army carried the rest on their horses.

Since in all of the extent of lands and provinces traversed in the course of the expedition land suitable to permit settlement and to augment our royal patrimony was not found, the captains and soldiers of the army asked and petitioned the general many times to bring them and return to Nueva España. They said that there they would be able to be of more service and there was better equipment for that. For this reason he came at length with the army [from] that province.

The statement referred to here, [made] on behalf of Francisco Vázquez de Coronado, and the one [made] on behalf of our fiscal were ordered published by our oidor, and they were so published. Likewise, a number of testimonies and declarations signed by our scribe Hernando Bermejo were presented on behalf of Francisco Vázquez. In them it is recorded and it appears that the captains and alférez of the army (having sufficient powers of attorney for themselves and the rest of the people and soldiers) stated before the aforesaid scribe [17v] that they had petitioned and requested many different times that general Francisco Vázquez de Coronado bring and lead the army by the return route to Nueva España, whence it had set out. This was because it was lacking the foodstuffs necessary to sustain human life. Further, the [people] lacked ecclesiastics and ministers who would conduct holy religious services for them and administer the sacraments necessary for their souls, as well as the paraphernalia for doing so. Also because the army was in danger and in such a state that it might be lost, as well as for many other reasons that they stated and alleged in these declarations.

In response, a number of reasons and justifications conducive to our service and that of God Our Lord were presented on behalf of Francisco Vázquez. And still other statements and declarations concerning this matter were made by the same individuals, in which they stated that it was fitting that the army had returned to Nueva España since, they said, here there was more equipment with which we could be served than there was in those lands and provinces where they were and had traveled. This was the same as what was contained at greater length in the statements previously mentioned. Our oidor ordered that a copy of them be provided to our fiscal, on whose behalf it was declared [18r] and stated [to be] thoroughly proven. And in addition to that, the aforesaid legal proceeding was summarized.

With things in this state, our oidor issued a finding in which he stated in fact that, in keeping with what he had been ordered by us in our decree and commission (included herein), he was sending and did forward the case to our president and oidores of our audiencia. The record of the action was brought before them and presented. When they had reviewed it, together with all the records and merits of the case, they delivered and handed down a definitive decision in the case, the substance of which follows.

Item: In the criminal proceedings involving Cristóbal de Benavente (His Majesty's fiscal of the Royal Audiencia), as one party, and Francisco Vázquez de Coronado (formerly his majesty's governor of the province of Nueva Galicia and formerly named and designated as captain general of the province of Cíbola and the newly discovered land) and his attorney on his behalf, as the other party, having considered the records and merits of the case, we find that the fiscal licenciado Benavente has not proven the indictment and charges he lodged against Francisco Vázquez de Coronado for offenses he claimed the general committed and perpetrated [18v] in that newly discovered land. We decide and proclaim that they were not proven. Francisco Vázquez de Coronado has proven his defenses and rebuttals. We decide and proclaim that they have been fully proven. Therefore, we must and do absolve Francisco Vázquez of everything he has been and is accused of in this case by the fiscal. And we impose permanent silence on the fiscal, so that neither now nor in the future may he make any petition or lodge any complaint regarding anything dealt with in this case and by our final judgment. Finding it thus, we order and proclaim it.

don Antonio de Mendoza
licenciado Tello de Sandoval
licenciado Ceynos
licenciado Tejada
licenciado Santillán

This decision was rendered and proclaimed by the lords president and judges in public court in the city of Mexico on the nineteenth day of the month of February last year, one thousand five hundred and forty-six, in the presence of our fiscal. It was read to him and to the attorney for Francisco Vázquez in person. The decision was not appealed by either of the parties.

Shortly thereafter Francisco Vázquez de Coronado appeared before our president and oidores and petitioned and asked that, since the decision had not been appealed and stood as a settled determination, we order that he be issued [19r] our final judgment, so that it would be fulfilled and sustained. In addition to this he asked that we grant whatever would be our will.

Having reviewed [the petition], our president and oidores were agreed that we should order this letter delivered to you our justices for the reason [stated]. And we considered it well [to do so] (both the document itself and the signed copy, as it is said).

We order each and every one of you, in your posts and jurisdictions, to treat the definitive decision that was proclaimed and ordered by our president and oidores in the case between the parties regarding the aforesaid as proclaimed and ordered likewise by this, our final judgment. Further, you are ordered to sustain and fulfill it and to have it sustained and fulfilled completely and by all persons exactly as it is written. And at no time are you to go or proceed against its content or contrary to its form; nor are you to permit it to be contravened in any way. And none of you (neither some nor others) are to emend it under penalty of [withdrawal] of our favor and of two hundred gold pesos each [to be paid] to our council and treasury. Furthermore, we order [any] man to whom you show our final judgment and whom you summon, to appear in our audiencia before our president and oidores within thirty days from the date you issue the summons, under the aforesaid penalty. Under this penalty we order whatsoever public scribe who may be called for this purpose to show you testimony to which his sign is affixed, so that we may know [19v] in that way that our order is fulfilled.

Issued in the city of Mexico on the twentieth day of the month of December in the year of the birth of our savior Jesus Christ one thousand five hundred and forth-seven. I, Antonio de Turcios, chief scribe of the Audiencia and Royal Chancery of Nueva España and of its government for His Majesty, had this written by his order. Registered with the agreement of its president and oidores.

Pedro de Requena, for Chancellor Pedro López.
don Antonio de Mendoza
licenciado Tejada
licenciado Santillán
doctor Quesada

Item: This copy was made and extracted from the original final decision on file in the city of Mexico on the twenty-sixth day of the month of November in the year of the birth of our savior Jesus Christ one thousand five hundred and fifty-one. I, Antonio de Turcios, chief scribe of the audiencia of Nueva España and of its government for His Majesty, had this copy made at the request of Governor Francisco Vázquez de Coronado and at the direction of the president and oidores of the Royal Audiencia. For this purpose I state that the copy is necessary. In order to insure its correctness, these witnesses saw it corrected and reconciled: Agustín Pinto and Andrés Pérez, residents of this city.

Certifying this and in testimony of its truth, I affix my sign, which is thus {sign}.

Antonio de Turcios

A TRANSCRIPT
OF THE DECISIONS

Sentencia Definitiva[5]

[fol. 125r cont'd]

de la qual d*e la* ACusaçion fue mandado dar traslado al d*i*cho / Fran*ci*sco Vazquez el qual R*e*spondio A ella çiertas causas por don- / de pidio ser dado por libre y las p*ar*tes Fueron rresçibidas / Aprueba Con çierto termi*n*o dentro del q*ua*l hizieron çiertas / probanças y estando la causa Conclusa en difinitiVa el d*i*cho / señor liçençiado tejada rremityo el d*i*cho pleyto a la d*i*cha / Real audiençia y vista por los señores *presidente* E oydor*e*s de *e*lla / dieron E pr*o*nunçiaron En ella senty*n*çia difinitiVa su tenor de la / qual es este q*ue* se sigue

En el pleyto criminal que entre p*ar*t*e*s de la una el liçençiado *cristo*bal de / bena Vente fisCal por su mag*estad* En el rreal aud*iencia* E de la otra Fran*ci*sco Vazq*uez* / de Coronado gov*ernad*or q*ue* fue por su mag*estad* en la provinçia de la nueva galizia / e Capitan general q*ue* fue pr*o*Veydo y nonbrado para la provinçia de / Çibola y tierra nuevamente desqubierta E su pr*ocurad*or en su *nombr*e / FFallamos Atentos los autos y meritos de *e*ste pr*o*çeso que el d*i*cho liç*encia*do / benavente fiscal no probo su ACusaçion E Capitulos que dio contra el d*i*cho / Fran*ci*sco Vazquez de Coronado de los delitos que dixo *h*Aber hecho y Cometido

[fol. 125v]

En la d*i*cha tierra nuevamente desqubierta Damos los y pronun- / Çiamos por no probados E que el d*i*cho Fran*ci*sco Vazquez de Coronado / probo sus (h)exe(b)*p*çiones E defensiones damos las y pronunçiamos / las por bien probadas por ende que devemos a*b*solVer y a*b*solVemos / al d*i*cho Fran*ci*sco Vazquez de todo lo q*ue* En esta causa *h*a sido y es A- / Cusado por el d*i*cho Fiscal al qual ponemos perpetuo silençio p*ar*a / que agora ni de aqui Adelante sobre Razon de lo En ella conteni- / do no le pueda pedir ni aCusar Cosa alguna y por esta nuestra sentyncia difiniti- / Va juzgando Asy lo mandamos y pronunçiamos don antonio / de mendoça El liçençiado tello de sandoVal El liçençiado çey- / nos El liçençiado Tejada El liçençiado santillan

Dada y pronunciada Fue esta dicha sentyncia por los dichos señores / presidente E oydores Estando en publica audiençia Viernes / diez y nueve dias del mes de hebrero de myll E quinientos E quaren- / ta E seys Años En haz del fizcal E de Francisco Ramirez / procurador del dicho Governador a los quales Se les notifico / Antonio de turçios

En la çiudad de mexico treynta e Un dias del mes de março de myll e quynientos / E quarenta E siete años yo antonio de turçios escribano mayor de la aUdiencia / e chançilleria Real de la nueVa españa E govierno de ella por su magestad de mandamyento / del muy magnifico señor El liçençiado Francisco tello de sandoVaL del Consejo Real / de las yndias de su magestad E su Visytador en la dicha Real aUdiencia del / dicho proçeSo original que queda en my poder (F)hize dar lo suSo- / dicho por quanto dixo que (h)era nesçesario para la Visyta / que hAbia tomado testigos que lo Vieron corregir E conçertar / Juan munoz e pedro de Requena escribanos E martyn de olid

E Yo eL dicho Antonio de turçios escribano suSodicho que Fuy con los dichos / testigos a lo Ver corregir E conçertar E por / ende (F)hize Aqui este myo signo que (a)tal (F)hecho / Esta Signo de oFicio / {sign} / antonio de turçios [rubrica] / [no number]

[fol. 126r]
[blank]

[fol. 126v]
[blank]

Carta Executoria[6]

[fol. 5v]

[. . .] Por Virtud de / la q*ual* di*c*ha nuestra ca*r*ta y ProVision rre- / al suso*en*-
CorPorada y en cunplimy*ento* de ella / Pareçe q*ue* *e*l di*c*ho lic*enci*ado teJada
nu*est*ro oydor por / ante P*ed*ro de Requena n*uest*ro es*c*rivano a*Ç*er- / ca de lo
en ella contenydo hizo y to- / mo Çierta ynFormaçion de testigos / ansi en la
di*c*ha ÇiUdad de mexico como *en* la / ÇiUdad de guadalajara de la di*c*ha
nueVa / GaliZia la qual Por el Vista y la ConFision / que çerca de *e*llo
ansimysmo tomo al di*c*ho / Fran*cis*co Vazques de Coronado ma*n*do al
susodi*c*ho q*ue* / dentro de ÇinCuenta Dias Primeros siguy- / entes se Pre-
sentase P*er*(e)sonalm*ente* *en* la / di*c*ha aUdienÇia de mexico ante *e*l Presiden-
/ te e oydores de la di*c*ha n*uest*ra aUdienÇia q*ue* / en ella Reside y ansi Presentado tuViese por / car*Ç*el la q*ue* *e*llos le señalsen y no la q*ue*bran- / tase en
manera alguna so Pena de myll / Pesos de oro de mynas Para la n*uest*ra cama-
/ ra e Fisco la q*ual* Pareçe q*ue* Fue notiFicado / al di*c*ho Fran*cis*co Vazques de
coronado y en / cunplimy*ento* de *e*llo se presento P*er*(e)sonalmen- / te *en* la
di*c*ha aUdienÇia ante los di*c*hos / n*uest*ro Presidente e oydores desPues de / v

[fol. 6r]

Lo q*ual* Por el di*c*ho lic*enci*ado teJada n*uest*ro oydor Fue / mand*a*do al di*c*ho
Fran*cis*co Vazques de Coronado que / tuViese su casa por Car*Ç*el en Razon
de lo suso- / di*c*ho y no saliese de *e*lla ny la q*ue*brantase / sin su liçenÇia y
mandado so la di*c*ha pena / y que se diese la di*c*ha ynFormaçion al di*c*ho /
liÇinçiado *cristo*bal de benaVente n*uest*ro Fis- / cal que ante(l) el Pusiese el
aCusa- / çion al di*c*ho Fran*cis*co Vazques de aqu*e*llo que por / ella contra el
Resultaba y por lo dem*a*S / que Viese que a n*uest*ro serViçio y a la exe- /
cuçion de la n*uest*ra Justiçia conViene pa- / ra que ansi Puesta el le oyese e
ReÇibie- / se sus descargos y lo Remytiese a la di*c*ha / n*uest*ra aUdienÇia
como Por nos le *e*sta- / ba mandado Por la di*c*ha n*uest*ra carta E / ProVision
lo qual Pareçe q*ue* Fue noti- / FiCado al di*c*ho Fran*cis*co Vazques de Corona-
/ do desPues de lo qual a Veynti- / Un dias del mes de mar*Ç*o del año /
Pasad*o* de myll y quy*nient*os y quarenta y ÇinCo / años *en* Conplimy*ento* de

lo susod*i*cho el d*i*cho n*uest*ro / Fiscal Pareçio ante *e*l d*i*cho lic*encia*do teJada n*uest*ro / oydor y Por Un escrito que ante *e*l / Presento dixo que aCusaba e aCuso cri- / mynalm*e*nte al d*i*cho Fran*ci*sco Vazques de Corona- / do y contando el caso de la d*i*cha (^n*uest*ra) aCusa- / Çion Pr(o)*e*suPuestas las solemnydades del / {ojo} / d*e*rec*h*o (dixo que aCusaba e aCuso crimynalm*e*nte al d*i*cho / Fran*ci*sco Vazques de Coronado y Contando el caso / de la d*i*cha acusaçion PresuPuestas) / v

[fol. 6v]
(las solem*n*ydades del d*e*rec*h*o) dizia q*ue* ansi era que *h*abien- / do sido nonbrado ansi Por n*uest*ro Viso- / Rey como Por la d*i*cha n*uest*ra aUdienÇia de / la d*i*cha nueVa esPana Por caPitan / General de la tierra nueVamente des- / qubierta y Provinçia de Çibola y *h*abiendo- / le sido dadas n*uest*ras Reales Provisiones / e yn*s*truyÇiones Para descubrir y pa- / ÇiFicar y Poblar lo que ansi desqubri- / ese de las d*i*chas ProVinÇias hazia el Ponyen- / te y la orden que *h*abia de tener en hazer- / leS la (^caUsa) Guerra y Reduzirlos y atra- / erlos a conoÇimy*ent*o de n*uest*ra santa Fee ca- / tolica E a n*uest*ro rreal domynio E sub(^se)jeçion / {ojo} / E *h*abiendo lleVado Para ello exerÇito de / mas de dozientos *h*onbres de Caballo y otra / mu(n)cha Gente de Pie bien armada y / ProVeyda de lo neçesario Para E- / Fe*c*tuar el d*i*cho ViaJe el d*i*cho Fran*ci*sco Vazques / de Coronado Vinyendo contra lo que le / *h*abia sido cometido y mandado por las / d*i*chas n*uest*ras Reales cartas y ProVisiones / e ynStruyçiones *en* *e*l d*i*cho ViaJe *h*abia (f)*h*ec*h*o / y P*er*(e)P(r)etrado ansi el como sus capita- / nes y tenyentes Por su m*anda*do los delitos / siGuyentes Primeram*e*nte *en* la ProVin- / Çia de chiametla sin caUsa ny Razon / alGuna a lo menos que leGitima Fuese / Estando los naturales de *e*lla de paz *h*abia / tomado ocho yndios e yndias Poco / vj

[fol. 7r]
mas o menos e a los Unos *h*abia ahorCado y los otros / hecho quartos yten que *h*abiendo Poblado / Una Villa d*e* esPaño*l*es *en* *e*l Valle de los co- / raçones y debiendo dexar en ella Perso- / na de ReCado de ConFiança Para que ad- / mynystrase Justiçia y PaÇiFiCase la d*i*cha / ProVinÇia Por n(^y)o lo *h*aber

(f)*h*echo e CaUsa / de las malas obras e tratamy*ent*os q*ue* la Per- / sona e Personas que a(^y)lli *h*abia dexado *h*abian / {ojo} / hecho a los *dichos* naturales de
la d*ich*a ProVinçia / toda ella se *h*abia Rebelado e *h*abian muerto / mu(n)chos
esPañoleS e Se *h*abia desPoblado la / d*ich*a Villa y alçadose la gente de(l) la
co- / marCa de *e*lla Por *h*aber sido Remyso el d*ich*o / caPitan General e no
*h*aber dexado Perso- / na suFiÇiente que Gobernase la d*ich*a Villa y / Gente
de *e*lla yten que llegando que *h*a- / bia llegado el d*ich*o exerÇito y gente de la
/ (la) ProVinÇia de Çibola los naturales de la / cabeçera de *e*lla les *h*abian
salido de paz dando- / les comyda y mantinymy*ent*os neçesarios y el / d*ich*o
Franc*is*co Vazques sin caUsa q*ue* ligitima / Fuese y sus caPitanes les *h*abian
(c)hecho / GueRa y quemado el Pueblo y muer- / to mu(n)cha gente Por la
qual mu(n)cha / Parte de la d*ich*a ProVinÇia e gente de / *e*lla se *h*abia Rebelado y alçado yten yendo / el d*ich*o General y pasando sesenta o setenta /
leGuas adelante lleGado a la ProVinçia de / tiGuex y estando muy poblado
de gente y bas- / timentos y mu(n)chos ediFiçios hechos / a modo de *e*sPana
le *h*abian salido los / vj

[fol. 7v]
(los) naturales de *e*lla de paz y dado(^s) (no) nos la obidi- / enÇia y ProVeydo
al d*ich*o exerçito y gente de *e*l / de mu(n)cho mayz y aves y otros mantinymy*ent*os / y estando de paz e sin *h*aber caUsa ligitima el d*ich*o ge- / neral y
sus capitanes por su m*anda*do *h*abian aPeReado los / caçiques del d*ich*o
Pueblo y de las comarCas a el / echandoles los PeRos q*ue* les mordiesen los
qu*a*les / les *h*abian mordido de quya caUsa los d*ich*os caÇiques / y naturales
de los d*ich*os Pueblos y proVinÇias / se *h*abian alçado y Rebelado y para
tornarlos a / (a) hazer guerra de nueVo *h*abian destruydo y que- / mado
mu(n)chos de los d*ich*os Pueblos y en otros / se *h*abian hecho (s)*f*uertes Por
manera q*ue* la d*ich*a Pro- / VinÇia estando de paz se *h*abia Vuelto de guerra
/ y lo estado a el Presente a quya caUsa los d*ich*os / naturales *h*abian muerto
mu(n)chos esPanoles y / *h*abia estado todo el d*ich*o exerÇito a Punto / de se
Perder y sobre *e*llo *h*abian muerto a Fuego y / quchillo mu(n)chos de los
d*ich*os naturales yten / ansimysmo el d*ich*o general Prosiguyendo / su Viaje y
Jornada yendo mas adelante lle- / Gado que *h*obo a la ProVinÇia de quyVira

y lle- / Vando Por lengua y guya a Un yndio que / se dezia el turCo *h*abiendo descubierto la / di*c*ha ProVinçia que era muy RiCa y po- / blada e abundante de mantinymy*en*tos / y saliendole de paz los naturales de *e*lla / y dadoles Pro-Vision Para toda la gen- / te del di*c*ho exerÇito *h*abia mandado matar / a la di*c*ha Guya sin CaUsa ny Razon alguna E / caso q*ue* lo (e) *h*obiera *h*abia de ser el castiGo pu*b*lico / y no secreto como se *h*abia (F)*h*echo yten q*ue* / siendo las di*c*has ProVinçias muy pobladas y a- / bundosas de mantinymy*en*tos y de mu(n)chos ga- / vij

[fol. 8r]

nados de bacas salvaGinas y pudiendo poblar las di*c*has / ProVinçias no solamente no lo *h*abia (f)*h*echo mas al- / Gunos esPanoles que *h*abian querido poblarselo *h*abia es- / torbado y (en)*im*Pedido que lo hiziesen E *h*abia (f)*h*echo e / dexasen des(e)*m*anparadas y despobladas las di*c*has proVin- / Çias y alborotadas y de guerra *h*abiendo consumydo / y gastando todos los adereços ResCates / muniçiones y armas q*ue* le *h*abian sido dados para / la di*c*ha GueRa en todo lo qual el di*c*ho Fran*c*is*c*o Vaz- / ques de Coronado y sus capitanes *h*abian hecho y / cometido graVes delitos Por tanto q*ue* pedia / y Pidio al di*c*ho n*uest*ro oydor e juez de comysion / que *h*abiendo ynFormaçion de lo susodi*c*ho / mandase Proçeder y proçediese contra ellos / y Contra qualquyer de *e*llos q*ue* pareçiesen / qulpados condenandoles *en* las mayores y mas / GraVes Penas ÇeViles y cremynales en / tal Caso en d*erec*ho estableçidas mandandolas / exeCutar en sus Personas y bienes Por- / q*ue* los delitos no quedasen sin castigo sobre to- / do lo qual Pido ser le (f)*h*echo conplimy*en*to de justi- / Çia con las costas y hizo Presenta- / Çion de la di*c*ha ynFormaçion Por el / di*c*ho n*uest*ro oydor tomada y ReÇibida de q*ue* / de suso se haze mynÇion de todo lo qual / Por el di*c*ho n*uest*ro oydor e juez de Comysion Fue / mandado dar traslado al di*c*ho Fran-*c*is*c*o Vazques / de Coronado e que para la Primera aUdiençia / ResPondiese y alegase ÇerCa de *e*llo lo / que Viese q*ue* le conVinyese el qual ProÇeso / ante *e*l di*c*ho n*uest*ro oydor y Presento an- / te *e*l Un escrito de exeCuçiones que / vij

[fol. 8v]

dixo q*ue* la di*c*ha aCusaçion no Proçedia contra el / Porque no solamente no *h*abia acometido delito ny / (f)*h*echo cosa malhecha ny dexado de hazer cosa que cum- / Pliese a n*uest*ro Real serViçio que Fuese posible / hazer pero en la d*i*cha jornada el *h*abia hecho con muy / entera Voluntad y lealtad en serViçio de dios / n*uest*ro señor y n*uest*ro todo aq*ue*llo que en el *h*abia sido y / a otr(o)*a* qualquyer Persona Pudiera / ser posible ansi en el Regir y gobernar el / exerÇito y hazer todo aq*ue*llo q*ue* le *h*abia sido / mandado y encomendado Por n*uest*ras Reales / Pro*v*isiones e ynstruyÇiones como en poner / su Persona a los peligros en la guerra quando *h*a- / bia sido neçesario y pasar hanbres y trabaxos / y hazer en todo lo que debia {//} Por lo qual no so- / lamente no mereçia Pena Pero sus traba- / Jos y buenos serViÇios {//} (^y hazer en todo lo q*ue*) / {ojo} / (^debia) (Por lo qual no solamente no me- / reçia Pena pero sus trabajos y buenos serViçios) / eran di*g*nos de Remuneraçion como de nos lo es- / Peraba siendo ynFormados de la Verdad / y sa(s)ti*s*faziendo a la d*i*cha aCusaçion dezia que / debia de ser (e) suelto y dado Por libre y quyto / Por lo siguyente lo Uno Porq*ue* la d*i*cha acu- / saçion no era Puesta Por parte bastan- / te ny Contra parte culpada ny en tienPo ny en / Forma era errada y defe*c*tuosa y CareÇia / de la orden y solemnydades del d*erech*o y en / su Relaçion no era Verdadera y la negaba segun / y Como Por la Forma y manera que en / ella se contenya y en quanto al primer / capitulo de la d*i*cha aCusaÇion en que se con- / viij

[fol. 9r]

ten*i*a que en la ProVinÇia de chiametla (^ny) sin ca- / Usa alguna estando los naturales de *e*lla de paz / *h*abia mandado ahorCar y hazer quartos Çiertos / yndios dezia q*ue* por el d*i*cho art(r)iCulo no se podia / ny debia Proçeder contra el ny era obligado a Res- / Ponder Porq*ue en* la ResidenÇia que Por n*uest*ro / mandado se le *h*abia tomado del CarGo que *h*abia te- / nydo de Gobernador de la d*i*cha ProVinÇia çer- / ca de *e*llo se le *h*abian hecho cargos y le *h*abia sa(s)ti*s*fe- / cho a ellos *h*abiendo Una Vez (f)*h*echo Residen- / Çia y en el termyno que *h*abia sido obligado aq*ue*l / Pasado y acabada la d*i*cha Resydençia no / era obligado a hazerla otra Vez y ansi Pid*i*o se de- / clarase En quanto al d*i*cho artiCulo y en caso q*ue* / Fuese obligado a ResPonder y no de otra / manera dezia que (*en*) lo que en eFe*c*to de / Realidad (d)e Verdad Pasaba açerca

de lo con- / tenydo En el d*i*cho capitulo era que el tienPo q*ue* / En n*uest*ro Real
nonbre el *h*abia ydo a Gobernar en / la d*i*cha ProVinçia de la nueVa galizia la
d*i*cha / ProVinçia de chiamet(a)l*a* estaba de Guerra / y en la proVinçia de
CuliaCan estaban mu(n)- / chos Pueblos alçados y Rebelados q*ue* la ca- / Usa
de *e*llo *h*abia sido Un yndio nonbrado aya- / Pin el qual andaba conduziendo
e trayendo / a los naturales de los d*i*chos Pueblos a q*ue* / se alçasen y Rebelasen
y Viendo que / al serViçio de n*uest*ro señor y n*uest*ro conVenya po- / ner çerCa
de *e*llo con toda breVedad el re- / medio neçesario el *h*abia ydo en Persona a
po- / nerlo y pasando por la d*i*cha ProVinçia de chi- / ametla *h*abia hallado los
naturales de *e*lla / alçados y Rebelados y para efe*c*to de los / viij

[fol. 9v]
PaÇiFiCar y Red(i)*u*zir a n*uest*ra santa Fee catoli*c*a / y a n*uest*ro serViçio y
senorio *h*abia enViado çier- / ta Gente de a Caballo de los q*ue* Con el yban /
entre los quales *h*abia sido Uno de *e*llos loPe / de samanyeGo maestre de
canpo del d*i*cho / exerÇito q*ue* Con el yba Para q*ue* les hyzie- / se los
Requyrimy*ent*os neçesarios y *h*abiendo / salido a el los d*i*chos naturales de
Guerra y / herido mu(n)cha Gente algunos de ellos *h*a- / bian sido Presos y
se los *h*abian traydo y no / solamente no les *h*abia (f)*h*echo ny m*a*nd*a*do hazer
alg*u*n / mal Pero antes el *h*abia hecho buen trata- / my*ent*o y los *h*abia vestido
y hecho dar Ropa y he- / cho d*ecir* Por lenGuas de ynterPretes / que dixesen
a los yndios de la d*i*cha proVin- / Çia que se Reduxesen a n*uest*ra santa Fee
catoli- / ca y a n*uest*ro Real señorio asegurandolos que / nenGun m*a*l-
tratamy*ent*o les seria hecho y *h*abien- / do ydo los d*i*chos naturales a d*ecir* y
mane- / Festar a los demas de la d*i*cha proVin- / Çia que ansi estaban alçados
el d*i*cho men- / saje y *h*abiendolos Requerido el d*i*cho lope / de samanyeGo y
los demas q*ue* Con el yban *h*an / inviado lo susod*i*cho no solamente no /
*h*abian querido venyr de paz Pero *h*abian venydo / sobre ellos de guerra y
muerto al d*i*cho maestre / de CanPo E a otra mu(n)cha gente y hecho mu(n)-
/ cho daño Para el Remedio de lo qual *h*abia con- / Venydo ProsiGuyendo la
d*i*cha Jornada q*ue* *e*l Fuese / como *h*abia ydo en Persona y paÇiFicado / la
d*i*cha ProVinÇia y (f)*h*echo justiçia de al- / gunos yndios que *en* lo Susod*i*cho
*h*abian / jx

[fol. 10r]

sido muy Culpados lo qual *h*abian (f)*h*echo con muy gran / tenplanÇa y menos daño que *h*abia podido ser / y ÇerCa de *e*llo no *h*abia (f)*h*echo exceso que se le Pudiese / ynputar y en quanto al segundo capitulo de la / d*i*cha aCusaçion dezia que contra el no Proçedia / Porque *e*ra sin culpa de lo q*ue* por el era aCusado / Porq*ue* *e*l tienPo q*ue* *e*L *h*abia Pasado Por el / d*i*cho Valle de los coraçones lo *h*abia hallado / Poblado y *h*abia sido ynFormado y teny- / do notiÇia que en la coma*r*Ca de *e*l *h*abia can- / tidad de yndios e Con aquerdo conseJo e delebera- / çion la *h*abia Pareçido q*ue* para Reduzir los na- / turales de *e*l al conoÇimy*ent*o de n*ues*tra santa Fee catoli- / ca y al n*ues*tro Real domynyo y Fundamento / e Perpetuaçion de la d*i*cha tierra conVenya / que se poblase alli Un Pueblo de *es*Panoles y / que atraxesen los d*i*chos naturales al Conoçimy*ent*o / de dios n*ues*tro señor y de n*ues*tra santa Fee catolica / e los conserVase *en* e(n)lla e Con el d*i*cho ynten- / to y entendiendo que ansi con- Venia *h*abia / ordenado que se poblase alli Una Villa *h*abian / Puesto en ella Por CaPitan alcal(l)d*e* mayor / a Un melchor diaz Persona *h*onRada / y de buena Razon y entendimy*ent*o y buen / cristiano abil y suFiçiente Para el d*i*cho / cargo y *h*onbre muy esPerimentado / *en* las cosas de la guerra y de prud(i)en- / Çia y muy ynclinado a la conVer(sa)Çion / y bien de los natu- rales y al tienpo q*ue* *e*l / *h*abia ordenado lo susod*i*cho *h*abia (F)*h*echo to- / do lo que en el *h*abia sido y le *h*abia pare- / Çido ser Util y ConVinyente y si despues / jx

[fol. 10v]

los d*i*chos yndios se *h*abian alÇado no *h*abia sido / Por su culpa mayormente que al tien- / Po que se d*ez*ia q*ue* los naturales de la d*i*cha / Villa se *h*abian alÇado y (e) *h*abian despoblado el es- / taba aUsente y mas de trezientas leguas la tierra / adentro y en quanto al terçero capitulo en que en eFec- / to era aCu- sado que en lle(a)gando a la provinçia de / Çibola la gente de la Cabeçera la *h*abia salido de paz / y dado lo neçesario e que sin caUsa les *h*abia he- / cho Guerra y quemado el d*i*cho Pueblo y muer- / to mu(n)cha gente a cuya caUsa se *h*abia alÇado mu(n)- / cha gente de la d*i*cha ProVinÇia dezia que / no era en Culpa de lo susod*i*cho y que *en* lo que / Verdad Pasaba era que desde la proVin- / Çia de CuliaCan el se *h*abia adelantado con Çier- / ta Parte del exerÇito y llegado asentar Re- / al tres leguas de la d*i*cha ProVinÇia de Çibola / Poco mas o menos e sin *h*aber dad*o* nynGuna oCa- / sion *h*abian Venydo los naturales de *e*lla de Gue- / Ra sobre don garÇi*a* loPez maestre de Canpo / del d*i*cho exerÇito que *e*staba media legua a- / delante de *e*l guardando Un Paso q*ue* Le(e) *h*abia / mandado que era a *h*esPero e si el no PreVi- / nyera que se Guardara el d*i*cho egerÇito Re- / Çibiera muy Gran dano los naturales / que *e*staban de GueRa *h*abian dado de / noche sobre ellos e los *h*abian Flechado e herido / algunos caballos el neGo como lo *h*abia sabido / Para poner Remedio en ello *h*abia / camynando con su Gente y enViado del(e)*a*n- / te Çiertos Religiosos y al maestr(o)*e* de*l* d*i*cho / canPo y Con ellos Un escribano para q*ue* / Requyriesen a los d*i*chos naturales que Vinye- / x

[fol. 11r]

sen de paz y nos diesen la obidienÇia y que / haziendo lo ansi no ReÇibirian m*a*ltratamy*ent*o / y el se *h*abia adelantado y juntado con los d*i*chos / Religiosos y por lenguas de ynterpr*e*tes y senas / les *h*abian hecho mu(n)chas Vezes los Requy- / rymy*ent*os neçesarios conForme a lo que Çer- / ca de *e*llo Por nos estaba mandado e proVeydo / y estandoles haziendo los d*i*chos Requyrimy*ent*os / los d*i*chos naturales *h*abian Flechado y herido / mu(n)cha Gente y Caballos del d*i*cho exeÇito / entre los quales *h*abian Flechado a Fray / luys Uno de los Religiosos q*ue* les hazian / los d*i*chos Requyrimy*ent*os de quya CaUsa *h*a- / bia conVenydo entrarles Por Guerra / la qual se les *h*abia hecho y tomado El / Primer pueblo y del conbate que se *h*abia da- / (da)do el *h*abia salido con tres malas heridas en / el Rostro y otros Go(s)*l*Pes heridas y pe- / dradas y Con todo su maltratamy*ent*o y el / que se *h*abian hecho a la demas Gente / no se *h*abia (f)*h*e*c*ho (^y) ny el *h*abia permetido / que se hiziese m*a*ltratamy*ent*o a los d*i*chos / yndios naturales ny se les *h*abia Pues- / to Fuego como Por la Parte contra- / ria diz(e)*i*a antes le*s* *h*abian hecho y man- / dado hazer buen tratamy*ent*o atrayen- / dolos Por bien y toda la d*i*cha ProVin- / Çia *h*abia Venydo de paz y dadonos las obi- / dienÇia y en quanto al quarto cargo / que era aCusado dezia que ansimysmo / era sin culpa de *e*llo *en* *e*l con-tenydo porq*ue* todo / el tienPo q*ue* los d*i*chos naturales *h*abian / x

[fol. 11v]

estado de paZ y en nuestra obidienÇia habian / sido muy bien tratados y
faVoreÇidos has- / ta tanto que habian trato y conçertado / entre si de se alçar
y Rebelar y lo habian / Puesto en eFecto alçandose y Re- / belandose e Una
noche habian Flechado qua- / renta caballos e mulas e azemylas de las / del
dicho exerÇito Poco(s) mas o menos / y muerto çiertos yndios de los amy- /
Gos que ConsiGo lleVaban y se habian hecho / Fuertes en los Pueblos y estando
/ ansi alÇados y Rebelados el los habia enVia- / do a Requyrir mu(n)chas Vezes
que VolViesen / de paz E a nuestra obidienÇia e aseGurandoles / y dandoles
çertiFicaÇion que haziendolo / ansi serian Perdonados e muy bien trata- / dos
e que no se les haria mal ninGuno ny Re- / Çibirian dano e que de otra manera
se les / hazer Guerra con todo Rigor lo qual se les / haber dado muy bien a
entender Por len- / Guas de ynterpretes y los dichos natura- / les no habian
querido Venyr de paz ny dar- / nos la obidienÇia e Vista su Rebelion con /
acuer(e)do y ConseJo deliberado de los Religio- / sos e ofiçiales nuestros e otras
Personas habian / convenydo hazerles la guerra y se les habia he- / cho con el
menos dano que se les habia podi- / do hazer sin que se les hiziese (a)exçeso
alGuno por / lo qual no era en culpa alguna en quanto al / dicho caPitulo y en
quanto a lo demas que / era aCusado Por el quynto capitulo de la / dicha
aCusaçion dezia que habia de ser / dado Por libre y quyto de lo en el con- / xj

[fol. 12r]

tenydo porque no era en Culpa de ninguna cosa de lo / que en el se contenya
por que el dicho yndio llama- / do tur(o)co guyando habia traydo enganando
el / dicho exerÇito con palabras Falsas diziendo / que sabia de Una tierra muy
Rica e muy pobla- / da y que guyaria a ella y Con las dichas fal- / sedades y
engaños habia guyado el exerÇito / Por despobaldos Por los quales toda la
gen- / te de el habia coRido muy Gran PeliGro / y padeÇido muy gran
neçesidad y hanbre y sed / lo qual el dicho yndio llamado turco ha- / bia
(F)hecho Falsa y enganosamente en eFec- / to que toda la gente del dicho
exerÇito muriese / y PereÇiese de hanbre y sed y ConoÇiendo / notoriamente
mentiras engaños E Falseda- / des del dicho yndio ynquyriendo de el la /

Verdad la *h*abia di*c*ho y ConFesado sin pre- / mya alGuna que enganosa-me*nt*e *h*aber traydo el / di*c*ho exerÇito Por las di*c*has Partes a efec- / to q*ue* la gente muriese y pereÇiese lo qual / *h*abia sido notorio y ansimysmo *h*abia pare- / Çidose y aVeriGuadose q*ue* *e*l di*c*ho yndio dezia y yn- / duzia a los naturales de la di*c*ha ProvinÇia / de quyVira que mat(e)*a*sen los caballos sena- / landoles los meJores diziendoles que ma(n)- / tando los caballos FaÇilmente matari- / an a los esPanoles que eran Pocos lo q*ua*l / todo *h*abiendo Venydo a su notiÇia e Viendo / q*ue* ConVenya Poner Remedio çerca ello / *h*abia man-dado a diego loPez que a la sazon / era maestre de Canpo que se ynForma- / se muy bien de lo q*ue* pasaba çerca de lo suso- / xj

[fol. 12v]
di*c*ho Para que se hiziese JustiÇia el qual *h*abiendo- / se ynFormado e que *h*abia Pareçido e a- / Veriguadose ser notorio como tal ma- / estre de CanPo *h*abia mandado hazer jus- / tiÇia del di*c*ho yndio e le *h*abia pareçido q*ue* *e*l / castigo Fuese secreto por ser como era / natural de aqu*e*lla ProVinçia e porq*ue* los de- / mas naturales no se alterasen E aUnq*ue* *e*l / no lo *h*abia mandado matar esp(a)*e*ÇiFicam*ent*e / mas de mandar al di*c*ho maestre de canpo que / aVeriguase la verdad Para hazer justiÇia / e desPues de hecha Por la Relaçion / e ynFormaÇion que *h*abia tenydo le *h*abia / Pareçido q*ue* *e*l di*c*ho maestre de Canpo *h*abia he- / cho lo q*ue* ConVenya Porq*ue* por las di*c*has False- / dades y engaños el di*c*ho yndio *h*abia mere- / çido muy bien la di*c*ha muerte que se le *h*abia dado an- / si para su Castigo como Para eVitar muy gran- / des daños que se pudieran Recreçer en el / di*c*ho exerÇito *h*abiendo de hallado el di*c*ho yndio / Falso y traydor y sabiendo las cosas y par- / tiCularidades de *e*l y los aVisos q*ue* pudiera / dar a los enemigos Por lo qual no era en cul- / Pa de lo contenydo en el di*c*ho quynto ca- / Pitulo y en quanto a lo demas de que *e*ra / acusado que *h*abiendo hallado mu(n)chas pro- / VinÇias muy pobladas y abundosas de man- / tinymy*ent*os no solamente no las *h*abian hecho / Poblar Pero lo *h*abia *h*abitado a otros / {ojo} / q*ue* lo *h*abian querido hazer Por lo qual *h*abian / quedado des*m*anParados alçados y de gue- / Ra dezia que no era en culpa de lo conte- / nydo en el di*c*ho caPitulo y la CaUsa por / xij

[fol. 13r]

que eL no habia Poblado ny hecho Poblar las / dichas ProVinÇias habia sido
Porque / no eran tales como la Parte con- / traria dezia Por no haber en ellas
oper- / tunydad Para Poderse mantener / y sustentar la Gente ny que se
hobiese / ProVecho ny aUmento nuestro rreal patri- / monyo Porque las dichas
tierras / las Unas eran demasiadamente Frias / y esteriles y otras de muy poca
gen- / te y mantinymyentos y en la Parte don- / de se habian hallado las VaCas
salVajines / habian sido disyertas y donde no ha- / bia Gente sino algunos
yndios caça- / dores que en cantidad de trezientas / leGuas que habia andado
Por despo- / blados no se habian hallado trezientos hon- / bres y Con deseo
yntento de poblar / acreÇentar y aumentar nuestro Real / Patrimonyo e
viendo que en toda la / distanÇia que habia andado no habia / hallado TieRa
que tuViese las calida- / des que Convenya para poder Poblar / habia enViado
Por mu(n)chas y di- / Versas Partes capitanes con ynstru- / yÇiones y Gente
con ellos Por- / que descubriesen tieRas Para que / (que) se poblasen los
quales habian ydo y no / habian hallado tierras conVenyentes / Para el dicho
eFecto ny de ellas no habian / tenydo notiÇia no enbarGante que ha- / xij

[fol. 13v]

bia Pasado mas de quynyentas Leguas / adelante de Çibola que era la tieRa /
de que habia dado RelaÇion Fray marcos / de nyça Por donde se habian habido
a yr el dicho / exerÇito yendo sienPre Por yer- / mos y desPoblados e la mayor
parte de tie- / Ras esteriles donde ansi el como la(os) de- / mas Gente que
Con el yba habian pasado / mu(n)chas y muy Grandes trabajos e han- / bre y
sed y si algun mantinymyento habian te- / nydo habia sido el que se habia lle-
Vado a Cues- / tas Para la Gente del dicho exerÇito e ha- / bian habido tanta
falta de el que sienpre / ansi el como todo el dicho exerÇito habian / comydo
Por onças el mayz y nunca se habian / hallado tierra que le pareçiese que se
debia po- / blar ny sustentar ny en que nuestro Real pa- / trimonyo se pudiera
aUmentar Porque Con- / llevar consiGo a quyVira solamente hasta / treynta
y ÇinCo o quarenta honbres habian / PadeÇido mu(n)cha neçesidad Por fal-
/ ta de mantinymyento mayormente que / nunCa a el se le habia Pedido Por
nenGuna / Persona que querian Poblar ny habia pa- / ra ello dispusiçion antes

sienPre / se le *h*abia pedido lo contrario diziendole E / Requyriendole que
Pues no se *h*abia hallado / tieRa q*ue* poder Poblar y la Gente del / exerÇito
PeresÇia q*ue* los VolViese la via / de la nueVa esPana y Viendo como *h*abia /
andado y PereGrinado mu(n)cho tienpo / xiij

[fol. 14r]
Y Cantidad de myll leguas de camyno en per- / sona desde la ÇiUdad de
mexico de donde / *h*abia salido sin otr(o)*a*s mu(n)ch(o)*a*s l(u)*e*g(are)*ua*s de /
(^donde *h*abia salido) Camynos que sus capitanes / {ojo} / *h*abian andado Por
su mandado descubrien- / do e que se *h*abian muerto e de Cada dia muria*n* /
mu(n)chos caballos y la gente del d*i*cho E- / xerÇito adoleçian que no tenyan
Re- / medio ny para el alma ny para el cuerPo / Por no *h*aber ça(r)cerdote que
se *h*abian todos / Vuelto ny medico y Cada dia el d*i*cho exerÇito / Venya e
Podia Venyr en dimynu(y)çion / se *h*abia Vuelto Porque la Gente no pe- /
reçiese y en efe*c*to *en* la d*i*cha Jornada / le *h*abia hecho todo lo que en el *h*abia
sido po- / sible ansi en serViçio de dios n*uest*ro senor / como n*uest*ro y no era
en culpa ny mereÇi / Pena antes ser de nos Remunerado / y Gratificado de
los grandes gastos y / trabajos que *en* n*uest*ro serViÇio *h*abia (f)*h*echo y pa- /
deçido en la d*i*cha Jornada de los quales / si no se *h*abia sacado el fruto y suçeso
q*ue* *e*l / deseaba no *h*abia sido a su culpa ny Causa / Por tanto que Pedia
suplicaba / se declarase el d*i*cho n*uest*ro Fiscal Por no / Parte y su aCusaÇion
Por (h)errada / y deFe*c*tuosa E no *h*abia lugar contra / el declarado no *h*aber
(f)*h*echo ny cometido deli- / to alguno abssolviendole y dandole por / libre y
quyto de todo aquello de que / era aCusado declarandole Por buen ge- / xiii

[fol. 14v]
neral y CaPitan n*uest*ro y Como tal deba ser / Remunerado gratificado de sus
serviÇios / encomendandole cosas y Cargos tocan- / tes a n*uest*ro Real
serViÇio sobre todo lo / que *e*l pido serle hecho conplimy*ent*o de just*i*cia / con
las costas sobre lo qual Fue el d*i*cho ple- / yto con(t)*d*enso el qual Por el d*i*cho
n*uest*ro oy- / dor E Juez de Comysion Visto dio E pronun- / Çio en la sentenÇia Por la qual en efe*c*- / to Reçibio a las d*i*chas Partes aprue- / ba en çierta
Forma e con çierto ter- / myno dentro del qual ambas las d*i*chas / Partes

hizieron sus Probanças y las / Presentaron ante *el* d*i*cho n*uest*ro oydor / e por
la Probança Por parte del d*i*cho / Franc*is*co vazques de Coronado hecha
consto / y pareÇio Por numero de testiGos / como Por el d*i*cho n*uest*ro
VisoRey pre- / sidente E oydores de la d*i*cha n*uest*ra aUd*ienci*a / de la nueva
esPaña *h*abia sido nonbra- / do y elegido Por Capitan general del d*i*cho /
exerÇito que en n*uest*ro serviÇio se *h*abia en- / Viado a las d*i*chas tierras de
Çibola nueva- / mente descubiertas para la conquysta / e PaçificaÇion de *e*llas
e para seGuridad / y anParo de los naturales y Re- / ligiosos que yban a
entender *en* la / conversion de los naturales de las d*i*chas / ProVinÇias Por ser
el d*i*cho Franc*is*co Vaz- / ques caballero hiJodalgo y persona de / xiiij

[fol. 15r]
conçi*en*Çia y ConfianÇa en q*ue* Concorrian las calidades / neçesarias Para
semeJantes cargos y que nos / *h*abia serVido en otros cargos y oFiçios Prevy-
/ n*i*entes y a la sazon nos serVia de n*uest*ro gobernad*or* / de la d*i*cha nueVa
galizia e que Para la d*i*cha Jor- / nada e viaje *h*abia Vendido mu(n)chas Partes
d*e* sus / bienes y hazienda e adeUdandose en mu(n)cha / cantidad de Pesos
de oro e armas caballos / neGros e azemylas e otros adereços neçesarios / Para
ella y en mu(n)chos criados que con- / siGo *h*abia lleVado bien armados enca-
balgados / E adereçados de Guerra en todo lo qual *h*abia / hecho muy
Grandes Gastos en muy gran can- / tidad de Pesos de oro y todaVia se estaba
/ adeUdado y enPenado e que al t*iem*Po / que *h*abia açertado el d*i*cho cargo
era casado y en / la d*i*cha ÇiUdad de mexico tenya su casa y mu- / Ger y
asiento y muy buenas haziendas e gran- / Gerias e que todo *e*l tienPo que
*h*abia tenydo / el d*i*cho carGo *h*abia tenydo el d*i*cho exerçito / muy bien
coRegido e Conçertado tinyendo / en el muy gran orden de guerra Vela y Vi-
/ Gilançia en ella e sienPre Por la GentE / de *e*l *h*abia sido amado tenydo e
ReVerençiado / e obedeÇido y que entre otras ProVi- / d(i)enÇias que *h*abia
tenydo en el d*i*cho ViaJe / e conquysta *h*abia ProVeydo y mandado / esPeçial-
mente q*ue* todas las PersonaS / del d*i*cho exerçito ViVie(n)sen como buenos
c*r*is- / tianos (^como) Ponyendo muy grandes Pen*a*S / Para eVitar que no se
blasFemase de dyos / n*uest*ro senor ny de n*uest*ra senora su Gloriosa madre /
ny de los santos e que no *h*oViese aman- / xiiij

[fol. 15v]

Çebados ny otros Pecados Publicos ynquy- / riendolo y mandandolo ynquyrir y saber para / lo castigar y poner Remedio en ello e quan- / do alGuna cosa se *h*abia ofreçido de Recado / Pu*b*lico que *h*obiese Venydo a su notiçia *h*abia pues- / to en ello el rremedio neçesario tenyendo sien- / Pre espeçial quydado ansimysmo en man- / dar so GraVes Penas que todos los naturales de las / di*c*has tierras Por donde *h*abian andado Fuesen muy / bien tratados e no se les tomase cosa suya contra / su Voluntad e sin se la Pagar ny les Fuese hecho otro / maltratamy*ent*o alguno haziendo y mandando pre- / Gonar ansi ÇerCa de *e*llo como de otras cosas tocan- / tes al serViÇio de dios n*uest*ro señor y n*ue*s*t*ro y bien del / di*c*ho exerÇito y de los di*c*hos naturales mu(n)chas / y muy buenas ordenanças las quales se *h*abian guardado / y quando *h*abia Venydo a su notiÇia que *h*obiese / q*ue*brantamy*ent*o de ellas lo *h*abia Castigado o hecho / castigar e que si en la ComarCa del Valle(e) de los / coraÇones los naturales de algunos lugares se *h*a- / bian alçado y Rebelado no *h*abia sido a su / caUsa ny culpa Porque a la sazon estaba *en* la tie- / Ra adentro mu(n)cha distanÇia e que todo el t*iem*po / q*ue* los naturales de las di*c*has ProVinÇias por / dond*e* *h*abia andado *h*abian estado de paz y en n*uest*ra obi- / dienÇia y domynio Real *h*abian sido muy bien / tratados y faVoreçidos ansi de *e*l como de los / caPitanes y gente del di*c*ho exerÇito e quando / alGunos se *h*abian Rebelado les *h*abia (F)*h*echo / los Requyrimy*ent*os neçesarios Por lenguas de / ynterP*r*etes y que si del di*c*ho yndio turco / se *h*abia (f)*h*echo JustiÇia Por el maestre de can- / Po del di*c*ho exerÇito *h*abia sido Por mu(n)chos / engaños y trayçiones que *h*abia (f)*h*echo y Co- / xv

[fol. 16r]

metido a los quales *h*abia Puesto en mu(n)chas / hanbres y(^e) neçesidades el di*c*ho exerÇito a eFe*c*to q*ue* / Pereçiese toda la Jente de *e*l como se *h*abia visto / Por esPir*i*enÇia y la justiçia que se le *h*a- / bia hecho *h*abia convenydo a n*ue*s*t*ro Real serViÇio y bien / del di*c*ho exerÇito que se hiziese ansi e que si no *h*abia / Poblado en nenGuna Parte de las di*c*has Par- / tes y tierras y proVinÇias Por donde *h*a- / bia andado *h*abia sido caUsa de ello no *h*aber / hallado tierra que se Pudiese poblar y sus- / tentar en ella la gente del di*c*ho exerçito

/ Por ser las *unas* tierras desPobladas de gentes / y otras yn*h*abitables y de Calidad muy Frias / y esteriles y fal(l)tas de mantinymy*en*tos / y no conVinyentes Para el di*c*ho eFe*c*to / e no enbarGante q*ue* Con deseo de Poblar y acre- / Çentar n*uest*ro Real Patrimonyo *h*abia en- / Viado Por mu(n)chas Partes capita- / nes con Gente para que descubriesen algunas / tieRas que se pudiesen Poblar y q*ue* *e*l en / Persona(s) *h*abia ydo adelante de la di*c*ha / ProVinçia de Çibola cantidad de mas de / quynyentas leguas Por yr mas des- / Poblados y tierras yn*h*abitables y no / *h*abia tenydo notiçia de *e*llo a Cuya CaUsa / se *h*abian Vuelto los Religiosos que en el di*c*ho / exerÇito *h*abian ydo sin quedar saçerdote / q*ue* a la Gente de *e*l Pudiese conFesar / la q*ua*l *h*abia llegado a estrema neÇesidad / de hanbre y enFermedades a CaUsa de no *h*aber / nenGun Relij*i*oso ny saçerdote mu(n)chas / Personas *h*abian muerto sin conFision / e sin *a*segurados Por no *h*aber ansimysmo / xv

[fol. 16v]
medicos ny mydiçinas Por lo qual *h*abia sido / neçesario Volverse el di*c*ho exerçito como se *h*a- / bia Vuelto a la di*c*ha nueVa esPana por- / que se *h*abia tenydo Por Çierto que como *h*a- / zerse ansi toda la gente de *e*l Pereçiera / Por que *h*abia llegado a termynos ansi el como / todos los demas a Comer el pan por onças e an- / simysmo consto el di*c*ho Franc*isc*o Vazques *en* los traba- / Jos de la di*c*ha guerra Velas y entradas y otras / cosas de *e*lla Ponerse Por su persona ansi a ellos / como *en* las batallas que se *h*abian ofreçido pu- / nyendose en la dela*n*tera Por lo qual / *h*abia sido mu(n)chas Vezes muy mal herido y tra*t*a- / do su Persona y que sienPre *h*abia guar- / dado y Cunplido n*uest*ras Reales ynstruyçiones / q*ue* Tiene*n* n*uest*ros mandad(a)*o*s guardar a los capita- / nes que yban a descobrir y Conquystar / *en* las Partes de n*uest*ras yndias y tieRas / nueVas Las quales ansimysmo *h*abia hecho / Guardar a los demas caPitanes de di*c*ho / exerÇito haziendolas leer Para el di*c*ho efe*c*to / E que en nenguna entrada conquysta ny descubrimy*en*to / que se *h*abia (F)*h*echo *en* las di*c*has ProVinÇias nunCa / se *h*abia (f)*h*echo esclaVo ny herrado nengun natural / de *e*llas aUnque se les *h*abia (F)*h*echo guerra por / no *h*abernos querido dar la obidienÇia habien- / do sido Para ello Requeridos conForme / a las di*c*has n*uest*ras yntruyçiones e *h*aber- / se alGuno de *e*llos Re(^l)^*b*elado

desPues / de habernos dado la dicha obidienÇia y Come- / tidos graVes
delitos E que ansimysmo el y sus / capitanes que para el dicho efecto habia
enViado habia / descubierto tieRas y poblaÇiones que nun- / ca habian sido
descubiertas ny hasta entonçes se / xvj

[fol. 17r]
tenya notiçia de ellas los naturales de las quales nos / habian dado la obidienÇia e quedado en ella e que no en- / barGante que se habia tenydo Por
Costunbre en los / descubrimyentos que se habian (F)hecho Por tieRa / ansi
en la dicha nueVa esPana como en las / yslas y tierra Firme lleVar las armas
artill(y)- / eria E munyçion e (^de) las demas cosas neçesarias / en (n)honbros
de yndios e en la dicha Jornada nunCa habia / consentido que se cargasen
yndios con nenguna / de las dichas cosas Porque la dicha artill(i)eria se / habia
lleVado en bestias y lo demas lo habia lle- / Vado la Gente del dicho exerÇito
en sus caballos E / que a caUsa de no haber hallado en toda la distan- / Çia
de tierras y ProVinÇias que en la dicha en- / trada se habia andado tieRa
suFiÇiente para po- / der Poblar y acreçentar nuestro Real Patri- / monyo los
caPitanes y soldados del dicho exerçito / le habian Pedido y Requerido
mu(n)chas Vezes los / traxese y VolViese a la dicha nueVa esPana dizi- / endo
que en ella Podrian meJor serVir / E habia para ello mejor aParejo a Cuya
CaUsa / se habia Venydo con el dicho exerÇito segun que / mas largamente
Por la dicha ProVinÇia por / Parte del dicho Francisco Vazques de Coronado
/ hecha se contiene de la qual y de la hecha Por / Parte del dicho nuestro Fiscal
Por el dicho nuestro oydor / Fue mandado hazer y Fue hecha Publicaçion / y
Por Parte del dicho Francisco Vazques Fue- / ron Presentados ansimysmo
Çiertos testimo- / nyos e Requyrimyentos signados de hernando bermejo /
nuestro escribano Por los quales en eFecto cons- / ta y pareÇe que los caPitanes y alFeres del / dicho exerÇito Por sy e por las demas PersonaS / y soldados de el de los quales dixeron tener / Poderes bastantes Por ante el dicho
escryvano / xvj

[fol. 17v]
Pidieron y Requyrieron mu(n)chas y diVersas / Vezes al dicho general Fran-

*cis*co Vazques de Co- / ronado traxese y VolViese en el d*i*cho exerçi- / to la
Via de la d*i*cha nueVa esPaña de don- / de lo *h*abia sacado Porq*ue* Careçian
ansi de / los mantinymy*ent*os neçesarios a la susten- / taçion de la Vida
*h*Umana como de saçerdo- / tes y mynystros e ynstrumentos que E / con que
les çelebrasen el culto diVino e comu- / nyCasen los sacramentos neçesarios
al any- / ma y Por estar el d*i*cho exerÇito a peligro y Con- / diÇion de se
Perder e por otras mu(n)chas / caUsas que dixeron e alegaron Por los / d*i*cho*s*
Requyrimy*ent*os a los quales Pareçe q*ue* / Por el d*i*cho Fran*cis*co vazques Fue
ResPon- / dido çiertas caUsas y Razones conplide- / ras al serViçio de dios
n*uest*ro señor y n*uest*ro y / todaVia Por los susod*i*chos le Fueron hechos / otros
Requyrimy*ent*os y protestaçiones çer- / ca de *e*llo y dadas mu(n)chas caUsas
por donde / dixeron q*ue* ConVenya q*ue* *e*l d*i*cho exerÇito Fuese / Vuelto a la
d*i*cha nueVa esPaña porque / en ella dezian que *h*abia mas aParejo para / nos
Poder serVir que *en* las d*i*chas tie- / Ras y ProVinÇias donde estaban y *h*abia*n*
/ andado como (^los) mas largam*ent*e *en* los d*i*chos / Requyrimy*ent*os de que
de suso se haze myn- / Çion se Contiene de los quales el d*i*cho n*uest*ro / oydor
mando dar traslado al d*i*cho n*uest*ro / Fiscal Por parte del qual Fue d*i*cho / xvij

[fol. 18r]
E alegado de bien Probado y sobre ello Fue / el d*i*cho Pleyto con(t)*d*enso y
estan- / do en este estado el d*i*cho n*uest*ro oydor pro- / nunÇio Un aUto en
que en eF*e*cto dixo / q*ue* ConForme a lo que Por nos le *h*abia / sido mandado
Por la d*i*cha n*uest*ra ca*r*ta / y proVision de Comysion suso*en*Cor- / Porada el
Remytia y rremytio la de- / termynaçion de la d*i*cha caUsa a los d*i*chos n*ue*-
*st*r*o*s / Presidente e oydores de la d*i*cha n*uest*ra / aUdienÇia ante los quales Fue
y tra- / ydo y presentado el Proçeso de *e*lla / el qual Por ellos Visto y todos los
aU- / tos y meritos de *e*l dieron y pronunçiaron / en *e*l sentenÇia diFinytiVa
e*l* tenor de la / qual es este que se siGue / {*ytem*}[7] / En el pleyto crimynal que
entre partes / de la Una el lic*enci*ado *cris*tobal de benaVente Fis- / cal Por su
m*a*g*estad* en esta Real aUdiençia y de / la otra Fran*cis*co Vazques de Coronado
/ Gobernador q*ue* Fue Por su m*a*g*estad* en la proVin- / Çia de la nueVa galizia y CaPitan ge- / neral q*ue* Fue ProVeydo y nonbrado para / la ProvinÇia
de Çibola y tierra nueVa- / mente descubierta e su procurador en su non- /

bre FFallamos atentios los aUtos y meri- / tos de este Proçeso que el dicho liçinçiado bena- / Vente Fiscal no Probo su aCusaçion y Capi- / tulos que dio contra el dicho Francisco Vazques / de Coronado de los delitos que dixo haber (F)hecho / xvii

[fol. 18v]
y Cometido en la dicha tierra nueVamente des- / cubierta damos los y pronunÇiamos los por / no Probados e que el dicho Francisco Vazques de Co- / ronado Probo sus exce(b)pçiones y diFinsiones / damos las y pronunçiamos las Por bien / Probadas Por ende que debemos absoL- / Ver e absulVemos al dicho Francisco vazques / de todo lo que en esta CaUsa ha sido y es aCusado / Por el dicho Fiscal al qual Ponemos per- / Petuo silenÇio Para que agora ny de / aquy adelante sobre Razon de lo en / ella contenydo no se Pueda Pedir ny / aCusar Cosa alguna e Por esta nuestra senten- / Çia diFinytiVa Jusgando ansi lo Pronun- / çiamos y mandamos don antonyo de / mendoÇa el llicenciado tello de sandoval el liçin- / çiado çaynos el licenciado tejada el licenciado santillan

la qual dicha sentenÇia Por los dichos nuestro pre- / sidente e oydores dieron e pronunçiaron en la / dicha ÇiUdad de mexico estando haziendo aUdiencia / PubliCa diez y nueVe dias del mes de hebrero / del año Proximo Pasado de myll y quynientos E / quarenta y seys años estando Presente / el dicho nuestro Procurador Fiscal al qual y al procurador del dicho / Francisco Vazques Fue notiFicado en sus per- / sonas de la qual dicha sentenÇia por nen- / guna de las dichas Partes Fue suplicado E / agora el dicho Francisco Vazques de Coro- / nado pare- / Çio ante los dichos nuestro Presidente oydores / e nos Pidio e suplico que Pues que de la / dicha sentenÇia no se habia suplicado y era pa- / sada en cosa Juzgada le mandasemos dar / xviij

[fol. 19r]
nuestra carta executoria Para que le Fuese guardada / y Cunplida e que sobre ello ProVeyesemos co- / mo la nuestra merced Fuese lo qual Por los dichos nue- / stro / Presidente e oydores Visto Fue aCordado / que debiamos de mandar

(dar) dar Esta nuestra carta / Para Vos las dichas nuestras Justiçias en la dicha
rra- / zon e nos tuVimos lo Por bien Por la qual / Por el dicho su traslado signado como dicho es Vos / mandamos a todos e Cada Uno de Vos en los dichos
/ Vuestros lugares e jurisdiçiones que Veays la dicha / sentenÇia diFinytiVa
que ansi en el dicho / Pleyto entre las dichas Partes ÇerCa de lo / susodicho
por los dichos nuestro Presidente e oydores / Fue dada y pronunçiada que de
suso en esta nuestra / carta executoria Va ynCorPorada e la / Guardeys y
Cumplays y hagays guardar y Cum- / Plir en todo y por todo sigun y Como
en ella / se Contiene y Contra el tenor y Forma de / lo en ella contenydo no
Vays ny paseys ny con- / sintays yr ny pasar en tienPo alguno ny por / alGuna
manera e los Unos ny los otros ni haga- / des ny hagan endere so Pena de la
nuestra merced / E de Cada dozientos Pesos de oro Para la nuestra ca- / mara
e Fisco ademas mandamos al honvre que / Vos esta nuestra carta executoria
mostrare que / vos enplaze que paresc(a)idos en La dicha nuestra aUdiencia /
ante los dichos nuestro Presidente e oydores del / dia que Vos enplazare hasta
treynta dias pri- / meros siguyentes so la dicha Pena so la qual man- / damos
a qualquyer escrivano PubIico que para esto Fue- / re llamado que de ende a
el que Vos mostrare / testimonyo signado con su signo Porque nos se- / xviij

[fol. 19v]
Pamos en Como se Cunple nuestro mandado dada en / la Çiudad de (^Con-
Postela) mexico a Veynte / dias del mes de dizienbre año del naÇimyento de
/ nuestro salVador Jesu cristo de myll y quynientos y quaren- / ta y siete años
yo antonyo de turçios escryvano / mayor de la aUdiençia e chançelleria rreal
de la / nueVa esPana y Gobernaçion de ella por / su magestad la (F)hize
escribir Por su mandado con / aCuerdo de su Presidente e oydores registrada
pe- / dro de Requena Por chançeller pero / loPez don antonyo de mendoça el
licinciado te- / Jada el licenciado santillan el doctor quesada / {ytem} / (F)hecho
e sacado Fue este dicho traslado de la dicha carta / exeCutoria original susen-
Corporada en la / ÇiUdad de mexico a Veyntiseys dias del mes / de
noVienbre ano del naçimyento de nuestro saIVador / Jesu cristo de myll y
quynientos e Çincuenta y Un años / el qual dicho traslado yo antonyo de
turÇios / escrybano mayor de la aUdienÇia Real de esta nue- / Va esPana e

gobernaçion de *e*lla por su / m*a*ge*s*t*ad* hize saCar de pedimy*ent*o del d*i*ch*o* gobernador Fr*a*nci*s*co / vazques de Coronado e de mandamy*ent*o de los se*ñore*s / Presidente y oydores de la d*i*cha Real aUdi*enci*a / por quanto dixo tener necesidad del d*i*ch*o* tras- / lado Para *a*Segurar de su d*e*rec*h*o testigos / q*ue* lo Vieron coRegir y Conçertar agustin / Pinto e andres Peres estantes en esta / ÇiUdad En Fee de lo qual (F)*h*izo aquy este / myo signo que *e*s (a)tal En testim*o*nyo / *de la* Verdad antonyo de turÇios

Chapter 25

Partisan Testimony
as Source Material for History

The Witnesses as Typical Members
of the Expedition

During the pesquisa into treatment of indigenous peoples by the expedition to Tierra Nueva, 21 witnesses testified, 14 de oficio and 7 de parte. Neither group was randomly summoned. As would be expected, the de parte witnesses were selected and called because they would support the defense claims of Vázquez de Coronado. More surprisingly, so were the de oficio witnesses. In other words, the investigation carried out by Lorenzo de Tejada was essentially a *pro forma* exercise, orchestrated to clear the captain general and, more importantly, his sponsor and superior, the viceroy, of directly contravening royal orders and instructions. As has previously been remarked, at the time, Viceroy Mendoza was facing a very aggressive challenge to his right to office mounted by Hernán Cortés and carried out by the visitador general Francisco Tello de Sandoval. The charges raised against the leaders of the expedition to Tierra Nueva, if proven, would have fallen to Mendoza's responsibility, a dangerous possibility in light of the many other charges raised by Tello de Sandoval.

Mendoza and his supporters, therefore, managed to insure that as little damage as possible accrued to the viceroy as a result of the investigation of the expedition. That successful effort began with securing appointment of Lorenzo de Tejada as investigating judge, rather than having the charges concerning the expedition's treatment of Indians simply added to those to be investigated by Tello de Sandoval. The close personal relationship between Tejada and Mendoza has already been detailed in Chapter 3 and need not be reviewed here. Certainly Tejada's partisan stance is revealed in his lack of pursuit of evidence of possible wrongdoing by Vázquez de Coronado, such as the assertion by Cristóbal de Escobar that the captain general had ordered the killing and maiming of as many as 150 Tiguex prisoners during the siege of Pueblo del Cerco and, in a more systematic way, by his selection of witnesses to be called for the investigation.

In several ways the group of 14 witnesses whom Tejada called was typical of the European contingent of the expedition as a whole. The total number of known non-Indian, lay participants in the expedition to Tierra Nueva continues to grow as more and more documents arising from the expedition are examined. To date, the names of 370 non-Indian, lay expedition members are known.[1] Of these, data have been compiled on 115 (or 31.1%) concerning their places of origin, their ages in 1540, and the length of their tenure in the New World/Nueva España as of 1540. In terms of the geography of modern Spain, the largest component of the 96 members of the expedition to Tierra Nueva for whom place of origin data are available originated from the *comunidad* of Castilla-León, as did Vázquez de Coronado (24 individuals, 25.0%). Not far behind were Extremadura (19 individuals, 19.8%) and Andalucía (18 individuals, 18.7%). The only other modern comunidad boasting a significant number of expedition members from this sample is Castilla-La Mancha (11 individuals, 11.5%).[2] As with other Spanish expeditions of that era in the New World that have been studied in this regard, the members of the expedition to Tierra Nueva, thus, hailed predominantly (75%) from western and southern Spain.[3] The remaining 15 Spanish members of the expedition in this sample were natives of seven other areas in Spain with no one area being home to more than three individuals.[4] In addition, the sample includes six individuals born in Europe but outside of Spain and three born in the Americas.

The 14 de oficio witnesses called by licenciado Tejada conformed to the dominant pattern of the expedition as a whole, with regard to place of origin. Four were from Castilla-León, four from Castilla-La Mancha, three from Extremadura, and three from Andalucía. In this respect they were representative of the mass of the expedition.

It appears, on the basis of this study, that the majority of non-Indian, lay members of the expedition to Tierra Nueva were in their twenties when the entrada began in 1540. Age data are more scarce than is information on place of origin and, as a consequence, the ages of only 67 non-Indian, lay expedition members are known. Of those, 18 (26.9%) were less than 20 years old in 1540, 39 (58.2%) were 20–29, and 9 (13.4%) were older than 29.[5] If this age distribution holds for the expedition as a whole, then the expedition to Tierra Nueva included a somewhat larger than usual cohort of teenagers, though not outside the range of other mid-century expeditions.[6] The de oficio witnesses in the 1544 investigation, included a similarly sized component of individuals who had been teenagers at the time of the expedition, three out of the total of the 14 witnesses (22.2%). The remainder of the witnesses, though, was more heavily weighted, than was the expedition as a whole, toward those who in 1540 had been 30 or older. There were five such witnesses (35.7% of the total). There were also five witnesses who had been in their twenties at the time the expedition began (35.7% of the total). And the age of one of the 14 witnesses, Juan de Contreras, is unknown.

Despite the significant component of teenagers in the expedition to Tierra Nueva, more than three-fourths of the 71 expedition members for whom data are available on their tenure in Nueva España[7] prior to the expedition had been in the viceroyalty three years or more.[8] And 22 (31.0% of the sample) had been in Nueva España at least 10 years.[9] Many of them (including three of the de oficio witnesses during Tejada's investigation) had participated in the conquest of Nueva Galicia under Nuño Beltrán de Guzmán. Compared with the Pizarro expedition in Peru and the expeditions to Nueva Granada, the expedition to Tierra Nueva was, thus, heavier with experienced personnel.[10]

Among the de oficio witnesses during the 1544 investigation, the distribution according to years of experience in Nueva España (or the New World) is comparable to that of the sample from the full expedition. Three (22.2%) had less than 3 years experience; 5 (35.7%) had 3–5 years experience; 1 (7.1%) had 6–10 years experience; and 5 (35.7%) had more than 10 years experience in Nueva España prior to the expedition.

It must be noted that, although it was completely legal and feasible, no American natives, either from among the allies or from Tierra Nueva, were called to testify. In the latter group, Juan Troyano's Pueblo wife would have been a likely choice.

Distinguishing Status and Vínculos

With regard to place of origin, age in 1540, and tenure in Nueva España prior to 1540, the de oficio witnesses called by Tejada in 1544 were generally representative of the 115 members of the expedition for whom data are available. On two important points, however, they exhibited traits that suggest they had reasons to testify uniformly in support of the former captain general Francisco Vázquez de Coronado, as they did. First, their economic status was among the middle to upper ranks of their colonial society, as indicated by the number of horses they took with them on the expedition, the money they expended on outfitting for the expedition, the number of slaves they owned, and their receipt of administrative positions and encomiendas. Second, they had direct personal links or vínculos with Vázquez de Coronado, Viceroy Mendoza, and the family of Alonso de Estrada (Vázquez de Coronado's in-laws), the chief underwriters of the expedition to Tierra Nueva.

Relevant to the matter of economic status, it can be said that of the 13 de oficio witnesses called by Tejada (excluding Vázquez de Coronado) only Alonso Álvarez can be said with certainty to have taken no horses along on the expedition. His service for the better part of a year as Vázquez de Coronado's standard bearer suggests, however, that his social status, if not his economic condition, was not of the meanest. His eventual establishment as a vecino at Chiametla also argues for his being of at least lower-middle economic status. Concerning three other de oficio witnesses, no information is available about horses they took on the expedition: Juan Troyano, Rodrigo Ximón, and Juan de Zaldívar. Troyano, a man-at-arms supported by Viceroy Mendoza, may well have been of humble economic status, though he later became a vecino of Mexico City and built and operated at least one bergantine that operated on Lake Texcoco. As for Rodrigo Ximón, he held encomiendas both in Nueva Galicia and elsewhere in Nueva España prior to the expedition to Tierra Nueva and for that reason, if no other, probably ought to be viewed as having a more than modest economic position. Meanwhile, Juan de Zaldívar, appointed regidor of Guadalajara by Vázquez de Coronado, spent at least 5,000–6,000 pesos to go on the expedition to Tierra Nueva, making him quite a wealthy individual, a status he later improved upon further. All nine remaining de oficio witnesses each took three or more horses or, in one case, two horses and a servant, on the expedition. Melchior Pérez and Alonso Sánchez (with his wife Francisca de Hozes and his unnamed son) each took seven horses; Juan Gómez de Paradinas and Pedro de Ledesma each took five; Domingo Martín took four; both Juan de Contreras and Rodrigo de Frías took three; and Cristóbal de Escobar took two horses and one servant. Besides his seven horses, Pérez also took servants with him to Tierra Nueva. This placed each of the nine well above the middle range of economic status for the expedition.[11]

In addition, Escobar and Martín together expended a substantial sum to take livestock on the expedition, as did Pérez, probably in both cases as speculative investments. Several witnesses held positions of responsibility and honor in the expedition, indicative of their above average status. Zaldívar was one of the captains of the expedition. Pérez and Gómez de Paradinas served as alguaciles mayores; Contreras was Vázquez de Coronado's head groom; and, as already mentioned, Álvarez served as the captain general's standard bearer. Additionally, five de oficio witnesses were encomenderos at the time of the expedition or became encomenderos thereafter: Martín, Ximón, Pérez, Ledesma, and Zaldívar. Ledesma and Zaldívar also served as regidores of

Guadalajara. And Cristóbal de Escobar was appointed corregidor of several Indian communities, beginning at about the time of his testimony before Tejada. It is also of note that all but one of the 13 de oficio witnesses (Francisca de Hozes) were literate enough to sign the statements they made before licenciado Tejada. As James Lockhart has observed, "The person who . . . could sign decently, had invariably been exposed to a year or two of education of the grammar-school type, with corresponding effects on his values, manners, and ambitions." Such individuals were "not at the very lowest level of Spanish society."[12]

All this is to say that all, or nearly all, the de oficio witnesses were at least relatively well off economically and were economically active. Thus they could be expected to exhibit general sympathy and shared attitudes regarding Indians with official instigators and engineers of colonial economic enterprise such as Francisco Vázquez de Coronado and Antonio de Mendoza. That is because in the middle decades of the sixteenth century and for long afterwards the large-scale colonial enterprises of wealth accumulation (tribute collection; mining; livestock raising; sugar, silk, dye, and textile production) derived from or depended on the indigenous peoples of the Americas.

The connections between the de oficio witnesses and the actual and potential targets of the investigation, though, were not solely those of shared economic position in colonial society. Such connections were reinforced and rendered all but constitutional by direct, personal links with the principal sponsors of the expedition to Tierra Nueva, those most likely to be penalized should the expedition's leadership be found responsible for wholesale, wanton mistreatment of the native peoples it encountered. Personal linkages or vínculos have already been detailed when discussing each witness individually, but the pattern for the group of de oficio witnesses as a whole emerges unmistakably in recapitulating those relationships briefly.

First, three of the witnesses, Pedro de Ledesma, Juan de Contreras, and Alonso Álvarez, were members of Vázquez de Coronado's personal household and nearly always with him, filling the roles of factotum, head groom, and standard bearer respectively. Four others, Juan Troyano, Rodrigo de Frías, Domingo Martín, and Cristóbal de Escobar, while not constantly in the captain general's presence during the expedition, were selected by Vázquez de Coronado to accompany him whenever he moved in advance of the body of the expedition. And three more witnesses, Juan de Zaldívar, Melchior Pérez, and Juan Gómez de Paradinas, were appointed to or confirmed in the positions they held during the expedition by the captain general. Gómez de Paradinas was trebly linked with the captain general, not only serving as alguacil mayor by his appointment, but coming from Vázquez de Coronado's home province of Salamanca in Spain and mustering into the expedition in the company captained by an uncle or cousin of Beatriz de Estrada, the captain general's wife. Zaldívar had been appointed regidor of Guadalajara in 1538 by Vázquez de Coronado, and Pérez had been spared the possibility of financial responsibility for his father's misdeeds as governor of Nueva Galicia because Vázquez de Coronado decided not to pursue a residencia investigation against the father. And Zaldívar was, of course, the nephew of Vázquez de Coronado's lieutenant governor of Nueva Galicia, Cristóbal de Oñate. Furthermore, Troyano, Ledesma, and Gómez de Paradinas had been associated with the captain general since at least 1535, when they all traveled to Nueva España in the entourage of Viceroy Mendoza. Juan de Contreras, prior to his service in the captain general's household, had been a member of the viceroy's personal guard. Finally, Domingo Martín, Alonso Sánchez, and Francisca de Hozes were potentially linked with Alonso de Estrada because of their places of origin: Martín from Las Brozas in the jurisdiction of Cáceres, where Estrada had served as corregidor; Sánchez and Hozes from Estrada's hometown of Ciudad Real.[13] Estrada, in his capacity as lieutenant governor of Nueva España, was directly involved in conferring and preserving encomiendas held by Domingo Martín and Rodrigo Ximón. In addition to their tenuous geographical link with Alonso de Estrada, Alonso Sánchez and Francisca de Hozes maintained a long-term relationship with Melchior Pérez (a stalwart supporter of Vázquez de Coronado). And, too, their apparent economic success following the 1544 pesquisa suggests there may have been a more profound connection with the sponsors of the expedition. Certainly their testimony was not at all critical of the captain general regarding his treatment of the Indians.

All 13 de oficio witnesses (ignoring the captain general), therefore, had personal links with one or more of the principal investors in the expedition. Most often those connections made them beholden to the investors for their livelihood, social or political position, or both. Certainly that established conditions under which the witnesses would be highly likely to testify in ways not detrimental to their sponsors or patrons.

Partisan Testimony and Foregone Conclusions

As has previously been pointed out in discussing the testimony of individual witnesses, the tenor of the statements of the de oficio witnesses as a group was one of almost uninterrupted ratification and justification of the actions of Vázquez de Coronado concerning indigenous peoples. In this respect there is little to distinguish the statements of the de oficio witnesses from those of the de parte witnesses. The testimony of all the witnesses, whether called by Tejada or by Vázquez de Coronado's representatives, conformed to the defense strategy of Vázquez de Coronado as evident in the interrogatorio used in his name at the mines in Culiacán province. That strategy was to insist that all actions against native peoples taken or authorized by the captain general were fully justified and carried out only after consultation with the lay and religious leaders of the expedition. For instance, all 12 de oficio witnesses who were asked about the killing of El Turco agreed that justice was done in his execution because he had deceived the people of the expedition and repeatedly had put them at peril. The witnesses seemed aware of the specific issues about which Tejada would ask even before they began their statements and they frequently volunteered information in support of the captain general. Rarely did they mention anything that could be construed as an accusation against Vázquez de Coronado.[14] This situation is, in itself, a strong argument that the decision in the case was a foregone conclusion. Moreover, the investigating judge was not at all aggressive in following up suggestions of wrongdoing by the captain general. Nor, evidently, did he call as witnesses any of the unnamed persons whom the king said had denounced Vázquez de Coronado's conduct.

Who were the less favorable witnesses the investigating judge could have called before him? To date, no documentary evidence has come to light regarding the names of specific individuals publicly critical at the time of Vázquez de Coronado's treatment of Indians in Tierra Nueva. Nevertheless, given his previous writing on the subject of abuse of Indians, one would have expected an aggressive investigator to call fray Marcos de Niza. Though Marcos could have been summoned to testify from Jalapa, where he was then residing, he was not; nor is there evidence that Tejada consulted with the outspoken cleric.[15] It might have been expected that Tejada would call either of the two friars who returned with the expedition, fray Antonio de Castilblanco or fray Daniel. Theirs would have been crucial testimony. Furthermore, in light of several critical statements Pedro de Castañeda made in his report written in the 1560s, he might well have been sought out by Tejada to provide support for the accusations made to the king.

Partisan selection of witnesses and orchestration of official inquiries such as that carried out by Lorenzo de Tejada were not unheard of. Very similar conditions prevailed during an investigation and residencia conducted in 1537 concerning, along with other charges, abuse of the Indians of Pánuco by Nuño de Guzmán. As Donald Chipman wrote:

> Throughout the entire residencia, not one person gave what might be regarded as a balanced testimony; every deponent was either strongly pro- or anti-Guzmán. In residencia proceedings following the conclusion of the pesquisa secreta, all persons giving evidence were pro-Guzmán for they were hand-picked by his procurador. Therefore, had Castañeda [the pesquisa judge] not chosen those with a grudge as witnesses in the pesquisa secreta, there would have been virtually no adverse criticism of Guzmán in the entire residencia.[16]

Lorenzo de Tejada was clearly careful to summon as witnesses in the pesquisa into the expedition to Tierra Nueva only persons known to be sympathetic to Vázquez de Coronado and Tejada's close associate, Viceroy Mendoza, that is, closely linked with and dependent on them. As the former captain general later testified, it came, therefore, as a bombshell when the fiscal Benavente lodged charges against Vázquez de Coronado based on the investigation record compiled by Tejada. By the time the audiencia announced its decision in the case, however, Benavente had been brought into line and he filed no appeal.

Cultural Bias and Associational Slant

The partisan character of the depositions taken during and in the wake of Tejada's investigation raises the question of the usefulness of the pesquisa record for study, more than 450 years later, of relations and interaction between the expedition to Tierra Nueva and the native peoples of that region. Since the testimony record comprises only selected evidence offered solely by Spanish members of the expedition who, furthermore, had an interest in protecting the political future of the investigation's principal target, is the record tainted and flawed so as to be of minimal worth? Worse yet, is it an inextricable tangle of misinformation and candid observation and opinion?

In short, the answer is no; while the investigation record may be colored when it comes to the issue of Vázquez de Coronado's personal responsibility for outrages committed against Indians, the testimony covers many collateral matters which there was little or no reason to purposely misrepresent or distort. Thus, for example, it was beside the point of Tejada's interest whether Pueblo del Cerco was situated on a height, whether Querechos transported tents and other possessions using dogs, or whether people from several different Zuni pueblos were at Cíbola on the day the expedition arrived. Even on the subject of relations between the expedition and indigenous peoples much of what was recorded by Pedro de Requena must be forthright, as far as it goes. Which is not to say that the testimony provides full and faultless accounts of what transpired in Tierra Nueva between spring 1540 and summer 1542. But there was fundamental agreement between those who denounced the expedition and the witnesses called by Tejada regarding what the Spaniards saw as harm done to Indians, inasmuch as there was virtually no dispute by the witnesses of the scenarios spelled out in Tejada's questions, neither in general outline nor in detail. Whatever biases those scenarios incorporated were widely shared by European members of the expedition; that is to say, they were cultural rather than associational or partisan. Furthermore, there is broad congruence between the version of events reported by the pesquisa witnesses and that provided by other contemporary documentary sources. As only one of countless examples, both Juan de Jaramillo, in a narrative written in the 1560s, and Pedro de Castañeda, in a very long narrative also written in the 1560s, recounted the same story told by many of the 1544 de oficio witnesses regarding El Turco's deceitfulness and collusion with the people of Quivira and his consequent execution by garrote.[17] The accounts from the pesquisa record, however, are often much richer in detail than are those from other sources.

It must be remembered that, even at its best, though, the testimony of the 1544 witnesses, is only a partial picture. Lacking is evidence from the religious members of the expedition, lay individuals who were critical of its conduct, the Mexican Indian allies, the corps of servants and slaves, and, most especially, the native peoples of Tierra Nueva. Evidence from archeology and indigenous oral traditions provides a small corrective, but the available record remains distinctly one-sided. Nevertheless, with the proviso that the proceedings of Tejada's investigation (like any other group of documents) are culturally filtered and selected, it remains what Bolton called it, "a priceless source of knowledge."

Summary of the Testimony concerning Brutality and Cruelty[18]

Ostensibly, the central aim of the pesquisa conducted by Lorenzo de Tejada was to determine who was responsible for brutal and inhumane acts committed by the expedition to Tierra Nueva against the native peoples it encountered. As has been observed, the trustworthiness of the testimony taken on that issue is highly questionable. In the course of addressing the question of responsibility, however, both de oficio and de parte witnesses confirmed and offered much information about exactly what brutal acts had occurred. Furthermore, they gave accounts of a variety of interactions between the expedition and indigenous peoples and provided a wealth of incidental detail about conduct of the expedition and the social configuration of the Greater Southwest.

Although the various witnesses sometimes disagreed on details,[19] there was broad consensus on the following outline of events during 1540–1542. Not long after departure of the expedition from Compostela there was a conflict with Indians in the Chiametla area. During the conflict the expedition's maestre de campo Lope de Samaniego was killed, perhaps in retaliation for his earlier violence against natives of the area. In punishment for the maestre de campo's death, a group of eight native men and women of Chiametla was drawn and quartered. Word of that administration of "justice" may have inspired more accommodation among native groups as the expedition moved north. At any rate, no further hostilities were mentioned by witnesses until the expedition approached Cíbola, its immediate goal. For example, at the Ópata urban center on the Río Sonora known to Spaniards as Corazones, the people acquiesced to establishment of an expeditionary base camp and nascent town called San Gerónimo.

Within days of Cíbola, however, several residents of that reputedly wealthy city were taken by force by the expedition and dispatched to their home with what the Spaniards thought was a pacific message, announcing their arrival. The Cíbolans did not respond. On slightly closer approach, Mexican Indian allies were sent to Cíbola with a similar message. They returned with a reply to the effect that the Spaniards were not welcome. When the advance guard had gotten within sight of the pueblo, a small group was sent forward to relay the mandatory requerimiento, demanding submission of Cíbola and threatening violence if the residents chose not to comply. Despite manifest rejection of the Spanish demand and the offering of hostile gestures by the Cíbolans, a priest read the requerimiento aloud twice more. By means of manual signs, Indians accompanying the expedition attempted to communicate the gist of the summons to the people of Cíbola and the other Zuni pueblos who had gathered there. They were unmoved and even sallied from the pueblo, advancing toward the Spaniards and their allies, voicing their displeasure, and launching arrows. In response, the Spanish-led party attacked. Within a matter of hours it had overrun Cíbola. A dozen or so Zunis had been killed and a number of Spaniards wounded, including the captain general. The resident natives were allowed to depart without their food stores, of which the advance guard had sore need.

Within days, representatives from all of the Zuni pueblos offered the gesture of submission. For the next 21 months the majority of Cíbolans (including nearly all the women) occupied fortified positions atop the mesa known as Dowa Yalane while some of the men interacted with units and individuals of the expedition. From July until December 1540 the pueblo of Cíbola was occupied by the expedition. While Vázquez de Coronado and his advance guard rested there, a group of emissaries from Cicuique or Pecos Pueblo arrived to solicit a military alliance. The captain general was invited to send representatives to Cicuique by way of the Rio Grande pueblos.

In the course of the resulting reconnaissance, a tour was made of many of the pueblos. With the mediation of a leader from Cicuique (whom the Spaniards called Bigotes), all but two of the pueblos complied with Spanish instruction and performed acts of submission. The remaining two were forced to abandon resistance. Pursuing stories of wild cattle on the plains to the east of the Pueblo area, the reconnaissance party ventured eastward. While among the bison herds, a native guide supplied by Bigotes (a Plains Indian referred to as El Turco by the Spaniards) told of Quivira, a city wealthy in gold and silver much farther to the east. El Turco also accused Bigotes and others from Cicuique of having stolen jewelry from him, jewelry that would confirm the truth of what he said about Quivira.

The reconnaissance party returned to Cicuique, from where it joined warriors in an abortive assault on another pueblo (according to the 1544 testimony, called Nanapagua). The party's leader, Hernando de Alvarado, questioned Bigotes about the missing jewelry. Bigotes said he knew nothing about the jewelry and that El Turco was making up stories. Unsatisfied, Alvarado took Bigotes and "the cacique," another leader from Cicuique, prisoner and conveyed them to the expedition's winter quarters, which in the meantime had been established in one of the Tiguex pueblos on the Rio Grande.

Having been detailed by the captain general to prepare housing for the expedition along the Rio Grande, Maestre de Campo García López de Cárdenas directed erection of shelters of brush and cornfield stubble. With the forceful arrival of winter, though, it became obvious that such shelter would be inadequate. López de Cárdenas therefore compelled the residents of the nearby pueblo of Coofor to surrender it to the expedition for its principal quarters. It was, thus, to Coofor that Hernando de Alvarado transported his prisoners. There Bigotes and the cacique were interrogated and tortured in an effort by the Spaniards to discover the whereabouts of the jewelry El Turco had described. Even under duress, the Cicuique natives continued to deny the existence of golden bracelets and the wealth of Quivira.

As winter advanced, the insufficiency of the expedition's wardrobe became painfully apparent. To allay the extreme shortage of winter clothing, Vázquez de Coronado detached squads to the neighboring pueblos to trade for woven mantas, bison hides, and fur robes. Often peaceful exchanges occurred, but increasingly the supply parties resorted to thievery and armed robbery to secure sorely needed clothing. Dwindling food supplies and the drive for satisfaction of sexual desire led to further confrontations between expedition members and the Pueblos. These included a case in which a brother of one of the captain general's fellow councilmen on the cabildo of Mexico City attacked a woman at Pueblo del Arenal.

Shortly after this rape and the levying of clothing, Tiguex raiders attacked the Spanish horse herd that had been grazing in their harvested fields, killing at least one Nahua guard, as well as some three dozen horses. The Tiguex then took refuge in three of their twelve pueblos and fortified themselves there. In response, the captain general sent López de Cárdenas and others to nearby Pueblo del Arenal to formally summon the Tiguex to resubmit to Spanish rule and return to amicability. When three summonses failed to draw the Tiguex out, several companies of the expedition launched an attack on Pueblo del Arenal, which turned into a campaign of days. During the campaign at least 60 Indian prisoners were taken, including some who had surrendered under a pledge of security. At the conclusion of hostilities a group of those prisoners was tied to stakes and burned alive. The remaining prisoners then attacked their guards, killing one. That brought down on them the wrath of the Spaniards, who attacked and slaughtered all of the Tiguex who remained alive.

In a near replay of events at Pueblo del Arenal, Vázquez de Coronado next directed a siege of Pueblo del Cerco. After an initial unsuccessful attack against this very strong pueblo, the investment lasted two months. At the end of that time the Pueblo defenders made a break from their stronghold one night. Their flight was detected and Spanish horsemen chased down and killed many of the men.

Captured women and children were subsequently distributed as servants among members of the expedition. Before the pueblo was finally captured, the captain general had one or two of its defenders set upon by dogs and the noses and hands of another ten cut off. These maimed individuals were then sent to their home pueblos to inspire fear in their families and fellows. During the siege five or six Spaniards were killed and many men-at-arms were wounded.

Members of the expedition burned and plundered many of the pueblos that had been abandoned by the Tiguex. Vigas and other roofing materials were used as firewood, and stores of corn and other produce brought relief to the hungry expedition.

When finally winter gave way to warmer weather, the entire expedition left behind a devastated Tiguex world and marched east under the guidance of El Turco. The new goal was Quivira. After meeting Querechos and Teyas, nomadic Plains dwellers and bison hunters, the expedition's leadership concluded El Turco was leading them astray. He was made captive and was taken with a select group of 50 who continued the pursuit of Quivira. The bulk of the expedition was sent back to Coofor. Along the Rio Grande the returnees found one Tiguex pueblo refurbished. They demolished it and confiscated its supply of corn, which supported the expedition through the winter of 1541–1542.

At long last Vázquez de Coronado and his select corps reached Quivira, only to be disappointed again. Of all the storied precious metal and gems, they saw only a single piece of copper. El Turco, accused of trying to stir up the Quivirans to kill the Spaniards, was executed. The captain general and his men rejoined the remainder of the expedition along the Rio Grande. Plans were made, though, to return east the following spring in search of still other wealthy, but more distant, indigenous communities.

Early in 1542, however, came word that the Ópata at San Gerónimo (the location of which had already been moved twice apparently because of hostility of the native people) had risen up, destroyed the town, and killed many of the Spaniards there. With communication to Nueva Galicia cut and after another difficult winter, Vázquez de Coronado and the other leaders of the expedition decided to abandon the enterprise and return south. Two friars and their assistants, along with some 60 other members of the expedition, petitioned to be allowed to remain in Tierra Nueva. Although the friars could be neither stopped nor dissuaded, the 60 aspiring lay settlers were threatened, confined as prisoners, and taken by force back to Nueva Galicia. The expedition departed from the Rio Grande the first of April 1542, and at least some members were in Mexico City by September. On the way, the expedition ran the gauntlet of the hostile Ópata country, engaging in skirmishes and reprisals as it went.

Chapter 26

Results and Repercussions
of the Expedition to Tierra Nueva
from Documentary and
Archeological Sources

Requerimiento and Response

E vidence from the 1544 investigation of the expedition to Tierra Nueva confirms that the prevailing attitudes of the European members of the expedition differed little from those manifested by the majority of members of other Spanish expeditions of that era when it came to the indigenous peoples they encountered and intended to bring under royal dominion. Attitudes of unquestioned superiority of all European and Christian things, persons, and forms over their American counterparts were the root cause of pervasive hostility between the expedition and the native peoples it sojourned among, be they Ópata or Zuni, Tiguex or Teya.[1] The assumption of superiority by sixteenth-century Spaniards is epitomized by the formal summons to submission or requerimiento read repeatedly by lay and religious members of the expedition to newly encountered or "rebellious" Indians. "We ask and require ... that you acknowledge the Church as the ruler and superior of the whole world, and the high priest called Pope, and in his name the king and queen ... our lords, in his place, as superiors and lords and kings of these islands and this mainland. ..."[2] Drafted in 1513, the requerimiento remained the official statement of Spanish authority over the New World until 1573.[3]

To be sure, all but the most skeptical of sixteenth-century Spaniards sincerely believed that the Catholic rite and Spanish culture they sought to impart to the natives of the New World were positive goods of universal value, necessary for ultimate salvation and commodious existence in this life. In exchange for such inestimable benefits it was beyond doubting that the peoples of the New World ought to be grateful and express that gratitude, in part, by paying tribute or tax to their generous benefactors. In the case of the expedition to Tierra Nueva that translated into an expectation that Ópatas, Pueblos, Querechos, Teyas, and Quivirans would willingly support and supply the 2,000 members of the expedition with food, clothing, and shelter, when possible "paid" for with glass beads, articles of fancy clothing, and metal objects.[4] Furthermore, it was assumed that the worth of this commerce in culture would be patently obvious to whatever peoples the expedition encountered and that they would readily abandon their own "benighted" customs in favor of the "true and right" way, begging to be taught and led by their clear "preceptors and masters." Such expectations are apparent in an outraged letter written to the king in 1545 by Mexico City resident and contemporary of the expedition to Tierra Nueva Gerónimo López:

When we had conquered the land, there was no Indian, *principal,* or cacique who would dare raise his eyes to look at a Spaniard's face while talking to him, let alone oppose or contradict him in anything he said. So much was this the case that if a Spaniard traveled on the roads, he could walk all over the land alone and would be served, feared, respected, and obeyed in the name of Your Majesty.[5]

No less an advocate of Indian rights than Bartolomé de las Casas still envisioned American natives as necessarily under the tutelage of European priests so as "to be taught about the Catholic faith and to be admitted to the holy sacraments."[6] Such assured confidence with regard both to the universal value of their culture and religion and the willingness of Indians to accept their transfer was typical of the sixteenth-century agents of Spanish occupation of the Americas. In the actual event, though, Native Americans were generally far from certain of the worth of the Spanish offer and more often than not strongly resisted attempts to impose the touted arrangement on them. Such was generally the case with the native peoples met by the expedition to Tierra Nueva. Surely the Pueblo response to such demands paraphrased in Vázquez de Coronado's interrogatorio of 1544 and 1545, if not literally authentic, must convey some of the natural astonishment and outrage with which native people routinely reacted: "that they were not familiar with his majesty nor did they want to be his subjects or serve him or any other Christian."[7]

The demands of the requerimiento and corollary pressures exerted by the expedition, both overt and tacit, were met by a variety of initial indigenous responses. At Corazones the Ópata welcomed the arrival of the advance party of the expedition, expecting benign effects such as those they had experienced when Álvar Núñez Cabeza de Vaca and his tiny party passed through their community nearly four years previously. And certainly they had heard of the harmless passage of fray Marcos de Niza through the region the year before. At any rate, as many witnesses during the 1544 investigation testified, they supplied provisions to the expedition and even permitted the establishment of a small settlement adjacent to or within their community. Accommodation of Spanish wishes did not last long, though. Hostility from the people of Corazones over demands for women and supplies prompted movement of the Spanish settlement of San Gerónimo to the next valley north. There again friction finally ignited conflict, and San Gerónimo was moved once more, to the extreme northern limit of Ópata territory. There a full-scale uprising early in 1542 killed many Spaniards and scattered the survivors, some retreating to Culiacán, others fleeing north to join the main body of the expedition.

At Cíbola, on the contrary, the reading of the requerimiento was met by immediate armed defense. The late Zuni anthropologist Edmund Ladd suggested that the hostility of the Cíbolans owed in part to the timing of the arrival of the expedition, during the major summer ceremonial.[8] It seems unlikely, however, that even at another time the Zuni people would have welcomed the expedition with pleasure, given their experience with Estevan de

Dorantes, whom they had killed the previous year, and the repeated demands of the expedition for their submission to an unknown overlord. After brief heavy fighting the Cíbolans nominally submitted to Spanish rule, but never fully reinhabited their occupied town, as they were invited to do.

Knowing of the outcome of open resistance to the expedition's demands at Cíbola, the people of Tiguex, three months later, seemed guardedly compliant with requests from the Spaniards, acquiescing to occupation of a pueblo by the expedition and furnishing food supplies in exchange for trade items. Within a month of the arrival of the first contingent of the expedition, though, the Tiguex were openly expressing discontent. At least one Indian woman had been raped,[9] food and clothing demands had become onerous, and Spanish livestock was consuming the fuel supply. The Pueblos withdrew to their towns and prepared defenses. The sequel was what has come to be called the Tiguex War, which resulted in the death and injury of many Tiguex people, forced servitude of many others, and the withdrawal of the remainder out of range of the expedition.

The nearest indigenous neighbors of the Tiguex, the people of Chia to the west, managed to tight-rope-walk between withdrawal and allying with the expedition. They supplied food and clothing to the newcomers even while the Tiguex War raged and agreed to store pieces of ordnance for the Spaniards, but never actually joined the expedition as combatants against the Tiguex.

To the east of the Tiguex area, though, the people of Cicuique initiated a diplomatic mission to the expedition soon after its occupation of Cíbola. They offered friendship and facilitation of relations with the other Pueblos. In exchange, they expected Spanish military aid against a pueblo with which they were in conflict. Relations soured quickly when leaders from Cicuique were taken prisoner and tortured by members of the expedition in order to learn the whereabouts of gold. Thereafter, the people of Cicuique maintained cool but nominally supportive relations with the expedition, giving excuses for their unwillingness to provide outright manpower support. Finally, even that cold facade dissolved into a skirmish at the pueblo itself.

The semi-nomadic peoples of the southern Great Plains, the Querechos and Teyas, adopted the strategy of putting as much distance as possible between themselves and the expedition, without ever resorting to belligerence. The first Querechos the expedition met, for instance, after a single night camped adjacent to the expedition, folded up their tents, loaded their dogs, and moved off in a direction contrary to that the expedition was pursuing. The Teyas, after suffering the theft of a large stock of bison hides by the expedition, offered to lead the strangers to good hunting grounds outside of their home territory and, thus, rid themselves of unwelcome guests that way.

The more settled agricultural Quivirans hid food and refused to supply it to Vázquez de Coronado and the small contingent of the expedition that reached their homeland with him. Armed conflict never developed, possibly because, for once, the expedition members were badly outnumbered and hundreds of miles from friendly support of any kind. Instead, the captain general decided to rejoin the bulk of his expeditionary force in the abandoned Tiguex pueblos along the Rio Grande.

Whether armed conflict ensued or not between the expedition and any particular indigenous group, its constant threat made for a climate of high tension and strain. At any moment an upward ratcheting of coercion, expansion of levies, or simple acts of overweening arrogance could set off a violent storm.

Corollary Pressures

Ultimately, issues of sovereignty and autonomy that even today loom large for Native Americans of all tribal affiliations underlay virtually all of the tension and conflict between the expedition to Tierra Nueva and the natives of the areas through which it passed. But each conflict also had a more proximate cause or trigger.

A sense of divinely conferred superiority, combined with the youth and dominantly male gender of the expedition to Tierra Nueva, together with its unmistakable numerical advantage over the native groups it met, set the stage for frequent sexual pressure and assault against native women. The Spanish documents agree that both at the communications base of San Gerónimo and among the Tiguex pueblos seizure of Indian women for sexual purposes was a major factor in bringing the expedition into conflict with indigenous communities.[10] This was a situation endemic to enterprises of armed European expansion throughout the hemisphere. As Mary Karasch has remarked about eighteenth- and nineteenth-century Brazil, "As is true of most frontiers, one characteristic of the Goiano outpost was intense male competition for female labor and companionship . . . One of the principal causes of conflict between Luso-Brazilian, Afro-Brazilian, and Indian men was raids for women."[11]

Like members of many other expeditions of the period, those of the expedition to Tierra Nueva expected also to benefit from the employment of native women as servants. As Diego López testified in 1545 in Culiacán province, while the expedition was in Tiguex he saw many men asking the captain general to requisition servants from the neighboring pueblos, something that Vázquez de Coronado was reluctant to do, so as not to annoy the Pueblo people. The wishes of many members of the expedition were fulfilled, however, once warfare broke out, since prisoners could then be pressed into domestic service legally. And many were.[12] Certainly there must have been expedition members who for this reason, if for no other, were pleased to have hostilities begin.

The expedition to Tierra Nueva was extremely ill-prepared to provide the necessities of life for its members in a land far removed from any customary source of supply. Although information on the severity of winters in the north, for instance, had been received from Melchor Díaz and Juan de Zaldívar while the expedition was still within Nueva Galicia, no provision for adequate clothing was made.[13] When winter arrived the expedition was forced to try to "buy" warm clothing from the Tiguex of New Mexico. This put incredible strains on the native population which simply did not have a surplus sufficient to clothe the huge group of Mexican Indian, European, and African adults who made up the expedition. The clothing shortage became a decisive factor in relations between the indigenous people and the new arrivals. Forced purchases were made and, when that failed to supply the necessary quantity of clothing, mantas and other articles of native apparel were taken by force.

With regard to food supply, the expedition was somewhat better prepared, though still not by any means provisioned so as to be self-sufficient. Thousands of meat animals (cattle, sheep, and hogs) accompanied the expedition, apparently adequate for more than a year and a half. Fortunately, before that supply was exhausted, the expedition encountered the immense bison herds of the southern Great Plains. That allowed the expedition to replenish its meat supply, spending two solid weeks hunting bison and preparing bison meat for transportation and storage. Fruits, vegetables, and grains were another matter altogether.[14] There is no evidence in any of the surviving documents related to the expedition that it carried either seeds or implements for cultivating crops. In this regard it was typical of Spanish New World expeditions of the sixteenth century. A study of 26 such expeditions showed that very few agricultural implements were carried by any of them, by the expedition to Tierra Nueva none at all that can be positively assigned to agricultural purposes.[15] Nor are seeds mentioned in the contemporary documents as being carried by the expedition.[16] It is clear that, even in its organization, it was assumed that cultivated foods would and could be obtained from the native peoples.[17] As I have previously written, "This situation calls into question the sustainability of the expedition even from its conception."[18] As with the issue of servants, the onset of warfare between the expedition and the Tiguex made acquisition of foodstuffs much easier than it was in times of peace. According to Lorenzo Álvarez in his 1545 testimony, "Nothing, neither corn nor anything else, was taken from peaceful Indians, only those at war."

To provide shelter from intense sunshine and inclement weather, the European members of the expedition carried pavilion tents and tools for erecting more substantial makeshift structures. The rest of the expedition was left to fend for itself. And while on the march most members of the expedition often camped without shelter. For instance, as the body of the expedition made its way from Cíbola to Tiguex in December 1540 most people slept outside unprotected, despite daily snowfall.[19] Once arrived at native settlements, though, the expedition appropriated space there in existing buildings. At Cíbola both accommodations and food were secured by outright attack, while in Tiguex only an implied threat of force was evidently necessary to persuade the people of the pueblo of Coofor to surrender it for the use of the expedition.[20] Eventually, the expedition occupied at least one other Tiguex pueblo, probably Pueblo de la Alameda, most likely after it was abandoned in the wake of armed assault on another nearby pueblo, Pueblo del Arenal.[21] As in the case of food supplies, the leadership and most other members of the expedition to Tierra Nueva assumed that shelter would be provided by the native people of the region.

Another consequence of absolute certainty of members of the expedition in their superiority was disregard and disparagement of indigenous practice by the expedition as a whole and its persistent employment of Spanish conventions to the detriment of newly submitted "vassals." The use of cornfield stubble among the Tiguex pueblos is a case in point. One night during the winter of 1540–1541 Tiguex people attacked the horse herd of the expedition to Tierra Nueva, driving off some 60 or more horses, which they later killed. According to Juan Troyano in his testimony before Tejada, the Tiguex rose up because the "horses were eating their planted fields." The Spaniards were outraged, feeling that the Tiguex had acted completely without reason or provocation. After all, the Spaniards were simply following the time-honored custom of grazing their livestock in harvested fields. In Spain of the later Middle Ages and Renaissance such land was, by law, available for the grazing of livestock by anyone once the crops were out of the fields.[22]

In contrast, the Tiguex, lacking domesticated grazing animals throughout prehistory and at the time of the expedition to Tierra Nueva, had another altogether different use for cornfield "waste." As examination of thousands of prehistoric middens or trash dumps across the Southwest has revealed, corncobs and cornstalks were for centuries an important and renewable source of fuel to the sedentary indigenous peoples of the region and remained so for the Tiguex in the mid sixteenth century.[23] Thus, cornstalks standing in their harvested fields in the winter of 1540–1541, were an abundant and much-relied-upon source of fuel for the Tiguex, certainly to be defended against marauding Spanish livestock.[24] Though neither Tiguex nor Spaniards seemed aware of the other group's expectations and assumptions for "proper use" of field stubble, the collision of such culturally based assumptions put the two groups almost inevitably in conflict, probably to everyone's bewilderment and consternation.

A Sunday School Picnic?

The immediate and most obvious result of the arrival of the expedition to Tierra Nueva among the sedentary native peoples of the far north was war. Assessment of the numerical impact of casualties on both sides must be imprecise at best. Pedro de Castañeda, the most thorough contemporary chronicler of the expedition, reported more than 401 Indians killed by the expedition and 21 European members of the expedition killed in turn by Indians, at Cíbola and the Tiguex pueblos (Pueblo del Arenal and Pueblo del Cerco).[25] Indian casualties were probably significantly higher than the figure reported by Castañeda, all but perhaps two dozen of whom died during the fighting in the Tiguex area. Even using Castañeda's very conservative figures, this means that the Tiguex suffered fatalities during the warfare of 1540–1541 in excess of ten percent of their total population,[26] with losses heavily weighted in the adult and young adult male segments of their population. The numbers of European and Indian casualties reported by Castañeda do not include the large number killed at San Gerónimo. Nor do other contemporary documents provide estimates. In addition, an unknown number of the expedition's approximately 1,300 Nahua and other Mexican Indian allies were killed, including between two and five on the night horses were stolen and killed in Tiguex.[27] In the course of his testimony during Viceroy Mendoza's residencia, Vázquez de Coronado estimated that fewer than 30 Indian allies had died while on the expedition.[28] Many more individuals on both sides were wounded. For instance, Francisco Martín, in his 1544 testimony, swore that 70 or 80 Spaniards were wounded during the fighting at Pueblo del Arenal alone. Others, including the captain general, were wounded at Cíbola and the Tiguex pueblos.[29] And expedition members are reported as rounding up wounded Tiguex after their attempt to flee from Pueblo del Cerco. How many Indians later died from their wounds or com-

plications therefrom out of sight and knowledge of the expedition is information now wholly inaccessible.

The effects of war death and incapacity among the Tiguex were surely
devastating. Defense and ceremonial capacities were seriously diminished, as
was the agricultural labor force. As Carroll Riley has put it, "Not only had
numbers of people been killed or wounded, but the Indians had lost their
pueblos, their stores of food and clothing, and use of their land."[30] While not
as catastrophic for the expedition to Tierra Nueva, deaths and debilitating
injuries were certainly disheartening and figured in the ultimate decision to
abandon the enterprise altogether.

Despite the heavy toll taken among the Tiguex and Ópata during warfare
with the expedition to Tierra Nueva, historians, led by Herbert Bolton, have
generally contrasted a supposed relative non-violence of the expedition with
the malevolence of other contemporary entradas, especially the expedition
through La Florida led by Hernando de Soto and the conquest of Nueva
Galicia by Nuño Belrán de Guzmán. In Bolton's words, "compared with de
Soto's swashbuckling raid, in the matter of human relations Coronado's expedition to Quivira was a Sunday school picnic."[31] The record of Lorenzo de
Tejada's investigation, together with other contemporary documentary evidence, however, reveals Bolton's appraisal as a gross misstatement. Detailed
comparison of the longest and most detailed narrative accounts of each of the
two expeditions[32] has shown that the number of native deaths resulting from
the two expeditions was very similar.[33] Additionally, both expeditions equally
frequently resorted to torture of native prisoners and other acts of terror and
were similarly reluctant to punish their own members for abuse of indigenous
people. Tellingly, neither expedition enjoyed a reputation for benevolence
among the natives it encountered; in fact, quite the opposite. For example, as
far away from the Tiguex territory as the Pacific coast Indians told members of
a sea-going party led by Juan Rodríguez Cabrillo in 1542 that "further inland
men like us [of the expedition to Tierra Nueva] moved about . . . they killed
many Indians and that is why they are afraid."[34] Nevertheless, the Soto expedition *was* more often engaged in hostilities with indigenous peoples than was

the expedition to Tierra Nueva. That greater frequency of violent clashes was due to two principal factors: 1) the very much greater and denser native population of the interior of what is now the southeastern United States compared to the Greater Southwest and 2) Soto's decision to rely on native load bearers for transport of equipment and provisions, which brought the expedition and indigenous groups into almost daily conflict.

It is worthy of note also that although it has been written that there was no overlap in personnel between the Guzmán entrada and the expedition to Tierra Nueva,[35] in fact, at least a dozen individuals participated in both. More significant still, five of the captains of the expedition to Tierra Nueva had been with Guzmán (Melchor Díaz, Diego de Alcaraz, Juan de Zaldívar, Pedro de Tovar, and Diego López) and the original maestre de campo of the expedition, Lope de Samaniego (appointed directly by the viceroy), had served as a captain under Guzmán. These individuals had participated in what are usually considered some of the darkest chapters in the history of European occupation of the New World, the wholesale slaughter and enslavement of indigenous peoples of northwestern Mexico in the early 1530s.[36] In all likelihood the killing of Samaniego by Indians near Chiametla early in the expedition to Tierra Nueva was retaliation for his earlier activities in the same area and not solely a refusal to supply food to the expedition, though that is what Pedro de Castañeda later reported.[37] With such individuals in command under Vázquez de Coronado, it is little wonder that the captain general was often kept in the dark about what was really transpiring between the expedition and the native peoples. Still, the inclusion of veterans of the Guzmán entrada in positions of leadership of the expedition to Tierra Nueva indicates an acceptance or tolerance by Viceroy Mendoza of some of Guzmán's brutal methods and tactics.

In an effort to frighten Indians into submission and quiescence, the Spaniards of the expedition to Tierra Nueva from time to time perpetrated acts of terror, subjecting individuals to torture to extract information, drawing and quartering Indians at Chiametla, and cutting off hands and noses of Pueblo captives then releasing them as objects of horror.[38] The setting of dogs on the leaders from Cicuique, Bigotes and the cacique, by members of the expedition in an effort to learn about the existence of precious metals is very reminiscent of torture applied for the same purpose to the Cazonci (leader) of Michoacán in 1530 by the expedition led by Guzmán[39] and extortion of information from captives by burning their comrades alive, which was done by the Soto expedition.[40]

Furthermore, whether intended to inspire terror or not, the systematic dismantling of Tiguex towns following their abandonment by the Tiguex themselves (as confirmed by many witnesses during the 1544 investigation) had a cruel impact. The psychological effect of torture and calculated disfigurement, combined with grief over death of relatives and loss of homes, was excruciating. In the Pueblo world the winter weather, which in 1540–1541 and again the following year was extraordinarily severe, added further stress. It can only be suggested that these strains and pressures weakened many Tiguex to the point of death. Certainly the expedition, even without generally suffering loss of family members or destruction and despoliation of homes, was hard pressed to cope with the situation in Tiguex, especially during the second winter. "Many Spaniards were ill and dying at Tiguex," testified Lorenzo Álvarez in 1544.

Despite the fact that there may have been potentially extenuating circumstances (including two abnormally cold winters and failure to be resupplied from the ships of Hernando de Alarcón), the demands made by the expedition to Tierra Nueva on local native peoples for food and clothing, the seizure of women, and the use of torture and terror tactics were unequivocally consistent with sixteenth-century Spanish expeditionary/settlement behavior throughout the New World. There is almost no evidence of especially benevolent behavior on the part of the expedition to Tierra Nueva, with the single possible exception that the expedition, abiding by specific instructions from the king and viceroy, did not make chattel slaves of any of the Indians from the north. The expedition did, however, press native women and children into extended involuntary servitude (that is, for the duration of its sojourn in Tierra Nueva). Undoubtedly, the technical distinction between chattel slavery and open-ended servitude would not have been appreciated by the women who, against their will, were cooking, cleaning, and providing sexual release for members of the expedition.

A New Social Configuration
in the Middle Rio Grande Valley

In the Pueblo area of what is now central New Mexico, the expedition employed a favorite strategy that dated back at least to the reconquest of the Iberian Peninsula from Muslims who had crossed from North Africa: to exploit regional rivalries and pit neighbors against neighbors.[41] In this case, the tactic enjoyed only the most minimal success. To be sure, territorial rivalries existed among the indigenous peoples of the Rio Grande and adjacent valleys. For centuries Towa, Tano, and Keres groups had been crowding in closer to the homeland of the Tiguex, the oldest Pueblo group of the region.[42] The equable climate and abundant water and arable land drove slow encroachment. As Pedro de Castañeda characterized the Tiguex area, it was the center or heart of the land of pueblos.[43] According to Vázquez de Coronado's 1544 testimony before Lorenzo de Tejada, the people of Cicuique agreed to send fighting men to battle the Tiguex on the side of the Spanish expedition, if they were given a pueblo in that area to ease the population pressure and land shortage at Cicuique. Nevertheless, neither Cicuique nor the Keres pueblo of Chia ever supplied fighters against the Tiguex. And, in fact, the people of Cicuique, at least, eventually became hostile to the expedition.

With the outbreak of hostilities, the Tiguex first sought to defend themselves against the insistent demands of the expedition by congregating in two easily defensible pueblos. When this expedient failed, they abandoned their home territory completely except for carrying out occasional ambushes of stray expedition members. It is likely they were granted asylum with neighboring Tanos, Tewas, Piros, Tompiros, or even Keres, in turn burdening their supplies of stored food. Between April and July 1541 some Tiguex reoccupied and repaired several of their pueblos. But when the expedition returned unexpectedly to take up residence again, they fled once more.

A crucial result of the nearly two-year abandonment of Tiguex territory, for both the Tiguex and the expedition, was that the Middle Rio Grande Valley went unplanted. Cristóbal de Escobar, testifying before Lorenzo de Tejada in 1544, stated that the Spaniards "would have died of cold and hunger if it had not been for the supplies and wood that they got from the pueblos [the Indians] had repaired and rebuilt."

The Tiguex, though they reoccupied most of their home territory after retreat of the expedition to Mexico in spring 1542, never did reoccupy all of it. In fact, the people of Chia and other Keres pueblos, the passive allies of the expedition during its conflict with the Tiguex, opportunistically established new pueblos in the northern fringe of what, prior to 1540, had been Tiguex and Tano territory. When the next Spanish expedition, led by fray Agustín Rodríguez, arrived in New Mexico in 1581, it encountered in the vicinity of the confluence of the Rio Grande and Jemez River five permanently inhabited Keres pueblos, where in 1540 there had been only one, Chia. In 1581, besides Chia, there were Castilleja (probably ancestral San Felipe), Guatitlán (Santa Ana), and La Guarda and La Rinconada (between Zia and Santa Ana).[44] It may be that in the wake of the horrific wintertime fighting early in 1541 at Pueblo del Cerco in this area and the resultant loss of life, the Tiguex did not contest the use right over the territory around the Jemez River–Rio Grande junction with the encroaching Keres.[45] Furthermore, in the Galisteo Basin to the northeast of the Tiguex area Pedro de Castañeda of the expedition to Tierra Nueva reported three pueblos in the early 1540s, only one of which was fully inhabited. Forty years later the Rodríguez-Chamuscado expedition visited four inhabited pueblos in the same area.[46] The additional pueblo in the Galisteo Basin in the 1580s was the one called Malpartida by the Rodríguez-Chamuscado expedition, usually identified as San Marcos Pueblo near the aboriginally exploited turquoise and lead mines. San Marcos is considered by ethnohistorians and archeologists to have been a Keres pueblo and, indeed, its ruins today are associated with the Keres pueblo of Cochiti.[47] Once again this suggests an intrusion of Keres people following the disruptions caused by the expedition to Tierra Nueva.[48]

Although lacking in temporal precision, oral traditions among the Keres people of modern Cochiti and San Felipe include an account of the ancestors of San Felipe leaving their cultural brethren at a pueblo known as Kuapa and migrating southward into the Tiguex area. There they were received with hostility by the people of Sandia Pueblo and moved on eastward where they took up residence among the Tanos. Later they left the Tanos and established a pueblo on the west bank of the Rio Grande not far from modern San Felipe.[49]

Transmission of Pathogens, Transplantation of People, and Acquisition of Knowledge

The question, often posed about early European contact in other areas of the Western Hemisphere, as to whether deadly Old World disease pathogens were introduced into the Greater Southwest by the expedition to Tierra Nueva must be considered. Certainly none of the known contemporary documents arising from the expedition to Tierra Nueva refers to illnesses among any of the native groups it contacted. But since some sickness was present among at least the European contingent of the expedition during the winter of 1541–1542,[50] the possibility exists that it was influenza or one of the other Old World maladies that proved extraordinarily lethal to Indians in the New World. Between the expedition to Tierra Nueva and the Rodríguez-Chamuscado expedition forty years later, however, there seems to have been very little change in total Pueblo population as estimated by Spanish observers. The total number of Pueblo communities remained all but constant not only between 1540 and 1581, but until establishment of a permanent Spanish colony in 1598.[51] Nevertheless, the source data are so scanty and dissimilar as to provide no unambiguous answer as to whether the Pueblos were significantly impacted by Old World diseases as a result of the expedition to Tierra Nueva.[52] More conclusively, Daniel Reff, in studying episodes of European disease in the sixteenth-century Ópata territory of central and northern Sonora, where the shifting base of San Gerónimo was located, has found that "there is little or no evidence that De Niza's or Coronado's expeditions were responsible for the introduction of acute and chronic infectious diseases."[53] Part of the explanation for lack of transmission of serious disease by the expedition to Tierra Nueva is the minimal amount of communication and direct contact between it and individuals from the established Spanish settlements in Nueva España and Nueva Galicia during its two-year sojourn in the north.

While the expedition may not have served as a conduit of disease, it did transplant people from central and western Mexico into the Upper Southwest. Of the thousand-plus Nahuatl-, Tarascan-, and Caxcán-speaking Indians who participated in the expedition to Tierra Nueva, an unknown number remained behind in the Greater Southwest when the expedition returned south. For instance, during the first few days of the expedition's return trek people from Cíbola followed along behind salvaging discarded equipment and welcoming Nahuas and other Indian allies who decided to stay behind.[54] In the Cíbola/Zuni area 40 years later, the expedition led by Antonio de Espejo found "Mexican Indians, and also a number from Guadalajara, some of those that Coronado had brought."[55] Carroll Riley has suggested that the most significant impact of the Nahuas and other Mexican Indians who remained in the north was "to reinforce the Mesoamerican element in Southwestern culture, and to introduce certain Spanish traits and ideas."[56] While the cultural effect of the Mexican Indians who stayed to live among the Pueblos may not have been great, they certainly were a valuable source of knowledge about European expectations and behavior, which conditioned Pueblo responses to subsequent Spanish entradas.

In a material way, the Mexican Indian members of the expedition had a major effect on the European contingent. More than 90% of the European men-at-war carried solely or primarily arms and armament characteristic of indigenous central Mexico, rather than or in addition to European gear.[57] In food and food preparation, too, the European members of the expedition relied heavily on the central Mexican staple, corn, and on indigenous culinary methods and utensils. For their part, the Mexican Indians continued to learn and employ Spanish techniques and customs regarding organization, warfare, livestock tending, diplomacy, engineering, and a raft of other facets of expeditionary and colonial life.

In the end it may be that the acquisition of knowledge and opinion by each group about the others was the most lasting result of the expedition for all parties. Specifics are difficult to find and extract from the documentary record, but many things are easily inferred. Indians throughout the Greater Southwest became familiar with the formalism and legal punctiliousness of the Europeans and their penchant for making written records. European reverence for the cross and its efficacy as a shield for beleaguered indigenous peoples was clear, despite abrogation of a cross-warranted promise at Pueblo del Arenal. European reliance on livestock and the limitations and liabilities that imposed were open for all to remark. Reports of the brutality of many European actions were repeatedly confirmed, reports that had been received for years prior to the coming of the expedition through the network of trade that linked all parts of the Greater Southwest and tied it to Mesoamerica and other areas.

For Europeans, on the other hand, ideas of Old-World-style kingdoms governed by monarchs and a class of elites had to be abandoned when considering the far north. The failure of the expedition to Tierra Nueva to locate large hierarchical states with accumulations of precious metals and jewels hastened a shift in Spanish attitudes about natives of the Americas in general. That shift, all but complete by mid-century, was from expectations of Indians as potential wealthy payers of "money" tribute to Indians as a labor force for Spanish economic enterprises, often the extraction of precious metals. While human similarities between Europeans and Native Americans were obvious, so was the existence of gulfs and chasms that circumscribed possibilities for effortless interaction. In many ways each group confirmed preconceived stereotypes of the others, especially since behavior in times of stress and conflict (as was often the case for all parties in the course of the expedition to Tierra Nueva) tends toward the routinized and habitual, resulting in self-generated caricatures. This explains in part why attitudes toward the indigenous peoples of Tierra Nueva expressed by the witnesses in Tejada's investigation tended to be so negative and so self-justificatory toward the actions of the expedition.

Although, as Janet Lecompte has observed, following its return from Tierra Nueva the "expedition was all but forgotten,"[58] its effects lingered, becoming part of the general lore and common knowledge that each group held about the others and passed to succeeding generations.

Herbert Bolton was quick to point toward increased geographical knowledge for Spaniards stemming from the expedition to Tierra Nueva. As

Robert Weddle has recently written, information gained during the Pacific coast voyages associated with the Coronado expedition figured in the opening of trade between Nueva España and the Far East.[59] Nevertheless, as Bolton himself pointed out, much of the geographical knowledge stemming from the expedition was forgotten or misinterpreted.[60] Not forgotten, however, was the absence of wealthy European-style cities in the north and the financial hardship chasing that chimera had caused.[61]

Most European expedition members for whom records survive complained, sometimes bitterly, that the trek to Tierra Nueva had seriously impoverished them. While such complaints were part of the standard application for reward and preferment by the Spanish king, there is considerable evidence that because the expected wealth was not found in the north many individuals lost their entire investments and were a long time in recovering from that blow. It was probably to stave off the eventuality of ruined investments that some 60 members of the expedition agitated obstinately to be allowed to remain in Tierra Nueva after the departure of the majority of the expedition.[62] After all, if they returned to Nueva España, they would be destitute and competing for resources with thousands of other ambitious Europeans. Whereas, by remaining in the north there was still the hope of wresting a living from the native peoples there and always the possibility that the original reports of wealth would be substantiated. Even among the principal investors, the financial losses resulting from the expedition to Tierra Nueva were debilitating. After 1542 Antonio de Mendoza, for instance, never again undertook sponsorship of a major expedition, turning his energies and resources instead increasingly to more prosaic economic development within Nueva España.

The return of the expedition to Tierra Nueva from the north in 1542 provided an influx of Spanish population into the Culiacán area, attracted by indications of ores of precious metals that had been located during Vázquez de Coronado's abortive entrada to Topira in the Sierra Madre Occidental and during the expedition to Tierra Nueva itself. According to seventeenth-century historian fray Antonio Tello, Vázquez de Coronado returned to Compostela with nearly the whole expedition dispersed because some men-at-arms had remained in Culiacán and others had gone on to Mexico City.[63] This did much to reverse the trend that Vázquez de Coronado had lamented as governor, when he found in 1538 that Culiacán was being abandoned.[64]

Departure of the expedition in 1540, though, had temporarily but dangerously reduced the population of Nueva Galicia, a fact not lost on the native peoples of that ten-year-old province. Within ten months a widespread uprising against Spanish presence and domination in Nueva Galicia was under way. Certainly the most serious threat to Spanish claims of sovereignty in the New World during the sixteenth century, the uprising, often referred to as the Mixtón War, was not put down until early 1542. Even then it was brought to an end only after a massive armed force was raised in central Mexico and led by the viceroy himself against the many fortified Indian towns of Nueva Galicia. The launching of the expedition to Tierra Nueva, thus, opened the door to a nearly successful challenge to Spanish rule in the whole of the viceroyalty of Nueva España.[65]

Conclusion

The pesquisa into the treatment of indigenous peoples by the expedition to Tierra Nueva was initiated as an expression of the sincere convictions of a powerful group agitating for Indian rights during the middle third of the sixteenth century in Spain. It was triggered by denunciations made to the king either directly or indirectly by unidentified persons who participated in the expedition. Because of the political ramifications of culpability for brutality for Francisco Vázquez de Coronado and Antonio de Mendoza, the viceroy's rival Hernán Cortés lobbied that such an investigation be conducted. But, precisely because of the political danger to the viceroy, individuals within the upper echelons of the colonial administration of Nueva España worked together to satisfy the outrage of the Indian rights faction in Spain while lodging blame for manifest brutality as far from the viceroy as possible. In this the colonial administration was successful. Responsibility for outrages committed among the Ópatas and Pueblos was fixed on the former maestre de campo of the expedition, García López de Cárdenas. Vázquez de Coronado and, by extension, Viceroy Mendoza were exonerated. Even López de Cárdenas was largely shielded from punishment.

The resulting investigation record is one of testimony heavily weighted in favor of the former captain general of the expedition. Despite this orchestration of the testimony, though, the witnesses revealed much about the complex motives and forces that determined the course of contact between the expedition to Tierra Nueva and the indigenous peoples of the Greater Southwest. Together with archeological and ethnographic evidence, their testimony has allowed detailed delineation of many effects of this "failed" expedition, both on its own members and on natives of the Greater Southwest.

It cannot be stressed strongly enough that all the groups and individuals who encountered and interacted with each other during the expedition to Tierra Nueva were governed by intricate constellations of principles, drives, and desires sometimes internally in conflict. The expedition was a diverse multitude ranging from black slaves to powerful members of the Spanish colonial elite, from sons and daughters of the Mexica to visionary Catholic friars, from individuals fresh off the boat from the Old World to long-time veterans of frontier life in the New. This assemblage of people intruded into the homelands of scores of equally heterogeneous indigenous peoples, from the sedentary people of Chiametla already ravaged for years by colonial slaving to fully nomadic Querechos without previous experience of Spaniards and their allies, from town-dwelling Cíbolans to Teyas whose encampments might vanish overnight, from long-distance traders in precious exotic commodities to grinders of cornmeal and curers of hides. Only a sample of the complexity of contact between such divergent and dissimilar peoples has been offered here.

For Europeans and Mexican Indian allies the results of the expedition to Tierra Nueva were very different from those anticipated during the heady days of recruitment in the fall of 1539. And the unintended repercussions of the entrada on both its own members and the indigenous peoples it came into contact and had commerce with were largely unforeseen. Those repercussions were, nevertheless, decisive in the lives of thousands of individuals and helped determine the course of future interaction between native peoples of the

Greater Southwest and European-led interlopers from the south. Hundreds died, hundreds more were injured, thousands were impoverished and deprived of their homes and livelihoods. Significant population shifts occurred. Spaniards from central Mexico were relocated to the far northern fringes of colonial settlement, assuring the slow but relentless expansion of Spanish dominance. In New Mexico, Keres groups took another step in a centuries-old encroachment on their neighbors the Tiguex. All across the Greater Southwest and throughout the New World Spanish empire (to which the members of the expedition dispersed) conclusions about foreign groups were drawn and solidified. Wariness and suspicion increased among all the groups concerned.

Afterword

This book has focused on the violent events of the Coronado expedition that figured in the investigation conducted by Lorenzo de Tejada in 1544. Those events were denounced to the king of Spain as wantonly brutal, and punishment of the responsible leaders was sought. Evidence was presented that, indeed, interaction between the expedition and the native peoples it encountered often seemed excessively violent. Certainly by standards at the beginning of the twenty-first century the Coronado expedition systematically disregarded and violated the rights of the native peoples it encountered to self-rule and other basic freedoms. It employed torture and terror to enforce control over populations subjugated by force. It compelled service and sex from non-consenting natives of the Greater Southwest throughout its sojourn there. It was routinely blind to the humanity and legitimacy of the customs and lifeways of Ópatas, Pueblos, Querechos, Teyas, and Quivirans.

By and large, the Native Americans brought into contact with the expedition expressed, mostly by actions, their view of the Europeans and their allies as unprincipled aggressors. There were occasional exceptions to that perception, however. The people of Chia, for example, evidently had a less harsh appraisal.

The expedition was manifestly not a non-aggressive geographical exploration or mineral prospecting party. The people of Tierra Nueva and their supposed wealth were the raison d'etre of the expedition. The documents demonstrate that the expedition was sent explicitly 1) to subjugate (*conquistar*) the peoples of Tierra Nueva; 2) to convert (*traer en conocimiento*) them to the Catholic faith; and 3) to establish Spanish settlement (*poblar*) in Tierra Nueva. The ultimate aim of most members of the expedition was enrichment from precious metals. They were expecting, however, that those precious metals would already be exploited by a sophisticated native population. Tribute and encomienda were the means the expedition had for tapping into that expected wealth. That required establishment of political control over the diverse populations of Corazones, Suya, Cíbola, Tiguex, Chia, Cicuique, and Quivira, with their voluntary acceptance or not.

That said, it must be noted that by the prevailing standards of the day in Spain, and Europe more generally, many of the acts that we view with horror and condemnation today were not seen in that way at the time. Most of the members of the expedition were not actively or intentionally cruel. They certainly did not see themselves as cruel, though some of their compatriots did. Just as certainly, most of them saw themselves as naturally superior to the native peoples they met. As so often happens, that sense of superiority generated pervasive insensitivity and frequent abuse. One result was some very bloody deeds undertaken with a sense of righteous justification.

Was the Coronado expedition unique in its resort to force in order to incorporate Native Americans and their resources into the Spanish sphere? The answer must be a resounding, "No." In fact, there were contemporary expeditions much more notorious for inhumane treatment of Indians. Nor were Spaniards of the era generally more prone to forcibly imposing their religious, economic, and political structures on the wider world than have been many other powerful, prosperous peoples throughout history.

Despite the brutality of the Coronado expedition and the sixteenth-century conquest of the Americas in general, we can point with some pride to the energetic activism of a group of contemporary Spaniards who led Europe in the first modern national debates on human rights. It was their efforts that led conquistadores like Francisco Vázquez de Coronado and Garcia López de Cárdenas to be called to account.

Appendices

Appendix 1

Origins, Ages, and Arrival of 115 Members of the Expedition to Tierra Nueva

*Information shown in boldface pertains to witnesses
in the pesquisa concerning treatment of Indians by the expedition.*

Name	Origin	Age in 1540	Year of arrival in Nueva España
Alba, H.	Salamanca (Cast-León)	?	?
Alonso, M.	Manzanilla (?)	?	?
Alvarado, H.	Santander	24±	1520
Álvarez, Al.	**Badajoz (Extrem)**	**14+**	**1537 or 38**
Arce, J.	Santander	?	1537
Arias de Saavedra, H.	Sevilla (And)	?	?
Barrionuevo, F.	Granada (And)	?	?
Bermejo, H.	Badajoz (Extrem)	?	?
Bermejo, J.	Tor de Laguna (Madrid)	?	?
Bertao, C.	Ruan (France)	?	1537
Beteta, J.	Beteta (Cast-La Mancha)	23±	1538 or 39
Blaque, T.	Scotland	21±	?
Botello, H.	Alcántara (Extrem)	?	1537
Caballero, L.	Galicia	?	1535
Cadena, H.	Medellín (Extrem)	25+	?
Campo, A. do	Portugal	?	?
Caravajal, F.	Utrera (And)	?	?

Name	Origin	Age in 1540	Year of arrival in Nueva España
Castañeda, A.	Vizcaya (Basq)	?	1528
Castillo, G.	Sevilla (And)	19+	?
Cepeda, J.	Toledo (Cast-La Mancha)	?	?
Cervantes, J.	Sevilla (And)	?	before 1526
Cepedes, J.	?	?	1532
Contreras, J.	**Huelva (And)**	?	**1538**
Cornejo, F.	Salamanca (Cast-León)?	1527	
Cuevas, J.	Aranda de Duero (Cast-León)	?	1525
Díaz, F.	?	14	1537 or 38
Entrambasagus, M.	Burgos (Cast-León)	33±	1537 or 38
Escobar, C.	**Huelva (And)**	**18+**	**1538**
Fernández, D.	Oviedo (Asturias)	?	?
Figueredo, L.	?	**25±**	?
Fioz, J.	Germany	23±	?
Frías, R.	**Toledo (Cast-La Mancha)**	**23±**	**1536**
Gallas, J.	Almendralejo (Extrem)	23±	?
Gallego, J.	Coruña (Gal)	?	1520
Garnica, J.	Vizcaya	?	?
Garrido, B.	Huelva (And)	?	1521
Gómez de la Peña, H.	?	?	1533
Gómez de Paradinas	**Salamanca (Cast-León)**	**18+**	**1535**
Gómez de Salazar, J.	?	20	?
González, F. or H.	Santo Domingo	?	?
González, R.	Villanueva de Fresno (Extrem)	?	1520
Gorbalán, F.	Guadalajara (Cast-La Mancha)	29±	?
Guevara, D.	?	19±	?
Hernández, J.	Asturias	?	1531
Hernández de Arriba	?	37±	?
Hozes, F.	**Ciudad Real (Cast-La Mancha)** (inferred)	**29+**	**1522**
Huerta, F.	Badajoz (Extrem)	?	1535
Jaramillo, J.	Villanueva de Barcarota (Extrem)	23+ or 30+	?
Jiménez, A.	?	?	1533
Jiménez, J.	Sevilla (And)	?	?
Ledesma, P.	**Zamora (Cast-León)**	**26±**	**1535**
López, A.	Córdoba (And)	?	?
López, D.	**Sevilla (And)**	**25±**	**1538**

Name	Origin	Age in 1540	Year of arrival in Nueva España
López, G.	?	25±	1536
López de la Rosa	Sayago (Cast-León)	?	?
López de la Cárdenas	Madrid	?	1535
Luna y Arellano	Borovia (Cast-León)	26±	1530 or 31
Madrid Avendaño	Toledo (Cast-La Mancha)	29±	1535
Maldonado, C.	Burgillos (Extrem)	?	1532 (New World)
Maldonado, R.	**Salamanca (Cast-León)**	**24±**	**1538**
Manrique, A.	Valladolid (Cast-León)	?	1535
Martín, D.	**Brozas (Extrem)**	**38+**	**by 1517**
Martín, E.	?	14+	?
Mayorga, C.	Benavente (Cast-León)	18+	before 1530
Melgosa, P.	Burgos (Cast-León)	24±	?
Mercado de Sotomayor	Sevilla (And)	?	1529
Muñoz, F.	Granja (Extrem)	21+	1533
Navarro, J.	Aragón	?	?
Navarro, P.	Estella (Navarra)	30+	?
Nieto, P.	?	20+	?
Olivares, F.	Béjar de Castañar (Cast-León)	?	1528
Ordoñez, F.	Alhanje (Extrem)	?	1524
Orduña, H.	Burgos (Cast-León)	18+	?
Orejón, A.	Ávila (Cast-León)	?	before 1537
Páez, F.	Villafranca (Portugal)	21±	?
Paniagua, J.	Écija (And)	?	1532 (New World)
Paradinas, A.	Salamanca (Cast-León)	?	1535
Peñas, J.	?	?	1533
Pérez, A.	?	21±	?
Pérez, M.	**Badajoz (Extrem)**	**28± or 26±**	**1531**
Pérez Buscavida, A.	Comil (Extrem)	?	1535
Puelles, D.	Miranda de Ebro (Cast-León)	?	1539
Quesada, C.	Sevilla (And)	?	1535
Ramírez de Vargas, L.	?	18+	?
Robles, M.	Antequera (Andalucía)	25±	?
Rodríquez, G.	**Alcaraz or Alcázar (Cast-La Mancha)**	**18+**	**1538 or 39**
Rodríguez de Alanje	Alanje (Extrem)	?	1535

Name	Origin	Age in 1540	Year of arrival in Nueva España
Rodríguez Parra, A.	Santibañez de Mascores (Extrem)	?	1534
Roxo Loro, F.	Sicily	?	1523
Roxo Loro, F.	Sicily	14	n / a
Ruiz, J.	Hispaniola	13+	1536
Salamanca, G.	?	20-	?
Saldaña, G.	**Guadalajara (Cast-La Mancha)**	**18+**	**?**
Sánchez, A.	Ciudad Real (Cast-La Mancha) (inferred)	29+	1522
Sánchez, R.	Azuaga (Extrem)	?	1532
Santillana, F.	?	?	shortly before 1540
Sayavedra, A.	?	15±	1533
Simón, D.	Huelva (And)	?	?
Simón, R.	**Huelva (And)**	**33±**	**1523**
Sotomayor, G.	Sevilla (And)	18±	?
Tamarán, R.	Castañedo or Espinosa de los Monteros (Santander)	?	1527
Temiño, F.	?	?	1531
Toro, A.	Alcalá de Henares (Madrid)	23±	1535
Torres, F.	Trujillo (Extrem)	?	1529
Tovar, P.	León (Cast-León)	22±	before 1529
Troyano, J.	**Medina de Rioseco (Cast-León)**	**44**	**1535**
Trujillo, R.	Veracruz (Mex)	?	n / a
Valderreina, A.	Astorga (Cast-León)	38	?
Valle, C.	Aranda de Duero (Cast-León)	?	1536
Valle, H.	Olmedo (Cast-León)	23+	1529
Vargas, L.	?	18+	?
Vásquez de Corondo	**Salamanca (Cast-León)**	**29±**	**1535**
Villareal, J.	Agudo (Cast-La Mancha)	?	1531
Villegas, J.	Badajoz (Extrem)	?	1538
Vitoria, J.	Burgos (Cast-León)	25±	?
Zaldívar, J.	**Guadalajara (Cast-La Mancha)**	**25±**	**by 1529**

Appendix 2

Biographical Data

Alarcón, Hernando de

Claimed as a native of Trujillo in Extremadura, Hernando de Alarcón came to the New World in the company of the newly appointed viceroy Antonio de Mendoza in 1535. From January 1538 until early 1540 he served as *escudero* or squire in the viceroy's personal guard. In 1540 and again in 1541 he was dispatched by the viceroy to lead sea-borne support for the expedition to Tierra Nueva. In both cases, the planned rendezvous with the land expedition led by Vázquez de Coronado never occurred, frustrated by the realities of North American geography and the Mixtón War, a massive native uprising in Jalisco.

Display, Convento de la Coria, Trujillo, Extremadura, Spain, May 1998; Bermúdez Plata, *Pasajeros*, 2: no. 1261; AGI, Justicia, 259, Pieza 2; New York Public Library, Rich Collection, no. 63, Primera Parte, Capítulo 6; Biblioteca del Escorial, Códice &-II-7, Doc. no. LXVII.

Alcaraz, Diego de

During the expedition to Tierra Nueva, Diego de Alcaraz was left in command of the Spanish settlement of San Gerónimo by Melchor Díaz in 1540. His behavior there aroused the ire of the Indians of the area, who in 1541 attacked and destroyed the town, killing Alcaraz and several other Spaniards. One of the charges eventually lodged against Vázquez de Coronado was that he had allowed such an unsuitable person to be put in charge at San Gerónimo.

Prior to the expedition, Diego de Alcaraz and his brother Juan had both been residents of Culiacán. In 1536, while captain of a slaving patrol, probably in modern northern Sinaloa, he had met and treated roughly the survivors of the Narváez expedition to La Florida and their large following of indigenous people.

New York Public Library, Rich Collection, no. 63, Primera Parte, Capítulo 10 and Tercera Parte, Capítulo 3; Hammond and Rey, *Narratives*, 104; Bolton, *Coronado*, 12.

Alvarado, Hernando de

Hernando de Alvarado was captain of artillery during the expedition to Tierra Nueva. In September 1540, Vázquez de Coronado gave Alvarado an eighty-day commission to take 20 men and go to Tiguex, Cicuique, and the buffalo plains. It was Alvarado and his ecclesiastical companion fray Juan de Padilla who recommended that the expedition winter at Tiguex. And it was he who first heard the stories of wealth at Quivira. In an effort to learn the truth about Quivira, he held the Indians Bigotes, the cacique, El Turco, and Ysopete captive. He was accused of having set dogs on Bigotes. As a result of Lorenzo de Tejada's investigation, charges stemming from the attack were recommended against Alvarado. However, none is known to have been filed.

Alvarado was born in 1516 in La Montaña, Santander, Spain, and died July 16, 1550. He arrived in Nueva España in 1528 with the returning Hernán Cortés. In 1547 he testified in Mexico City on behalf of García López de Cárdenas during the Council of the Indies's investigation of his conduct during the expedition to Tierra Nueva. At that time, Alvarado was a vecino of Mexico City.

AGI, Guadalajara, 5, R. 1, N. 7; New York Public Library, Rich Collection, no. 63, Primera Parte, Capítulo 12; Victor M. Álvarez, *Diccionario de Conquistadores* (México: Instituto Nacional de Antropología y Historia, 1975), 1:25; AGI, Justicia, 1021, N. 2, Pieza 6; AGI, Justicia, 1021, N. 2, Pieza 5; Icaza, *Conquistadores y Pobladores,* 2: no. 1221.

Arellano, Tristán de [Luna y]

Don Tristán de Luna y Arellano, known as Arellano during the expedition to Tierra Nueva, was in charge of the body of the expedition. In this role, he led the bulk of the Spaniards, their livestock, and many of the Mexican Indians from Culiacán to Cíbola, from Cíbola to Tiguex, and from the buffalo plains back to Tiguex. He established the Spanish outpost of San Gerónimo at Corazones and later moved it to the Valley of Señora. Arellano became maestre de campo of the entire expedition following the injury of García López de Cárdenas in a fall in the summer of 1541.

Arellano was born at Borobia in Castile, Spain, about 1514. He came to Nueva España in 1527. In 1547 he married the wealthy widow doña Isabel de Rojas. Through her, he acquired several encomiendas. He also had at least one sugar mill and an estancia. In 1559–1561 Luna y Arellano served as captain general of an expedition to La Florida that ended in fiasco. He died in poverty in Mexico City before February 1, 1571.

New York Public Library, Rich Collection, no. 63, Primera Parte, Capítulo 8, Capítulo 9, Capítulo 13, Capítulo 20; Boyd-Bowman, *Cuarenta Mil Pobladores,* 2: no. 10523; Priestley, *The Luna Papers,* 1: xxv, xxvii–lxvii; Icaza, *Conquistadores y Pobladores,* 2: no. 516; Álvarez, *Diccionario,* 1: 38–40.

Ayapín

As early as 1538, Vázquez de Coronado claimed that Ayapín was a leader and fomenter of unrest among the native peoples of the Culiacán area. By 1542, he was evidently much farther south in Nueva Galicia in the vicinity of Compostela among the Tecoxquines.

AGI, Guadalajara 5, R. 1, N. 5.

Barrionuevo, Velasco de

From September 1537 until at least the end of 1539 Velasco de Barrionuevo served in Viceroy Mendoza's personal guard. Velasco and his brother Rodrigo Barrionuevo mustered into the expedition to Tierra Nueva as horsemen in February 1540. Later in the year Velasco was appointed maestre de campo of the body of the expedition at Culiacán, under Tristán de Arellano. Velasco was present during the siege of the Pueblo del Cerco. During the summer of 1541, Arellano sent a Francisco de Barrionuevo (probably this is Velasco, since there is no other mention of Francisco among Coronado expedition documents) north from Tiguex to Jemez, Yuque-Yunque, and Brava to get supplies. Velasco was a native of Granada, Spain.

AGI, Justicia, 259, Pieza 2; AGI, Guadalajara, 5, R. 1, N. 7; Bolton, *Coronado*, 208; New York Public Library, Rich Collection, no. 63, Primera Parte, Capítulo 5.

Bartolomé

Bartolomé was an Indian boy from Petatlán, who accompanied fray Marcos de Niza and Esteban de Dorantes north from Vacapa in 1539, seeking confirmation of the existence of wealthy cities. He was with Esteban at Cíbola and remained there after the Moor was killed. He was demanded by and returned to Vázquez de Coronado at Cíbola in July 1540. Bartolomé, who knew Nahuatl, served as an interpreter for the expedition at Cíbola.

Giovanni Battista Ramusio, *Terzo Volume delle Navigationi et Viaggi* (Venice: La Stamperia de Giunti, 1565), 363.

Bermejo, Hernando

Hernando Bermejo, a native of Fuente del Arco in Badajoz, Spain, evidently traveled in the same fleet that carried Antonio de Mendoza to Nueva España in 1535. At Compostela in February 1540, he passed muster as a horseman. During the expedition to Tierra Nueva, he served as principal scribe and secretary to Vázquez de Coronado.

Bermúdez Plata, *Pasajeros*, 2: no. 2201; Hammond and Rey, *Narratives*, 101 n76; AGI, Guadalajara 5, R. 1, N. 7; AGI, Contratación, 5575, N. 24.

Bigotes

Bigotes was one of a party of three or four Indians from the pueblo of Cicuique who arrived at Cíbola in July 1540 shortly after its capture by the expedition to Tierra Nueva. His mustaches, being unusual among the Pueblos, attracted attention and occasioned application by the Spaniards of the sobriquet Bigotes. What he was called in his own community is unknown. Though a young man, he was apparently an important person, said by the Spaniards to be both a captain and a cacique. He may have been a war chief or society chief, and the party he was with may have been a trading party, though it is also possible that its mission was primarily diplomatic.

He offered alliance with the Spaniards and conducted Hernando de Alvarado and a small party to Tiguex and Cicuique. Through Bigotes's good offices, the Spaniards were well received. He furnished a Plains Indian, El Turco, as guide for Alvarado's 1540 trip to the buffalo plains. El Turco told Alvarado that Bigotes had a gold bracelet and other jewelry of his. As a result, Bigotes was seized and kept prisoner for six months in the expedition's camp at Tiguex. He was tortured by dog attack in order to extract information, but was allowed to return to his home at Cicuique in spring 1541 and was not seen by the Spaniards thereafter. Following his return, the people of Cicuique were openly hostile toward the expedition.

New York Public Library, Rich Collection, no. 63, Primera Parte, Capítulo 12, Capítulo 13, Capítulo 18, and Capítulo 22; Carroll L. Riley, "Pecos and Trade," in *Across the Chichimec Sea, Papers in Honor of J. Charles Kelley,* ed. Carroll L. Riley and Basil C. Hedrick (Carbondale and Edwardsville, Illinois: Southern Illinois University Press, 1978), 55; Riley, *Rio del Norte,* 163–64.

Blaque, Tomás

Tomás Blaque, or Thomas Blake, was one of the considerable number of non-Spanish members of the expedition to Tierra Nueva. He was born in Scotland about 1519 and arrived in Nueva España in 1532 after participating in a conquest at Cartagena. He was a member of the expedition to Tierra Nueva, though he is not mentioned in any of the existing narrative documents dealing with the entrada. By 1547, he was a vecino of Mexico City and married to Francisca de Rivera, widow of an early settler of the city, Cristóbal de Canyego. In 1553 he was repaid a small debt by Francisca de Hozes, the widow of fellow expedition member Alonso Sánchez. Six years later he testified on behalf of Tristán de Luna y Arellano, stating that he had known the former maestre de campo since 1536.

AGI, Mexico, 97, R. 1, proof of service of Tristán de Luna y Arellano, Mexico City, 1559 and Icaza, *Conquistadores y Pobladores,* 2: no. 738.

The Cacique

"Cacique," an Arawak title meaning "headman," was applied by the Spaniards of the expedition to Tierra Nueva to an elderly and important man from the pueblo of Cicuique. He was also called "governor." He may have been with Bigotes in the trading/diplomatic party that arrived at Cíbola in July 1540 and offered alliance with the Spaniards. He may also have been a leader of that party and an important individual among the religious hierarchy of Cicuique.

When Hernando de Alvarado was told of the gold bracelet by El Turco, he took the cacique in chains to Tiguex, along with Bigotes, El Turco, and Ysopete. The cacique was kept prisoner there throughout the fall and winter of 1540 and then returned to Cicuique as a gesture of goodwill. It is possible that, while at Tiguex, dogs were set on the cacique, as they were on Bigotes.

New York Public Library, Rich Collection, no. 63, Primera Parte, Capítulo 13, Capítulo 15, and Capítulo 18; Riley, *Rio del Norte,* 163, 176; Bolton, *Coronado,* 200.

Castilblanco, fray Antonio de

The exact number of ecclesiastical members of the expedition to Tierra Nueva is not known with certainty, but there were at least six, all Franciscans. Fray Antonio de Castilblanco was one of those six. He arrived in Nueva España in 1538, coming from the Franciscan province of Los Angeles in Castile. He was assigned to northern Nueva Galicia, where he developed a close relationship with the new governor, Francisco Vázquez de Coronado, becoming his personal confessor. Following his two years with the expedition to Tierra Nueva, fray Antonio became guardian at Xochimilco, where fray Marcos de Niza was in residence. After a sojourn of several years in Peru, fray Antonio returned to the Mexico City area, where he died before 1559.

Hammond and Rey, *Narratives*, 9; Fray Angelico Chavez, *Coronado's Friars* (Washington, D.C.: Academy of American Franciscan History, 1968), 30–31, 76–77.

fray Daniel

Another of the Franciscans accompanying the expedition to Tierra Nueva was fray Daniel, an Italian lay brother. He may have arrived in Nueva España as early as 1525. He was fluent in Nahuatl, was a famous embroiderer, and his penitential behavior was renowned among his confreres. Before leaving for Tierra Nueva, fray Daniel was in residence at Tuxpán, as was fray Juan de la Cruz, his fellow evangelist to Cíbola and the rest of the far north. They both returned to Nueva España after the capture of Cíbola. Fray Daniel died about 1567 at Guadalajara.

Chavez, *Coronado's Friars*, 37–39, 78–81.

Díaz, Melchor

In 1539 Melchor Díaz, with Juan de Zaldívar and 12 others, was dispatched north by Viceroy Mendoza, to verify the reports of Cíbola by fray Marcos de Niza. They got as far as the large ruin known as Chichilticale. This detachment apparently had no conflict with native peoples. Díaz returned south in time to meet the expedition to Tierra Nueva at Chiametla with discouraging news at variance with fray Marcos's reports.

Vázquez de Coronado appointed Díaz alcalde mayor or chief judge and administrator of the Spanish outpost of San Gerónimo and then sent him, with 25 men, to the coast of the Mar del Sur to look for supply ships under Hernando de Alarcón. In his absence, Díaz left Diego de Alcaraz in charge at San Gerónimo. While in modern northern Sonora or southern California, Díaz died of an accidental wound from his own lance, in late 1540 or early 1541.

Prior to the expedition, Díaz had been alcalde mayor of Culiacán. As such, he was the official who first received the survivors of the Narváez expedition to La Florida there in 1536. While alcalde at Culiacán, Díaz allegedly sent three Indian women as servants to Vázquez de Coronado's wife Beatriz in Mexico City. Vázquez de Coronado was later found to have acted improperly in accepting the servants.

New York Public Library, Rich Collection, no. 63, Primera Parte, Capítulo 7, Capítulo 10, and Capítulo 17; AGI, Patronato, 184, R. 31, letter, Antonio de Mendoza to the king, Mexico City, April 17, 1540; Bolton, *Coronado*, 12; Hammond and Rey, *Narratives*, 106 n97; AGI, Justicia, 339, N. 1, R. 1.

Écija, Bartolomé de

At the time of Lorenzo de Tejada's investigation of the expedition to Tierra Nueva, Juan Troyano was living in Mexico City in the home of fellow artilleryman Bartolomé de Écija. Bartolomé, not himself a member of the expedition to Tierra Nueva, was probably a relative of Pedro de Écija, who was listed on the 1540 muster near Melchior Pérez, Domingo Martín, and Pedro de Ledesma, all witnesses before Tejada in 1544. This is a further indication of the social connection of this group of witnesses.

Bartolomé de Écija was a native of Granada, Spain, the son of an artilleryman. He arrived in Nueva España in 1535, possibly in the entourage of Viceroy Mendoza, also from Granada.

Guadalajara 5, R. 1, N. 7 and Icaza, *Conquistadores y Pobladores*, 2: no. 834.

Estepa, Martín de

All that is known about Martín de Estepa, besides the accusations made against him before Tejada in 1544 by Alonso Sánchez, is that he was a horsemen in the expedition to Tierra Nueva, probably of relatively low status.

Guadalajara 5, R. 1, N. 7.

Gallego, Juan

A veteran of two decades of conquest in Nueva España by the time of the expedition to Tierra Nueva and a native of Coruña in Galicia, Spain, Juan Gallego had been part of the Pánfilo de Narváez expedition of 1520, designed to rein in the renegade Hernán Cortés. Like most of Narváez's followers, once the captain general had been overthrown by Cortés, Gallego joined the victor and then participated in the final conquest of México-Tenochtitlán. Subsequently, he participated in Cortés's march to Honduras and Nuño de Guzmán's conquest of Nueva Galicia.

He was among the first individuals to muster before Viceroy Mendoza for the expedition to Tierra Nueva, indicative of his relatively high social status, which is further confirmed by the large number of horses he took with him, seven. Gallego put those horses to heavy use since, after the capture of Cíbola, Vázquez de Coronado dispatched him to carry messages to the viceroy and escort fray Marcos de Niza on his return to Mexico City. Gallego turned about and went north again with additional men and supplies in 1542 and met the returning expedition near Chichilticale.

Following the return of the expedition from Tierra Nueva, Gallego settled for several years in Nueva Galicia, becoming a vecino of Purificación. During that time he was encomendero of the towns of Chamela, Guamuchal, Mera, and Pazapanoa, along the Pacific coast. By 1554, though, Gallego had already served several years as an interpreter for the audiencia of Nueva España. As such, he resided in Mexico City.

Hammond and Rey, *Narratives*, 88 n7; AGI, Mexico, 204, N. 36; Guadalajara 5, R. 1, N. 7; New York Public Library, Rich Collection, no. 63, Primera Parte, Capítulo 10 and Tercera Parte, Capítulo 5; Icaza, *Conquistadores y Pobladores*, 2: no. 1186; Gerhard, *North Frontier*, 119.

Gómez de la Peña, Hernando

In addition to being the scribe who recorded the de parte testimony taken at the mines of Nuestra Señora de los Remedios in 1545, Hernando Gómez de la Peña was himself a member of the expedition to Tierra Nueva.

AGI, Contratación, 5575, N. 24.

The Guaches, Guaces, Guales, Guaes

Writing more than 20 years after the expedition to Tierra Nueva, Pedro de Castañeda, one of its members, wrote that El Turco claimed that there were precious metals in Quivira, but not as much as in "Arehe y los guaes." It has been suggested that the Guaes, Guaches, or Guaces were a tribal people living north and east of Quivira, perhaps to the west of the great bend of the Missouri River.

New York Public Library, Rich Collection, no. 63, Primera Parte, Capítulo 18 and Bolton, *Coronado*, 233.

Guevara, Diego de

Don Diego de Guevara was captain of a company of horsemen during the expedition to Tierra Nueva. According to Pedro de Castañeda, another member of the expedition, Guevara, with Juan de Zaldívar, was in command of the siege of one of the Tiguex towns during winter 1540–1541. Herbert Bolton called this Pueblo X, half a league from Moho or Pueblo del Cerco. The 1544 testimony before licenciado Tejada, on the other hand, indicated that Guevara was under the command of García López de Cárdenas at the siege of Pueblo del Cerco.

As early as 1539, Viceroy Mendoza was directed by the king to provide Guevara with a position as corregidor. Guevara, appointed alcalde mayor of Nueva Galicia in 1547, was a son of the conde de Oñate and was married to doña Isabel de Barrios, daughter of Andrés de Barrios, a first conqueror of Nueva España. When his father-in-law died in 1548, Guevara became encomendero of half of Meztitlán north of Mexico City. The other half of Meztitlán was controlled for a time by fellow expedition member Rodrigo Maldonado. In the 1550s Guevara and the other encomenderos of Meztitlán were accused of mistreatment of Indians, and the encomienda was temporarily placed directly under royal jurisdiction.

Guadalajara 5, R. 1, N. 7; New York Public Library, Rich Collection, no. 63, Primera Parte, Capítulo 16; Bolton, *Coronado*, 218; AGI, Justicia, 259, Pieza 2; Hammond and Rey, *Narratives*, 94 n35; AGI, Mexico, 97, letter, Francisco Morales to the king, Mexico City, May 19, 1563; Gerhard, *Historical Geography of New Spain*, 184; Velasco, *Relación de las Encomiendas*, 34–35; Paso y Troncoso, *Epistolario*, 7: 64–126.

Jumena, Juan Eman, or Juan Alemán

A principal at the Tiguex pueblo of Coofor, Jumena (also called Juan Eman and Juan Alemán) was thoroughly disenchanted with the members of the expedition to Tierra Nueva. It has been suggested that his Tiwa name was Xauian. Months after the abandonment of Coofor by its residents, he took part in an attempt at Pueblo del Cerco or Moho to kill Maestre de Campo García López de Cárdenas.

Riley, *Rio del Norte*, 176 and New York Public Library, Rich Collection, no. 63, Primera Parte, Capítulo 15 and Capítulo 16.

fray Luis [de Úbeda]

After arriving in Nueva España in 1533, the Franciscan lay brother fray Luis de Úbeda served in the household of the first bishop of Mexico, fray Juan de Zumárraga. Upon joining the expedition to Tierra Nueva, fray Luis was responsible for erecting crosses in the indigenous communities through which it passed. When it was determined that the expedition would return to Nueva España, he remained in the north, going to Cicuique with the hope of converting its population. Within a short time he was killed. Historian Fray Angelico Chavez determined that the fray Luis de Escalona referred to by expedition member Juan de Jaramillo in his memoir was the same individual and that Escalona was a name erroneously assigned to him.

Chavez, *Coronado's Friars*, 28–29; New York Public Library, Rich Collection, no. 63, Tercera Parte, Capítulo 4; AGI, Patronato, 20, N. 5, R. 8, narrative of Juan de Jaramillo, n.p., [1560s].

Manrique [de Lara], Alonso

Don Alonso Manrique hailed from Valladolid in Spain. He journeyed to the New World in the expedition of Pedro de Mendoza to the Río de la Plata in 1535. By 1536, however, he had made his way north to Nueva España. An hidalgo, he joined the expedition to Tierra Nueva as a horseman. Like many other members of the expedition, he claimed to have been impoverished by his expenditures because of it. Following his service in the expedition, Manrique went with Ruy López de Villalobos to the Philippines and returned afterwards to Nueva España. There he was alcalde mayor of Coatzacoalco and Tabasco in 1550.

Icaza, *Conquistadores y Pobladores*, 2: no. 1369; Guadalajara 5, R. 1, N. 7; Boyd-Bowman, *Cuarenta Mil Pobladores*, 2: no. 12150.

fray Marcos de Niza

The Franciscan friar Marcos de Niza was born in Nice in Savoy in a region often disputed between France and Italy. He departed for the New World in 1531, intending to go to Nueva España. En route, however, he was diverted, eventually arriving in Peru shortly after the initial conquest of the Incas. He was horrified by what he saw to be frequent wanton violence perpetrated against the natives of Peru. In reaction, he authored a summary account of the horrors he witnessed in Peru which fray Bartolomé de las Casas included in his sensational *Brevísima Relación de la Destrucción de las Indias*.

Marcos finally arrived in Nueva España in 1536, where he was evidently well-liked by Viceroy Mendoza and his own provincial, fray Antonio de Ciudad Rodrigo. The two designated fray Marcos to journey to the north in 1538, with Esteban de Dorantes as a guide, to verify the news given by Álvar Núñez Cabeza de Vaca and other survivors of the expedition of Pánfilo de Narváez about wealthy, populous places far in that direction. After making the round trip, fray Marcos submitted a restrained official report about the town-dwelling peoples of Cíbola. That report and other stories that circulated without the friar's denial stimulated a rush to join the expedition bound for the newly discovered land. Historians still debate whether fray Marcos actually saw all the things he reported. Whether he did or not, the members of the expedition to Tierra Nueva found the land to be radically different than they had been led to believe. In fear for his life, fray Marcos, who had retraced his steps to Cíbola with the expedition, returned hurriedly to Mexico City.

There he continued to serve as provincial of the order, but then lapsed into semi-retirement, perhaps hastened by illness acquired on his long journey. He died about 1558.

Fray Pedro Oroz, *The Oroz Codex*, ed. and trans. Angelico Chavez (Washington, D.C.: Academy of American Franciscan History, 1972) 130–32; Fray Toribio de [Benavente], *Motolinía's History of the Indians of New Spain*, trans. Francis Borgia Steck (Washington, D.C.: Academy of American Franciscan History, 1951), 255; AGI, Patronato, 20, N. 5, R. 10, report of Marcos de Niza, Mexico City, September 2, 1539; New York Public Library, Rich Collection, no. 63, Tercera Parte, Capítulo 2, Capítulo 3, and Capítulo 9; Boyd-Bowman, *Cuarenta Mil Pobladores*, 2: no. 13383.

Martín, Francisco

Two Francisco Martíns were listed during the muster of the expedition to Tierra Nueva. One was a horseman, the other a crossbowman. During Tejada's investigation of the expedition, Alonso Sánchez testified that one Martín, a meat cutter by trade, choked the guide El Turco to death, on orders from Diego López. Herbert Bolton asserted that this was Francisco Martín the crossbowman and that during Tejada's investigation he was sought as a witness, but did not appear. Also according to Bolton, he was from Mexico City, but took up residence in Culiacán upon the expedition's return from Tierra Nueva. There were so many individuals by this name in Nueva España at the time, Bolton's contentions are difficult to confirm.

Guadalajara 5, R. 1, N. 7 and Bolton, *Coronado,* 283, 303, 349.

Mayorga, Cristóbal de

Cristóbal de Mayorga, originally from Benavente in the jurisdiction of Zamora in Spain, arrived in Nueva España in 1529. The following year he accompanied Nuño de Guzmán in the conquest of Nueva Galicia. He was a settler of Compostela and then of Espíritu Santo in the province of Chiametla, where he was granted an encomienda. Because the income from the encomienda was smaller than he wanted, he joined the expedition to Tierra Nueva as a horseman, taking with him just two horses.

After the end of the expedition he went to Mexico City, where, as late as 1547, he claimed to be in debt as a result of the journey to Tierra Nueva. He served as a de oficio witness in the investigation of García López de Cárdenas's conduct during the expedition. In the course of his testimony he told of Indians being executed as traitors after the siege of Pueblo del Arenal.

Icaza, *Conquistadores y Pobladores,* 2: no. 1377 and AGI, Justicia, 1021, N. 2, Pieza 6.

Melgosa, Pablos de

Pablos de Melgosa was born in Burgos in Spain about 1516. He had returned there from Nueva España when, as a vecino of Burgos, he testified on behalf of García López de Cárdenas in October 1546. During the expedition to Tierra Nueva, Melgosa was captain of the footmen. He served under López de Cárdenas during both the march to Tusayán in summer 1540 and the siege of Pueblo del Arenal that winter. According to Pedro de Castañeda, it was Melgosa, along with Diego López, who gave assurances of safety to people fleeing from that pueblo, which were later ignored when captives were burned and lanced.

AGI, Justicia 1021, N. 2, Pieza 5; Guadalajara 5, R. 1, N. 7; New York Public Library, Rich Collection, no. 63, Primera Parte, Capítulo 15.

Mendoza, Antonio de

Don Antonio de Mendoza was the first viceroy of Nueva España, from 1535 to 1550, although he had first been offered the post in 1529. The new viceroy took a sizeable entourage with him to Nueva España, including Francisco Vázquez de Coronado. At least 13 individuals who received licenses to travel to Nueva España between April 17 and September 26, 1535, stated that they were accompanying the viceroy. More than 170 others were granted such licenses during that period, many of whom were also in Mendoza's entourage. In 1536 he received the survivors of the Narváez expedition to La Florida and heard their reports of populous and wealthy towns far to the north. A little over two years later, he dispatched Esteban de Dorantes (one of the Narváez survivors) and fray Marcos de Niza to confirm those reports. Then, he assigned Francisco Vázquez de Coronado, governor of Nueva Galicia, to lead a full-scale expedition to the Tierra Nueva reported by fray Marcos. As has been pointed out earlier,

Mendoza was reported to have spent at least 60,000 pesos as one of the expedition's four principal financial backers. According to seventeenth-century historian fray Antonio Tello, Mendoza provided 30 pesos of aid to each horseman and 20 pesos to each footman. In 1545, he claimed still to be in debt because of his expenses for the expedition. In Vázquez de Coronado's absence while in Tierra Nueva, Mendoza led a very large force of Indians and Spaniards to suppress a serious native uprising in Nueva Galicia known as the Mixtón War.

Mendoza also served as president of the audiencia of Nueva España. In that role, he was a party to the decision exonerating Vázquez de Coronado following Tejada's investigation. At the instigation of Hernán Cortés, from 1544 to 1546 a sweeping visita was conducted of the performance in office of the viceroy and all the royal officials of Nueva España. The visitador, Francisco Tello de Sandoval, very much in accord with Cortés's complaints and perhaps with the hope of replacing the viceroy himself, determinedly sought indications of malfeasance by Mendoza. Tello de Sandoval eventually lodged 44 mostly petty charges against the viceroy. Mendoza, in turn, responded with a massive documentary defense. In 1545, the viceroy's half-brother Luis Hurtado de Mendoza became president of the Council of the Indies. Under his pressure, the king recalled Tello de Sandoval to Spain. And in 1548 the Council of the Indies absolved the viceroy and chastised the former visitador. In 1550 Antonio de Mendoza, though suffering from ill health, was ordered transferred to the Viceroyalty of Peru, in an effort to put a definitive end to the civil unrest there. Mendoza served briefly in Peru, until his death in 1552.

Like his sometime business partner Lorenzo de Tejada, Antonio de Mendoza used his official position in Nueva España to further private business as part of a general effort toward economic development. He owned at least one *obraje* or weaving shop, a sugar mill, and several estancias. Through third parties, especially his son Francisco, he controlled the supply of livestock and equipment used in the several enterprises of exploration he sponsored and he also shipped horses to Peru for sale. Nevertheless, historical judgement has been almost uniformly that Mendoza was the most capable and effective viceroy that Nueva España ever had.

Mendoza was a native of Granada, Spain, having been born in 1490 or 1491. His father was Iñigo López de Mendoza, the conde de Tendilla, marqués de Mondéjar, and *alcaide* or warden of the Alhambra. His mother was Francisca Pacheco, second wife of López de Mendoza and daughter of the marqués de Villena. Antonio's half-brother Luis Hurtado de Mendoza, in addition to serving as president of the Council of the Indies, succeeded to his father's titles, including that of captain general of Granada.

Antonio de Mendoza was married to Catalina de Vargas. Before becoming viceroy, he led royal forces at Huéscar during the Comunero Revolt. He had also served as ambassador to Hungary and as the queen's chamberlain. He was a knight of the Order of Santiago.

Aiton, *Antonio de Mendoza* ; AGI, Mexico, 1088, L. 1, royal cédula, Madrid, November 9, 1529; Bermúdez Plata, *Pasajeros,* 2: nos. 913–2213; AGI, Patronato, 57, N. 2, R. 1; Tello, *Crónica Miscelanea,* 2:126; Aiton, "The Secret Visita Against Viceroy Mendoza," in *New Spain and the Anglo-American West: Historical Contributions Presented to Herbert Eugene Bolton,* vol. 1, (Los Angeles: privately printed, 1932), 1–7; Ruiz Medrano, "La Política del Virrey Mendoza," 162–205; Lewis Hanke, "Antonio de Mendoza (1535–1550), Bibliografía" in *Los Virreyes Españoles en América durante el Gobierno de la Casa de Austria,* vol. 1, *Mexico,* vol. 273, Biblioteca de Autores Españoles desde la Formación del Lenguaje hasta Nuestros Dias (Madrid: Atlas Ediciones, 1976), 18.

Nahuas, Indian allies

As was common practice in the course of Spanish imperial expansion from at least the late fifteenth century, the expedition to Tierra Nueva included a large number of people only recently brought under Spanish dominion themselves. In the case of the expedition led by Francisco Vázquez de Coronado, the recently subdued members were principally speakers of Nahuatl, the dominant language of central Mexico at the time of Spanish conquest. The scant evidence that exists indicates that the Nahuas of the expedition were mainly from the immediate vicinity of Tenochtitlán-México. There were also some non-Nahuatl speakers: Tecuexes from Zapotlán and the Guadalajara area. A little over a century after the expedition fray Antonio Tello wrote that it included more than a thousand Indian allies from the environs of Mexico City, and the provinces of Michoacán and Ávalos (extreme southern modern Jalisco). He also specifically mentioned the presence of Indian women in the expedition, taken along "to make tortillas."

Despite their infrequent mention in the surviving documents relating to the expedition to Tierra Nueva, Nahuas and other Indian allies or auxiliaries comprised 1,000 to 1,300 individuals, about three fourths of the entire group. During the expedition they served as emissaries and intermediaries, as herders, and, certainly most importantly, as warriors. It may even be that, as Inga Clendinnen has suggested of the Tlaxcalan allies of Cortés during the conquest of Tenochtitlán in 1521, the Mexican Indians who accompanied the expedition to Tierra Nueva saw themselves as "co-venturers with the Spaniards, associates in no way subordinate."

New York Public Library, Rich Collection, no. 63, Primera Parte, Capítulo 4, Capítulo 15, Segunda Parte, Capítulo 8, and Tercera Parte, Capítulo 8; Riley, *Rio del Norte*, 155; Bolton, *Coronado*, 68; Tello, *Crónica Miscelanea*, 2:130; George P. Hammond and Agapito Rey, "Report of Antonio de Espejo," in *The Rediscovery of New Mexico, 1580–1594: The Explorations of Chamuscado, Espejo, Castaño de Sosa, Morlete, and Leyva de Bonilla and Humaña* (Albuquerque: The University of New Mexico Press, 1966), 184, 225; Oroz, *The Oroz Codex*, 314; Inga Clendinnen, "'Fierce and Unnatural Cruelty': Cortés and the Conquest of Mexico," *Representations* 33 (winter 1991): 92.

Padilla, fray Juan de

Fray Juan de Padilla was in Nueva España at least as early as 1529, arriving there from Andalucía in Spain. He served as guardian of the Franciscan *conventos* at Tulancingo and Zapotlán before the expedition to Tierra Nueva was mounted. Fray Juan was deeply interested in, if not obsessed by, stories of the Seven Cities of Antillia. So when the organization of the expedition was announced, he sought out Vázquez de Coronado and asked to join. Fray Juan was the senior ecclesiastic with the expedition after the return of fray Marcos de Niza to Mexico City. As head of the religious component of the expedition, fray Juan was frequently consulted by the captain general when questions of the proper course of action arose. He supported attacks on the pueblos of Cíbola and Tiguex, recommended interrogation of Bigotes, and confirmed the decision to execute El Turco. His reported approval of those actions was certainly an important factor in the later decisions by the audiencia and the Council of the Indies to exonerate Vázquez de Coronado. When it was decided that the expedition would leave Tierra Nueva, fray Juan insisted on remaining to preach to the people of Quivira. He traveled there with a Portuguese, a Black, a mestizo, and two Indian *donados* or lay assistants dedicated during their youth, but was killed within a short time.

Boyd-Bowman, *Cuarenta Mil Pobladores*, 2: no. 12928a; New York Public Library, Rich Collection, no. 63, Tercera Parte, Capítulo 4 and Capítulo 9; Chavez, *Coronado's Friars*, 14–27.

Pilo or Pilón, Francisco

Francisco Pilo was the son of licenciado Pilón, alcalde mayor of Sevilla in Spain. He was in Nueva España by at least 1539, when a royal cédula was issued authorizing that he be assigned a corregimiento. In 1544 he was a resident of Culiacán, when he was given Vázquez de Coronado's power of attorney to have testimony taken there on his behalf. By the late 1540s he was a resident of Guadalajara and encomendero of Tequila, northwest of that town. He held Tequila in encomienda until his death about 1550.

AGI, Mexico, 1088, L. 3, royal cédula, Valladolid, 1539; Biblioteca del Escorial, Códice &-II-7, Doc. no. LXXIX; Gerhard, *North Frontier,* 147.

Querechos

The Querechos were a nomadic Apachean people of the northern and western Llano Estacado of modern eastern New Mexico and the Texas Panhandle encountered in summer 1541 by the expedition to Tierra Nueva. Like their neighbors to the south and east, the Teyas, they subsisted primarily by hunting bison, lived in hide tents, used the dog travois, and traded regularly with the Pueblo Indians of the Rio Grande region. They are thought to be the people responsible for the remains identified archeologically as the Tierra Blanca Complex. They had little interaction with the expedition to Tierra Nueva, packing up and moving off soon after their encounters.

Judith A. Habicht-Mauche, "Coronado's Querechos and Teyas in the Archaeological Record of the Texas Panhandle," *Plains Anthropologist* 140 (1992): 247–59; New York Public Library, Rich Collection, no. 63, Primera Parte, Capítulo 19 and Segunda Parte, Capítulo 7.

Ruiz de Haro, Pedro

Pedro Ruiz de Haro was born in Peñaranda de Duero in the jurisdiction of Burgos, Spain, about 1515 and arrived in Nueva España in 1526. He participated in the conquest of Nueva Galicia with Nuño de Guzmán. From at least the early 1540s to the early 1550s, he served as Francisco Vázquez de Coronado's attorney. He was a public scribe at Compostela from 1533 or earlier till as late as 1552 and also served as scribe of the cabildo there. Still alive in 1570, he had been encomendero of the town of Otomistlán in the jurisdiction of Tepíc since about 1548.

Boyd-Bowman, *Cuarenta Mil Pobladores,* 2: no. 2539; Icaza, *Conquistadores y Pobladores,* 2: no. 1177; AGI, Patronato, 61, N. 2, R. 9; AGI, Justicia, 339, N. 1, R. 1; AGI, Justicia, 336, N. 1, R. 3; AGI, Guadalajara, 30, N. 1, letter, cabildo of Compostela to the king, Compostela, February 19, 1533; Gerhard, *North Frontier,* 141.

Samaniego, Lope de

Viceroy Mendoza appointed long-time veteran of Nueva España, regidor of Mexico City, and its alcaide, Lope de Samaniego, as maestre de campo of the expedition to Tierra Nueva. Indicative of his status within the expedition and Nueva España more generally were the sixteen or seventeen horses Samaniego took with him.

A native of Segovia in Spain, Samaniego served on the cabildo of Mexico City from about 1529 until his death in the province of Chiametla in 1540 while trying to commandeer supplies from the Indians there. He had been a captain under Nuño de Guzmán in the conquest of Nueva Galicia and had been sent by Guzmán to pacify Chiametla. It is quite likely that his killing there in 1540 was an act of revenge for his earlier violence against the natives.

When Francisco Vázquez de Coronado joined the Mexico City cabildo in June 1538, Samaniego signed as a witness. He was married to Isabel Flaces and had at least one son. For a short time he was encomendero of Calimaya, Metepec, and Tepemaxalco southwest of Mexico City.

Boyd-Bowman, *Cuarenta Mil Pobladores*, 2: no. 8024, Guadalajara 5, R. 1, N. 7; AGI, Mexico, 203, N. 13, report concerning Lope de Samaniego, Mexico City, 1531; *Cuarto Libro de las Actas*, 131–33; Bermúdez Plata, Cristóbal, ed., *1560–1566*, vol. 4, *Catálogo de Pasajeros a Indias durante los Siglos XVI, XVII y XVIII* (Sevilla: Editorial de la Gavida, 1942), no. 2406; "Cuarta Relación Anónima de la Jornada de Nuño de Guzmán," in *Colección de Documentos para la Historia de México*, 2nd facsimile ed., ed. Joaquín García Icazbalceta (Mexico City: Editorial Porrua, S.A., 1980), 2: 472; Himmerich y Valencia, *Encomenderos*, 123.

Suárez de Figueroa, Gómez

Gómez Suárez de Figueroa mustered into the expedition to Tierra Nueva as a horseman, in a group including Melchior Pérez and Domingo Martín, each of whom had three to five horses. He was wounded by an arrow at Cíbola.

Guadalajara 5, R. 1, N. 7 and Ramusio, *Navigationi et Viaggi*, 373–80.

Tecoxquines

Speaking a language related to Nahuatl, the Tecoxquines inhabited mountains in western Nueva Galicia in the 1530s. There they lived in scattered rancherías, farming and hunting. After the Mixtón War, Vázquez de Coronado, recently returned from Tierra Nueva, assembled and led an armed force into the region and compelled many of the Tecoxquines to move to lowland plains near Compostela.

Gerhard, *North Frontier*, 43, 49, 92–93.

Tello de Sandoval, Francisco

Licenciado Francisco Tello de Sandoval was canon of the cathedral in Sevilla, Spain, and a member of the Council of the Indies from 1543 until 1558, when he became president of that body. By cédulas of May and June 1543 he was directed to conduct a visita of all the royal officials of Nueva España. After storm delays he departed for the New World on November 3. With him he took Indians improperly taken from their homeland, to be returned there.

In Nueva España his investigations from 1544 through 1546 raised the ire of many and, according to Lorenzo de Tejada, split the viceroyalty into rancorous factions. The visitador eventually brought charges against the president and three oidores of the audiencia, as well as numerous lesser functionaries. In 1546, the king recalled Tello de Sandoval to Spain under pressure from the viceroy's brother Luis Hurtado de Mendoza, who had become president of the Council of the Indies. Two years later the Council absolved the viceroy and chastised the former visitador.

Ernesto Schäfer, *Las Rúbricas del Consejo Real y Supremo de las Indias desde la Fundación del Consejo en 1524 hasta la Terminación del Reinado de los Austrias* (Sevilla: n.p., 1934; reprint, Nendeln, Liechtenstein: Klaus Reprint, 1975), 4; Aiton, "Secret Visita," 1–7; AGI, Indiferente, 1093, R. 2, N. 16, letter, Tello de Sandoval to the king, San Lucar de Barrameda, November 3, 1543; AGI, Mexico, 68, R. 13, N. 38; Pilar Arregui Zamorano, "Quejas sobre Incumplimiento de Oficio," in *La Audiencia de México según los Visitadores (Siglos XVI y XVII)* (Mexico City: Universidad Nacional Autónoma de México, 1981), 111–60.

Teyas, Teyvas

Like their fellow nomads of the Plains and some-time enemies the Querechos, with whom they shared the Llano Estacado, the Teyas lived by hunting bison, gathering wild plants, and trading bison products with the Pueblos of modern New Mexico. They may also, however, have done some farming. Archeologically identified village sites on the southeastern margin of the Llano Estacado, labeled the Garza Complex, are attributed to the Teyas. It has been suggested that the Teyas spoke either a Caddoan dialect or a language related to that of the Piro Pueblos.

According to members of the expedition to Tierra Nueva, Teyas routinely spent the winters at or in the vicinity of the easternmost pueblos, especially Cicuique. This did not prevent occasional hostility between Teyas and Pueblos. For instance, members of the expedition to Tierra Nueva were told that Teyas had destroyed a pueblo in New Mexico's Galisteo Basin only a few years earlier. Although the expedition stole a large number of bison hides from Teyas encountered in a *barranca* at the edge of the buffalo plains, relations between the two groups during their brief encounter seem not to have been openly hostile.

Habicht-Mauche, "Coronado's Querechos and Teyas," 247–59; Carroll L. Riley, "The Teya Indians of the Southwestern Plains," in *The Coronado Expedition to Tierra Nueva*, 320–43; New York Public Library, Rich Collection, no. 63, Primera Parte, Capítulo 19, Capítulo 20, Capítulo 21 and Segunda Parte, Capítulo 5.

Torquemada, Juan de

Juan de Torquemada mustered into the expedition to Tierra Nueva with five horses, marking him as a relatively high-status individual.

Guadalajara 5, R. 1, N. 7.

Turco, El Turco

A native of Quivira offered to the expedition as a guide at Cicuique was called El Turco by the Spaniards because, according to Pedro de Castañeda, "he resembled one in appearance." He is usually presumed to have been a member of an ancestral Wichita band from modern central Kansas, although it has been suggested that his homeland was Arahe, beyond Quivira, and that he was, thus, a member of a proto-Pawnee people. Members of the expedition understood him to say that precious metals were abundant in Quivira, which was governed by a wealthy elite. As proof of his statements he pointed to the existence of a gold bracelet and other jewelry that had supposedly been stolen from him at Cicuique by Bigotes. In an effort to confirm El Turco's story and retrieve his jewelry, dogs were set on Bigotes, but the gold never was seen.

El Turco, along with two other Plains Indians, Ysopete and Xabe, accompanied the expedition throughout the summer of 1541 for the purpose of guiding it to Quivira. After more than a month's travel, the Spaniards determined that El Turco was misleading them. Acting on Ysopete's advice, Vázquez de Coronado led a small party in a radically different direction, ultimately reaching Quivira in another month. While in his home territory, El Turco was accused of conspiring to kill the Spaniards and was executed.

Communication between the Spaniards and El Turco was imperfect at best, relying as it did primarily on hand signs. So, it is likely that the Spaniards never did understand exactly what El Turco said about Quivira or why he led them as he did. It is even remotely possible that, as Mildred Mott Wedel suggested almost twenty years ago, El Turco's goal was the great tributary chiefdoms of the lower Mississippi Valley. More recently, Jane Walsh has raised the possibility that the name El Turco was applied to the guide *ex post facto* in reference to his lying. Under this suggestion he was seen as "evil" like the Turks, enemies of the Christians of the time.

Riley, *Rio del Norte*, 169; New York Public Library, Rich Collection, no. 63, Primera Parte, Capítulo 12, Capítulo 13, Capítulo 18, Capítulo 20, and Capítulo 21; Mildred Mott Wedel, "The Indian They Called *Turco*," in *Pathways to Plains Prehistory: Anthropological Perspectives of Plains Natives and Their Pasts*, ed. Don G. Wyckoff and Jack L. Hofman (Duncan, Oklahoma: The Cross Timbers Press, 1982), 153–62; Jane MacLaren Walsh, "Myth and Imagination in the American Story: The Coronado Expedition, 1540–1542" (Ph.D. diss., The Catholic University of America, 1993), 207–08.

Urrea, Lope de

Although don Lope de Urrea was the fourth person to muster into the expedition to Tierra Nueva, behind Vázquez de Coronado, Lope de Samaniego, and Pedro de Tovar, and thus clearly an important individual, very little is known about him. According to Pedro de Castañeda, he was an hidalgo from Aragón in Spain. His high status is confirmed by the five horses he took on the expedition. During the siege of Pueblo del Cerco it is said that don Lope shuttled from the pueblo women and children who were surrendered for their safety. The women and children subsequently became servants of members of the expedition for the next year and more, until the expedition departed from Tierra Nueva, when most, at least, were allowed to return to their families.

Guadalajara 5, R. 1, N. 7 and New York Public Library, Rich Collection, no. 63, Primera Parte, Capítulo 5 and Capítulo 16.

Villalobos, Juan de

Licenciado Juan de Villalobos was fiscal of the Council of the Indies from 1530 until his death in 1550. He pursued the case against García López de Cárdenas. Villalobos engaged Cristóbal de Benavente, fiscal of the audiencia of Nueva España, to transport a royal grant of gold for him from the New World. His heirs sued Benavente for 250 pesos of that sum, which they claimed he had not delivered.

Schäfer, *Las Rúbricas,* 5; AGI, Justicia, 1010, N. 3, R. 1, proceeding of the heirs of licenciado Villalobos against licenciado Cristóbal de Benavente, Valladolid, 1551; AGI, Patronato, 281, N. 1, R. 121.

Villegas, Juan de

Juan de Villegas, a native of Zafra, in Badajoz in Spain, joined the expedition to Tierra Nueva as a horseman, taking three horses with him. He had arrived in Nueva España in 1538. Villegas was said to have assaulted a Pueblo woman at Pueblo del Arenal near the expedition's winter quarters in fall 1540. The woman's husband identified Villegas's horse, but was not able to pick out Villegas himself as the culprit. Maestre de Campo López de Cárdenas claimed later that the husband's hand signs had been unclear. Francisco Vázquez de Coronado denied hearing of the incident until his return to Mexico. Juan de Contreras, however, testified during Tejada's investigation that Villegas was not punished because his brother, Pedro de Villegas, was a regidor of Mexico City and as such served on the cabildo with Vázquez de Coronado. The rape doubtless contributed to friction between the people of Tiguex and the expedition.

Bermúdez Plata, *Pasajeros,* 2: no. 4946; Guadalajara 5, R. 1, N. 7; New York Public Library, Rich Collection, no. 63, Primera Parte, Capítulo 15.

Xabe, Xebe

A young Quivira native residing at Cicuique, Xabe was one of the three guides provided by Bigotes to Vázquez de Coronado in late spring 1541. He confirmed El Turco's reports of precious metals in Quivira. When the main body of the expedition returned to Tiguex that summer, he accompanied it. There he continued to maintain that the captain general would find gold in his homeland. Even after Vázquez de Coronado returned empty-handed, Xabe persisted in telling of gold in Quivira. Partly for that reason, the captain general planned to make another foray onto the Plains when warm weather returned in 1542.

Whether Xabe was this boy's name in his native tongue is not known. The Spaniards, however, commonly assigned names of their own to native people they dealt with, and there were a number of Arabic borrowings current in sixteenth-century Spanish that had "xabe" as a major element; these have to do with nets and catching with nets.

New York Public Library, Rich Collection, no. 63, Primera Parte, Capítulo 18 and Capítulo 22 and Covarrubias Orozco, *Tesoro,* 675.

Ysopete, Sopete

Ysopete was a native of Quivira, perhaps a member of a Wichita band, who in 1540 was at the town of Cicuique. Pedro de Castañeda described him as a "painted Indian," evidently in reference to tattooing. By modern historians he is often said to have been a slave of Bigotes and the cacique, who had captured him on the buffalo plains. Ysopete repeatedly told members of the expedition to Tierra Nueva that the stories of gold at Quivira, told by El Turco, were false.

With El Turco, he accompanied the expedition onto the buffalo plains in summer 1541. He said that El Turco was misguiding the Spaniards. That was confirmed by Teyas Indians on the Plains. Once El Turco was discredited, Francisco Vázquez de Coronado followed Ysopete and Teyas guides to Quivira. There El Turco was garrotted, about which Ysopete was said to be pleased. In August 1541, Ysopete was allowed to stay in Quivira when the expedition returned to Tiguex for the winter of 1541–1542.

As with his companions El Turco and Xabe, Ysopete's name may indicate the attitudes of expedition members toward him. Jane Walsh has pointed out that Ysopete was a common Spanish variant of the name of the fable teller of classical antiquity Aesop. Its use by the Spaniards as a name for a Wichita guide suggests a perceived similarity with Aesop, perhaps in physical deformity or as a spinner of tales.

Hammond and Rey, *Narratives*, 237 n4; New York Public Library, Rich Collection, no. 63, Primera Parte, Capítulo 19, Capítulo 20, and Capítulo 21; Riley, *Rio del Norte*, 169; Bolton, *Coronado*, 188; AGI, Patronato, 20, N. 5, R. 8; Walsh, "Myth and Imagination," 202.

Yupo and Zamarilla

In his testimony before licenciado Tejada, Juan Troyano referred to a Zamarilla who was a Plains Indian supplied, along with El Turco, by Bigotes as a guide for Hernando de Alvarado's 1540 trip to the buffalo plains. When testifying on behalf of Vázquez de Coronado at Nuestra Señora de los Remedios, Gaspar de Saldaña mentioned an individual called Yupo, also with El Turco. These are the only known references to individuals named Yupo and Zamarilla in Coronado expedition documents. Both names probably refer to Ysopete.

Appendix 3

Geographical Data

Aqucui, Acus, Acuco

Aqucui, Acus, and Acuco are renderings of the Keresan *ák'u,* the native name of the New Mexico pueblo now usually referred to as Acoma. The pueblo in modern Cíbola County is today only lightly populated on a full-time basis. Notable now as in the sixteenth century, Acoma occupies the top of an isolated 350-foot-high, sheer-walled mesa in Acoma Valley. The pueblo has been occupied since at least the 1100s. At long distance and unbeknownst to the people of Acoma, in 1539 fray Marcos de Niza took symbolic possession of Acus for the king of Spain. Its population in 1540 included an estimated 200 adult males. Contact between Acoma and the expedition to Tierra Nueva was minimal.

Velma García-Mason, "Acoma Pueblo," in *Southwest,* vol. 9 of *Handbook of North American Indians,* ed. Alfonso Ortiz (Washington, D.C.: Smithsonian Institution, 1979), 450, 456; Robert Julyan, *The Place Names of New Mexico* (Albuquerque: University of New Mexico Press, 1996), 3; AGI, Patronato, 20, N. 5, R. 10.

Arahe

Members of the expedition to Tierra Nueva were told of a land to the east, and possibly north, of Quivira called Arahe or Harahey. It was supposed to be wealthier in precious metals than Quivira. It is thought by most students of the subject that Arahe was a region of ancestral Pawnee settlements in modern eastern Nebraska. Had the expedition to Tierra Nueva continued another year, Arahe would have been among its destinations.

New York Public Library, Rich Collection, no. 63, Primera Parte, Capítulo 18 and Tercera Parte, Capítulo 2; Riley, *Rio del Norte,* 196; Bolton, *Coronado,* 233.

The Barrancas

Narratives of the expedition to Tierra Nueva refer to two barrancas on the edge of the buffalo plains visited by the expedition in mid summer 1541. The first was inhabited by Teyas

Indians in a settlement of hide tents. No human occupation was reported in the second and larger barranca, indicating that it may have been in a buffer zone between Teyas and Querechos. In the last five years one of those barrancas has been identified archeologically as Blanco Canyon in southern Floyd County and northern Crosby County, Texas. I have contended that Blanco Canyon is the first barranca, where the expedition was hit by a powerful hail storm. Part of the support for this view is the presence within the canyon of several large Garza Complex settlements that appear to have been occupied during the middle sixteenth century. Nevertheless, the archeologist excavating a likely campsite of the expedition in Blanco Canyon and a number of other scholars hold that Blanco Canyon represents the second barranca.

New York Public Library, Rich Collection, no. 63, Primera Parte, Capítulo 19 and Capítulo 20; Richard Flint, "A Coronado Campsite in Blanco Canyon, Texas," *Wagon Tracks, Santa Fe Trail Association Quarterly* 11 (August 1997), 3–4; Donald J. Blakeslee, Richard Flint, and Jack T. Hughes, "Una Barranca Grande: Recent Archeological Evidence and a Discussion of Its Place in the Coronado Route," in *The Coronado Expedition to Tierra Nueva*, 370–83.

Betuco, Batuco

On its return route from Tierra Nueva the expedition passed through Batuco, where the people provided supplies, despite the ongoing disturbance in the nearby Señora Valley. No mention of Batuco was made in accounts of the northbound journey, giving rise to the possibility that the return route was somewhat different. Of the two settlements named Batuco in modern Sonora, it is probably the one on the Río Moctezuma that was visited by the expedition in 1542.

New York Public Library, Rich Collection, no. 63, Tercera Parte, Capítulo 5; Jerry Gurulé, "Francisco Vázquez de Coronado's Northward Trek Through Sonora," in *The Coronado Expedition to Tierra Nueva*, 160.

Brava, Braba, Uraba

Brava or Braba has been identified as modern Taos Pueblo, a northern Tiwa community, situated now, as in 1540–1542, along Taos Creek, a small tributary flowing into the Rio Grande from the east in Taos County, New Mexico. It was in the sixteenth century and still is the northernmost Pueblo community. It was apparently visited only twice by the expedition, evidently without incident. It was given the name Valladolid by the Spaniards. The name Brava was also occasionally written as Uraba and, in several of Tejada's 1544 questions, was inadvertently mislocated in Sonora.

Albert H. Schroeder, "Pueblos Abandoned in Historic Times," in *Southwest*, vol. 9, 251; New York Public Library, Rich Collection, no. 63, Primera Parte, Capítulo 22.

Chia, Zia

During the expedition to Tierra Nueva's sojourn in the Tiguex area of the Rio Grande Valley during the winters of 1540–1541 and 1541–1542 hostility was avoided with the people of Chia to the northwest, although there were repeated contacts between Chia and the expedition. Four or six small cannon were even left at Chia while the expedition pursued the chimera of gold in Quivira. And the people of Chia supplied both food and clothing to the expedition. Chia has been identified with Old Zia Pueblo, the ruins of which lie along the lower Jemez River in Sandoval County, New Mexico. The expedition to Tierra Nueva did not visit or make note of any other pueblos along the Jemez River affiliated with Chia. Conspicuous by its absence is any mention of the pueblo later known as Santa Ana. In fact, it seems likely that Santa Ana did not come into existence until after the departure of the expedition to Tierra Nueva.

New York Public Library, Rich Collection, no. 63, Primera Parte, Capítulo 18 and Segunda Parte, Capítulo 4, Capítulo 6; Schroeder, "Pueblos Abandoned," 244.

Chiametla, Chametla

Characterized as a province by Nuño de Guzmán when he reached it late in 1530, Chiametla or Chametlán was a region densely populated by speakers of a Nahuatl-like language, Totorame. Farmers and fishermen, they suffered heavy depredations from slave raiders in the early 1530s and were devastated by an intense outbreak of measles in 1536. People of Chiametla killed former Guzmán captain Lope de Samaniego and wounded several other members of the expedition to Tierra Nueva when they attempted to commandeer food there early in 1540. In retaliation for the killing, Vázquez de Coronado had at least eight Chiametlans hung and drawn and quartered.

Chiametla comprised the coastal plain along the Río Baluarte in modern southern Sinaloa. Like so many names used to refer to social entities in the Americas during the era of conquest, "Chiametla" was applied to both a region and a specific settlement within that region. That settlement may have been at a site known more recently as Cocoyolitos on the north side of the Río Baluarte less than five miles from its mouth. For many years the river was known as the Río Chametla (spelled without an "i").

Gerhard, *North Frontier,* 270–71; New York Public Library, Rich Collection, no. 63, Primera Parte, Capítulo 7; Isabel Kelly, *Excavations at Chametla, Sinaloa, Ibero-Americana,* 14 (Berkeley: University of California Press, 1938), 4.

Chichitequecale, Chichilticale

A landmark and stopover point for travelers between Sonora and the Pueblo region of New Mexico, both prehistorically and at the time of the expedition to Tierra Nueva, Chichilticale was a ruined town constructed of red earth. The name also applied to the region of the town. Melchor Díaz and Juan de Zaldívar, with a small reconnaissance party, spent the winter of 1539–1540 there. They had been sent north to verify the reports of fray Marcos de Niza. Later in 1540, the full expedition camped at Chichilticale, and it saw occasional traffic between the expedition among the Pueblos and its shifting supply base at San Gerónimo in Sonora over the course of the next two years. The town of Chichilticale itself had been abandoned for more than 100 years, and the surrounding region was unsettled.

Researchers have differed widely in locating the site of Chichilticale, placing it at several points in modern southeastern Arizona, southwestern New Mexico, and northern Sonora. In 1940, Herbert Bolton and archeologist Emil Haury concluded that several Salado pueblo ruins in the Sulphur Springs Valley of Graham County, Arizona, were prime candidates for Chichilticale. That idea has gained new credence since recent reexamination of one of those ruins by William Duffen, William Hartmann, and Gayle Harrison Hartmann.

New York Public Library, Rich Collection, no. 63, Primera Parte, Capítulo 7 and

Segunda Parte, Capítulo 3; William A. Duffen and William K. Hartmann, "The 76 Ranch Ruin and the Location of Chichilticale," in *The Coronado Expedition to Tierra Nueva*, 190–211.

Cíbola

The original goal of the expedition to Tierra Nueva, Cíbola had been heard of and possibly seen by fray Marcos de Niza in 1539. Marcos's guide Esteban de Dorantes was killed there. It was stories of the reputed size and wealth of Cíbola that launched the expedition. And, in fact, Cíbola was at the time an important center of trade in turquoise, bison hides, and tropical feathers and shells between the Pueblo world and the northern fringes of Mesoamerica. The name referred to a group of related pueblos and also to the principal pueblo of the group. When Vázquez de Coronado and the advance unit of the expedition arrived there in July 1540, violence quickly flared when the people of Cíbola refused to allow the armed force to enter the principal pueblo. In a short time the expedition overran the pueblo and its residents abandoned it. The pueblo was renamed Granada by the Spaniards. For the next two years a tense peace existed between the Cíbolans and the expedition. Probably as a result of news received by the Pueblos of Spanish slaving habits in the Chiametla and Culiacán areas, women and children were kept largely out of sight while the expedition was in Cíbola.

Cíbola has for more than a century been identified as the Zunian-speaking culture area located in modern west-central New Mexico. In 1540–1542 it comprised six or seven towns along the Zuni River in modern western McKinley and Cibola counties. Also, in 1540–1542 the name was applied to the most southwesterly town within the area, now usually identified as the ruined pueblo of Hawikkuh, about 12 miles southwest of modern Zuni. As identified by modern archeology, the Cíbolan pueblos of 1540 were Hawikkuh, Kechiba:wa, Kwa'ki'na, Kyaki:ma, Mats'a:kya, Halona:wa north, and possibly Chalo:wa.

Information, presented during testimony concerning the conduct of the expedition, that Vázquez de Coronado approached the first pueblo of Cíbola from the west, all but rules out the possibility that the ruined pueblo of Kyaki:ma was the pueblo attacked and overrun by the expedition.

AGI, Patronato, 20, N. 5, R. 10; Riley, *Rio del Norte*, 113–14; New York Public Library, Rich Collection, no. 63, Primera Parte, Capítulo 9 and Segunda Parte, Capítulo 3; J[ames] H. Simpson, "Coronado's March in Search of the 'Seven Cities of Cibola' and Discussion of their Probable Location," in *Annual Report of the Board of Regents of the Smithsonian Institution for 1869* (Washington, D.C.: n.p., 1872), 309–40; Roger Anyon, "The Late Prehistoric and Early Historic Periods in the Zuni-Cibola Area, A.D. 1400–1680," in *Current Research on the Late Prehistory and Early History of New Mexico*, ed. Bradley J. Vierra (Albuquerque: New Mexico Archaeological Council, 1992), 77; Madeleine Turrell Rodack, "Cíbola, from Fray Marcos to Coronado," in *The Coronado Expedition to Tierra Nueva*, 112–14.

Cicuique, Cicarique

Accepting the offer of friendship from a trading or diplomatic party from Cicuique in summer 1540, Vázquez de Coronado detailed Hernando de Alvarado to conduct a reconnaissance of the pueblos east of Cíbola and of the buffalo plains beyond. Alvarado imprisoned and tortured a principal of Cicuique in an effort to verify reports of a wealthy population center much farther east called Quivira. Initially willing to link themselves with the expedition to

Tierra Nueva, the people of Cicuique became increasingly hostile, finally openly attacking a group under Tristán de Arellano in early fall 1541. When the expedition departed from the Pueblo world, two Franciscan friars remained behind in the hope of converting the native people. One of them was fray Luis de Úbeda, who went to Cicuique and was later killed nearby.

Cicuique was a Towa-speaking pueblo situated in the upper Pecos River Valley in what is now extreme western San Miguel County, New Mexico. It had been inhabited since the 1300s. In 1540–1542, it was the most populous of the pueblos and one with extensive trade contact with buffalo-hunting Indians of the Great Plains. Now known as Pecos Pueblo, it has been abandoned since the 1830s.

New York Public Library, Rich Collection, no. 63, Primera Parte, Capítulo 12, Capítulo 13, Capítulo 22 and Segunda Parte, Capítulo 5 and Tercera Parte, Capítulo 4; John L. Kessell, *Kiva, Cross, and Crown: the Pecos Indians and New Mexico, 1540–1840*, 2nd ed. (Albuquerque: University of New Mexico Press, 1987), 10–12, 459.

Comulpa

According to Alonso Sánchez, in his 1544 testimony before Tejada, Diego de Alcaraz and others from the settlement of San Gerónimo took women and girls from the town of Señora and the valley of Comulpa. This latter place is probably the valley of the modern Río Oposura, the next river valley east of the Río Sonora in east-central Sonora. In the 1600s there was a native settlement on the Río Oposura called Cúmupas, surely cognate with the name used by Sánchez and the name Comu used by Castañeda.

Gerhard, *North Frontier*, 280, 283; New York Public Library, Rich Collection, no. 63, Segunda Parte, Capítulo 2.

Coofer, Coofor, Alcanfor

Also known as Alcanfor, Coafor, and Tiguex, the pueblo of Coofor was, in 1540, one of the largest, if not the largest, of the dozen or so Tiguex pueblos. The various names used by the Spaniards for this pueblo probably derive from the Tiwa name, *ghufoor* (meaning parched corn). It was in the pueblo of Coofor that the expedition to Tierra Nueva took up quarters, after its maestre de campo "asked" that its native residents vacate it. There was quite evident bitterness on the part of the people of Coofor over this removal, which certainly contributed to hostility that erupted in warfare during the winter of 1540–1541. This despite the fact that no members of the expedition are known to have acknowledged the forced removal as a contributing cause of violence. Following the fruitless quest for gold in Quivira, at least part of the expedition took up quarters again at Coofor, spending the winter of 1541–1542 there.

There has been considerable disagreement among historians and archeologists about which of the several ruins of Southern Tiwa pueblos represents Coofor. What can be said with assurance is that it was on the west side of the Río de Tiguex, or modern Rio Grande, in what is now northern Bernalillo County or southern Sandoval County, New Mexico.

The discovery and archeological investigation in 1987 of part of a campsite likely associated with the expedition to Tierra Nueva has once again focused attention on nearby Santiago Pueblo as the most likely candidate. And the information on distances between the various Tiguex pueblos provided during Tejada's investigation supports that possibility. Melchior Pérez stated that Coofor was next to the river and Vázquez de Coronado indicated that other pueblos were one-half, one, two, and three leagues from Coofor. Juan Troyano said that Coofor was one or two leagues from the pueblo besieged by López de Cárdenas, Pueblo del Arenal. Castañeda stated, more precisely, that Arenal and Coofor were one league apart. Furthermore, Pedro de Ledesma declared that Pueblo de la Alameda was "between" Coofor and Pueblo del Arenal, meaning intermediate in distance between the two. Together, these statements imply that there was a cluster of at least three pueblos, including Coofor, that were in very close proximity, two of them being only half a league apart, while the third was no more than one league from one of the others, which was on the west bank of the Rio Grande. In addition, that cluster must comprise the pueblos called Coofor, Alameda, and Arenal by the expedition members, with Coofor somewhat closer to Alameda than to Arenal (since Vázquez de Coronado and López de Cárdenas were to meet at Alameda which was "between" the other two).

Of the known pueblo ruins with mid-sixteenth-century occupations in the Southern Tiwa area, there is only one such tight cluster, the ruins known as Santiago, Kuaua, and Watche near and within Bernalillo, New Mexico. On this reasoning, Santiago would be Coofor, Watche would be Alameda, and Kuaua would be Arenal.

Albert Schroeder's 1992 identification of Santiago as the site of Pueblo del Cerco or Moho must be incorrect, given the 1545 statement of Lorenzo Álvarez that Pueblo del Cerco was on a height, which Santiago decidedly is not; being in the flood plain, much of it has been lost to the Rio Grande. Further, although Schroeder referred to the clustering of Coofor, Alameda, and Arenal, the archeological sites he identified them with are not clustered in that way at all.

In 1999 a collector and metal detector from Valencia County came forward with a group of 21 copper crossbow boltheads and a dozen fired lead shot he had recovered from the immediate vicinity of the ruins of Santiago Pueblo. Both the shot and several of the boltheads give evidence of having made impact, probably with the adobe of the pueblo. This suggests that fighting occurred between the Coronado expedition and residents of Santiago. In turn, this raises the possibility that Santiago may be the Pueblo del Arenal of the Coronado expedition documents. If so, then Kuaua would be Coofor.

Riley, *Rio del Norte*, 170; New York Public Library, Rich Collection, no. 63, Primera Parte, Capítulo 12, Capítulo 15 and Segunda Parte, Capítulo 4, Capítulo 6; Bradley J. Vierra, *A Sixteenth-Century Spanish Campsite in the Tiguex Province*, Laboratory of Anthropology Notes 475 (Santa Fe: Museum of New Mexico, Research Section, 1989); Bradley J. Vierra and Stanley M. Hordes, "Let the Dust Settle: A Review of the Coronado Campsite in the Tiguex Province," in *The Coronado Expedition to Tierra Nueva*, 249–61; Archeological Records Management System (ARMS) site files for LA 187, Kuaua Pueblo; LA 288, Corrales Pueblo; LA 289, Calabacillas Pueblo; LA 290, Piedras Marcadas Pueblo; LA 294, Sandia Pueblo; LA 326, Santiago Pueblo; LA 421, Alameda Pueblo; LA 677, Watche Pueblo; LA 716; LA 717, Maigua Pueblo; and LA 22765, Chamisal Pueblo, unpublished files, Laboratory of Anthropology, Museum of New Mexico, Santa Fe; Albert H. Schroeder, "Vásquez de Coronado and the Southern Tiwa Pueblos," in *Archaeology, Art, and Anthropology: Papers in Honor of J. J. Brody*, The Archaeological Society of New Mexico, no. 18, ed. Meliha S. Duran and David T. Kirkpatrick (Albuquerque: The Archaeological Society of New Mexico, 1992), 185–91.

Corazones

As with a number of other places referred to by members of the expedition to Tierra Nueva, both a town and a region were called by the name Corazones. In 1536, the four survivors of the expedition of Pánfilo de Narváez were feasted on dear hearts at this town and, thus, applied the name Corazones to it. Under the leadership of Tristán de Arellano, the main body of the expedition to Tierra Nueva established a town there early in 1540, naming it San Gerónimo. The town was later moved to a neighboring valley or another part of the same valley, called Señora by the Spaniards. Afterwards, the town was moved yet again to the Suya or Fuya Valley. The results of archeological survey of the Río Sonora Valley support the proposition that Corazones was downstream from the Ures Gorge along the Río Sonora in modern central Sonora. This would place Corazones in what has come to be known as the Pimería Bajo or Lower Pima culture area. At the time of the expedition to Tierra Nueva the ancestral Lower Pima maintained a sophisticated culture much influenced by their proximity to the northern reaches of Mesoamerica. Their population, though heavily agricultural, clustered in substantial towns that also participated in long-distance trade. Exposure to European diseases decimated the Lower Pima population and radically altered their lifeway after the 1540s.

Álvar Núñez Cabeza de Vaca, *Naufragios y Comentarios con Dos Cartas*, Colección Austral, 304, 9th ed. (Mexico City: Espasa-Calpe, Mexicana, S.A., 1985), 94; New York Public Library, Rich Collection, no. 63, Primera Parte, Capítulo 9 and Segunda Parte, Capítulo 2; Richard A. Pailes, "An Archaeological Perspective on the Sonoran Entrada," in *The Coronado Expedition to Tierra Nueva*, 186; Carroll L. Riley, *The Frontier People: the Greater Southwest in the Protohistoric Period*, rev. and expanded ed. (Albuquerque: University of New Mexico Press, 1987), 68–76; Timothy Dunnigan, "Lower Pima," in *Southwest*, vol. 10 of *Handbook of North American Indians* ed. Alfonso Ortiz (Washington, D.C.: Smithsonian Institution, 1983), 218; Daniel T. Reff, *Disease, Depopulation, and Culture Change in Northwestern New Spain, 1518–1764* (Salt Lake City: University of Utah Press, 1991), 57, 59–60, 245.

Culiacán and San Miguel de Culiacán

In 1540, San Miguel de Culiacán was the northernmost Spanish settlement in Nueva Galicia. The site visited by the expedition to Tierra Nueva was the town's second location, on the Río San Lorenzo, roughly ten miles upstream from its mouth, in the west central part of what is now the Mexican state of Sinaloa. Founded in 1531 by Nuño de Guzmán, San Miguel's population in 1540 was comprised overwhelmingly of Indians transplanted from central Mexico, a number of whom joined the expedition to Tierra Nueva. The indigenous Taracahitan-speaking population of the region (called the province of Culiacán by the Spaniards) had been ravaged by slave hunters and disease. The Spanish citizenry of Culiacán was well represented in the expedition, including such captains as Diego de Alcaraz, Melchor Díaz, Diego López, and Pedro de Tovar.

New York Public Library, Rich Collection, no. 63, Segunda Parte, Capítulo 2; Gerhard, *North Frontier*, 256–262.

Fuyas, Fuya, Suya

Rendered as Suya in other documents relating to the expedition to Tierra Nueva, the name of this valley and region visited by the expedition is unequivocally spelled Fuya in the documents relating to Tejada's investigation. The spelling Fuya is evidently a scribal error (an easy confusion of "f" and "s") since it renders the indigenous (presumably Ópata) name of the area, and there was no "f" phoneme in the now extinct Ópata language.

The final outpost of the expedition to be called San Gerónimo was established in the Suya Valley, some 40 leagues, or about 100 miles, from the Señora Valley. It was here that, in 1542, an uprising of the native peoples, in response to abuses by Diego de Alcaraz and others, destroyed the town, which helped precipitate the retreat of the expedition from Tierra Nueva. Later that year, Juan Gallego, traveling north with reinforcements for the expedition, captured and hung many people at Suya as punishment for their uprising. To the members of the expedition the people at Suya seemed culturally and physically the same as those at Señora. This is in agreement with current understanding of the ancestral Ópata culture area that occupied much of what is now central Sonora at the time. Like their neighbors to the south, the Lower Pima, the Ópata were devastated by European disease in the century following the expedition to Tierra Nueva.

It is unclear exactly where Suya was, although Carroll Riley has suggested it was in extreme northern modern Sonora, perhaps along the headwaters of the Río San Pedro. More recently Daniel Reff has said flatly that it was in the area of Bacoachi in northern Sonora, but still on the Río Sonora.

Campbell W. Pennington, "Bosquejo Grammática y Vocabulario de la Lengua Ópata, Sacada de un Obra de Natal Lombardo, S.J., que Sirve dentro los Ópatas de Sonora durante las Últimas Décadas del Siglo Diecisiete," unpublished book manuscript, Library, Laboratory of Anthropology, Museum of New Mexico, Santa Fe; New York Public Library, Rich Collection, no. 63, Segunda Parte, Capítulo 2 and Tercera Parte, Capítulo 7; Thomas B. Hinton, "Southern Periphery: West," in *Southwest*, vol. 10, 317; Reff, *Disease, Depopulation, and Culture Change*, 245 ; Riley, *Frontier People*, 72; Daniel T. Reff, "The Relevance of Ethnology to the Routing of the Coronado Expedition in Sonora," in *The Coronado Expedition to Tierra Nueva*, 168.

Mar del Sur

Mar del Sur was the sixteenth-century designation for what is now called the Pacific Ocean and the Gulf of California.

Moha, Noha, Pueblo de Macha, Pueblo de Mocha

(See Pueblo del Cerco)

Nanapagua

Nanapagua was an Indian community at least two days' travel from Cicuique, with which it was at war in 1540. Nanapagua's identity has not been established. However, on the basis of syllable count and vowel sequence, as well as its reported distance from Cicuique, it is possible that it was the so-called Ubates pueblo of Acacagua, at the north end of the Sandia Mountains in today's southeast Sandoval County, New Mexico. This is a very shadowy and little-known area of Pueblo occupation.

Schroeder, "Pueblos Abandoned," 249.

Petatlán

On his way north in March 1539, fray Marcos de Niza stopped for three days at the Indian community of Petatlán. He was received there very cordially and from there on was joined by a large group of Petatleños. Likewise, the expedition to Tierra Nueva experienced no conflict at Petatlán, where it also stopped for a rest of several days on its return to the south in 1542. Petatlán was the home of Bartolomé, the young companion of Esteban de Dorantes, who later served as interpreter for the expedition because he knew both Nahuatl and perhaps Ópata

Castañeda's description of Petatlán indicates a series of ranchería settlements on the coastal plain along a river either 20 or 30 leagues from Culiacán. The name of the extended community derived from the *petates* or mats that walled most of the houses. Herbert Bolton put Petatlán in today's state of Sinaloa along the Río Sinaloa, of which the modern Río Petatlán is a tributary. This would conform with Castañeda's longer estimate of 30 leagues from Culiacán to Petatlán. Charles DiPeso, on the other hand, placed Petatlán on the Río Evora de Mocorito, some 30 miles (about 12 leagues) south of the Río Sinaloa, which seems to be a better fit with Castañeda's lower figure of 20 leagues from Culiacán.

AGI, Patronato, 20, N. 5, R. 10; New York Public Library, Rich Collection, no. 63, Segunda Parte, Capítulo 2 and Tercera Parte, Capítulo 5; Bolton, *Coronado,* 26; Charles C. DiPeso, John B. Rinaldo, and Gloria J. Fenner, *Architecture and Dating Methods,* vol. 4 of *Casas Grandes, A Fallen Trading Center of the Gran Chichimeca* (Dragoon, Arizona: The Amerind Foundation, 1974), 93.

Pueblo del Arenal

In late fall 1540, a member of the expedition to Tierra Nueva, possibly Juan de Villegas, assaulted a Pueblo woman who was a resident of Pueblo del Arenal. As winter set in, clothing was asked for and sometimes stolen from Tiguex pueblos in the vicinity of Coofor, including Arenal. The day after the commandeering of clothing, according to Pedro de Ledesma in his testimony before Tejada, Pueblos attacked the Spaniards' horse herd, killing several dozen horses. The people of Arenal were said to have done the greatest part of the killing. In reprisal, Vázquez de Coronado ordered his maestre de campo to attack Pueblo del Arenal. In the course of the fighting there, part of the pueblo was burned. Despite assurances of safety to some refugees from the pueblo, a large group of captives was burned and slaughtered. It was this event for which the maestre de campo was eventually found responsible.

Pueblo del Arenal was one of the 12 or so active Tiguex pueblos at the time of the expedition to Tierra Nueva. (See the entry dealing with Coofor for an argument that the ruins known today as Kuaua are those of Arenal, a proposition made even stronger by the existence of large burned section in Kuaua.)

New York Public Library, Rich Collection, no. 63, Primera Parte, Capítulo 15; ARMS site files for LA 187, Kuaua Pueblo, unpublished files, Laboratory of Anthropology, Museum of New Mexico, Santa Fe.

Pueblo del Cerco

More a description than a name, Pueblo del Cerco (the besieged pueblo), was applied by witnesses in the 1544 investigation to two distinct Tiguex pueblos. Usually, Pueblo del Cerco referred to the pueblo that was also called Moho, Mohi, Pueblo de Macha, and Pueblo de Mocha, the pueblo invested directly under the leadership of Vázquez de Coronado during the winter months of early 1541. Tiguex people gathered there and took refuge after the fighting at Pueblo del Arenal, including one of the leaders of the people who had vacated Coofor at the Spaniards' behest. Such withdrawal from contact with sixteenth-century Spanish authorities was seen by them as rebellion calling for disciplinary action, if a summons to return to Spanish dominion was rejected. Thus, following refusal of the Tiguex of Pueblo del Cerco to submit, a siege was laid.

This Pueblo del Cerco was said by Lorenzo Álvarez to have been situated on a height. Clearly it was a very strong pueblo, owing at least partly to that elevated location, since the siege lasted at least 50 days and possibly as many as 80 days during the winter of 1540–1541. Several times snowfall provided critically needed water to the Tiguex within. Finally, though, one night they attempted to flee. The besieging camp was aroused and many of the fleeing people were killed, both as they ran across the land and when they attempted to swim the nearby frigid river. Those who survived were taken captive and distributed as servants among members of the expedition.

Given its elevated location away from long-term availability of water, very different from the other known Tiguex pueblos, Pueblo del Cerco was most likely an accustomed but temporary defensive refuge. Resort to such elevated strongholds was common among the various Pueblo groups from prehistoric times through at least the end of the seventeenth century. When confronted by the expedition to Tierra Nueva, not only Tiguex but also Cíbolans and Tewas withdrew to such refuges. In the case of the Cíbolans it was to a pueblo atop Dowa Yalanne or Corn Mountain. The Tewas in the area of the junction of the Rio Grande and Chama River abandoned their valley pueblos in favor of what Pedro de Castañeda termed, "four very strong pueblos" in the sierra.

The exact location of Pueblo del Cerco is much more problematic than that of Coofor, Alameda, and Arenal. Rodrigo de Frias, testifying before licenciado Tejada in 1544, reported that it was three leagues from Pueblo del Cerco to Coofor, where Pedro de Tovar had been left in charge during the siege. A little over a hundred years later, fray Antonio Tello, writing with the benefit of Tovar's now missing papers, described it as a little less than four leagues from Coofor to Pueblo del Cerco. He also echoed Álvarez's statement that Pueblo del Cerco was located on a height and then added that it was separated from the river by a strip of land. That strip must have been quite narrow to allow those running from the pueblo to reach the river when pursued by Spanish horsemen.

Pueblo del Cerco's elevated position and relative proximity to the Rio Grande rule out all the known large structural archeological sites thought to have been occupied in the Tiguex area during the mid-sixteenth century. That area is thought to have extended in 1540, much as it had 200 years earlier, along the Rio Grande from approximately the mouth of the Jemez River southward perhaps as far as the mouth of the Rio Puerco. In terms of modern communities, the north-south extent of the area was from approximately Angosturas south to Contreras, within the greater Albuquerque area. The basaltic mesa west of the Rio Grande in the immediate vicinity of modern Albuquerque known as Volcano Cliffs, the only real candidate for a significant height in the traditionally-conceived Tiguex area, approaches no closer than about one and a half miles to the Rio Grande, a very long distance, indeed, for defenders of Pueblo del Cerco to run pursued by Spanish horsemen.

However, if one looks just north of the Tiguex area as understood until now, another basaltic mesa, Santa Ana Mesa or Black Mesa of San Felipe, occupying much of the wedge of territory between the lower Jemez River and the Rio Grande, conforms very well to fray Antonio Tello's description. The distance from the foot of the mesa to the Rio Grande just north of modern San Felipe Pueblo, for example, is no more than 400 yards. In addition, the ruins of several very strong defensive pueblos stand on the southeastern rim of Santa Ana mesa, one called Canjillon Pueblo (LA 2029), 3 1/2 miles west of modern Algodones, another known as Basalt Point Pueblo (LA 2047), half a mile north of San Felipe, and a third assigned the designation LA 2049. Any one of these fits very well the contemporary descriptions of Pueblo del Cerco. Florence Hawley Ellis suggested that LA 2049 was built about 1515, making it, and perhaps LA 2047 and LA 2029 also, contemporaneous with the Coronado expedition. Their distances from Santiago Pueblo-Coofor are approximately 12 miles for Basalt Point, slightly over the four leagues reported in the Spanish documents, based on 2.63 miles to the league, and about two leagues for Canjillon. In 1995, Carroll Riley also suggested that ruins in this general area might well represent those of Pueblo del Cerco. It should be noted that the Keres pueblo now known as San Felipe evidently did not exist at the time of the expedition to Tierra Nueva. According to Pedro de Castañeda, the nearest Keres pueblos were then seven leagues north of Tiguex, considerably north of the junction of the modern Jemez River and Rio Grande. (For further discussion of the equation of Basalt Point Pueblo or Canjillon Pueblo with Pueblo del Cerco and its ramifications for understanding the dynamic relationship between the Keres and Tiguex of the 1540s, see Chapter 26.)

The name Pueblo del Cerco was also used by Vázquez de Coronado and Juan Troyano, during their 1544 testimony before Tejada, in referring to Pueblo del Arenal. Indeed, it also was attacked and in that sense besieged by a unit from the expedition to Tierra Nueva.

New York Public Library, Rich Collection, no. 63, Primera Parte, Capítulo 16, Capítulo 22 and Segunda Parte, Capítulo 4; AGI, Patronato, 20, N. 5, R. 8, relación del suceso, n.p., 1540s; Hammond and Rey, *Narratives*, 174–75; Tello, *Crónica Miscelanea*, 2:261; Riley, *Rio del Norte*, 103, 177–78; Teresa Mueller and Robin Ransom, *New Mexico Highway Geologic Map* (Socorro, New Mexico: New Mexico Geological Society, 1982); ARMS site files for LA 2047, Basalt Point Pueblo, and LA 2049, Canjillon Pueblo, unpublished files, Laboratory of Anthropology, Museum of New Mexico, Santa Fe; Bayer, *Santa Ana*, 259; Florence Hawley Ellis, "Anthropological Evidence Supporting the Land Claim of the Pueblos of Zia, Santa Ana, and Jemez" (Albuquerque: University of Albuquerque, Native American Bilingual Teacher Education Program, 1956), 16; Roland Chardon, "The Linear League in North America," *Annals of the Association of American Geographers* 70 (1980): 129–53.

Pueblo de la Alameda, Pueblo del Almeneda

Other than the fact that Vázquez de Coronado and García López de Cárdenas conferred at Pueblo de la Alameda during the fighting at Pueblo del Arenal, as reported during the 1544 investigation, little is known of events that occurred there during 1540–1542. It was one of the Tiguex pueblos of the time that was deserted from late fall 1540 at least until after the expedition to Tierra Nueva withdrew to Nueva España in spring 1542. Like Coofor, it may have been occupied by part of the expedition. Melchior Pérez, in his 1544 testimony, reported that in late fall 1540 he and others from the expedition were housed in a pueblo on another part (side) of the river. This could easily refer to Alameda, since its remains are likely those of Watche which stand on the east side of the Rio Grande, while Coofor/Santiago is on the west. (See the entry dealing with Coofor for a discussion of Pueblo de la Alameda's location.)

Pueblo de la Cruz

During his 1544 testimony, Rodrigo de Frias reported that members of the expedition to Tierra Nueva took three pueblos by force: Pueblo de la Alameda (evidently an error for Pueblo del Arenal), Pueblo del Cerco, and Pueblo de la Cruz. Since this is the only known use of the name Pueblo de la Cruz in contemporary documents, its modern identity is unknown. Only one other witness before Tejada, Juan de Contreras, and the chronicler of the expedition Pedro de Castañeda, mentioned a third Tiguex pueblo taken by violence, a pueblo one half league from Pueblo del Cerco. If these three reports about fighting at a third pueblo are accurate, then Pueblo de la Cruz may be represented by one of the archeological sites situated on Santa Ana Mesa. (See the entry concerning Pueblo del Cerco.)

New York Public Library, Rich Collection, no. 63, Primera Parte, Capítulo 16.

Pueblo Quemado

In responding to questions in the province of Culiacán in 1545 about Pueblo del Arenal, Pedro de Tovar called it Pueblo Quemado, or the burned pueblo. (See the entry dealing with Pueblo del Arenal.)

Quivira, Quevira

Quivira, in 1540–1542, was a "province" or culture area along the middle Arkansas River in what is now central Kansas, especially in Rice and McPherson counties. It was described as a well-settled area of six or seven towns of up to 200 round straw houses each in 1541. It was the "most remote land seen" by the expedition to Tierra Nueva. The people there, Caddoan-speaking ancestors of the Wichita, dry-farmed a number of crops, most significantly corn, and lived in permanent round, grass-thatched houses (a characteristic of protohistoric Caddoes of the central Plains). Both El Turco and Ysopete were probably natives of Quivira. Some of the people of Quivira were said to have conspired with El Turco to kill Vázquez de Coronado and his select party who arrived there in summer 1541. Nevertheless, the various Spanish accounts give little indication and no specifics about hostility between the Quivirans and members of the expedition to Tierra Nueva. When the expedition returned to Nueva España, fray Juan de Padilla, together with a Portuguese, a Black, a mestizo, and two Indian lay assistants, journeyed back to Quivira to preach the Catholic faith. Fray Juan was soon killed, but the others returned eventually to central Mexico.

Waldo R. Wedel, "Coronado, Quivira, and Kansas: An Archeologist's View," lecture delivered November 3, 1990, Coronado-Quivira Museum, Lyons, Kansas; Waldo R. Wedel, *Archeological Remains in Central Kansas and Their Possible Bearing on the Location of Quivira* (Washington, D.C.: Smithsonian Institution, 1942); New York Public Library, Rich Collection, no. 63, Segunda Parte, Capítulo 8 and Tercera Parte, Capítulo 4, Capítulo 9; AGI, Patronato, 20, N. 5, R. 8; AGI, Patronato, 20, N. 5, R. 8.

Río de Tiguex

In 1540, as now, the Río de Tiguex, the modern Rio Grande, was the focus of human settlement in what has become New Mexico. Its reliability as a source of abundant water was crucial to the success of irrigated crops of squash, cotton, beans, and corn among the Tewa, Keres, Tiguex, and Piro peoples who lived along its middle reaches.

Señora, Sonora

In the 1540s, a town, an area, a river, and a valley all went by an indigenous name recorded as Senora by members of the expedition to Tierra Nueva. The name was transmuted by the Spaniards into Señora and has become Sonora in more recent times. In the mid-sixteenth century the area of Señora was one densely populated by Ópata peoples along the middle portion of today's Río Sonora. The region was very prosperous agriculturally. The ruins of the town of Señora, likely the largest of the region, may now lie beneath Baviácora or Aconchi along the Río Sonora in modern central Sonora. As at Suya, the indigenous people of Señora and most of the other Ópata rose up in early 1542 and expelled the members of the expedition to Tierra Nueva who had been left there. Retaliation was soon to come when Juan Gallego made lightning strikes the whole length of Ópata country on his way north to join the expedition.

Pailes, "An Archaeological Perspective," 187; New York Public Library, Rich Collection, no. 63, Segunda Parte, Capítulo 2 and Tercera Parte, Capítulo 7.

Tabas

Herbert Bolton, writing in 1949, had this to say about the Quiviran town of Tabas: "I have recently acquired the significant eyewitness testimony that the last settlement reached by Vázquez de Coronado was called Tabás, which is but another spelling for Towásh or Taováyas, the well-known name of a Wichita group at a later date." He even went so far as to identify the location of Tabas as "near Lindsborg [Kansas] on Smoky Hill River." This assertion derives from archeological findings of Waldo R. Wedel. According to Domingo Martín's 1544 testimony, Tabas was the town where El Turco was executed.

Bolton, *Coronado*, 293, 299; Wedel, "Coronado, Quivira, and Kansas," 8–9.

Tiguex

Tiguex was a "province" or culture area in 1540 comprising 12 or 13 Tiwa-speaking pueblos situated in the middle Rio Grande Valley in modern central New Mexico. Tiguex pueblos of the sixteenth century were located on both sides of the Rio Grande from south of modern Isleta Pueblo (northern Valencia County) north to the confluence of the Rio Grande and the Jemez River, and perhaps slightly farther north (in southeast Sandoval County). (See entries dealing with Coofor, Pueblo del Arenal, Pueblo de la Alameda, and Pueblo del Cerco, the four Tiguex pueblos, the locations of which can be postulated.)

The Tiguex had been in the middle Rio Grande Valley for over 500 years when the expedition to Tierra Nueva arrived and were the first of the Puebloan peoples to live along the Rio

Grande. It is no accident that their middle Rio Grande homeland has proved enduringly attractive to humans. A relative abundance of water and a mild climate in an area largely sheltered from frigid cold that can grip New Mexico's eastern plains and just on the northern margin of the land of blistering summers made it probably the prime real estate of sixteenth-century New Mexico. And there is abundant archeological evidence that other agricultural peoples had been nibbling at the edges of Tiguex territory and actually intruding for hundreds of years.

In 1540 the Tiguex area was the most populous of the areas settled by town-dwelling agricultural peoples along and adjacent to the Rio Grande. Immediately to the west and north of Tiguex were the Keres Pueblos, to the east the Tano Pueblos, and to the south the Piro Pueblos. Farther north were the Tewas and more Tiwas; beyond the Keres to the west, the Jemez; to the east beyond the Tanos, the people of Cicuique; and to the east and southeast, the Tompiros and the enigmatic and perhaps illusory Ubates. Though often unified under the name Puebloans these peoples spoke distinct languages, essentially mutually unintelligible. Despite the language differences, though, the Puebloan groups of the sixteenth century shared broad cultural similarity, including government by councils of elders and complex religious practices involving solicitation of activity on the part of deified ancestors in bringing beneficial weather and otherwise supporting the living. This similarity was noticed and commented on by members of the expedition to Tierra Nueva such as Pedro de Castañeda. There was clearly much contact and interchange between the various Puebloan groups.

Francisco Vázquez de Coronado directed that winter quarters for the expedition be established at Tiguex during 1540–1541 and 1541–1542. Conflict between the newcomers and the natives resulted almost immediately once it was evident that the Spaniards and their associates meant to stay. The Spaniards, Mexican Indians, Blacks, and others needed shelter, food, and clothing; expected to receive significant wealth; desired the feeling of dominance over their new neighbors; and preyed on Pueblo women. Each of these needs and wants repeatedly aroused hostility. The first winter had barely begun when open defiance of the demands and expectations of the newcomers brought on violence. After assaults on two or three pueblos by the expedition, the Tiguex abandoned all their pueblos and did not return to them for the better part of two years.

Schroeder, "Pueblos Abandoned," 238, 240; Elinore M. Barrett, *The Geography of Rio Grande Pueblos Revealed by Spanish Explorers, 1540–1598*, Latin American Institute Research Paper Series, no. 30 (Albuquerque: Latin American Institute, University of New Mexico, 1997), 7–11; New York Public Library, Rich Collection, no. 63, Primera Parte, Capítulo 12, Capítulo 15, Capítulo 16 and Segunda Parte, Capítulo 4; Riley, *Rio del Norte*, 99–102; Marc Simmons, "History of Pueblo-Spanish Relations to 1821," in *Southwest*, vol. 9, 178–79; Edward P. Dozier, *The Pueblo Indians of North America* (New York: Holt, Rinehart and Winston, Inc, 1970; reprint, Prospect Heights, Illinois: Waveland Press, Inc., 1983), 43–44, 200 (page citations are to the reprint edition).

Topira

Stories of the Seven Cities of Cíbola were not the only stimulus for expeditions in search of precious metals northwest of Mexico City in the late 1530s. Much nearer to the seat of

Vázquez de Coronado's administration in Nueva Galicia was Topira, or Topia, where the natives were rumored to wear ornaments of gold and precious jewels. In mid April 1539, the governor departed from Culiacán with a force of at least 350 for the valleys of Topira in the Sierra Madre Occidental to the northeast. The ruggedness of the Sierra Madre and lack of confirmation of the reports of precious metals caused abandonment of the expedition. By the 1590s, though, silver veins were discovered in the region and as a result Topia came fully under Spanish control. Topia comprised an area in the extreme west of the modern state of Durango along tributary valleys of the Río Culiacán.

Giovanni Battista Ramusio, "Copia delle Lettere di Francesco Vazquez di Coronado...date in San Michiel di Culuacan, a gli otto di Marzo MDXXXIX," in *Terzo Volume delle Navigationi et Viaggi* (Venice: Stamperia de Giunti, 1565), fols. 354v–355r; New York Public Library, Rich Collection, no. 63, Primera Parte, Capítulo 4; Gerhard, *North Frontier*, 238–39.

Totonqueade, Totonqueates, Totonqueantes, Totonteac

The place called Totonqueade, Totonqueates, and Totonqueantes during the investigation of the conduct of the expedition to Tierra Nueva is the Totonteac of which fray Marcos de Niza was told in Sonora. It was said to be a very large "kingdom" southwest of Cíbola. Within a few months of Marcos's learning of Totonteac, Melchor Díaz and Juan de Zaldívar heard similar stories about 12 pueblos, each larger than those at Cíbola at a distance of seven short days' travel from there, to which the same name was applied. After his arrival in Cíbola, Vázquez de Coronado was told that Totonteac was a hot spring where there were only five or six houses. By the time of the 1544 investigation, Totonteac was described as a hot spring only. Where that hot spring was is not now known. In recent years, some researchers have concluded that Totonteac was a name applied to the Hopi pueblos of modern Arizona, but that does not agree with the statements of members of the expedition. It is quite likely that two similar names were conflated in what fray Marcos heard and reported.

AGI, Patronato, 20, N. 5, R. 10; AGI, Patronato 184, R. 31; Giovanni Battista Ramusio, "Relatione che Mando Francesco Vazquez di Coronado...MDXL," in *Terzo Volume delle Navigationi et Viaggi*, fols. 359v–363r; Bolton, *Coronado*, 36; John C. Connelly, "Hopi Social Organization," in *Southwest*, vol. 9, 551.

Tusayán

Tusayán is a name used by members of the expedition to Tierra Nueva for the Hopi pueblos of modern north-central Arizona. The name either dropped out of use after the 1540s or had been misunderstood in the first place. At any rate, the name was not used again until the late 1800s when it was resurrected by anthropologists who had become familiar with some the sixteenth-century Spanish documents.

After the initial disappointment of finding Cíbola to be a small unremarkable pueblo, Vázquez de Coronado dispatched two reconnaissance parties to the seven pueblos of Tusayán, one led by Pedro de Tovar and the other by García López de Cárdenas. At the first of the Tusayán/Hopi pueblos to be contacted by Tovar, thought to be Awatovi, the people blocked entrance to the Spaniards, and some tense discussion ensued followed by a brief skirmish.

Other residents of Awatovi intervened, calming the situation, after which leaders made the formal act of submission as required by the Spaniards and the two groups engaged in trade. Within a couple of weeks, López de Cárdenas was received peacefully at Tusayán en route to a great river the Spaniards had been told about, the Colorado River. There was no further contact between the Hopi and the expedition to Tierra Nueva.

    John C. Connelly, "Hopi Social Organization," 551; New York Public Library, Rich Collection, no. 63, Primera Parte, Capítulo 9, Capítulo 11; J[ohn] O. Brew, "Hopi Prehistory and History to 1850," in *Southwest,* vol. 9, 519.

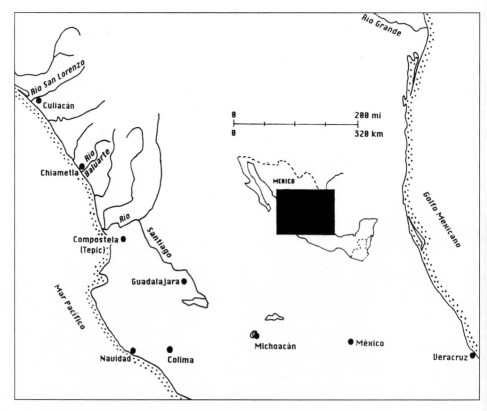

FIGURE 16.
Map of Central and western Nueva España, 1540

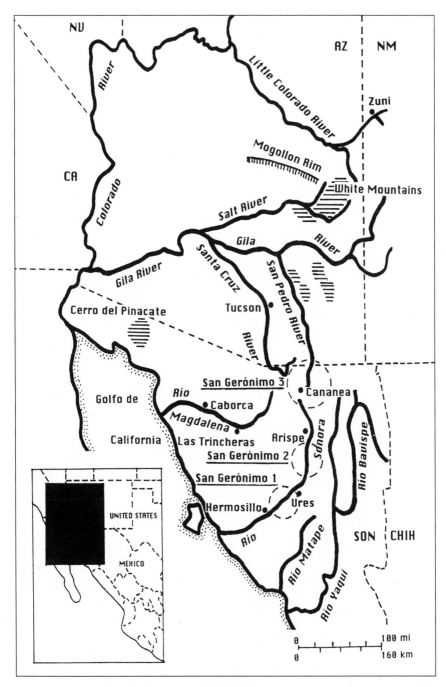

FIGURE 17.
Map of Possible locales of San Geronimo, 1540–1542

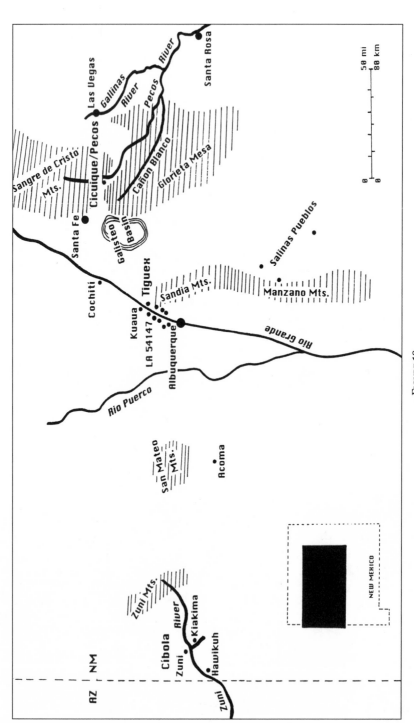

FIGURE 18.
Map of Cíbola, the Tiguex Pueblos, and Cicuique

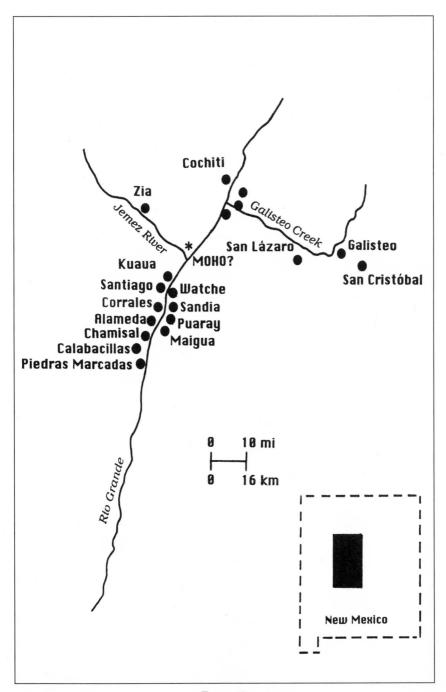

FIGURE 19.
Map of Pueblos of the Middle Rio Grande and Adjacent Areas, 1540–1542

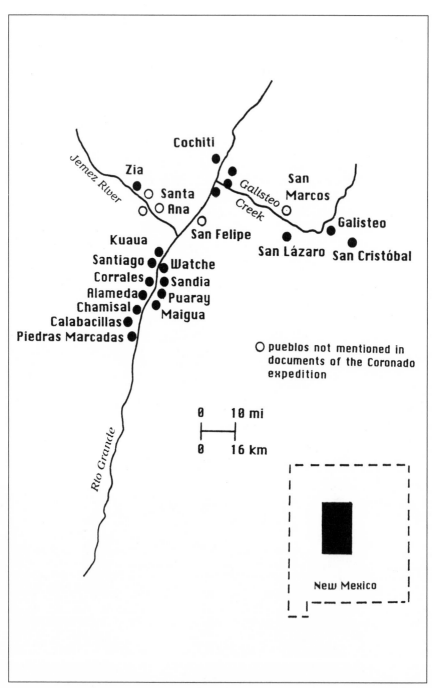

FIGURE 20.
Map of Pueblos of the Middle Rio Grande and Adjacent Areas, 1580–1581

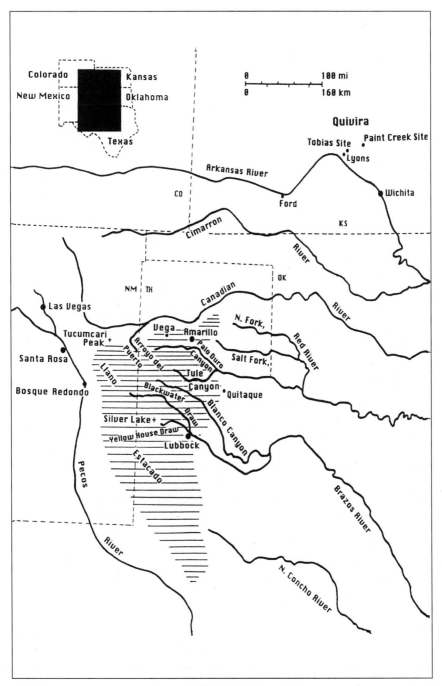

FIGURE 21.
Map of The Barrancas and Quivira

Glossary

adelantado - perpetual governor; the office was assumed to be inheritable

alcaide - warden or commander of a fortress

alcalde mayor - chief judge and administrator of a cabildo or other entity

alcalde ordinario - judge/legislator of a cabildo

alférez mayor - chief lieutenant or standard bearer

alguacil - law enforcement officer, constable

alguacil mayor - chief law enforcement officer, constable

audiencia - the governing body of a province-sized jurisdiction within the Spanish Empire, having judicial, legislative, and limited executive power

barranca - canyon or ravine

caballería - a standard unit of agricultural land

cabildo - the governing council of an urban area and its surroundings

cacique - Arawak word meaning "headman", widely used in Spanish America

cédula - a written order, often from the king or the royal court

ciudad - status conferred on a settlement by the king indicating its relatively large size and great importance

comendador - high officer in one of the military orders

comunidad - a geo-political unit in modern Spain roughly equivalent to a state in the United States of America

convento - a monastery

corregidor - royally appointed official who administered an encomienda or other jurisdiction held directly by the crown

corregimiento - an encomienda or other jurisdiction held directly by the crown

criado - literally "servant", but more often a henchman or retainer

de parte - pertaining to a private party in a legal proceeding

de oficio - pertaining to a governmental entity in a legal proceeding

despoblado - an extensive area without permanent settlements
donado - a servant in a religious order
encomendero - a person holding and exercising an encomienda
encomienda - a grant of the right to collect tribute and/or labor from an indigenous community, usually granted by the king as reward for service
entrada - an expedition penetrating new territory
escribano - a combination secretary, scribe, and notary
estancia - a livestock ranch
fiscal - court official roughly equivalent to a prosecuting attorney
interrogatorio - questionnaire for interrogating witnesses
juez de residencia - investigating judge charged with conducting a residencia
juez visitador - investigating judge conducting a visita
ladino - culturally Hispanic though of another ethnic origin
licenciado - university graduate, roughly equivalent to modern master's level
maestre de campo - field commander
manta - shawl-like article of indigenous clothing common during and before the Spanish Colonial Period
oidor - judge/legislator of an audiencia
peso de oro de minas - gold coin with standard value of 450 *maravedís*
peso de oro común - unminted gold coin valued at roughly 2/3 a peso de oro de minas
pesquisa - an official investigation or judicial inquiry
pesquisador - investigating judge conducting a pesquisa
principal - an indigenous leader
procurador - legal representative or agent
pueblo - status conferred on a settlement and its hinterland by the king indicating its intermediate size and importance; the term is still used to refer to the communities of a number of indigenous groups in New Mexico and Arizona
regidor - a member of the cabildo of a municipality (ciudad, pueblo, or villa)
requerimiento - formal summons to submit to the authority of the king of Spain
residencia - judicial review of the performance of a royal official held at the end of the term in office
secreta - when applied to testimony, taken out of the presence of other witnesses
solar - a house lot
Tierra Nueva - the newly discovered land, in Nueva España during the 1540s applied exclusively to what is now the Greater American Southwest
tomín - a *real* or 1/8 of a peso
vecino - a person with full political rights in a municipality; such rights were not automatic but granted by the cabildo after payment of a fee and pledge to establish and maintain a residence for a certain length of time; residents without full political rights were *estantes*
villa - status conferred on a settlement and its hinterland by the king indicating its inferior size and importance
visita - extraordinary judicial review of performance of officials
visitador - investigating judge assigned to conduct a visita

Notes

Introduction

1. Herbert E. Bolton, *Coronado, Knight of Pueblos and Plains* (New York, London, and Toronto: Whittlesey House, McGraw-Hill Book Company, Inc; Albuquerque: University of New Mexico Press, 1949), 393, 401.

Chapter 1, The Historical Background

1. Traditionally, Melchor has been considered the proper Spanish spelling of this given name. All known contemporary documents referring to Pérez, however, spell his name with an "i," making it Melchior. Thus, in writing about him I maintain consistency with the documents. When referring to other individuals such as Melchor Díaz, I use the more "standard" spelling without the "i."

Chapter 2, The Texts and Editorial Protocols

1. George P. Hammond and Agapito Rey, *Narratives of the Coronado Expedition, 1540–1542*, vol. 2 of Coronado Cuarto Centennial Publications (Albuquerque: University of New Mexico Press, 1940).
2. Bolton cited only the manuscript document, though he acknowledged Rey's work, writing, "A large body of these documents which Hammond and Rey acquired but did not publish they generously turned over to me, and they have been used for the first time in the writing of this book. The difficult paleographic work of transcribing them from the original sixteenth-century manuscripts has been done by expert Professor Agapito Rey, of the University of Indiana." Particularly when transcribing difficult passages or words, I consulted Rey's rendition, which was often very helpful, though I did not always agree with Rey's decisions. Rey rendered his transcript in lightly edited modern Spanish. It is curated in the Herbert E. Bolton Collection of the Bancroft Library as Item 393, C-B 840, Part I. Bolton, *Coronado*, 423–24.
3. Constance Carter, "Finding Aid, Spain, Archivo General de Indias, Vol. 34," unpublished finding aid, Bancroft Library, University of California at Berkeley, Berkeley, California.
4. Three of these are virtually identical, "y firmolo de su nombre" or variations, at the end of testimonies.
5. Confirmation of the absence of wheeled artillery carriages or wagons is provided by the king's *carta executoria* or final decision included in AGI, Justicia, 336. It reads in part [fol. 17r], "la dicha artilleria se habia llevado en bestias [the artillery had been carried on beasts of burden]."
   The use of pack horses rather than wheeled vehicles to transport the small artillery pieces was also reported by fray Antonio Tello writing in the mid-1600s. Antonio Tello, *Crónica Miscelanea de la Sancta Provincia de Xalisco, Libro Segundo* (Guadalajara: Gobierno del Estado de Jalisco and Universidad de Guadalajara, 1968), 2:130.
6. Bolton, *Coronado*, 319.
7. See Chapter 4 for further discussion of this issue.
8. Examples of the kind of shorthand probably used to record testimony can often be seen in the bottom margins of documents, where the scribe lists the corrections he had to make on the page. Often these are all but incomprehensible except with close and patient study. I know of no surviving example, though, of a sixteenth-century stenographic record of testimony. Nevertheless, such abbreviated documents were most certainly a routine part of scribal work.
   Vicenta Cortés Alonso, in her work on sixteenth- and seventeenth-century Spanish paleography, mentions in passing the preparation of such *minutas* or *notas* as a necessary first step in drafting an "original" document. Vicenta Cortés Alonso, *La Escritura y Lo Escrito: Paleografía y Diplomática de España y América en los siglos XVI y XVII* (Madrid: Ediciones Cultura Hispanica, Instituto de Cooperación Iberoamericana, 1986), 51.
9. AGI, Justicia, 339, N. 1, R. 3, investigation concerning certain Indian towns, Guadalajara, fall 1544.
10. Hammond and Rey, *Narratives*, 337–65, 366–67, 367–68.
11. See the references for a complete listing.
12. In 1611, Sebastián de Covarrubias Orozco in the first formal dictionary of Spanish remarked that *notarios* or scribes had formerly been able to write very rapidly using many abbreviations. Sebastián de Covarrubias Orozco, *Tesoro de la Lengua Castellana o Española*, 2nd rev. ed., ed. Felipe C.R. Maldonado (Madrid: Editorial Castalia, S.A., 1995), 780.
13. Bolton, *Coronado*, 377.
14. Herbert Ingram Priestley, ed. and trans., *The Luna Papers: Documents Relating to the Expedition of don Tristán de Luna y Arellano for the Conquest of La Florida in 1559–1561* (DeLand, Florida: The Florida

State Historical Society, 1928; reprint, Freeport, New York: Books for Libraries Press, 1971), 1:xv (page citations are to the reprint edition).

Chapter 3, Lorenzo de Tejada and the Beginning of the Investigation

1. Linda A. Newson, Indian Population Patterns in Colonial Spanish America, *Latin American Research Review* 20(3) (1985):46–47.
2. Lewis Hanke, *The Spanish Struggle for Justice in the Conquest of America* (Boston: Little, Brown and Company, 1965), 17–19, 23–24.
3. John H. Parry and Robert G. Keith, comps., 1512–1513. The Laws of Burgos. In *The Conquerors and the Conquered*, Vol. 1, *New Iberian World* (New York: Times Books and Hector & Rose, 1984), 336–47.
4. Charles Gibson, ed., *The Spanish Tradition in America* (Columbia: University of South Carolina Press, 1968), 58–60.
5. John H. Elliot, *Imperial Spain, 1469–1716* (London: Edward Arnold, 1963; reprint, London: Penquin Books, 1990), 73.
6. Hanke, *Spanish Struggle for Justice*, 91. See also the facsimile reprint of the 1543 publication of the New Laws in Henry Stevens, *The New Laws for the Indies* (London: privately printed, 1893).
7. Joaquín García Icazbalceta, *Colección de Documentos para la Historia de México* (Mexico City: Antigua Librería, 1866), 2:204.
8. Peter Bakewell, *A History of Latin America: Empires and Sequels, 1450–1930* (Malden, Massachusetts and Oxford, England: Blackwell Publishers, 1997), 125.
9. Chipman, *Guzmán*, 295.
10. David A. Howard, *Conquistador in Chains: Cabeza de Vaca and the Indians of the Americas* (Tuscaloosa and London: University of Alabama Press, 1997), 187–90.
11. An enigmatic entry on the verso of a folio in AGI, Justicia, 1021, N. 2, Pieza 6 suggested that one of the complainants may have been an Hernán González Párraga, who after the expedition went on to Castilla de Oro in hopes of better luck there. That possibility is raised by an undated, incomplete, and possibly unrelated document of seven lines, a cédula to the governor of Castilla de Oro and an escribano in Nombre de Dios, referring to a *petición de acusación* submitted by "Hernán Gonçález de Párraga, presently in the royal court." The muster role of the Coronado expedition lists two Hernán/Fernán Gonzálezes, about whom very little is known except that one of them was from Santo Domingo. These may represent only one individual named twice, since the entries are all but identical.

A number of documents survive relating to the Hernán González of Castilla de Oro, all dealing with events in Panama and Peru, to which he is said to have gone in 1543. In a *probanza* prepared in 1551 he says that he is a native of Carmona and does not refer to service in the expedition to Tierra Nueva or in Nueva España, making it unlikely that he was one of the complainants about treatment of Indians in Cíbola and other places in the north. Still, it is curious that the seven lines in AGI, Justicia, 1021, N. 2, Pieza 6 were not struck out or otherwise deleted, if they had nothing to do with the investigation of the Coronado expedition.

AGI, Guadalajara, 5, R. 1, N. 7, muster roll of the expedition, Compostela, February 22, 1540; Francisco A. de Icaza, *Conquistadores y Pobladores de Nueva España: Diccionario Autobiográfico Sacado de los Textos Originales* (Madrid: n.p., 1923), 2: no. 696; AGI, Indiferente, 737, N. 69 b, proof of service of Fernand González de Párraga, Castilla de Oro, 1551.
12. In 1542, while the Coronado expedition was still in the field, las Casas had read a draft of his powerful and extremely influential *Brevísima Relación de la Destrucción de las Indias* before the Spanish court. In it he narrated lurid and gory stories of what he had seen and been told while in the Indies concerning murder and enslavement of natives.
13. Cargos de Hernán Cortés contra el virrey Antonio de Mendoza y sus criados y solicitud de juicio de residencia, Madrid, hacia 1543, *Documentos Cortesianos*, ed. José Luis Martínez (Mexico City: Universidad Nacional Autónoma de México, 1992), 4:249.
14. It is probably more accurate to refer to the expedition as the Mendoza-Coronado-Estrada-Alvarado expedition. It was the viceroy, after all, who received license to make the entrada, was the largest investor in it (followed closely by Vázquez de Coronado, through the dowry of his wife Beatriz de Estrada), and entered into partnership with Pedro de Alvarado formally incorporating the expedition into a larger program of exploration and conquest and apportioning its expected profits. AGI, Patronato, 21, N. 3, R. 2, contract between Antonio de Mendoza and the adelantado Pedro de Alvarado, Mexico City, November 29, 1540.
15. Alonso de Villadiego Vascuñana y Montoya, *Instrucción Política y Práctica Judicial Conforme al Estilo de*

los Consejos, Audiencias, y Tribunales de Corte, y Otros Ordinarios del Reyno Utilissima para los Governadores, y Corregidores, y otros Jueces Ordinarios, y de Comisión, y para los Abogados, Escrivanos, Procuradores, y Litigantes (Madrid: Oficina de Antonio Marin, 1766), 62.

The procedure of a pesquisa secreta was parallel to that followed in ordinary criminal cases, having three phases analogous to the *sumaria, plenario,* and *sentencia.* For a full description, see Charles R. Cutter, *The Legal Culture of Northern New Spain, 1700–1810* (Albuquerque: University of New Mexico Press, 1995), 105–46.

16. Mendoza referred to this investigation using the term pesquisa during his visita before Tello de Sandoval. Vázquez de Coronado referred to the investigation as a pesquisa and pesquisa secreta. AGI, Justicia, 259, Pieza 3, fol. 9v, administrative review of don Antonio de Mendoza, Mexico City, 1544–1546; AGI, Justicia, 260, Pieza 4, fol. 5r, administrative review of licenciado Cristóbal de Benavente, Mexico City, 1546.

17. AGI, Justicia, 267, proceedings of the secret review of the officials of the royal audiencia of Mexico, Mexico City, 1546; AGI, Contratación, 5787, N. 1, L. 4, royal cédula, Valladolid, 1537.

18. Ethelia Ruiz Medrano, "El Oidor como Empresario: El Caso del Licenciado Lorenzo de Tejada (1537–1550)" in *Gobierno y Sociedad en Nueva España: Segunda Audiencia y Antonio de Mendoza* (Zamora, Michoacán: El Colegio de Michoacán and Gobierno de Michoacán, 1991), 210.

19. AGI, Indiferente, 425, L. 23, fol. 421v, royal cédula, Madrid, 1559.

20. Francisco del Paso y Troncoso, ed., *Epistolario de Nueva España, 1505–1818,* 2nd series (Mexico City: José Porrua e Hijos, 1939–1942), 4: 132.

21. AGI, Patronato 284, N. 2, R. 24, final decision in the administrative review by Doctor Montealegre, oidor, and the administrative review by licenciado Francisco Tello de Sandoval, Valladolid, 1558.

22. AGI, Mexico, 68, R. 13, N. 38, letter, Lorenzo de Tejada to the marqués de Mondéjar, Mexico City, April 24, 1547.

23. AGI, Justicia, 259, Pieza 2, folios 234r and 234v, royal cédula, Madrid, 1540.

24. Arthur Scott Aiton, *Antonio de Mendoza, First Viceroy of New Spain* (Durham, North Carolina: Duke University Press, 1927), 113.

25. Probably by coincidence, Juan Troyano, a de oficio witness in the 1544 investigation, became involved more than 15 years later with several communities of Indians transplanted from the Valley of Mexico to Tlalmanalco, perhaps some that Tejada had been instrumental in moving.

26. Ruiz Medrano, "El Oidor como Empresario," 209–339. For a description of Tejada's stores, see Francisco Cervantes de Salazar, *México en 1554,* ed. Julio Jiménez Rueda, trans. Joaquín García Icazbalceta (Mexico City: Universidad Nacional Autónoma de México, 1984), 62–63. This group of three dialogs in Latin presents a tour of Mexico City and environs in 1554, when its author was professor of Latin in the new Real y Pontificia Universidad.

27. Ethelia Ruiz Medrano, "La Política del Virrey Mendoza: Encomienda y Corregimineto. El Virrey como Empresario en México (1535–1550)," in *Gobierno y Sociedad en Nueva España: Segunda Audiencia y Antonio de Mendoza* (Zamora, Michoacán: El Colegio de Michoacán and Gobierno de Michoacán: 1991), 168–69.

28. AGI, Mexico, 68, R. 13, N. 38.

29. AGI, Mexico, 68, R. 12, N. 29, letter, Lorenzo de Tejada to the king, Mexico City, March 12, 1545.

30. AGI, Mexico, 68, R. 11, N. 25, letter, Lorenzo de Tejada to the prince, Mexico City, May 24, 1544.

31. AGI, Justicia, 267.

32. AGI, Mexico, 204, N. 36, investigation of Juan Gallego, Mexico City, 1558.

33. *Códice Franciscano, Siglo XVI,* ed. Joaquín García Icazbalceta (Mexico City: Francisco Díaz de León, 1889), 250, 270.

34. AGI, Justicia, 260, Pieza 4, charges and rebuttals, Lorenzo de Tejada, Mexico City, 1546.

35. *Quinto Libro de Actas de la Ciudad de México,* ed. Antonio Espinosa de los Monteros ([Mexico City]: n.p., 1862), 205.

36. AGI, Mexico, 68, R. 12, N. 29.

37. AGI, Mexico, 68, R. 13, N. 38.

38. AGI, Mexico, 68, R. 12, N. 29.

39. Many of the questions to each witness were multifaceted, consisting of several run-on interrogatives. The numbers stated here refer to such lengthy, rambling questions, rather than to the many queries into which they are resolved in English translation.

40. From AGI, Justicia, 267.

41. The king and emperor had left Spain in May 1543 and was not to return for fourteen years while he attempted to stabilize the northern countries of his European empire. By summer his son Felipe was

signing official documents, including this one. Henry Kamen, *Philip of Spain* (New Haven and London: Yale University Press, 1997), 10, 14.
42. Supplied from AGI, Mexico, 68, R. 11, N. 25.
43. From AGI, Justicia, 267.
44. Although the last name of this witness is omitted in both AGI, Justicia, 267 and AGI, Justicia, 1021, N. 2, Pieza 4, it is supplied by AGI, Justicia, 1021, N. 2, Pieza 6.
45. From AGI, Justicia, 267.
46. Supplied from AGI, Mexico, 68, R. 11, N. 25.
47. Return to AGI, Justicia, 267.
48. Although the last name of this witness is omitted in both AGI, Justicia, 267 and AGI, Justicia, 1021, N. 2, Pieza 4, it is supplied by AGI, Justicia, 1021, N. 2, Pieza 6.

Chapter 4, The First de Oficio Witnesses, Francisca de Hozes and Alonso Sánchez

1. Peter Boyd-Bowman, *Indice Geobiográfico de Cuarenta Mil Pobladores Españoles de América en el Siglo XVI* (Mexico City: Editorial Jus, 1968), 2: no. 3672, no. 3726.
2. AGI, Patronato, 21, N. 2, R. 3, investigation of the persons who are going with Francisco Vázquez de Coronado, Compostela, February 1540.
3. In 1553 six adult children of the couple were alive: Alonso de la Cámara, Francisco de la Serna, Juan de Hozes, Catalina de Hozes, María de Hozes, and Isabel de Hozes. Which one of the sons it was who went to Tierra Nueva is not known. AGnot, 1, Diego de Isla, IV, distribution of inheritance from Alonso Sánchez, Mexico City, 1553; Boyd-Bowman, *Cuarenta Mil Pobladores*, 2:no. 3726; and Icaza, *Conquistadores y Pobladores*, 2:no. 762.
4. The "información," Requena's copy of the investigation record refers on folio 12v to "*hijos*," whereas both other copies of the record (folio 14v of the "proceso and AGI, Justicia, 1021, N. 2, Pieza 6) agree on only one "hijo." Bolton, *Coronado*, 319.
5. Most typically, members of the expedition had one horse, and more than half of all the members of the expedition had two horses or fewer. AGI, Guadalajara, 5, R. 1, N. 7.
6. Sánchez owed Tomás Blaque three pesos when he died and Melchior Pérez witnessed the settlement of Sánchez's estate proposed by his son Francisco de la Serna. AGnot, 1, Diego de Isla, IV.
7. Bolton, *Coronado*, 117, 238.
8. From AGI, Justicia, 267.
9. From AGI, Justicia, 267.
10. AGI, Justicia, 1021, N. 2, Pieza 4, fol. 17r has *enbaydor* or *embaidor* in modern spelling.

Chapter 5, Juan Gómez de Paradinas, the Third de Oficio Witness

1. AGI, Patronato, 63, R. 5, proof of service of Juan Gómez de Paradinas, Mexico City, June 6, 1560.
2. AGI, Guadalajara, 5, R. 1, N. 7.
3. *Quinto Libro de Actas*, 44.
4. Icaza, *Pobladores y Conquistadores*, 2:no. 837.
5. Biblioteca del Escorial, Códice &-II-7, Doc. no. LXXVIII, settlers without Indians, n.p., [late 1540s].
6. AGI, Patronato, 63, R. 5.
7. AGI, Patronato, 79, N. 3, R. 2, proof of service of Francisco de Santillán, Madrid, December 14, 1598.
8. From AGI, Justicia, 267.
9. From AGI, Justicia, 267.

Chapter 6, Domingo Martín, the Fourth de Oficio Witness

1. AGI, Guadalajara 5, R. 1, N. 7.
2. AGI, Justicia, 1021, N. 2, Pieza 5, affidavit prepared at the request of don García López de Cárdenas, Mexico City, end of 1547 and early 1548 and AGI, Justicia, 1021 N. 2, Pieza 6, affidavit prepared for the fiscal Juan de Villalobos, Mexico City, January 10, 1547.
3. AGI, Patronato, 21, N. 2, R. 3.
4. Boyd-Bowman, *Cuarenta Mil Pobladores*, 2:no. 884.
5. AGI, Justicia, 124, N. 2, legal action between Domingo Martín and Gómez Nieto, Valladolid, June 28, 1542.

6. AGI, Justicia, 260, Pieza 4.
7. *Cuarto Libro de las Actas de Cabildo de la Ciudad de México, comprende de Primero de Enero de 1536 a 30 de Agosto de 1543*, ed. D. Manuel (Mexico City: Orozco y Berra, 1859), 100.
8. AGI, Mexico, 204, N. 14, proof of service of Cristóbal de Escobar, Mexico City, November 21, 1543.
9. Of course, those horses may represent some of the livestock he took along as a small merchant. AGI, Guadalajara, 5, R. 1, N. 7.
10. From AGI, Justicia, 267.
11. In AGI, Justicia, 1021 it is very unclear whether the name is Fuya(s) or Suya(s). In his draft transcription of 1021, Agapito Rey also indicated both possibilities. In AGI, Justicia, 267, however, the name is clearly and consistently Fuya(s). See the entry on Fuyas in Appendix 3.
12. Supplied by AGI, Justicia, 1021, N. 2, Pieza 4, fol. 19v.
13. Almost certainly this refers to turkeys.
14. Supplied by AGI, Justicia, 1021, N. 2, Pieza 4, fol. 22r.
15. From AGI, Justicia, 267.

Chapter 7, Juan de Contreras, the Fifth de Oficio Witness

1. Cristóbal Bermúdez Plata, ed, *1535–1538*, vol. 2 of *Catálogo de Pasajeros a Indias durante los Siglos XVI, XVII y XVIII* (Sevilla: Editorial de la Gavida, 1942), no. 5617.
2. AGI, Justicia, 259, Pieza 2, administrative review of Antonio de Mendoza, Mexico City, 1544–1546.
3. AGI, Guadalajara, 5, R. 1, N. 7.
4. AGnot, 1, Luis Sánchez, proceedings concerning Baltasar Dorantes de Carranza, San Juan Teotihuacan, August 8, 1582.
5. Petition from Sebastián Rodríguez, Valladolid, January 7, 1550, in AGI, Justicia, 1021, N. 2, Pieza 1, accusation against Ramírez de Cárdenas, Madrid, 1546–1547.
6. From AGI, Justicia, 267.
7. From AGI, Justicia, 267.

Chapter 8, Rodrigo Ximón, the Sixth de Oficio Witness

1. Icaza, *Pobladores y Conquistadores*, 1: no. 176; AGI, Patronato, 287, R. 57, final decision concerning certain Indians, Bosque de Segovia, 1562.
2. AGI, Justicia, 1021, N. 2, Pieza 6; Biblioteca del Escorial, Códice &-II-7, Doc. no. LXXVIII.
3. AGI, Patronato, 287, R. 57.
4. From AGI, Justicia, 267.
5. Supplied by AGI, Justicia, 1021, N. 2, Pieza 4, fol. 33v.
6. From AGI, Justicia, 267.

Chapter 9, Crisóbal de Escobar, the Seventh de Oficio Witness

1. AGI, Mexico, 204, N. 14; AGI, Indiferente, 423, Libro 18, F 65r, permission to Cristóbal de Escobar to transport one black slave to the Indies, Sevilla, December 30, 1537.
2. Icaza, *Pobladores y Conquistadores*, 2: no. 640; Bermúdez Plata, *1535–1538*, no. 4370.
3. AGI, Justicia, 1021, N. 2.
4. AGI, Mexico, 204, N. 14 and AGI, Mexico, 206, N. 35, investigation of Cristóbal de Escobar, Mexico City, February 1, 1561.
5. Biblioteca del Escorial, Códice &-II-7, Doc. no. LXXVIII.
6. La Sociedad de Bibliófilos Españoles, *Nobilario de Conquistadores de Indias* (Madrid: M. Tello, 1892), 112–13.
7. Despite Escobar's own statement to this effect, Peter Gerhard does not list Escobar among the corregidores of either Xicotepeque or any of the three pueblos called Xilotepeque. AGI, Mexico, 206, N. 35 and Peter Gerhard, *A Guide to the Historical Geography of New Spain*, rev. ed. (Norman and London: University of Oklahoma Press, 1993).
8. AGI, Mexico, 206, N. 35.
9. *Quinto Libro de Actas*, 155.
10. AGI, Mexico, 204, N. 14.
11. From AGI, Justicia, 267.

12. Supplied by AGI, Justicia, 1021, N. 2, Pieza 4, fol. 36v.
13. Supplied from AGI, Justicia, 1021, N. 2, Pieza 4, fol. 38r.
14. From AGI, Justicia, 267.

Chapter 10, Juan Troyano, the Eighth de Oficio Witness

1. AGI, Mexico, 206, N. 12, proof of service of Juan Troyano, Mexico City, February 20, 1560.
2. AGI, Mexico, 168, letter, Juan Troyano to the king, Mexico City, December 20, 1568.
3. AGI, Mexico, 206, N. 12.
4. AGI, Mexico, 206, N. 12 and New York Public Library, Rich Collection, no. 63, Pedro de Castañeda, *Relación de la Jornada de Cibola....*, Sevilla, 1596, Primera Parte, Capítulo 8.
5. AGI, Justicia, 1021, N. 2, Pieza 1.
6. AGI, Mexico, 206, N. 12.
7. Though it may never be known for sure, this woman was most likely from one of the New Mexico pueblos, since Troyano spent far more time among them than anywhere else during the journey. It is possible she was one of the many captives distributed to members of the expedition as servants. Carroll Riley has suggested that she was a woman called doña Inés, who returned to the Pueblo world in 1598 with Juan de Oñate. Carroll L. Riley, *Rio del Norte: People of the Upper Rio Grande from Earliest Times to the Pueblo Revolt* (Salt Lake City: University of Utah Press, 1995), 206.
8. AGI, Mexico, 168.
9. AGI, Mexico, 98, N. 33e, letter, Juan Troyano to the viceroy, Mexico City, 1569.
10. AGI, Mexico, 206, N. 12.
11. It is tempting to imagine that the population of these eight *sujetos* of Tlalmanalco represented some of the Indian allies of the expedition to Tierra Nueva resettled outside the growing Spanish and Indian city of Mexico, which might explain Troyano's connection with them. AGI, Mexico, 98, N. 33, investigation of Juan Troyano, Mexico City, 1569.
12. AGI, Indiferente, 2055, N. 10, license to travel to Nueva España, Sevilla, 1574.
13. From AGI, Justicia, 267.
14. Lienzos. This may refer to painted books like the ones the Spaniards would have been familiar with from central Mexico. Definitions from 1611, however, do not include that possibility, but suggest that the reference may be to painted pictures. Covarrubias Orozco, *Tesoro* , 715.
15. The Spanish terms are *perro* and *barril*. In his draft translation of AGI, Justicia, 1021, N. 2, Pieza 4, p. 63, Agapito Rey suggested that these might be scribal errors for *perla* (pearl) and *berilo* (beryl). This possibility seems less likely now that the current document (AGI, Justicia, 267) has been thoroughly examined. It is far less riddled with obvious scribal errors and on this point agrees with AGI, Justicia, 1021, N. 2, Pieza 4 .
16. Supplied by AGI, Justicia, 1021, N. 2, Pieza 4, fol. 49r.
17. Supplied by AGI, Justicia, 1021, N. 2, Pieza 4, fol. 52v.
18. Supplied by AGI, Justicia, 1021, N. 2, Pieza 4, fol. 53v.
19. From AGI, Justicia, 267.

Chapter 11, Rodrigo de Frías, the Ninth de Oficio Witness

1. Peter Gerhard, *The North Frontier of New Spain*, rev. ed. (Norman and London: University of Oklahoma Press, 1993), 106.
2. Bermúdez Plata, *Pasajeros*, 2: no. 2587; AGI, Justicia, 1021, N. 2, Pieza 6.
3. AGI, Guadalajara, 5, R. 1, N. 7.
4. AGI, Justicia, 1021, N. 2, Pieza 5.
5. From AGI, Justicia, 267.
6. From AGI, Justicia, 267.

Chapter 12, Melchior Pérez, the Tenth de Oficio Witness

1. Icaza, *Pobladores y Conquistadores*, 2: no. 1059.
2. AGI, Guadalajara, 5, R. 1, N. 5, letter, Francisco Vázquez de Coronado to the viceroy, Compostela, December 15, 1538.
3. Boyd-Bowman, *Cuarenta Mil Pobladores*, 2: no. 1861; Icaza, *Pobladores y Conquistadores*, 2: no. 1059.

4. AGI, Mexico, 207, N. 39, proof of service of Melchior Pérez, Mexico City, 1563.
5. Bancroft Library, University of California, Berkeley, M-M 1714, proof of service of Melchior Pérez, Mexico City, January 30, 1551.
6. Biblioteca del Escorial, Códice &-II-7, Doc. no. LXXIX, list of the persons, conquerors, and settlers of Nueva Galicia, n.p., [late 1540s].
7. AGI, Patronato, 60, N. 5, R. 4, proof of service of Juan de Zaldívar, Guadalajara, February 1566.
8. Biblioteca del Escorial, Códice &-II-7, Doc. no. LXXIX and Gerhard, North Frontier, 133.
9. Bancroft Library, M-M 1714.
10. AGI, Justicia, 336, N. 1, testimony concerning certain pueblos, Compostela, spring 1552.
11. AGI, Mexico, 207, N. 39.
12. AGI, Patronato, 60, N. 5, R. 4.
13. AGI, Patronato, 60, N. 5, R. 4.
14. Bancroft Library, M-M 1714.
15. AGI, Justicia, 1021, N. 2, Pieza 1.
16. From AGI, Justicia, 267.
17. Supplied by AGI, Justicia, 1021, N. 2, Pieza 4, fol. 60v.
18. Supplied by AGI, Justicia, 1021, N. 2, Pieza 4, fol. 61v.
19. Supplied by AGI, Justicia, 1021, N. 2, Pieza 4, fol. 61v.
20. Possibly "on the other side of the river."
21. Supplied by AGI, Justicia, 1021, N. 2, Pieza 4, fol. 69r.
22. From AGI, Justicia, 267.

Chapter 13, Pedro de Ledesma, the Eleventh de Oficio Witness

1. AGI, Justicia, 336, N. 1; Bermúdez Plata, Pasajeros, 2:no. 1255.
2. AGI, Justicia, 339, N. 1, R. 1, residencia of Francisco Vázquez de Coronado, Guadalajara, 1544–45 and AGI, Patronato, 60, N. 5, R. 4.
3. AGI, Guadalajara, 5, R. 1, N. 7.
4. AGI, Justicia ,1021, N. 2, Pieza 6.
5. AGI, Justicia, 336, N. 1.
6. Biblioteca del Escorial, Códice &-II-7, Doc. no. LXXIX and Gerhard, North Frontier, 133.
7. AGI, Patronato, 63, R. 5.
8. AGI, Justicia, 336, N. 2, suit concerning distribution of Indians to Diego de Colio, Guadalajara, 1565.
9. AGI, Patronato, 60, N. 5, R. 4.
10. From AGI, Justicia, 267.
11. From AGI, Justicia, 267.

Chapter 14, Juan de Zaldívar, the Twelfth de Oficio Witness

1. AGI, Patronato 60, N. 5, R. 4.
2. Marc Simmons, The Last Conquistador: Juan de Oñate and the Settling of the Far Southwest (Norman: University of Oklahoma Press, 1991), 22, 23.
3. However, Peter Boyd-Bowman writes that Zaldívar participated in the conquest of Nueva Galicia in 1530 with Nuño Beltrán de Guzmán. AGI, Patronato 60, N. 5, R. 4; Boyd-Bowman, Cuarenta Mil Pobladores , 2: no. 13623.
4. Antonio Tello, Crónica Miscelanea de la Sancta Provincia de Xalisco, Libro Segundo (Guadalajara: Gobierno del Estado de Jalisco and Universidad de Guadalajara, 1968), 2: 94.
5. AGI, Justicia, 336, N. 2.
6. AGI, Patronato, 60, N. 5, R. 4.
7. AGI, Patronato, 76, N. 1, R. 5, proof of service of Francisco de Zaldívar, Mexico City, March 29, 1580; Gerhard, North Frontier , 136.
8. AGI, Patronato, 76, N. 1, R. 5.
9. AGI, Patronato, 60, N. 5, R. 4.
10. From AGI, Justicia, 267.
11. Supplied by AGI, Justicia, 1021, N. 2, Pieza 4, fol. 77r.
12. Supplied by AGI, Justicia, 1021, N. 2, Pieza 4, fol. 79v.
13. Supplied by AGI, Justicia, 1021, N. 2, Pieza 4, fol. 80v.
14. Supplied by AGI, Justicia, 1021, N. 2, Pieza 4, fol. 81r.

15. AGI, Justicia 267 has sesenta, but since AGI, Justicia, 1021, N. 2, Pieza 4, fol. 81v and AGI, Justicia, 1021, N. 2, Pieza 6 both have setenta, I have accepted that figure.
16. Supplied by AGI, Justicia, 1021, N. 2, Pieza 4, fol. 81v.
17. Supplied by AGI, Justicia, 1021, N. 2, Pieza 4, fol. 82r.
18. Supplied by AGI, Justicia, 1021, N. 2, Pieza 4, fol. 82v.
19. Supplied by AGI, Justicia, 1021, N. 2, Pieza 4, fol. 84r.
20. Supplied by AGI, Justicia, 1021, N. 2, Pieza 4, fol. 84r.
21. From AGI, Justicia, 267.

Chapter 15, The Nominal Target of the Investigation, Francisco Vázquez de Coronado

1. The viceroy's appointment of Vázquez de Coronado, Michoacán, January 6, 1540, in AGI, Justicia, 339, N. 1, R. 1; AGI, Justicia, 213, N. 4, lawsuit regarding Teocaluyacan and Cayuca, Cuernavaca, 1551.
2. Mendoza was said to have spent more than 60,000 pesos. Icaza, *Pobladores y Conquistadores*, 1: no. 364; Francisco López de Gómara, *Historia General de las Indias*, facsimile ed. (Lima: Comisión Nacional del V Centenario del Descubrimiento de América-Encuentro de Dos Mundos, 1993), fol. 95v.
   Marc Simmons has stated that Cristóbal de Oñate also invested 50,000 pesos in the expedition to Tierra Nueva. As a well-to-do friend and lieutenant governor of Vázquez de Coronado, Oñate well might have been expected to make such an investment. Documentary basis for Simmons's remark has not been located, however. In fact, on several occasions when Oñate himself or his descendants might have appropriately boasted of such an expenditure, they did not, suggesting that the investment was never made. Simmons himself has suggested it not be referred to unless a firm documentary foundation can be verified. Simmons, *The Last Conquistador*, 22; AGI, Patronato, 75, R. 3, N. 1, investigation into the services of Cristóbal de Oñate, Mexico City, 1577; AGI, Patronato, 78, R.1, N.1, proof of service of Cristóbal de Oñate, Mexico City, 1584.
3. James Lockhart, *The Men of Cajamarca: A Social and Biographical Study of the First Conquerors of Peru* (Austin: University of Texas Press, 1972), 96.
4. AGI, Patronato, 21, N. 3, R. 2.
5. Letter, archbishop of Sevilla to don Antonio de Mendoza, Madrid, June 10, 1540, in AGI, Justicia, 259, Pieza 2.
6. By late summer 1539, however, it was public knowledge in Mexico City that Vázquez de Coronado would lead the expedition. Bolton, *Coronado*, 53, 54; AGI, Patronato, 21, N. 2, R. 4, testimony about fray Marcos's discovery, Havana, November 1539.
   More than a century later, fray Antonio Tello remarked that at first the viceroy had planned to lead the expedition himself. Tello, *Crónica Miscelanea*, 2:127.
7. Icaza, *Pobladores y Conquistadores*, 1: no. 364; AGI, Indiferente, 422, L. 16, F. 205, license to Francisco Vázquez de Coronado to take a black slave to the Indies, Sevilla, May 31, 1535; Arthur S. Aiton and Agapito Rey, "Coronado's Testimony in the Viceroy Mendoza Residencia," *New Mexico Historical Review* 12(3) (July 1937), 296.
8. AGI, Justicia, 259, Pieza 4, certification of suit concerning Tlapa, Mexico City, 1544; AHN, Ordenes Militares, 304, Expillo. 13408, order of San Juan to Juan Vázquez de Coronado, n.p., n.d.
9. Joaquín F. Pacheco and Francisco de Cárdenas, *Colección de Documentos Inéditos Relativos al Descubrimiento, Conquista y Organización de las Antiguas Posesiones Españolas de América y Oceania*, series 1, 42 vols. (Madrid: n.p., 1864–1884) 2: 198–99.
10. Two mine operators, Alonso de Soto and Gonzalo Guisado, were accused of disobeying the existing ordinances for good treatment of Indians. More specifically, the charges against them included compelling Indians from Matalcingo, Michoacán, to carry large loads of ore to the furnaces; to dismantle mines against their will; to work the bellows for processing ore; to work night and day, as well as Sundays and religious holidays; and to cut, split, and carry firewood. Free Indian women were required to bake bread for mine slaves, and none of the Indian workers were being taught Church doctrine and ritual. Furthermore, Soto and Guisado were said to have hit their Indian workers with sticks and not to have given them necessary food. As a result many Indians died and were ill. After taking testimony from 46 Indian witnesses, Vázquez de Coronado decided that there was sufficient evidence to warrant lodging complaints before the audiencia. When it had deliberated, the audiencia found Soto and Guidaso guilty and imposed a fine of 1,885 pesos. The verdict and fine were appealed. Unfortunately, no record of the final decision exists in the surviving case file.
    AGI, Justicia 127, N. 2, summary of investigation of treatment of Indians at Sultepec, Mexico City, February and March 1537.

11. *Cuarto Libro de las Actas de Cabildo*, 130–33; Bolton, *Coronado*, 405; *Libro del Cabildo e Ayuntamiento desta Ynsigne e Muy Leal Ciudad de Tenuxtitan Mexico desta Nueba España que Comenzo a Primero Dia del Mes de Dizienbre del 1550 Años Fenece a Fin de Dizienbre de 1561 Años* (Mexico City: n.p., n.d.), 152.

12. AGI, Guadalajara, 5, R. 1, N. 5.

13. The charges in this case were familiar ones: that Indians were made to mine gold and carry heavy loads long distances without being fed well. Also it was said that Indians in Nueva Galicia were being sold as slaves. After his investigation of the treatment of Indians in his province, Vázquez de Coronado decided that actually the Indians were being worked only moderately, and those in the mines were the only ones who had any knowledge of Christianity. As a result, he decided to leave things as they were.
AGI, Guadalajara, 5, R. 1, N. 5.

14. AGS, Camara de Castilla, 121–146, petition of Juan Vázquez de Coronado, Granada, December 5, 1516; and Aiton, *Mendoza*, 9.

15. Herbert Bolton erroneously stated that Vázquez de Coronado was sent a second time to consult the viceroy at Huastepec on July 5, 1549. In fact, payment for his expenses during the February trip was authorized on that day, rather than a second trip, although a marginal note refers to payment of twice the amount mentioned in the cabildo minutes themselves. Bolton, *Coronado*, 404 and *Quinto Libro de Actas*, 249, 262.

16. *Quinto Libro de Actas*, 305–06.

17. Ruiz Medrano, "La Política," 169, 172.

18. Here, Pedro de Castañeda's assertion that Vázquez de Coronado returned to Mexico City primarily because he missed his young wife and children is vastly over simplified and ignores the perilous situation of the expedition in Tierra Nueva, sick and running out of food and with its supply and communication line cut at San Gerónimo. New York Public Library, Rich Collection, no. 63, Tercera Parte, Capítulo 2.

19. AGI, Justicia, 1021, N. 2. Pieza 6.

20. AGI, Patronato, 60, N. 5, R. 4.

21. AGI, Mexico, 124, R. 5, proof of service of Francisco Pacheco de Córdova y Bocanegra, Mexico City, 1605.

22. Francisco Fernández de Bethencourt, *Historia Genealógica y Heráldica de la Monarquía Española Casa Real y Grandes de España* (Madrid: Jaime Ratés, 1912), 9: 502; and AGI, Patronato, 74, N. 1, R. 1, proof of service of Francisco Pacheco de Córdova y Bocanegra, Madrid, 1624.

23. AGI, Justicia 339, N. 1, R. 1.

24. Biblioteca del Escorial, Códice &-II-7, Document no. LXVII, instructions to Hernando de Alarcón, Mexico City, May 31, 1541.

25. AGI, Justicia, 260, Pieza 2, administrative review of the fiscal Cristóbal de Benavente, Mexico City, 1547.

26. In the twelve years following his return from Tierra Nueva he was in regular attendance at meetings of the Mexico City cabildo and was named several times as its *procurador mayor*, or legal agent, and *diputado*, or representative, both jobs not to be assigned to someone mentally incapable of responsibility as has sometimes been implied. Bolton, *Coronado*, 404; Day, *Coronado's Quest*, 307, 310; Aiton, *Mendoza*, 128 n24; *Quinto Libro de Actas*, 78, 165–66; and *Libro del Cabildo e Ayuntamiento*, 15, 32.

27. Most scholarly attention to communicable diseases in Nueva España has been paid to their effects on the indigenous population. In that regard, the year 1554 has not been linked to an epidemic episode. Nevertheless, repeated and frequent outbreaks of disease among the European colonists of the Americas were a fact of life. As Luis de Figueredo testified before Tejada, disease was expected wherever there were groups of people. Hanns J. Prem, "Disease Outbreaks in Central Mexico During the Sixteenth Century," in Noble David Cook and W. George Lovell, eds., *"Secret Judgments of God": Old World Disease in Colonial Spanish America* (Norman and London: University of Oklahoma Press, 1991), 20–48.

28. Sosa's death is mentioned as having occurred in September 1554. AGI, Mexico, 168, letter, don Pedro Ladrón de Guevara to the prince, Puebla de los Angeles, October 30, 1554, transcribed in Paso y Troncoso, *Espistolario*, 276–277.

29. The five ill regidores were Bernaldino Vázquez de Tapia, Gonzalo Ruiz, Antonio de Carbajal, Bernardino de Albornoz, and García de Vega. *Libro del Cabildo e Ayuntamiento*, 152.

30. From AGI, Justicia, 267.

31. Supplied by AGI, Justicia, 1021, N. 2, Pieza 4, fol. 84v.

32. Supplied by AGI, Justicia, 1021, N. 2, Pieza 4, fol. 86v.

33. AGI, Justicia 267 has "xacobe," but since both AGI, Justicia, 1021, N. 2, Pieza 4 and AGI, Justicia, 1021, N. 2, Pieza 6 have "xabe," I have used that form.

34. Supplied by AGI, Justicia, 1021, N. 2, Pieza 4, fol. 90r.
35. Supplied by AGI, Justicia, 1021, N. 2, Pieza 4, fol. 90r.
36. Supplied by AGI, Justicia, 1021, N. 2, Pieza 4, fol. 90v.
37. Supplied by AGI, Justicia, 1021, N. 2, Pieza 4, fol. 91r.
38. Supplied by AGI, Justicia, 1021, N. 2, Pieza 4, fol. 91v.
39. Supplied by AGI, Justicia, 1021, N. 2, Pieza 4, fol. 100r.
40. From AGI, Justicia, 267.

Chapter 16, Alonso Álvarez, the Fourteenth de Oficio Witness

1. AGI, Contratación, 5575, N. 24, disposal of the estate of Juan Jiménez, Puebla de los Angeles, 1550.
2. AGI, Guadalajara, 5, N. 1, R. 7.
3. George Hammond and Agapito Rey claimed that Álvarez was from Villanueva de la Serena. This reference is apparently to Alonso Álvarez de Espinosa, an older man who had participated in the conquest of Nueva Galicia under Nuño Beltrán de Guzmán and was subsequently a vecino of Compostela. Hammond and Rey, *Narratives*, 103 n81; Bermúdez Plata, *Pasajeros*, 2: no. 3193; AGI, Patronato 61, N. 2, R. 9, proof of service of Alonso Álvarez de Espinosa, Mexico City, January 27, 1558; Icaza, *Pobladores y Conquistadores*, 2: no. 1206.
4. AGI, Patronato, 74, N. 2, R. 2, proofs of service of Alonso y Juan Rodríguez, San Sebastián, 1576.
5. AGI, Mexico, 204, N. 14.
6. AGI, Patronato, 74, N. 2, R. 2.
7. From AGI, Justicia, 267.
8. Supplied by AGI, Justicia, 1021, N. 2, Pieza 4, fol. 101r.
9. Supplied by AGI, Justicia, 1021, N. 2, Pieza 4, fol. 103v.
10. Supplied by AGI, Justicia, 1021, N. 2, Pieza 4, fol. 104r.
11. From AGI, Justicia, 267.

Chapter 17, The Fiscal's Accusations against Vázquez de Coronado

1. AGI, Patronato, 57, N. 2, R. 1, proof of service of Antonio de Mendoza, Mexico City, March 1545.
2. AGI, Indiferente, 1382A, petition of Cristóbal de Benavente, Antequera, July 19, 1529.
3. AGI, Justicia, 267, proceedings.
4. AGI, Patronato, 57, N. 2, R. 1.
5. *Quinto Libro de Actas*, 212.
6. AGI, Patronato, 281, N. 1, R. 121, summons of Cristóbal de Benavente, Madrid, May 27, 1551.
7. AGI, Justicia, 260, Pieza 2.
8. Ida Altman, *Emigrants and Society: Extremadura and Spanish America in the Sixteenth Century* (Berkeley: University of California Press, 1989), 74.
9. New York Public Library, Rich Collection, no. 63, Primera Parte, Capítulo 7.
10. From AGI, Justicia, 267.
11. Supplied by AGI, Justicia, 1021, N. 2, pieza 4, fol. 104r.
12. This is the captain who first learned the story of Quivira from El Turco and took him captive. According to many witness he was also involved in setting dogs on Bigotes.
13. From AGI, Justicia, 267.
14. From AGI, Justicia, 267.
15. Supplied by AGI, Justicia, 1021, N. 2, Pieza 4.
16. Agapito Rey in his transcription of AGI, Justicia, 1021, N. 2, Pieza 4 interpolated the word "veinte" into the text, making the potential fine 20,000 pesos. Where the "veinte" came from was completely unexplained. Bancroft Library, Bolton Papers, Item 393, C-B 840, Part 1, 131.
17. From AGI, Justicia, 267.

Chapter 18, The Maestre de Campo Held Responsible

1. Sworn statement of don García Ramírez, Pinto, February 20, 1546, in AGI, Justicia, 1021, N. 2, Pieza 1.
2. New York Public Library, Rich Collection, no. 63, Tercera Parte, Capítulo 1.
3. Bermúdez Plata, *Pasajeros*, 2: no. 1064.
4. Royal cédula, Valladolid, July 24, 1536, in AGI, Justicia, 259, Pieza 2.

5. AGI, Justicia, 1021, N. 2, Pieza 1.
6. AGI, Patronato, 277, N. 4, R. 36, appointment of López de Cárdenas, Mexico City, April 8, 1538.
7. AGI, Justicia, 1021, N. 2, Pieza 1.
8. AGI, Guadalajara, 5, R.1, N.7 and AGI, Justicia, 1021, N. 2, Pieza 5.
9. New York Public Library, Rich Collection, no. 63, Primera Parte, Capítulo 7.
10. AGI, Justicia, 1021, N. 2, Pieza 5.
11. AGI, Justicia, 1021, N. 2, Pieza 1.
12. Now known as the Torre de Eboli, Ramírez de Cárdenas's gray prison still stands, almost windowless and about three stories tall, not far from the center of Pinto, obscured by more modern buildings.
13. AGI, Justicia, 1021, N. 2, Pieza 1.
14. Petition from Sebastián Rodríguez, Valladolid, January 1547, in AGI, Justicia, 1021, N. 2, Pieza 1.
15. Decision of the Council of the Indies, Madrid, April 2, 1546, in AGI, Justicia, 1021, N. 2, Pieza 1.
16. At Villalobos's request, testimony was taken from 14 witnesses in Nueva España, including six who had previously been examined by Tejada. Seventeen witnesses were called to testify on behalf of García Ramírez de Cárdenas, both in Nueva España and in Burgos, including three who had testified before Tejada. The witnesses called by the two parties included five who gave testimony for both sides in the dispute: Hernando de Alvarado, Pedro de Ledesma, Rodrigo de Frías, Domingo Martín, and Gaspar de Saldaña.
    AGI, Justicia 1021, N. 2, Pieza 3, report extracted from the affidavit prepared for licenciado Villalobos, n.p, n.d. and AGI, Justicia, 1021, N. 2, Pieza 2, report extracted from the affidavit prepared for don García Ramírez de Cárdenas, n.p., n.d.
17. Sentence of don García López de Cárdenas, Valladolid, December 20, 1549, in AGI, Justicia, 1021, N. 2, Pieza 1.
18. AGI, Patronato, 281, N. 1, R. 34, final decision in the case of Ramírez de Cárdenas, Valladolid, September 1551.
19. Royal cédula, Madrid, November 10, 1551, in AGI, Indiferente, 424, L. 22.
20. Hammond and Rey, *Narratives*, 340 n2.
21. Herbert Bolton wrote, "Thus, counting the time spent in jail or out under bond, he [Ramírez de Cárdenas] had been a prisoner for some seven years. He had paid a high price for his treasure hunt in Tierra Nueva." While the former maestre de campo's movements were restricted for the seven years Bolton referred to, he was by no means in jail as we would know it. He moved around the country attending to his private business, including his marriage, and when not away by permission of the Council of the Indies was at his own house in Madrid. Furthermore, the service he was required to render to the king was performed within the jurisdiction of a relative in Andalucía, where he himself had a hacienda.
    Bolton, *Coronado,*, 393 and order of the Council of the Indies, Madrid, October 2, 1546, in AGI, Justicia, 1021, N. 2, Pieza 1.
22. Supplied by AGI, Justicia, 1021, N. 2, Pieza 4.
23. Supplied by AGI, Justicia, 1021, N. 2, pieza 4, fols. 104v and 105r.
24. Supplied by AGI, Justicia, 1021, N. 2, Pieza 4.

Chapter 19, Defense Offered by Vázquez de Coronado

1. AGI, Justicia, 339, N. 1, R. 1.
2. AGI, Guadalajara, 5, N. 1, R. 7.
3. Supplied by AGI, Patronato, 216, R. 2, investigation concerning Núño de Cháves, Mexico City, 1566.
4. Vázquez de Coronado's power of attorney to Francisco Pilo is placed here out of its order in the original document. The foliation numbers reflect its original position.
5. *Celemines*. Each celemín was one *almud* or a twelfth of a fanega. Manuel Carrera Stampa, "The Evolution of Weights and Measures in New Spain," *The Hispanic American Historical Review* 29 (February 1949): 16.
6. The word in the original appears to be "Pellexo" or "Piesxo," meaning an animal skin and referring to a wineskin, in this case being utilized as a dry measure. Covarrubias Orozco, *Tesoro*, 812, 822.
7. Supplied by AGI, Patronato, 216, R. 2, investigation concerning Núño de Cháves, Mexico City, 1566.
8. Ad perpetuam rey memoriam. Peter Boyd-Bowman, *Lexico Hispanoamericano del Siglo XVI* (London: Tamesis Books Limited, 1971), 23–4. See also John L. Kessell, Rick Hendricks, and Meredith Dodge, eds., *Blood on the Boulders: The Journals of Don Diego de Vargas, New Mexico, 1694–97* (Albuquerque: University of New Mexico Press, 1998), 460 n162 and Real Academia Española, *Diccionario de la Lengua Española*, 21st ed., 2 vols. (Madrid: Real Academia Española, 1992), 2:1164.

9. Vázquez de Coronado's power of attorney to Francisco Pilo is placed here out of its order in the original document. The foliation numbers reflect its original position.
10. Or *piesxos.*

Chapter 20, Diego López, the Second de Parte Witness

1. For several decades this seat on the city council of Sevilla was occupied by members of López's family, all with the given name Diego. AGS, Guerra y Marina, 37–136, resignation of doctor Gonzalo de Zúñiga as regidor, Sevilla, August 13, 1551 and AGS, Cámara de Castilla, 121–7, petition from Diego López, Sevilla, 1517.
2. AGI, Guadalajara, 5, N. 1, R. 7.
3. Tello, *Crónica Miscelanea,* 1: 185.
4. Biblioteca del Escorial, Códice &-II-7, Doc. no. LXXX, list of vecinos of Culiacán, n.p., [late 1540s].
5. Bermúdez Plata, *Pasajeros,* 2: no. 4804 and Bermúdez Plata, *Pasajeros,* 3: no. 3218.
6. Charles W. Hackett, *Historical Documents relating to New Mexico, Nueva Vizcaya, and Approaches Thereto, to 1773,* Carnegie Institution of Washington Publications no. 330, 3 vols. (Washington, D.C.: Carnegie Institution of Washington, 1923), 1: 95.
7. Supplied by AGI, Patronato, 216, R. 2.
8. Several times throughout López's testimony a scribe inserted marginal highlighting to call attention to certain details of the witness's statement.
9. Supplied by AGI, Patronato, 216, R. 2.

Chapter 21, Luis de Figueredo, the Third de Parte Witness

1. The closest match is an individual named Luis de Pigredo, about whom nothing else is known. AGI, Guadalajara, 5, N. 1, R. 7.
2. Supplied by AGI, Patronato, 216, R. 2.
3. Supplied by AGI, Patronato, 216, R. 2.

Chapter 22, Pedro de Tovar, the Fourth de Parte Witness

1. AGI, Guadalajara, 5, R. 1, N. 7.
2. The other seven are don Diego de Guevara, don Tristán de Arellano, don García López, don Rodrigo Maldonado, don Alonso Manrique, don Francisco Vázquez de Coronado, and don Lope de Urrea. Tello, *Crónica Miscelanea,* 1: 185.
3. Gerhard, *North Frontier,* 258.
4. Boyd-Bowman, *Cuarenta Mil Pobladores,* 2: 182.
5. Tello, *Crónica Miscelanea,* 1: 185, 2: 355.
6. Tello, *Crónica Miscelanea,* 2: 355.
7. Tello, *Crónica Miscelanea,* 2: 247, 373.
8. Tello, *Crónica Miscelanea,* 2: 415.
9. The location of this pueblo is not known. Biblioteca del Escorial, Códice &-II-7, Doc. no. LXXX.
10. Gerhard, *North Frontier,* 258, 274.
11. Tello, *Crónica Miscelanea,* 2: 355; A. Grove Day, "Mota Padilla on the Coronado Expedition," *The Hispanic American Historical Review* 20, no. 1 (February 1940): 89.
12. Supplied by AGI, Patronato, 216, R. 2.
13. The power of attorney from Vázquez de Coronado to Francisco Pilo is included in Chapter 19. Its original location was here on folios 35r to 37v.
14. Supplied by AGI, Patronato, 216, R. 2.
15. The power of attorney from Vázquez de Coronado to Francisco Pilo is included in Chapter 19. Its original location was here on folios 35r to 37v.

Chapter 23, Further Defense

1. Although the document itself does not say that the questioning was conducted in Mexico City, all three witnesses were vecinos of that city. See: AGI, Justicia, 1021, N. 2, Pieza 5; AGI, Justicia, 1021, N. 2, Pieza 6; AGI, Mexico, 206, N. 12.

2. Boyd-Bowman, *Cuarenta Mil Pobladores*, 2: no. 3552; Icaza, *Pobladores y Conquistadores*, 2: no. 1312; AGI, Justicia, 1021, N. 2, Pieza 6; AGI, Patronato, 87, N. 1, R. 5, proof of service of García Rodríguez and his grandson, Mexico City, April 26, 1617.
3. AGI, Patronato, 87, N. 1, R. 5.
4. AGI, Guadalajara, 5, N. 1, R. 7.
5. AGI, Patronato, 87, N. 1, R. 5.
6. AGI, Justicia, 1021, N. 2, Pieza 5 and AGI, Justicia, 1021, N. 2, Pieza 6.
7. AGI, Justicia, 259, Pieza 2.
8. New York Public Library, Rich Collection, no. 63, Primera Parte, Capítulo 5; Icaza, *Pobladores y Conquistadores*, 1: 127; Robert Himmerich y Valencia, *The Encomenderos of New Spain, 1521–1555* (Austin: University of Texas Press, 1991), 152.
9. AGI, Justicia, 260, Pieza 1, charges and rebuttals of Lorenzo de Tejada, Mexico City, 1546.
10. AGI, Guadalajara, 5, N. 1, R. 7.
11. New York Public Library, Rich Collection, no. 63, Primera Parte, Capítulo 9.
12. Himmerich y Valencia, *The Encomenderos of New Spain*, 152.
13. Luis de Velasco, *Relación de las Encomiendas. . . .*, ed. France V. Scholes and Eleanor B. Adams (Mexico City: José Porrúa e hijos, 1955), 34–35.
14. Pacheco de Bocanegra was married to Isabel de Luján, Francisco Vázquez de Coronado and Beatriz de Estrada's daughter; Dávila Alvarado was husband to María de Sosa, daughter of Juan Alonso de Sosa and Ana de Estrada, Beatriz's sister. AGI, Mexico, 168, letter, ten vecinos to the king, Mexico City, February 17, 1564.
15. Supplied by AGI, Justicia, 1021, N. 2, Pieza 2.
16. There is no "Question 1" included in this summary. According to standard form, it would have inquired whether the witnesses were familiar with Vázquez de Coronado and his captains.
17. The summary of Maldonado's testimony breaks off here without explanation.
18. Supplied by AGI, Justicia, 1021, N. 2, Pieza 2.
19. The summary of Maldonado's testimony breaks off here.

Chapter 24, A Final and Definitive Decision

1. AGI, Justicia, 260, Pieza 4.
2. AGI, Mexico, 124, R. 5.
3. Return to AGI, Justicia, 267.
4. Supplied by AGI, Justicia, 336, N. 1.
5. From AGI, Justicia, 267.
6. Supplied by AGI, Justicia, 336, N. 1.
7. With minor variations the decision included here is the same as that recorded in AGI, Justicia, 267, fol. 125r.

Chapter 25, Partisan Testimony as Source Material for History

1. This number is likely to include some individuals who are duplicated because they are cited in the documents in different instances by slightly different names. Also there are several cases in which a single name seems to apply to more than one individual, but without location of further data that cannot be determined unequivocally. All previous counts suffer from the same difficulties. The current research project has added the names of 12 individuals not previously known to have participated in the expedition.
    In 1949 Herbert Bolton reported 336 male, non-Indian members of the expedition; more than three decades later, Douglas Inglis determined the count to be 338. Bolton, *Coronado*, 68; G. Douglas Inglis, "The Men of Cíbola: New Investigations on the Francisco Vázquez de Coronado Expedition," *Panhandle-Plains Historical Review* 55 (1982): 4.
2. These figures are at significant variance with those provided by Douglas Inglis during his 1982 study of the place of origin of 85 members of the expedition. He showed 23.7% of the individuals he studied as being from New Castile (roughly equivalent to modern Castilla-La Mancha), 18.4% from Old Castile and León (equivalent to modern Castilla-León), 17.1% from Extremadura, and 15.8% from Andalucía. Unfortunately, because the data base which Inglis used was lost during his move to Spain and is no longer known to exist, the list of individuals included in his study cannot be compared with the list used in the current study in an effort to ascertain where the differences or discrepancies lie. Apparently,

though, Inglis's figures for New Castile are reversed with those for Old Castile and León. If those figures are now switched, Inglis's data and those of the current study are more consonant.

Inglis, "The Men of Cíbola," 7; G. Douglas Inglis, Sevilla, to Richard Flint, April 27, 1995, original in author's collection.

3. Nearly 90% of the members of the expedition that conquered the Inca in Peru in 1532, for example, were from the same four western and southern *comunidades*. Some 71% of the 240 survivors of the Soto expedition through the modern southeastern United States from 1538 to 1543 for whom data are available were natives of those four comunidades. Of the members of six expeditions that traveled to Nueva Granada in what is now Colombia between 1536 and 1542, 77% were born in Castilla-León, Castilla-La Mancha, Extremadura, and Andalucía.

James Lockhart, The Men of Cajamarca, 28; [José] Ignacio Avellaneda, *Los Sobrevivientes de la Florida: The Survivors of the De Soto Expedition*, Research Publications of the P.K. Yonge Library of Florida History, 2 (Gainesville: University of Florida Libraries, 1990), 68; José Ignacio Avellaneda, *The Conquerors of the New Kingdom of Granada* (Albuquerque: University of New Mexico Press, 1995), 60.

4. Madrid (3 individuals, 3.1%); Santander (3 individuals, 3.1%); Basque (2 individuals, 2.1%); Galicia (2 individuals, 2.1%); Asturias (2 individuals, 2.1%); Navarra (1 individual, 1.0%); Aragón (1 individual, 1.0%); and one individual (1.0%) for whom the exact place of origin within Spain is undeterminable. See Appendix 3 for full data on the 115 individuals considered in this study.

5. In addition, information on the age of one individual, Juan de Jaramillo, is ambiguous. According to documentary evidence, he may have been either in his twenties or over thirty in 1540. AGI, Justicia, 1021, N. 2, Pieza 6; AGI, Patronato, 87, N. 1, R. 5.

6. For comparison, the teenage members of the expedition that conquered the Inca in 1532 comprised only 4.7% of the whole group. Among the survivors of the Soto expedition fully 26.3% had been younger than 20 when the expedition began. Avellaneda's study of the expeditions to Nueva Granada of the late 1530s and early 1540s has yielded a composite figure of 7.3% for those less than 20 years old. The range of teenage presence for the six Nueva Granada expeditions, however, was quite broad, from 0.0% to 20.0%.

Lockhart, *The Men of Cajamarca*, 26; Avellaneda, *Los Sobrevivientes de la Florida*, 69; Avellaneda, *The Conquerors of the New Kingdom of Granada*, 62, 63.

7. In several cases information on tenure in Nueva España is not available, but information on tenure in the Americas is. In those cases, American tenure has been considered equivalent to experience in Nueva España, especially in regard to formation of attitudes and opinions concerning Native Americans.

8. It should be noted that the largest single group among the 71 individuals for which tenure data are available arrived in Nueva España in 1535, presumably with Viceroy Mendoza. This group comprised 14 individuals or 19.7% of the sample.

9. The full distributional information on these 71 expedition members is as follows. Sixteen (22.5%) had been in Nueva España less than 3 years when the expedition began; 18 (25.3%), 3–5 years; 15 (21.1%), 6–10 years; and 22 (31.0%), more than 10 years.

10. For the Pizarro expedition, 23.8% of the participants had 10 years or more experience in the Indies prior to the expedition. The corresponding figure for the six Nueva Granada expeditions is 17.5%. Comparable data for the Soto expedition are not available. Lockhart, *The Men of Cajamarca*," 23; Avellaneda, *The Conquerors of the New Kingdom of Granada*, 79.

11. See Chapter 4 for a discussion of the number of horses as an indicator of economic status.

12. Lockhart, *The Men of Cajamarca*, 34–35.

13. There is, however, no known documentary evidence that this geographical connection resulted in frequent social contact between any of the three and Estrada.

14. Apparently without suspecting an orchestrated investigation, Bolton marveled that the testimony "was put in phrases that leave no doubt of the loyalty and admiration of [Vázquez de Coronado's] followers." Bolton, *Coronado*, 403.

15. Bolton, *Coronado*, 407; Chavez, *Coronado's Friars*, 64.

16. Donald E. Chipman, *Nuño de Guzmán and the Province of Pánuco in New Spain, 1518–1533*, Spain in the West, vol. 10 (Glendale, California: The Arthur H. Clark Company, 1967), 259.

17. AGI, Patronato, 20, N. 5, R. 8; New York Public Library, Rich Collection, no. 63, Primera Parte, Capítulo 21.

18. This summary derives from the testimony of the 14 de oficio and 7 de parte witnesses contained in AGI, Justicia, 267; AGI, Patronato, 216, R. 2; and AGI, Justicia, 1021, N. 2, Pieza 2.

19. As, for instance, on the number of Tiguex pueblos that were burned and demolished.

Chapter 26, Results and Repercusions of the Expedition to Tierra Nueva from Documentary and Archeological Sources

1. Arrogance and unquestioned confidence in the superiority of invaders were not unique to Spaniards nor to the sixteenth century. In fact, they characterized the majority of colonial expansion around the world and projects in political, economic, and religious hegemony. Sadly, they are currently apparent in modern attempts to blanket the globe with "free-market" economies and Western values.

Richard Slatta has recently characterized dominant Spanish colonial attitudes as a "Eurocentric ideology" that "demanded total victory of Spanish 'civilization' over Indian 'barbarism.'"

In the Spanish world at the time of the expedition to Tierra Nueva, belief in divine election of Spain had already been widespread for generations. As Peggy Liss has recently written regarding the Spain of Fernando and Isabel, a generation before the expedition, "Monarchs and nobles shared the belief of Spain having been chosen and directed by God."

The notion that all Catholic Spaniards were unquestionably superior to non-Catholics and non-Spaniards was fostered, if not engendered, by the sporadic eight-century-long military victory of Castilian forces over the Islamic states of the Iberian Peninsula. And it is significant that Vázquez de Coronado and other members of the expedition to Tierra Nueva saw it as an extension of the reconquest of Iberia. The captain general, himself, explicitly drew the parallel by renaming the subjugated pueblo of Cíbola after Granada in Spain, the site of the final capitulation of Islamic sovereignty on the peninsula only slightly over 40 years earlier.

Richard W. Slatta, "Spanish Colonial Military Strategy and Ideology," in *Contested Ground: Comparative Frontiers on the Northern and Southern Edges of the Spanish Empire*, ed. Donna J. Guy and Thomas E. Sheridan (Tucson: The University of Arizona Press, 1998), 96; Peggy K. Liss, *Isabel the Queen: Life and Times* (New York and Oxford: Oxford University Press, 1992), 358; "Letter of Coronado to Mendoza, August 3, 1540," in Hammond and Rey, *Narratives*, 170.

2. Charles Gibson, *The Spanish Tradition in America* (Columbia: University of South Carolina Press, 1968), 59.

For a detailed recent analysis of the coersive nature of the requerimineto and its demand for submission to a "superior" culture and religion, see Patricia Seed, *Ceremonies of Possession in Europe's Conquest of the New World, 1492–1640* (Cambridge: Cambridge University Press, 1995), 69–99.

3. David J. Weber, *The Spanish Frontier in North America* (New Haven and London: Yale University Press, 1992), 388 n70.

4. Almost without exception, similar expectations were manifested by all Spanish expeditions and settlements throughout the Americas. As Elizabeth Reitz and Bonnie McEwan have written recently about sixteenth-century Spanish activities in the circum-Caribbean area, "Both in Spanish Florida and at Puerto Real, demands were made upon local peoples for food, and these requests were so burdensome to the natives that they frequently rebelled." Elizabeth J. Reitz and Bonnie G. McEwan, "Animals, Environment, and the Spanish Diet at Puerto Real," in *Puerto Real: The Archaeology of a Sixteenth-Century Spanish Town in Hispaniola*, ed. Kathleen Deagan (Gainesville: University Press of Florida, 1995), 332.

5. Gerónimo López to the King, on native policy, in John H. Parry and Robert G. Keith, comps., *Central America and Mexico*, vol. 3, *New Iberian World* (New York: Times Books and Hector & Rose, 1984), 447. A transcription of the full Spanish text of the letter is in Francisco del Paso y Troncoso, comp., *Epistolario de Nueva España, 1505–1818* (Mexico City: 1939–42), 4: 151–79.

6. Bartolomé de las Casas, *In Defense of the Indians*, trans. Stafford Poole (DeKalb, Illinois: Northern Illinois University Press, 1992), 42.

7. No implication of comprehension by Indians of the demands of the requeriminto is made here. In fact, given the highly abstract nature of the concepts employed in the requerimiento and the near impossibility of translating them adequately into the native spoken tongues or, as was often the case, sign language, thorough lack of literal comprehension must be assumed. Nevertheless, the Spaniards' intent to dominate and control was clear from their actions.

8. Edmund J. Ladd, "Zuni on the Day the Men in Metal Arrived," in *The Coronado Expedition to Tierra Nueva: The 1540–1542 Route Across the Southwest*, ed. Richard Flint and Shirley Cushing Flint (Niwot, Colorado: University Press of Colorado, 1997), 225–33.

9. Almost certainly there were more than one. Francisca de Hozes in her statement before Tejada referred to "wives and daughters" having been taken by force at Tiguex and Cicuique.

10. The threat to Indian women was clear to the indigenous people of Cíbola for, as Vázquez de Coronado wrote to the viceroy in August 1540, "I am unable to give your lordship any certain information

about the dress of the women, because the Indians keep them guarded so carefully that I have not seen any, except two old ones."

In his cursory assessment of the effects of the expedition to Tierra Nueva, Ramón Gutiérrez rightly brings attention to sexual pressure on Pueblo women as a cause of the Tiguex war, but he also oversimplifies a very complex situation by asserting that this was the sole or at least principal cause. Furthermore, he gratuitously and wholly without foundation implies that there would have been no hostility if only the expedition members had adequately compensated the Pueblo women or their male relatives for their sexual activities. Hammond and Rey, *Narratives*, 177; Ramón A. Gutiérrez, *When Jesus Came, the Corn Mothers Went Away: Marriage, Sexuality, and Power in New Mexico, 1500–1846* (Stanford: Stanford University Press, 1991), 45.

11. Mary Karasch, "Interethnic Conflict and Resistance on the Brazilian Frontier of Goiás, 1750–1890," in *Contested Ground: Comparative Frontiers on the Northern and Southern Edges of the Spanish Empire*, ed. Donna J. Guy and Thomas E. Sheridan (Tucson: The University of Arizona Press, 1998), 122.

12. New York Public Library, Rich Collection, no. 63, Primera Parte, Capítulo 16.

13. The ships of Hernando de Alarcón carried personal belongings which members of the expedition could not carry themselves, with the plan of rendezvousing with the overland group en route. Precisely what items Alarcón carried is unknown. Even assuming that the ships transported sufficient warm clothing for the nearly 2,000 members of the expedition, when the anticipated rendezvous failed to happen, the expedition went on with apparent unconcern over inevitable cold weather.

14. Less than 50 years after Columbus's landfall in the New World, corn or maize was considered a necessity of life, in the absence of wheat, for all members of the expedition to Tierra Nueva, European, Native American, and African, as well as for their livestock.

15. Richard Flint, "The Pattern of Coronado Expedition Material Culture" (M.A. thesis, New Mexico Highlands University, 1992), 79.

16. There is, nevertheless, the possibility that seeds were carried by the expedition, as Bernardo de Vargas Machuca recommended at the end of the sixteenth century in his manual for expedition leaders. Further, it is possible that melons seen in the Sonora Valley by Baltasar de Obregón in the 1560s descended from seeds left by the expedition to Tierra Nueva. Bernardo de Vargas Machuca, *Milicia y Descripción de las Indias*, vol. 1 (Madrid: Librería de Victoriano Suárez, 1892), 157; Baltasar de Obregón, *Historia de los Descubrimientos Antiguos y Modernos de la Nueva España, Escrita por el Conquistador en el Año de 1584* (Mexico City: Editorial Porrúa, S.A., 1988), 146.

17. Such expectations were typical of New World expeditions of the sixteenth century. As but one example, here is Pedro de Cieza de León's formulation of the native assessment of the attitudes and behavior of the 1532 Pizarro expedition in Peru: "Those bearded idlers did not plant, but went from place to place eating and stealing whatever they found." Pedro de Cieza de León, *The Discovery and Conquest of Peru*, ed. and trans, Alexandra Parma Cook and Noble David Cook (Durham and London: Duke University Press, 1998), 187.

18. Flint, "Pattern," 79.

19. New York Public Library, Rich Collection, no. 63, Primera Parte, Capítulo 14.

20. Pedro de Castañeda remarked that the Indians of Tiguex were required to vacate a pueblo for the expedition's use. García López de Cárdenas, who was in charge of establishing winter quarters among the Tiguex, put it less harshly, testifying that he "begged" the residents of Coofor to hand over their pueblo. New York Public Library, Rich Collection, no. 63, Primera Parte, Capítulo 12; AGI, Justicia, 1021, N. 2, Pieza 1.

21. AGI, Contratación, 5575, N. 24.

22. During the late Middle Ages the Spanish *mesta* or livestock growers' guild had secured royal recognition of extensive grazing rights, including prohibition of the fencing of fields and blanket permission to graze flocks on fallow land. Marcelin Defourneaux, *Daily Life in Spain in the Golden Age*, tr. Newton Branch (Stanford: Stanford University Press, 1979), 101.

23. About the twelfth-century Bis sa'ani community of the San Juan Basin, for instance, Marcia Donaldson and Mollie Toll have written, "That cobs divested of their kernels [were] often used as fuel explains the presence of burned cobs and cob fragments (cupules) in hearths and ash dumps." Similarly, in discussing the excavation of LA 54147, a sixteenth-century Spanish campsite in the Middle Rio Grande Valley, Toll contrasted the habitual protohistoric Pueblo practice of utilizing cornfield residue, saying, "Cobs stripped of their kernels were recycled as fuel, and cob fragments are ordinarily ubiquitous in Pueblo hearths." Marcia L. Donaldson and Mollie S. Toll, "Prehistoric Subsistence in the Bis sa'ani Area: Evidence from Flotation, Macrobotanical Remains, and Wood Identification," in *Bis sa'ani: A Late Bonito Phase Community on Escavada Wash, Northwest New Mexico*, Navajo Nation Papers in Anthropology Number 14,

ed. Cory Dale Breternitz, David E. Doyel, and Michael P. Marshall (Window Rock, Arizona: Navajo Nation Cultural Resource Management Program, 1982), 3: 1130; Mollie S. Toll, "Paleofloral Materials," in Bradley J. Vierra, *A Sixteenth-Century Spanish Campsite in the Tiguex Province*, Laboratory of Anthropology Notes 475 (Santa Fe: Museum of New Mexico, 1989), 160.

24. There may also have been a directly human assault on the Tiguex fuel supply earlier when, upon establishing a camp near Coofor, García López de Cárdenas directed that thatched huts (*ranchos de paja*) be erected. Although "paja" is usually translated as "straw," its use in the Americas in the sixteenth century also included reference to cornstalks and corn husks. The harvesting of cornstalks by expedition members for use as building material may well have provided additional reason for the residents of Coofor to consent to vacating their pueblo so that it could be used for accommodating the expedition. AGI, Justicia, 1021, N. 2, Pieza 6.

For a clear reference to paja de maiz, see Archivo General de la Nación/Buenos Aires, Census records of Río de la Plata, 13-17-5-1, review of Sisicaya [Peru], Lima, 1588.

25. Richard Flint, "The Coronado and de Soto Expeditions: A Contrast in Attitudes or Difference in External Conditions? Part 1: Relative Humanity of the Expeditions," *El Viaje* 1 (April 1992): 6–7.

26. On the basis of an average of 300 persons per pueblo throughout the Pueblo area, as supplied by Castañeda. New York Public Library, Rich Collection, no. 63, Segunda Parte, Capítulo 6.

27. This is according to the testimony of Vázquez de Coronado and Pedro de Ledesma before licenciado Tejada in 1544.

28. Aiton and Rey, "Coronado's Testimony," 316.

29. While on guard duty during the siege of Pueblo del Cerco, blacksmith Francisco de Santillana was struck by an arrow in the right shoulder. As a result, he was never again able to pursue his trade. AGI, Patronato, 79, N. 3, R. 2.

30. Carroll L. Riley, "Puaray and Coronado's Tiguex," in *Collected Papers in Honor of Erik K. Reed*, Papers of the Archaeological Society of New Mexico, 6, ed. Albert H. Schroeder (Albuquerque: Archaeological Society Press, 1981), 209.

31. Bolton, *Coronado*, 275.

32. That of Pedro de Castañeda for the expedition to Tierra Nueva (New York Public Library, Rich Collection, no. 63) and that of the anonymous hidalgo of Elvas for the Soto expedition, "The Account by a Gentleman from Elvas," in Lawrence A. Clayton; Vernon James Knight, Jr.; and Edward C. Moore, ed., *The De Soto Chronicles: The Expedition of Hernando de Soto to North America in 1539–1543* (Tuscaloosa and London: The University of Alabama Press, 1993), 1:19–219.

33. For a lengthy discussion of this comparison, see Flint, "The Coronado and de Soto Expeditions."

The most thorough treatment of the impact of the Soto expedition of the indigenous peoples of the Southeast is Charles Hudson, *Knights of Spain, Warriors of the Sun: Hernando de Soto and the South's Ancient Chiefdoms* (Athens, Georgia and London: University of Georgia Press, 1997).

34. See also Andrés Urdaneta, "An Account of the Voyage," trans. Thomas E. Chase in *An Account of the Voyage of Juan Rodríguez Cabrillo* (San Diego: Cabrillo National Monument Foundation, 1999), 65. Juan Páez, "Relation of the Voyage of Juan Rodríguez Cabrillo, 1542–1543," in Herbert E. Bolton, ed., *Spanish Explorations in the Southwest, 1542–1706* (New York: Charles Scribner and Sons, 1916), 23.

35. "And even though Nuño de Guzmán had only recently conquered New Galicia, his soldiers did not pass into the ranks of Vázquez de Coronado's army." Inglis, "The Men of Cíbola," 6.

36. For example, Bartolomé de las Casas, *The Devastation of the Indies: A Brief Account*, tr. Herma Briffault (Baltimore and London: The Johns Hopkins University Press, 1992), 74–79; Bolton, *Coronado*, 20–21; Thomas Calvo, Eustaquio Celestino, Magdalena Gómez, Jean Meyer, and Ricardo Xochitemol, *Xalisco, la voz de un pueblo en el siglo XVI* (Mexico City: Centro de Investigaciones y Estudios Superiores en Antropología Social and Centro de Estudios Mexicanos y Centroamericanos, 1993), 15–19; Gerhard, *North Frontier*, 5.

37. New York Public Library, Rich Collection, no. 63, Primera Parte, Capítulo 7.

38. The practice of cutting off hands and noses was not uncommon. In 1550 Pedro de Valdivia in Chile inflicted such punishment on some 200 natives there. Tzvetan Todorov, *The Conquest of America* (New York: HarperCollins Publishers, 1985), 148.

Peter Bakewell has rightly characterized such terrorism as "a prime Spanish tool of conquest." Bakewell, *History of Latin America*, 79.

39. Eugene R. Craine and Reginald C. Reindorp, ed. and trans., *The Chronicles of Michoacán* (Norman: University of Oklahoma Press, 1970), 96.

J. Benedict Warren suggests that Guzmán's reasons for having the Cazonci tortured may have been more complex. Among those reasons may have been the Cazonci's "interference" in tribute collection by encomenderos. Warren admits, however, that "Guzmán was a very greedy man, willing to do almost anything to the natives to enrich himself." J. Benedict Warren, *The Conquest of Michoacán: The Spanish Domination of the Tarascan Kingdom in Western Mexico, 1521–1530* (Norman: University of Oklahoma Press, 1985): 221, 241.

40. Clayton, Knight, and Moore, *The De Soto Chronicles*, 1: 82.

Writing in the 1560s, Bishop Diego de Landa of Yucatán expressed shock and horror at the cruelty of the Spanish conquerors of the Maya in burning alive several of their leaders. Diego de Landa, *Yucatán Before and After the Conquest*, ed. and trans. William Gates (Mérida: Editorial Dante, 1986): 46.

41. Most recently, Mathew Restall has detailed the nearly seemless continuity from prehistory into the Spanish colonial period of competition and aggression among the Maya of Yucatán and adjacent areas. In the documents Restall presents, we witness developments from Maya perspectives in which the Spanish conquistadores served to strengthen the position of some Maya groups against centuries-old rivals. See especially Mathew Restall, *Maya Conquistador* (Boston: Beacon Press, 1998), 40, 48–49.

42. Riley, *Rio del Norte*, 99–102; E. Adamson Hoebel, "Zia Pueblo," in *Southwest*, vol. 9 of *Handbook of North American Indians*, ed. Alfonso Ortiz (Washington, D.C.: Smithsonian Institution, 1979), 408; Joe Sando, "Jemez Pueblo," in *Southwest*, 418; Kessell, *Kiva, Cross, and Crown*, 10–12.

43. *Riñon.* New York Public Library, Rich Collection, no. 63, Segunda Parte, Capítulo 6.

For a discussion of Castañeda's use of the word riñón, see Clevy Lloyd Strout, "A Linguistic Study of the Journals of the Coronado Expedition" (Ph.D. diss., University of Colorado, 1958), 808–09.

44. Barrett, *The Geography of Rio Grande Pueblos*, 12–13.

45. See the entry dealing with Pueblo del Cerco in Appendix 3 for a discussion of its location.

46. New York Public Library, Rich Collection, no. 63, Segunda Parte, Capítulo 5; Hammond and Rey, *Rediscovery of New Mexico*, 106.

47. Schroeder, "Pueblos Abandoned in Historic Times," 244–47.

48. Important new archeological investigation of San Marcos has recently begun under the direction of Ann F. Ramenofsky, which may clarify the occupational history of that pueblo.

Geographer Elinore Barrett has written conservatively that the differing reports of Castañeda and Hernán Gallegos (of the Rodríguez-Chamuscado expedition) indicate "that the pueblos of Coronado's time had been rebuilt and enlarged." Barrett, *The Geography of Rio Grande Pueblos*, 17.

49. Adolph F. Bandelier, *Final Report of Investigations among the Indians of the Southwestern United States, Carried On Mainly in the Years from 1880 to 1885*, Papers of the Archaeological Institute of America, American Series, 4 (Cambridge, Mass.: Archaeological Institute of America, 1892), 162–66, 188.

Similar Keres migration accounts are still current at Santa Ana Pueblo. Laura Bayer, *Santa Ana: The People, the Pueblo, and the History of Tamaya* (Albuquerque: University of New Mexico Press, 1994), 3–11.

50. Richard Flint and Shirley Cushing Flint, "A Death in Tiguex, 1542," *New Mexico Historical Review* 74(3) (July 1999): 247–70.

51. Albert H. Schroeder, "Protohistoric Pueblo Demographic Changes," in *Current Research on the Late Prehistory and Early History of New Mexico*, ed. Bradley J. Vierra (Albuquerque: New Mexico Archaeological Council, 1992), 29–35; Barrett, *Geography of Rio Grande Pueblos*, 23.

52. Ann F. Ramenofsky, "The Problem of Introduced Infectious Diseases in New Mexico: A.D. 1540–1680," *Journal of Anthropological Research* 52 (1996): 161–84.

53. Reff, *Disease, Depopulation, and Culture Change*, 114.

Recently, though, Heidi Roberts and Richard Ahlstrom have suggested that spread of malaria as far north as southern Arizona by the time of the expedition to Tierra Nueva should not be ruled out. Heidi Roberts and Richard V.N. Ahlstrom, "Malaria, Microbes, and Mechanisms of Change," *Kiva* 63(2) (fall 1997): 117–35.

54. New York Public Library, Rich Collection, no. 63, Tercera Parte, Capítulo 5.

55. "Diego Pérez de Luxán's Account of the Antonio de Espejo Expedition into New Mexico, 1582," in *The Rediscovery of New Mexico, 1580–1594: The Explorations of Chamuscado, Espejo, Castaño de Sosa, Morlete, and Leyva de Bonilla and Humaña*, George P. Hammond and Agapito Rey (Albuquerque: The University of New Mexico Press, 1966), 184.

56. Carroll L. Riley, "Mesoamerican Indians in the Early Southwest," *Ethnohistory* 21 (winter 1974): 33.

57. Richard Flint, *"Armas de la Tierra* : The Mexican Indian Component of Coronado Expedition Material Culture," in *The Coronado Expedition to Tierra Nueva*, 57–70.

58. Janet Lecompte, "Coronado and Conquest," *New Mexico Historical Review* 64 (July 1989): 303.

59. Robert S. Weddle, "Coastal Exploration and Mapping, A Concomitant of the Entradas," in *The Mapping of the Entradas into the Greater Southwest*, ed. Dennis Reinhartz and Gerald D. Saxon (Norman: University of Oklahoma Press, 1998),126.

60. Bolton, *Coronado*, 395–98.
61. A. Grove Day, *Coronado's Quest* (Berkeley and Los Angeles: University of California Press, 1940), 318–19.
62. Very similar motives spurred the Pizarro expedition to persist in the face of disappointment and hardship. As Pedro de Cieza de León wrote, Francisco Pizarro exhorted his companions by saying "because they had already begun and were in debt, it would not be expedient to give up." Cieza de León, *Discovery and Conquest of Peru*, 69.
63. Tello, *Crónica Miscelanea*, 2: 349.
    The expedition members known to have taken up residence in or near Culiacán include Pedro de Nájera, Alonso Rodríguez, Pedro de Tovar, Diego López, Luis de Figueredo, Lorenzo Álvarez, Hernando Gómez de la Peña, Rodrigo Tamarán, Graviel López, Juan Paniagua, Juan Pastor, Hernando Arias de Saavedra, and Francisco Martín. AGI, Guadalajara, 46, N. 8, report by the cabildo of Culiacán, Culiacán, November 12, 1566; AGI, Patronato, 74, N. 2, R. 2; AGI, Patronato, 216, R. 2; Icaza, *Conquistadores y Pobladores*, no. 1103, no. 1320, no. 1378; Hammond and Rey, *Narratives*, 98 n60, 105 n84; 1544 testimony of Alonso Sánchez.
64. AGI, Guadalajara, 5, R. 1, N. 5.
65. See Aiton, *Antonio de Mendoza*, 137–57; Obregón, *Historia*, 31–38.

References

Archival Material

AGI, Contratación, 5575, N. 24, disposal of the estate of Juan Jiménez, Puebla de los Angeles, 1550.

AGI, Contratación, 5787, N. 1, L. 4, royal cédula, Valladolid, 1537.

AGI, Guadalajara, 5, R. 1, N. 5, letter, Francisco Vázquez de Coronado to the viceroy, Compostela, December 15, 1538.

AGI, Guadalajara, 5, R. 1, N. 7, muster roll of the expedition, Compostela, February 22, 1540.

AGI, Guadalajara, 30, N. 1, letter, cabildo of Compostela to the king, Compostela, February 19, 1533.

AGI, Guadalajara, 46, N. 8, report by the cabildo of Culiacán, Culiacán, November 12, 1566.

AGI, Indiferente, 422, L. 16, F. 205, license to Francisco Vázquez de Coronado to take a black slave to the Indies, Sevilla, May 31, 1535.

AGI, Indiferente, 423, L. 18, F 65r, permission to Cristóbal de Escobar to transport one black slave to the Indies, Sevilla, December 30, 1537.

AGI, Indiferente, 424, L. 22, royal cédula, Madrid, November 10, 1551.

AGI, Indiferente, 425, L. 23, fol. 421v, royal cédula, Madrid, 1559.

AGI, Indiferente, 737, N. 69 b, proof of service of Fernand González de Párraga, Castilla de Oro, 1551.

AGI, Indiferente, 1093, R. 2, N. 16, letter, Tello de Sandoval to the king, San Lucar de Barrameda, November 3, 1543.

AGI, Indiferente, 1382A, petition of Cristóbal de Benavente, Antequera, July 19, 1529.

AGI, Indiferente, 2055, N. 10, license to travel to Nueva España, Sevilla, 1574.

AGI, Justicia, 124, N. 2, legal action between Domingo Martín and Gómez Nieto, Valladolid, June 28, 1542.

AGI, Justicia 127, N. 2, summary of investigation of treatment of Indians at Sultepec, Mexico City, February and March 1537.

AGI, Justicia, 213, N. 4, lawsuit regarding Teocaluyacan and Cayuca, Cuernavaca, 1551.

AGI, Justicia, 259, Pieza 2, administrative review of Antonio de Mendoza, Mexico City, 1544–1546.

AGI, Justicia, 259, Pieza 2, letter, archbishop of Sevilla to don Antonio de Mendoza, Madrid, June 10, 1540.

AGI, Justicia, 259, Pieza 2, folios 234r and 234v, royal cédula, Madrid 1540.

AGI, Justicia, 259, Pieza 4, certification of suit concerning Tlapa, Mexico City, 1544

AGI, Justicia, 260, Pieza 1, charges and rebuttals of Lorenzo de Tejada, Mexico City, 1546.

AGI, Justicia, 260, Pieza 2, administrative review of the fiscal Cristóbal de Benavente, Mexico City, 1547.

AGI, Justicia, 260, Pieza 4, fol. 5r, administrative review of licenciado Cristóbal de Benavente, Mexico City, 1546.

AGI, Justicia, 260, Pieza 4, charges and rebuttals, Lorenzo de Tejada, Mexico City, 1546.

AGI, Justicia, 267, proceedings of the secret review of the officials of the Royal Audiencia of Mexico, Mexico City, 1546.

AGI, Justicia, 267, N. 3, proceso de Francisco Vázquez, copy by unidentified scribes, Mexico City, March 1547.

AGI, Justicia, 336, N. 1, R. 3, testimony concerning certain pueblos, Compostela, spring 1552.

AGI, Justicia, 336, N. 2, suit concerning distribution of Indians to Diego de Colio, Guadalajara, 1565.

AGI, Justicia, 339, N. 1, R. 1, residencia of Francisco Vázquez de Coronado, Guadalajara, 1544–45.

AGI, Justicia, 339, N. 1, R. 3, investigation concerning certain Indian towns, Guadalajara, fall 1544.

AGI, Justicia, 1010, N. 3, R. 1, proceeding of the heirs of licenciado Villalobos against licenciado Cristóbal de Benavente, Valladolid, 1551.

AGI, Justicia, 1021, N. 2, Pieza 1, accusation against Ramírez de Cárdenas, Madrid, 1546–1547.

AGI, Justicia, 1021, N. 2, Pieza 2, report extracted from the affidavit prepared for don García Ramírez de Cárdenas, n.p., n.d.

AGI, Justicia 1021, N. 2, Pieza 3, report extracted from the affidavit prepared for licenciado Villalobos, n.p, n.d.

AGI, Justicia, 1021, N. 2, Pieza 4, información contra Coronado, copy by Pedro de Requena, Mexico City, March 11, 1545.

AGI, Justicia, 1021, N. 2, Pieza 5, affidavit prepared at the request of don García López de Cárdenas, Mexico City, end of 1547 and early 1548.

AGI, Justicia, 1021 N. 2, Pieza 6, affidavit prepared for the fiscal Juan de Villalobos, Mexico City, January 10, 1547.

AGI, Justicia, 1021, N. 2, Pieza 6, record of 1544 investigation Lorenzo de Tejada, copy by Sancho López de Agurto, Mexico City, January 1547.

AGI, Mexico, 68, R. 11, N. 25, letter, Lorenzo de Tejada to the prince, Mexico City, May 24, 1544.

AGI, Mexico, 68, R. 12, N. 29, letter, Lorenzo de Tejada to the king, Mexico City, March 12, 1545.

AGI, Mexico, 68, R. 13, N. 38, letter, Lorenzo de Tejada to the marqués de Mondéjar, Mexico City, April 24, 1547.

AGI, Mexico, 97, letter, Francisco Morales to the king, Mexico City, May 19, 1563.

AGI, Mexico, 97, R. 1, proof of service of Tristán de Luna y Arellano, Mexico City, 1559.

AGI, Mexico, 98, N. 33, investigation of Juan Troyano, Mexico City, 1569.

AGI, Mexico, 98, N. 33e, letter, Juan Troyano to the viceroy, Mexico City, 1569.

AGI, Mexico, 124, R. 5, proof of service of Francisco Pacheco de Córdova y Bocanegra, Mexico City, 1605.

AGI, Mexico, 168, letter, Juan Troyano to the king, Mexico City, December 20, 1568.

AGI, Mexico, 203, N. 13, report concerning Lope de Samaniego, Mexico City, 1531.

AGI, Mexico, 204, N. 14, proof of service of Cristóbal de Escobar, Mexico City, November 21, 1543.

AGI, Mexico, 204, N. 36, investigation of Juan Gallego, Mexico City, 1558.

AGI, Mexico, 206, N. 12, proof of service of Juan Troyano, Mexico City, February 20, 1560.

AGI, Mexico, 206, N. 35, investigation of Cristóbal de Escobar, Mexico City, February 1, 1561.

AGI, Mexico, 207, N. 39, proof of service of Melchor Pérez, Mexico City, 1563.

AGI, Mexico, 1088, L. 1, royal cédula, Madrid, November 9, 1529.

AGI, Mexico, 1088, L. 3, royal cédula, Valladolid, 1539.

AGI, Patronato, 20, N. 5, R. 8, narrative of Juan de Jaramillo, n.p., [1560s].

AGI, Patronato, 20, N. 5, R. 8, relación del suceso, n.p., 1540s.

AGI, Patronato, 20, N. 5, R. 10, report of Marcos de Niza, Mexico City, September 2, 1539.

AGI, Patronato, 21, N. 2, R. 3, investigation of the persons who are going with Francisco Vázquez de Coronado, Compostela, February 1540.

AGI, Patronato, 21, N. 2, R. 4, testimony about fray Marcos's discovery, Havana, November 1539.

AGI, Patronato, 21, N. 3, R. 2, contract between Antonio de Mendoza and the adelantado Pedro de Alvarado, Mexico City, November 29, 1540.

AGI, Patronato, 57, N. 2, R. 1, proof of service of Antonio de Mendoza, Mexico City, March 1545.

AGI, Patronato, 60, N. 5, R. 4, proof of service of Juan de Zaldívar, Guadalajara, February 1566.

AGI, Patronato 61, N. 2, R. 9, proof of service of Alonso Alvarez de Espinosa, Mexico City, January 27, 1558.

AGI, Patronato, 63, R. 5, proof of service of Juan Gómez de Paradinas, Mexico City, June 6, 1560.

AGI, Patronato, 74, N. 1, R. 1, proof of service of Francisco Pacheco de Córdova y Bocanegra, Madrid, 1624.

AGI, Patronato, 74, N. 2, R. 2, proofs of service of Alonso y Juan Rodríguez, San Sebastián, 1576.

AGI, Patronato, 75, R. 3, N. 1, investigation into the services of Cristóbal de Oñate, Mexico City, 1577.

AGI, Patronato, 76, N. 1, R. 5, proof of service of Francisco de Zaldívar, Mexico City, March 29, 1580.

AGI, Patronato, 78, R.1, N.1, proof of service of Cristóbal de Oñate, Mexico City, 1584.

AGI, Patronato, 79, N. 3, R. 2, proof of service of Francisco de Santillán, Madrid, December 14, 1598.

AGI, Patronato, 87, N. 1, R. 5, proof of service of García Rodríguez and his grandson, Mexico City, April 26, 1617.

AGI, Patronato, 184, R. 31, letter, Antonio de Mendoza to the king, Mexico City, April 17, 1540.

AGI, Patronato, 216, R. 2, investigation concerning Núño de Cháves, Mexico City, 1566.

AGI, Patronato, 277, N. 4, R. 36, appointment of López de Cárdenas, Mexico City, April 8, 1538.

AGI, Patronato, 281, N. 1, R. 34, final decision in the case of Ramírez de Cárdenas, Valladolid, September 1551.

AGI, Patronato, 281, N. 1, R. 121, summons of Cristóbal de Benavente, Madrid, May 27, 1551.

AGI, Patronato 284, N. 2, R. 24, final decision in the administrative review by Doctor Montealegre, oidor, and the administrative review by licenciado Francisco Tello de Sandoval, Valladolid, 1558.

AGI, Patronato, 287, R. 57, final decision concerning certain Indians, Bosque de Segovia, 1562.

AGnot, 1, Diego de Isla, IV, distribution of inheritance from Alonso Sánchez, Mexico City, 1553.

AGnot, 1, Luis Sánchez, proceedings concerning Baltasar Dorantes de Carranza, San Juan Teotihuacan, August 8, 1582.

AGS, Cámara de Castilla, 121–7, petition from Diego López, Sevilla, 1517.

AGS, Camara de Castilla, 121–146, petition of Juan Vázquez de Coronado, Granada, December 5, 1516.

AGS, Guerra y Marina, 37–136, resignation of doctor Gonzalo de Zúñiga as regidor, Sevilla, August 13, 1551.

AHN, Ordenes Militares, 304, Expillo. 13408, order of San Juan to Juan Vázquez de Coronado, n.p., n.d.

Archivo General de la Nación/Buenos Aires, Census records of Río de la Plata, 13-17-5-1, review of Sisicaya [Peru], Lima, 1588.

Archeological Records Management System (ARMS) site files for LA 187, Kuaua Pueblo; LA 288, Corrales Pueblo; LA 289, Calabacillas Pueblo; LA 290, Piedras Marcadas Pueblo; LA 294, Sandia Pueblo; LA 326, Santiago Pueblo; LA 421, Alameda Pueblo; LA 677, Watche Pueblo; LA 716; LA 717, Maigua Pueblo; and LA 22765, Chamisal Pueblo. Unpublished files. Laboratory of Anthropology, Museum of New Mexico, Santa Fe.

ARMS site files for LA 2047, Basalt Point Pueblo, and LA 2049, Canjillon Pueblo. Unpublished files. Laboratory of Anthropology, Museum of New Mexico, Santa Fe.

Bancroft Library, University of California, Berkeley, Herbert E. Bolton Collection, Item 393, C-B 840, Part I, draft transcription and draft English translation of AGI, Justicia, 1021, N. 2, Pieza 4, by Agapito Rey, Bloomington, Indiana, 1930s.

Bancroft Library, University of California, Berkeley, M-M 1714, proof of service of Melchior Pérez, Mexico City, January 30, 1551.

Biblioteca del Escorial, Códice &-II-7, Document no. LXVII, instructions to Hernando de Alarcón, Mexico City, May 31, 1541.

Biblioteca del Escorial, Códice &-II-7, Doc. no. LXXVIII, settlers without Indians, n.p., [late 1540s].

Biblioteca del Escorial, Códice &-II-7, Doc. no. LXXIX, list of the persons, conquerors, and settlers of Nueva Galicia, n.p., [late 1540s].

Biblioteca del Escorial, Códice &-II-7, Doc. no. LXXX, list of vecinos of Culiacán, n.p., [late 1540s].

New York Public Library, Rich Collection, no. 63, Pedro de Castañeda, *Relación de la Jornada de Cibola....*, Sevilla, 1596.

Published Material

Aiton, Arthur Scott. *Antonio de Mendoza, First Viceroy of New Spain.* Durham, North Carolina: Duke University Press, 1927.

_____. "The Secret Visita Against Viceroy Mendoza." In *New Spain, New Spain and the Anglo-American West: Historical Contributions Presented to Herbert Eugene Bolton*, vol. 1, 1–22. Los Angeles: privately printed, 1932.

_____, and Agapito Rey. "Coronado's Testimony in the Viceroy Mendoza Residencia," *New Mexico Historical Review* 12(3) (July 1937): 288–329.

Altman, Ida. *Emigrants and Society: Extremadura and Spanish America in the Sixteenth Century.* Berkeley: University of California Press, 1989.

Álvarez, Victor M. *Diccionario de Conquistadores*, 2 vols. Mexico City: Instituto Nacional de Antropología y Historia, 1975.

Anyon, Roger. "The Late Prehistoric and Early Historic Periods in the Zuni-Cibola Area, A.D. 1400–1680." In *Current Research on the Late Prehistory and Early History of New Mexico*, ed. Bradley J. Vierra, 75–83. Albuquerque: New Mexico Archaeological Council, 1992.

Arregui Zamorano, Pilar. "Quejas sobre Incumplimiento de Oficio." In *La Audiencia de México según los Visitadores (Siglos XVI y XVII)*, 111–60. Mexico City: Universidad Nacional Autónoma de México, 1981.

Avellaneda, José Ignacio. *The Conquerors of the New Kingdom of Granada.* Albuquerque: University of New Mexico Press, 1995.

_____. *Los Sobrevivientes de la Florida: The Survivors of the De Soto Expedition*, Research Publications of the P.K. Yonge Library of Florida History, 2. Gainesville: University of Florida Libraries, 1990.

Bakewell, Peter. *A History of Latin America: Empires and Sequels, 1450–1930.* Malden, Massachusetts and Oxford, England: Blackwell Publishers, 1997.

Bandelier, Adolph F. *Final Report of Investigations among the Indians of the Southwestern United States, Carried On Mainly in the Years from 1880 to 1885*, Papers of the Archaeological Institute of America, American Series, 4. Cambridge, Mass.: Archaeological Institute of America, 1892.

Barrett, Elinore M. *The Geography of Rio Grande Pueblos Revealed by Spanish Explorers, 1540–1598,* Latin American Institute Research Paper Series, no. 30. Albuquerque: Latin American Institute, University of New Mexico, 1997.

Bayer, Laura. *Santa Ana: The People, the Pueblo, and the History of Tamaya.* Albuquerque: University of New Mexico Press, 1994.

[Benavente], fray Toribio de. *Motolinía's History of the Indians of New Spain.* Translated by Francis Borgia Steck. Washington, D.C.: Academy of American Franciscan History, 1951.

Bermúdez Plata, Cristóbal, ed. *1535–1538,* vol. 2, *Catálogo de Pasajeros a Indias durante los Siglos XVI, XVII y XVIII.* Sevilla: Editorial de la Gavida, 1942.

_____. *1539–1559,* vol. 3, *Catálogo de Pasajeros a Indias durante los Siglos XVI, XVII y XVIII.* Sevilla: Editorial de la Gavida, 1946.

_____. *1560–1566,* vol. 4, *Catálogo de Pasajeros a Indias durante los Siglos XVI, XVII y XVIII.* Sevilla: Editorial de la Gavida, 1946.

Blakeslee, Donald J., Richard Flint, and Jack T. Hughes. "Una Barranca Grande: Recent Archeological Evidence and a Discussion of Its Place in the Coronado Route." In *The Coronado Expedition to Tierra Nueva: The 1540–1542 Route Across the Southwest,* ed. Richard Flint and Shirley Cushing Flint, 370–83. Niwot, Colorado: University Press of Colorado, 1997.

Bolton, Herbert E. *Coronado, Knight of Pueblos and Plains.* New York, London, and Toronto: Whittlesey House, McGraw-Hill Book Company, Inc; Albuquerque: University of New Mexico Press, 1949.

_____, ed. *Spanish Explorations in the Southwest, 1542–1706.* New York: Charles Scribner and Sons, 1916.

Boyd-Bowman, Peter. *Indice Geobiográfico de Cuarenta Mil Pobladores Españoles de América en el Siglo XVI,* 2 vols. Bogota: Instituto Caro y Cuervo, 1964; Mexico City: Editorial Jus, 1968.

_____. *Lexico Hispanoamericano del Siglo XVI.* London: Tamesis Books Limited, 1971.

Brew, J[ohn] O. "Hopi Prehistory and History to 1850." In *Southwest,* vol. 9 of *Handbook of North American Indians,* ed. Alfonso Ortiz, 514–23. Washington, D.C.: Smithsonian Institution, 1979.

Calvo, Thomas, Eustaquio Celestino, Magdalena Gómez, Jean Meyer, and Ricardo Xochitemol. *Xalisco, la voz de un pueblo en el siglo XVI.* Mexico City: Centro de Investigaciones y Estudios Superiores en Antropología Social and Centro de Estudios Mexicanos y Centroamericanos, 1993.

Carrera Stampa, Manuel. "The Evolution of Weights and Measures in New Spain," *The Hispanic American Historical Review* 29 (February 1949): 2–24.

Cervantes de Salazar, Francisco. *México en 1554.* Edited by Julio Jiménez Rueda, translated by Joaquín García Icazbalceta. Mexico City: Universidad Nacional Autónoma de México, 1984.

Chardon, Roland. "The Linear League in North America," *Annals of the Association of American Geographers* 70 (1980): 129–53.

Chavez, Fray Angelico. *Coronado's Friars.* Washington, D.C.: Academy of American Franciscan History, 1968.

Chipman, Donald E. *Nuño de Guzmán and the Province of Pánuco in New Spain, 1518–1533.* Spain in the West, vol. 10. Glendale, California: The Arthur H. Clark Company, 1967.

Cieza de León, Pedro de. *The Discovery and Conquest of Peru*. Edited and translated by Alexandra Parma Cook and Noble David Cook. Durham and London: Duke University Press, 1998.

Clayton, Lawrence A.; Vernon James Knight, Jr.; and Edward C. Moore, ed. *The De Soto Chronicles: The Expedition of Hernando de Soto to North America in 1539–1543*, 2 vols. Tuscaloosa and London: The University of Alabama Press, 1993.

Clendinnen, Inga. "'Fierce and Unnatural Cruelty': Cortés and the Conquest of Mexico," *Representations* 33 (winter 1991): 65–100.

Códice Franciscano, Siglo XVI. Edited by Joaquín García Icazbalceta. Mexico City: Francisco Díaz de León, 1889.

Connelly, John C. "Hopi Social Organization." In *Southwest*, vol. 9 of *Handbook of North American Indians*, ed. Alfonso Ortiz, 539–53. Washington, D.C.: Smithsonian Institution, 1979.

Cortés Alonso, Vicenta. *La Escritura y Lo Escrito: Paleografía y Diplomática de España y América en los siglos XVI y XVII*. Madrid: Ediciones Cultura Hispanica, Instituto de Cooperación Iberoamericana, 1986

Covarrubias Orozco, Sebastián de. *Tesoro de la Lengua Castellana o Española*, 2nd rev. ed. Edited by Felipe C.R. Maldonado. Madrid: Editorial Castalia, S.A., 1995.

Craine, Eugene R., and Reginald C. Reindorp, ed. and trans. *The Chronicles of Michoacán*. Norman: University of Oklahoma Press, 1970.

"Cuarta Relación Anónima de la Jornada de Nuño de Guzmán." In vol. 2 of *Colección de Documentos para la Historia de México*, 2nd facsimile ed., 472–83. Edited by Joaquín García Icazbalceta. Mexico City: Editorial Porrua, S.A., 1980.

Cuarto Libro de las Actas de Cabildo de la Ciudad de México, comprende de Primero de Enero de 1536 a 30 de Agosto de 1543. Edited by D. Manuel. Mexico City: Orozco y Berra, 1859.

Cutter, Charles R. *The Legal Culture of Northern New Spain, 1700–1810*. Albuquerque: University of New Mexico Press, 1995.

Day, A. Grove. *Coronado's Quest*. Berkeley and Los Angeles: University of California Press, 1940.

_____. "Mota Padilla on the Coronado Expedition," *The Hispanic American Historical Review* 20(1) (February 1940): 88–110.

Defourneaux, Marcelin. *Daily Life in Spain in the Golden Age*. Translated by Newton Branch. Stanford: Stanford University Press, 1979.

del Paso y Troncoso, Francisco, ed. *Epistolario de Nueva España, 1505–1818*, 2nd series, 16 vols. Mexico City: José Porrua e Hijos, 1939–1942.

DiPeso, Charles C., John B. Rinaldo, and Gloria J. Fenner. *Architecture and Dating Methods*, vol. 4 of *Casas Grandes, A Fallen Trading Center of the Gran Chichimeca*. Dragoon, Arizona: The Amerind Foundation, 1974.

Donaldson, Marcia L., and Mollie S. Toll. "Prehistoric Subsistence in the Bis sa'ani Area: Evidence from Flotation, Macrobotanical Remains, and Wood Identification." In *Bis sa'ani: A Late Bonito Phase Community on Escavada Wash, Northwest New Mexico*, Navajo Nation Papers in Anthropology Number 14, ed. Cory Dale Breternitz, David E. Doyel, and Michael P. Marshall, 3: 1015–65. Window Rock, Arizona: Navajo Nation Cultural Resource Management Program, 1982.

Dozier, Edward P. *The Pueblo Indians of North America*. New York: Holt, Rinehart and Winston, Inc, 1970. Reprint, Prospect Heights, Illinois: Waveland Press, Inc., 1983.

Duffen, William A., and William K. Hartmann. "The 76 Ranch Ruin and the Location of Chichilticale." In *The Coronado Expedition to Tierra Nueva: The 1540–1542 Route Across the Southwest*, ed. Richard Flint and Shirley Cushing Flint, 190–211. Niwot, Colorado: University Press of Colorado, 1997.

Dunnigan, Timothy. "Lower Pima." In *Southwest*, vol. 10 of *Handbook of North American Indians*, ed. Alfonso Ortiz, 217–29. Washington, D.C.: Smithsonian Institution, 1983.

Elliot, John H. *Imperial Spain, 1469–1716* London: Edward Arnold, 1963; reprint, London: Penquin Books, 1990.

Ellis, Florence Hawley. "Anthropological Evidence Supporting the Land Claim of the Pueblos of Zia, Santa Ana, and Jemez." Albuquerque: Univesity of Albuquerque, Native American Bilingual Teacher Education Program, 1956.

Fernández de Bethencourt, Francisco. *Historia Genealógica y Heráldica de la Monarquía Española Casa Real y Grandes de España*. Madrid: Jaime Ratés, 1912.

Flint, Richard. "*Armas de la Tierra* : The Mexican Indian Component of Coronado Expedition Material Culture." In *The Coronado Expedition to Tierra Nueva: The 1540–1542 Route Across the Southwest*, ed. Richard Flint and Shirley Cushing Flint, 57–70. Niwot, Colorado: University Press of Colorado, 1997.

———. "The Coronado and de Soto Expeditions: A Contrast in Attitudes or Difference in External Conditions? Part 1: Relative Humanity of the Expeditions," *El Viaje*, Coronado Trail Association Newsletter 1(2) (April 1992): 4–8.

———. "A Coronado Campsite in Blanco Canyon, Texas," *Wagon Tracks*, Santa Fe Trail Association Quarterly 1 (August 1997): 3–4.

———, and Shirley Cushing Flint. "A Death in Tiguex, 1542," *New Mexico Historical Review* 74(3) (July 1999): 247–70.

García Icazbalceta, Joaquín. *Colección de Documentos para la Historia de México*. Vol. 2. Mexico City: Antigua Librería, 1866.

García-Mason, Velma. "Acoma Pueblo." In *Southwest*, vol. 9 of *Handbook of North American Indians*, ed. Alfonso Ortiz, 450–66. Washington, D.C.: Smithsonian Institution, 1979.

Gerhard, Peter. *A Guide to the Historical Geography of New Spain*, rev. ed. Norman and London: University of Oklahoma Press, 1993.

———. *The North Frontier of New Spain*, rev. ed. Norman and London: University of Oklahoma Press, 1993.

Gibson, Charles. *The Spanish Tradition in America*. Columbia: University of South Carolina Press, 1968.

Gurulé, Jerry. "Francisco Vázquez de Coronado's Northward Trek Through Sonora." In *The Coronado Expedition to Tierra Nueva: The 1540–1542 Route Across the Southwest*, ed. Richard Flint and Shirley Cushing Flint, 149–64. Niwot, Colorado: University Press of Colorado, 1997.

Gutiérrez, Ramón A. *When Jesus Came, the Corn Mothers Went Away: Marriage, Sexuality, and Power in New Mexico, 1500–1846*. Stanford: Stanford University Press, 1991.

Habicht-Mauche, Judith A. "Coronado's Querechos and Teyas in the Archaeological Record of the Texas Panhandle," *Plains Anthropologist* 140 (1992): 247–59.

Hackett, Charles W. *Historical Documents relating to New Mexico, Nueva Vizcaya, and Approaches Thereto, to 1773*, Carnegie Institution of Washington Publications no. 330, 3 vols. Washington, D.C.: Carnegie Institution of Washington, 1923–37.

Hammond, George P., and Agapito Rey. *Narratives of the Coronado Expedition, 1540–1542.* Vol. 2, Coronado Cuarto Centennial Publications. Albuquerque: University of New Mexico Press, 1940.

_____. *The Rediscovery of New Mexico, 1580–1594: The Explorations of Chamuscado, Espejo, Castaño de Sosa, Morlete, and Leyva de Bonilla and Humaña.* Albuquerque: University of New Mexico Press, 1966.

Hanke, Lewis. "Antonio de Mendoza (1535–1550), Bibliografía." In *Los Virreyes Españoles en América durante el Gobierno de la Casa de Austria*, vol. 1, *Mexico*, vol. 273, Biblioteca de Autores Españoles desde la Formación del Lenguaje hasta Nuestros Dias, 17–20. Madrid: Atlas Ediciones, 1976.

_____. *The Spanish Struggle for Justice in the Conquest of America.* Boston: Little, Brown and Company, 1965.

Himmerich y Valencia, Robert. *The Encomenderos of New Spain, 1521–1555.* Austin: University of Texas Press, 1991.

Hinton, Thomas B. "Southern Periphery: West." In *Southwest*, vol. 10 of *Handbook of North American Indians*, ed. Alfonso Ortiz, 315–28. Washington, D.C.: Smithsonian Institution, 1983.

Hoebel, E. Adamson. "Zia Pueblo." In *Southwest*, vol. 9 of *Handbook of North American Indians*, ed. Alfonso Ortiz, 407–17. Washington, D.C.: Smithsonian Institution, 1979.

Howard, David A. *Conquistador in Chains: Cabeza de Vaca and the Indians of the Americas.* Tuscaloosa and London: University of Alabama Press, 1997.

Hudson, Charles. *Knights of Spain, Warriors of the Sun: Hernando de Soto and the South's Ancient Chiefdoms.* Athens, Georgia and London: University of Georgia Press, 1997.

Icaza, Francisco A. de. *Conquistadores y Pobladores de Nueva España: Diccionario Autobiográfico Sacado de los Textos Originales*, 2 vols. Madrid: n.p., 1923.

Inglis, G. Douglas. "The Men of Cíbola: New Investigations on the Francisco Vázquez de Coronado Expedition," *Panhandle-Plains Historical Review* 55 (1982): 1–24.

Julyan, Robert. *The Place Names of New Mexico.* Albuquerque: University of New Mexico Press, 1996.

Kamen, Henry. *Philip of Spain.* New Haven and London: Yale University Press, 1997.

Karasch, Mary. "Interethnic Conflict and Resistance on the Brazilian Frontier of Goiás, 1750–1890." In *Contested Ground: Comparative Frontiers on the Northern and Southern Edges of the Spanish Empire*, ed. Donna J. Guy and Thomas E. Sheridan, 115–34. Tucson: The University of Arizona Press, 1998.

Kelly, Isabel. *Excavations at Chametla, Sinaloa, Ibero-Americana*, 14. Berkeley: University of California Press, 1938.

Kessell, John L. *Kiva, Cross, and Crown: the Pecos Indians and New Mexico, 1540–1840*, 2nd ed. Albuquerque: University of New Mexico Press, 1987.

_____, Rick Hendricks, and Meredith Dodge, eds. *Blood on the Boulders: The Journals of Don Diego de Vargas, New Mexico, 1694–97.* Albuquerque: University of New Mexico Press, 1998.

Ladd, Edmund J. "Zuni on the Day the Men in Metal Arrived." In *The Coronado Expedition to Tierra Nueva: The 1540–1542 Route Across the Southwest*, ed. Richard Flint and Shirley Cushing Flint, 225–33. Niwot, Colorado: University Press of Colorado, 1997.

Landa, Diego de. *Yucatán Before and After the Conquest*. Edited and translated by William Gates. Mérida: Editorial Dante, 1986.

Las Casas, Bartolomé de. *In Defense of the Indians*. Translated by Stafford Poole. DeKalb, Illinois: Northern Illinois University Press, 1992.

————. *The Devastation of the Indies: A Brief Account*. Translated by Herma Briffault. Baltimore and London: The Johns Hopkins University Press, 1992.

La Sociedad de Bibliófilos Españoles. *Nobilario de Conquistadores de Indias*. Madrid: M. Tello, 1892.

Lecompte, Janet. "Coronado and Conquest," *New Mexico Historical Review* 64(3) (July 1989): 279–304.

Libro del Cabildo e Ayuntamiento desta Ynsigne e Muy Leal Ciudad de Tenuxtitan Mexico desta Nueba España que Comenzo a Primero Dia del Mes de Dizienbre de 1550 Años Fenece a Fin de Dizienbre de 1561 Años. Mexico City: n.p., n.d.

Liss, Peggy K. *Isabel the Queen: Life and Times*. New York and Oxford: Oxford University Press, 1992.

Lockhart, James. *The Men of Cajamarca: A Social and Biographical Study of the First Conquerors of Peru*, Institute of Latin American Studies, Latin American Monographs, 27. Austin and London: The University of Texas Press, 1972.

López de Gómara, Francisco. *Historia General de las Indias*, facsimile ed. Lima: Comisión Nacional del V Centenario del Descubrimiento de América–Encuentro de Dos Mundos, 1993.

Martínez, José Luis, ed. *Documentos Cortesianos*, 4 vols. Mexico City: Universidad Nacional Autónoma de México, 1992.

Mueller, Teresa, and Robin Ransom. *New Mexico Highway Geologic Map*. Socorro, New Mexico: New Mexico Geological Society, 1982.

Newson, Linda A. Indian Population Patterns in Colonial Spanish America, *Latin American Research Review* 20(3) (1985): 41–74.

Núñez Cabeza de Vaca, Álvar. *Naufragios y Comentarios con Dos Cartas*, Colección Austral, 304, 9th ed. Mexico City: Espasa-Calpe, Mexicana, S.A., 1985.

Obregón, Baltasar de. *Historia de los Descubrimientos Antiguos y Modernos de la Nueva España, Escrita por el Conquistador en el Año de 1584*. Mexico City: Editorial Porrúa, S.A., 1988.

Oroz, Fray Pedro. *The Oroz Codex*. Edited and translated by Angelico Chavez. Washington, D.C.: Academy of American Franciscan History, 1972.

Pacheco, Joaquín F., and Francisco de Cárdenas, ed. *Colección de Documentos Inéditos Relativos al Descubrimiento, Conquista y Organización de las Antiguas Posesiones Españolas de América y Oceania*, series 1, 42 vols. Madrid: n.p., 1864–1884.

Pailes, Richard A. "An Archaeological Perspective on the Sonoran Entrada." In *The Coronado Expedition to Tierra Nueva: The 1540–1542 Route Across the Southwest*, ed. Richard Flint and Shirley Cushing Flint, 177–189. Niwot, Colorado: University Press of Colorado, 1997.

Parry, John H. and Robert G. Keith, comps. *Central America and Mexico*, Vol. 3, *New Iberian World*. New York: Times Books and Hector & Rose, 1984.

_____. *The Conquerors and the Conquered*, Vol. 1, *New Iberian World*. New York: Times Books and Hector & Rose, 1984.

Prem, Hanns J. "Disease Outbreaks in Central Mexico During the Sixteenth Century." In *"Secret Judgements of God": Old World Disease in Colonial Spanish America*, ed. Noble David Cook and W. George Lovell, 20–48. Norman and London: University of Oklahoma Press, 1991.

Priestley, Herbert Ingram, ed. and trans. *The Luna Papers: Documents Relating to the Expedition of don Tristán de Luna y Arellano for the Conquest of La Florida in 1559–1561*, 2 vols. DeLand, Florida: The Florida State Historical Society, 1928. Reprint, Freeport, New York: Books for Libraries Press, 1971.

Quinto Libro de Actas de la Ciudad de México. Edited by Antonio Espinosa de los Monteros. [Mexico City]: n.p., 1862.

Ramenofsky, Ann F. "The Problem of Introduced Infectious Diseases in New Mexico: A.D. 1540–1680," *Journal of Anthropological Research* 52 (1996): 161–84.

Ramusio, Giovanni Battista. *Terzo Volume delle Navigationi et Viaggi*. Venice: La Stamperia de Giunti, 1565.

Real Academia Española. *Diccionario de la Lengua Española*, 21st ed., 2 vols. Madrid: Real Academia Española, 1992.

Reff, Daniel T. *Disease, Depopulation, and Culture Change in Northwestern New Spain, 1518–1764*. Salt Lake City: University of Utah Press, 1991.

_____. "The Relevance of Ethnology to the Routing of the Coronado Expedition in Sonora." In *The Coronado Expedition to Tierra Nueva: The 1540–1542 Route Across the Southwest*, ed. Richard Flint and Shirley Cushing Flint, 165–76. Niwot, Colorado: University Press of Colorado, 1997.

Reitz, Elizabeth J., and Bonnie G. McEwan. "Animals, Environment, and the Spanish Diet at Puerto Real." In *Puerto Real: The Archaeology of a Sixteenth-Century Spanish Town in Hispaniola*, ed. Kathleen Deagan, 287–334. Gainesville: University Press of Florida, 1995.

Restall, Mathew. *Maya Conquistador*. Boston: Beacon Press, 1998.

Riley, Carroll L. *The Frontier People: the Greater Southwest in the Protohistoric Period*, rev. and expanded ed. Albuquerque: University of New Mexico Press, 1987.

_____. "Mesoamerican Indians in the Early Southwest," *Ethnohistory* 21 (winter 1974): 25–36.

_____. "Pecos and Trade." In *Across the Chichimec Sea, Papers in Honor of J. Charles Kelley*, ed. Carroll L. Riley and Basil C. Hedrick, 53–64. Carbondale and Edwardsville, Illinois: Southern Illinois University Press, 1978.

_____. "Puaray and Coronado's Tiguex." In *Collected Papers in Honor of Erik K. Reed*, Papers of the Archaeological Society of New Mexico, 6, ed. Albert H. Schroeder, 197–210. Albuquerque: Archaeological Society Press, 1981.

_____. *Rio del Norte: People of the Upper Rio Grande from Earliest Times to the Pueblo Revolt*. Salt Lake City: University of Utah Press, 1995.

_____. "The Teya Indians of the Southwestern Plains." In *The Coronado Expedition to Tierra Nueva: The 1540–1542 Route Across the Southwest*, ed. Richard Flint and Shirley Cushing Flint, 320–43. Niwot, Colorado: University Press of Colorado, 1997.

Roberts, Heidi, and Richard V.N. Ahlstrom. "Malaria, Microbes, and Mechanisms of Change." *Kiva* 63(2) (fall 1997): 117–35.

Rodack, Madeleine Turrell. "Cíbola, from Fray Marcos to Coronado." In *The Coronado Expedition to Tierra Nueva: The 1540–1542 Route Across the Southwest*, ed. Richard Flint and Shirley Cushing Flint, 102–15. Niwot, Colorado: University Press of Colorado, 1997.

Ruiz Medrano, Ethelia. "El Oidor como Empresario: El Caso del Licenciado Lorenzo de Tejada (1537–1550)." In *Gobierno y Sociedad en Nueva España: Segunda Audiencia y Antonio de Mendoza*, 209–339. Zamora, Michoacán: El Colegio de Michoacán and Gobierno de Michoacán, 1991.

_____. "La Política del Virrey Mendoza: Encomienda y Corregimineto. El Virrey como Empresario en México (1535–1550)." In *Gobierno y Sociedad en Nueva España: Segunda Audiencia y Antonio de Mendoza*, 115–205. Zamora, Michoacán: El Colegio de Michoacán and Gobierno de Michoacán: 1991.

Sando, Joe. "Jemez Pueblo." In *Southwest*, vol. 9 of *Handbook of North American Indians*, ed. Alfonso Ortiz, 418–29. Washington, D.C.: Smithsonian Institution, 1979.

Schäfer, Ernesto. *Las Rúbricas del Consejo Real y Supremo de las Indias desde la Fundación del Consejo en 1524 hasta la Terminación del Reinado de los Austrias*. Sevilla: n.p., 1934. Reprint, Nendeln, Liechtenstein: Klaus Reprint, 1975.

Schroeder, Albert H. "Protohistoric Pueblo Demographic Changes." In *Current Research on the Late Prehistory and Early History of New Mexico*, ed. Bradley J. Vierra, 29–35. Albuquerque: New Mexico Archaeological Council, 1992.

_____. "Pueblos Abandoned in Historic Times." In *Southwest*, vol. 9 of *Handbook of North American Indians*, ed. Alfonso Ortiz, 236–54. Washington, D.C.: Smithsonian Institution, 1979.

_____. "Vásquez de Coronado and the Southern Tiwa Pueblos." In *Archaeology, Art, and Anthropology: Papers in Honor of J. J. Brody*, The Archaeological Society of New Mexico, no. 18, ed. Meliha S. Duran and David T. Kirkpatrick, 185–91. Albuquerque: The Archaeological Society of New Mexico, 1992.

Seed, Patricia. *Ceremonies of Possession in Europe's Conquest of the New World, 1492–1640*. Cambridge: Cambridge University Press, 1995.

Simmons, Marc. "History of Pueblo-Spanish Relations to 1821." In *Southwest*, vol. 9 of *Handbook of North American Indians*, ed. Alfonso Ortiz, 178–93. Washington, D.C.: Smithsonian Institution, 1979.

_____. *The Last Conquistador: Juan de Oñate and the Settling of the Far Southwest*. Norman: University of Oklahoma Press, 1991.

Simpson, J[ames] H. "Coronado's March in Search of the 'Seven Cities of Cibola and Discussion of their Probable Location." In *Annual Report of the Board of Regents of the Smithsonian Institution for 1869*, 309–40. Washington, D.C.: n.p., 1872.

Slatta, Richard W. "Spanish Colonial Military Strategy and Ideology." In *Contested Ground: Comparative Frontiers on the Northern and Southern Edges of the Spanish Empire*, ed. Donna J. Guy and Thomas E. Sheridan, 83–96. Tucson: The University of Arizona Press, 1998.

Stevens, Henry. *The New Laws of the Indies*. London: privately printed, 1893.

Tello, Antonio. *Crónica Miscelanea de la Sancta Provincia de Xalisco, Libro Segundo*. Guadalajara: Gobierno del Estado de Jalisco and Universidad de Guadalajara, 1968.

Todorov, Tzvetan. *The Conquest of America*. New York: HarperCollins Publishers, 1985.

Toll, Mollie S. "Paleofloral Materials." In *A Sixteenth-Century Spanish Campsite in the Tiguex Province*, Laboratory of Anthropology Notes 475, Bradley J. Vierra, 151–67. Santa Fe: Museum of New Mexico, 1989.

Urdaneta, Andrés. "An Account of the Voyage," trans. Thomas E. Chase. In *An Account of the Voyage of Juan Rodríguez Cabrillo*, 49–87. San Diego: Cabrillo National Monument Foundation, 1999.

Vargas Machuca, Bernardo de. *Milicia y Descripción de las Indias*, vol. 1. Madrid: Librería de Victoriano Suárez, 1892.

Velasco, Luis de. *Relación de las Encomiendas.* . . . Edited by France V. Scholes and Eleanor B. Adams. Mexico City: José Porrúa e hijos, 1955.

Vierra, Bradley J. *A Sixteenth-Century Spanish Campsite in the Tiguex Province*, Laboratory of Anthropology Notes 475. Santa Fe: Museum of New Mexico, Research Section, 1989.

_____, and Stanley M. Hordes. "Let the Dust Settle: A Review of the Coronado Campsite in the Tiguex Province." In *The Coronado Expedition to Tierra Nueva: The 1540–1542 Route Across the Southwest*, ed. Richard Flint and Shirley Cushing Flint, 249–61. Niwot, Colorado: University Press of Colorado, 1997.

Villadiego Vascuñana y Montoya, Alonso de. *Instrucción Política y Práctica Judicial Conforme al Estilo de los Consejos, Audiencias, y Tribunales de Corte, y Otros Ordinarios del Reyno Utilissima para los Governadores, y Corregidores, y otros Jueces Ordinarios, y de Comisión, y para los Abogados, Escrivanos, Procuradores, y Litigantes*. Madrid: Oficina de Antonio Marin, 1766.

Warren, J. Benedict. *The Conquest of Michoacán: The Spanish Domination of the Tarascan Kingdom in Western Mexico, 1521–1530*. Norman: University of Oklahoma Press, 1985.

Weber, David J. *The Spanish Frontier in North America*. New Haven and London: Yale University Press, 1992.

Weddle, Robert S. "Coastal Exploration and Mapping, A Concomitant of the Entradas." In *The Mapping of the Entradas into the Greater Southwest*, ed. Dennis Reinhartz and Gerald D. Saxon, 107–31. Norman: University of Oklahoma Press, 1998.

Wedel, Mildred Mott. "The Indian They Called *Turco*." In *Pathways to Plains Prehistory: Anthropological Perspectives of Plains Natives and Their Pasts*, ed. Don G. Wyckoff and Jack L. Hofman, 153–62. Duncan, Oklahoma: The Cross Timbers Press, 1982.

Wedel, Waldo R. *Archeological Remains in Central Kansas and Their Possible Bearing on the Location of Quivira*. Washington, D.C.: Smithsonian Institution, 1942.

Unpublished, Non-Archival Material

Carter, Constance. "Finding Aid, Spain, Archivo General de Indias, Vol. 34." Typescript. Bancroft Library, University of California, Berkeley.

Display, Convento de la Coria, Trujillo, Extremadura, Spain, May 1997.

Flint, Richard. "The Pattern of Coronado Expedition Material Culture." M.A. thesis, New Mexico Highlands University, 1992.

Inglis, G. Douglas, Sevilla, to Richard Flint, April 27, 1995, original in author's collection.

Pennington, Campbell W. "Bosquejo Grammática y Vocabulario de la Lengua Ópata, Sacada de un Obra de Natal Lombardo, S.J., que Sirve dentro los Ópatas de Sonora durante las Últimas Décadas del Siglo Diecisiete." Typescript. Library, Laboratory of Anthropology, Museum of New Mexico, Santa Fe.

Strout, Clevy Lloyd. "A Linguistic Study of the Journals of the Coronado Expedition." Ph.D. diss., University of Colorado, 1958.

Walsh, Jane MacLaren. "Myth and Imagination in the American Story: The Coronado Expedition, 1540–1542." Ph.D. diss., The Catholic University of America, 1993.

Wedel, Waldo R. "Coronado, Quivira, and Kansas: An Archeologist's View," lecture delivered November 3, 1990, Coronado-Quivira Museum, Lyons, Kansas. Photocopy. In author's collection.

Index

Vázquez de Coronado, 273; returned to Vázquez de Coronado, 273

Enslavement of Indians and taking of servants by expedition: no servants said to have been taken, 390, 392, 399; prisoners became servants, 355, 376, 516, 523; prohibition against enslavement by king, 529; slaves not taken, 355, 363, 376, 384, 420, 427; women and children pressed into service, 529

Escobar, Cristóbal de (de oficio witness): 3; able to sign his name, 151, 160; age of, 141; associated with Alonso Álvarez, 141, 142, 312; associated with Domingo Martín, 142, 312; assessment of testimony of, 142-143; carried supplies to the expedition from Corazones, 141; corregidor of Xicotepeque (Xilotepeque), 142, 507, 592ch9n7; denied mistreatment of Indians in Sonora, 145, 153; formed company with Domingo Martín, 89, 506; granted a coat of arms, 142; husband of Isabel Ortiz, 141; member of advance guard, 507-508; native of Aracena, Huelva, Spain, 141; oath of, 45, 53; on the expedition to Tierra Nueva, 144, 152; participated in entrada to Yuparo and Betuco, 141; owned at least one slave, 141; served as tasador of Indian tribute, 142; served in Vázquez de Coronado's company, 141, 145, 153; testimony of, 144-151, 152-160; took a servant and two horses on expedition to Tierra Nueva, 141, 506; vecino of Mexico City, 45, 53, 142; went to Mar del Sur with Melchor Díaz, 141; wounded during expedition, 141

Espejo, Antonio: found Indian allies of expedition at Cíbola (1580s), 533

Esteban [de Dorantes] (black slave): 520-521; killed at Cíbola, 168, 180, 521; with Marcos de Niza, 168, 180, 272

Estepa, Martín de (a footman): accused of abuse of Indians, 56; accused of setting dogs on Indians, 64, 72; bio., 551

Estimate of number casualties of conflict between Indians and expedition, 526-527

Estrada, Alonso de: 505; associated with Domingo Martín and Rodrigo Ximón, 508; brought his family from Spain, 54; came to New World (1523), 54; corregidor of Cáceres, 89; daughter, Beatriz de Estrada, 271; father-in-law of Vázquez de Coronado, 54, 89, 271; from Ciudad Real, 54, 508; gave permission to Domingo

Martín to return to Spain, 89; governor of Nueva España, 126; granted encomiendas to Rodrigo Ximón, 126; lieutenant governor of Nueva España, 89; royal treasurer, 54, 271

Estrada, Beatriz de: daughter of Alonso de Estrada and Marina Gutiérrez de la Caballería, 271; invested heavily in expedition, 270; received encomienda of Tlapa as dowry, 271; relative of Diego Gutiérrez de la Caballería, 75, 508; wife of Vázquez de Coronado, 75, 271, 508

Evidence, sixteenth-century standards of: 56

Execution of Indians by the expedition: at Pueblo del Cerco, 363, 384; by hanging, 327, illus., 327, 463, 483; by Juan Gallego in the region of San Gerónimo, 8; by quartering, at Chiametla, 327, 463, 483, 513; of El Turco, 7, 36, 64, 73, 81, 86, 97, 106, 115, 124, 151, 159, 174, 186, 197, 205, 217, 228; Vázquez de Coronado charged with executing Indians at Chiametla, 326, 330, 334, 463, 483; Vázquez de Coronado charged with executing El Turco illegally, 327, 331, 335

Expedition to Tierra Nueva (Coronado Expedition): 589ch3n14; authorized, 1; carried primarily native arms and armor, 533; chronology of, 5-8; composition of, 2, 537; contrasted with Soto expedition, 527; denounced to king, 3; departed from Compostela (February 1540), 5, 277, 294; disbanded on return route, 29, 535-536; included dozens of veterans of Guzmán's conquest of Nueva Galicia, 528; expected to tap into wealth of sophisticated native population, 540; a native view of, 527; goals: to subjugate, convert, and settle, 540; investors in, 270-271; joint venture, 271; knowledge and opinion major result of, 534-535; land settled as result of, 434; led by Vázquez de Coronado, 1, 5, 38, 46, 270, 277, 294, 463, 473, 483, 494, 595ch15n6; members impoverished as result, 535; mines discovered as result of, 434; not a benign exploring or mineral prospecting party, 539; not prepared to raise crops, 524, 603ch26n16, 603ch26n17; not unique in use of force and brutality, 540; part of larger program of exploration and conquest, 271; practices of vis-a-vis native peoples consistent with those of other expeditions, 529; provided influx of settlers

402, 420, 426, 441, 442, 451, 452; maestre de campo, 277-278, 295; named Juan de Contreras, Juan Troyano, and Melchior Pérez as his enemies, 108, 162, 208; native of Madrid, Spain, 336; ordered to join expedition to Tierra Nueva, 337; prepared winter quarters, 337, 440, 449-450, 515; punishment of, very light, 4, 339, 537; relative of Antonio de Mendoza, 339; replaced Lope de Samaniego as maestre de campo, 337; present at killing of Indians by dog attack, 114, 123; warned about breaking his promise, 338; burned Indians by Vázquez de Coronado's order, 131-132, 138, 318, 323-324; mutilated Indians by Vázquez de Coronado's order, 318, 323; ordered Indians burned, 81, 86, 113, 122, 172, 185, 216, 217, 227, 251, 259, 267, 442, 451; set dogs on Bigotes, 238, 246; sentence against, 4, 339; sentence reduced, 9, 339; sent to Cíbola to deliver requerimiento, 93, 101, 280, 298, 468, 489; sent to find Mar del Sur, 357, 364, 385, 446, 455; sent to pueblo of Tiguex to deliver requerimiento, 95, 104, 441, 442, 451, 452, 515; sent to reconnoiter dangerous pass, 235, 243, 280, 297, 468, 489; sent to solicit clothing from pueblos, 238, 246, 287, 305, 337; served king in Spain and Italy, 337; sought and gained release from prison, 338-339; summary of defense of, 338; took many horses, servants, and slaves on expedition, 337; wounded at Cíbola, 93, 102; wounded at Pueblo del Cerco, 395, 402, 420, 427, 443, 452

Luis [de Úbeda], fray: bio., 552; remained at Cicuique, 8; sent to Cíbola to deliver requerimiento, 280, 298, 468, 489; wounded at Cíbola, 280, 298, 468, 489

Luyando, Ochoa de (*oficial mayor* of the Council of the Indies): 41, 49

Madrid (Spain): home of García López de Cárdenas, 336

Maldonado, María: accompanied husband Juan Gómez de Paradinas on expedition, 75; associated with Pedro de Ledesma, 231; her service contributed to her husband's receipt of a grant, 75; nursed the sick on the expedition, 75

Maldonado, Rodrigo (de parte witness): 19, 432; age of, 435; associated with Antonio de Mendoza, 435; brother-in-law of the duque del Infantado, 435; captain of horsemen, 277, 294, 435; native of Guadalajara, Spain, 435; signed plea for perpetual encomiendas with Vázquez de Coronado, Bernaldino Pacheco de Bocanegra, Alonso Dávila Alvarado, 435; present at burning of Indians, 81, 86, 216, 227; burned pueblos, 151, 159, 257, 265, 289, 307, 435; ordered to burn and dismantle pueblos by Vázquez de Coronado, 313, 317, 323; sent to deliver requerimiento to Pueblo del Cerco, 290, 308, 363, 383, 420, 427, 442, 452; sent to Mar del Sur, 435; shared encomienda of Mextitlán with Diego de Guevara, 436; summary of testimony of incomplete, 435, 438, 448; went to Quivira, 444, 454

Malpartida (possibly San Marcos Pueblo, New Mexico): map, 582; pueblo populated or repopulated in Galisteo Basin between 1540 and 1581, 531, 605ch26n48

Manrique [de Lara], Alonso: bio., 553; present at killing of Indians by dog attack, 114, 123;

Marcos, fray, de Niza: 422, 429, 437, 447, 471, 492, 520; as possible accuser of the expedition, 30; at Jalapa, 510; bio., 553; dispatched to check rumors of wealth (1539), 5, 272; left expedition (August 1540), 6; not called to testify, 510; reports not heard directly, 418, 425; reports of Cíbola not confirmed, 273, 364, 385; returned from reconnaissance with favorable news (1539), 5; sent to Cíbola to deliver requerimiento, 93, 101; sent Esteban ahead toward Cíbola, 168, 180; thought to have lied, 396, 403;

Mar del Sur: geo. data, 570; López de Cárdenas sent to find, 357, 364, 385; reconnaissance to, made by Melchor Díaz, 92, 100, 141; Rodrigo de Maldonado sent to, 435

Martín, Domingo (de oficio witness): 3; able to sign his name, 98, 106; age of, 89; apologist for expedition, 90; assessment of testimony of, 90; associated with Alonso Álvarez, 312; associated with Alonso de Estrada, 508; associated with Cristóbal de Escobar, 142, 312; associated with Hernán Pérez de Bocanegra, 89; associated with Vázquez de Coronado, 88-89, 91, 99; encomendero of Yagualicán, 89, 506; formed company with Cristóbal de Escobar, 89, 506; gave lengthy and detailed

Shirley Cushing Flint

Raised in South Dakota, RICHARD FLINT has lived for most of his life in northern New Mexico. He received a Ph.D. in colonial Latin American history and history of the U.S. West from the University of New Mexico. Under a 1997-98 Fulbright grant, Flint did research in Sevilla, Spain, which has culminated in this book.

Dr. Flint and his wife Shirley Cushing Flint, also a historian, are among the foremost authorities on the Coronado expedition. Most recently they edited *The Coronado Expedition to Tierra Nueva, the 1540-1542 Route across the Southwest.* Currently they are at work on a dual-language edition of Coronado expedition documents titled *'They Were Not Familiar with His Majesty, Nor Did They Want To Be His Subjects': Documents of the Coronado Expedition, 1540-42.*